PETERSON'S

LAW
SCHOOLS

*A Comprehensive
Guide to All 181
Accredited U.S.
Law Schools*

PETERSON'S
Princeton, New Jersey

Visit Peterson's Education Center on the Internet (World Wide Web) at
www.petersons.com

Editorial inquiries concerning this book should be addressed to the Editor at
Peterson's, P.O. Box 2123, Princeton, New Jersey 08543-2123.

ISSN 1521-8015

ISBN 0-7689-0011-5

Printed in the United States of America

10 9 8 7 6 5 4 3 2 1

CONTENTS

Contents

PREFACE

hese articles are designed to give the reader a comprehensive account of how to go about preparing and applying for law school. Information about deadlines and other procedural matter is important in preventing the applicant from making a fatal mistake, such as not taking the Law School Admissions Test in time to be used in a recruitment season. At the end the article section, you will find a comprehensive timetable for accomplishing the many tasks associated with applying to law school.

When reading these chapters, keeping mind that the probability of your acceptance at any law school is largely determined by your GPA and LSAT score, and there are only minimal actions you can take to distort that probability to any degree in your favor. So many of the strategies discussed here must be viewed in the context of your comprehensive record. With this caveat out of the way, it is important to add that this does not mean you should not pay attention to these strategies. Sometimes, what separates an offer of admission from a rejection is blessed little.

William Weaver received his J.D. and Ph.D. from the University of Virginia. He has advised prelaw students at three different colleges throughout the last decade and currently teaches at the University of Texas at El Paso where he is codirector of UTEP's Law School Preparation Institute.

THE ABSOLUTE BASICS

WHAT IS LAW SCHOOL?

Law school is normally three years long (six semesters) of full-time classes. There are about 180 schools that are accredited by the American Bar Association (ABA). Accreditation through this body is extremely demanding and requires a school to have minimum resources in areas such as faculty, materials, and classroom space. Additionally, the ABA maintains close supervision over the curriculum requirements of accredited schools. These requirements are most stringent for first-year courses. Today, it is absolutely crucial that you attend an ABA-accredited law school. In many jurisdictions a law graduate's ability to practice law is severely limited if he or she has not received a law degree from an ABA-accredited law school. And in today's employment climate it may be all but impossible for graduates of non-ABA-accredited schools to find a job.

WHEN DOES LAW SCHOOL START?

All ABA-accredited full-time law programs start in the fall semester. A few schools have programs directed at ethnic minority, nontraditional, or provisional students that begin in the summer prior to the normal first-year fall session. These programs are generally for students who do not meet normal admission requirements for the school and are a way of determining if a student, despite not having strong enough numbers, can still excel in a law school environment. These programs, however, are extraordinary and irrelevant for most law school applicants.

Some schools also allow students to attend full-time twelve months a year. The advantage of such a program is that students graduate in roughly two years rather than the normal three. The disadvantages, though, can be serious. Such a program means that a student will not engage in summer employment—often crucial in obtaining a job offer. Without summer employment, students look less attractive to prospective law firms. Additionally, many job offers to law students come from firms and institutions that the students work for in the summer. Obviously, if you have no summer employment you will not receive such offers. Again, schools that offer twelve-month programs are few in number, and where they are offered they are optional. Some institutions cater to part-time students and

William Weaver, J.D., Ph.D., Department of Political Science, University of Texas at El Paso

may allow these students to be admitted in the fall or spring or even the summer. Again, though, unless you absolutely must attend law school part-time, you should enroll in the normal program of study, starting with full-time fall admission.

WHAT DO YOU NEED TO APPLY TO LAW SCHOOL?

In order to apply to law school the applicant must have a four-year degree from an accredited college or university. No particular undergraduate major or course of study is required, and applicants from the so-called "hard" sciences are welcomed by law schools. Law schools mainly look for students who have taken a rigorous track in undergraduate school and who have demonstrated writing and critical thinking abilities. No law-related courses at the undergraduate level are required in order to apply to law school.

HOW MUCH DOES IT COST TO APPLY?

Registration for the LSAT is about $80, and Law School Data Assembly Service (explanations of these services can be found in the application booklet—available from your prelaw adviser or on line—see contact information on page 93) registration for a dozen schools or so is another hundred. But these expenses are just the beginning. If you intend to take a professionally administered preparation course for the LSAT the fee can be up to $850. Additionally, law schools charge application fees that can range from $20 to $70. If a person applies to a dozen law schools and takes a professional preparation course for the LSAT, the final bill for the law school application process could easily be more than $2000. Some law schools will wave fees for members of minority groups under certain circumstances, and the LSAS gives test fee waivers and application fee waivers for participating schools when an applicant is in dire financial need. Talk to your prelaw adviser for information and forms concerning fee waivers, or contact the LSAS on the World Wide Web or by phone at the number found on page 93.

HOW DO LAW SCHOOLS DECIDE WHICH STUDENTS TO ACCEPT?

Law school admissions committees generally make their decisions based on two factors: undergraduate GPA and

LSAT scores. Most schools transform an applicant's GPA and LSAT score into an index score, a single number that is then used to compare the applicant to the rest of the applicant pool. Some schools require extremely high GPAs and LSATs, while other schools are more flexible in their approach. Typically, the highest ranked law schools require superior performance in terms of both grades and LSAT scores. We will discuss these matters at greater length later in this book.

WHEN SHOULD YOU TALK TO A PRELAW ADVISER?

You should talk to a prelaw adviser as soon as you recognize that you may have an interest in applying to law school. Even your first-year of undergraduate school is not too early to talk to an adviser. Many students have strange misconceptions about law school and the applications process, and these should be cleared up as soon as possible. See your prelaw adviser!

HOW MUCH MONEY MIGHT YOU MAKE AS A LAWYER?

Many people imagine that attorneys make vast sums of money and lead endlessly interesting lives. In reality, most attorneys earn a solid middle-class living. Fully one third of attorneys are in solo practice and many times they—like other small business owners—are just barely scraping by. And while lawyers often work on interesting cases or projects, they are just as likely to be laboring away on excruciatingly boring material. Unlike on TV, most attorneys never try a major case in court, and eye strain and back pain are the main hazards of the average attorney's life. Being an attorney usually means extremely long working hours—60 hours a week is not unusual—and sometimes coming into contact with extremely unpleasant people and circumstances.

ARE YOU SMART ENOUGH TO BE A LAWYER?

Of course, law school requires dedication and serious work, but any person of average intelligence and above-average persistence should make it through with little trouble. Perhaps the most important skills you can take to law school are the abilities to analyze and write quickly, clearly, and in a direct and nonelliptical manner. After all, all attorneys have are words. So the better you are at writing and analysis the better you will be prepared for law school. With this in mind, you should make sure that you take undergraduate courses that require significant amounts of writing and analysis.

HOW CAN YOU AFFORD LAW SCHOOL?

Most law school students survive on student loans, and loan debt can easily exceed $100,000 for undergraduate and law school expenses combined. Do not over worry about this aspect of legal education. At any rate, be assured that if you are admitted to an ABA-approved law school you will be eligible for sufficient loans to pay for school and survive (barely, perhaps)—provided you are not delinquent in any other school loans. Law school is big business, and most schools have a staff that exclusively handles financial aid matters. Some students can get through with filling out a minimal amount of paperwork, and a few weeks later being summoned to an office to sign over a hunk of money to the school with a smaller hunk doled out to make rent, etc. The process is relatively painless. Notice, however, that financial aid practices are meant to make things easy for the school, not necessarily the student. This means that a student may not receive financial aid until well after the start of the semester and may receive only two or three disbursements for the entire school year. This requires students to manage their money very carefully. At any rate, you should arrive at law school with enough financial wherewithal to make sure that you can pay rent, buy books, and eat for the first few months of school. With luck, things will go smoothly, but prepare for the worst.

STRATEGIES AND CONSIDERATIONS

SHOULD YOU GO TO LAW SCHOOL?

Law school is a lengthy, arduous, annoying, expensive, and anxiety-inducing experience. Common wisdom would probably dictate that it is something to be withstood only if one has clear reasons and goals for withstanding it. However, on this point, most law students depart a great distance from this assumption. Few law school students end up doing anything remotely resembling what they thought they would be doing before they entered law school. The truth is that before you go to law school you are woefully equipped to make judgments about what areas of law or what types of jobs you will be interested in. Even if a family member or friend is an attorney, it is still difficult to get enough of a bead on the myriad possibilities in legal practice to make your mind up about what it is you want to do after graduation. If you simply have a generalized, largely unjustified desire to go to law school, do not second-guess yourself. Do it! As long as you know what you are getting into, law school is not such a bad place, even if you do not know what you want to do with your life. Law school is an oftentimes whirlwind experience where you are constantly being exposed to new ideas and new people from many areas of business and law. If you cannot figure out a direction to follow in life from such an environment then you will not have an easy time of it anywhere.

The adventure potential in law school is high. One week you may have convinced yourself that you are not going to be offered summer employment and the next you have been hired by a large law firm to spend the summer in its Salzburg, Austria, office. So do not worry if your life goals are indefinite, and do not mentally strap yourself down before going to law school. Leave all of your options open and do not be afraid to experiment.

WHAT SHOULD YOU DO IN COLLEGE PRIOR TO LAW SCHOOL?

Many students labor under misconceptions about what in their undergraduate record will make them more attractive

---

William Weaver, J.D., Ph.D., Department of Political Science, University of Texas at El Paso

law school candidates. These misconceptions generally fall into one of three categories: selection of major, course selection, or extracurricular activities.

Major

Perhaps the most pervasive misconception of potential law school applicants is that majoring in certain disciplines provides an advantage in the law school admissions process. Virtually no school has a "prelaw" undergraduate major, so many students believe that political science is the prelaw major. The actuality is that any rigorous program of study, from anthropology to zoology, is fine. You should major in an area you enjoy, since you are more likely to do better working at a subject you like than working at one you simply think will open a door for you. People in the so-called "hard" sciences should take special note. Engineering or physics majors frequently may think that they cannot or should not apply to law school because they lack a liberal arts degree. This perception is dead wrong. Law schools are happy to receive applications from engineers, physics majors, and chemists.

Course Selection

Further, students often believe that they need to, or should take, law courses in the undergraduate curriculum to prepare for law school. This perception is also false. By all means, take courses in public law or business law if you are interested in those areas, but don't feel compelled to take these courses simply because you are applying to law school. In fact, while it is not a crucial point, law schools often frown on student records that show lots of courses in law-related areas. Law schools don't want students coming in with preconceived notions about the law, because such students are less open to the pervasive "world-changing" effects of law school. You cannot "learn" the law in undergraduate school, so don't worry about "preparing" for law school in this substantive way. The best tools to take to law school are the abilities to write and analyze quickly, well, and with economy. If you are a "hard" science major make sure that you take courses that require sufficient writing so that you are not handicapped in law school. Conversely, liberal arts majors should take courses requiring logical analysis. For example, "hard" science majors should consider taking courses in philosophy or critical writing as electives. Likewise, liberal arts majors should consider taking math all the way through the calculus or advanced courses in the physical sciences.

Extracurricular Activities

Finally, evidence of extracurricular activities are useful in the admissions process in that they can tell a story about your commitment to community and those who are friendless and resourceless. But do not undertake these activities merely to have something to put on your application. Do these things because your heart tells you to. The difference that extracurricular activities make in gaining admission to law school is insufficient to warrant undertaking them unless you are really inclined to such activity. Certain types of activities say more than others. It may be nice that you were on the governing board of your social fraternity, but it says more about you from the law school perspective if you spent your weekends as a research volunteer for the Legal Aid Society or helped fix up the local battered spouse's shelter.

THE LSAT

The LSAT is a half-day long exam given in six parts with a writing sample requirement. The exam is given four times a year, usually in June, September or October, December, and February. By and large, the test carries much more weight in the admissions process than the applicant's GPA. for this reason, all those applying to law school should definitely prepare for the test and consider taking a professional preparation course. Some courses utilize live instruction, while others supply extensive materials without classroom instruction and, as a result, are more flexible. Your preparation for the LSAT should be extensive. Here are a few tips.

TIPS FOR TAKING THE LSAT

· Try to sign up for the June administration of the exam just prior to the fall semester in which you plan to apply to law school.
· Do not prepare for the exam months ahead of time. The LSAT is not a knowledge-based examination, but rather is meant to test the way in which you solve problems. Therefore, the test does not require months and months of preparation. In fact, over preparation is a problem. If you over prepare you lose your edge.
· Devote an intense period of four to six weeks preparing for the exam. Order back examinations from the LSAS corporation (may be ordered using forms in the information and registration booklet or on line). If you can afford it, take a professional preparation course. Otherwise, buy self-help books from reputable publishers.
· Take your practice exams under test conditions. That is, time yourself and take a full examination each time.
· Take one or two practice exams under less-than-ideal conditions. Take an exam in a cafeteria or other location that is likely to be noisy. LSAT test conditions are as quiet as can be possibly achieved under the circumstances, but that does not mean that they are as quiet as a library special collections room. People get up and move around during the exam. Many people are concentrating so hard during the exam that they do not realize that they are making noises by shaking their legs or groaning.
· If you drink coffee, quit. Coffee will only accentuate the anxiety associated with the exam. Further, it may cause you to make a trip to the bathroom during the exam—a catastrophic event—which will make you worry even more about how you are doing.
· Visit the room where the exam will be given before the day of the examination. Select several seats that appear to be satisfactory. Don't sit next to a window or in an aisle seat. Things going on outside the windows might distract you, and if you sit in an aisle seat, anybody who gets up in your row will have to climb past you. The corner seat farthest from the entrance to the room is usually a fine choice.
· Wear loose clothing and after you sit down spend a few seconds taking several deep breaths and think of something restful.
· Prepare for the LSAT as you would prepare yourself for a sporting event—psych yourself up and be "high," but controlled.

Two practice LSAT tests appear on page 9 and 38. For advice and practice to boost your LSAT test scores, *LSAT Success* with diagnostic CD-ROM test feedback is available in your local bookstore or directly through http://www.petersons.com.

William Weaver, J.D., Ph.D., Department of Political Science, University of Texas at El Paso

LSAT PRACTICE TESTS

LAW SCHOOL ADMISSION TEST SIMULATIONS

On the following pages are two examples of what a real LSAT is like. According to the test-taking strategies you have developed during the course of your training, you may use these tests in one of two ways.

First, you could work only on those sections of the tests that you feel require additional practice. Use the individual section-tests of this simulation as if each is a pretest, employing the 9-12-18 system to sharpen your test-taking techniques (Sections 1 and 3 contain Relationships problems, Sections 2 and 5 contain Arguments problems, and Section 4 contains Passages problems). Review the sessions on the particular question type before beginning, and be sure to follow the instructions for each section-test carefully.

The second way to approach these simulated tests is to treat them as if you were taking an actual LSAT. In this case, you would spend 30 minutes on the Writing Sample and 35 minutes on each of the five section-tests (remember the experimental section?), in effect putting the 9-12-18 system through a dry run in preparation for this 3-hour-and-25-minute test. Work only on one section during the 35 minutes allowed, and do not work on or review other sections. Take a 15-minute break between Sections 3 and 4 of the test.

Whichever method of working through the questions you choose, mark the best answers in the book, and, when you have finished a question set, transfer your choices to the answer sheet (on the facing page for Practice Test 1; on page 185 for Practice Test 2). For ease of use, you might want to photocopy the answer sheet before working on the questions.

Quick-Score Answers to the two LSAT Practice Tests are found on pages 67 and 68, while Explanatory Answers begin on page 69.

Excerpted from *LSAT Success 1998* © 1996 by Thomas O. White

Law School Admission Test Simulation Answer Sheet

SECTION 1	SECTION 2	SECTION 3	SECTION 4	SECTION 5
1. A B C D E	1. A B C D E	1. A B C D E	1. A B C D E	1. A B C D E
2. A B C D E	2. A B C D E	2. A B C D E	2. A B C D E	2. A B C D E
3. A B C D E	3. A B C D E	3. A B C D E	3. A B C D E	3. A B C D E
4. A B C D E	4. A B C D E	4. A B C D E	4. A B C D E	4. A B C D E
5. A B C D E	5. A B C D E	5. A B C D E	5. A B C D E	5. A B C D E
6. A B C D E	6. A B C D E	6. A B C D E	6. A B C D E	6. A B C D E
7. A B C D E	7. A B C D E	7. A B C D E	7. A B C D E	7. A B C D E
8. A B C D E	8. A B C D E	8. A B C D E	8. A B C D E	8. A B C D E
9. A B C D E	9. A B C D E	9. A B C D E	9. A B C D E	9. A B C D E
10. A B C D E	10. A B C D E	10. A B C D E	10. A B C D E	10. A B C D E
11. A B C D E	11. A B C D E	11. A B C D E	11. A B C D E	11. A B C D E
12. A B C D E	12. A B C D E	12. A B C D E	12. A B C D E	12. A B C D E
13. A B C D E	13. A B C D E	13. A B C D E	13. A B C D E	13. A B C D E
14. A B C D E	14. A B C D E	14. A B C D E	14. A B C D E	14. A B C D E
15. A B C D E	15. A B C D E	15. A B C D E	15. A B C D E	15. A B C D E
16. A B C D E	16. A B C D E	16. A B C D E	16. A B C D E	16. A B C D E
17. A B C D E	17. A B C D E	17. A B C D E	17. A B C D E	17. A B C D E
18. A B C D E	18. A B C D E	18. A B C D E	18. A B C D E	18. A B C D E
19. A B C D E	19. A B C D E	19. A B C D E	19. A B C D E	19. A B C D E
20. A B C D E	20. A B C D E	20. A B C D E	20. A B C D E	20. A B C D E
21. A B C D E	21. A B C D E	21. A B C D E	21. A B C D E	21. A B C D E
22. A B C D E	22. A B C D E	22. A B C D E	22. A B C D E	22. A B C D E
23. A B C D E	23. A B C D E	23. A B C D E	23. A B C D E	23. A B C D E
24. A B C D E	24. A B C D E	24. A B C D E	24. A B C D E	24. A B C D E
25. A B C D E	25. A B C D E	25. A B C D E	25. A B C D E	25. A B C D E
26. A B C D E	26. A B C D E	26. A B C D E	26. A B C D E	26. A B C D E
27. A B C D E	27. A B C D E	27. A B C D E	27. A B C D E	27. A B C D E
28. A B C D E	28. A B C D E	28. A B C D E	28. A B C D E	28. A B C D E
29. A B C D E	29. A B C D E	29. A B C D E	29. A B C D E	29. A B C D E
30. A B C D E	30. A B C D E	30. A B C D E	30. A B C D E	30. A B C D E

Excerpted from *LSAT Success 1998* © 1996 by Thomas O. White

Peterson's Law Schools

PRACTICE TEST 1

LSAT WRITING SAMPLE TOPIC

Complete the short writing exercise on the topic that follows. You have only 30 minutes to plan, organize, and write your sample. WRITE ONLY ON THE TOPIC SPECIFIED.

Alice Anderson is a senior at John Paul Jones University. She has been offered two positions as a result of her outstanding record in her major, television and radio broadcasting. As her counselor, you are to write an argument favoring one of the two offers. Two considerations guide your decision:

- Alice has a large student-loan debt that she has to begin to repay immediately upon graduation.
- Alice has as her career goal a position as a network-news anchorperson.

WAND is the only television station serving a large area located some 250 miles north of the capital of the state. The station has offered Alice a job as a reporter whose principal assignments would be to cover the activities of local governments, politics, and business. In addition to her assigned stories, Alice would have the opportunity to independently prepare stories for possible broadcast. Because the station is small, has a very stable staff, and has limited growth prospects, Alice's chances for advancement are not good. WAND's owner is a former network executive who purchased the station in order to get away from the pressures of broadcasting in major markets. Alice would get only a modest salary at WAND, and she would have to supplement her income with outside work.

KBSC is one of three television stations located in the state capital. The station has offered Alice a job as a production assistant in the news department. She would primarily do background research and check facts and sources for the producers and reporters. Production assistants who work hard are promoted to positions as special-assignment reporters in about two years. There are many special-assignment reporters competing for assignments, most of which involve covering minor events such as political dinners, award ceremonies, and concerts and writing human-interest stories. Most special-assignment reporters spend at least five years covering minor events before moving into a position as a general report-anchorperson. KBSC would pay Alice a salary in excess of the amount she would need to live comfortably in the city.

Excerpted from *LSAT Success 1998* © 1996 by Thomas O. White

Excerpted from *LSAT Success 1998* © 1996 by Thomas O. White

| SECTION **1** | TIME—35 MINUTES | 24 QUESTIONS |

The questions in this section are based on a set of conditions. A diagram may be helpful in the answer selection process. Select the best answer to each question, and mark the corresponding space on the answer sheet.

Questions 1–6

A student is preparing a report on statehood. The source material is incomplete, but the following is known.

Wyoming became a state before Ohio.
Kansas became a state before Wyoming.
Ohio became a state after Maine.

1. Which of the following CANNOT be true?

   (A) Kansas was a state before Maine.
   (B) Maine was a state before Wyoming.
   (C) Ohio was a state before Kansas.
   (D) Wyoming was a state before Maine.
   (E) Kansas was a state before Ohio.

2. Which of the following must be true?

   (A) Kansas was a state before Maine.
   (B) Wyoming was a state before Kansas.
   (C) Maine was a state before Kansas.
   (D) Ohio was a state before Maine.
   (E) Kansas was a state before Ohio.

3. If Texas was a state before Maine, which of the following must be true?

   (A) Texas was a state first.
   (B) Texas was a state before Kansas.
   (C) Wyoming was a state before Texas.
   (D) Texas was a state before Ohio.
   (E) Maine was a state before Texas.

4. If Kansas became a state before Maine, Wyoming became a state after Maine, and Vermont was last to become a state, which of the following must be the order of statehood, first to last?

   (A) Vermont, Wyoming, Maine, Ohio, Kansas
   (B) Wyoming, Ohio, Kansas, Vermont, Maine
   (C) Maine, Kansas, Ohio, Vermont, Wyoming
   (D) Kansas, Maine, Wyoming, Ohio, Vermont
   (E) Ohio, Wyoming, Vermont, Kansas, Maine

5. If Utah became a state before Ohio, and Florida became a state after Wyoming, which of the following CANNOT be true if Maine became a state after Utah and before Florida?

   (A) Utah was a state before Wyoming.
   (B) Florida was a state before Ohio.
   (C) Florida was a state before Kansas.
   (D) Maine was a state before Ohio.
   (E) Wyoming was a state before Florida.

6. If Alaska became a state after Iowa and Wyoming, which of the following must be true?

   (A) Alaska was a state before Maine.
   (B) Iowa was a state before Wyoming.
   (C) Iowa was a state before Ohio.
   (D) Alaska was a state before Ohio.
   (E) Kansas was a state before Alaska.

Questions 7–12

T lives in a smaller house than her brother.
T lives in a larger house than her parents.
T's children live with T.
T has no other relatives.

7. If four females and two males live in smaller houses than T's brother, how many of T's children are boys and girls, respectively?

   (A) 1, 0
   (B) 0, 1
   (C) 2, 1
   (D) 1, 2
   (E) 2, 0

Excerpted from *LSAT Success 1998* © 1996 by Thomas O. White

8. If T's relative U lives in a larger house than her relative S, and both U and S are the same sex, what relationship could U be to S?

   (A) father to son
   (B) mother to daughter
   (C) daughter to mother
   (D) grandfather to grandson
   (E) son to father

9. If T's relative U lives in a larger house than T's relative S, all of the following may be true EXCEPT

   (A) S is U's son
   (B) S is U's mother
   (C) U is younger than S
   (D) S is younger than U
   (E) U and S are both female

10. If T's relative U is not as old as T, who is not as old as her relative V, what relationship can U NOT be to V?

   (A) grandson
   (B) uncle
   (C) nephew
   (D) son
   (E) granddaughter

11. If, of all T's relatives who could possibly be either older or younger than T, none are the same age or older, how many of T's relatives must be younger than T?

   (A) less than 2
   (B) 2
   (C) 2 or 3
   (D) 3
   (E) more than 3

12. If the number of males related to T equals the number of females related to T, which of the following can be true?

   (A) T has exactly 4 children.
   (B) T has exactly 3 children.
   (C) T has exactly 1 child.
   (D) T has exactly 6 children.
   (E) T has exactly 2 children.

Questions 13–18

Busses 1, 2, and 3 make one trip each day, and they are the only ones that riders A, B, C, D, E, F, and G take to work.

   Neither E nor G takes bus 1 on a day when B does.
   G does not take bus 2 on a day when D does.
   When A and F take the same bus, it is always bus 3.
   C always takes bus 3.

13. Which of the following groups consists of riders who CANNOT take bus 1 to work on the same day?

   (A) A, D, G
   (B) D, E, F
   (C) D, E, G
   (D) E, F, G
   (E) B, D, G

14. Traveling together to work, B, C, and G could take which of the same busses on a given day?

   (A) 1 only
   (B) 2 only
   (C) 3 only
   (D) 2 and 3 only
   (E) 1, 2, and 3

15. The maximum number of riders who could take bus 2 to work on a given day must be

   (A) 3
   (B) 4
   (C) 5
   (D) 6
   (E) 7

16. Traveling together to work, B, D, E, F, and G could take which of the same busses on a given day?

   (A) 1 only
   (B) 2 only
   (C) 3 only
   (D) 1 and 3 only
   (E) 2 and 3 only

Excerpted from *LSAT Success 1998* © 1996 by Thomas O. White

17. On a day when each of the riders takes one of the three busses to work, exactly how many riders CANNOT take any bus other than bus 2?

    (A) 0
    (B) 1
    (C) 2
    (D) 3
    (E) 4

18. Which of the following could be a group of riders that takes bus 1 to work on a given day?

    (A) A, C, E, G
    (B) A, D, E, G
    (C) A, E, F, G
    (D) B, D, E, F
    (E) B, D, E, G

Questions 19–24

Angela, Bruce, Cora, Dora, and Elmer live at different points along a straight east-west highway.

   Angela lives 5 miles away from Bruce.
   Cora lives 7 miles away from Dora.
   Elmer lives 2 miles away from Cora.
   Bruce lives 3 miles away from Cora.
   The distance between houses is measured by straight line only.

19. Which of the following could be true?

    (A) Dora lives 9 miles from Elmer.
    (B) Dora lives 2 miles from Bruce.
    (C) Angela lives 5 miles from Cora.
    (D) Elmer lives 2 miles from Bruce.
    (E) Angela lives 18 miles from Dora.

20. Which of the following must be true?

    (A) The distance between Elmer's and Bruce's houses is greater than the distance between Cora's and Angela's houses.
    (B) The distance between Bruce's and Elmer's houses is shorter than the distance between Cora's and Dora's houses.
    (C) Of the group, Dora lives farthest from Cora.
    (D) Cora lives closer to Dora than she does to Angela.
    (E) Elmer lives closer to Cora than Angela does.

21. Which of the following statements must be FALSE?

    (A) Angela and Cora live 12 miles apart.
    (B) Angela and Dora live 5 miles apart.
    (C) Bruce and Dora live 10 miles apart.
    (D) Elmer and Dora live 9 miles apart.
    (E) Elmer and Bruce live 5 miles apart.

22. If Bruce and Dora live east of Cora, which of the following must be the distance between Bruce's and Dora's houses?

    (A) 10 miles
    (B) 8 miles
    (C) 5 miles
    (D) 4 miles
    (E) 2 miles

23. If Bruce and Elmer live east of Cora, and Dora lives west of Cora, which of the following must be true?

    (A) Dora lives closer to Elmer than Cora does to Bruce.
    (B) Cora lives closer to Dora than Elmer does to Bruce.
    (C) Elmer lives closer to Cora than Bruce does to Elmer.
    (D) Bruce lives closer to Elmer than Cora does to Dora.
    (E) Angela lives closer to Bruce than Cora does to Elmer.

24. If Cora, starting from her house, visits Dora, Bruce, and Elmer in that order and then returns home, what is the smallest number of miles she walks?

    (A) 14
    (B) 15
    (C) 16
    (D) 17
    (E) 18

Excerpted from *LSAT Success 1998* © 1996 by Thomas O. White

Evaluate the reasoning contained in the brief statements, and select the best answer. Do not make implausible, superfluous, or incompatible assumptions. Select the best answer to each question, and mark the corresponding space on the answer sheet.

1. Well-designed clothing was once described as the hallmark of a stylish person. We agree, and our clothing is designed for stylish people. Their lifestyles are well-defined. They do everything in good taste. And they search out well-designed clothing as the guarantee of good workmanship.

   This advertisement is intended to suggest which of the following conclusions?

   (A) Well-designed clothing defines a lifestyle.
   (B) Good taste is important in clothing design.
   (C) Workmanship guarantees good design.
   (D) Purchasers of this brand of clothing will be stylish.
   (E) Appearance is the hallmark of purchasers of this brand of clothing.

2. Native American tribes seeking monetary reparations from the government are often told, "There is neither wealth nor wisdom enough in the world to compensate in money for all the wrongs in history."

   Which of the following most weakens the argument above?

   (A) Prior wrongs should not be permitted as a justification for present wrongs.
   (B) Even though all wrongs cannot be compensated for, some wrongs can be.
   (C) Since most people committed wrongs, the government should compensate for wrongs with money.
   (D) Monetary reparations upset social order less than other forms of reparation.
   (E) Since money is the basic cause of the wrongs, should it not be the cure?

3. A mother told her daughter, "You lie too much. You cannot be believed. When you start telling me the truth, I will start believing you."

   Which of the following is assumed by the mother's statement?

   (A) The mother has explained what is wrong about lying.
   (B) The mother has determined that her daughter knows what a lie is.
   (C) The mother knows when the daughter has been truthful.
   (D) The mother is routinely truthful with her daughter.
   (E) The mother believes her daughter ultimately will tell the truth.

4. Manufacturing products using glass made from sand rather than materials made from other natural resources can save energy, despite the fact that the initial cost is high.

   Which of the following, if true, does NOT support the above argument?

   (A) Manufacturing wood and metal products requires energy that could have been more efficiently used to make glass.
   (B) Unlike metal and wood products, those made from glass must be discarded rather than repaired when they break.
   (C) Aluminum products require much more energy to produce than do those made of glass.
   (D) Fiberglass insulation is much more energy efficient than insulation made with other materials.
   (E) Glass cookware transfers heat more efficiently than that made from metal.

Excerpted from *LSAT Success 1998* © 1996 by Thomas O. White

5. The United States gets 5 percent of its oil from Mexico. If Mexico raises the price of its oil by 20 percent, that will result in an increase of 1 percent (5 percent times 20 percent) in the price of oil products in the United States.

Which of the following is an assumption upon which the above argument depends?

(A) Oil prices in the United States are not affected by inflation in Mexico.

(B) Other countries will not increase oil exports to the United States.

(C) The price increase will not result in a decrease in the sales of Mexican oil products.

(D) People will not substitute other products for those made from Mexican oil.

(E) A 1 percent price increase in oil products will not be recognized by the buying public.

6. Historians, by trade, describe events that are confused as to motive and significance. Therefore, historians, however well-intentioned, primarily traffic in half-truths and lies. But novelists are free from such burdens. Even though they relate many things that are untrue, their characterizations are not offered as true and, therefore, are not half-truths or lies.

Which of the following, if true, would be an extension of the argument above?

(A) Historians and novelists, by trade, characterize events and, therefore, are required to deal in half-truths and lies.

(B) Poets offer their writing as truth in perception and, thus, do not deal in half-truths and lies.

(C) Journalists report on motives and the significance of events and, like historians, traffic primarily in half-truths and lies.

(D) Nonfiction writers select information to support their point and, thus, deal in half-truths.

(E) Economists characterize statistics and, therefore, do not deal in half-truths and lies.

7. The policy of equal pay for women continues to erode the importance of the mother's role in society.

The above argument can be criticized for which of the following reasons?

(A) The importance of a role is not related to the pay for that role.

(B) Equal pay for women is unrelated to motherhood.

(C) All women are not mothers.

(D) Society continues to devalue motherhood.

(E) When someone gains in a society, someone else loses.

8. The Earth receives energy in the form of heat from the sun and discharges heat energy into space by its own emissions. The heat energy received undergoes many transformations. But in the long run, no significant amount of heat energy is stored on the Earth, and there is no continuing trend toward higher or lower temperatures.

Which of the following sentences provides the most logical continuation of this paragraph?

(A) It is obvious, therefore, that much of the heat energy that reaches the Earth is transformed by some means not yet understood.

(B) Thus, it is imperative that we develop a way to use solar energy before it is dissipated into outer space.

(C) As a result, the amount of heat energy lost by the Earth must closely approximate the amount gained from the sun.

(D) The Earth would become as hot as the sun without the many transformations of heat energy.

(E) The Earth's slow but persistent receding from the sun prevents it from overheating.

Questions 9–10

Lecturer: On average, the majority of Americans enjoy the highest standard of living of any people in the world.

Critic: There are thousands of Americans who have annual incomes of less than $3,000 per year.

9. Which of the following best describes the critic's response?

   (A) It is not inconsistent with the lecturer's statement.
   (B) It cites data confirming the lecturer's statement.
   (C) It fails to distinguish between cause and effect.
   (D) It generalizes from too small a number of cases.
   (E) It resorts to emotional language.

10. A logical criticism of the lecturer's statement would focus on the existence of

    (A) a country in which the majority of people enjoy a higher standard of living than that of the American people
    (B) a country with a higher level of employment than America
    (C) poor Americans who receive federal aid
    (D) a higher level of inflation in America than in other countries
    (E) many poor American families that are so isolated that they are not included in statistical surveys

Questions 11–12

The position that the prohibition of morally offensive works is wrong in principle is hardly tenable. There certainly are circumstances in which censorship could be desirable. If it were shown that all or most people of a certain type who saw a film thereafter committed a burglary or murder that they would not otherwise have committed, no one would deny that public exhibition of the film should be prohibited. To admit this is to admit that censorship is not wrong in principle. But to approve the principle of censorship on these grounds does not, of course, commit one to approve censorship in every form.

11. Which of the following can be inferred from the paragraph above?

    (A) No film affects any 2 individuals in the same way.
    (B) The causal connection between specific acts and exposure to specific films is not established.
    (C) We cannot anticipate the abuses to which censorship may lead.
    (D) People not exposed to morally offensive works will commit socially offensive acts.
    (E) There can be no relationship between a general principle and specific practices.

12. The paragraph questions the position that censorship is wrong in principle by

    (A) pointing out the ambiguity of a key term
    (B) rehearsing facts that are not generally known
    (C) questioning the truth of a factual generalization
    (D) exposing a logical inconsistency
    (E) presenting a hypothetical case

13. No Vikings carried watches. Some Vikings were explorers. Therefore, some explorers did not carry watches.

    Which of the following is logically most similar to the argument above?

    (A) Everyone who eats too much candy will be sick. I do not eat too much candy and will, therefore, probably avoid sickness.
    (B) All dogs are excluded from this motel, but many dogs are friendly. Therefore, some friendly animals are kept out of this motel.
    (C) People who want to avoid the pain of dental work will see the dentist twice a year. My children refuse to have their cavities filled. Therefore, my children like pain.
    (D) Some who are athletic are young people, and all young people can run. Therefore, everyone who can run is young.
    (E) Hawaii is a beautiful place. Some Hawaiians emigrate to California. Therefore, California is a beautiful place.

Excerpted from *LSAT Success 1998* © 1996 by Thomas O. White

14. Many people confuse reasons and causes. Any justification for performing an action is a reason. Anything that makes performing an action necessary is a cause—for example, a strong urge, hunger, an intense desire, social pressure, or some brain disorder. Those people who believe that the same thing may be both a reason for performing an action and its cause are clearly mistaken.

Which of the above examples of a cause that makes an action necessary best fits the description of a cause of an action rather than a justification for it?

(A) "hunger"
(B) "some brain disorder"
(C) "social pressure"
(D) "a strong urge"
(E) "an intense desire"

15. One form of reasoning holds that by eliminating all possible explanations until only one remains, that one should be accepted. Critics argue that the flaw in this form of reasoning is that one cannot know about all possible explanations.

Which of the following examples best supports this criticism?

(A) the possible causes of heart disease
(B) the possible results of rolling dice
(C) the possible family members who left the house unlocked
(D) the possible candidates running for mayor of Atlanta, Georgia
(E) the possible countries with nuclear weapons

16. Doctor: The law of genetics holds that if both parents have brown eyes, then they can have only brown-eyed children.

Patient: That is not true; my mother has blue eyes, and I have brown eyes.

The patient has misinterpreted the doctor's statement to mean that

(A) only brown-eyed people can have blue-eyed children
(B) brown-eyed people cannot have blue-eyed children
(C) people with blue eyes invariably have blue-eyed children
(D) parents with the same eye color have children with a different eye color
(E) parents with different eye colors have children with the same eye color

17. Certain similarities between prehistoric art and the art of children has led some people to the mistaken conclusion that either early humans had the mentality of children or that they were as unskilled as children. These conclusions assume which of the following?

(A) Art that is considered sophisticated today must always have been considered sophisticated.
(B) What is easy for humans today must always have been easy.
(C) The significance of art is consistent over time.
(D) Prehistoric humans painted in the same way that children now paint.
(E) Modern humans have learned from prehistoric man.

18. During the cultural revolution in China under Chairman Mao, thousands of "enemies of the republic" were killed. When Mao's critics accused him of confusing his personal enemies with enemies of the republic, he responded, "I deny the accusation, and the proof is that you are still alive."

Which of the following assumptions was Mao making?

(A) All the enemies of the republic are dead.
(B) His critics are his personal enemies.
(C) Some personal enemies are also enemies of the republic.
(D) Enemies of the republic are not personal critics.
(E) Those killed were personal enemies.

Excerpted from *LSAT Success 1998* © 1996 by Thomas O. White

19. Today, neither scientists nor the pharmaceutical companies for which they work are willing to run the risk of being wrong. In the past, these scientists were encouraged to experiment with imaginative hypotheses that had a high probability of failure. If this situation continues, the country's drug-development work will come to a standstill.

    The point of the argument above is that

    (A) scientists are too concerned about failure
    (B) scientists are not concerned about the outcome of experimentation
    (C) risk should be an issue in experimental research
    (D) scientific advances repay extensive experimentation
    (E) support for drug research is vanishing

20. In his latest book, John does some clever writing, but even he might have been encouraged to use more everyday language.

    Which of the following has a logical structure most like that of the above statement?

    (A) The fertilizer serves some valuable purposes, but the smell of it when it is used is offensive.
    (B) The latest sermon was effective as inspirational writing, but it did not offer the path to realizing the objectives it outlined.
    (C) The star's last movie contained the usual bit of impressive acting, but her director should have advised her to act more like an average person.
    (D) The chef at the resort makes wonderful desserts, but the manager should explain how to portion them more reasonably.
    (E) Cage was a brilliant composer, but only a few people are able to understand his music.

21. The end of overcrowding at colleges and universities provides them with the opportunity to improve the quality of the educational services they offer. As enrollment declines, services and campus facilities should better serve student needs.

    If true, which of the following statements most weakens the above conclusion?

    (A) The quality of educational services does not depend on the variety of services offered.
    (B) Fees paid by students are the major source of funding for educational services.
    (C) Educational services are a critical factor in a student's choice of school.
    (D) As campus facilities grow older, their maintenance becomes more expensive.
    (E) Student needs are different than they were when colleges and universities were overcrowded.

22. When pregnant laboratory rats are given caffeine equivalent to the amount a human would consume by drinking six cups of coffee per day, an increase in the incidence of birth defects results. When asked if the government would require warning labels on products containing caffeine, a spokesperson stated that it would not, because if the finding of these studies were to be refuted in the future, the government would lose credibility.

    Which of the following is most strongly suggested by the government's statement above?

    (A) A warning that applies to a small population is inappropriate.
    (B) Very few people drink as many as six cups of coffee a day.
    (C) There are doubts about the conclusive nature of studies on animals.
    (D) Studies on rats provide little data about human birth defects.
    (E) The seriousness of birth defects involving caffeine is not clear.

Excerpted from *LSAT Success 1998* © 1996 by Thomas O. White

23. The Mercers are avid sailors. They have a child who will never be able to accompany them sailing because he is afraid of water.

   Upon which of the following assumptions does the conclusion above depend?

   (A) The Mercers will not take their child sailing.
   (B) Avid sailors are not afraid of water.
   (C) The Mercer's child will never want to sail.
   (D) Sailors cannot be afraid of water.
   (E) The Mercer's child may overcome his fear of water.

24. Sam: Olive oil can help prevent heart attacks, according to physicians.

   Betty: It cannot. My mother cooked with olive oil her entire life, and she died of a heart attack last year.

   Betty's statement can best be countered by pointing out that

   (A) Betty's mother was an exception
   (B) other factors could have nullified the influence of the olive oil
   (C) Betty does not know that her mother always cooked with olive oil
   (D) It has never been scientifically proven that olive oil causes heart attacks
   (E) Betty's mother might have used olive oil irregularly

Excerpted from *LSAT Success 1998* © 1996 by Thomas O. White

| SECTION **3** | TIME—35 MINUTES | 24 QUESTIONS |

Questions 1-6

A restaurant franchise has several locations in Ames County that are designated by the letters A, B, C, D, etc. The restaurants have the following relationships to the Central Office and one another:

A is northwest of the Central Office.
B is northeast of the Central Office.
C is northeast of the Central Office, but C is located farther east than B.
D is south (but not necessarily due south) of the Central Office.
E is southwest of the Central Office.
A is farther north than C and farther west than D.
E is farther west than A.
G is southeast of the Central Office and farther east than B.

1. If a delivery truck travels in a straight line from E to the Central Office and continues in exactly the same direction, it could pass directly by which of the following?

   (A) the northwest corner of D
   (B) the southeast corner of G
   (C) the northwest corner of A
   (D) the west side of A
   (E) the east side of G

2. If F is located due north of the Central Office, which of the following could be true?

   (A) F is located due north of G.
   (B) F is located west of E.
   (C) F is located east of B.
   (D) F is located due west of C.
   (E) F is located due north of E.

3. A restaurant located precisely midway between C and G must be

   (A) farther east than B
   (B) north of the Central Office
   (C) farther south than B
   (D) farther south than A
   (E) south of the Central Office

4. Which of the following CANNOT be the location of D?

   (A) southwest of A
   (B) northeast of C
   (C) southeast of E
   (D) southeast of G
   (E) northwest of G

5. Which of the following CANNOT be true?

   (A) B is precisely midway between E and G.
   (B) B is precisely midway between C and D.
   (C) B is precisely midway between C and E.
   (D) G is precisely midway between C and E.
   (E) D is precisely midway between C and E.

6. If G is southeast of D, and D is farther east than B, which of the following must be true?

   (A) The Central Office is closer to D than to G.
   (B) E is closer to D than to G.
   (C) E is closer to G than to D.
   (D) E is closer to the Central Office than to G.
   (E) C is closer to D than to G.

Questions 7–12

Six college officers—H, I, J, K, L, and M—are seated at equal distances around a circular table according to a list of personal preferences submitted by each officer.

The secretary and the treasurer have no preference as to where they sit.
The president must be seated directly opposite the vice president.
The 2 trustees may not sit together.
H must sit next to either J or K.

While it is unclear who occupies which office, M is neither the president nor a trustee.
The vice president is either L or J.
Either H or I or both are trustees.

7. If, in satisfying all of the above conditions, the officers are seated around the table in the order K, I, J, H, L, and M, all of the following may be true EXCEPT

   (A) J is the vice president
   (B) H is a trustee
   (C) I is the president
   (D) K is the treasurer
   (E) M is the secretary

8. If H is seated between K and L, and M is seated opposite H, what is a complete and accurate listing of every officer who could be sitting next to M?

   (A) president, vice president
   (B) president, vice president, secretary
   (C) president, vice president, trustee, secretary, treasurer
   (D) trustee, secretary, treasurer
   (E) vice president, trustee, secretary, treasurer

9. If J, the secretary, must sit across from one of the trustees, how might the officers be arranged clockwise in order to satisfy all conditions?

   (A) L, M, I, K, J, H
   (B) K, M, J, L, H, I
   (C) J, K, L, H, M, I
   (D) K, I, H, J, M, L
   (E) I, J, K, M, H, L

10. If the president has M to her right and H to her left, which is NOT an acceptable arrangement for the other three officers, assuming that their order starts with H and goes around the table clockwise?

    (A) J, K, L
    (B) I, J, L
    (C) K, J, I
    (D) K, L, I
    (E) L, J, K

11. If the officers are seated around the table clockwise in the order J, H, I, K, M, and L, and I is the treasurer, who are the 2 trustees?

    (A) I and K
    (B) H and J
    (C) H and K
    (D) I and J
    (E) H and L

12. If the officers are seated around the table clockwise in the order H, J, K, L, M, and I, all of the following must be true EXCEPT

    (A) M is the secretary
    (B) H is not the treasurer
    (C) J is not the vice president
    (D) I is a trustee
    (E) either J or K is a trustee

Questions 13–18

Holly Hauling has six vehicles. The Kenworth, Mack, and White are trucks; the Chevrolet, Dodge, and Ford are vans.

Holly always fuels and washes the trucks before the vans.
Within the respective groups, Holly fuels the vehicles that hold comparatively more fuel before she fuels those that hold comparatively less.
Holly washes the vehicles in their respective groups in the opposite order of their fueling.

The White holds more fuel than the Chevrolet, and no vehicle holds both more than the Chevrolet and less than the White.
The Dodge holds more than the Mack, and no vehicle holds both less than the Dodge and more than the Mack.
Only the Ford and the Kenworth hold the same amount of fuel.

13. If the Kenworth is fueled first and the White third, which of the following must be true?

    (A) The Ford is fueled fifth.
    (B) The Ford is fueled last.
    (C) The Chevrolet is fueled fifth.
    (D) The Chevrolet is fueled last.
    (E) The Dodge is fueled fourth.

Excerpted from *LSAT Success 1998* © 1996 by Thomas O. White

14. If the White is washed first, which of the following could NOT be possible?

    (A) The Kenworth is fueled before the White.
    (B) The Mack is fueled before the Kenworth.
    (C) The Chevrolet is fueled before the Ford.
    (D) The Dodge is fueled after the Ford.
    (E) The Ford is fueled before the Chevrolet.

15. If the Mack is fueled first and the White third, which of the following must be true?

    (A) The Ford is washed first.
    (B) The Dodge is washed second.
    (C) The Kenworth is washed second.
    (D) The White is washed third.
    (E) The Chevrolet is washed third.

16. Which of the following is NOT a possible order in which the vehicles are washed?

    (A) Kenworth, White, Mack, Ford, Chevrolet, Dodge
    (B) Mack, Kenworth, White, Dodge, Ford, Chevrolet
    (C) Mack, White, Kenworth, Dodge, Chevrolet, Ford
    (D) White, Kenworth, Mack, Chevrolet, Ford, Dodge
    (E) White, Mack, Kenworth, Ford, Dodge, Chevrolet

17. Suppose Holly does not wash the trucks first but alternates by washing a van and then a truck. If the Mack is fueled first, it would NOT be possible for which pair of vehicles to be washed sequentially?

    (A) the Kenworth immediately before the Chevrolet
    (B) the Chevrolet immediately before the White
    (C) the White immediately before the Ford
    (D) the Dodge immediately before the Mack
    (E) the Ford immediately before the Dodge

18. If Holly fuels the trucks after the vans on a day the White is washed second and the Dodge is washed fourth, the order of fueling must be

    (A) Chevrolet, Dodge, Ford, White, Mack, Kenworth
    (B) Chevrolet, Ford, Dodge, White, Kenworth, Mack
    (C) Ford, Chevrolet, Dodge, Kenworth, White, Mack
    (D) Ford, Dodge, Chevrolet, Kenworth, Mack, White
    (E) Dodge, Chevrolet, Ford, Mack, White, Kenworth

Questions 19–24

There are six distinct building groups in a large office complex. From smallest to largest, respectively, the groups are constructed of aluminum, brick, concrete, glass, stone, and wood. The building groups are designated Groups 1 through 6.

Group 1, which is not stone, is larger than Group 3.
Group 2 is larger than Group 5 and Group 6.
Group 2 is smaller than Group 4.
Group 3 is larger than Group 6.

19. What material must Group 6 be made of if Group 3 is smaller than Group 5?

    (A) aluminum
    (B) brick
    (C) concrete
    (D) glass
    (E) stone

20. From smallest to largest, which of the following is a possible arrangement of the groups?

    (A) 5, 3, 6, 1, 2, 4
    (B) 6, 3, 1, 5, 2, 4
    (C) 6, 3, 1, 2, 5, 4
    (D) 6, 3, 5, 2, 1, 4
    (E) 6, 5, 3, 2, 1, 4

21. If Group 1 is concrete, Group 3 must be which of the following?

    (A) aluminum
    (B) brick
    (C) glass
    (D) stone
    (E) wood

Excerpted from *LSAT Success 1998* © 1996 by Thomas O. White

22. Which of the following CANNOT be a possible arrangement of the groups from smallest to largest?

(A) 5, 6, 3, 1, 2, 4
(B) 5, 6, 3, 2, 4, 1
(C) 6, 5, 2, 4, 3, 1
(D) 6, 5, 3, 1, 2, 4
(E) 6, 5, 4, 3, 2, 1

23. If Group 5 is glass, Group 2 could be made of which of the following materials?

(A) concrete
(B) stone
(C) wood
(D) brick
(E) aluminum

24. If Group 4 is stone, Group 1 could be made of which of the following materials?

(A) concrete
(B) glass
(C) brick
(D) aluminum
(E) wood

Excerpted from *LSAT Success 1998* © 1996 by Thomas O. White

<table>
<tr><td>SECTION **4**</td><td>TIME—35 MINUTES</td><td>28 QUESTIONS</td></tr>
</table>

The questions in this section are based on what is stated or implied in the passage. Select the best answer to each question, and mark the corresponding space on the answer sheet.

Line A. L. Macfie makes the distinction between what he calls the Scottish method, characteristic of Adam Smith's approach to problems of social policy, and the scientific
5 or analytical method, which is more familiar to modern social scientists. In the former, the center of attention lay in the society as observed rather than in the idealized version of the society considered as an
10 abstraction. Smith did have an underlying model or paradigm for social interaction; he could scarcely have discussed reforms without one. But his interest was in making the existing social structure "work better,"
15 in terms of the norms that he laid down, rather than in evaluating the possible limitations of the structure as it might work ideally if organized on specific principles.

    Frank Knight suggested that critics of
20 the free-enterprise system are seldom clear as to whether they object to the system because it does not work in accordance with its idealized principles or because it does, in fact, work in some approximation
25 to these principles. There is no such uncertainty with respect to Adam Smith. He was critical of the economic order of his time because it did not work in accordance with the principles of natural liberty. He
30 was not, and need not have been, overly concerned with some ultimate evaluation of an idealized structure.

    Smith's methodology has been turned on its head by many modern scientists. The
35 post-Pigovian theory of welfare economics has largely, if not entirely, consisted of a search for conceptual flaws in the working of an idealized competitive economic order, conceived independently of the flawed and
40 imperfect order that may be observed to exist. Partial correctives are offered in both the theory of the second-best and in the still-emerging theory of public choice, but the perfect-competition paradigm continues
45 to dominate applied economic policy discussions.

    This methodological distinction is important in our examination of Smith's conception of justice. In one sense, John
50 Rawls's efforts in defining and delineating "a theory of justice" are akin to those of the neoclassical economists who first described the idealized competitive economy. By contrast, Adam Smith saw no
55 need for defining in great detail the idealized operation of a market system and for evaluating this system in terms of strict efficiency criteria. Similarly, he would have seen no need for elaborating in detail a
60 complete "theory of justice" for defining those principles that must be operative in a society that would be adjudged to be "just." In comparing Smith with Rawls, therefore, we must somehow bridge the
65 contrasting methodologies. We can make an attempt to infer from Smith's applied discussion of real problems what his idealized principles of justice might have embodied. Or we can infer from John
70 Rawls's treatment of idealized principles what his particular application of these might be in an institutional context.

1. Which of the following best describes the passage's objective?

  (A) distinguishing between the Scottish and Pigovian theories of justice

  (B) supporting Adam Smith's concept of justice

  (C) comparing Smith's and Rawls's views of a just society

  (D) supporting John Rawls's theory of justice

  (E) analyzing the contrasting methodologies of Smith and Rawls

Excerpted from *LSAT Success 1998* © 1996 by Thomas O. White

2. According to the passage, all of the following are methods used to explain social policy EXCEPT

   (A) the Scottish method
   (B) the theory of welfare economics
   (C) the perfect-competition paradigm
   (D) the scientific method
   (E) the principles of natural liberty

3. According to the passage, John Rawls's "theory of justice" is similar to which of the following?

   (A) the description of the free-enterprise system
   (B) the description of the efficiency of the market system
   (C) the description of the idealized structure of natural liberty
   (D) the description of the idealized competitive economy
   (E) the description of the society considered as an abstraction

4. It can be inferred from the passage that Adam Smith was

   (A) not interested in achieving a just society
   (B) concerned with improving the operation of society
   (C) not worried about efficiency in the operation of society
   (D) indifferent to the economic operation of society
   (E) anxious to achieve an idealized operation of society

5. The author of the passage is presenting which of the following?

   (A) a recitation of methods of approaching social problems
   (B) an analysis of various economic systems
   (C) a comparison of the theories of Knight, Rawls, and Smith
   (D) an exposition of various theories of justice
   (E) an argument supporting idealized versions of social order

6. Which of the following is most likely to be the next sentence of the passage?

   (A) Since Smith planned a book on jurisprudence, there is a reason to develop his theory of justice.
   (B) The practical application of theories of what is "just" is guided by principles of natural justice.
   (C) In what follows, both of these routes will be explored.
   (D) Neither Rawls nor Smith was successful in dealing with real problems.
   (E) Rawls's "theory of justice" is difficult to apply to questions of natural liberty.

7. The author's purpose in finding a bridge between the Rawls and Smith methodologies (lines 63–65) is to

   (A) facilitate understanding of their philosophies
   (B) identify principles that each feels are just
   (C) explore their views toward an idealized market system
   (D) permit comparison of their concepts of justice
   (E) support their attempts to reform society

Excerpted from *LSAT Success 1998* © 1996 by Thomas O. White

Line Many, perhaps most, well-disposed,
practical people would, if they had to
designate a philosophy that comes closest
to expressing their unstated principles, pick
5 utilitarianism. The philosophy that pro-
claims as its sovereign criterion the
procuring of the greatest good for the
greatest number has indeed served as a
powerful engine of legal reform and
10 rationalization. And it is a crucial feature of
utilitarianism that it is consequences that
count. Now it is interesting that some
judgments that are actually made in the law
and elsewhere do not appear to accord
15 with this thoroughgoing consequentialism.
For instance, both in law and morals there
are many instances of a distinction being
made between direct and indirect inten-
tion—i.e., the distinction between, on the
20 one hand, the doing of evil as an end in
itself or, on the other hand, bringing about
the same evil result as a consequence of
one's direct ends or means. So also the
distinction is drawn between the conse-
25 quences that we bring about by our actions
and consequences that come about through
our failures to act. Also, when bad consequences ensue from our actions and what
was done was in the exercise of a right or
30 privilege, the law is less likely to lay those
bad consequences at our doorstep. And,
finally, if the only way to prevent some
great harm would be by inflicting a lesser
harm on ourselves or on others, then too
35 the law is inclined to absolve us of responsibility for that avoidable greater harm. It is
as if the net value of the consequences
were not crucial, at least where net benefit
is procured by the intentional infliction of
40 harm.

Not only are these distinctions drawn
in some moral systems, but there are
numerous places in the law where they are
made regularly. Since in utilitarianism and
45 consequentialism in general the ultimate
questions must always be whether and to
what extent the valued end-state (be it
happiness or possession of true knowledge)
is obtained at a particular moment, it is
50 inevitable that the judgments on the human
agencies that may affect this end-state must
be wholly instrumental: Human actions can
be judged only by their tendency to
produce the relevant end-states.

55 Indeed, it may well be that even the
point and contents of normative judgments—whether legal or moral—are
concerned not just with particular end-
states of the world but also with how
60 end-states are brought about. These kinds
of substantive judgments take the form:
There are some things one should just
never do—kill an innocent person, falsely
accuse a defendant in a criminal proceed-
65 ing, engage in sex for pay. These are to be
contrasted to judgments that this or that is
an unfortunate, perhaps terrible, result that
(other things being equal) one would want
to avoid. The former are—very generally—
70 judgments of right and wrong. It is wrong
to do this or that, even if the balance of
advantages favors it; a person is right to do
some particular thing (help a friend, protect
his client's interests) even though more
good will come if he does not.

8. The author's point in the passage is
primarily that

(A) law and utilitarianism are not always
compatible
(B) utilitarianism is the operating philosophy of most people
(C) consequentialism is the basis for legal
reform
(D) direct and indirect intentions lead to
different end-states
(E) judgments about human actions can
be made only by the resulting end-
states

9. Which of the following is NOT a feature of
utilitarianism?

(A) Results are considered important.
(B) Consequences are considered important.
(C) The valued end-state is considered
important.
(D) The means of achieving results are
considered important.
(E) The net value of consequences is
considered important.

Excerpted from *LSAT Success 1998* © 1996 by Thomas O. White

10. Which of the following is an example of judgments that may conflict with the utilitarian philosophy?

    (A) It is legally acceptable to base judgements on the net consequences of acts.
    (B) It is legally acceptable to act for the greatest good to the greatest number.
    (C) It is legally acceptable for human actions that produce more harm than good to be punished.
    (D) It is legally acceptable for bad consequences to flow from the exercise of an individual's right or privilege.
    (E) It is not legally acceptable to avoid a small harm to oneself, even if the result is a great harm to another.

11. The point of the last paragraph is to

    (A) explain the differences between utilitarianism and consequentialism
    (B) contrast judgments of right and wrong with other types of judgments
    (C) discuss the role of intention in both law and words
    (D) distinguish between the results of actions and inaction
    (E) develop a rationale upon which to judge human actions

12. It can be inferred from the passage that the author is concerned with which of the following?

    (A) legal reform
    (B) false accusations
    (C) results of human inaction
    (D) means used to produce results
    (E) aspirations producing human action

13. The passage suggests that utilitarianism

    (A) explains all legal and moral judgments
    (B) explains only judgments of right and wrong
    (C) explains some judgments in law and morals
    (D) explains judgments of direct and indirect intentions
    (E) explains judgments of right and privilege

14. The author's attitude about utilitarianism as a philosophy is best described as

    (A) somewhat critical
    (B) generally supportive
    (C) mostly accepting
    (D) totally convinced
    (E) nearly convinced

Excerpted from *LSAT Success 1998* © 1996 by Thomas O. White

Line Although lawyers frequently reason in
terms of models, they tend to reason, in
Henry Steiner's terms, in *prose* models. I
think there are some real advantages of the
5   symbolic-logic type of reasoning in the law.
Although lawyers pride themselves on their
method of argumentation and on being
logicians, actually a lot of their arguments
are very flabby. One way of teasing them is
10 to say, "Well, let's write this problem down
in formal terms and abstract systems; let's
agree on a rigorous abstract definition of
this concept or behavioral principle and
derive its logical implications." And then
15 you allege that two situations they consider
as absolutely distinct are really formally
identical. That is what the model says. And
if they are not formally identical, what
really is the distinction? How has the model
20 been misspecified? You ask them whether
they may be making a distinction without a
difference.
    I think that the benefit of formal logic
is that it sets out very nakedly, with all of
25 its warts and pimples exposed, whatever
difficulties there are in the argumentation.
By using prose, a lot of that is swept under
the carpet. Lawyers invoke the forces of
"equity" and "fairness" on both sides of
30 precisely the same set of facts. Two
arguments produce equity and fairness
"clearly or obviously," as they put it, while
pointing in different directions.
    Formal models can be built assuming
35 that all people act in accord with the
Kantian categorical imperative—or pick any
principle you want. The desirable thing is
to write it down, to define your terms as
well as you can, say what you mean, and
40 then argue about it.
    Those of us who have been making
models for a long time realize that all
models are bad, but some models are worse
than others. Part of the seduction of
45 mathematical models is that they look
much more rigorous than they are. They
are always abstractions; there is always
something wrong with them, something left
out of consideration. But I think that this is
50 no less true in the physical sciences, where
the models are supposed to be very good.
My chemist friends tell me that the
fundamental laws of chemistry are contra-
dicted every day in the laboratory. In the

55 last analysis, I think the way one ought to
look at this is as a method of argumentation. I feel that for a lot of uses in the law,
it will demonstrate to you problems you did
not think existed, inconsistencies, and
60 incidences of illogic. Although we are never
going to get all of the answers from formal
models, we would be foolish not to take
them for what they are worth.
    And if the Landes and Posner thesis
65 stimulated this argument, that is precisely
what "writing it down" is supposed to
accomplish.

15. The passage can best be summarized as

   (A) an analysis of law as a social science
   (B) a comparison of formal and flabby
       models
   (C) an argument for the use of formal
       models by lawyers
   (D) a criticism of the method of argumen-
       tation of lawyers
   (E) a challenge to the value of models in
       the sciences

16. According to the passage, which of the
    following applies to both prose models and
    formal models?

   (A) expose all imperfections
   (B) require precise definition of terms
   (C) appear to be more rigorous than they
       are
   (D) not demonstrably useful in the law
   (E) a method of argumentation

17. The author contends that all of the follow-
    ing are benefits of using formal models
    EXCEPT

   (A) determining that an argument is
       making a distinction without a
       difference
   (B) locating something left out of consid-
       eration
   (C) demonstrating inconsistencies in an
       argument
   (D) setting out difficulties with the form of
       argumentation
   (E) assisting in the derivation of the
       logical implications of an argument

Excerpted from *LSAT Success 1998* © 1996 by Thomas O. White

18. The author defines a "flabby" argument (line 9) as one that

    (A) is not internally contradicted
    (B) is presented in prose
    (C) is too abstract
    (D) is not logically rigorous
    (E) is formally identical to another

19. According to the passage, the primary purpose of "writing it down" is to

    (A) avoid contradictions in arguments
    (B) pick the principle for the model
    (C) provide the basis for argumentation
    (D) determine the worth of an argument
    (E) identify distinctions without differences

20. The passage indicates that models are used as all of the following EXCEPT

    (A) as a method of argumentation
    (B) as a source of answers to problems
    (C) as a form of reasoning used by lawyers
    (D) as a method to identify problems with logic
    (E) as a technique to ensure equity

21. Which of the following, if true, most weakens the author's argument about formal models?

    (A) Abstract symbols are the same as words.
    (B) Behavioral principles are hard to reduce to abstract symbols.
    (C) Models are regularly contradicted by facts.
    (D) Formal models are as illogical as prose models.
    (E) Prose models are routinely used by scientists.

22. Which of the following is implied by the author of the passage?

    (A) Symbols are inefficient expressions of behavioral principles.
    (B) A lawyer should not use an argument on both sides of a set of facts.
    (C) Prose is not a useful form of argumentation.
    (D) Omissions are a problem with formal models.
    (E) Mathematical inconsistencies are a problem with formal models.

Excerpted from *LSAT Success 1998* © 1996 by Thomas O. White

Line Applying communications theory to legal
discourse has foundered on a lack of clear
conception of what the theory means in
the context of law and can tell attorneys
5   about the legal process. Communications
theory is not a unified body of thought. It
has three quite distinct branches. The first,
"syntactics," is concerned with the logical
arrangement, transmission, and receipt of
10   signals or signs. The second is "semantics,"
which is concerned with the meaning of
signals to people. The third is "pragmatics," which is the study of the impact of
signal transmission on human behavior.

15   The key concepts of syntactics are
"information," "redundancy," and "feedback," of which the first two are best
discussed together. For the telegraphic
engineer, information is the content of the
20   signal that could not have been predicted
by the receiver; it is a probability concept.
The more probable the transmission of a
given sign, the less information its actual
transmission conveys. "Redundancy" is the
25   opposite of information. It is the introduction of repetition or pattern into the
message. If the telegrapher sends each
message twice, his second sending is
redundant and contains less information
30   than his first.

            The ideal transmission, then, in terms
of pure "information," would contain no
repetition and no pattern. The engineer
finds it wise, however, to introduce
35   redundancy at the cost of reducing the
information content of the message,
because otherwise, any loss of information
due to malfunctions in the transmission
system would be undetectable and irreme-
40   diable. It is only when we can predict, at
least partially, what message we are going
to receive that we can spot an erroneous
transmission or substitution in the message
and call for its correction. The ideal
45   message, then, will contain the highest
proportion of information and the lowest
proportion of redundancy necessary to
identify and correct errors in transmission.

            Thus it will be seen that redundancy
50   and information, in syntactic terms, are
reciprocals of each other. But the situation
is more complicated when we consider the
semantic dimension of communication, for
both information and redundancy convey

55   meaning. And the line is even more blurred
when we consider the pragmatics of
communication. Weakland has said, "There
is no redundancy," his point being, of
course, that repetitions and patterns in
60   messages do have significance to participants in the communication process. Such
redundancies carry a freight of meaning,
knowledge, and stimuli to the receiver and
in this important sense are not redundant.

65   In the law, the strongest argument
that an attorney can make is that the
current case is "on all fours" with many
previous cases, all of which were decided
by repeatedly applying the same legal
70   principle. So it is that, in terms of communications theory, the rules of legal discourse
seem to require attorneys to suppress as
much information and transmit as much
redundancy as possible.

23. The passage can best be characterized as

(A) an explanation of the principles of
communications theory
(B) a description of conflict between
information and redundancy
(C) an interpretation of syntactics applied
to aspects of legal discourse
(D) an exposition of redundancy
(E) a review of the branches of thought in
communications theory

24. According to the passage, which of the
following describes an ideal transmission in
terms of pure information?

(A) A, 2, #, +, s, ?, c, p, %, $
(B) A, C, A, E, A, G, A, I, A, K
(C) 1, 2, 3, 4, 5, 6, 5, 4, 3, 2, 1
(D) @, %, &, @, %, &, @, %, &
(E) 8, 1, 9, 1, 7, 1, 6, 1, 5, 1, 4, 1

Excerpted from *LSAT Success 1998* © 1996 by Thomas O. White

25. According to the passage, which of the following is an unambiguous example of syntactic redundancy?

    (A) the transmission of the dash in dot-dot-dash
    (B) the transmission of the dash in dot-dot-dash when two dots are always followed by a dash
    (C) the transmission of a dot in dot-dot-dash
    (D) the transmission of a dot when two dashes are never followed by a dot
    (E) the transmission of the dash in dot-dot-dash when two dots are never followed by a dash

26. In the context of the passage, "on all fours" (line 67) most likely refers to

    (A) a type of information in terms of communications theory
    (B) a legal principle that is applied to many different cases
    (C) the most recent example in a series of cases
    (D) a type of argument lawyers use to distinguish one case from another
    (E) a case that is exactly the same as previous cases

27. According to the passage, which of the following is NOT true?

    (A) Patterns in messages are significant to communicating.
    (B) Legal discourse requires maximum redundancy.
    (C) Information in a message can be predicted by a telegraphic engineer.
    (D) Redundancy in a message reduces the information transmitted.
    (E) Information is the opposite of redundancy.

28. Which of the following best reflects the author's view about the application of communications theory to legal discourse?

    (A) Syntactics tell lawyers very little about the legal process.
    (B) Redundancy accounts for the difference between strong and weak legal arguments.
    (C) Engineering, not law, has been the profession making use of communications theory.
    (D) Communications theory is too difficult for lawyers to understand clearly.
    (E) Legal discourse is dominated by the attempt to present pure information.

Excerpted from *LSAT Success 1998* © 1996 by Thomas O. White

| **SECTION 5** | TIME—35 MINUTES | 24 QUESTIONS |

Evaluate the reasoning contained in the brief statements, and select the best answer. Do not make implausible, superfluous, or incompatible assumptions. Select the best answer to each question, and mark the corresponding space on the answer sheet.

1. There are no great writers in Largo because freedom of expression does not exist there.

   The conclusion above depends upon which of the following assumptions?

   (A) In the absence of freedom of expression, great writers do not develop.
   (B) If there is freedom of expression, there will be many great writers.
   (C) Where there is no freedom of expression, great writers turn to politics.
   (D) Great writers leave places that do not have freedom of expression.
   (E) Great writers must express themselves freely.

2. Archaeologists have determined that the bison was the primary source of meat for the cave dwellers, but their caves also contained the bones of birds, snakes, and fish, which indicates that they also liked to eat these animals.

   Which of the following, if true, would weaken the conclusion reached in the statement above?

   (A) Drawings of snakes and fish were made by cave dwellers.
   (B) Cave dwellers were not always able to eat what they liked.
   (C) Birds, rather than cave dwellers, may have brought snakes and fish to the caves to eat.
   (D) Cave dwellers ate grains and berries.
   (E) The bones of birds, snakes, and fish found in the caves were from small animals.

3. Some psychologists believe that humans, like porpoises, are benevolent creatures by nature. These psychologists assume that human nature is essentially disposed to benevolent conduct. To account for social evils, psychologists have to blame institutions that corrupt the native disposition of humans.

   The psychologists' argument described above would be most strengthened if it were to explain how

   (A) a way of life consistent with benevolent ideals is possible in the modern world
   (B) people can be persuaded to abandon technology, urbanization, and mass production
   (C) benevolent conduct can result from humans living in accordance with their own natural dispositions
   (D) benevolent dispositions give rise to evil institutions
   (E) corrupt institutions can be eliminated or reformed

4. Whenever the sky is cloudy and rain is falling, Bob wears his slicker. Whenever the sky is cloudy and rain is not falling, Bob ties his slicker around his waist. Sometimes rain falls when the sky is not cloudy.

   If the statements above are true, and it is true that Bob is not wearing his slicker, which of the following must also be true?

   (A) Bob has tied his slicker around his waist.
   (B) The sky is not overcast.
   (C) The sky is not cloudy, and rain is not falling.
   (D) The sky is cloudy, and/or rain is not falling.
   (E) The sky is not cloudy, and/or rain is not falling.

Excerpted from *LSAT Success 1998* © 1996 by Thomas O. White

5. Only excellent musicians can be professors at Juilliard. No insensitive people are great lovers of poetry. No one who is not sensitive can be a lover. There are no excellent musicians who are not great lovers of poetry. Therefore, all Juilliard professors are lovers.

   Which of the following inferences leading to the conclusion above is NOT valid?

   (A) All Juilliard professors are excellent musicians.
   (B) Juilliard professors are sensitive people.
   (C) Sensitive people are lovers.
   (D) Great lovers of poetry are sensitive people.
   (E) Excellent musicians are great lovers of poetry.

6. Since plaznium evaporates in air, and this cube did not evaporate when it was exposed to air, it is not plaznium.

   Which of the following is most like the argument above?

   (A) Since no cats have hooves, and Fifi is a cat, Fifi does not have hooves.
   (B) Since owls feed only at night, the bird feeding in daylight is not an owl.
   (C) Since this box is made of brass, and boxes not made of brass are better than brass boxes, this brass box is not as good as a box not made of brass.
   (D) Since chicks are never furry, and this animal is not furry, it is not a chick.
   (E) Since every Canarbik dog is black or white, and Fido is a Canarbik, Fido cannot be gray.

7. Some ocean-liner captains are alcoholics. Ocean-liner captains who are alcoholics are dangerous. Every captain of an ocean liner is responsible for the care of the passengers.

   The above leads to which of the following conclusions?

   (A) All ocean-liner passengers are in the care of an alcoholic.
   (B) Some ocean-liner passengers are dangerous when they drink.
   (C) Some ocean-liner passengers are in the care of a dangerous person.
   (D) All ocean-liner captains are dangerous when they drink.

   (E) Some ocean-liner captains are dangerous when they drink.

8. Because coal is a nonrenewable resource, states that produce coal will experience problems that will never be faced by the lumber-processing industry.

   Which of the following, if true, most weakens this argument?

   (A) The resources required to log forests cannot be replenished.
   (B) States with economies dominated by coal are trying to develop forest products.
   (C) Lumber-producing states must secure much of the food they require from other states.
   (D) Renewable resources are a significant part of the economies of coal-producing states.
   (E) Coal-producing states depend on money from coal sales to buy lumber.

9. A criminal justice study has found that 82 percent of people presented with eyewitness testimony regarding a crime were willing to convict the accused. However, only 58 percent of the same people were willing to convict the accused when presented with lie-detector, fingerprint, and handwriting evidence from experts.

   Which of the following conclusions is most reasonably supported by the above study results?

   (A) Most crimes do not involve eyewitness and expert testimony.
   (B) An accused can only be convicted by evidence that eliminates all reasonable doubt.
   (C) Most people do not understand expert evidence.
   (D) Prosecutors can ensure conviction by presenting both eyewitness and expert testimony.
   (E) Jurors think eyewitness testimony leaves less room for doubt than does expert testimony.

Excerpted from *LSAT Success 1998* © 1996 by Thomas O. White

10. By 1997, the number of 18-year-olds will be dramatically lower than it was in 1961, when population growth in the United States reached its highest point. This decline in the number of potential college students will result in large enrollment decreases at colleges in the United States.

   If true, which of the following would most weaken the conclusion of the above argument?

   (A) Colleges prospered in the 1950s with lower enrollments than there are today.
   (B) By 1997, there will be more colleges than there are today.
   (C) Colleges will compete more aggressively for students when the number of 18-year-olds declines sharply.
   (D) In the future, more older students will enter college than ever before.
   (E) College enrollments in the 1960s were inflated by students avoiding the draft.

11. The contemporary film is a form of mass entertainment rather than an important art form. It fascinates, amuses, and distracts but fails to elevate the human spirit and deepen awareness. Film can be ignored if one is looking for art rather than escape.

   Which of the following is NOT implied by the argument above?

   (A) When looking for art, film can be ignored.
   (B) Contemporary film is not an important art form.
   (C) Film is an amusement.
   (D) In the past, film was an important art form.
   (E) Film is a form of escape.

Questions 12–13

Critics who claim that the sale of U.S. military equipment to other countries is destabilizing and leads to war take a narrow view of history. War occurs when one country gains a military advantage over another. By selling arms, the United States can ensure that the military balance among countries is maintained and war avoided.

12. The above argument depends on which of the following assumptions?

   (A) Arms sales by the United States do not lead to wars between countries.
   (B) Critics do not understand military history.
   (C) Countries can accurately determine one another's military strength.
   (D) Arms imbalances stimulate conflict between countries.
   (E) Critics misunderstand the principle of military balance between countries.

13. Which of the following, if true, most weakens the above argument?

   (A) Military equipment is usually used to intimidate rather than to actually conduct war.
   (B) A country's military strength depends on military equipment rather than on the expertise of military commanders.
   (C) The sale and delivery of military equipment is usually known only by the two countries involved.
   (D) The military advantages of all countries are well known by the United States.
   (E) Military equipment sold by the United States to other countries is less sophisticated than the equipment it produces for itself.

14. A study by the motor-vehicle bureau shows that only 3 percent of all cars fail the annual safety inspection because of defective lights. Consequently, the bureau has decided to discontinue inspecting lights, because the benefit is not worth the expense involved.

   Which of the following, if true, is the greatest weakness in the decision of the bureau?

   (A) Studies in other states show that a larger percentage of cars have defective lights.
   (B) Cars with defective lights often have safety problems that are not part of the inspection.
   (C) Lights are maintained in good working order because of the inspection requirement.
   (D) Most cars fail inspection for more than one defect.
   (E) Inspecting for defective lights costs less than 2 percent of the annual budget of the motor-vehicle bureau.

Excerpted from *LSAT Success 1998* © 1996 by Thomas O. White

Questions 15–16

The public's right to know is an inadequate justification for exposing people's private lives to public scrutiny. Only when the public welfare is involved does the public have a right to know information about a person's private life.

15. Which of the following, if true, most weakens the position taken in the above argument?

    (A) The public seldom knows which activities promote its welfare.
    (B) The public seldom wants much of the information exposed to it.
    (C) It is seldom possible to discover the most intimate details of someone's personal life.
    (D) The public seldom understands the implications of the information exposed to it.
    (E) It is seldom possible to determine which information involves the public welfare.

16. Which of the following best expresses the underlying point of the above argument?

    (A) Public welfare is the greatest good.
    (B) A justification is not a reason.
    (C) Personal privacy is an important right.
    (D) The common good is an insufficient justification.
    (E) Public rights supersede individual privacy.

17. A study shows that there is a strong positive relationship between voting and political involvement.

    Which of the following CANNOT be inferred from this finding?

    (A) Political involvement and voting appear to be interrelated.
    (B) People who are not involved in politics are less likely to vote than those who are involved.
    (C) After people become involved in politics, they vote more frequently than before.
    (D) People who vote are more likely to be involved in politics.
    (E) Voting is a form of political involvement.

Questions 18–19

A survey of students concludes that some students prefer physics to history; all students prefer history to geometry; no students prefer history to economics; and all students prefer biology to history.

18. Based on the survey results, which of the following must represent students' preferences?

    (A) Some students prefer geometry to physics.
    (B) Some students prefer physics to geometry.
    (C) Some students prefer biology to economics.
    (D) Some students prefer geometry to economics.
    (E) Some students prefer physics to economics.

19. Based on the survey results, which of the following CANNOT represent students' preferences?

    (A) Some students prefer geometry to physics.
    (B) Some students prefer physics to geometry.
    (C) Some students prefer biology to economics.
    (D) Some students prefer economics to biology.
    (E) Some students prefer physics to economics.

20. Voters who complain about a trusted politician's betrayal remind me of the tale of the man who nursed a starving snake back to health. Afterward, the snake bit the man, who then complained about the snake's ingratitude. The snake responded to the complaint by saying, "You knew I was a snake when you saved me."

    Which of the following can be derived from the argument above?

    (A) Don't cut off your nose to spite your face.
    (B) Things are not always what they seem.
    (C) Chickens always come home to roost.
    (D) Nature cannot be changed.
    (E) Take the bitter with the sweet.

Excerpted from *LSAT Success 1998* © 1996 by Thomas O. White

21. Representatives of dairy producers say that government subsidies are needed to ensure that milk processors produce sufficient amounts for children. If there are no milk-price subsidies, processors will attempt to meet the demand for cheese and butter before producing milk.

Which of the following can be inferred from the above argument?

(A) The demand for milk is volatile, often leading to underproduction and shortages.

(B) Processors have produced sufficient milk in the past because they understood the needs of hungry children.

(C) Cheese and butter produce greater profits for processors than does milk.

(D) Representatives of dairies have a lobby that is powerful enough to ensure the passage of favorable subsidies.

(E) Dairy representatives are trying to avoid a surplus of cheese and butter.

22. The sculpture of the woman was carved during the early Greek period. The shape of the fingers, the style of hair, and the design of her sandals indicate the early period. The tilt of the chin and the closed eyes are frequently found in early Greek sculpture.

Which of the following is an assumption upon which this argument is based?

(A) The period of a work of art can be established with certainty.

(B) Certain attributes of works of art are typical of specific periods.

(C) Tilted chins and closed eyes always appear together in Greek sculpture.

(D) Sculptures of women first appeared in the early Greek period.

(E) Closed eyes are characteristic of early art.

23. The village is overrun by poisonous snakes. The mayor argues that paying a $10 bounty for each dead snake turned in by a villager will result in ridding the village of snakes.

Which of the following does NOT weaken the mayor's argument?

(A) The bounty ensures that breeding the snakes is in the economic interest of the villagers.

(B) Village taxes will triple if the mayor's proposal is implemented.

(C) The villagers do not trust the mayor.

(D) The snakes control the rat population, so the villagers will not kill the snakes.

(E) A drug company pays villagers $15 for each live snake delivered to it.

24. Spring Lake does not appear to be good for sailing. I have gone to the lake many times this year, and each time the water was too rough for sailing.

Which of the following most closely parallels the above argument?

(A) It appears that we will move to Spring Lake this year. The city is simply too rough for safe living.

(B) Economy-grade gasoline apparently does not prevent my car from running rough. It appears that a good grade of fuel is required.

(C) It appears that the cost of housing at Spring Lake is prohibitive. I looked at a number of houses last month, and they cost much more than I could afford.

(D) I am withdrawing from Spring Lake College. Two months at school was sufficient to prove that college was too rough for me.

(E) It appears that I will never play the clarinet. I began lessons many times, but each time, I quit.

Excerpted from *LSAT Success 1998* © 1996 by Thomas O. White

Law School Admission Test Simulation Answer Sheet

SECTION 1	SECTION 2	SECTION 3	SECTION 4	SECTION 5
1. Ⓐ Ⓑ Ⓒ Ⓓ Ⓔ	1. Ⓐ Ⓑ Ⓒ Ⓓ Ⓔ	1. Ⓐ Ⓑ Ⓒ Ⓓ Ⓔ	1. Ⓐ Ⓑ Ⓒ Ⓓ Ⓔ	1. Ⓐ Ⓑ Ⓒ Ⓓ Ⓔ
2. Ⓐ Ⓑ Ⓒ Ⓓ Ⓔ	2. Ⓐ Ⓑ Ⓒ Ⓓ Ⓔ	2. Ⓐ Ⓑ Ⓒ Ⓓ Ⓔ	2. Ⓐ Ⓑ Ⓒ Ⓓ Ⓔ	2. Ⓐ Ⓑ Ⓒ Ⓓ Ⓔ
3. Ⓐ Ⓑ Ⓒ Ⓓ Ⓔ	3. Ⓐ Ⓑ Ⓒ Ⓓ Ⓔ	3. Ⓐ Ⓑ Ⓒ Ⓓ Ⓔ	3. Ⓐ Ⓑ Ⓒ Ⓓ Ⓔ	3. Ⓐ Ⓑ Ⓒ Ⓓ Ⓔ
4. Ⓐ Ⓑ Ⓒ Ⓓ Ⓔ	4. Ⓐ Ⓑ Ⓒ Ⓓ Ⓔ	4. Ⓐ Ⓑ Ⓒ Ⓓ Ⓔ	4. Ⓐ Ⓑ Ⓒ Ⓓ Ⓔ	4. Ⓐ Ⓑ Ⓒ Ⓓ Ⓔ
5. Ⓐ Ⓑ Ⓒ Ⓓ Ⓔ	5. Ⓐ Ⓑ Ⓒ Ⓓ Ⓔ	5. Ⓐ Ⓑ Ⓒ Ⓓ Ⓔ	5. Ⓐ Ⓑ Ⓒ Ⓓ Ⓔ	5. Ⓐ Ⓑ Ⓒ Ⓓ Ⓔ
6. Ⓐ Ⓑ Ⓒ Ⓓ Ⓔ	6. Ⓐ Ⓑ Ⓒ Ⓓ Ⓔ	6. Ⓐ Ⓑ Ⓒ Ⓓ Ⓔ	6. Ⓐ Ⓑ Ⓒ Ⓓ Ⓔ	6. Ⓐ Ⓑ Ⓒ Ⓓ Ⓔ
7. Ⓐ Ⓑ Ⓒ Ⓓ Ⓔ	7. Ⓐ Ⓑ Ⓒ Ⓓ Ⓔ	7. Ⓐ Ⓑ Ⓒ Ⓓ Ⓔ	7. Ⓐ Ⓑ Ⓒ Ⓓ Ⓔ	7. Ⓐ Ⓑ Ⓒ Ⓓ Ⓔ
8. Ⓐ Ⓑ Ⓒ Ⓓ Ⓔ	8. Ⓐ Ⓑ Ⓒ Ⓓ Ⓔ	8. Ⓐ Ⓑ Ⓒ Ⓓ Ⓔ	8. Ⓐ Ⓑ Ⓒ Ⓓ Ⓔ	8. Ⓐ Ⓑ Ⓒ Ⓓ Ⓔ
9. Ⓐ Ⓑ Ⓒ Ⓓ Ⓔ	9. Ⓐ Ⓑ Ⓒ Ⓓ Ⓔ	9. Ⓐ Ⓑ Ⓒ Ⓓ Ⓔ	9. Ⓐ Ⓑ Ⓒ Ⓓ Ⓔ	9. Ⓐ Ⓑ Ⓒ Ⓓ Ⓔ
10. Ⓐ Ⓑ Ⓒ Ⓓ Ⓔ	10. Ⓐ Ⓑ Ⓒ Ⓓ Ⓔ	10. Ⓐ Ⓑ Ⓒ Ⓓ Ⓔ	10. Ⓐ Ⓑ Ⓒ Ⓓ Ⓔ	10. Ⓐ Ⓑ Ⓒ Ⓓ Ⓔ
11. Ⓐ Ⓑ Ⓒ Ⓓ Ⓔ	11. Ⓐ Ⓑ Ⓒ Ⓓ Ⓔ	11. Ⓐ Ⓑ Ⓒ Ⓓ Ⓔ	11. Ⓐ Ⓑ Ⓒ Ⓓ Ⓔ	11. Ⓐ Ⓑ Ⓒ Ⓓ Ⓔ
12. Ⓐ Ⓑ Ⓒ Ⓓ Ⓔ	12. Ⓐ Ⓑ Ⓒ Ⓓ Ⓔ	12. Ⓐ Ⓑ Ⓒ Ⓓ Ⓔ	12. Ⓐ Ⓑ Ⓒ Ⓓ Ⓔ	12. Ⓐ Ⓑ Ⓒ Ⓓ Ⓔ
13. Ⓐ Ⓑ Ⓒ Ⓓ Ⓔ	13. Ⓐ Ⓑ Ⓒ Ⓓ Ⓔ	13. Ⓐ Ⓑ Ⓒ Ⓓ Ⓔ	13. Ⓐ Ⓑ Ⓒ Ⓓ Ⓔ	13. Ⓐ Ⓑ Ⓒ Ⓓ Ⓔ
14. Ⓐ Ⓑ Ⓒ Ⓓ Ⓔ	14. Ⓐ Ⓑ Ⓒ Ⓓ Ⓔ	14. Ⓐ Ⓑ Ⓒ Ⓓ Ⓔ	14. Ⓐ Ⓑ Ⓒ Ⓓ Ⓔ	14. Ⓐ Ⓑ Ⓒ Ⓓ Ⓔ
15. Ⓐ Ⓑ Ⓒ Ⓓ Ⓔ	15. Ⓐ Ⓑ Ⓒ Ⓓ Ⓔ	15. Ⓐ Ⓑ Ⓒ Ⓓ Ⓔ	15. Ⓐ Ⓑ Ⓒ Ⓓ Ⓔ	15. Ⓐ Ⓑ Ⓒ Ⓓ Ⓔ
16. Ⓐ Ⓑ Ⓒ Ⓓ Ⓔ	16. Ⓐ Ⓑ Ⓒ Ⓓ Ⓔ	16. Ⓐ Ⓑ Ⓒ Ⓓ Ⓔ	16. Ⓐ Ⓑ Ⓒ Ⓓ Ⓔ	16. Ⓐ Ⓑ Ⓒ Ⓓ Ⓔ
17. Ⓐ Ⓑ Ⓒ Ⓓ Ⓔ	17. Ⓐ Ⓑ Ⓒ Ⓓ Ⓔ	17. Ⓐ Ⓑ Ⓒ Ⓓ Ⓔ	17. Ⓐ Ⓑ Ⓒ Ⓓ Ⓔ	17. Ⓐ Ⓑ Ⓒ Ⓓ Ⓔ
18. Ⓐ Ⓑ Ⓒ Ⓓ Ⓔ	18. Ⓐ Ⓑ Ⓒ Ⓓ Ⓔ	18. Ⓐ Ⓑ Ⓒ Ⓓ Ⓔ	18. Ⓐ Ⓑ Ⓒ Ⓓ Ⓔ	18. Ⓐ Ⓑ Ⓒ Ⓓ Ⓔ
19. Ⓐ Ⓑ Ⓒ Ⓓ Ⓔ	19. Ⓐ Ⓑ Ⓒ Ⓓ Ⓔ	19. Ⓐ Ⓑ Ⓒ Ⓓ Ⓔ	19. Ⓐ Ⓑ Ⓒ Ⓓ Ⓔ	19. Ⓐ Ⓑ Ⓒ Ⓓ Ⓔ
20. Ⓐ Ⓑ Ⓒ Ⓓ Ⓔ	20. Ⓐ Ⓑ Ⓒ Ⓓ Ⓔ	20. Ⓐ Ⓑ Ⓒ Ⓓ Ⓔ	20. Ⓐ Ⓑ Ⓒ Ⓓ Ⓔ	20. Ⓐ Ⓑ Ⓒ Ⓓ Ⓔ
21. Ⓐ Ⓑ Ⓒ Ⓓ Ⓔ	21. Ⓐ Ⓑ Ⓒ Ⓓ Ⓔ	21. Ⓐ Ⓑ Ⓒ Ⓓ Ⓔ	21. Ⓐ Ⓑ Ⓒ Ⓓ Ⓔ	21. Ⓐ Ⓑ Ⓒ Ⓓ Ⓔ
22. Ⓐ Ⓑ Ⓒ Ⓓ Ⓔ	22. Ⓐ Ⓑ Ⓒ Ⓓ Ⓔ	22. Ⓐ Ⓑ Ⓒ Ⓓ Ⓔ	22. Ⓐ Ⓑ Ⓒ Ⓓ Ⓔ	22. Ⓐ Ⓑ Ⓒ Ⓓ Ⓔ
23. Ⓐ Ⓑ Ⓒ Ⓓ Ⓔ	23. Ⓐ Ⓑ Ⓒ Ⓓ Ⓔ	23. Ⓐ Ⓑ Ⓒ Ⓓ Ⓔ	23. Ⓐ Ⓑ Ⓒ Ⓓ Ⓔ	23. Ⓐ Ⓑ Ⓒ Ⓓ Ⓔ
24. Ⓐ Ⓑ Ⓒ Ⓓ Ⓔ	24. Ⓐ Ⓑ Ⓒ Ⓓ Ⓔ	24. Ⓐ Ⓑ Ⓒ Ⓓ Ⓔ	24. Ⓐ Ⓑ Ⓒ Ⓓ Ⓔ	24. Ⓐ Ⓑ Ⓒ Ⓓ Ⓔ
25. Ⓐ Ⓑ Ⓒ Ⓓ Ⓔ	25. Ⓐ Ⓑ Ⓒ Ⓓ Ⓔ	25. Ⓐ Ⓑ Ⓒ Ⓓ Ⓔ	25. Ⓐ Ⓑ Ⓒ Ⓓ Ⓔ	25. Ⓐ Ⓑ Ⓒ Ⓓ Ⓔ
26. Ⓐ Ⓑ Ⓒ Ⓓ Ⓔ	26. Ⓐ Ⓑ Ⓒ Ⓓ Ⓔ	26. Ⓐ Ⓑ Ⓒ Ⓓ Ⓔ	26. Ⓐ Ⓑ Ⓒ Ⓓ Ⓔ	26. Ⓐ Ⓑ Ⓒ Ⓓ Ⓔ
27. Ⓐ Ⓑ Ⓒ Ⓓ Ⓔ	27. Ⓐ Ⓑ Ⓒ Ⓓ Ⓔ	27. Ⓐ Ⓑ Ⓒ Ⓓ Ⓔ	27. Ⓐ Ⓑ Ⓒ Ⓓ Ⓔ	27. Ⓐ Ⓑ Ⓒ Ⓓ Ⓔ
28. Ⓐ Ⓑ Ⓒ Ⓓ Ⓔ	28. Ⓐ Ⓑ Ⓒ Ⓓ Ⓔ	28. Ⓐ Ⓑ Ⓒ Ⓓ Ⓔ	28. Ⓐ Ⓑ Ⓒ Ⓓ Ⓔ	28. Ⓐ Ⓑ Ⓒ Ⓓ Ⓔ
29. Ⓐ Ⓑ Ⓒ Ⓓ Ⓔ	29. Ⓐ Ⓑ Ⓒ Ⓓ Ⓔ	29. Ⓐ Ⓑ Ⓒ Ⓓ Ⓔ	29. Ⓐ Ⓑ Ⓒ Ⓓ Ⓔ	29. Ⓐ Ⓑ Ⓒ Ⓓ Ⓔ
30. Ⓐ Ⓑ Ⓒ Ⓓ Ⓔ	30. Ⓐ Ⓑ Ⓒ Ⓓ Ⓔ	30. Ⓐ Ⓑ Ⓒ Ⓓ Ⓔ	30. Ⓐ Ⓑ Ⓒ Ⓓ Ⓔ	30. Ⓐ Ⓑ Ⓒ Ⓓ Ⓔ

Excerpted from *LSAT Success 1998* © 1996 by Thomas O. White

PRACTICE TEST 2

LSAT WRITING SAMPLE TOPIC

Complete the short writing exercise on the topic that follows. You have only 30 minutes to plan, organize, and write your sample. WRITE ONLY ON THE TOPIC SPECIFIED.

As the director of the Carthage University Press, you must recommend to the board of managers a long-range plan to counteract the Press's financial decline. You must choose between merging with a high-quality publisher or changing your publishing policy in a way that would greatly increase income. Two considerations guide your decision:

- The plan must provide a relatively permanent solution to the financial problems of the Press.
- The Press must maintain its tradition of only publishing work of the highest quality, using the very best paper, printing, and binding.

By merging with Lisle & Fish, Ltd., savings would result from combined sales, advertising, management, and printing, and a strong financial future would be ensured. Lisle & Fish has an impeccable reputation in the industry, and its taste is fastidious. If the companies merged, however, Carthage would lose its autonomy, and Lisle & Fish policies would control, including the use of somewhat lower-quality paper, printing, and binding.

On the other hand, by changing the Carthage publishing policy and introducing a series of annotated works of Shakespeare for use in high school and college courses, a permanently enlarged market would result. Professor Barth, the series' editor, produces popular and effective material but is not a highly respected scholar. And the Shakespeare series would require Carthage to publish in paperback form, which Carthage has refused to do for decades because it felt its reputation would suffer.

Excerpted from *LSAT Success 1998* © 1996 by Thomas O. White

Excerpted from *LSAT Success 1998* © 1996 by Thomas O. White

SECTION 1	**TIME—35 MINUTES**	**24 QUESTIONS**

The questions are based on a set of conditions. A diagram may be helpful in the answer selection process. Select the best answer to each question, and mark the corresponding space on the answer sheet.

Questions 1–6

Five golfers, C, D, E, F, and G, play a series of matches in which the following are always true of the results.

Either C is last and G is first or C is first and G is last.

D finishes ahead of E.

Every golfer plays in and finishes every match.

There are no ties in any match; that is, no 2 players ever finish in the same position in a match.

1. If exactly 1 golfer finishes between C and D, which of the following must be true?

   (A) C finishes first.
   (B) G finishes first.
   (C) F finishes third.
   (D) D finishes fourth.
   (E) E finishes fourth.

2. Which of the following CANNOT be true?

   (A) E finishes second.
   (B) F finishes second.
   (C) F finishes third.
   (D) E finishes ahead of F.
   (E) F finishes ahead of D.

3. If D finishes third, which of the following must be true?

   (A) G finishes first.
   (B) C finishes first.
   (C) E finishes ahead of F.
   (D) F finishes ahead of E.
   (E) F finishes behind D.

4. If C finishes first, in how many different orders is it possible for the other golfers to finish?

   (A) 1
   (B) 2
   (C) 3
   (D) 4
   (E) 5

5. Which of the following additional conditions makes it certain that F finishes second?

   (A) C finishes ahead of D.
   (B) D finishes ahead of F.
   (C) F finishes ahead of D.
   (D) D finishes behind G.
   (E) G finishes behind F.

6. If a sixth golfer, H, enters a match and finishes ahead of F and behind D, which of the following CANNOT be true?

   (A) D finishes ahead of G.
   (B) H finishes ahead of E.
   (C) E finishes third.
   (D) F finishes fourth.
   (E) H finishes fifth.

Questions 7–12

The state presidents of the Half Century Club are comparing ages at the Club's annual meeting.

The Kansas president is older than the Wyoming president.

The Ohio president is younger than the Maine president.

7. If the president from Ohio is younger than the president from Wyoming, which of the following CANNOT be true?

   (A) The Kansas president is younger than the Maine president.
   (B) The Maine president is younger than the Wyoming president.
   (C) The Ohio president is younger than the Kansas president.
   (D) The Wyoming president is younger than the Maine president.
   (E) The Kansas president is younger than the Ohio president.

Excerpted from *LSAT Success 1998* © 1996 by Thomas O. White

8. If the president from Wyoming is older than the president from Ohio, which of the following must be true?

   (A) The Kansas president is older than the Maine president.
   (B) The Wyoming president is older than the Kansas president.
   (C) The Maine president is older than the Kansas president.
   (D) The Wyoming president is older than the Maine president.
   (E) The Kansas president is older than the Ohio president.

9. If the Texas president is older than the Maine president, which of the following must be true?

   (A) The Texas president is the oldest president.
   (B) The Texas president is older than the Kansas president.
   (C) The Wyoming president is older than the Texas president.
   (D) The Texas president is older than the Ohio president.
   (E) The Kansas president is older than the Texas president.

10. If the Vermont president is younger than the Maine president, the Wyoming president is older than the Maine president, and the Ohio president is the youngest, which of the following is the second-oldest president?

   (A) Vermont
   (B) Wyoming
   (C) Maine
   (D) Kansas
   (E) Ohio

11. If the Utah president is older than the Ohio president and the Florida president is younger than the Wyoming president, which of the following CANNOT be true if the age of the Maine president is between the ages of the Utah and Florida presidents?

   (A) The Utah president is older than the Wyoming president.
   (B) The Florida president is older than the Ohio president.

   (C) The Florida president is older than the Kansas president.
   (D) The Maine president is older than the Ohio president.
   (E) The Wyoming president is older than the Florida president.

12. If the Alaska president is older than the Iowa, Maine, and Wyoming presidents, which of the following must be true?

   (A) The Iowa president is older than the Maine president.
   (B) The Iowa president is older than the Wyoming president.
   (C) The Iowa president is older than the Ohio president.
   (D) The Alaska president is older than the Ohio president.
   (E) The Kansas president is older than the Alaska president.

Questions 13–18

There are four parallel train tracks at a railroad station, numbered 1 through 4 from left to right. Tracks 1 and 2 are northbound, tracks 3 and 4 are southbound. A train coming from the north will arrive on a southbound track. A train coming from the south will arrive on a northbound track.

   A round-trip train must arrive on a track adjacent to a track going the other direction.
   A local train can only arrive immediately after either an express or a metroliner.
   Two consecutive trains cannot use the same track.

13. If three trains, P, Q, and R, arrive at the station on tracks 2, 4, and 1, respectively, and in that order, what could be true about the trains?

   I. P is an express.

   II. P and R are metroliners.

   III. Q and R are locals.

   (A) I only
   (B) II only
   (C) III only
   (D) I and II only
   (E) I, II, and III

14. If two northbound locals, a southbound express, and a round-trip metroliner coming from the north are all approaching the station, what is the order in which the tracks can be used, from first to last?

    (A) 2,3,4,1
    (B) 1,2,3,4
    (C) 3,2,1,4
    (D) 1,3,2,4
    (E) 4,1,3,2

15. If five trains arrive on tracks 1,3,1,4, and 2, in that order, and the second train to arrive is not a local, what is the maximum number of trains that could be locals?

    (A) 1
    (B) 2
    (C) 3
    (D) 4
    (E) 5

16. Train Q, a northbound express; train R, a round-trip express coming from the south; train S, a northbound metroliner; and trains T and U, both southbound locals, are arriving at the station, though not necessarily in that order.

    In what order and on what track can each train arrive?

    (A) S on track 1, U on track 4, Q on track 2, T on track 4, R on track 3
    (B) R on track 2, T on track 3, S on track 1, Q on track 1, U on track 4
    (C) R on track 2, U on track 3, S on track 1, T on track 3, Q on track 2
    (D) Q on track 2, T on track 4, R on track 3, U on track 4, S on track 1
    (E) T on track 3, Q on track 2, S on track 1, U on track 4, R on track 2

17. If six trains arrive on tracks 1,2,1,3,4,3, in that order, and there are two locals, what are the maximum and minimum numbers, respectively, of trains that could be expresses?

    (A) 3,0
    (B) 3,2
    (C) 4,2
    (D) 2,1
    (E) 4,0

18. If four trains arrive at the station, and none of them arrives on track 3, what must be true about the trains?

    (A) None are round-trip trains.
    (B) Two of the trains are not northbound locals.
    (C) The number of locals equals the number of southbound trains.
    (D) There are more northbound trains than there are southbound trains.
    (E) The greatest number of locals cannot exceed the greatest number of express trains.

Questions 19–24

Five friends, Carol, Ed, Jenny, Rick, and Walt, go to the beach. Each person either brings something (food, blankets, or umbrella) or does something for the trip (drives or pays the tolls along the route).

Two people are brother and sister. They are the only two of the group of friends who are related to each other.

One person meets the others on the beach when they arrive. This person brings the umbrella. The driver of the group that meets the person on the beach is male.

When Ed brings the food, Walt does not drive.

The brother pays the tolls.

When Carol or Jenny brings the blankets, Rick drives.

19. If Ed brings the food, which of the following must be true?

    (A) Carol brings the blankets.
    (B) Rick drives.
    (C) Jenny does not bring the blankets.
    (D) Carol does not bring the umbrella.
    (E) Jenny meets the others at the beach.

20. If Rick drives, what CANNOT be true?

    (A) Jenny brings the umbrella.
    (B) Ed pays the tolls.
    (C) Ed brings the food.
    (D) Walt is Jenny's brother.
    (E) Carol is Rick's sister.

21. If Walt brings the food, Rick CANNOT

    (A) drive
    (B) be Jenny's brother
    (C) bring the umbrella
    (D) be Carol's brother
    (E) pay the tolls

Excerpted from *LSAT Success 1998* © 1996 by Thomas O. White

22. If Carol brings the umbrella, which of the following CANNOT be true?

(A) Carol is Rick's sister.
(B) Ed pays no tolls.
(C) Jenny brings neither blankets nor food.
(D) Ed brings the food.
(E) Jenny does not bring the blankets.

23. If Ed brings the food, Rick must

(A) drive
(B) pay tolls
(C) bring the blankets
(D) bring the umbrella
(E) be someone's brother

24. If Jenny brings the blankets, which two people CANNOT be related?

(A) Carol and Ed
(B) Carol and Rick
(C) Jenny and Walt
(D) Carol and Walt
(E) Jenny and Ed

Excerpted from *LSAT Success 1998* © 1996 by Thomas O. White

SECTION **2**	TIME—35 MINUTES	**24 QUESTIONS**

Evaluate the reasoning contained in the brief statements, and select the best answer. Do not make implausible, superfluous, or incompatible assumptions. Select the best answer to each question, and mark the corresponding space on the answer sheet.

1. All quiet people are harmless.

   No harmless people are easily identified.

   The premises above lead to which of the following conclusions?

   (A) Quiet people are not easily identified.
   (B) Most people who are easily identified are harmless.
   (C) No harmless people are quiet.
   (D) Some easily identified people are quiet.
   (E) All quiet people are easily identified.

2. I don't believe that ambitious people are good parents. Of course, there are some parents who have successful careers and well-raised children. But these parents are not really ambitious. Were they ambitious, they could not devote the necessary time and energy to raising their children well.

   Which of the following best explains the flawed reasoning in the author's argument?

   (A) It relies on a word with two different meanings.
   (B) It bases an absolute conclusion upon relative evidence.
   (C) It assumes the conclusion.
   (D) It generalizes from inappropriate specifics.
   (E) It depends on a false analogy.

3. Arthritis specialists understand that effective treatment must do more than relieve pain. So, the medicine arthritis specialists prescribe most has both an anti-pain and anti-inflammation ingredient. These same ingredients are found in Arthrelief. Use Arthrelief to combat arthritic pain.

   The advertisement above does NOT assume which of the following?

   (A) Arthritis specialists provide authoritative information on effective medication for arthritis.
   (B) Arthritis specialists use Arthrelief because it contains anti-inflammation medicine.
   (C) A medicine containing ingredients prescribed for arthritis will be effective.
   (D) Arthrelief only combats arthritic pain.
   (E) Arthritis specialists prescribe Arthrelief most.

4. Testing the reasoning abilities of illiterate people has proven to be particularly challenging to psychologists. When illiterate people are given tasks that are designed to require them to reason to a conclusion, they are relatively successful when the mechanical devices used in the test are familiar ones. But if the devices used in the test are unfamiliar to the illiterate person, they are relatively unsuccessful at performing analogous tasks.

   Which of the following conclusions can be reasonably drawn from the information above?

   (A) Reasoning abilities of illiterate people should not be tested using tasks that do not involve familiar devices.
   (B) Literacy is required in order to test the reasoning abilities of people through the use of mechanical devices.
   (C) Testing illiterate people for reasoning abilities is relatively unsuccessful.
   (D) Mechanical devices are a poor substitute for words in reasoning to a conclusion.
   (E) Unfamiliar tasks provide a better measure of reasoning ability than do familiar tasks.

Excerpted from *LSAT Success 1998* © 1996 by Thomas O. White

5. Japanese workers exercise each day in their workplaces. American employers do not require daily exercise, and, as a result, American workers are more overweight and much less fit and suffer more sickness and injuries than their Japanese counterparts. American workers will only become as productive as the Japanese if they are required to exercise on a daily basis.

Which of the following, if true, most weakens the above argument?

(A) Daily exercise does not reduce or prevent incidents of sickness.
(B) Daily exercise does not reduce the severity of on-the-job injuries.
(C) Daily exercise does not contribute greatly to Japanese worker fitness.
(D) Daily exercise does not contribute greatly to Japanese worker productivity.
(E) Daily exercise does not result in significant weight loss.

6. Dictatorships or centralized governments result from the political indifference of a country's people. If people were not politically indifferent, all governments would be democratic or decentralized.

Which of the following could NOT be inferred from the above argument?

(A) Democratic governments result from politically active people.
(B) Dictatorships only exist in countries whose people are politically indifferent.
(C) Politically active people are responsible for decentralized governments.
(D) A country with a democratic government must have politically active people.
(E) Centralized governments are the responsibility of the politically indifferent.

7. Question

I. By reducing its standard of living the United States can conserve energy.
II. Yet, the United States aspires to energy independence.
III. Studies confirm that the only certain path to energy independence is through conservation.
IV. More than 20 percent of the energy consumed by the United States is imported.

Which is the most logical arrangement of the above sentences?

(A) I, II, III, IV
(B) I, III, IV, II
(C) II, III, IV, I
(D) III, IV, I, II
(E) IV, II, III, I

8. Dr. Bartels concludes that governments waste the money they spend in support of higher education. His argument is based on longitudinal research that shows that fewer than 20 percent of persons with college degrees are working in the field of their training five years after receiving their degrees.

Dr. Bartels makes the assumption that

(A) higher education in a field is valuable training only for that field
(B) what is desirable at one time will continue into another
(C) higher education can be valued only in degrees awarded
(D) work areas are directly related to college-degree areas
(E) higher education should not be a governmental concern

Excerpted from *LSAT Success 1998* © 1996 by Thomas O. White

9. Ninety percent of the students taking as few as two Alert tablets daily got better grades in school. Improve your grades, get Alert today!

Which of the following could be offered as a valid criticism of the advertisement above?

(A) It does not state that Alert tablets cause grade improvement.
(B) Using medication to get good grades is cheating.
(C) Taking more Alert will result in greater grade improvement.
(D) It suggests that only 10 percent of students do not use Alert daily.
(E) Being alert in school does not always result in improved grades.

10. According to dog lovers, the principal virtue of the dog is its general friendliness toward all people. According to cat lovers, the principal virtue of the cat is its exclusive friendliness toward its provider.

Which of the following is true of the claims of both dog and cat lovers?

(A) Pet friendliness toward a provider is unworthy.
(B) They come from sources that apply the same standard.
(C) Animals cannot be judged by standards for human behavior.
(D) Animal lovers are friendly.
(E) Friendliness is a virtue.

11. In Canada, a family can stay overnight in a litter-free public campground on a clear lake for less than it costs to spend a day at a filthy public beach in the United States. Why must public beaches in the United States be so expensive and dirty?

Which of the following, if true, most weakens the above argument?

(A) Campgrounds in Canada are little used.
(B) Beaches in the United States are intensely used.
(C) There are more public campgrounds in Canada than there are public beaches in the United States.
(D) There are more public beaches in the United States than there are public campgrounds in Canada.
(E) Public beaches in Canada are no cleaner or cheaper than those in the United States.

12. Computers have been programmed to play poker. Because of the way they are programmed, computers reproduce human strategies, such as bluffing. Apparently, they make decisions for the same reasons as human players.

The author of this note

(A) uses scientific evidence to support the conclusion
(B) proposes a common cause for similar effects
(C) grounds the argument on the double meaning of the word "reason"
(D) states a conclusion and then explains how it was reached
(E) argues from an analogy to reconcile an apparent contradiction

13. The Department of Agriculture will stop inspecting milk processing plants because no citations have been issued in the past two years.

If true, which of the following most strengthens the decision?

(A) Processors will cut corners if the threat of inspection is removed.
(B) Milk processing is very automated.
(C) The source of milk is known, so compensation can be had for any problem that occurs.
(D) The Department budget has been cut by 30 percent.
(E) The industry association has standards that exceed the legal requirements.

Excerpted from *LSAT Success 1998* © 1996 by Thomas O. White

14. Rites of adulthood are more frequently found in societies where the differences between adults and children are not clear. The purpose of such rites is to formally impose adult responsibilities on participants.

    The above argument would be most strengthened if it were found that

    (A) children do not generally behave as adults prior to the rites
    (B) children generally accept the rites without question
    (C) adults generally approve of the rites
    (D) formal rites are prevalent in such societies
    (E) children do not generally accept adult responsibilities prior to the rites

15. Attempts to make public-transportation facilities accessible to physically challenged people are misguided. Only the most athletic of the physically challenged are able to get to the stops and stations where it is possible for them to take advantage of special devices installed on buses and trains.

    Which of the following most strengthens the argument above?

    (A) It is extremely expensive to install special devices on buses and trains to accommodate the physically challenged.
    (B) More physically challenged people have access to motorized wheelchairs than ever before.
    (C) Very few physically challenged people use facilities in the places where they have been installed.
    (D) Special-access facilities to public buildings have increased their use by physically challenged people.
    (E) Physically challenged people on buses and trains are at greater safety risk than others.

Questions 16–17

Every time a business grants financial credit to an individual, the business assumes the risk of the individual not being able to make all the agreed-upon payments. Credit bureaus assist businesses in their efforts to evaluate the risks involved with the extension of credit to individual purchasers. The financial history of individuals is maintained and reported on by credit bureaus. Credit bureaus assist debtors as well as creditors by preventing them from assuming greater debt resulting from the work of credit bureaus, which holds losses and prices down and, thus, benefits consumers generally. The few concerns for individual privacy that have been raised about credit bureaus hardly offset their financial value to business and consumer alike.

16. Which of the following is assumed by the above argument?

    (A) Business would have no way to make credit decisions without credit bureaus.
    (B) Risk of nonpayment is difficult for most businesses to assess.
    (C) Purchasers attempt to secure more credit than they can afford.
    (D) Credit bureaus seldom make errors in their reports about individuals' financial histories.
    (E) Financial histories are complex and difficult to develop and maintain.

17. According to the above argument, harm that results from the use of credit bureaus by businesses is

    (A) offset by the need for individual financial histories
    (B) minimal, because so few errors are made in their reports
    (C) acceptable, because business requires financial histories
    (D) justified by the economic value to business and society
    (E) essential to the effective extension of credit to individuals

Excerpted from *LSAT Success 1998* © 1996 by Thomas O. White

18. Harold is a better writer of short stories than Stan and a better novelist, too. Thus, Harold is indubitably a better playwright as well.

    Given the information in the passage, which of the following is a belief about Harold that can be most justifiably attributed to the speaker?

    (A) Harold is more versatile than Stan.
    (B) Harold is a better writer than Stan.
    (C) Harold is altogether more effective than Stan.
    (D) Harold is more cultivated than Stan.
    (E) Harold is more artistically talented than Stan.

19. The average salary of a college graduate is only 22 percent greater than that of a high school graduate. In 1969, the difference was 55 percent. In addition, college graduates' salaries have not kept up with inflation. For most, the rewards of a college education will not justify the cost of tuition and lost income while getting a degree.

    Which of the following, if true, most weakens the above argument?

    (A) Since 1969, the incomes of few groups have kept pace with inflation.
    (B) Since 1969, college education costs have outpaced inflation by nearly 100 percent.
    (C) Since 1969, more high school graduates have decided to seek a college degree.
    (D) Since 1969, the unemployment rate for college graduates is lower than that for high school graduates.
    (E) Since 1969, there has been a steady decline in the number of high school graduates in the job market.

20. Genetic engineering places the nature-versus-nurture argument in stark relief. Not only will physical qualities (nature) of individuals be altered by manufacturing processes, but intellectual, emotional, and spiritual qualities will be modified as well. Those who argue that the altering of human qualities violates the laws of nature ignore the reality that people are already the result of engineering in the form of their manufactured education, socialization, and environment (nurture).

Which of the following, if true, supports the above argument?

    (A) Manufacturing techniques do not alter spiritual qualities of individuals.
    (B) By definition, the laws of nature cannot be altered.
    (C) Manufacturing of education and intellect are markedly different.
    (D) Engineering of genes and environment are virtually the same.
    (E) Qualities of individuals and societies are virtually the same.

Questions 21–22

There is an inherent fallacy in the reasoning of Shea, who suggests that all of his readers ought to attend the retrospective of Beatles music offered by the Springfield Pops because "the Beatles have had as great an influence on the musical development of our day as Beethoven had on his." Stalin had great influence on the political development of his time, but no one suggests that people should rush to Moscow to pay homage at his tomb.

21. The point of the above argument is that

    (A) Shea confuses influence with merit
    (B) Shea confuses politics with music
    (C) Shea confuses the Beatles with Beethoven
    (D) Shea confuses honor with attendance
    (E) Shea confuses popularity with importance

22. Which of the following is analogous to Stalin's tomb in the argument above?

    (A) the Springfield Pops
    (B) musical influence
    (C) Beethoven
    (D) attendance at the Beatles retrospective
    (E) Shea's readers

Excerpted from *LSAT Success 1998* © 1996 by Thomas O. White

23. Ann has vacationed at three different Florida resorts and has enjoyed each of them very much. Thus, Ann is confident that she will enjoy vacationing at the newly opened resort in the Florida keys.

    Which of the following statements does NOT alter the probability that vacationing at the new Florida resort will be enjoyable?

    (A) All three resorts Ann previously visited are in north Miami Beach, and the new resort is in south Miami Beach.
    (B) The new resort was unfavorably reviewed in a national travel magazine.
    (C) The manager of the new resort was trained at the same hotel-management school as 2 of the 3 managers of the other three resorts.
    (D) The owner of the new resort has been in the resort business for thirty years.
    (E) The architect of the other three resorts did not design the new resort.

24. A recent survey has found that the number of high school students that attend a house of worship regularly has increased 60 percent in the past decade. This increase in religious exposure appears to have significantly reduced cheating on tests and improved class participation.

    Which of the following, if true, most weakens the inference made above?

    (A) Religious leaders frequently speak out for academic honesty.
    (B) Not all students responded to the survey.
    (C) Recently the high school changed from proctored exams to an honor system.
    (D) Social reasons account for the attendance of most students at services.
    (E) Cheating is not considered to be a major problem by most teachers.

Excerpted from *LSAT Success 1998* © 1996 by Thomas O. White

SECTION 3	TIME—35 MINUTES	24 QUESTIONS

The questions are based on a set of conditions. A diagram may be helpful in the answer selection process. Select the best answer to each question, and mark the corresponding space on the answer sheet.

Questions 1–6

Six building contractors—L, M, N, O, P, and Q—bid on the construction of a new school. Each submits one bid stating the total price for constructing the building. The school board must award the job to the lowest bidder.

P bids less than N but more than Q.
O bids less than P but more than M.
Q bids less than N but more than L.
No two bids are equal to each other.

1. Which of the following could be the ranking of the contractors' bids?

   (A) M, Q, O, P, L, N
   (B) M, L, O, Q, P, N
   (C) L, Q, M, P, O, N
   (D) Q, M, O, L, P, N
   (E) L, M, Q, N, P, O

2. If O submits the third-highest bid, which of the following contractors could get the job?

   (A) M only
   (B) L only
   (C) Q or M
   (D) M or L
   (E) Q or L

3. If O submits one of the lowest two bids, which of the following must be true?

   (A) N submits the second-highest bid.
   (B) L submits the third-lowest bid.
   (C) P submits the third-highest bid.
   (D) Q submits the fourth-highest bid.
   (E) L submits the fourth-lowest bid.

4. If L submits the lowest bid, all of the following must be true EXCEPT

   (A) M submits a lower bid than O
   (B) Q submits a higher bid than M
   (C) Q submits a lower bid than P
   (D) P submits a higher bid than O
   (E) M submits a lower bid than P

5. If M submits the second-lowest bid, which of the following can be a ranking of the contractors' bids?

   (A) L, M, Q, O, P, N
   (B) Q, M, L, O, P, N
   (C) O, M, L, Q, P, N
   (D) L, M, Q, P, O, N
   (E) L, M, P, O, Q, N

6. Which of the following contractors could submit the lowest bid and the second-lowest bid, respectively?

   (A) Q and N
   (B) M and Q
   (C) Q and L
   (D) L and P
   (E) Q and M

Questions 7–12

Ten students—L, M, N, O, P, Q, R, S, T, and U graduated from Naquapaug High School in the years 1971–1975, two students per year.

M graduated the year before Q.
P and R graduated together before 1975.
Q and N did not graduate in the same year S and T graduated together.

7. All of the following are possible orders of graduation, starting with the 1971 pair of graduates EXCEPT

   (A) S, T; P, R; M, O; Q, N; L, U
   (B) S, T; P, R; M, N; Q, O; L, U
   (C) O, U; M, N; Q, L; P, R; S, T
   (D) P, R; M, U; Q, L; N, O; S, T
   (E) L, U; M, N; Q, O; P, R; S, T

8. Which of the following could be in the pairs that graduated in 1971, 1973, and 1975, respectively?

   (A) O, U, N
   (B) O, L, U
   (C) L, N, S
   (D) S, N, P
   (E) L, O, U

9. If Q, T, and U graduated in 1972, 1973, and 1975, respectively, and O and M graduated together, which of the following must be true?

   (A) L graduated in 1972.
   (B) N graduated in 1974.
   (C) P graduated two years before N.
   (D) R graduated before 1974.
   (E) S graduated the year before O.

10. If O and U graduated together, and Q graduated in 1974, which of the following must be true?

    (A) N graduated in 1974.
    (B) N graduated in 1972.
    (C) L graduated in 1974.
    (D) R graduated in 1972.
    (E) T graduated in 1971.

11. If P graduated in 1973, and L and O graduated together, which of the following are the only years in which N could be one of the pair of graduates?

    (A) 1971 and 1972
    (B) 1971 and 1974
    (C) 1971 and 1975
    (D) 1972 and 1974
    (E) 1972 and 1975

12. If L, O, and U each graduated in an even-numbered year, which of the following must be true?

    (A) P graduated in 1971.
    (B) O graduated in 1972.
    (C) Q graduated in 1972.
    (D) N graduated in 1973.
    (E) S graduated in 1975.

Questions 13–18

On any day their schedules permit, Adam, Beth, Cary, Dana, and Edith each set up a sales table at a flea market.

Edith will set up only when Cary does not.
Dana will set up only when Adam does not.
Cary will set up only when Dana does.
Beth will set up only when Edith does.
Adam will always set up.

13. Who will set up on a day when the schedules of only Adam, Beth, and Cary permit them to sell?

    (A) Adam only
    (B) Beth only
    (C) Cary only
    (D) Adam and Beth only
    (E) Beth and Cary only

14. How many will set up on a day when the schedules of only Adam, Beth, and Cary permit them to sell?

    (A) one
    (B) two
    (C) three
    (D) four
    (E) five

15. Which of the following groups of people could set up on the same day?

    (A) Adam, Beth, and Cary
    (B) Adam, Cary, and Dana
    (C) Cary, Dana, and Edith
    (D) Beth, Dana, and Edith
    (E) Beth, Cary, and Edith

16. If a buyer wanted to be certain that both Beth and Cary were set up on the same day, which of the following must be set up also?

    (A) Dana and Edith
    (B) Adam
    (C) Edith
    (D) Adam and Dana
    (E) Adam and Edith

17. Which of the following could set up on a day when the schedules of only Beth, Cary, and Edith permit them to sell?

    (A) Beth only
    (B) Cary only
    (C) Edith only
    (D) Cary and Edith only
    (E) Beth and Edith only

Excerpted from *LSAT Success 1998* © 1996 by Thomas O. White

18. How many will set up on a day when the schedules of only Beth, Cary, and Dana permit them to sell?

(A) Zero
(B) One
(C) Two
(D) Three
(E) Four

Questions 19–24

A, B, and C are dentists and S, T, U, and V are hygienists assigned to work for them.

A and B each have exactly two hygienists assigned to them.
C sometimes is assigned one hygienist and sometimes two.
T is assigned to A and one other dentist.
Each hygienist is assigned to at least one dentist.

19. If S and T are assigned to the same two dentists, V must work for

(A) both A and B
(B) both A and C
(C) either A or B
(D) either A or C
(E) either B or C

20. If V is assigned to both B and C, which of the following must be true?

(A) U is assigned to B.
(B) S is assigned to A.
(C) T and U are assigned to the same dentist.
(D) S and T are assigned to the same dentist.
(E) U is assigned to only one dentist.

21. If T and V both are assigned to the same two dentists, S must work for

(A) both A and B
(B) both A and C
(C) either A or B
(D) either A or C
(E) either B or C

22. If U is assigned to B and C, and V is assigned to B, S must work for

(A) A only
(B) B only
(C) C only
(D) both A and B
(E) both A and C

23. Whenever S is assigned to only one dentist and C is assigned only one hygienist, which of the following must be true?

(A) S is assigned to C.
(B) V is assigned to two dentists.
(C) U is assigned to only one dentist.
(D) T is assigned to C.
(E) U is assigned to A.

24. If S is assigned to both B and C, which of the following must be true?

(A) T and V are assigned to the same dentist.
(B) V is assigned to A.
(C) U and V are assigned to the same dentist.
(D) U is assigned to B.
(E) U is assigned to only one dentist.

Excerpted from *LSAT Success 1998* © 1996 by Thomas O. White

| SECTION **4** | TIME—35 MINUTES | 28 QUESTIONS |

Line Without a doubt, the role of firearms in American violence is much greater today than a decade ago. Rates of gun violence and the proportion of violent acts that are
5 committed by guns have increased substantially, even after the Gun Control Act went into effect. Behind these increases lies the probability that handgun ownership has become at least a subcultural institution in
10 the big cities that are the main arena of American violence. During this period, regional differences in gun ownership and use have been moderated as the large Northeastern cities that were traditionally
15 areas of low ownership and use have experienced large increases in handgun use.

The special role of the handgun in urban violence is one of the more obvious
20 lessons of the data that are reported. Over the past ten years, rates of handgun homicide have increased more than three times as much as homicides by all other means. The data reported suggest, but do
25 not compel, other conclusions about patterns of handgun ownership and violence in the United States. First, the sharp rise in the proportion of violence attributable to handguns in Northeastern
30 cities may lead to modification of the hypothesis that general patterns of handgun ownership determine the extent to which handguns are used in violent episodes. While it is still true that those regions with
35 the highest general levels of gun ownership have the highest proportion of gun use in violence, the past decade has produced an increase in handgun use in the Northeast that leaves cities in that region closer to but
40 still below the average handgun share of violence. This could be due to a substantial rise in handgun ownership in the general population in these cities, but that would

45 mean that a vast Northeastern urban handgun arsenal has been accumulating during the past ten years. It is more likely that handgun ownership increased substantially among subcultural groups disproportionately associated with violence without
50 necessarily affecting other parts of the population.

If one adopts a "subcultural" explanation of the relationship between gun ownership and violence, hypotheses about
55 the effect of increases or decreases in handgun ownership on handgun violence should take a slightly more complicated form. One would predict that high levels of handgun ownership produce high levels of
60 handgun violence for two reasons: More handguns are available at a moment of perceived need, and high ownership rates necessarily suggest high levels of handgun availability to all potential consumers. Low
65 general levels of handgun ownership, on the other hand, become the necessary but not sufficient condition of low levels of handgun violence. If the lower-than-average general ownership levels are still high
70 enough to create relatively easy handgun availability and if both handgun ownership and propensity for violence are concentrated in discrete subpopulations, lower-than-average general ownership is an
75 inadequate insurance policy against increases in handgun violence. It is only when ownership levels are low enough to have an impact on handgun availability that low aggregate ownership will depress
80 handgun involvement in rates of subcultural violence. Efforts to limit handgun supply on a national basis by limiting legitimate production, or imports, or both will not require a large federal street police force.
85 At the point when market controls make illicit gun production profitable, some police work will obviously be needed, along the lines of controls on illicit liquor production.

Excerpted from *LSAT Success 1998* © 1996 by Thomas O. White

1. The primary purpose of the passage is to

   (A) criticize the Gun Control Act
   (B) describe the role of the handgun in urban violence
   (C) advocate limiting handgun availability
   (D) explain the growth of handgun violence
   (E) point out the increase in the urban handgun arsenal

2. If true, the "subcultural" explanation of gun ownership and violence means that

   (A) all parts of the population own more guns
   (B) general patterns of gun ownership determine their use in violent episodes
   (C) higher levels of gun ownership produce higher levels of violence
   (D) gun ownership by people associated with violence has greatly increased
   (E) guns are now primarily owned by the violent elements of urban society

3. The author refers to the Gun Control Act to

   (A) dramatize the increase in gun-related violence
   (B) criticize the government for gun-related violence
   (C) point out the statute's total ineffectiveness
   (D) minimize the importance of gun-control legislation
   (E) argue for more enforcement of the statute

4. Which of the following, if true, would most weaken the author's argument concerning handgun ownership in Northeastern cities?

   (A) Handgun ownership among Boston drug dealers has increased 300 percent in the last ten years.
   (B) Handgun ownership among organized crime figures in New Jersey has increased dramatically in the last ten years.
   (C) Handgun ownership among convicted criminals has increased in the last ten years.
   (D) Handgun ownership among middle-class New Yorkers has increased fourfold in the last ten years.
   (E) Handgun ownership among middle-class Philadelphians has increased slightly in the last ten years.

5. Which of the following may be inferred from the passage?

   (A) The rate of growth in gun ownership in the Northeast is greater than that of other regions.
   (B) Gun ownership in the Northeast is greater than that of other regions.
   (C) There is little data available concerning the growth of gun ownership in urban areas.
   (D) High levels of handgun ownership do not necessarily result in increased violence.
   (E) High levels of handgun ownership in urban areas do not necessarily result in increased violence.

6. The passage suggests which of the following?

   (A) High levels of handgun ownership are not related to perceived needs among consumers.
   (B) More violent acts are committed by means other than handguns.
   (C) Urban violence is due to subcultural differences among residents.
   (D) The number of homicides not involving handguns has increased in the past ten years.
   (E) Lower-than-average handgun ownership will result in lower violence.

7. The author would likely disagree that which of the following would reduce handgun violence?

   (A) regulation of handgun imports
   (B) reduction of handgun ownership in certain subcultural groups
   (C) regulation of handgun possession
   (D) reduction of handgun ownership levels
   (E) regulation of handgun production

Excerpted from *LSAT Success 1998* © 1996 by Thomas O. White

Line Software is like hardware in that it causes
machines to perform tasks. Software is
merely a replacement for hardware
components that could otherwise perform
5 the same function. Software is often
embedded in hardware and part of an
overall hardware system. Like hardware,
software can often serve as a tool for
creating other items. Like hardware,
10 software needs maintenance work from
time to time to operate properly.

Software is unlike hardware, however,
in a great many ways. Software is, for
example, easy and cheap to replicate as
15 compared with hardware. Once the first
copy has been produced, software can be
almost endlessly replicated at almost no
cost, regardless of how complex it is. One
of the consequences of this characteristic is
20 that the government tends to think that
additional copies of software ought to be
deliverable at a very low cost, whereas
industry, which is concerned about
recouping its research and development
25 costs and which tends to regard the sale of
software as the sale of a production facility
(as if one bought a General Motors factory
when one bought a truck produced by
GM), thinks that sales at higher price levels
30 are necessary to make the software
business viable. A second consequence of
low-cost replicability is that the software
industry, for the most part, tends to make
its products available only on a highly
35 restrictive licensing basis, rather than
selling copies outright.

Another important difference between
software and hardware is that software may
be wholly subject to a very lengthy lawful
40 monopoly (i.e., a copyright) as well as
being held as a trade secret, whereas
hardware may be subject to a much shorter
monopoly (i.e., a patent) and most often
cannot be held as a trade secret. Moreover,
45 quite often hardware is either not patented
at all or only subject to partial patent
protection. A high standard of inventiveness
is required for patent, while copyright
requires only the most minimal originality.
50 Hardware, unlike software, cannot be
copyrighted at all. As a result, it tends to be
much harder to get competition for
software procurements and maintenance
than for hardware, which means that it is

55 even easier for the government to find itself
in a sole-source position as to software than
as to hardware. Moreover, because software
engineering is still in the early stages of
development, it is generally more difficult
60 to specify how software, as opposed to
hardware, should be developed for particular functions and to estimate the cost and
development schedule for it.

Software, which consists of a stream
65 of electrical impulses, is also virtually
"invisible" as compared with hardware,
which means that it is more difficult to
detect if someone delivers very similar or
nearly identical software on a second
70 development contract. Again, because
software engineering is a developing art,
software is likely to contain many undetec-
ted defects that will need to be corrected
while in the user's possession.

75 Unlike hardware, software is readily
changeable; that is, new capabilities can be
added to software without additional plant
or material costs. Often, all that is required
is some intellectual labor. All of these
80 factors tend to make software maintenance
and enhancement a much bigger part of
computer system life-cycle planning than is
the case with hardware.

8. The passage is primarily concerned with

   (A) correcting misimpressions about
       hardware and software
   (B) explaining the nature of software
   (C) minimizing apparent difficulties with
       software
   (D) comparing hardware and software
   (E) describing computer system life-cycle
       planning

9. According to the passage, which of the
   following is true?

   (A) Hardware and software cannot
       perform the same functions.
   (B) Software can make hardware cheaper.
   (C) Software can be located within
       hardware.
   (D) Software cannot be copyrighted.
   (E) Hardware is readily changeable.

Excerpted from *LSAT Success 1998* © 1996 by Thomas O. White

10. According to the passage all of the follow-
    ing is true EXCEPT

    (A) the cost of duplicating software is low
    (B) very little software is sold outright
    (C) hardware is often not patented
    (D) software requires minimal originality
    (E) hardware is readily changeable

11. According to the passage, which of the
    following characteristics does NOT apply to
    both hardware and software?

    (A) It can be held as a trade secret.
    (B) It can be copyrighted.
    (C) It can create other items.
    (D) It can be subject to a monopoly.
    (E) It can be maintained.

12. Which of the following can be inferred
    from the passage?

    (A) Hardware is more expensive than
        software.
    (B) It is more profitable to sell copies of
        software than hardware.
    (C) Software maintenance is a relatively
        competitive business.
    (D) Procurement of hardware is not a
        competitive business.
    (E) Software is licensed because it is too
        expensive to buy.

13. Which of the following can be inferred
    from the passage?

    (A) Ownership rights in software can be
        better protected than those in
        hardware.
    (B) Copyrighted software requires greater
        inventiveness than does hardware.
    (C) Ownership rights in hardware can be
        better protected than those in
        software.
    (D) Patented hardware requires greater
        inventiveness than does software.
    (E) Patented hardware is difficult to
        specify for particular functions.

14. The argument that one purchased the
    factory when one purchased a truck made
    at the factory (lines 27–29) is most like
    which of the following?

    (A) One purchased the typewriter when
        one purchased the book that prepared
        the manuscript.
    (B) One purchased the cruise when one
        purchased the cruise ship.
    (C) One purchased the restaurant when
        one purchased the dinner prepared
        there.
    (D) One purchased the office building
        when one leased an office located in
        the building.
    (E) One purchased the health club when
        one purchased a membership to use
        the club facilities.

Line We customarily identify the concept of
status with its conventional indices, such as
wealth, title, and occupation. But there is
nothing sacred about these indices; they are
5 merely the most convenient and concrete
manifestations in everyday life of different
social positions. If every member of society
routinely tested his strength in court several
times each year instead of once or twice a
10 lifetime, we would immediately recognize
court performance as a direct measure of
social position, perhaps even more reveal-
ing of the pecking order than conventional
indices, such as power.

15   Of course, in no society, not even a
litigious one like premodern New Haven,
does the court play so vital a role as this in
the life of the community. Nevertheless, if
other societies show the same positive
20 correlation between status and court
performance found in New Haven, we will
be compelled to admit that individual court
appearances—infrequent though they
are—are revelatory of group status when
25 treated collectively. Of course, one cannot
assume on the basis of this one study of a
single society that court performance is
always and everywhere a reliable index of
status. Only a considerable accumulation of
30 confirmatory studies of other communities
and courts could justify the use of the
voluntary appearance ratio as an independent measure of status. But if, as in the case
of New Haven, it can be shown for a given
35 community that court performance is
strongly correlated with the more conventional indices of status over a long period of
time, then it seems reasonable to treat
court performance itself as an index of
40 status in that community. Doing so may be
extremely advantageous because, unlike
most indices of status, court performance
can be reconstructed on a year-to-year
basis.

45   If court performance can be shown to
reflect the static distribution of power and
advantage in the community—as has been
done for New Haven—then by tracing
court performance through time, on a
50 year-to-year basis, it should be possible to
reveal shifts of power and advantage as
they take place. Court records exploited in
this manner might serve as a weather vane
of social change. The gentry controversy in

55 English history stands as the classic
illustration of the difficulty of reconstructing an account through time of the relative
position of two classes, using only economic and demographic data. Of all the
60 kinds of data relating to group status, none
is more likely to be recorded and be
preserved in as complete a form as court
records. A continuous year-by-year account
of group status would be virtually impos-
65 sible to reconstruct from surviving economic data, but such an account may be
feasible for societies with complete court
records. Such a methodological tool should
be useful to any historian who wants to test
70 hypotheses postulating the rise or fall of a
class or other large group.

15. The author views court records primarily as

(A) surviving other available records about
    society
(B) a source of more reliable data about
    society
(C) reflecting distribution of power in
    society
(D) a means of tracing changes in group
    status in society
(E) reporting on tests of strength within a
    society

16. The term "positive correlation" in lines
19–20 refers to which of the following?

(A) the relationship between individual
    and group status
(B) the relationship between group status
    and frequency of court appearance
(C) the relationship between individual
    court appearance and social position
(D) the relationship between the pecking
    order and group status in the commu-
    nity
(E) the relationship between power shifts
    and frequency of court appearance

17. The passage suggests that which of the
following is an indication of individual
social status?

(A) wealth
(B) occupation
(C) title
(D) court performance
(E) power

Excerpted from *LSAT Success 1998* © 1996 by Thomas O. White

18. Which of the following, if true, would most weaken the author's thesis?

    (A) There is an inverse relationship between wealth and court appearances.
    (B) There is a negative relationship between age and court appearances.
    (C) There is a random relationship between occupation and court appearances.
    (D) There is a positive relationship between title and court appearances.
    (E) There is a direct relationship between land ownership and court appearances.

19. If true, which of the following would best support the author's thesis?

    (A) There is little correlation between the New Haven findings and those of other towns.
    (B) There is a positive correlation between the New Haven findings and those of other towns.
    (C) There is a positive correlation between wealth and court appearances in New Haven and those of other towns.
    (D) There is little correlation between occupations and court appearances in New Haven and those of other towns.
    (E) There is a direct relationship between land ownership in New Haven and ten surrounding towns.

20. Which of the following is most likely the author of the passage?

    (A) a sociologist
    (B) a genealogist
    (C) a heraldrist
    (D) an anthropologist
    (E) a legal historian

21. The passage suggests that all of the following would be advantages of using court records and performance as a means of social status determination EXCEPT

    (A) court records can be reconstructed over long periods of time
    (B) court appearances change with status within the society
    (C) court records are generally preserved in most jurisdictions
    (D) court appearances can be treated collectively to reflect status
    (E) court procedures remain the same over long periods of time

Excerpted from *LSAT Success 1998* © 1996 by Thomas O. White

Line Much advertising is patently uninformative: Rational consumers should not care what sort of breakfast cereal is eaten by famous baseball players. Nonetheless, advertisers
5   spend large sums of money on these sorts of messages as well as many others of equal value as information. Rational consumers should not be influenced by such messages, and rational advertisers should not spend
10   money on messages without influence.

There are two types of goods: search goods and experience goods. A search good is one whose salient characteristics can be ascertained by presale inspection (e.g., the
15   comfort of a pair of shoes); experience goods are those that must be consumed to be evaluated (e.g., the taste of a candy bar). The role of advertising differs depending on which type of good is involved. In the case
20   of search goods, where the consumer can and will easily determine for himself whether the goods are what he wants, advertisers have little incentive to misrepresent the quality of their goods. Thus,
25   advertisers simply urge the consumer to make the inspection, and their message should be largely informative and truthful. In the case of the experience good, the consumer can determine quality only by
30   purchasing and using the good. The function of advertising, therefore, is to get the consumer to try the product. Here, advertisers might have an incentive to mislead and make false claims.
35   With respect to advertising, then, the characteristics of goods and services form a continuum, from those in which it is very easy to detect the truth or falsity of advertising claims (search goods: The truth
40   of the claim can be ascertained before purchase) through experience goods (where the truth of the claim can be detected only after purchase and use) through credence goods (where the validity
45   of advertisements may never be determined).

As we move along this continuum from search to credence characteristics, misrepresentation becomes relatively more
50   profitable, since detection by consumers becomes more expensive. Nonetheless, it is in the case of credence characteristics that self-protection becomes most difficult and

in which some legal remedy would seem
55   most important.

For any one purchase where credence qualities are involved, the consumer cannot be sure that he is getting a desirable good; i.e., there is a low probability of his finding
60   out whether claims about any one good are true or false. However, if the consumer buys many goods from the same source, the probability of ascertaining that claims about one of those goods are false would
65   be increased. In this situation, claims about individual goods have credence characteristics; but the reputation of the seller of all of the goods is an experience characteristic. It may be that consumer trust in the reputa-
70   tion of the intermediary is misplaced in the situation of mail-order advertisements carried by magazines. Although the consumer may rely on the publisher of the magazine to police their advertisers,
75   Consumers Union claims that in fact such policing is minimal or nonexistent.

22. Which of the following best states the primary objective of the passage?

(A) to point out that advertising reliability varies by type of good

(B) to contrast advertising purposes for three types of goods

(C) to differentiate between advertising for two types of goods

(D) to discuss the role of advertising as information

(E) to question the trustworthiness of magazine mail-order advertising

23. According to the passage, the consumer can determine the quality of experience goods by which of the following?

(A) advertising

(B) inspection

(C) consumption

(D) policing

(E) reputation

Excerpted from *LSAT Success 1998* © 1996 by Thomas O. White

24. According to the passage, each of the following is true EXCEPT which statement?

(A) Search-goods advertising is likely to be informative and truthful.

(B) Mail-order advertising in magazines is not likely to be truthful.

(C) Experience-goods advertisers have incentive to mislead.

(D) Credence-goods advertisements may never be determined to be valid.

(E) Advertisers spend large sums of money on informative messages.

25. Which of the following articles is the most likely source of the passage?

(A) "The Economics of Advertising"

(B) "The Law of False Advertising"

(C) "Advertising by Type of Good"

(D) "Analysis of the Function of Advertising"

(E) "Advertising and the Quality of Goods"

26. It can be inferred from the passage that which of the following are credence goods?

(A) auto transmission oil

(B) vitamin pills

(C) plant fertilizer

(D) eyeglasses

(E) air conditioner

27. Which of the following best describes the author's attitude toward advertising?

(A) Many advertisers and consumers do not act rationally.

(B) Many advertisers spend too much money on ads.

(C) Many consumers are influenced by advertising.

(D) Many advertisers are not interested in informing consumers.

(E) Many consumers use advertising to determine the quality of goods.

28. The author implies which of the following in the passage?

(A) Search-goods consumers are easily misled by advertising.

(B) Experience-goods consumers purchase by mail order.

(C) Credence-goods consumers require statutory protection.

(D) Experience-goods consumers ascertain value by inspection.

(E) Credence-goods consumers depend on seller credibility.

Excerpted from *LSAT Success 1998* © 1996 by Thomas O. White

SECTION 5   TIME—35 MINUTES   24 QUESTIONS

Evaluate the reasoning contained in the brief statements, and select the best answer. Do not make implausible, superfluous, or incompatible assumptions. Select the best answer to each question, and mark the corresponding space on the answer sheet.

1. Hitler was born in 1889 and became chancellor of Germany in 1933. On December 7, 1941, he was 52 years old and had been in power for 8 years. Hirohito was born in 1901 and became emperor of Japan in 1926. On December 7, 1941, he was 40 years old and had been in power for 15 years. The four underlined figures for each man total 3,882.

   Which of the following most accurately describes the total 3,882?

   (A) It is significant, but its meaning is not clear.
   (B) It is insignificant and coincidental.
   (C) Important leaders share significant events and figures.
   (D) It is politically significant only.
   (E) There is more significance in figures than is usually acknowledged.

2. It is acceptable to support one corrupt faction in a war against another in Nicaragua. And it is acceptable to send troops to Grenada to oust a Communist leader. But it is unacceptable to use force to get food to thousands of isolated and starving people in Sudan because it would interfere with that nation's internal affairs.

   The author makes a point by

   (A) identifying incongruities in the use of force
   (B) analyzing evidence of the use of force
   (C) attacking proprieties in the use of force
   (D) complaining about irrationality in the use of force
   (E) arguing for a more pervasive use of force

3. "Return my pocket watch!"

   "How did you get it?"

   "My father gave it to me."

   "How did your father get it?"

   "His father gave it to him."

   "How did your grandfather get it?"

   "He won it in a poker game."

   "Good, we will play poker for it."

   Which of the following is best inferred from the statement, "Good, we will play poker for it"?

   (A) Gambling achieves objectives effectively.
   (B) Past practice validates future action.
   (C) Meaningful customs transcend generations.
   (D) Possession is a privilege not a right.
   (E) Wanting another's possessions is instinctive.

4. Kaminski's disparaging reviews of the book call her abilities as a critic into question since the book became an immediate best-seller.

   Which of the following, if true, would most weaken the author's questioning of Kaminski's critical ability?

   (A) Immediate success of books is quickly forgotten.
   (B) Book critics often disagree with each other.
   (C) Sales of a book are not always indicative of its value.
   (D) The significance of a book is not known for years.
   (E) Critics often change their views about books.

Excerpted from *LSAT Success 1998* © 1996 by Thomas O. White

Questions 5–6

If a writer is truly emotional, his writing will comprise his deepest feelings about the world; and one would expect such feelings to appear in his work, if not dominate it. Many societies and people are very emotional, and their writing has as its principal function the expression and integration of deep feeling. This suggests that writing must be either emotional or trivial, that only emotional people can be great writers, and that writing cannot flourish in a technical society.

5. The writing of emotional people demon-strates

    (A) feelings are not integrated in other ways
    (B) only emotional writing can be great
    (C) the expression of deep feeling
    (D) writing cannot flourish in a technical society
    (E) one type of writing is better than another

6. On which of the following assumptions is the author's position based?

    (A) Great writers must be emotional.
    (B) Societies must be emotional or technical.
    (C) Feelings dominate an emotional writer's work.
    (D) Writing is emotional or trivial.
    (E) A writer's purpose is to express emotion.

Questions 7–8

It is almost as safe to assume that an artist of any dignity is against his country, i.e., against the environment in which God hath placed him, as it is to assume that his country is against the artist. He differs from the rest of us mainly because he reacts sharply and in an uncommon manner to phenomena that leave the rest of us unmoved, or, at most, merely annoy us vaguely. Therefore, he takes to artistic endeavor, which is at once a criticism of life and an attempt to escape from life.

The more the facts are studied, the more they bear out these generalizations. In those fields of art, at all events, which concern themselves with ideas as well as with sensations, it is almost impossible to find any trace of an artist who was not actively hostile to his environ-ment and, thus, an indifferent patriot. From Dante to Tolstoy and from Shakespeare to Mark Twain, the story is ever the same. Names suggest themselves instantly: Goethe, Shelley, Byron, Balzac, Cervantes, Swift, Dostoevsky, Carlyle, Moliere, and Pope were each a bitter critic of his time and nation.

7. Which of the following, if true, would most strongly refute the author's argument?

    (A) Artists are generally honored by their countries.
    (B) Artists best recognize life's difficulties.
    (C) Artists usually escape from their countries.
    (D) Artists generally venerate their countries.
    (E) Artists are best known in their own countries.

8. The author's argument most depends upon which of the following assumptions?

    (A) Most people are annoyed by phenom-ena that make an artist hostile.
    (B) Art defines in the abstract events and sensations that are uncommon.
    (C) The purpose of art is to both find fault with and escape from life.
    (D) In order to be an artist of dignity, a person must be an indifferent patriot.
    (E) Life is actively hostile to the artistic endeavors of most artists.

9. In a recent survey, the majority of respon-dents answered "no" to the question, "Should free hypodermic needles be provided by the government to drug addicts on welfare?"

    The survey results can be best criticized because the question structure

    (A) presented more than one issue to respondents
    (B) presented a choice that suggested a negative reply
    (C) presented respondents an impossible value judgment
    (D) presented an issue to largely unaf-fected respondents
    (E) presented a controversial issue out of context

Excerpted from *LSAT Success 1998* © 1996 by Thomas O. White

10. When it rains, the crops grow; but it hasn't rained recently, so the crops must not be growing.

   Which of the following arguments is logically most similar to the one above?

   (A) When people are old, they complain about their health; but our town has no health problems, so it must have no old people.
   (B) When a town has health problems, so it must also have many old people.
   (C) When people are old, they complain about their health; but one can complain about one's health and yet not be old.
   (D) When people complain about their health, they get old; but no one is complaining about their health, so we must have no people getting old.
   (E) When a town has people complaining about their health, it must also have old people; our town has many people complaining about their health, so it must have many old people.

Questions 11–12

The proposal to divert one third of the flow of the Delaware River to supply New York City with water ought to be a matter of great concern to the people who live in the Delaware Valley. The interests of the people of the Delaware Valley are being put aside so that growth can continue in an already overdeveloped area. Fresh water is a natural resource in the same sense that oil and coal are natural resources. Do Texas and Alaska give away their oil? Does West Virginia give away its coal? Why should Pennsylvania and New Jersey supply New York or any other place with fresh water? If the growth of New York is capped by limited fresh water, so much the better.

11. The author assumes which of the following to be fact rather than opinion?

   (A) Diverting the Delaware River is a matter of great concern to people in the Delaware Valley.
   (B) Oil, coal, and fresh water are natural resources.
   (C) The purpose of diverting the Delaware River is to allow New York City to continue to grow.

   (D) The interests of New York and the Delaware Valley conflict.
   (E) The Delaware River supplies New York with water.

12. Which of the following, if true, would most weaken the author's argument?

   (A) New York City is permanently committed to zero growth.
   (B) The diversion will not reduce water availability to people in the Delaware Valley.
   (C) New York City will pay Pennsylvania and New Jersey for each gallon of water diverted.
   (D) The diversion will reduce the risk of flooding in the Delaware Valley.
   (E) New York City will get water from Vermont if the Delaware River is not diverted.

13. If the present moment contains no living and creative choice and is totally and mechanically the product of the matter and moment of the moment before, so, then, was that moment the mechanical effect of the moment that preceded it and so on until we arrive at a single cause of every later event, of every act and suffering of man.

   Which of the following would NOT be supported by the above argument?

   (A) a theory postulating a mechanistic origin of the universe
   (B) a theory postulating suffering as a requisite for creativity
   (C) a theory postulating a deterministic explanation of history
   (D) a theory postulating that there are no choices in the present moment
   (E) a theory postulating a single cause of all events

Excerpted from *LSAT Success 1998* © 1996 by Thomas O. White

14. Baxter defends paternal authority and the preservation of the family in her most recent work. But other aspects of her thinking more convincingly demonstrate that she cannot be considered a feminist. For example, she fails to appreciate that the full realization of a woman's capacities depends on her securing the same political, economic, and civil rights as those afforded me.

Which of the following inferences is NOT supported by the above argument?

(A) Paternal authority is not generally supported by feminists.
(B) The family is not generally supported by feminists.
(C) Baxter feels that women do not need rights equal to men's.
(D) Women's capacities have not been fully realized.
(E) Baxter feels that women and men have unequal capacities.

15. Many children in urban schools are forced to learn in dilapidated classrooms with few modern teaching aids. Compared to children in suburban schools with their computers, labs, and the latest advances in educational resources, the urban student is truly deprived.

The point of the author's argument is best stated by which of the following?

(A) Modern educational aids should be provided for urban children.
(B) Urban and suburban children should be educated in the same schools.
(C) Urban schoolchildren should not be required to compete with suburban schoolchildren.
(D) Unequal resources for urban and suburban children should be investigated.
(E) Suburban school resources should be combined with those of urban schools if an ideal education is to be achieved.

16. A philosopher makes arguments that frequently are not logical in order to demonstrate that rationality is not as valuable as irrationality to us humans. Consequently, the philosopher should not be expected to use the same arguments as those whose positions are rationally based.

The argument above is most similar to which of the following?

(A) A philosopher's arguments focus on the flaws in logical reasoning of those who oppose her.
(B) A writer often uses great restraint when describing mayhem.
(C) A female author was not taken seriously, so she used a male pseudonym when establishing her reputation.
(D) A novel is judged to be boring because it describes a boring situation.
(E) A philosopher's reasoning is complicated because he was trained in a tradition that often uses complicated reasoning.

Question 17–18

United States treaty negotiations with Japan about trade involve the basic question, "Can the Japanese be trusted?" But treaties are based on self-interest rather than on trust. There would be no need to have treaties if countries trusted one another. A treaty is an alternative to trust; one that formally recognizes that each country finds an advantage in the agreement.

17. Which of the following is an argument made above?

(A) If the Japanese can be trusted, the United States should negotiate treaties with Japan.
(B) If the Japanese cannot be trusted, the United States should not negotiate treaties with Japan.
(C) If Japan and the United States have common trade interests, a treaty between the countries should be negotiated.
(D) If Japan and the United States sign a treaty, interests of each will be served by the agreement.
(E) If Japanese and United States interests are different, a treaty dealing with those interests will not be signed.

Excerpted from *LSAT Success 1998* © 1996 by Thomas O. White

18. Which of the following is NOT supported by the author's argument above?

    (A) Treaties are made only between countries that trust one another.
    (B) Treaties further the self-interest of countries.
    (C) Treaties formally recognize an advantage one country has over another.
    (D) Treaties do not serve mutual interests of countries.
    (E) Treaties serve as reasonable alternatives to trust.

19. Tests done on the employees of a chemical plant showed that 28 percent had abnormal chromosome patterns. Chemical fumes, radiation, and airborne particulates are among the causes of abnormal chromosome patterns.

    Which of the following would most support the conclusion that chemical fumes were responsible for employees' abnormal chromosome patterns?

    (A) Abnormal chromosome patterns can be altered.
    (B) Nonemployees in the area also develop abnormal chromosome patterns.
    (C) Employees of other chemical plants do not develop abnormal chromosome patterns.
    (D) Abnormal chromosome patterns are not necessarily harmful.
    (E) Employees of most chemical plants develop abnormal chromosome patterns.

20. "None of the legislators we polled are in favor of this bill?"

    "That cannot be true. There are six legislators who introduced the bill and support it."

    Which of the following can be inferred from the above exchange?

    (A) Legislators who do not favor the bill may support it.
    (B) The only legislators who favor the bill are those who introduced it.
    (C) Only legislators who do not favor the bill were polled.
    (D) Some legislators refused to participate in the poll.
    (E) Legislators might indicate that they favor a bill when they do not.

21. The Audubon Society Falcon Watch reports that there were 2,487 more falcon sightings in 1988 than there were in 1987. This proves that an increase in the falcon population has finally been realized.

    Which of the following, if true, most weakens the above argument?

    (A) Falcons regularly move from area to area in search of food.
    (B) Falcons have been introduced into urban environments.
    (C) Development in falcon nesting areas is being restricted.
    (D) The Society intensified its falcon sighting program in 1988.
    (E) The Society database about falcons improved in 1988.

22. The following notice was received by Mary Castle, a scientist.

    "We regret that your article cannot be accepted. Page limitations in the *Journal* force the editor to return many worthy and well-written articles."

    All of the following may be inferred from the above, EXCEPT

    (A) only well-written articles were accepted for publication
    (B) Castle's article was considered to be well-written
    (C) Castle's article was found to be too long for the *Journal*
    (D) Castle's article was considered to be worthy of publication
    (E) writing was not the only factor in deciding which articles to publish

Excerpted from *LSAT Success 1998* © 1996 by Thomas O. White

Questions 23–24

The drug Thalidomide caused unforeseen birth defects in thousands of babies; therefore, thorough testing of the effects of all new drugs should be required before release to the public.

23. Which of the following is an assumption made in the argument above?

    (A) Birth defects caused by Thalidomide could have been prevented by testing.
    (B) Thalidomide produced more harmful birth defects than any drug before it.
    (C) The benefits of Thalidomide are not outweighed by its harmful side effects.
    (D) Thalidomide producers acted irresponsibly in putting such a dangerous drug on the market.
    (E) Less harmful drugs were available to treat the problems treated by Thalidomide.

24. The argument above is most similar to which of the following?

    (A) Exposure to loud music has been shown to be harmful to teenage hearing; therefore, teens should not be permitted to listen to loud music.
    (B) The value of research is hard to determine; therefore, amounts spent for research should be reduced.
    (C) The Ford Pinto has been found to have a design defect; therefore, it should be replaced by the manufacturer.
    (D) Teenage drivers have caused some of the worst auto accidents; therefore, driving tests for teenagers should be more rigorous than for others.
    (E) Generic drugs are less expensive than brand-name drugs; therefore, doctors should prescribe only generic drugs.

QUICK-SCORE ANSWERS

ANSWERS FOR PRACTICE TEST 1

Section 1	Section 2	Section 3	Section 4	Section 5
1. C	1. D	1. A	1. C	1. A
2. E	2. B	2. D	2. B	2. C
3. D	3. C	3. A	3. D	3. B
4. D	4. B	4. B	4. B	4. C
5. C	5. C	5. A	5. A	5. C
6. E	6. C	6. A	6. C	6. B
7. D	7. C	7. A	7. D	7. C
8. E	8. C	8. C	8. E	8. A
9. A	9. A	9. D	9. E	9. E
10. B	10. A	10. A	10. D	10. D
11. D	11. E	11. B	11. B	11. D
12. B	12. E	12. A	12. D	12. C
13. E	13. B	13. C	13. C	13. C
14. C	14. C	14. C	14. A	14. C
15. B	15. A	15. C	15. C	15. E
16. C	16. C	16. E	16. E	16. C
17. A	17. C	17. E	17. B	17. E
18. B	18. A	18. C	18. D	18. A
19. A	19. A	19. A	19. C	19. A
20. B	20. C	20. B	20. E	20. D
21. A	21. B	21. B	21. D	21. C
22. D	22. C	22. E	22. D	22. B
23. D	23. D	23. B	23. C	23. C
24. A	24. B	24. E	24. A	24. C
			25. B	
			26. E	
			27. D	
			28. B	

Excerpted from *LSAT Success 1998* © 1996 by Thomas O. White

QUICK-SCORE ANSWERS

ANSWERS FOR PRACTICE TEST 2

Section 1	Section 2	Section 3	Section 4	Section 5
1. E	1. A	1. B	1. C	1. B
2. A	2. C	2. D	2. D	2. A
3. D	3. A	3. B	3. A	3. B
4. C	4. A	4. B	4. D	4. C
5. C	5. D	5. A	5. A	5. C
6. D	6. D	6. C	6. C	6. B
7. E	7. E	7. A	7. C	7. D
8. E	8. D	8. C	8. D	8. C
9. D	9. A	9. A	9. C	9. A
10. B	10. E	10. D	10. E	10. D
11. C	11. E	11. B	11. B	11. B
12. D	12. B	12. E	12. B	12. C
13. D	13. E	13. A	13. D	13. B
14. E	14. E	14. A	14. C	14. E
15. B	15. C	15. D	15. D	15. A
16. C	16. C	16. A	16. B	16. E
17. E	17. D	17. E	17. D	17. D
18. E	18. B	18. C	18. A	18. D
19. B	19. C	19. E	19. B	19. E
20. E	20. D	20. E	20. E	20. C
21. C	21. A	21. E	21. E	21. D
22. C	22. A	22. A	22. A	22. E
23. A	23. A	23. C	23. C	23. A
24. B	24. D	24. E	24. E	24. D
			25. D	
			26. A	
			27. A	
			28. C	

Excerpted from *LSAT Success 1998* © 1996 by Thomas O. White

EXPLANATORY ANSWERS FOR PRACTICE TESTS 1 AND 2

PRACTICE TEST 1

In the following answer guide, the credited responses appear in bold type and the visualizations that make the credited response clear appear before the answers to each question set. Use the visualization to guide you in determining the credited answer.

Section 1

Questions 1-6

Statehood   A,F,K,M,O,T,V,W

Earlier   Later
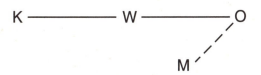

1. **(C) Ohio was a state before Kansas.**

2. **(E) Kansas was a state before Ohio.**

3. **(D) Texas was a state before Ohio.**

4. **(D) Kansas, Maine, Wyoming, Ohio, Vermont**

5. **(C) Florida was a state before Kansas.**

6. **(E) Kansas was a state before Alaska.**

Questions 7-12

Houses   T
                T's Children
                Brother
                Parents

Smaller   Larger

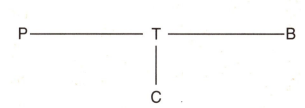

7. **(D) 1, 2**

8. **(E) son to father**

9. **(A) S is U's son.**

10. **(B) uncle**

11. **(D) 3**

12. **(B) T has exactly 3 children.**

Excerpted from *LSAT Success 1998* © 1996 by Thomas O. White

Questions 13-18

Riders-A,B,C,D,E,F,G

Busses-1,2,3

Bus

　　1 if B then no E or G

　　2 if D then no G

　　3 C always

　　3 when A and F take the same bus

13. (E) B, D, G

14. (C) 3 only

15. (B) 4

16. (C) 3 only

17. (A) 0

18. (B) A, D, E, G

Questions 19-24

W ◄────────────────► E

```
B ◄──5── A ──5─► B
D ◄──7── C ──7─► D
E ◄──2── C ──2─► E
B ◄──3── C ──3─► B
```

19. (A) Dora lives 9 miles from Elmer.

20. (B) The distance between Bruce's and Elmer's houses is shorter than the distance between Cora's and Dora's houses.

21. (A) Angela and Cora live 12 miles apart.

22. (D) 4 miles

23. (D) Bruce lives closer to Elmer than Cora does to Dora.

24. (A) 14

Section 2

In the following answer guide, the credited responses appear in bold type and the guide that directs you toward the credited response appears within the answer-choice context. The first reference is to the point of the argument and the second is to the nature of the issue involved.

1. (D) Purchasers of this brand of clothing will be stylish.

Point—Stylish people wear well-designed clothing.

Issue—Extension question/conclusion

2. (B) Even though all wrongs cannot be compensated for, some wrongs can be.

Point—Money cannot compensate for historic wrongs.

Issue—Extension question/assumption

3. (C) The mother knows when the daughter has been truthful.

Point—Tell the truth and I will believe you.

Issue—Extension question/assumption

4. (B) Unlike metal and wood products, those made from glass must be discarded rather than repaired when they break.

Point—Products made from glass can save energy.

Issue—Extension question/weakening evidence

5. (C) The price increase will not result in a decrease in the sales of Mexican oil products.

Point—Raising oil prices 20 percent will cause a 1 percent increase in the U.S.

Issue—Extension question/assumption

6. (C) Journalists report on motives and the significance of events and, like historians, traffic primarily in half-truths and lies.

Point—Those who try to describe events engage in half-truths and lies.

Issue—Extension question/conclusion

Excerpted from *LSAT Success 1998* © 1996 by Thomas O. White

7. **(C) All women are not mothers.**

    Point—Equal pay for women detracts from motherhood.

    Issue—Extension question/weakening evidence

8. **(C) As a result, the amount of heat energy lost by the Earth must closely approximate the amount gained from the sun.**

    Point—The Earth does not store energy.

    Issue—Extension question/conclusion

9. **(A) It is not inconsistent with the lecturer's statement.**

    Point—All Americans do not enjoy a high standard of living.

    Issue—Description question/nature of response

10. **(A) a country in which the majority of people enjoy a higher standard of living than that of the American people**

    Point—All Americans do not enjoy a high standard of living.

    Issue—Extension question/weakening evidence

11. **(E) There can be no relationship between a general principle and specific practices.**

    Point—Censorship is appropriate in some circumstances.

    Issue—Extension question/conclusion

12. **(E) presenting a hypothetical case**

    Point—Censorship is appropriate in some circumstances.

    Issue—Description question/tactic

13. **(B) All dogs are excluded from this motel, but many dogs are friendly. Therefore, some friendly animals are kept out of this motel.**

    Point—All have one attribute, some have another attribute; therefore, some have both attributes.

    Issue—Extension question/same point, new context

14. **(C) "social pressure"**

    Point—Causes require actions; reasons justify actions.

    Issue—Extension question/conclusion

15. **(A) the possible causes of heart disease**

    Point—Accepting the only explanation does not take all possible explanations into account.

    Issue—Description question/example

16. **(C) people with blue eyes invariably have blue-eyed children**

    Point—Children have the same color eyes as their parent(s)

    Issue—Extension question/conclusion

17. **(C) The significance of art is consistent over time.**

    Point—Similar results connote similar causes, regardless of context.

    Issue—Extension question/assumption

18. **(A) All the enemies of the republic are dead.**

    Point—Any living critic proves that Mao did not have personal enemies killed.

    Issue—Extension question/assumption

19. **(A) scientists are too concerned about failure**

    Point—Risking failure is no longer tolerated in drug development.

    Issue—Extension question/conclusion

20. **(C) The star's last movie contained the usual bit of impressive acting, but her director should have advised her to act more like an average person.**

    Point—Those producing exceptional work should use more common devices.

    Issue—Extension question/same point, new context

Excerpted from *LSAT Success 1998* © 1996 by Thomas O. White

21. **(B) Fees paid by students are the major source of funding for educational services.**

    Point—As demands on resources decrease, services and facilities should improve.

    Issue—Extension question/weakening evidence

22. **(C) There are doubts about the conclusive nature of studies on animals.**

    Point—If the government acts prematurely, it loses credibility.

    Issue—Extension question/conclusion

23. **(D) Sailors cannot be afraid of water.**

    Point—The Mercer child will not sail because of his fear of water.

    Issue—Extension question/conclusion

24. **(B) other factors could have nullified the influence of the olive oil**

    Point—Olive oil did not prevent heart attack in Betty's mother.

    Issue—Extension question/weakening evidence

Section 3

In the following answer guide, the credited responses appear in bold type and the visualizations that make the credited response clear appear before the answers to each question set. Use the visualization to guide you in determining the credited answer.

Questions 1-6

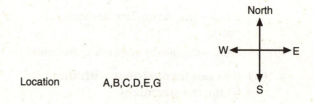

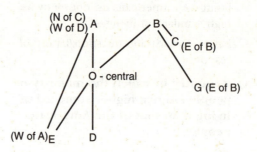

1. **(A) the northwest corner of D**

2. **(D) F is located due west of C.**

3. **(A) farther east than B**

4. **(B) northeast of C**

5. **(A) B is precisely midway between E and G.**

6. **(A) The Central Office is closer to D than to G.**

Excerpted from *LSAT Success 1998* © 1996 by Thomas O. White

Questions 7-12

Seating   H,I,J,K,L,M

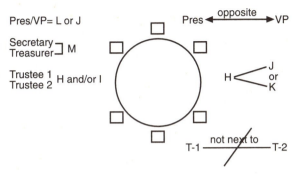

Pres/VP= L or J

Secretary
Treasurer ⌐ M

Trustee 1
Trustee 2   H and/or I

7. (A) J is the vice president

8. (C) president, vice president, trustee, secretary, treasurer

9. (D) K, I, H, J, M, L

10. (A) J, K, L

11. (B) H and J

12. (A) M is the secretary

Questions 13-18

Trucks - K, M, W   Fuel and wash - trucks before vans
                       Fuel larger tanks before smaller
Vans - C, D, F   Wash smaller before larger

Tank Size

Larger ——————————————————— Small

K

equals ——————D———M——————W more than C

F

13. (C) The Chevrolet is fueled fifth.

14. (C) The Chevrolet is fueled before the Ford.

15. (C) The Kenworth is washed second.

16. (E) White, Mack, Kenworth, Ford, Dodge, Chevrolet

17. (E) the Ford immediately before the Dodge

18. (C) Ford, Chevrolet, Dodge, Kenworth, White, Mack

Questions 19-24

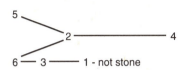

Alum, Brick, Concrete, Glass, Stone, Wood

Groups 1- 6

19. (A) aluminum

20. (B) 6, 3, 1, 5, 2, 4

21. (B) brick

22. (E) 6, 5, 4, 3, 2, 1

23. (B) stone

24. (E) wood

Section 4

In the following answer guide, the credited responses appear in bold type and the guide that directs you to the place in the passage that accounts for the credited response appears within the answer-choice context. The first reference is to the paragraph number in the passage that accounts for the credited response and the second number refers to the relevant sentence in the paragraph. The reference will appear as 2/4 for example. This means paragraph 2 and sentence 4 within paragraph 2.

1. (C) **comparing Smith's and Rawls's views of a just society**—Paragraph 4/Sentence 5

2. (B) **the theory of welfare economics** For (A) *the Scottish method* and (D) *the scientific method*, see 1/1; for (C) *the perfect-competition paradigm*, see 3/3; and for (E) *the principles of natural liberty*, see 2/3.

3. (D) **the description of the idealized competitive economy**—Paragraph 4/Sentence 2

4. (B) **concerned with improving the operation of society**—Paragraph 1/Sentence 4

Excerpted from *LSAT Success 1998* © 1996 by Thomas O. White

5. **(A)** **a recitation of methods of approaching social problems**—Most inclusive of the five answer choices

6. **(C)** **In what follows, both of these routes will be explored.**—Paragraph 4/Sentence 7

7. **(D)** **permit comparison of their concepts of justice**—Paragraph 4/Sentences 6 and 7

8. **(E)** **judgments about human actions can be made only by the resulting end-states**—Paragraph 2/Sentence 2

9. **(E)** **The net value of consequences is considered important.** Only (A), (B), (C), and (D) are mentioned as features of utilitarianism. See the importance of (A) *results*, 3/3; (B) *consequences*, 1/3; (C) *valued end-state*, 2/2; and (D) *means of achieving results*, 3/1.

10. **(D)** **It is legally acceptable for bad consequences to flow from the exercise of an individual's right or privilege.**—Paragraph 1/Sentence 8

11. **(B)** **contrast judgments of right and wrong with other types of judgments**—Paragraph 4/Sentence 5

12. **(D)** **means used to produce results**—Paragraph 3/Sentence 1 and Paragraph 2/Sentence 2

13. **(C)** **explains some judgments in law and morals**—Paragraph 1/Sentence 2

14. **(A)** **somewhat critical**—Paragraph 1/Sentence 4

15. **(C)** **an argument for the use of formal models by lawyers**—Paragraph 1/Sentence 8

16. **(E)** **a method of argumentation**—Paragraph 1/Sentence 6

17. **(B)** **locating something left out of consideration** Only (A), (C), (D), and (E) are benefits of using formal models. For (A) *determining that an argument is making a distinction without a difference*, see 1/8; for (C) *demonstrating inconsistencies in an argument*, see 4/7; for (D) *setting out difficulties with the form of argumentation*, see 2/1; and for (E) *assisting in the derivation of the logical implications of an argument*, see 1/4.

18. **(D)** **is not logically rigorous**—Paragraph 1/Sentence 4

19. **(C)** **provide the basis for argumentation**—Paragraph 3/Sentence 2

20. **(E)** **as a technique to ensure equity** Only (A), (B), (C), and (D) describe uses for models as argued in the passage. For models used (A) *as a method of argumentation*, see 4/7; (B) *as a source of answers to problems*, see 4/8; (C) *as a form of reasoning used by lawyers*, see 1/1; and (D) *as a method to identify problems with logic*, see 4/7.

21. **(D)** **Formal models are as illogical as prose models.**—Paragraph 2/Sentences 1 and 2

22. **(D)** **Omissions are a problem with formal models.**—Paragraph 4/Sentence 3

23. **(C)** **an interpretation of syntactics applied to aspects of legal discourse**—Paragraph 1/Sentence 1

24. **(A)** **A, 2, #, +, s, ?, c, p, %, $**—Paragraph 3/Sentence 1

25. **(B)** **the transmission of the dash in dot-dot-dash when two dots are always followed by a dash**—Paragraph 2/Sentence 6

26. **(E)** **a case that is exactly the same as previous cases**—Paragraph 5/Sentence 1

Excerpted from *LSAT Success 1998* © 1996 by Thomas O. White

27. **(D) Redundancy in a message reduces the information transmitted.**— Paragraph 4/Sentence 4

28. **(B) Redundancy accounts for the difference between strong and weak legal arguments.**—Paragraph 5/Sentence 2

Section 5

In the following answer guide, the credited responses appear in bold type and the guide that directs you toward the credited response appears within the answer-choice context. The first reference is to the point of the argument and the second is to the nature of the issue involved.

1. **(A) In the absence of freedom of expression, great writers do not develop.**

    Point—Neither great writers nor freedom of expression exist in Largo.

    Issue—Extension question/assumption

2. **(C) Birds, rather than cave dwellers, may have brought snakes and fish to the caves to eat.**

    Point—Cavemen ate bison, birds, snakes, and fish.

    Issue—Extension question/weakening evidence

3. **(B) people can be persuaded to abandon technology, urbanization, and mass production**

    Point—The natural benevolence of people is corrupted by institutions.

    Issue—Extension question/strengthening evidence

4. **(C) The sky is not cloudy, and rain is not falling.**

    Point—Bob is not in the slicker he wears when it is cloudy and rainy.

    Issue—Extension question/conclusion

5. **(C) Sensitive people are lovers.**

    Point—Excellent musicians love poetry.
    Issue—Description question/Sensitivity not involved in argument

6. **(B) Since owls feed only at night, the bird feeding in daylight is not an owl.**

    Point—Reasoning from properties of plazium to a conclusion

    Issue—Description question/structure of argument

7. **(C) Some ocean-liner passengers are in the care of a dangerous person.**

    Point—Captains who care for passengers may be dangerous alcoholics.

    Issue—Extension question/conclusion

8. **(A) The resources required to log forests cannot be replenished.**

    Point—Coal is a nonrenewable resource—trees are a renewable resource.

    Issue—Extension question/weakening evidence

9. **(E) Jurors think eyewitness testimony leaves less room for doubt than does expert testimony.**

    Point—Jurors find expert testimony less persuasive than eyewitness testimony.

    Issue—Extension question/conclusion

10. **(D) In the future, more older students will enter college than ever before.**

    Point—College enrollment will decline when the number of 18-year-olds declines.

    Issue—Extension question/weakening evidence

11. **(D) In the past, film was an important art form.**

    Point—Contemporary film is not an art form.

    Issue—Extension question/unsupported conclusion

Excerpted from *LSAT Success 1998* © 1996 by Thomas O. White

12. (C) **Countries can accurately determine one another's military strength.**

    Point—U. S. can assure military balance of power by selling arms to other countries.

    Issue—Extension question/assumption

13. (C) **The sale and delivery of military equipment is usually known only by the two countries involved.**

    Point—U. S. can assure military balance of power by selling arms to other countries.

    Issue—Extension question/weakening evidence

14. (C) **Lights are maintained in good working order because of the inspection requirement.**

    Point—Turn-signal inspection identifies few defective lights.

    Issue—Extension question/weakening evidence

15. (E) **It is seldom possible to determine which information involves the public welfare.**

    Point—Public welfare is the only justification for exposing people's private lives.

    Issue—Extension question/weakening evidence

16. (C) **Personal privacy is an important right.**

    Point—Public welfare is the only justification for exposing people's private lives.

    Issue—Extension question/conclusion

17. (E) **Voting is a form of political involvement.**

    Point—Voting and political involvement have a strong relationship.

    Issue—Extension question/conclusion

18. (A) **Some students prefer geometry to physics.**

    Point—All prefer history to geometry— some prefer physics to history.

    Issue—Extension question/conclusion

19. (A) **Some students prefer geometry to physics.**

    Point—All prefer history to geometry— some prefer physics to history.

    Issue—Extension question/conclusion

20. (D) **Nature cannot be changed.**

    Point—A snake will bite a hand that fed it.

    Issue—Extension question/conclusion

21. (C) **Cheese and butter produce greater profits for processors than does milk.**

    Point—Without government subsidies, more milk would be used for cheese and butter.

    Issue—Extension question/conclusion

22. (B) **Certain attributes of works of art are typical of specific periods.**

    Point—Many characteristics differentiate early Greek period sculpture.

    Issue—Extension question/assumption

23. (C) **The villagers do not trust the mayor.**

    Point—By paying a bounty for snakes, the mayor will rid the town of them.

    Issue—Extension question/NOT weakening evidence

24. (C) **It appears that the cost of housing at Spring Lake is prohibitive. I looked at a number of houses last month, and they cost much more than I could afford.**

    Point—Spring Lake is too rough for sailing.

    Issue—Description question/structure of argument

Excerpted from *LSAT Success 1998* © 1996 by Thomas O. White

PRACTICE TEST 2

In the following answer guide, the credited responses appear in bold type, and the visualization that makes the credited response clear appears before the question set. Use the visualization to guide you in determining the credited answer.

Section 1

Questions 1–6

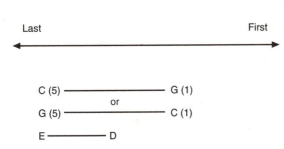

Golf   C, D, E, F, G

1. **(E) E finishes fourth.**

2. **(A) E finishes second.**

3. **(D) F finishes ahead of E.**

4. **(C) 3**

5. **(C) F finishes ahead of D.**

6. **(D) F finishes fourth.**

Questions 7–12

Ages   A, F, I, K, M, O, T, U, V, W

7. **(E) The Kansas president is younger than the Ohio president.**

8. **(E) The Kansas president is older than the Ohio president.**

9. **(D) The Texas president is older than the Ohio president.**

10. **(B) Wyoming**

11. **(C) The Florida president is older than the Kansas president.**

12. **(D) The Alaska president is older than the Ohio president.**

Questions 13–18

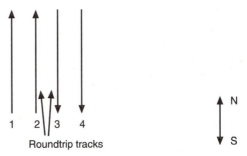

2 consecutive trains cannot use same track

Local after express or metro

13. **(D) I and II only**

14. **(E) 4, 1, 3, 2**

15. **(B) 2**

16. **(C) R on track 2, U on track 3, S on track 1, T on track 3, Q on track 2**

17. **(E) 4, 0**

18. **(E) The greatest number of locals cannot exceed the greatest number of express trains.**

Excerpted from *LSAT Success 1998* © 1996 by Thomas O. White

Questions 19–24

Beach   C, E, J, R, W
               Food, Blankets, Umbrella, Drives, Pays

Brother—Sister
First brings umbrella
Driver = male
Brother pays
When E brings food—W not drive
When C or J brings blankets—R drives

19. **(B) Rick drives.**

20. **(E) Carol is Rick's sister.**

21. **(C) bring the umbrella**

22. **(C) Jenny brings neither blankets nor food.**

23. **(A) drive**

24. **(B) Carol and Rick**

Section 2

In the following answer guide, the credited responses appear in bold type, and the guide that directs you toward the credited response appears within the answer choice context. The first reference is to the point of the argument and the second is to the nature of the issue involved.

1. **(A) Quiet people are not easily identified.**

    Point—All people have one attribute. All with the one attribute have a second attribute.

    Issue—Extension question/conclusion

2. **(C) It assumes the conclusion.**

    Point—Ambitious people are not good parents. Good parents are not ambitious people.

    Issue—Description question/tactic

3. **(A) Arthritis specialists provide authoritative information on effective medication for arthritis.**

    Point—Connect Arthrelief to the most prescribed medicine.

    Issue—Extension question/NOT assumption

4. **(A) Reasoning abilities of illiterate people should not be tested using tasks that do not involve familiar devices.**

    Point—Testing results for illiterates vary by the devices used to test.

    Issue—Extension question/conclusion

5. **(D) Daily exercise does not contribute greatly to Japanese worker productivity.**

    Point—Americans and Japanese vary in terms of daily exercise and productivity.

    Issue—Extension question/weakening evidence

6. **(D) A country with a democratic government must have a politically active people.**

    Point—Political indifference is required by dictators and central governments.

    Issue—Extension question/conclusion

7. **(E) IV, II, III, I**

    Point—The path to follow to U. S. energy independence

    Issue—Extension question/order of evidence to conclusion

8. **(D) work areas are directly related to college degree areas**

    Point—It is wasteful to spend for training that is little used.

    Issue—Extension question/assumption

9. **(A) It does not state that Alert tablets cause grade improvement.**

    Point—Students who use Alert get good grades.

    Issue—Extension question/strengthening conclusion

10. **(E) Friendliness is a virtue.**

    Point—Dogs and cats express friendliness differently.

    Issue—Extension question/conclusion

Excerpted from *LSAT Success 1998* © 1996 by Thomas O. White

11. **(E) Public beaches in Canada are no cleaner or cheaper than those in the United States.**

    Point—Canadian public campgrounds compare favorably with U. S. public beaches.

    Issue—Extension question/weakening evidence

12. **(B) proposes a common cause for similar effects**

    Point—Computers and people play poker in the same way.

    Issue—Description question/tactic

13. **(E) The industry association has standards that exceed the legal requirements.**

    Point—Inspections identify no violations.

    Issue—Extension question/conclusion

14. **(E) children do not generally accept adult responsibilities prior to the rites**

    Point—Rites that formally impose adult responsibilities are found in societies with unclear differences between adults and children.

    Issue—Extension question/strengthening evidence

15. **(C) Very few physically challenged people use facilities in the places where they have been installed.**

    Point—Devices to help the physically impaired use public transportation help only very athletic people.

    Issue—Extension question/strengthening evidence

Questions 16–17

16. **(C) Purchasers attempt to secure more credit than they can afford.**

    Point—Credit bureaus provide valuable services with little personal intrusion by reducing business losses and preventing consumers from overextending their financial obligations.

    Issue—Extension question/assumption of behavior

17. **(D) justified by the economic value to business and society**

    Point—Credit bureaus provide valuable services with little personal intrusion by reducing business losses and preventing consumers from overextending their financial obligations.

    Issue—Extension question/conclusion

18. **(B) Harold is a better writer than Stan.**

    Point—Harold writes better short stories and novels than does Stan.

    Issue—Extension question/conclusion

19. **(C) Since 1969, more high school graduates have decided to seek a college degree.**

    Point—The value of a college education has dropped significantly over time.

    Issue—Extension question/weakening evidence

20. **(D) Engineering of genes and environment are virtually the same.**

    Point—Engineering produces change in many characteristics of people.

    Issue—Extension question/strengthening evidence

Questions 21–22

21. **(A) Shea confuses influence with merit**

    Point—Similar influence requires similar recognition.

    Issue—Extension question/conclusion

22. **(A) the Springfield Pops**

    Point—Similar influence requires similar recognition.

    Issue—Extension question/same structure/new context

23. **(A) All three resorts Ann previously visited are in north Miami Beach, and the new resort is in south Miami Beach.**

    Point—Florida resorts are enjoyable to Ann.

    Issue—Extension question/insignificant evidence

Excerpted from *LSAT Success 1998* © 1996 by Thomas O. White

24. (D) Social reasons account for the attendance of most students at services.

Point—There is an inverse relationship between cheating and religious exposure.

Issue—Extension question/weakening evidence

Section 3

In the following answer guide, the credited responses appear in bold type, and the visualization that makes the credited response clear appears before each question set. Use the visualization to guide you in determining the credited answer.

Questions 1–6

Bids   L, M, N, O, P, Q

Lowest   Highest

K——Q——P——N

M——O——P

1. (B) M, L, O, Q, P, N

2. (D) M or L

3. (B) L submits the third-lowest bid.

4. (D) Q submits a higher bid than M

5. (A) L, M, Q, O, P, N

6. (C) Q and L

Questions 7–12

Graduation   L, M, N, O, P, Q, R, S, T, U

1971 - 1975 - Two per year

1971   1975

M———Q
   1

P and Q in '71 to '74

S and T together

Q not with N

7. (A) S, T; P, R; M, O; Q, N; L, U

8. (C) L, N, S

9. (A) L graduated in 1972.

10. (D) R graduated in 1972.

11. (B) 1971 and 1974

12. (E) S graduated in 1975.

Questions 13–18

Table set-ups   A,B,C,D,E

B must E
C must D
E not with C
D not with A
A always sets up

13. (A) Adam only

14. (A) one

15. (D) Beth, Dana, and Edith

16. (A) Dana and Edith

17. (E) Beth and Edith only

18. (C) two

Questions 19–24

Dentists - A, B, C   Hygienists all assigned
Hygienists - S, T, U, V

A and B - 2 hygienists each
C - 1 or 2 hygienists
T assign A and B or C

19. (E) either B or C

20. (E) U is assigned to only one dentist.

21. (E) either B or C

22. (A) A only

23. (C) U is assigned to only one dentist.

24. (E) U is assigned to only one dentist.

Excerpted from *LSAT Success 1998* © 1996 by Thomas O. White

Section 4

In the following answer guide, the credited responses appear in bold type, and the guide that directs you to the place in the passage that accounts for the credited response appears within the answer choice context. The first reference is to the paragraph number in the passage that accounts for the credited response and the second number refers to the relevant sentence in the paragraph. The reference will appear as 2/4 for example. This means paragraph 2 and sentence 4 within paragraph 2.

1. (C) **advocate limiting handgun availability**—Paragraph 3/Sentence 6

2. (D) **gun ownership by people associated with violence has greatly increased**—Paragraph 2/Sentence 7

3. (A) **dramatize the increase in gun-related violence**—Paragraph 1/Sentence 2

4. (D) **Handgun ownership among middle-class New Yorkers has increased fourfold in the last ten years.**—Paragraph 2/Sentences 6 and 7

5. (A) **The rate of growth in gun ownership in the Northeast is greater than that of other regions**—Paragraph 2/Sentence 5

6. (C) **Urban violence is due to subcultural differences among residents.**—Paragraph 1/Sentences 3 and 4

7. (C) **regulation of handgun possession**—Paragraph 3/Sentence 4

8. (D) **comparing hardware and software**—Paragraph 1/Sentence 1; Paragraph 2/Sentence 1

9. (C) **Software can be located within hardware.**—Paragraph 1/Sentence 3

10. (E) **hardware is readily changeable** According to the passage, choices (A), (B), (C), and (D) are all true. For (A) the cost of duplicating software is low, see 2/1; for (B) very little software is sold outright, see 2/5; for (C) hardware is often not patented, see 3/2; and for (D) software requires minimal originality, see 3/3.

11. (B) **It can be copyrighted.**—Paragraph 3/Sentence 1

12. (B) **It is more profitable to sell copies of software than hardware.**—Paragraph 2/Sentences 2 and 4

13. (D) **Patented hardware requires greater inventiveness than does software.**—Paragraph 3/Sentence 3

14. (C) **One purchased the restaurant when one purchased the dinner prepared there.**—Production Capacity/Production Result

15. (D) **a means of tracing changes in group status in society**—Paragraph 1/Sentence 3

16. (B) **the relationship between group status and frequency of court appearance**—Paragraph 2/Sentence 2

17. (D) **court performance**—Paragraph 2/Sentence 5

18. (A) **There is an inverse relationship between wealth and court appearances.**—Paragraph 2/Sentence 5

19. (B) **There is a positive correlation between the New Haven findings and those of other towns.**—Paragraph 2/Sentence 4

20. (E) **a legal historian**—Paragraph 5/Sentence 6

21. (E) **court procedures remain the same over long periods of time** According to the passage, choices (A), (B), (C), and (D) are all true. For (A) court records can be constructed over long periods of time, see 3/5; for (B) court appearances change with status within the society, see 3/1; for (C) court records are generally preserved in most jurisdictions, see 3/4; and for (D) court appearances can be treated collectively to reflect status, see 3/5.

22. (A) **to point out that advertising reliability varies by type of good**—Paragraph 2/Sentence 3

23. (C) **consumption**—Paragraph 2/Sentence 2

Excerpted from *LSAT Success 1998* © 1996 by Thomas O. White

24. **(E) Advertisers spend large sums of money on informative messages.**
    According to the passage, choices (A), (B), (C), and (D) are all true. For (A) Search goods advertising is likely to be informative and truthful, see 2/5; for (B) Mail order advertising in magazines is not likely to be truthful, see 5/4; for (C) Experienced goods advertisers have incentive to mislead, see 3/1; and for (D) Credence goods advertisements may never be determined to be valid, see 3/1.

25. **(D) "Analysis of the Function of Advertising"—Paragraph 1/Sentence 1**

26. **(A) auto transmission oil—Paragraph 3/Sentence 1**

27. **(A) Many advertisers and consumers do not act rationally.—Paragraph 1/Sentence 3**

28. **(C) Credence-goods consumers require statutory protection.—Paragraph 4/Sentence 2**

Section 5

In the following answer guide, the credited responses appear in bold type, and the guide that directs you toward the credited response appears within the answer choice context. The first reference is to the point of the argument and the second is to the nature of the issue involved.

1. **(B) It is insignificant and coincidental.**

    Point—Significant figures in two peoples lives total the same number.

    Issue—Description question/characterize the number

2. **(A) identifying incongruities in the use of force**

    Point—The acceptable use of force varies by context.

    Issue—Description question/tactic

3. **(B) Past practice validates future action.**

    Point—Past is prologue

    Issue—Extension question/conclusion

4. **(C) Sales of a book are not always indicative of its value.**

    Point—Able criticism anticipates the market reaction.

    Issue—Extension question/weakening evidence

Questions 5–6

5. **(C) the expression of deep feeling**

    Point—Emotional societies produce better writing than technical societies.

    Issue—Description question/rephrasing

6. **(B) Societies must be emotional or technical.**

    Point—Emotional societies produce better writing than technical societies.

    Issue—Extension question/assumption

Questions 7–8

7. **(D) Artists generally venerate their countries.**

    Point—Artists oppose their environments.

    Issue—Extension question/weakening evidence

8. **(C) The purpose of art is to both find fault with and escape from life.**

    Point—Artists oppose their environments.

    Issue—Extension question/assumption

9. **(A) presented more than one issue to respondents**

    Point—Drug addicts on welfare should not get free needles.

    Issue—Description question/tactic

10. **(D) When people complain about their health, they get old; but no one is complaining about their health, so we must have no people getting old.**

    Point—If : then—Not if : not then

    Issue—Extension question/same structure/new context

Excerpted from *LSAT Success 1998* © 1996 by Thomas O. White

Questions 11–12

11. **(B) Oil, coal, and fresh water are natural resources.**

    Point—Natural resources should not be given away by a state.

    Issue—Extension question/assumption

12. **(C) New York City will pay Pennsylvania and New Jersey for each gallon of water diverted.**

    Point—Natural resources should not be given away by a state.

    Issue—Extension question/weakening evidence

13. **(B) a theory postulating suffering as a requisite for creativity**

    Point—Excluding matters of choice, the present is the product of past actions.

    Issue—Extension question/NOT conclusion

14. **(E) Baxter feels that women and men have unequal capacities.**

    Point—For various reasons Baxter is not a feminist.

    Issue—Extension question/NOT conclusion

15. **(A) Modern educational aids should be provided for urban children.**

    Point—Suburban students have more educational resources than urban students.

    Issue—Extension question/conclusion

16. **(E) A philosopher's reasoning is complicated because he was trained in a tradition that often uses complicated reasoning.**

    Point—Because they do not, they should not be expected to.

    Issue—Extension question/same structure/new context

Questions 17–18

17. **(D) If Japan and the United States sign a treaty, interests of each will be served by the agreement.**

    Point—Treaties serve self-interest, not trust.

    Issue—Extension question/conclusion

18. **(D) Treaties do not serve mutual interests of countries.**

    Point—Treaties serve self-interest, not trust.

    Issue—Extension question/NOT conclusion

19. **(E) Employees of most chemical plants develop abnormal chromosome patterns.**

    Point—Plant environment may produce abnormal chromosome patterns in workers.

    Issue—Extension question/strengthening evidence

20. **(C) Only legislators who do not favor the bill were polled.**

    Point—Some legislators support the bills and some do not.

    Issue—Extension question/conclusion

21. **(D) The Society intensified its falcon sighting program in 1988.**

    Point—More sightings result from more falcons.

    Issue—Extension question/weakening evidence

22. **(E) writing was not the only factor in deciding which articles to publish**

    Point—Worthy and well-written articles are not always published.

    Issue—Extension question/conclusion

Questions 23–24

23. **(A) Birth defects caused by Thalidomide could have been prevented by testing.**

    Point—Testing will detect unforeseen effects in new drugs.

    Issue—Extension question/assumption

24. **(D) Teenage drivers have caused some of the worst auto accidents; therefore, driving tests for teenagers should be more rigorous than for others.**

    Point—Testing will detect unforeseen effects in new drugs.

    Issue—Extension question/same structure/new context

Excerpted from *LSAT Success 1998* © 1996 by Thomas O. White

THE APPLICATION: INSIDER'S TIPS

THE PERSONAL STATEMENT

All law schools require or allow you to submit some sort of personal statement with your application, and nothing gives students more trouble than this seemingly simple task. People become nervous and disconcerted when asked to write about themselves and tend to make two general types of mistakes when constructing their personal statements. The first is the "why-I'm-so-great mistake." The brightest, most humble student will end up writing a personal statement that would make people with Napoleon complexes blush in embarrassment. The second type of mistake is the "laundry-list" mistake. Your personal statement should not be a grab bag of all the things you have done in your life. Information about charitable work, club membership, offices held, etc., should appear in the application proper. Nearly all schools have sections for extracurricular activities and charitable work.

Think of the personal statement as a mini-paper or a short story about some feature of your life. It should have a thesis—though an implied thesis works better in this situation—a development phase, and a conclusion. It should be no more than 450 words and, if possible, should fit on a single sheet of paper. Do not, however, make the font so small as to be unreadable in trying to reduce it to one page in length. Try to make the opening sentence catchy, but don't make it sound ridiculous or pompous. A short account of some important event in your life is perfectly fine for the personal statement. The idea is to tell the law school a lot about yourself without duplicating information that should be found elsewhere in the application.

The personal statement is usually not a terribly important part of the application, but it is the kind of thing that if very badly done and then read by committee members can result in serious harm. On some occasions, though, a personal statement can be so charming, moving, or painfully forthright that it can make the difference between admission and rejection, so you must give the personal statement careful attention.

LETTERS OF RECOMMENDATION

You should arrange for at least three letters of recommendation. Two of these letters should come from academics; preferably from professors of classes you have done

extremely well in. Don't be concerned that the professor won't remember you. Just give her a brief resume, a list of when you took her class and the final grade in the class, and any papers you might still have from the course. It is not required that recommending professors know you well; only that they can comment on your class performance relative to other students. Then ask the professor directly whether or not she can write you a good recommendation. If there is some reluctance on the part of the professor, thank her and move on.

With rare exceptions, a recommender will write one letter addressed generically to law school admission committees. This letter will then be sent to all of the law schools to which you apply. Tell your professors early that you will be needing a letter of recommendation. This means notifying potential recommenders in September of the year you are applying to law school. Also give your recommenders a deadline for when to have the letters ready. Let them have three or so weeks, but definitely track down for the letters if you have not received them by the middle of October.

Give all of the materials to the professor at the same time; don't string out requests for letters two or three at a time. Include envelopes addressed to either yourself or the law school, depending on what the application requires (explained at the end of this heading). This means that you must have all of your applications by mid September. Waiver forms allow you to waive your right to see your letters of recommendation. If schools ask, your best course is usually to waive your right to see your letters of recommendation. Make sure any waiver forms are correctly filled in with your signature. Without such a waiver the law school will place less credence in the recommender's statements, believing that the recommender will not be as forthcoming if she thinks the student will have access to her evaluation.

Law schools receive letters of recommendation in one of three ways. First, they may ask the recommender to send the letter directly to the law school. In this case, make sure that the envelopes are correctly made out and that all the forms are attached by a paper clip to the appropriate envelopes. Second, some schools ask that recommenders enclose their letters in an envelope, sign it across the back seal, and then give the envelope back to the student who is to enclose it in the application. Make sure you know which school does things which way and keep the two piles separate when giving them to the recommender. Third, you can place your letters on file, for a fee, with the LSAS and it

---

William Weaver, J.D., Ph.D., Department of Political Science, University of Texas at El Paso

will send the letters out to schools requesting your test scores. It is important to recognize that very few college professors or employers know how to write an effective letter of recommendation for law school. You should delicately suggest to your recommenders that they approach the letter in the following way. First, they should use specifics rather than rely on generalizations. Rather than saying that "Roger X was a wonderful student who earned an 'A' in my class in American literature" and leaving the matter there, it would make a big difference if we knew, say, that historically only 5 percent of his American literature students receive "A" grades. Also, citing specifics about class performance can be helpful, especially if the student demonstrated exceptional rhetorical skills or helped substantially in making the class successful. Likewise, detailed comments about written work submitted for the course are preferable to general statements about ability. Letters should concentrate on three things. First, they should address your dependability in performing the assignments and keeping up with the course readings. Second, the analytical skills of the student should be addressed. And, finally, the student's communicative skills should be discussed. Additional comments, where appropriate, about a student's integrity or personal information are welcomed.

One additional question that is frequently asked concerns letters of recommendation and whether or not the student should use the recommendation of a famous friend or relative or a family member or friend who is a judge or attorney. Use only recommenders who know you well enough to write intelligently about your character and abilities. If a famous person or judge meets this requirement, then by all means ask that person to recommend you.

TO HOW MANY SCHOOLS SHOULD YOU APPLY?

One of the worst mistakes a prospective law student can make is to apply to too few schools. As a general rule, apply to no less than twelve institutions. Under certain circumstances, students should apply to upward of twenty schools. Those circumstances are discussed below.

If you apply to a dozen schools you should divide these schools up into four groups. Three of the schools you apply to should be institutions where your chances of admission are slim. Obviously, what counts as slim depends on your numbers. If you have a 3.0 GPA and score in the 70th percentile on the LSAT, then UT Austin, Duke, Cornell, Wisconsin, Minnesota, etc., are all slim possibilities for admission. The second three schools should be institutions where you probably will not be admitted, but stand, say, a 25 percent chance of getting in. The third set

of three schools should be institutions where you stand a 40 percent chance or better of admission. Finally, you should have three schools where you stand a very high chance of admission. Many times students get "boxed out," left without an offer of admission because they applied to too few schools or applied only to schools beyond their reach. Bear in mind that at schools such as Stanford, Yale, Harvard, Chicago, and Columbia you cannot count on admission even if you have a 3.9 GPA and score above the 95th percentile on the LSAT. All applicants should apply to a range of schools. This book contains bar graphs for most schools that show the total enrollment, percentage of students admitted, average LSAT score and average GPA of students, and average student debt upon graduation. You can use the information in these graphs to estimate your chances of admission to a particular school.

There are basically three circumstances where students should apply to up to twenty law schools. The first is when students have extremely low numbers—say a 2.5 GPA and a 30th percentile on the LSAT. In this circumstance, students should apply to fifteen schools that are considered to be in the bottom tier of law schools. Five applications should be directed at third-tier (one tier up from the bottom) law schools. Remember, all ABA-accredited law schools deliver a first-rate education, and whether or not you are a good lawyer often has little to do with grades or where you went to law school. Prospective clients do not ask F. Lee Bailey where he went to law school or what sort of grades he made.

The second circumstance that justifies higher numbers of applications is when an applicant has very good numbers but not quite good enough for top-tier institutions. If you are Anglo and have a 3.5 GPA and score in the 80th percentile on the LSAT you should make twelve applications to schools that seem just beyond your reach—schools ranging in rank from number five to twenty-five.

The final circumstance that justifies increased numbers of applications is when the applicant is a member of a minority group favored by law school admission committees and has "mixed" or good but marginal numbers. For example, a student who has a 3.8 GPA but scores in the 50th percentile on the LSAT may want to still use the four category approach, but triple the normal number of applications for the first tier or schools where the student perceives he or she has a "slim" chance of admission. The same goes for an applicant who is a member of a minority group favored for admission by law schools and has, say, a 3.4 GPA and scores in the 80th percentile on the LSAT. The reason applicants in these categories should increase the number of applications is because admission of members of minority groups is often idiosyncratic and not measured against the standard applicant pool. These students should risk a few more applications to schools that seem out of their range.

GEOGRAPHIC CONSIDERATIONS

There is a slight admissions edge given to candidates who live farther away from the school to which they applied. Schools seek to formulate a diverse student body that includes representation of as many states as possible. Since most law schools receive the majority of their applications from relatively nearby, candidates across the country might get a slight break in admissions decisions. This favoring may be the subconscious desire on the part of the evaluator to introduce some degree of novelty in the class, or may even specifically be an item for consideration. Also, one should realize that it is usually more difficult to gain admission to one's undergraduate alma mater, simply because the law school receives a very large number of applicants from the "home" school. Additionally, a lot of students are under the misconception that one will have to practice law near where one attends law school. After graduating from an ABA-accredited school you may take the bar in any jurisdiction in the United States. And rarely do people attending law school in the jurisdiction to which you wish to move have any decided advantage in passing the bar. So do not think, for example, that you must go to law school in Texas in order to practice in Texas.

ELECTRONIC APPLICATIONS

As would be expected, more and more schools are allowing candidates to submit applications electronically over the Internet. Obviously, there is no admissions advantage to electronically submitted applications, and until the entire applications process becomes electronically integrated—letters of recommendation and other matter to be appended to the application may be submitted via file attachment, document scanner, or other electronic means. The traditional paper method, in fact, may be preferable because it allows the student to have everything together in one place to be submitted. It is easier to keep track of what is missing from a packet and what further actions need to be taken. If you are applying both online and through the traditional method, you will just have more items to keep track of. You will already have a lot to follow anyway, making sure your letters of recommendation are turned in, your personal statement is included, your LSAT score is requested for each school from the LSDAS, and so forth. Filing with some schools online simply adds another layer—and an avoidable layer—of complexity.

Second, there is a different mind-set when filling out paper forms than that used when submitting information via a computer. There is a penumbra of informality,

spontaneity, fuzzy edges, however one wishes to put it, when communicating electronically over the Internet. This can be readily seen in the difference in grammar and syntax found on the Internet when compared to typewriting. You may not be as alert to mistakes, colloquialisms, idiosyncratic phrasing, syntactical errors when submitting an electronic application as when you must think about answers before committing them to paper.

When the LSAS has moved to an integrated application procedure, where all major items of the application may be submitted electronically at all of the participating institutions, applying online should be more appealing than it presently is.

DEAN CERTIFICATION FORMS

Some law schools still require that you have the dean of your school at your undergraduate institution fill out a certification form. This sometimes confuses students, since they often do not know the dean of their school or what a dean even does. Generally, the forms are used to make sure that the student formally is held in good character or integrity by the student's undergraduate college and institution. Disciplinary action for cheating and violation of laws are the sorts of thing that the form is meant to elicit from the applicant's dean's office. Just take the form to the dean of your school—ask any professor in your department where that is—and they will know what to do with it.

THINGS TO CONSIDER: GENDER, ETHNICITY, AND EXPERIENCE

Law schools look to diversify their classes as much as possible. The most common law student tends to be about 23 years old, white, and male. Many law students have never had full-time jobs, and the first such job they will have will be as a lawyer. Consequently, law schools usually give slightly favorable admission breaks to students who are members of minority groups with favored admission status, nontraditional students, and applicants who have interesting experiences or backgrounds. If you fall into one of these categories your chances for admission at schools outside the range of your numbers increase, but such decisions become more idiosyncratic. In essence, if you have reasonable numbers you are no longer competing against the entire applicant pool for a school. You may be competing against other members of minority groups or nontraditional students. So, if you are a member of a minority group, a nontraditional student, or someone with unusual life experiences, shoot higher than you normally would.

Applicants who are members of minority groups ought not feel any guilt that they will be trading on their ethnicity to gain admission to law school. Perhaps your first lesson as an attorney is that you use whatever weapons you have available to win your case. Law schools give preferences to veterans, to women, to nontraditional students, to single mothers, and to a host of other "classes" of applicants. They do not do this because they are all run by bleeding hearts, they do this because it is the best thing for the school. Think about it. In three years a law school has to take a group of (mostly) young people, who often have never had a full-time job, and prepare them to take responsibility for the property, affairs, and sometimes the lives, of their clients. One aid in this process is to develop a diverse class with students of varying backgrounds and experiences. Preferences in admission are designed to help all law students mature and learn together.

Note that the registration form for the LSAT and LSDAS includes an ethnic identikit section. This section contains categories for Hispanic and Chicano applicants. Make sure that you indicate the proper category; do not simply glance and see Hispanic and check it. Also, make sure that you sign up for the Candidate Referral Service for ABA-accredited law schools (question 12), but do not bother to sign up for the Candidate Referral Service for non-ABA–approved law schools. The CRS allows schools to access a database looking for specific sorts of potential law applicants. Often times, as a result of these searches, a student will receive an application from an institution that he or she had not thought of applying to. Further, these invitations to apply often come with an application fee waiver.

Note further that the Fifth Circuit Court of Appeals held in Hopwood v. Texas that members of minority group status may not be used as a criterion in admitting students to law school. This decision is law for the states of Texas, Louisiana, and Mississippi.

HOW LAW SCHOOLS EVALUATE APPLICATIONS

Obviously the two most important items in your application are your undergraduate GPA and your LSAT score. All law schools have devised their own unique formula to give varying amounts of weight to these two items. These indexes are calculated by the LSDAS and are available upon demand. Initially, then, the index score of an applicant is the most crucial item in the application.

Based on the index number, many schools will have a score at which the applicant is presumptively admitted and, conversely, a score at which the applicant is presumptively rejected. Except for very unusual situations it is difficult to get out of the automatic rejection pile. The presumptive admit numbers usually do not come anywhere near the majority of admissions offers to be made. Most of the decisions of admission are made by considering further information in applications. Difficulty of course work, undergraduate institution, loads taken, full-time work during school, letters of recommendation, life experience, charitable work, and other items may affect decisions. Some evaluators go through each application in depth, while others stick mainly with the numbers.

Usually a file is looked at by a number of evaluators, and a sort of collective "grade" oftentimes determines whether or not to admit a candidate. Recently, some law schools have been moving back to the practice of granting interviews to applicants. For a period of years, few schools were willing to interview applicants. Now, however, schools such as University of Texas School of Law, and beginning this year, Texas Tech School of Law, are interviewing candidates. The primary reason these two schools moved to an interview method is a Fifth Circuit Court of Appeals decision forbidding the use of ethnic information in the admissions decisions of candidates to school programs. By moving to interviews, these institutions hope to be able to develop information leading to admissions of ethnically diverse candidates without violating the rule in Hopwood.

However, schools outside of the Fifth Circuit, and not governed by Hopwood, are also revisiting the interview as an admissions tool. If you are invited to interview at a school that you are very interested in, go on the interview. If you are broke and cannot pay for a trip, do not be bashful; tell the school you have no money to make a trip at the moment but that you would be willing to accept all help in this regard. The school will probably say there is no money available, but at least it knows that you declined the interview for financial reasons rather than for holding a negative opinion of the school. And, you never know, the school might come through with money for the trip. Be aware, though, that an interview is a double-edged sword. It can just as easily assure rejection as easily as it can advance the possibility of admission. Make sure you are up on your interview skills and dress appropriately. Your career counseling office will be able to help you in these matters.

LAW SCHOOL RESPONSES TO APPLICATIONS

WHICH OFFER TO ACCEPT

Deciding which offer of admission to accept is a relatively straightforward proposition, so long as you keep a few things in mind. The thing to keep in mind is that you are not shopping for a piece of art. You don't "buy" what you like or what "feels good" to you. You select a law school based on practical considerations. These considerations include the reputation of the school, its success at placing graduates, starting salary of graduates, its effective area of placement, and, if relevant, cost of attendance.

Let us begin by dividing law schools up into three classes: national, regional, and localized institutions. National institutions are law schools that have a reputation that allows their graduates to be competitive for employment almost anywhere in the United States. National institutions are usually, though not exclusively, the top twenty or thirty law schools in rankings lists.

Regional institutions are schools that have strong reputations within some relatively large but limited geographic area. Regional schools generally enjoy strong hiring patterns in their areas, but the further away one gets from these schools the weaker one's placement ability becomes as one encroaches on territory occupied by neighbor regional institutions.

Localized institutions are schools that have a fairly severely limited placement area. Sometimes these schools can be dramatically hemmed in by nearby more highly ranked schools. Law schools with lesser reputations within 250 miles of a dozen or more "national" law schools may be severely limited in where they can place their graduates.

There is no such thing as a bad ABA-approved law school. This is the truth. They are all high-quality institutions, and the training at Yale will be little different from the training at Nebraska. However, perhaps unfairly, though, certain things will hinge on where you attend law school.

Offers from National Schools

If you are lucky enough to have numbers that bring offers of admission from top-thirty institutions, your decision is, or should be, fairly easy: you simply accept admission at the law school that can demonstrate the greatest success in placing its graduates, as measured by high starting salaries, employment in large and prestigious law firms or major corporations, and location of employed graduates in the country's major urban centers. This rule is fairly hard and fast, but there are a couple of situations that might justify a deviation. Say you are accepted at the University of Texas at Austin and Vanderbilt University, but you are a Texas resident. Even though Vanderbilt can demonstrate a superior track record of placements based on your criteria, Texas has a much better placement record than the average law school and is extremely well regarded by judges and lawyers, and Vanderbilt's record is not so much better than that of Texas to justify the difference in the expense to attend. Here you must make your decision based on likelihoods. The likelihood of getting a job offer as a graduate of Texas, which is near or matches a job offer you would get coming out of Vanderbilt, is high enough to warrant sacrificing the few position difference in the rankings between the universities.

For some, the more interesting question might arise when they have been accepted by Texas and, say, Columbia. Generally, one should select Columbia. There may be a $50,000 (or more) difference in educational expenses, but there is a strong likelihood that if you attend Columbia, this difference will quickly be made up by higher starting salary or by a greater marketability that lets you practice law where you want. Do not be contrary just to be contrary. If given the choice between a law school whose graduates' beginning salaries are among the "top in the country" and a law school with starting average salaries for its graduates that are 30 percent or more less, which, nevertheless, you like better, keep in mind that although money may not be everything, you are considering investing considerable money, time, and effort in a career that is attractive in good part because it can promise affluence. Remember, if you have the opportunity to achieve the big numbers, keep your eye on the ball.

Offers from Regional Schools

If you don't get any offers from national schools, then your best bet is to attend a regional school with a strong placement record and bar passage. If you can do it, visit your two best options and try to get a feel for the area and the way the law school operates. Talk to law students and ask the placement office for detailed information on bar passage rates, starting salaries, percent placed in law-related

William Weaver, J.D., Ph.D., Department of Political Science, University of Texas at El Paso

positions within six months of graduation, and the number and kind of employers who come to campus to interview students. Just because you go to a regional school does not mean that you cannot get a job out of the school's region; it just means that the odds are more strongly against it as compared to national institutions. But if you are editor of the law review, no matter where you go to school, you will have opportunities all over the United States. So even if you go to a regional school, superior performance can make you sell like a graduate from a national institution.

Offers from Local Institutions

"Local" schools are those that have a very limited placement area for graduates. If you don't have offers from national or regional schools, then where you choose to go to law school becomes even more important than for the person trying to select from regional institutions. As with the regional choice, visit your most attractive offers and ask questions of students and obtain the information described above. Again, just because you have to go to a local institution does not mean that you cannot get a job across the country practicing law—it simply means you must work harder at such a prospect. And as mentioned previously for regional schools, superior performance can make up for a lot of the difference in marketability between the three divisions.

ACCEPTANCE, REJECTION, AND THE WAITING LIST

Law schools may do one of several things with your application. The two most obvious are that they may either reject you or make you an offer of admission. But law schools may also place you on a waiting list. Waiting lists are strange and obscure items that vary in length and purpose from school to school. Some schools have relatively short waiting lists that yield a high percentage of ultimate offers of admission, while others are tantamount to rejection. If you find yourself on the waiting list of a school you are really interested in attending, you must go on as if you had been rejected by the school. It would be unwise to place any reliance on your position on the waiting list. If you do make into the school from the waiting list, then be prepared to accept the offer and move immediately. You may not be notified that you are admitted, if indeed you are, until as late as the first day of class. Though this rarely occurs, the law school must make provisions for acceptees that cancel at the last minute.

POSITION DEPOSITS

Once you receive an acceptance from a law school, the school will ask you to send a specified amount of money to reserve your seat in the entering class—usually a couple of hundred dollars. By sending a law school a deposit, you are not promising to attend the law school. The deposit only reserves your right to attend the school and gives the law school an indication of how serious you might be about attending. These deposits are almost never refundable, but you should not think of them as a commitment to attend a particular school. When you receive your first acceptance, and if you have received no more acceptances from schools you deem more attractive by the time the deadline for deposit comes for the first school, make sure to send in the deposit. As other acceptances arrive, make sure that the deadline for the most attractive school among the acceptances does not pass without submission of a deposit. In the end you may lose some money on deposits, but it is better than being boxed out with no law school to attend in the fall.

WHAT TO DO BEFORE LAW SCHOOL BEGINS

Before beginning law school there are a number of things you can do to make your first semester easier. Do not arrive in town the day before classes or orientations are scheduled to begin. Try to arrive the last week in July or the first week in August to nail down your living quarters. If you have to have roommates, live with other law students—at least they will understand what you are going through. Avoid living with people who party or talk a lot. Living with nonlaw graduate students is OK, but by no means optimal. If you have the money, live by yourself the first year. The closer to school the better.

Certain things that did not annoy you before will begin to bug you in law school. One of those things is commute time and trying to find a parking place. Your time is so impacted in law school that the frittering away of minutes driving back and forth and looking for a spot to park can cause upset way out of proportion to the inconvenience. Become familiar with the arrangement of the law school. Become especially familiar with the library. Ask for a guide to the location of commonly used resources, and ask about any tours or orientations the library staff might give. Summer is a good time to ask library staff for "special" help. Maintain a good relationship with library staff members—they can be enormously helpful. Most students treat library staff members as their servants and rarely even know their names. Try to be someone who stands out to the staff members in a positive way—they are a tremendous resource that goes largely untapped. Also, most head librarians at law schools are lawyers as well as professional librarians, and they usually like to help students with interesting research problems.

Figure out where and when you will do your weekly shopping in advance. Do not do your shopping during popular shopping hours—as with commuting and other time-wasting endeavors you will just get aggravated. Shop late at night or early in the morning. Make a detailed weekly schedule for everything that you do. This includes exercise, movies, study time (a lot four hours per day minimum), class note entry, TV, etc. Try to schedule as much homework time as possible during breaks between classes during the day. Too many students talk the days away while they could be freeing up their evenings by studying for next day's assignments at school. Schedule at least one hour for lunch, and try to always have lunch with classmates.

Decide early on who the people are in your class that you really like and want to spend time with. As for the rest, even the ones that you sort of like, don't commit any time to them. If you are already at a function you budgeted time for, such as a class party, by all means be gregarious. But don't schedule your leisure time activities with people you don't really want to be with. Time is too short in law school.

Have a fund of several thousand dollars to see you through the first few months of school. Often times, financial aid disbursements are slow in coming. If you do not have cash, try to arrange something with relatives, or apply for credit cards or a line of credit with a bank.

Try not to fall in love while you are in law school. If you do you can kiss your schedule and orderly life goodbye. But, alas, if you must fall in love, try to make sure you fall in love with another law student—at least that way you can study together.

William Weaver, J.D., Ph.D., Department of Political Science, University of Texas at El Paso

WHAT IS FIRST-YEAR LAW SCHOOL LIKE?

First-year law school is a disorienting experience, and it is meant to be that way. In law school you don't so much learn law as you learn to speak and think like a lawyer—you learn the language of law. The type of logic and thinking that serves lawyers well is often very different from the patterns of thought students have acquired in their previous schooling. So, first-year law school often resembles and feels more like boot camp than like a purely intellectual endeavor. This analogy is apt in that law professors try to break down the presuppositions and pretensions of students and then build up the entire class in a singular understanding of a legal subject or area. The important thing to remember is that pretty much everyone feels the same way as you do—lost, somewhat depressed, a bit frightened, and wondering how they could ever have wanted to go to law school in the first place.

Law school is mostly about solving problems through the application of logic. Often, there is no "right" answer to a particular problem; there may be many satisfactory solutions or no satisfactory solutions. If you like playing with problems, often seemingly intractable problems, then you will be deluged to your heart's content in law school. If you don't like to play with such problems, or you find them hopelessly boring or trivial, you may want to talk to a prelaw adviser and dig a bit deeper into what exactly transpires in law school.

The first few weeks of law school are anxiety ridden. It is an uncomfortable time, but it can be made easier if you understand what is going to happen to you in that first semester. Most schools have orientations for new students, but there seems to be mixed reviews about whether these orientations do much good or merely increase anxiety. As with everything else, it depends on how it is done and who is doing it. So you should have a handle on what it is you will be doing and facing before you begin law school. You should find out as much as you can about how the school does things. You might also read some sources on law school education that can put you in the "proper" frame of mind. Two good sources are Scott Turow's *One L* and Karl Llewellyn's classic, *Bramble Bush*. First-semester first-year courses usually meet four times a week for an hour each time. Usually, these first-semester courses are torts, contracts, civil procedure, and criminal law or property. Along with these courses you will be required to take legal writing, a course that meets only a couple of hours a week, but is

extremely valuable. Pay close attention to what your legal writing instructors say and, even though such courses are often pass-fail, put in as much effort as possible on the legal writing assignments. Researching is much of a lawyer's stock in trade, so make sure that you understand how to use all of the tools you will be exposed to in legal writing.

Law school classes do not begin like undergraduate classes. There is no "slow start" or "class introduction," at least not usually. You will have assigned reading for the first day of class, and the instructor simply will come in and without further pause start grilling various students ready to hand about the day's reading. In many law schools there is a bulletin board where first-day assignments are posted. Make sure you get off to a good start, do your reading. However, you will not have yet learned how to "read" a case, so you can expect to be somewhat lost and intimidated in class. Expect that several times at the beginning of your first year you will be asking yourself "Is the instructor talking about the same case that I read last night?" Oftentimes it seems as if what you are supposed to get out of a case and what you do get out of a case are hopelessly irreconcilable. After a few weeks, though, you begin to get the hang of reading cases, and things start coming into focus. The important thing is not to panic, or come to the conclusion that you just can't make it. You can and will make it.

Students occasionally ask if they should join a study group in their first year of law school. Yes, but do not rely on the group to do any of your work. It's OK to get involved in a group outline (a detailed digest of a course's material and concepts used to prepare for the final exam—some outlines can be quite lengthy) of your courses, but make sure that you do your own outline from your own notes, using the group outline to fill in any gaps and holes in your personal outline. You should be rigorous in your schedule, in that you have a reserved time for entering your class notes into your class outline. If you don't already have one, you should purchase a computer prior to law school. Spend the hour or so it will take each day to enter that day's notes into your personal outlines. Students sometimes ask if they should purchase any commercial outlines for first year courses. Again, yes, but they should be used only to fill in holes in your personal

William Weaver, J.D., Ph.D., Department of Political Science, University of Texas at El Paso

outlines or to clear up areas of confusion. Buy the expansive, detailed outlines, not the cut-rate jobs. Remember, though, the emphases of your course will differ greatly from what is in the commercial outline since your instructor will tailor the course around his or her interests. There is no substitute for a good personal outline. Usually you will make the best grades in the courses in which you invest the time and effort to make a detailed, extensive outline from your course notes.

Make sure that you remember to set aside time in your schedule for fun and relaxation. Schedule a movie for Saturday night or an evening walk along a river during the week. Finally, realize that you are going to be insufferable for your family during the holiday season after your first semester. Law will have become your life, but it will not have become the life of your relatives. As hard as it might be, try to avoid talking about law while you are home on vacation.

TIMETABLE FOR THE LAW SCHOOL APPLICATION PROCESS

· See your prelaw adviser as soon as you *think you may* be interested in attending law school.

SPRING OF YOUR JUNIOR YEAR

· Collect the LSAS Law School Admissions Test application from your prelaw adviser or request a copy directly from LSAS by phone at 215-968-1001 or on the Web at http://www.lsas.org.
· Register for June LSAT. By taking the June administration you gain three advantages. First, you will know both your GPA and your LSAT before you must select to which schools to apply. This allows you to make a more informed choice about where to apply. Second, if anything goes wrong and you must cancel your test results or wish to retake the exam in October, you are no worse off than the vast majority of other candidates. Third, the June administration does not interfere with normal school time frames, so you are not dealing with both classwork and the LSAT.
· Register with Law School Data Assembly Service. Registration forms are found in the packet you received from your prelaw adviser.
· After the end of spring semester, begin preparation for LSAT. Prepare intensely for at least four weeks prior to examination.
· Begin identifying appropriate law schools based on your LSAT practice scores and your GPA.

SUMMER AFTER JUNIOR YEAR

· Take June LSAT.

· Write law schools for their catalogs and admissions materials (August).
· Receive LSAT score (four to six weeks after test).
· Begin receiving law school catalogs (September).
· Review law school choices in light of LSAT score.
· Register for October LSAT, if appropriate.
· If appropriate, request official school transcripts be sent to the Law School Data Assembly Service from all higher education institutions you attended.

FALL OF SENIOR YEAR

· Meet with prelaw adviser to review selection of schools.
· Request letters of recommendation.
· Take October LSAT, if appropriate.
· Prepare applications. Applications should be submitted well ahead of the deadlines. Try to have all of your applications submitted by December 1.

SPRING OF SENIOR YEAR

· If you have not received notification, call law schools to see if your applications are complete (February 1).
· Fill out required financial aid forms as soon as they become available.

William Weaver, J.D., Ph.D., Department of Political Science, University of Texas at El Paso

ADVICE FOR MEMBERS OF MINORITY GROUPS

As we approach the beginning of the third millennium, the legal profession still offers lifelong opportunities for professional challenge, community service, and professional satisfaction.

BACKGROUND

In 1997, the typical entering law school class was a little more than 20 percent members of minority groups. Thirty years ago, there were fewer than 800 law students nationally who were members of minority groups, accounting for fewer than 10 percent of an entering law school class. This nearly doubling of enrollment of members of minority groups would not have happened without the enhanced commitment of law schools to recruit, admit, retain, and graduate talented students who are members of minority groups into the legal profession. In June 1991, the Association of American Law Schools, the American Bar Association, and the Law School Admission Council issued a joint statement saying that "a student body diverse with respect to sex, ethnicity, race, economic, educational, and experiential backgrounds is essential to a quality legal education. Students must obtain a wide range of perspectives concerning the impact of law on various segments of our population and a deeper understanding of law and justice in an increasingly complex society." According to Carl Monk, the Executive Vice President of the Association of American Law Schools, the learned society representing law professors, "It is not possible in our increasingly diverse society and increasingly global economy to offer quality legal education without the many cultures of our society being adequately represented in the classroom."

Today, nearly forty years after the Supreme Court ruled in Sweatt v. Painter that maintenance of racially segregated law schools violated equal protection and while members of minority groups constitute more than 20 percent of the national population, they are still only 4 percent of all practicing lawyers. A *Personal Reflection on 30 Years in Legal Education* comes to us from Judge Harry Edwards. When he entered Michigan Law School in 1962, he was the only black student in his class and there were no black faculty members until 1970. He reports that the assumption thirty years ago was that he must be talented and had succeeded despite his race. Today, his son, a summa cum laude and Phi Beta Kappa graduate of Yale with a Ph.D. in comparative literature, frequently encounters people who assume he's made it only because of his race. Judge Edwards continues to support affirmative action efforts noting that the need is greater than the cost. As law professor Charles E. Daye recently wrote, "the challenges of the 1990s and beyond is best expressed by Native American leader Chief Seattle who observed "A great vision is hard to hold."

As our society becomes increasingly multicultural, the practice of law becomes increasingly transnational. Educating lawyers for the twenty-first century in an increasingly global economy requires introducing voices of different cultures and perspectives. In choosing lawyers for the twenty-first century, we must continue to be creative in our search for talent. Admissions professionals must learn about the variety of backgrounds from which future lawyers will come.

We must remember that students of color are still victims of diminished expectations. A recent newspaper article told the story of young Denise Sepulveda. When Denise glowingly told her inner-city high school guidance counselor of her dream of teaching at a university, the guidance counselor rolled her eyes in disbelief. The first African-American astronaut was told by a high school counselor that he was only smart enough for trade school. When I was considering applying to law school nearly twenty years ago, I was told by a college adviser that as a nontraditional student with children, I could never go to law school. I worked hard in school, worked part-time as a paralegal, and found others who believed in me and my ability to handle the difficult work of law school. Your job, as an applicant who is a member of a minority group, is to educate the admissions committee about hurdles that you have to clear before reaching our doors.

HOW TO PREPARE FOR LAW SCHOOL

Ideally, preparation for law school begins with a challenging course of study in undergraduate school. Build a solid academic foundation and do well. If you get off to a weak

---

Camille deJorna, Director of Admission and Assistant to the Dean, University of Iowa College of Law

start, work toward establishing an upward grade trend with a strong finish. Counter stereotypical expectations by taking rigorous courses, reading scholarly journals, and gaining critical writing experience. Know the academic reputation of your school and your department. This will help you to understand the value of your degree, your major, and your grade point average in the competitive world of law school admissions.

Augment your course work, if possible, with law-related internships that emphasize research and writing assignments, not just by observing trials. Consult with prelaw advisers. Take courses taught by faculty members who regularly teach students who go on to law school. They will be both a good source of advice and an opportunity for learning more about the rigors of law school.

HOW TO APPLY TO LAW SCHOOL

Plan to take the Law School Admission Test in June preceding your senior year or early in the fall of the year you plan to apply. The test is offered four times a year. While you may hear conflicting information on preparing for the LSAT, the best preparation begins with taking undergraduate courses that emphasize reasoning and problem-solving skills. The test is timed and the more exposure you have to the testing materials prior to the exam, the more intense your preparation, the better you are likely to do. Minority test takers must focus on finishing the exam.

Research shows that people who prepare do better that those who don't. Sample questions and other materials are available from the Law School Admission Council, the testing company that produces the test. Treat preparing for the LSAT as you would preparing for a marathon. Take the test under time conditions as often as you can, well in advance of the actual test. Consider investing in low-cost test-prep programs like those sponsored by the Puerto Rican Legal Defense Fund.

Students with poor histories of standardized testing should be prepared to document their claims and to offset them with an outstanding record of academic achievement. Sustained academic excellence with unusually strong letters of recommendation from faculty members who can compare you favorably with former students they have taught and who have done well in law school is the best antidote to less-than-stellar standardized test performance. Students in this situation may also take law school classes, where possible, and do well to establish their ability to handle the demanding work of law school, despite conflicting indicators.

Apply Broadly

Approach the application process for law school in a lawyerly fashion. Begin to gather information well in advance of the year that you plan to apply. Compile a list of law schools, including your dream or reach school, likely schools based on your credentials, and schools that would consider you a sure bet. Determine this strategy by gathering information on how many applicants for admission with your credentials a school selected in the preceding year. This information is available online and in various publications provided by the ABA and LSAC, for example. Your prelaw adviser may also have this data or may keep his or her own.

Apply broadly and your likelihood of success will improve. Fee waivers, both for the LSAT and for individual school application fees, may be available for students with need. Call the admissions office and ask for the names and telephone numbers of the leaders of the organizations for members of minority groups who may be more candid about the range of credentials at their institution. Ask if there is a minority recruiter for the law school or if a faculty member who is a member of a minority group is available to answer applicant questions about the admissions process and about life for students of color at the school. Often schools will keep a directory of alumni who are members of minority groups who are also willing to be helpful to future lawyers who are members of minority groups.

Once you know your undergraduate grade point average and LSAT score, plan on attending prelaw conferences and forums sponsored by colleges, LSAC, and others. Make a list of schools that you plan to visit at these events. They are often attended by directors of admission or faculty members from the admissions committee who are available to give you substantive advice about their process. Treat these encounters as mini-interviews. Introduce yourself, giving a quick summary of your credentials, and ask about the likelihood of success at their school for admission and for scholarship opportunities.

Determine rationally how competitive you are and proceed accordingly. If you are at the top of the pool, don't just apply to schools that you know. You may get full scholarship opportunities and more overall institutional support at schools with which you are less familiar. If you are in the great middle, complete your application early. Distinguish yourself. Describe your accomplishments. Put your performance in a context. If, for example, you worked 40 hours a week while in school to support yourself or your family and still maintained a good record of accomplishment, give the committee that information. If you are the first in your family to attend college, let them know!

Apply Early

Plan to have your personal statement completed by Thanksgiving and your application in by mid-December. Schools tend to have more flexibility earlier than later in the process. It also gives you time to gather additional information if the admissions committee requests it. December should also be the latest that you plan to take or retake the LSAT. Once you take the test, you may receive targeted mailings from the Candidate Referral Service. Read these letters carefully, since schools often encourage applications from students to whom they write. These letters may be accompanied by waivers of the school's application fee.

BEYOND THE NUMBERS IN LAW SCHOOL ADMISSIONS

What do we value beyond grade point average and performance on the Law School Admission Test? The American Bar Association suggests that in addition to critical-thinking, problem-solving, writing, and researching skills, "each member of the legal profession should be dedicated to serving others and promoting justice." I was recently inspired by Morris Dees, founder of the Southern Poverty Law Center to consider a "passion for justice" among these criteria. How do we measure a candidate's likelihood to devoting their efforts to others? May in law school admissions have been encouraging applicants to tell their stories, whether or not there is a box to check indicating your racial background.

For example, at a recent Society of American Law Teachers conference on "Affirming Action and Reconstructing Merit," Julie Su reported that her effective representation of Thai and Latina sweatshop workers required "strategizing with clients, engagement in their lives, and the comfort and flexibility to meet with clients where they lived." Describe your encounters with the legal system that inform your sense of justice. Describe experiences of injustice and remedies you pursued or how you plan to expand access to justice in your community. Describe experiences that will influence the kind of lawyer that you are likely to become. Law schools are looking for students who, in addition to being able to handle the work of law school, have overcome and won "personal battles of courage" making them more empathetic advocates for their clients.

FORMULATING PLAN B

If you did not take full advantage of college there are still options remaining. Plan to attend graduate school and aim to reach a GPA of 3.5 or better. Students who enter law school following another career or after a lengthy time away from an academic environment should contact the law school they are interested in to learn what they are likely to put more weight on in their selection process. Often you can think about your work life, think about law school, and establish that you have the skills for law school

based on transferable skills that you use in your current professional life. If you interact with lawyers or judges in the course of your employment, get to know them, let them know of your interest, and see if they might be willing to write a letter of recommendation.

Finally, you can also apply to schools with conditional admission programs. You should also consider conditional admit programs like CLEO, the Council on Legal Education Opportunity. If you are Native American, also consider applying to the American Indian Law Center's Pre-Law Summer Institute (PLSI) at the University of New Mexico Law School.

SELECTING A LAW SCHOOL

Select a law school where you are likely to thrive. Find out how many students, faculty members, and alumni are members of minority groups and how involved they all are in the life of the law school. Are there administrators or staff members who are also members of minority groups? Find out what resources are committed to students who are members of minority groups. How extensive is the financial aid budget? Is there an academic support program? What's the retention rate for members of minority groups? What's the placement rate for members of minority groups? The bar passage rate for members of minority groups? Is there a mentoring program for members of minority groups with the local minority bar association? What's the climate at the school like for members of minority groups day to day? Despite our best efforts and progress in the area of diversity, law schools are not sanctuaries from the realities of life for members of minority groups in the U.S. Law school can be an alienating and isolating experience for members of minority groups. Racially insensitive hypothetical posed by faculty, the absence of strong numbers of faculty members who are members of minority groups, and a more conservative student body mirror the challenges you can expect in practice.

Once you select a law school, take full advantage of the resources that the school offers to ensure that you do your best. Join the student organizations for members of minority groups, as well as other student organizations. Do not become isolated. Share your experiences with others. There is no monolithic minority experience of law school. As critical race scholar Mari Matsuda reminds us, "Issues of identity are not just of our own making, it's part of our history. Speak in your own voice in your professional life. Issues of race and gender in the academy, in legal education and in the profession are unavoidable."

Work hard, learn as much as you can, and hold onto your dreams so that you may join the next generation of lawyers, the women and men who will serve as leaders in the twenty-first century.

PAYING FOR SCHOOL—FINANCING YOUR GRADUATE EDUCATION

If you're considering attending graduate school but fear you don't have enough money, don't despair. Financial support for graduate study does exist, although, admittedly, the information about support sources can be difficult to find.

Support for graduate study can take many forms, depending upon the field of study and program you pursue. For example, some 60 percent of doctoral students receive support in the form of either grants/fellowships or assistantships, whereas most students in master's programs rely on loans to pay for their graduate study. In addition, doctoral candidates are more likely to receive grants/fellowships and assistantships than master's degree students, and students in the sciences are more likely to receive aid than those in the arts and humanities.

For those of you who have applied for financial aid as an undergraduate, there are some differences for graduate students you'll notice right away. For one, aid to undergraduates is based primarily on need (although the number of colleges that now offer undergraduate merit-based aid is increasing), but graduate aid is often based on academic merit. Second, as a graduate student, you are automatically declared "independent" for federal financial aid purposes, meaning your parents' income and asset information is not required in assessing your need for federal aid. Third, at some graduate schools, the awarding of aid may be administered by the academic departments or the graduate school itself, not the financial aid office. That means that at some schools, you may be involved with as many as three offices: a central financial aid office, the graduate school, *and* your academic department.

BE PREPARED

Being prepared for graduate school means you have to put together a financial plan. So, before you enter graduate school, you should have answers to these questions:

- What should I be doing now to prepare for the cost of my graduate education?
- What can I do to minimize my costs once I arrive on campus?
- What financial aid programs are available at each of the schools to which I am applying?
- What financial aid programs are available outside the university at the federal, state, or private level?

- What financing options do I have if I cannot pay the full cost from my own resources and those of my family?
- What should I know about the loans I am being offered?
- What impact will these loans have on me when I complete my program?

You'll find your answers in three guiding principles: think ahead, live within your means, and keep your head above water.

THINK AHEAD

The first step to putting together your financial plan comes from thinking about the future: the loss of your income while you're attending school, your projected income after you graduate, the annual rate of inflation, additional expenses you will incur as a student and after you graduate, and any loss of income you may experience later on from unintentional periods of unemployment, pregnancy, or disability. The cornerstone of thinking ahead is following a step-by-step process.

1. *Set your goals.* Decide what and where you want to study, whether you will go full- or part-time, whether you'll work while attending, and what an appropriate level of debt would be. Consider whether you would attend full-time if you had enough financial aid or whether keeping your full-time job is an important priority in your life. Keep in mind that many employers have tuition reimbursement plans for full-time employees.
2. *Take inventory.* Collect your financial information and add up your assets—bank accounts, stocks, bonds, real estate, business and personal property. Then subtract your liabilities—money owed on your assets, including credit card debt and car loans—to yield your net worth.
3. *Calculate your need.* Compare your net worth with the costs at the schools you are considering to get a rough estimate of how much of your assets you can use for your schooling.
4. *Create an action plan.* Determine how much you'll earn while in school, how much you think you will receive in grants and scholarships, and how much

you plan to borrow. Don't forget to consider inflation and possible life changes that could affect your overall financial plan.

5. *Review your plan regularly.* Measure the progress of your plan every year and make adjustments for such things as increases in salary or other changes in your goals or circumstances.

LIVE WITHIN YOUR MEANS

The second step in being prepared is knowing how much you spend now so you can determine how much you'll spend when you're in school. Use the standard cost of attendance budget published by your school as a guide, but don't be surprised if your estimated budget is higher than the one the school provides, especially if you've been out of school for a while. Once you've figured out your budget, see if you can pare down your current costs and financial obligations so the lean years of graduate school don't come as too large a shock.

KEEP YOUR HEAD ABOVE WATER

Finally, the third step is managing the debt you'll accrue as a graduate student. Debt is manageable only when considered in terms of five things:

1. Your future income
2. The amount of time it takes to repay the loan
3. The interest rate you are being charged
4. Your personal lifestyle and expenses after graduation
5. Unexpected circumstances that change your income or your ability to repay what you owe

To make sure your educational debt is manageable, you should borrow an amount that requires payments of no more than 8 percent of your starting salary.

The approximate monthly installments for repaying borrowed principal at 5, 8–10, and 12 percent are indicated below.

Estimated Loan Repayment Schedule Monthly Payments for Every $1000 Borrowed

Rate	5 years	10 years	15 years	20 years	25 years
5%	$18.87	$10.61	$ 7.91	$ 6.60	$ 5.85
8%	20.28	12.13	9.56	8.36	7.72
9%	20.76	12.67	10.14	9.00	8.39
10%	21.74	13.77	10.75	9.65	9.09
12%	22.24	14.35	12.00	11.01	10.53

You can use this table to estimate your monthly payments on a loan for any of the five repayment periods (5, 10, 15, 20, and 25 years). The amounts listed are the monthly payments for a $1000 loan for each of the interest rates. To estimate your monthly payment, choose the closest interest rate and multiply the amount of the payment listed by the total amount of your loan and then divide by 1,000. For example, for a total loan of $15,000 at 9 percent to be paid back over ten years, multiply $12.67 by 15,000 (190,050), divided by 1,000. This yields $190.05 per month.

If you're wondering just how much of a loan payment you can afford monthly without running into payment problems, consult the chart below.

Of course, the best way to manage your debt is to borrow less. While cutting your personal budget may be one option, there are a few others you may want to consider:

- *Ask Your Family for Help:* Although the federal government considers you "independent," your parents and family may still be willing and able to help pay for your graduate education. If your family is not open to just giving you money, they may be open to making a low-interest (or deferred-interest) loan. Family loans usually have more attractive interest rates and repayment terms than commercial loans. They may also have tax consequences, so you may want to check with a tax adviser.
- *Push to Graduate Early:* It's possible to reduce your total indebtedness by completing your program ahead of schedule. You can take more courses either per semester or during the summer. Keep in mind, though, that these options reduce the time you have available to work.
- *Work More, Attend Less:* Another alternative is to enroll part-time, leaving more time to work. Remember, though, to qualify for aid, you must be

How Much Can You Afford to Repay?

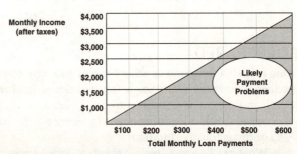

This graph shows the monthly cash-flow outlook based on your total monthly loan payments in comparison with your monthly income earned after taxes. Ideally, to eliminate likely payment problems, your monthly loan payment should be less than 15 percent of your monthly income.

enrolled at least half-time, which is usually considered 6 credits per term. And if you're enrolled less than half-time, you'll have to start repaying your loans once the grace period has expired.

Roll Your Loans into One

There's a good chance that as a graduate student you will have two or more loans included in your aid package, plus any money you borrowed as an undergraduate. That means when you start repaying, you could be making loan payments to several different lenders. Not only can the recordkeeping be a nightmare, but with each loan having a minimum payment, your total monthly payments may be more than you can handle. If that is the case, you may want to consider consolidating your federal loans.

There is no minimum or maximum on the amount of loans you must have in order to consolidate. Also, there is no consolidation fee. The interest rate varies annually, is adjusted every July 1, and is capped at 8.25 percent. Your repayment can also be extended to up to thirty years, depending on the total amount you borrow, which will make your monthly payments lower (of course, you'll also be paying more total interest). With a consolidated loan, some lenders offer graduated or income-sensitive repayment options. Consult with your lender or the U.S. Department of Education about the types of consolidation provisions offered.

Plastic Mania

Any section on managing debt would be incomplete if it didn't mention the responsible use of credit cards. Most graduate students hold one or more credit cards, and many students find themselves in financial difficulties because of them. Here are two suggestions: use credit cards only for convenience, never for extended credit; and, if you have more than one credit card, keep only the one that has the lowest finance charge and the lowest limit.

Credit: Don't Let Your Past Haunt You

Many schools will check your credit history before they process any private educational loans for you. To make sure your credit rating is accurate, you may want to request a copy of your credit report before you start graduate school. You can get a copy of your report by sending a signed, written request to one of the four national credit reporting agencies at the address listed on this page. Include your full name, social security number, current address, any previous addresses for the past five years, date of birth, and daytime phone number. Call the agency before you request your report so you know whether or not there is a fee for this report. Note that you are entitled to a free copy of your credit report if you have been denied credit within the last sixty days. In addition, Experian currently provides complimentary credit reports once every twelve months.

Credit criteria used to review and approve student loans can include the following:

· Absence of negative credit
· No bankruptcies, foreclosures, repossessions, charge-offs, or open judgments
· No prior educational loan defaults, unless paid in full or making satisfactory repayments
· Absence of excessive past due accounts; that is, no thirty-, sixty-, or ninety-day delinquencies on consumer loans or revolving charge accounts within the past two years

Types of Aid Available

There are three types of aid: money given to you (grants, scholarships, and fellowships), money you earn through work, and loans.

GRANTS, SCHOLARSHIPS, AND FELLOWSHIPS

Most grants, scholarships, and fellowships are outright awards that require no service in return. Often they provide the cost of tuition and fees plus a stipend to cover living expenses. Some are based exclusively on financial need, some exclusively on academic merit, and some on a combination of need and merit. As a rule, grants are awarded to those with financial need, although they may require the recipient to have expertise in a certain field.

Credit Reporting Agencies

Experian
P.O. Box 9530
Allen, Texas 75013
888-397-3742

Equifax
P.O. Box 105873
Atlanta, Georgia 30348
800-685-1111

CSC Credit Services
Consumer Assistance Center
P.O. Box 674402
Houston, Texas 77267-4402
800-759-5979

Trans Union Data Corporation
P.O. Box 390
Springfield, Pennsylvania 19064-0390
800-888-4213

Fellowships and scholarships often connote selectivity based on ability—financial need is usually not a factor.

Federal Support

Several federal agencies fund fellowship and trainee programs for graduate and professional students. The amounts and types of assistance offered vary considerably by field of study.

National Institutes of Health (NIH). NIH sponsors many different fellowship opportunities. For example, it offers training grants administered through schools' research departments. Training grants provide tuition plus a twelve-month stipend of $11,496. For more information, call 301-435-0714.

Veterans' Benefits. Veterans may use their educational benefits for training at the graduate and professional levels. Contact your regional office of the Veterans Administration for more details.

State Support

Some states offer grants for graduate study, with California, Michigan, New York, North Carolina, Texas, and Virginia offering the largest programs. States grant approximately $2.9 billion per year to graduate students. Due to fiscal constraints, however, some states have had to reduce or eliminate their financial aid programs for graduate study. To qualify for a particular state's aid you must be a resident of that state. Residency is established in most states after you have lived there for at least twelve consecutive months prior to enrolling in school. Many states provide funds for in-state students only; that is, funds are not transferable out of state. Contact your state scholarship office to determine what aid it offers.

Institutional Aid

Educational institutions using their own funds provide more than $3 billion in graduate assistance in the form of fellowships, tuition waivers, and assistantships. Consult each school's catalog for information about aid programs.

Corporate Aid

Many corporations provide graduate student support as part of the employee benefits package. Most employees who receive aid study at the master's level or take courses without enrolling in a particular degree program.

Aid from Foundations

Most foundations provide support in areas of interest to them. For example, for those studying for the Ph.D., the Howard Hughes Institute funds students in the biomedical sciences, while the Spencer Foundation funds dissertation research in the field of education. The Foundation Center of New York City publishes several reference books on foundation support for graduate study. For more information call 212-620-4230.

Financial Aid for Minorities and Women

Patricia Roberts Harris Fellowships. This federal award provides support for minorities and women. Awards are made to schools, and the schools decide who receives these funds. Fellows receive a stipend of $14,000 for up to four years, and their institutions receive up to $9493 per year. Consult the graduate school for more information. Funds for this program may be cut in the next federal budget. No funding is guaranteed beyond the 1998 fiscal year.

Bureau of Indian Affairs. The Bureau of Indian Affairs (BIA) offers aid to students who are at least one-quarter American Indian or native Alaskan and from a federally recognized tribe. Contact your tribal education officer, BIA area office, or call the Bureau of Indian Affairs at 202-208-3710.

The Ford Foundation Doctoral Fellowship for Minorities. Provides three-year doctoral fellowships and one-year dissertation fellowships. Predoctoral fellowships include an annual stipend of $14,000 to the fellow and an annual institutional grant of $7500 to the fellowship institution in lieu of tuition and fees. Dissertation fellows receive a stipend of $18,000 for a twelve-month period. Applications are due in early November. For more information, contact the Fellowship Office, National Research Council at 202-334-2872.

The Council on Legal Education Opportunity (CLEO) helps economically and educationally disadvantaged students attend law school. It also sponsors summer institutes for preparatory work. Contact the law school you want to attend and ask if the school participates in the CLEO program. In addition, below are some books available that describe financial aid opportunities for women and minorities.

The Directory of Financial Aids for Women, by Gail Ann Schlachter (Reference Service Press, 1997) lists sources of support and identifies foundations and other organizations interested in helping women secure funding for graduate study.

The Association for Women in Science publishes *Grants-at-a-Glance,* a booklet highlighting fellowships for women in science. It can be ordered by calling 202-326-8940, or visit their Web site at http://www.awis.org.

Books such as *Financial Aid for Minorities* (Garrett Park, Md.: Garrett Park Press, 1998) describe financial aid opportunities for minority students. For more information, call 301-946-2553.

Reference Service Press also publishes four directories specifically for minorities: *Financial Aid for African Americans, Financial Aid for Asian Americans, Financial Aid for Hispanic Americans,* and *Financial Aid for Native Americans.*

Also, visit the Minority On-Line Information Service (MOLIS) Web site at http://web.fie.com/web/mol/.

Disabled students are eligible to receive aid from a number of organizations. *Financial Aid for the Disabled and Their Families, 1996–98* by Gail Ann Schlachter and David R. Weber (Reference Service Press) lists aid opportunities for disabled students. The Vocational Rehabilitation Services in your home state can also provide information.

RESEARCHING GRANTS AND FELLOWSHIPS

The books listed below are good sources of information on grant and fellowship support for graduate education and should be consulted before you resort to borrowing. Keep in mind that grant support varies dramatically from field to field.

Annual Register of Grant Support: A Directory of Funding Sources, Wilmette, Ill.: National Register Publishing Co. This is a comprehensive guide to grants and awards from government agencies, foundations, and business and professional organizations.

Corporate Foundation Profiles, 10th ed. New York: Foundation Center, 1998. This is an in-depth, analytical profile of 250 of the largest company-sponsored foundations in the United States. Brief descriptions of all 700 company-sponsored foundations are also included. There is an index of subjects, types of support, and geographical locations.

The Foundation Directory, Edited by Stan Olsen. New York: Foundation Center, 1998. This directory, with a supplement, gives detailed information on U.S. foundations with brief descriptions of the purpose and activities of each.

The Grants Register 1998, 16th ed. Edited by Lisa Williams. New York: St. Martin's, 1998. This lists grant agencies alphabetically and gives information on awards available to graduate students, young professionals, and scholars for study and research.

Peterson's Grants for Graduate and Postdoctoral Study, 5th ed. Princeton: Peterson's, 1998. This book includes information on more than 1,400 grants, scholarships, awards, fellowships, and prizes. Originally compiled by the Office of Research Affairs at the Graduate School of the University of Massachusetts at Amherst, this guide is updated periodically by Peterson's.

Graduate schools sometimes publish listings of support sources in their catalogs, and some provide separate publications, such as the *Graduate Guide to Grants,* compiled by the Harvard Graduate School of Arts and Sciences. For more information, call 617-495-1814.

THE INTERNET AS A SOURCE OF FUNDING INFORMATION

If you have not explored the financial resources on the World Wide Web (the Web, for short), your research is not complete. Now available on the Web is a wealth of information ranging from loan and entrance applications to minority grants and scholarships.

University-Specific Information on the Web

Many universities have Web financial aid directories. Florida, Virginia Tech, Massachusetts, Emory, and Georgetown are just a few. Applications of admission can now be downloaded from the Web to start the graduate process. After that, detailed information can be obtained on financial aid processes, forms, and deadlines. University-specific grant and scholarship information can also be found, and more may be learned about financing by using the Web than by an actual visit. Questions can be asked on line.

Scholarships on the Web

When searching for scholarship opportunities, one can search the Web. Many benefactors and other scholarship donors have pages on the Web listing pertinent information with regard to their specific scholarship. You can reach this information through a variety of methods. For example, you can find a directory listing minority scholarships, quickly look at the information on line, decide if it applies to you, and then move on. New scholarship pages are being added to the Web daily. Library and Web resources are productive and—free.

The Web also lists many services that will look for scholarships for you. Some of these services cost money and advertise more scholarships per dollar than any other service. While some of these might be helpful, beware. Check references to make sure a bona fide service is being offered. Your best bet initially is to surf the Web and use the traditional library resources on available scholarships.

Bank and Loan Information on the Web

Banks and loan servicing centers have pages on the Web, making it easier to access loan information on the Web. Having the information on screen in front of you instantaneously is more convenient than being put on hold on the phone. Any loan information such as interest rate variations, descriptions of loans, loan consolidation programs, and repayment charts can all be found on the Web.

WORK PROGRAMS

Certain types of support, such as teaching, research, and administrative assistantships, require recipients to provide service to the university in exchange for a salary or stipend; sometimes tuition is also provided or waived.

Teaching Assistantships

Because science and engineering classes are taught at the undergraduate level, you stand a good chance of securing a teaching assistantship. These positions usually involve conducting small classes, delivering lectures, correcting class work, grading papers, counseling students, and supervising laboratory groups. Usually about 20 hours of work are required each week.

Teaching assistantships provide excellent educational experience as well as financial support. TAs generally receive a salary (now considered taxable income). Sometimes tuition is provided or waived as well. In addition, at some schools, TAs can be declared state residents, qualifying them for the in-state tuition rates. Appointments are based on academic qualifications and are subject to the availability of funds within a department. If you are interested in a teaching assistantship, contact the academic department. Ordinarily you are not considered for such positions until you have been admitted to the graduate school.

Research Assistantships

Research assistantships usually require that you assist in the research activities of a faculty member. Appointments are ordinarily made for the academic year. They are rarely offered to first-year students. Contact the academic department, describing your particular research interests. As is the case with teaching assistantships, research assistantships provide excellent academic training as well as practical experience and financial support.

Administrative Assistantships

These positions usually require 10 to 20 hours of work each week in an administrative office of the university. For example, those seeking a graduate degree in education may work in the admissions, financial aid, student affairs, or placement office of the school they are attending. Some administrative assistantships provide a tuition waiver, others a salary. Details concerning these positions can be found in the school catalog or by contacting the academic department directly.

Federal Work-Study Program (FWS)

This federally funded program provides eligible students with employment opportunities, usually in public and private nonprofit organizations. Federal funds pay up to 75 percent of the wages, with the remainder paid by the employing agency. FWS is available to graduate students who demonstrate financial need. Not all schools have these funds, and some only award undergraduates. Each school sets its application deadline and work-study earnings limits. Wages vary and are related to the type of work done.

Additional Employment Opportunities

Many schools provide on-campus employment opportunities that do not require demonstrated financial need. The student employment office on most campuses assists students in securing jobs both on and off the campus.

LOANS

Most needy graduate students, except those pursuing Ph.D.'s in certain fields, borrow to finance their graduate programs. There are two sources of student loans—the federal government and private loan programs. You should read and understand the terms of these loan programs before submitting your loan application.

Federal Loans

Federal Direct Loans Some schools are participating in the Department of Education's Direct Lending Program instead of offering Federal Stafford Loans. The two programs are essentially the same except that with Direct Loans, schools themselves originate the loans with funds provided from the Federal Government. Terms and interest rates are virtually the same except that there are a few more repayment options with Federal Direct Loans.

Federal Perkins Loans The Federal Perkins Loan is a long-term loan program available to graduate students demonstrating financial need and is administered directly by the school. Not all schools have these funds, and some may award them to undergraduates only. Eligibility is determined from the information you provide on the FAFSA. The school will notify you of your eligibility.

Eligible graduate students may borrow up to $5000 per year, up to a maximum of $30,000, including undergraduate borrowing (even if your previous Perkins Loans have been repaid). The interest rate for Federal Perkins Loans is 5 percent, and no interest accrues while you remain in school at least half-time. There are no guarantee, loan, or disbursement fees. Repayment begins nine months after your last enrollment on at least a half-time basis and may extend over a maximum of ten years with no prepayment penalty.

Supplemental Loans

Many lending institutions offer supplemental loan programs and other financing plans, such as the ones described below, to students seeking assistance in meeting their expected contribution toward educational expenses.

If you are considering borrowing through a supplemental loan program, you should carefully consider the terms of the program and be sure to "read the fine print." Check with the program sponsor for the most current terms that will be applicable to the amounts you intend to borrow for graduate study. Most supplemental loan programs for graduate study offer unsubsidized, credit-based loans. In general, a credit-ready borrower is one who has a satisfactory credit history or no credit history at all. A creditworthy borrower generally must pass a credit test to be eligible to borrow or act as a cosigner for the loan funds.

Many supplemental loan programs have a minimum annual loan limit and a maximum annual loan limit. Some offer amounts equal to the cost of attendance minus any other aid you will receive for graduate study. If you are planning to borrow for several years of graduate study, consider whether there is a cumulative or aggregate limit on the amount you may borrow. Often this cumulative or aggregate limit will include any amounts you borrowed and have not repaid for undergraduate or previous graduate study.

The combination of the annual interest rate, loan fees, and the repayment terms you choose will determine how much the amount is that you will repay over time. Compare these features in combination before you decide which loan program to use. Some loans offer interest rates that are adjusted monthly, some quarterly, some annually. Some offer interest rates that are lower during the in-school, grace, and deferment periods, and then increase when you begin repayment. Most programs include a loan "origination" fee, which is usually deducted from the principal amount you receive when the loan is disbursed, and must be repaid along with the interest and other principal when you graduate, withdraw from school, or drop below half-time study. Sometimes the loan fees are reduced if you borrow with a qualified cosigner. Some programs allow you to defer interest and/or principal payments while you are enrolled in graduate school. Many programs allow you to capitalize your interest payments; the interest due on your loan is added to the outstanding balance of your loan, so you don't have to repay immediately, but this increases the amount you owe. Other programs allow you to pay the interest as you go, which will reduce the amount you later have to repay.

For more information about supplemental loan programs or to obtain applications, call the customer service phone numbers of the organizations listed below, access the sponsor's site on the World Wide Web, or visit your school's financial aid office.

American Express Alternative Loan. An unsubsidized, credit-based loan for credit-ready graduate students enrolled at least half-time, sponsored by American Express/California Higher Education Loan Authority (800-255-8374).

CitiAssist Graduate Loan. An unsubsidized, credit-based loan for graduate students in all disciplines, sponsored by Citibank (800-745-5473 or 800-946-4019; World Wide Web: http://www.citibank.com/student).

CollegeReserve Loan. An unsubsidized, credit-based loan for credit-worthy graduate students enrolled at least half-time, sponsored by USA Group (800-538-8492; World Wide Web: http://www.usagroup.com).

EXCEL Loan. An unsubsidized, credit-based loan for borrowers who are not credit-ready or who would prefer to borrow with a creditworthy cosigner to obtain a more attractive interest rate, sponsored by Nellie Mae (888-2TUITION).

GradAchiever Loan. An unsubsidized, credit-based loan for graduate students enrolled at least half-time, sponsored by Key Education Resources (800-KEY-LEND; World Wide Web: http://www.key.com/education/grad.html).

GradEXCEL Loan. An unsubsidized, credit-based loan for credit-ready graduate students enrolled at least half-time, sponsored by Nellie Mae (888-2TUITION).

Graduate Access Loan. An unsubsidized, credit-based loan for creditworthy graduate students enrolled at least half-time, sponsored by the Access Group (800-282-1550; World Wide Web: http://www.accessgroup.org).

Signature Student Loan. An unsubsidized, credit-based loan for graduate students enrolled at least half-time, sponsored by Sallie Mae (888-272-5543; World Wide Web: http://www.salliemae.com).

Law Loans

Law Access Loans. The Access Group has a loan program that provides law students with access to private loans. The minimum loan amount is $500. The maximum total outstanding debt is $130,000 (including undergraduate and graduate debt). The interest rate varies quarterly based on the 91-Day U.S. Treasury Bill rate plus 2.9 percent. Interest is capitalized once—at repayment. The guarantee fee is 6 percent at disbursement. An additional fee of between 1.5 and 6.9 percent is added to the principal of the loan immediately prior to repayment. There is no origination fee. Repayment begins nine months after graduation, or when your student status drops to less than half-time, with up to twenty years to repay. For more information, call The Access Group at 800-282-1550.

LawEXCEL. The maximum total outstanding educational debt is $105,000. The interest rate is based on the prime rate. There is a guarantee fee of 7 percent with a co-borrower, 10 percent without a co-borrower. There is a 2 percent capitalization fee. With a co-borrower, you may borrow up to the total cost of attendance, and without a co-borrower, you may borrow up to $12,000. For more information, contact Nellie Mae at 800-FOR-TUITION. **LawLoans.** LawLoans provide up to the cost of education, with a cumulative LawLoans limit of $75,000 and a total educational debt limit of $150,000 with a cosigner, $125,000 without a cosigner. The interest rate is based on the 91-Day U.S. Treasury Bill rate plus 3.25 percent. For more information, call 800-366-5626.

International Education and Study Abroad

A variety of funding sources are offered for study abroad and for foreign nationals studying in the United States. The Institute of International Education in New York assists students in locating such aid. It publishes *Funding for U.S. Study—A Guide for International Students* and *Financial Resources for International Study,* a guide to organizations offering awards for overseas study. The Council on International Educational Exchange in New York publishes the *Student Travel Catalogue,* which lists fellowship sources and explains the council's services both for United States students traveling abroad and for international students coming to the United States.

The U.S. Department of Education administers programs that support fellowships related to international education. Foreign Language and Area Studies Fellowships and Fulbright-Hays Doctoral Dissertation Awards were established to promote knowledge and understanding of other countries and cultures. They offer support to graduate students interested in foreign languages and international relations. Discuss these and other foreign study opportunities with the financial aid officer or someone in the graduate school dean's office at the school you will attend.

How to Apply

All applicants for federal aid must complete the Free Application for Federal Student Aid (FAFSA). This application must be completed *after* January 1 preceding enrollment in the fall. It is a good idea to submit the FAFSA as soon as possible after this date. On this form you

Application Deadlines

Application deadlines vary. Some schools require you to apply for aid when applying for admission; others require that you be admitted before applying for aid. Aid application instructions and deadlines should be clearly stated in each school's application material. The FAFSA must be filed after January 1 of the year you are applying for aid but the Financial Aid PROFILE should be completed earlier, in October or November.

report your income and asset information for the preceding calendar year and specify which schools will receive the data. Two to four weeks later you'll receive an acknowledgment, the Student Aid Report (SAR), on which you can make any corrections. The schools you've designated will also receive the information and may begin asking you to send them documents, usually your U.S. income tax return, verifying what you reported.

In addition to the FAFSA, some graduate schools want additional information and will ask you to complete a new form, the CSS Financial Aid PROFILE. If your school requires this form, it will be listed in the PROFILE registration form available in college financial aid offices. Other schools use their own supplemental application. Check with your financial aid office to confirm which forms they require.

If you have already filed your federal income tax for the year, it will be much easier for you to complete these forms. If not, use estimates, but be certain to notify the financial aid office if your estimated figures differ from the actual ones once you have calculated them.

Determining Financial Need

Eligibility for need-based financial aid is based on your income during the calendar year prior to the academic year in which you apply for aid. Prior-year income is used because it is a good predictor of current-year income and is verifiable. If you have a significant reduction in income or assets after your aid application is completed, consult a financial aid counselor. If, for example, you are returning to school after working, you should let the financial aid counselor know your projected income for the year you will be in school. Aid counselors may use their "professional judgment" to revise your financial need, based on the actual income you will earn while you are in graduate school.

Need is determined by examining the difference between the cost of attendance at a given institution and the financial resources you bring to the table. Eligibility for aid is calculated by subtracting your resources from the total cost of attendance budget. These standard student budgets are generally on the low side of the norm. So if your expenses are higher because of medical bills, higher research travel, or more costly books, for example, a financial aid counselor can make an adjustment. Of course, you'll have to document any unusual expenses. Also, keep in mind that with limited grant and scholarship aid, a higher budget will probably mean either more loan or more working hours for you.

Tax Issues

Since the passage of the Tax Reform Act of 1986, grants, scholarships, and fellowships may be considered taxable income. That portion of the grant used for payment of tuition and course-required fees, books, supplies, and equipment is excludable from taxable income. Grant support for living expenses is taxable. A good rule of thumb for determining the tax liability for grants and scholarships is to view anything that exceeds the actual cost of tuition, required fees, books, supplies related to courses, and required equipment as taxable.

· If you are employed by an educational institution or other organization that gives tuition reimbursement, you must pay tax on the value that exceeds $5250.

· If your tuition is waived in exchange for working at the institution, the tuition waiver is taxable. This includes waivers that come with teaching or research assistantships.

· Other student support, such as stipends and wages paid to research assistants and teaching assistants, is also taxable income. Student loans, however, are not taxable.

· If you are an international student you may or may not owe taxes depending upon the agreement the U.S. has negotiated with your home country. The United States

has tax treaties with more than forty countries. You are responsible for making sure that the school you attend follows the terms of the tax treaty. If your country does not have a tax treaty with the U.S., you may have as much as 30 percent withheld from your paycheck.

A Final Note

While amounts and eligibility criteria vary from field to field as well as from year to year, with thorough research you can uncover many opportunities for graduate financial assistance. If you are interested in graduate study, discuss your plans with faculty members and advisers. Explore all options. Plan ahead, complete forms on time, and be tenacious in your search for support. No matter what your financial situation, if you are academically qualified and knowledgeable about the different sources of aid, you should be able to attend the graduate school of your choice.

Patricia McWade
Dean of Student Financial Services
Georgetown University

HOW TO USE THIS BOOK

Peterson's Law Schools provides detailed information, including more than 3,500 elective and clinical courses, for the 181 law schools that, as of October 1998, are accredited (approved) by the American Bar Association to confer the first degree in law. Law programs are described only for schools that have accreditation with national recognition. In addition to J.D. programs, other advanced degree programs in law, such as the LL.M., combined degree, and postdoctoral programs, are described for relevant institutions. These programs are offered only in the United States and its territories. Nineteen law schools have elected to provide additional information that should prove useful to students who are considering application options.

PROGRAM PROFILES

Profiles begin with the official school name, the name of the law unit (if applicable), and the primary address of the school.

Information Module

The left-hand column of the first page of the profile provides a defined section of basic school contact, student body, and application-related information.

Address and Contact

Address information appears within the first box. All this information is specific to the law school and is the preferred address for applicants to use to request information. Typically provided are the name of the person to whom application queries and applications should be addressed and the law school postal address, telephone and fax numbers, and World Wide Web and e-mail addresses.

Law Student Profile

Following the boxed information is the Law Student Profile. This is immediately appended with the date, in parentheses, for which this information is correct. The profile is segmented into four sections: full-time, part-time, racial or ethnic composition, and applicants and admittees.

The full-time section provides information on the full-time total enrollment in the law school as of the noted date and the percentage of women and men students.

The part-time section provides information on the part-time total enrollment in the law school as of the noted date and the percentage of women and men students.

The racial or ethnic composition section lists the percentage of students reported by the law school as fitting the four minority ethnic categories established by the U.S. Bureau of the Census (African American, Asian/Pacific Islander, Hispanic, American Indian) and the percentage of international students, meaning those students who are not U.S. citizens.

Applicants and Admittees

The applicants and admittees section lists the number of prospective students who applied to the law school, the number admitted, the percentage of those who applied that were accepted, the number of available seats (or openings available) for full-time students (law schools typically fill all their seats), the average LSAT score of entering students, and the average GPA of entering students. All of these figures are for the entering class of fall 1997.

At a Glance

At the bottom of the first page, five bar graphs represent key statistics. Each bar graph has numbers at the top and bottom that represent the ultimate end of each particular range. The bisecting line and figure to the right show the number reported by the institution being profiled. The bottom half of each bar is shaded to make viewing easier. The graphic presentation will help readers quickly zero in on answers to their most frequently asked questions: How large is the school? How hard is it to be accepted? What do I have to pay? The bar graphs also provide an easy way to compare schools in these areas. Total enrollment is the law school enrollment for fall 1997. Percentage admitted is the percentage of applicants accepted for fall 1997. Average LSAT scores and GPA are the averages of the entering class in fall 1997. Average debt on graduation is the figure reported by the schools.

Application Information

This section indicates what forms, fees, scores, or other items are required or recommended of applicants to the law school. Among these items are the **LSAT** (Law School Admissions Test), the **GRE** (Graduate Record Examinations), the **LSDAS** (use of the centralized Law School Data Assembly Service of the Law School Admissions Council), the **application form** specific to the law school, the **application fee**, the **minimum undergraduate GPA**, **letters of recommendation**, the **personal statement**, an **essay**, a **writing sample**, an **interview**, **college transcripts**, and a **resume**. If they are required, minimum LSAT scores, minimum GPA, application fee amount, and the number of letters of recommendation are specified immediately after the item. The application deadline indicates whether this is for fall entrance. If it is not a strict deadline, but a priority deadline, this is indicated. If applications are received and processed continually, the term *rolling* is used to show this.

Costs

Costs normally represent the tuition for the 1997–98 school year. If a different year is represented, or if the tuition is estimated rather than actual, this is indicated. Other tuition rates for part-time students and for out-of-state residents (where applicable) are specifically indicated.

Financial Aid

Financial aid indicates the percent of students in the law school who receive some form of financial aid, the number of fellowships awarded through the school to students at all levels and their total dollar value, the number of other types of awards and their total dollar value, and whether law-related internships, federal work-study, or institutionally sponsored loans are available. The average student debt on graduation is also indicated. The types of application forms for financial aid are indicated as is whether or not the law school participates in an LRAP (Loan Repayment Assistance Program), which is a state or institutionally supported low-interest or interest-free loan provided to help make payments on regular loans. The deadline for financial aid forms is indicated, as are the name, title, mailing address, phone and fax numbers, and e-mail address of the party to contact about financial aid.

The Law School Library

This paragraph provides the name of the law library; the total number of volumes and number of periodicals in the law library; the number of seats; the availability of WESTLAW, LEXIS-NEXIS, the World Wide Web, other online bibliographic retrieval services, CD-ROM players, and other kinds of resources through the law library; and names of any special law collections.

Degree Options

Highlighted in a box are the degrees offered by the law school. The acronym and name of the degree or joint degree are indicated in the left-hand column. The total credits or range of credits required to complete the degree are shown in the middle column. The usual length, or range, in years is shown in the right-hand column as is an indication of whether the degree program is offered full-time and part-time or full-time only. If the program is

available to part-time students, an indication is made of whether it is scheduled during the day, evenings, weekends, and/or summers.

First-Year Program

This portion of each profile reveals the average class size for first-year courses and what percentage of first-year courses are taught by full-time faculty members.

Upper-Level Programs

This section lists the average class size for upper-level (second- and third-year) courses and also lists many of the courses offered to students at this level. A star preceding the course indicates that the school has indicated that this course represents a subject that is given special emphasis or strength.

Clinical Courses

This provides information on clinical courses offered by the law school, whether they are required, how many hours may be required, and what some of the clinical offerings may be.

Internships and Special Programs

The final sentences of the second page of the profile provide information about special programs. The percentage of students who participate in internships is listed. Also, if an international exchange program is offered, this is indicated with the countries that participate.

In-Depth Description

Many of the law schools profiled have chosen to provide two pages of additional information about the special qualities, values, and attractions of their law school for prospective students. This information includes:

- A statement from the Dean of the law school
- The history of the school and a description of its location and physical facilities
- A description of the special qualities of the school
- A description of the integration of electronic and telecommunications into campus life and instruction
- A description of the school's financial aid efforts and of major scholarship and loan programs available through the college
- Special opportunities for students, including law reviews, moot court, extracurricular activities, special opportunities to enhance legal education, aspects of the institution with special interest for women and minorities, and special certificate programs
- Bar passage rates for graduates and states in which the greatest number practice
- Career services provided to graduates and alumni

• Percentages of graduates that placed in specific legal fields and their average salaries or average starting salaries

DATA COLLECTION PROCEDURES

Information contained in the program profile was collected in the spring and summer of 1998 through Peterson's Survey of ABA-Accredited Law Schools and Peterson's Annual Survey of Graduate Institutions. Questionnaires were sent to all U.S. institutions approved by the American Bar Association to confer the first degree in law. Information was requested from admissions officers or other appropriate personnel within these institutions in order to ensure accuracy. In some cases, this information was supplemented with data available from school catalogs and brochures and in some instances directly from the institution's Web site on the Internet in order to provide as much detail as possible on a particular law school's degree offerings.

The omission of any particular item from a profile, chart, or index entry indicates that the item was either not applicable, not available at the time of publication, or not provided by the institution. Users of this guide should check with specific colleges and universities at the time of application to verify figures such as tuition and fees that may have changed since the publication of this guide.

LAW SCHOOL PROFILES
AND INCLUSIONS

SAMFORD UNIVERSITY
CUMBERLAND SCHOOL OF LAW

Birmingham, Alabama

INFORMATION CONTACT

Dr. Barry A. Currier, Dean
800 Lakeshore Drive
Birmingham, AL 35229

Phone: 205-870-2704   Fax: 205-870-2673
E-mail: msdavis@samford.edu
Web site: http://cumberland.samford.edu/

LAW STUDENT PROFILE [1997–98]

FULL-TIME   Enrollment: 610
Women: 34%   Men: 66%

PART-TIME   Enrollment: 4
Women: 75%   Men: 25%

RACIAL or ETHNIC COMPOSITION
African American, 7%; Asian/Pacific Islander, 0.5%; Hispanic, 1%

APPLICANTS and ADMITTEES
Number applied: 999
Admitted: 592
Percentage accepted: 59%
Seats available: 205
Average LSAT score: 151
Average GPA: 3.0

Samford University Cumberland School of Law is a private institution that organizes classes on a semester calendar system. The campus is situated in a suburban setting. Founded in 1847, first ABA approved in 1949, and an AALS member, Samford University Cumberland School of Law offers JD, JD/MBA, JD/MDiv, JD/MPA, JD/MPAd, JD/MPH, JD/MS, and MCL degrees.

Faculty consists of 34 full-time and 26 part-time members in 1997–98. 7 full-time faculty members and 5 part-time faculty members are women. 100% of all faculty members have a JD; 21% have advanced law degrees. Of all faculty members, 2.9% are Asian/Pacific Islander, 8.8% are African American, 88.3% are white.

Application Information *Required:* LSAT, LSDAS, application form, application fee of $40, baccalaureate degree, 2 letters of recommendation, personal statement, writing sample, college transcripts. *Application deadline* for fall term is February 28.

Costs The 1997–98 tuition is $18,350 full-time; $612 per credit hour part-time.

Financial Aid In 1997–98, 82% of all students received some form of financial aid. 34 other awards were given. Loans, merit based grants/scholarships, and need-based grants/scholarships are also available. To apply for financial assistance, students must com-

AT a GLANCE

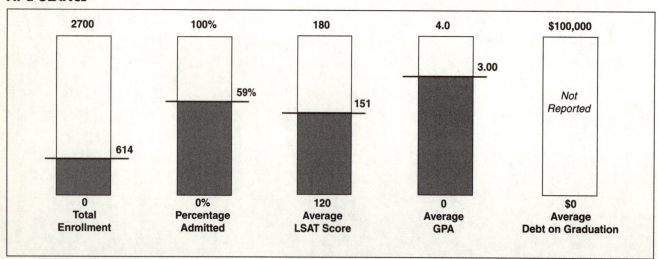

2700	100%	180	4.0	$100,000
			3.00	
	59%			Not Reported
		151		
614				
0	0%	120	0	$0
Total Enrollment	**Percentage Admitted**	**Average LSAT Score**	**Average GPA**	**Average Debt on Graduation**

Degree Options

Degree	Total Credits Required	Length of Program
JD–Doctor of Laws	90	3 yrs, full-time only [day, summer]
JD/MBA–Juris Doctor/Master of Business Administration–Dual-degree Program	102	4 yrs, full-time only [day, evening, summer]
JD/MDiv–Juris Doctor/Master of Divinity–Dual-degree Program	154	5 yrs, full-time only
JD/MPA–Juris Doctor/Master of Professional Accountancy–Dual-degree Program	99	3–4 yrs, full-time only [day, evening, summer]
JD/MPAd–Juris Doctor/Master of Public Administration–Dual-degree Program	111	4 yrs, full-time only [day]
JD/MPH–Juris Doctor/Master of Public Health–Dual-degree Program	120	4 yrs, full-time only [day, evening, summer]
JD/MS–Juris Doctor/Master of Science–Environmental Management Dual-degree Program	102	4 yrs, full-time only [day, evening]
MCL–Master of Comparative Law–International Jurists Program		full-time only

plete the Free Application for Federal Student Aid and institutional forms. Financial aid contact: Ane Peeples, Assistant Director of Financial Aid, 800 Lakeshore Drive, Birmingham, AL 35229. Phone: 800-888-7245 or toll-free 800-888-7213. Fax: 205-870-2673. E-mail: dclong@samford.edu. Completed financial aid forms should be received by March 1.

Law School Library Lucille Stewart Beeson Law Library has 7 professional staff members and contains more than 240,329 volumes and 2,703 periodicals. 474 seats are available in the library. When classes are in session, the library is open 107 hours per week.

WESTLAW and LEXIS-NEXIS are available, as are the World Wide Web, online bibliographic services, and CD-ROM players. 30 computer workstations are available to students in the library. Special law collections include the Brantley collection.

First-Year Program Class size in the average section is 65; 100% of the first-year courses are taught by full-time faculty.

Upper-Level Program Class size in the average section is 45. Among the electives are:

Administrative Law
★ Advocacy
Business and Corporate Law
Constitutional Law
Consumer Law
Criminal Law
Criminal Procedure

Education Law
Entertainment Law
★ Environmental Law
Family Law
Government/Regulation
★ Health Care/Human Services
Intellectual Property
★ International/Comparative Law
Jurisprudence
Labor Law
Land Use Law/Natural Resources
★ Law and Religion
★ Lawyering Skills
Legal History/Philosophy
★ Litigation
Maritime Law
Mediation
Probate Law
Public Interest
Securities
★ Tax Law
(★ indicates an area of special strength)

Clinical Courses Students receive degree credit for clinical courses. (Clinical practicum is not required.) Among the clinical areas offered are:

Corporate Law
Criminal Prosecution
General Practice
Government Litigation
Juvenile Law
Legal Externship
Public Interest
Tax Law

23% of the students participate in internship programs.

THE UNIVERSITY OF ALABAMA
SCHOOL OF LAW

School of Law

Tuscaloosa, Alabama

INFORMATION CONTACT
Kenneth C. Randall, Dean
Box 870382
Tuscaloosa, AL 35487

Phone: 205-348-5117   Fax: 205-348-3917
E-mail: admissions@law.ua.edu
Web site: http://www.ua.edu/

LAW STUDENT PROFILE [1997–98]

FULL-TIME   Enrollment: 568
Women: 41%   Men: 59%

RACIAL or ETHNIC COMPOSITION
African American, 6%; Asian/Pacific Islander, 1%; Hispanic, 0.4%; Native American, 1%

APPLICANTS and ADMITTEES
Number applied: 744
Admitted: 326
Percentage accepted: 44%
Seats available: 185
Average LSAT score: 158
Average GPA: 3.4

The University of Alabama School of Law is a public institution that organizes classes on a semester calendar system. The campus is situated in a small-town setting. Founded in 1872, first ABA approved in 1926, and an AALS member, The University of Alabama School of Law offers JD, JD/MBA, LLM, and MCL degrees.

Faculty consists of 30 full-time and 37 part-time members in 1997–98. 6 full-time faculty members and 9 part-time faculty members are women. 98% of all faculty members have a JD; 30% have advanced law degrees. Of all faculty members, 6% are African American, 94% are white.

Application Information *Required:* LSAT, LSDAS, application form, application fee of $25, baccalaureate degree, personal statement, essay, college transcripts. *Recommended:* recommendations. *Application deadline* for fall term is March 1.

Financial Aid In 1997–98, 60% of all students received some form of financial aid. 54 research assistantships, totaling $137,943, were awarded. Graduate assistantships, loans, merit-based grants/scholarships, need-based grants/scholarships, and federal work-study loans are also available. The average student debt at graduation is $12,000. To apply for financial assistance, students must complete the Free Application for Federal Student

AT a GLANCE

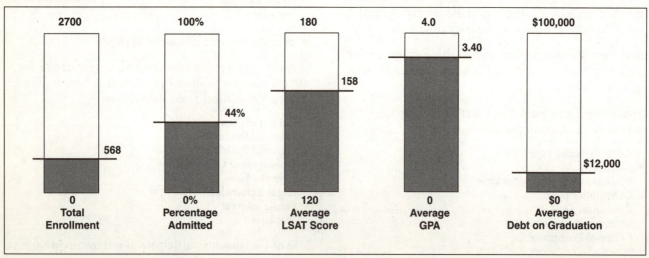

Degree Options

Degree	Total Credits Required	Length of Program
JD–Doctor of Laws	90	3–4 yrs, full-time only [day, summer]
JD/MBA–Juris Doctor/Master of Business Administration–Dual-degree Program	108	4–5 yrs, full-time only [day, summer]
LLM–Master of Laws–Taxation	24	2 yrs, part-time only [evening, weekend]
MCL–Master of Comparative Law	30	1 yr, full-time only [day]

Aid, institutional forms, and scholarship specific applications. Financial aid contact: Noah Funderburg, Assistant Dean for Administration, Box 870384, Tuscaloosa, AL 35487. Phone: 205-348-4508. Fax: 205-348-3917. E-mail: nfunderb@law.ua.edu. Completed financial aid forms should be received by March 15.

Law School Library Bounds Law Library has 10 professional staff members and contains more than 356,552 volumes and 3,148 periodicals. 562 seats are available in the library. When classes are in session, the library is open 102 hours per week.

WESTLAW and LEXIS-NEXIS are available, as are the World Wide Web, online bibliographic services, and CD-ROM players. 61 computer workstations are available to students in the library. Special law collections include Howell Heflins papers, Hugo Black papers.

First-Year Program Class size in the average section is 96; 100% of the first-year courses are taught by full-time faculty.

Upper-Level Program Class size in the average section is 40. Among the electives are:

Administrative Law
★ **Advocacy**
★ **Business and Corporate Law**
Consumer Law
Education Law
Entertainment Law

Environmental Law
Family Law
Government/Regulation
Health Care/Human Services
Intellectual Property
International/Comparative Law
Jurisprudence
Labor Law
Land Use Law/Natural Resources
★ **Lawyering Skills**
Legal History/Philosophy
★ **Litigation**
Maritime Law
Media Law
Mediation
Probate Law
Public Interest
Securities
★ **Tax Law**
(★ *indicates an area of special strength*)

Clinical Courses Students receive degree credit for clinical courses. (Clinical practicum is not required.) Among the clinical areas offered are:

Criminal Defense
Education
Elderly Advocacy
Pensions
Public Interest

20% of the students participate in internship programs. International exchange programs permit students to visit Switzerland.

DEAN'S STATEMENT . . .

The University of Alabama School of Law combines great traditions with great promise. For more than 120 years, our law school has educated premier lawyers, business and civic leaders, and state and federal judges. But never content with its past success, our law school today offers state-of-the-art facilities and technology, an updated curriculum, increased opportunity for skills training, and expanded career services for students. It is the only public law school in the state and is considered one of the best in the Southeast. National surveys consistently give the University of Alabama a fine ranking. Our student body of about 570 students is talented, diverse, academically strong, and friendly. The admissions process is rigorous; however, the Admissions Committee considers material beyond the LSAT and undergraduate GPAs. It also considers other factors that indicate a student will academically perform well in law school. The Admissions Committee looks for determination, diligence, the ability to solve problems and deal with difficult situations, and perseverance. The Admissions Committee also is sensitive to the idea that a diverse student body, a group with difficult life experience and from different academic and economic backgrounds, creates a stronger law school.

Come visit the University of Alabama. Meet our faculty, talk with our students, and sit in on classes. You will see that the University of Alabama School of Law is committed to providing the best legal education anywhere. Drawing upon our great traditions, we are working hard to create an even greater future for our law school and students.

—*Ken Randall, Dean and McMillan Professor of Law*

HISTORY, CAMPUS, AND LOCATION

The University of Alabama School of Law was established in 1872 and remains the only state-supported law school in Alabama. Under the direction of Dean Albert John Farrah, the School moved into its first permanent home, Farrah Hall, in 1913. Farrah Hall remained the academic building until 1978 when the Law Center was built. The Law Center is a modern, spacious building with lots of natural light and open spaces. Future construction plans include a new building to house clinical offices and to provide more classrooms and faculty offices. An expansion of the Bounds Law Library also is planned.

SPECIAL QUALITIES OF THE SCHOOL

The law faculty includes nationally known scholars from some of the best law schools in the United States, whose first priority is good classroom teaching. The faculty includes more women and members of minority groups than ever before.

From its beginning, the law school has been the place where Alabama's bar and community leaders are educated. Strong support from alumni resulted in the excellent success of a recent Capital Campaign where more than $23.3 million was raised, 40 percent more than the original goal of $16.5 million.

The University of Alabama School of Law provides a strong academic support program for students with lower numerical predictors and others who might face academic difficulties. This support includes offering a summer class that allows first-year students to take a reduced course load in the fall, a smaller section of a spring semester first-year class that includes emphasis on writing and analytical skills, special instruction from faculty members, and extra support tailored to students' needs.

TECHNOLOGY ON CAMPUS

The law school is substantially expanding and enhancing its information services and the technology available to students and faculty. A new multimedia classroom became functional in 1997, and another is planned during the next two years. Expansion plans for the Law Center include state-of-the-art technology in several new classrooms. Students, faculty, and staff may communicate through the School's network, and they also may access the network from their home computers through the School of Law's dial-in capabilities. The Bounds Law Library houses a large and up-to-date computer lab, and there are carrels in the library connected to the School network for laptop use. The School's LL.M. in taxation program is taught through interactive, distinctive learning through the University's IITS system.

SCHOLARSHIPS AND LOANS

Though tuition remains reasonable, at about $4500 a year for residents, the School provides more than $500,000 a year in student scholarships, financial aid, and upperclass student employment.

STUDENT ACTIVITIES AND OPPORTUNITIES

Law Review The law school publishes four legal journals that provide excellent opportunities for more than one third of the second- and third-year students to sharpen their skills in legal research, analysis, writing, and editing. The *Alabama Law Review* is ranked in the top 25 student journals in the country. The *Journal of the Legal Profession* was the nation's first periodical to explore legal ethics and problems confronting the profession. The *Law and Psychology Review* was among the first legal periodicals to combine the discipline of law with the behavioral sciences. The *American Journal of Tax Policy* is the official publication of the American College of Tax Counsel.

Moot Court Moot court is required in the first year. More than one third of the second-year students choose to participate in the Campbell Moot Court Competition. Top scorers in the competition are placed on the Campbell Moot Court Board, which conducts the next year's competition and assists the Legal Writing Lecturers in teaching first-year moot court. Members of the National Moot Court Team and the Jessup International Moot Court Team are selected from the Campbell Moot Team. The School of Law also sponsors a team in the Duberstein Bankruptcy Moot Competition and the Frederick Douglass Moot Court Competition. The School's appellate advocacy teams have been very successful over the years. Fifteen of the School's teams have advanced from regional to national competition in the last eight years. The 1997–98 Duberstein team won its national competition.

Special Opportunities The clinical programs at the School are extensive, varied, and of high quality, and externship opportunities are offered in the academic year and during the summer. Alabama's trial and appellate advocacy teams are among the nation's best and have won numerous awards. Ten trial advocacy teams from Alabama have advanced from regional competition to national competition in the last eight years. Ninety percent of the students at the law school enroll in at least one trial advocacy class. All instructors receive national training. The law school and the Manderson Graduate School of Business at the University of Alabama offer select students an opportunity to earn a joint M.B.A./J.D. degree in a four-year program of study. There is a summer program at the University of Fribourg that allows students to study other legal systems. Three endowed lecture series bring national judges and scholars to campus. These have included U.S. Supreme Court Justices Anthony Kennedy and Antonin Scalia.

Opportunities for Members of Minority Groups and Women Minority students participate in all extracurricular and clinical programs, law reviews, and student organizations. For example, in 1997–98 the president of the Student Bar and the Chief Justice of the Student Honor Court were both African Americans. The Black Law Student Association is very active, sponsoring activities during Black History Month and in celebration of Martin Luther King Jr.'s birthday, tutoring at a local elementary school, and providing support for entering first-year students.

BAR PASSAGE, CAREER SERVICES, AND PLACEMENT

In recent years, more than 90 percent of the Alabama graduates passed the bar exam on their first attempt. Ninety-five percent of the May 1997 graduates taking the Alabama bar exam passed it the first time.

The School of Law, through its Career Services Office, is committed to supporting its students' and alumni's career goals. The placement rate for Alabama is exceptional. Ninety-eight percent of the 1996–97 graduating class was employed in the legal sector within six months of graduating.

In addition to on-campus interviewing and resume forwarding programs, Careers Services offers an extensive library of career-planning resources, presents frequent seminars on resume writing and job search techniques, hosts speakers and panel discussions, sponsors several recruiting conferences, and maintains databases of employees seeking experienced attorneys and alumni who are interested in relocating.

Legal Field	Percentage of Graduates	Average Starting Salary
Academic	2%	n/a
Business	6%	$44,500
Government	8%	$30,320
Judicial Clerkships	14%	$32,200
Private Practice	68%	$49,850
Public Interest	2%	$25,000
Other	n/a	n/a

CORRESPONDENCE AND INFORMATION

Admissions Office
University of Alabama School of Law
Box 870382
Tuscaloosa, Alabama 35487-0382
Telephone: 205-348-5440
Fax: 205-348-3917
E-mail: admissions@law.ua.edu

ARIZONA STATE UNIVERSITY
COLLEGE OF LAW

Tempe, Arizona

LAW STUDENT PROFILE [1997–98]

FULL-TIME   Enrollment: 458
Women: 49%   Men: 51%

RACIAL or ETHNIC COMPOSITION
African American, 4%; Asian/Pacific Islander, 3%; Hispanic, 11%; Native American, 6%; International, 2%

APPLICANTS and ADMITTEES
Number applied: 1,754
Admitted: 391
Percentage accepted: 22%
Seats available: 150

Arizona State University College of Law is a public institution that organizes classes on a semester calendar system. The campus is situated in an urban setting. Founded in 1966, first ABA approved in 1969, and an AALS member, Arizona State University College of Law offers JD, JD/MBA, JD/MHA, and JD/PhD degrees.

Faculty consists of 35 full-time members in 1997–98.

Application Information *Required:* LSAT, LSDAS, application form, application fee of $45, baccalaureate degree, personal statement. *Recommended:* recommendations. *Application deadline* for fall term is March 1.

Costs The 1997–98 tuition is $4536 for state residents. Tuition is $11,488 for nonresidents.

Financial Aid 42 research assistantships, totaling $34,617, were awarded. 181 other awards were given. Loans, merit-based grants/scholarships, and need-based grants/scholarships are also available. To apply for financial assistance, students must complete the Free Application for Federal Student Aid. Financial aid contact: Student Financial Assistance Office, Arizona State University Law School, Box 870412, Tempe, AZ 85287-0412. Phone:

AT a GLANCE

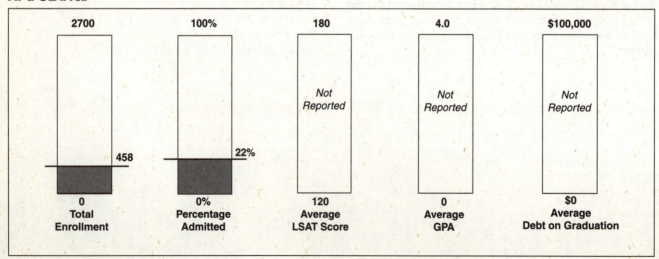

2700	100%	180	4.0	$100,000
		Not Reported	Not Reported	Not Reported
458	22%			
0	0%	120	0	$0
Total Enrollment	Percentage Admitted	Average LSAT Score	Average GPA	Average Debt on Graduation

Degree Options

Degree	Total Credits Required	Length of Program
JD–Doctor of Laws	87	
JD/MBA–Juris Doctor/Master of Business Administration		4 yrs, full-time only
JD/MHA–Juris Doctor/Master of Health Administration–Dual-degree Program Health Services Administration		4 yrs, full-time only
JD/PhD–Juris Doctor/Doctor of Philosophy–Dual-degree Program Justice Studies		

602-965-3355. Completed financial aid forms should be received by March 1.

Law School Library John J. Ross - William C. Blakley Law Library has 9 professional staff members and contains more than 359,471 volumes and 6,423 periodicals. 558 seats are available in the library. When classes are in session, the library is open 110 hours per week.

WESTLAW and LEXIS-NEXIS are available, as are CD-ROM players. 40 computer workstations are available to students in the library.

First-Year Program Class size in the average section is 135.

Upper-Level Program Among the electives are:

Business and Corporate Law
Civil Rights
Conflict of Laws
Constitutional Law
Criminal Procedure
Environmental Law
Evidence
Family Law
Government/Regulation
★ Indian/Tribal Law
Intellectual Property
Labor Law
Lawyering Skills
Legal History/Philosophy
Legislation
Water Law

(★ *indicates an area of special strength*)

Clinical Courses Among the clinical areas offered are:

Civil Litigation
Criminal Defense
Criminal Prosecution
General Practice
Indian/Tribal Law
Mediation

THE UNIVERSITY OF ARIZONA
COLLEGE OF LAW

Tucson, Arizona

INFORMATION CONTACT
Joel Seligman, Dean
James E. Rogers Law Center
PO Box 210176
Tucson, AZ 85721-0176

Phone: 520-621-1498   Fax: 520-621-9140
E-mail: holpert@nt.law.arizona.edu
Web site: http://www.law.arizona.edu/

LAW STUDENT PROFILE [1997–98]

FULL-TIME   Enrollment: 458
Women: 48%   Men: 52%

RACIAL or ETHNIC COMPOSITION
African American, 3%; Asian/Pacific Islander, 6%; Hispanic, 12%; Native American, 3%; International, 1%

APPLICANTS and ADMITTEES
Number applied: 4,863
Admitted: 1,459
Percentage accepted: 30%
Seats available: 150
Median LSAT score: 160
Median GPA: 3.4

The University of Arizona College of Law is a public institution that organizes classes on a semester calendar system. The campus is situated in an urban setting. Founded in 1915, first ABA approved in 1931, and an AALS member, The University of Arizona College of Law offers JD, JD/MA, JD/MBA, JD/MPAd, and JD/PhD degrees.

Faculty consists of 32 full-time and 50 part-time members in 1997–98. 8 full-time faculty members and 14 part-time faculty members are women. 100% of all faculty members have a JD; 40% have advanced law degrees. Of all faculty members, 3% are Native American, 10% are African American, 7% are Hispanic, 80% are white.

Application Information *Required:* LSAT, application form, application fee of $45, baccalaureate degree, 2 letters of recommendation, personal statement, writing sample, college transcripts, resume, LSDAS. *Application deadline* for fall term is March 1.

Costs The 1997–98 tuition is $4464 for state residents. Tuition is $11,416 for nonresidents. Fees: $74.

Financial Aid In 1997–98, 66% of all students received some form of financial aid. 300 other awards were given. Fellowships, loans, loan repay-

AT a GLANCE

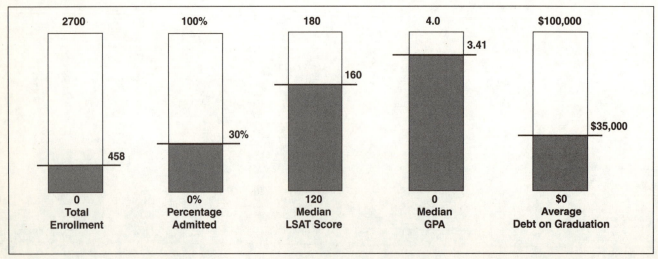

	Total Enrollment	Percentage Admitted	Median LSAT Score	Median GPA	Average Debt on Graduation
top	2700	100%	180	4.0	$100,000
value	458	30%	160	3.41	$35,000
bottom	0	0%	120	0	$0

Degree Options

Degree	Total Credits Required	Length of Program
JD–Juris Doctor	85	3 yrs, full-time only [day, summer]
JD/MA–Juris Doctor/Master of Arts–Economics	103	3 yrs, full-time only [day, summer]
JD/MA–Juris Doctor/Master of Arts–Indian Studies	106	4 yrs
JD/MBA–Juris Doctor/Master of Business Administration	113	4 yrs, full-time only [day, summer]
JD/MPAd–Juris Doctor/Master of Public Administration	112	4 yrs, full-time only [day, summer]
JD/PhD–Juris Doctor/Doctor of Philosophy–Psychology, Philosophy, or Economics	133	6 yrs, full-time only [day, summer]

ment assistance program (LRAP), merit-based grants/scholarships, need-based grants/scholarships, and federal work-study loans are also available. The average student debt at graduation is $35,000. To apply for financial assistance, students must complete the Free Application for Federal Student Aid. Financial aid contact: Henrietta Stover, Assistant Dean for Finance and Administration, PO Box 210176, Tuscon, AZ 85721-0176. Phone: 520-621-5433. Fax: 520-621-9140. E-mail: stover@nt.law.arizona.edu. Completed financial aid forms should be received by March 1.

Law School Library College of Law Library has 8 professional staff members and contains more than 371,000 volumes and 4,158 periodicals. 353 seats are available in the library. When classes are in session, the library is open 107 hours per week.

WESTLAW and LEXIS-NEXIS are available, as are the World Wide Web, online bibliographic services, and CD-ROM players. 25 computer workstations are available to students in the library. Special law collections include International/Mexican Law Collection, International Commercial Law Collection, Latin American Law Collection, Government Documents Repository.

First-Year Program Class size in the average section is 35; 100% of the first-year courses are taught by full-time faculty.

Upper-Level Program Class size in the average section is 30. Among the electives are:

Accounting

Advocacy
Business and Corporate Law
Constitutional Law
Environmental Law
Family Law
Health Care/Human Services
Immigration
Indian/Tribal Law
Intellectual Property
International/Comparative Law
Land Use Law/Natural Resources
Lawyering Skills
Legal History/Philosophy
Media Law
Mediation
Probate Law
Public Interest
Sports Law
Tax Law
Water Law

Clinical Courses Students receive degree credit for clinical courses. (Clinical practicum is not required.) Among the clinical areas offered are:

Children's Advocacy
Criminal Defense
Criminal Prosecution
Domestic Violence
Immigration
Indian/Tribal Law
International Law
Juvenile Law
Mediation

Internships are available.

UNIVERSITY OF ARKANSAS
SCHOOL OF LAW

Fayetteville, Arkansas

INFORMATION CONTACT
Leonard P. Strickman, Dean
Leflar Law Center
Fayettville, AR 72701

Phone: 501-575-5601   Fax: 501-575-3320
Web site: http://www.uark.edu/

LAW STUDENT PROFILE [1997–98]

FULL-TIME   Enrollment: 377
Women: 40%   Men: 60%

RACIAL or ETHNIC COMPOSITION
African American, 6%; Asian/Pacific Islander, 2%; Hispanic, 1%; Native American, 2%; International, 1%

APPLICANTS and ADMITTEES
Number applied: 647
Admitted: 317
Percentage accepted: 49%
Seats available: 135
Average LSAT score: 153
Average GPA: 3.3

University of Arkansas School of Law is a public institution that organizes classes on a semester calendar system. The campus is situated in a small-town setting. Founded in 1924, first ABA approved in 1926, and an AALS member, University of Arkansas School of Law offers JD, JD/MBA, and LLM degrees.

Faculty consists of 31 full-time and 11 part-time members in 1997–98. 8 full-time faculty members and 3 part-time faculty members are women. 100% of all faculty members have a JD; 29% have advanced law degrees. Of all faculty members, 2% are Native American, 6% are African American, 92% are white.

Application Information *Required:* LSAT, LSDAS, application form, baccalaureate degree. *Application deadline* for fall term is April 1.

Financial Aid Loans, merit-based grants/scholarships, need-based grants/scholarships, and federal work-study loans are available. The average student debt at graduation is $31,000. To apply for financial assistance, students must complete the Free Application for Federal Student Aid and institutional forms. Financial aid contact: James K. Miller, Associate Dean for Students, Le Flar Law Center, Fayetteville, AR 72701. Phone: 501-575-3102. Fax: 501-575-3320.

AT a GLANCE

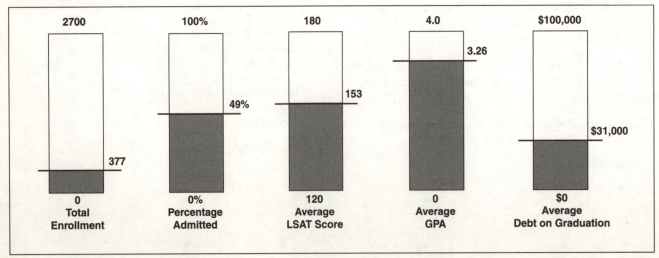

Degree Options		
Degree	**Total Credits Required**	**Length of Program**
JD–Doctor of Laws	90	3 yrs, full-time only [day, summer]
JD/MBA–Juris Doctor/Master of Business Administration–Joint Program		3 yrs, full-time only [day, summer]
LLM–Master of Laws–Agricultural Law	24	1 yr, full-time only [day, summer]

Completed financial aid forms should be received by April 1.

Law School Library Young Law Library has 7 professional staff members and contains more than 243,962 volumes and 2,240 periodicals. 355 seats are available in the library. When classes are in session, the library is open 107 hours per week.

WESTLAW and LEXIS-NEXIS are available, as are the World Wide Web, online bibliographic services, and CD-ROM players. 34 computer workstations are available to students in the library. Special law collections include Agricultural Law.

First-Year Program Class size in the average section is 25; 100% of the first-year courses are taught by full-time faculty.

Upper-Level Program Class size in the average section is 30. Among the electives are:

Administrative Law
Advocacy
Business and Corporate Law
Consumer Law
Education Law
Entertainment Law
Environmental Law
Family Law
Government/Regulation
Health Care/Human Services
Indian/Tribal Law
Intellectual Property
International/Comparative Law
Jurisprudence
Labor Law
Land Use Law/Natural Resources
Lawyering Skills
Legal History/Philosophy
Litigation
Media Law
Mediation
Probate Law
Public Interest
Securities
Tax Law

Clinical Courses Students receive degree credit for clinical courses. (Clinical practicum is not required.) Among the clinical areas offered are:

Civil Litigation
Criminal Defense
Criminal Prosecution
General Practice
Government Litigation
Juvenile Law

Internships are available.

UNIVERSITY OF ARKANSAS AT LITTLE ROCK
SCHOOL OF LAW

Little Rock, Arkansas

INFORMATION CONTACT

Rodney K. Smith, Dean
1201 McAlmont Street
Little Rock, AR 72202-5142

Phone: 501-324-9434   Fax: 501-324-9433
Web site: http://www.ualr.edu/~lawschool/

LAW STUDENT PROFILE [1997–98]

FULL-TIME   Enrollment: 253
Women: 53%   Men: 47%

PART-TIME   Enrollment: 151
Women: 41%   Men: 59%

RACIAL or ETHNIC COMPOSITION
African American, 8%; Asian/Pacific Islander, 1%; Hispanic, 2%; Native American, 1%

APPLICANTS and ADMITTEES
Number applied: 460
Admitted: 234
Percentage accepted: 51%
Seats available: 130
Average LSAT score: 151
Average GPA: 3.2

University of Arkansas at Little Rock School of Law is a public institution that organizes classes on a semester calendar system. The campus is situated in an urban setting. Founded in 1975, first ABA approved in 1969, and an AALS member, University of Arkansas at Little Rock School of Law offers JD and JD/MBA degrees.

Faculty consists of 26 full-time and 20 part-time members in 1997–98. 10 full-time faculty members and 5 part-time faculty members are women. 100% of all faculty members have a JD; 26% have advanced law degrees. Of all faculty members, 2% are Asian/Pacific Islander, 7% are African American, 91% are white.

Application Information *Required:* LSAT, LSDAS, application form, application fee of $40, baccalaureate degree, 2 letters of recommendation, personal statement, college transcripts. *Application deadline* for fall term is April 1.

Costs The 1997–98 tuition is $4500 full-time for state residents; $150 per credit hour part-time for state residents. Tuition is $10,200 full-time for nonresidents; $340 per credit hour part-time for nonresidents. Fees: $174 full-time; $54 per semester (minimum) part-time.

AT a GLANCE

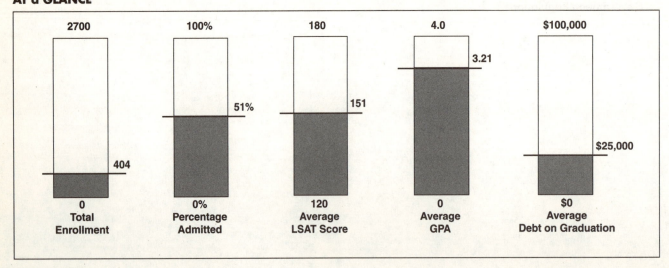

Degree Options

Degree	Total Credits Required	Length of Program
JD–Doctor of Laws	87	3–4 yrs, full-time or part-time [day, evening]
JD/MBA–Juris Doctor/Master of Business Administration–Joint Degree	102	4–6 yrs, full-time or part-time [day, evening]

Financial Aid In 1997–98, 63% of all students received some form of financial aid. 24 research assistantships were awarded. Loans, merit-based grants/scholarships, need-based grants/scholarships, and federal work-study loans are also available. The average student debt at graduation is $25,000. To apply for financial assistance, students must complete the Free Application for Federal Student Aid and institutional forms. Financial aid contact: Cari Wickliffe, Director, Student Financial Services, 2801 South University, Administration South 206, Little Rock, AR 72204. Phone: 501-569-3035. Fax: 501-324-9433. E-mail: cswickliffe@ualr.edu. Completed financial aid forms should be received by April 1.

Law School Library University of Arkansas at Little Rock Law Library has 6 professional staff members and contains more than 257,000 volumes and 2,711 periodicals. 385 seats are available in the library. When classes are in session, the library is open 99 hours per week.

WESTLAW and LEXIS-NEXIS are available, as are the World Wide Web, online bibliographic services, and CD-ROM players. 52 computer workstations are available to students in the library. Special law collections include Archive of Arkansas Supreme Court Records and Briefs.

First-Year Program Class size in the average section is 65; 100% of the first-year courses are taught by full-time faculty.

Upper-Level Program Class size in the average section is 26. Among the electives are:

Administrative Law

Advocacy
Business and Corporate Law
Consumer Law
★ Education Law
Employment Law
Environmental Law
★ Family Practice
Health Care/Human Services
Intellectual Property
International/Comparative Law
Jurisprudence
★ Juvenile Law
Labor Law
Land Use Law/Natural Resources
Lawyering Skills
Legal History/Philosophy
Litigation
Maritime Law
Media Law
★ Mediation
★ Mental Health and Law
Probate Law
Securities
Sports Law
★ Tax Law
(★ indicates an area of special strength)

Clinical Courses Students receive degree credit for clinical courses. (Clinical practicum is not required.) Among the clinical areas offered are:

Education
Family Practice
Juvenile Law
Mediation

CALIFORNIA WESTERN SCHOOL OF LAW

San Diego, California

INFORMATION CONTACT

Steven R. Smith, Dean
225 Cedar Street
San Diego, CA 92101-3090

Phone: 619-239-0391   Fax: 619-525-7092
E-mail: admissions@cwsl.edu
Web site: http://www.cwsl.edu/

LAW STUDENT PROFILE [1997–98]

FULL-TIME   Enrollment: 721
Women: 48%   Men: 52%

APPLICANTS and ADMITTEES
Number applied: 1,779
Admitted: 1,277
Percentage accepted: 72%
Seats available: 292

California Western School of Law is a private nonprofit institution that organizes classes on a trimester calendar system. The campus is situated in an urban setting. Founded in 1924, first ABA approved in 1962, and an AALS member, California Western School of Law offers JD, JD/MSW, LLM, and MCL degrees.

Faculty consists of 43 full-time and 48 part-time members in 1997–98. 18 full-time faculty members and 14 part-time faculty members are women. 100% of all faculty members have a JD; 20% have advanced law degrees. Of all faculty members, 4% are African American, 1% are Hispanic, 38% are white.

Application Information *Required:* LSAT, LSDAS, application form, application fee of $45, baccalaureate degree, 2 letters of recommendation, personal statement, college transcripts. *Recommended:* resume. *Application deadline* for fall term is May 1.

Financial Aid Fellowships, loans, merit-based grants/scholarships, need-based grants/scholarships, and federal work-study loans are available. The average student debt at graduation is $70,000. To apply for financial assistance, students must complete the Free Application for Federal Student Aid and institutional forms. Financial aid contact: Kyle C. Poston, Executive Director of Financial Aid, 225 Cedar Street, San Diego, CA 92101. Phone:

AT a GLANCE

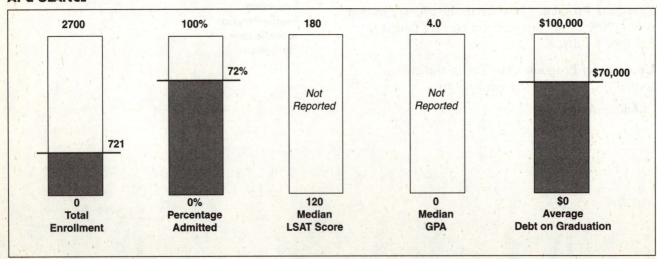

Degree Options

Degree	Total Credits Required	Length of Program
JD–Doctor of Law	89	2–5 yrs, full-time or part-time
JD/MSW–Juris Doctor/Master of Social Work–Dual-degree Program	149	4 yrs, full-time only
LLM–Master of Laws–Comparative Law		full-time only
MCL–Master of Comparative Law		full-time only

619-525-7060. Fax: 619-525-7092. E-mail: financial-aid@cwsl.edu. Completed financial aid forms should be received by March 20.

Law School Library California Western School of Law Library has 8 professional staff members and contains more than 262,039 volumes and 3,223 periodicals. 508 seats are available in the library. When classes are in session, the library is open 119 hours per week.

WESTLAW and LEXIS-NEXIS are available, as are the World Wide Web, online bibliographic services, and CD-ROM players. 66 computer workstations are available to students in the library. Special law collections include State Session Laws, CIS Legislative History (complete set), Pacific Island codes, Law of the Sea.

First-Year Program Class size in the average section is 85; 100% of the first-year courses are taught by full-time faculty.

Upper-Level Program Class size in the average section is 50. Among the electives are:

Administrative Law
★ Advocacy
★ Business and Corporate Law
Entertainment Law
Environmental Law
★ Family Practice
Health Care/Human Services
Intellectual Property
★ International/Comparative Law
Jurisprudence
Labor Law
Land Use Law/Natural Resources
Lawyering Skills
Legal History/Philosophy

Litigation
Maritime Law
Media Law
Mediation
Probate Law
Securities
Tax Law
(★ indicates an area of special strength)

Clinical Courses Students receive degree credit for clinical courses. (Clinical practicum is not required.) Among the clinical areas offered are:

Civil Litigation
Civil Rights
Corporate Law
Criminal Defense
Criminal Prosecution
Education
Elderly Advocacy
Entertainment Law
Environmental Law
Family Practice
General Practice
Government Litigation
Health
Immigration
Indian/Tribal Law
Intellectual Property
International Law
Juvenile Law
Land Rights/Natural Resource
Mediation
Public Interest
Sports Law
Tax Law
Telecommunications Law

70% of the students participate in internship programs.

CHAPMAN UNIVERSITY
SCHOOL OF LAW

Orange, California

INFORMATION CONTACT
Parham Williams, Dean
1240 South State College Boulevard
Anaheim, CA 92806

Phone: 714-517-0303   Fax: 714-517-0320
E-mail: jparamor@chapman.edu
Web site: http://www.chapman.edu/law/index.html

LAW STUDENT PROFILE [1997–98]

FULL-TIME   Enrollment: 160
Women: 43%   Men: 58%

PART-TIME   Enrollment: 100
Women: 44%   Men: 56%

APPLICANTS and ADMITTEES
Average LSAT score: 149
Average GPA: 3.1

Chapman University School of Law is a private institution that organizes classes on a semester calendar system. The campus is situated in a suburban setting. Founded in 1995, first ABA approved in 1998, Chapman University School of Law offers a JD degree.

Faculty consists of 18 full-time and 4 part-time members in 1997–98. 9 full-time faculty members are women. 100% of all faculty members have a JD degree. Of all faculty members, 7.5% are Asian/Pacific Islander, 7.5% are African American, 5% are Hispanic, 80% are white.

Application Information *Required:* LSAT, LSDAS, application form, application fee of $40, baccalaureate degree, 2 letters of recommendation, personal statement. *Recommended:* resume.

Financial Aid Graduate assistantships, loans, merit-based grants/scholarships, and federal work-study loans are available. To apply for financial assistance, students must complete the Free Application for Federal Student Aid and institutional forms. Financial aid contact: Peggy Crawford, Director of Financial Aid, 1240 South State College Boulevard, Anaheim, CA 92806. Phone: 714-517-0304 or toll-free 888-242-1913. Fax: 714-517-0320. E-mail: pcrawfor@chapman.edu. Completed financial aid forms should be received by March 1.

AT a GLANCE

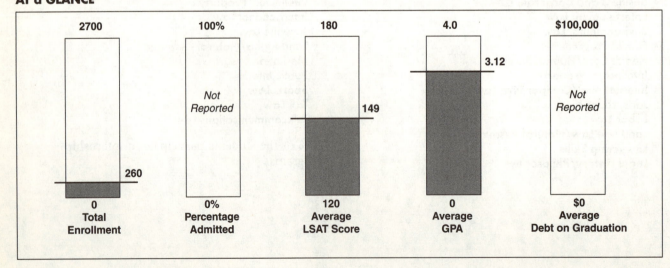

2700	100%	180	4.0	$100,000
	Not Reported		3.12	Not Reported
		149		
260				
0	0%	120	0	$0
Total Enrollment	Percentage Admitted	Average LSAT Score	Average GPA	Average Debt on Graduation

Degree Options

Degree	Total Credits Required	Length of Program
JD–Doctor of Laws	88	3–4 yrs, full-time or part-time [day, evening, weekend, summer]

Law School Library Chapman University Law Library has 6 professional staff members and contains more than 220,687 volumes and 502 periodicals. 162 seats are available in the library. When classes are in session, the library is open 95 hours per week.

WESTLAW and LEXIS-NEXIS are available, as are the World Wide Web and CD-ROM players. 20 computer workstations are available to students in the library.

First-Year Program Class size in the average section is 24; 100% of the first-year courses are taught by full-time faculty.

Upper-Level Program Class size in the average section is 12. Among the electives are:

Administrative Law
Advocacy
Business and Corporate Law
Consumer Law
Entertainment Law
★ Environmental Law

Family Law
Health Care/Human Services
Intellectual Property
International/Comparative Law
Jurisprudence
Labor Law
Land Use Law/Natural Resources
Lawyering Skills
Legal History/Philosophy
Litigation
Probate Law
Public Interest
★ Securities
Tax Law
(★ *indicates an area of special strength*)

Clinical Courses Students receive degree credit for clinical courses. (Clinical practicum is not required.) Among the clinical areas offered is:

Tax Law

11% of the students participate in internship programs.

GOLDEN GATE UNIVERSITY
SCHOOL OF LAW

San Francisco, California

INFORMATION CONTACT
Anthony J. Pagano, Dean
536 Mission Street
San Francisco, CA 94105

Phone: 415-442-6600   Fax: 415-442-6609
E-mail: lawadmit@ggu.edu
Web site: http://www.ggu.edu/law/

LAW STUDENT PROFILE [1997–98]

FULL-TIME   Enrollment: 534
Women: 58%   Men: 42%

PART-TIME   Enrollment: 326
Women: 46%   Men: 54%

RACIAL or ETHNIC COMPOSITION
African American, 4%; Asian/Pacific Islander, 12%; Hispanic, 8%; International, 6%

APPLICANTS and ADMITTEES
Number applied: 1,963
Admitted: 1,144
Percentage accepted: 58%
Seats available: 190
Average LSAT score: 153
Average GPA: 3.0

Golden Gate University School of Law is a private institution that organizes classes on a semester calendar system. The campus is situated in an urban setting. Founded in 1901, first ABA approved in 1956, and an AALS member, Golden Gate University School of Law offers JD, JD/MA, JD/MBA, JD/MPAd, JD/PhD, JSD, and LLM degrees.

Faculty consists of 35 full-time and 89 part-time members in 1997–98. 13 full-time faculty members and 37 part-time faculty members are women. 100% of all faculty members have a JD; 11% have advanced law degrees. Of all faculty members, 5% are Asian/Pacific Islander, 7% are African American, 2% are Hispanic, 86% are white.

Application Information *Required:* LSAT, LSDAS, application form, application fee of $40, baccalaureate degree, 1 recommendation, personal statement, college transcripts. *Recommended:* resume. *Application deadline* for fall term is April 15.

Costs The 1997–98 tuition is $19,981 full-time; $13,780 part-time. Fees: $224.

Financial Aid In 1997–98, 76% of all students received some form of financial aid. 3 fellowships, totaling $41,200, were awarded. Fellowships, graduate assistantships, loans, loan repayment assistance program (LRAP), merit-based grants/

AT a GLANCE

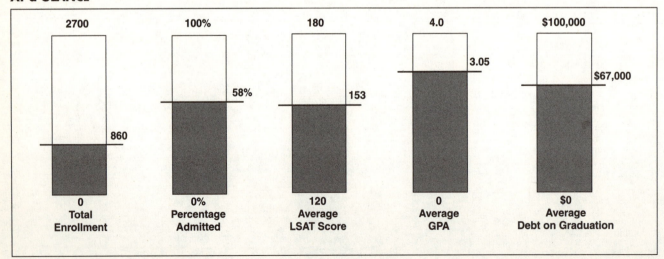

Degree Options

Degree	Total Credits Required	Length of Program
JD–Doctor of Laws	88	3–4 yrs, full-time or part-time [day, evening, summer]
JD/MA–Juris Doctor/Master of Arts–International Relations Combined-degree Program	106	3–5 yrs, full-time or part-time [day, evening, summer]
JD/MBA–Juris Doctor/Master of Business Administration–Combined-degree Program	100	3–5 yrs, full-time or part-time [day, evening, summer]
JD/MPAd–Juris Doctor/Master of Public Administration–Combined-degree Program	109	3–5 yrs, full-time or part-time [day, evening, summer]
JD/PhD–Juris Doctor/Doctor of Philosophy–Combined-degree Program		7 yrs, full-time or part-time [day, evening, summer]
JSD–Doctor of Juridical Science–International Legal Studies		3–5 yrs, full-time or part-time [day]
LLM–Master of Laws–Environmental Law, US Legal Studies, International Legal Studies, Taxation	24–26	1–2 yrs, full-time or part-time [day, evening, summer]

scholarships, need-based grants/scholarships, and federal work-study loans are also available. The average student debt at graduation is $67,000. To apply for financial assistance, students must complete the Free Application for Federal Student Aid and institutional forms. Financial aid contact: Cheryl Barnes, Assistant Director for Admissions and Financial Aid, 536 Mission Street, San Francisco, CA 94105. Phone: 415-442-6630. Fax: 415-442-6609. E-mail: lawfao@ggu.edu. Completed financial aid forms should be received by March 1.

Law School Library Golden Gate University School of Law Library has 6 professional staff members and contains more than 234,368 volumes and 3,917 periodicals. 336 seats are available in the library. When classes are in session, the library is open 91 hours per week.

WESTLAW and LEXIS-NEXIS are available, as are the World Wide Web and CD-ROM players. 58 computer workstations are available to students in the library. Special law collections include McDaniel Law and Literature Collection.

First-Year Program Class size in the average section is 38; 76% of the first-year courses are taught by full-time faculty.

Upper-Level Program Class size in the average section is 23. Among the electives are:

Administrative Law
★ Advocacy
★ Business and Corporate Law
Entertainment Law
★ Environmental Law
★ Family Law
Health Care/Human Services
Indian/Tribal Law
Intellectual Property
★ International/Comparative Law
Jurisprudence
★ Labor Law
Land Use Law/Natural Resources
Lawyering Skills
★ Litigation
Maritime Law
Media Law
Mediation
★ Public Interest
Securities
Tax Law
(★ *indicates an area of special strength*)

Clinical Courses Students receive degree credit for clinical courses. (Clinical practicum is not required.) Among the clinical areas offered are:

Civil Litigation
Corporate Law
Criminal Defense
Criminal Prosecution
Family Practice
General Practice
Government Litigation
Health
Intellectual Property
Judicial Externship
Juvenile Law
Tax Law

International exchange programs available.

DEAN'S STATEMENT . . .

Iinvite you to learn about the outstanding opportunities for the study of law at Golden Gate University. We provide students with a solid foundation in legal theory and the skills necessary to practice law successfully. As a student, you will be challenged to view law not merely as rules to be mastered but also as social policies to be explored and questioned.

One of Golden Gate's greatest assets has always been its dedicated faculty. The School of Law faculty has a strong commitment to teaching and being accessible to students. Combining excellent academic credentials with expertise gained through the practice of law, the faculty is uniquely qualified to bring to the classroom a practical dimension often lacking in American legal education. Our talented faculty has been instrumental in shaping legal doctrines, many of which have expanded individual rights.

There is no dichotomy between teaching and research at Golden Gate. Stimulating teaching generates new ideas, leading to serious scholarship that often involves faculty-student collaboration, and faculty scholarship brought to the classroom enriches the learning experience.

The ethic we share at Golden Gate University School of Law is that lawyering is an honorable profession, worthy of the public trust. Come join us.

—Dean Anthony J. Pagano

HISTORY, CAMPUS, AND LOCATION

Golden Gate University School of Law was founded in 1901 and is fully accredited by the American Bar Association (ABA) and the Committee of Bar Examiners of the State of California and is a member of the Association of American Law Schools (AALS). Graduates qualify to take the bar exam in all fifty states and in the District of Columbia.

Golden Gate University School of Law is located in the heart of downtown San Francisco, gateway to the Pacific Rim and one of the most beautiful cities in the world. With the legal and financial district on one side and the bustling South of Market area on the other, the School is a short walk from restaurants, shopping, and downtown plazas.

Golden Gate's 700 full- and part-time law students include working professionals and recent college graduates drawn from more than 100 undergraduate and graduate institutions. They come from across the United States and from a number of other nations and represent a wide spectrum of ethnic, economic, and cultural backgrounds.

SPECIAL QUALITIES OF THE SCHOOL

Golden Gate University is an urban law school that draws on the dynamic environment of the legal/business district of San Francisco. Students can enroll part-time or full-time, and full-time students can begin their studies in August or January. The low student-faculty ratio of 17:1 strengthens the bonds of communication between students and teachers. The Law School endowment of $3.2 million allows the School to attract an excellent faculty and provide generous financial aid to incoming and continuing students.

TECHNOLOGY ON CAMPUS

All first-year students complete training in the use of the LEXIS and WESTLAW online databases. The law library maintains online links to consortium law library catalogs. A computer lab in the library provides students across to the

Internet, various CD-ROM databases, Computer-Assisted Legal Instruction, word processing and spreadsheet applications, and GGU Online!, the Golden Gate University e-mail system that also provides access to the Internet. Every law student receives a GGU Online! account and an e-mail address.

SCHOLARSHIPS AND LOANS

To attract a highly qualified student body, the School of Law awards entering students a number of full and partial tuition scholarships based solely on academic merit. In addition, scholarships in the amount of $5000 are awarded to entering members of minority groups who have demonstrated leadership qualities.

All eligible first-year students are considered for several endowed scholarships. Entering students who are accepted to the Public Interest Scholars Program may be eligible for scholarship assistance. The School of Law also has a variety of scholarships for continuing students.

STUDENT ACTIVITIES AND OPPORTUNITIES

Law Review The *Golden Gate University Law Review* is written and edited by student members who are selected by academic standing or on the basis of a writing competition. Three issues of the *Law Review* are published annually: a survey of cases from the Ninth Circuit Court of Appeals; a Women's Law Forum; and a Notes and Comments issue on the environment. Students interested in International Legal Studies may work on the *Annual Survey of International and Comparative Law*.

Moot Court All second-year students are required to take Appellate Advocacy, a course in which they prepare appellate briefs and present oral arguments in a moot court program. Tryouts for interscholastic moot court teams are open to all students. Golden Gate regularly participates in the Jessup International Law, American Bar Association Appellate Advocacy, and Roger Traynor California Moot

Court Competitions. The School selects additional competitions based on demonstrated student interest.

Extracurricular Activities The Student Bar Association sponsors a variety of activities and events for all law students. In addition, there are more than fifteen other campus organizations that students can join.

Special Opportunities In addition to the standard J.D. program, Golden Gate offers the Integrated Professional Apprenticeship Curriculum, an innovative honors program in which students attend classes with other J.D. students but also participate in two full-time semester-long professional apprenticeships in law offices and other legal settings. These apprenticeships link work in the legal community with the theory, skills, and values learned in the classroom. In addition, Golden Gate University School of Law has one of the most extensive clinical programs in the country. Three on-site clinics and seven field-placement clinics offer students excellent opportunities to experience hands-on, practical legal training. The law school also has a comprehensive litigation program, with small classes that allow all students full participation in litigation skills training.

Opportunities for Members of Minority Groups and Women These opportunities include the Women's Employment Rights Clinic through which students represent clients in employment disputes and the Environmental Law and Justice Clinic through which students provide direct representation to community groups and environmental organizations in low-income and minority communities. A variety of scholarships are available for new and continuing women and minority students.

Special Certificate Programs J.D. students can earn specialization certificates in business law, criminal law, environmental law, international law, labor and employment law, litigation, public interest law, or real estate law. Students may also earn a combined J.D./M.B.A. with a focus in one of eleven business areas. Other combined degrees include a J.D./M.A. in international relations and a J.D./Ph.D. in clinical psychology.

In recent years, the law school has become a center for graduate legal study, offering four Master of Law (LL.M.) degree programs: international legal studies, environmental law, taxation, and United States legal studies. In addition, students with an LL.M. can earn a Doctor of Laws (S.J.D.) degree in international legal studies.

BAR PASSAGE, CAREER SERVICES, AND PLACEMENT

The first-time bar passage rate for 1996–97 graduates was 69 percent. Most graduates take the California bar exam.

The Golden Gate University Law Career and Alumni Services Office provides comprehensive services and support from the time students enter law school through graduation and beyond. All first-year students receive a one-on-one orientation session, a special resume and cover letter workshop, and a free Job Search Guide binder. Continuing students have access to print, online, and telephone job listings; career counseling; job search skills workshops; resume and cover letter review; special programs and job fairs; mock interviews with alumni; alumni mentors; recruitment programs; and many other services. Services and programs for graduates are also available. Recent graduates were employed as shown below.

Legal Field	Percentage of Graduates	Average Salary
Academic	0.9%	$28,000
Business	21.7%	$57,500
Government	8.7%	$45,300
Judicial Clerkship	4.3%	$38,000
Private Practice	56.5%	$48,700
Public Interest	6.1%	$34,000
Other	1.8%	n/a

CORRESPONDENCE AND INFORMATION

Admissions Office
Golden Gate University School of Law
536 Mission Street
San Francisco, California 94105-2968
Telephone: 415-442-6630
Fax: 415-442-6631
E-mail: lawadmit@ggu.edu
World Wide Web: http://www.ggu.edu/law

LOYOLA MARYMOUNT UNIVERSITY
LOYOLA LAW SCHOOL

Los Angeles, California

INFORMATION CONTACT
Gerald T. McLaughlin, Dean
919 South Albany Street
Los Angeles, CA 90028

Phone: 213-736-1435   Fax: 213-380-3769
E-mail: lawadmission@lmulaw.lmu.edu
Web site: http://www.lls.edu/

LAW STUDENT PROFILE [1997–98]

FULL-TIME   Enrollment: 927
Women: 47%   Men: 53%

PART-TIME   Enrollment: 393
Women: 44%   Men: 56%

RACIAL or ETHNIC COMPOSITION
African American, 5%; Asian/Pacific Islander, 20%; Hispanic, 13%; Native American, 1%; International, 0%

APPLICANTS and ADMITTEES
Number applied: 2,638
Admitted: 1,064
Percentage accepted: 40%
Seats available: 414
Median LSAT score: 158
Median GPA: 3.2

Loyola Marymount University Loyola Law School is a private institution that organizes classes on a semester calendar system. The campus is situated in an urban setting. Founded in 1920, first ABA approved in 1937, and an AALS member, Loyola Marymount University Loyola Law School offers JD and JD/MBA degrees.

Faculty consists of 63 full-time and 58 part-time members in 1997–98. 25 full-time faculty members and 12 part-time faculty members are women. 100% of all faculty members have a JD; 5% have advanced law degrees. Of all faculty members, 5% are Asian/Pacific Islander, 4% are African American, 7% are Hispanic, 84% are white.

Application Information *Required:* LSAT, LSDAS, application form, application fee of $50, baccalaureate degree, 2 letters of recommendation, personal statement, college transcripts. *Application deadline* for fall term is February 1.

Costs The 1997–98 tuition is $21,488 full-time; $14,368 part-time. Fees: $218 full-time; $198 part-time.

Financial Aid In 1997–98, 88% of all students received some form of financial aid. Loans, loan repayment assistance program (LRAP), merit based grants/scholarships, and federal work-study loans are also available. The average student debt at gradua-

AT a GLANCE

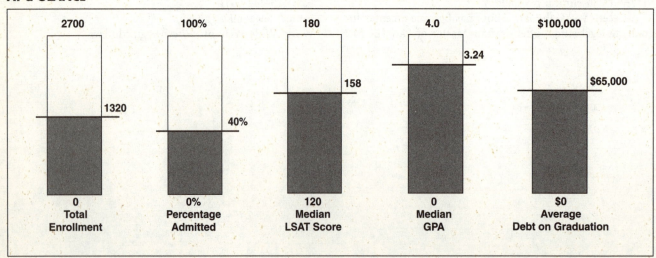

Degree Options

Degree	Total Credits Required	Length of Program
JD–Doctor of Laws	87	3–4 yrs, full-time or part-time [day, evening, summer]
JD/MBA–Juris Doctor/Master of Business Administration–Dual-degree Program		4–5 yrs, full-time only [day, summer]

tion is $65,000. To apply for financial assistance, students must complete the Free Application for Federal Student Aid. Financial aid contact: Ciel Senechal, Deputy Director of Financial Aid, 919 South Albany Street, Los Angeles, CA 90015. Phone: 213-736-1140. Fax: 213-380-3769. E-mail: ciel.senechal@lls.edu. Completed financial aid forms should be received by March 2.

Law School Library William M. Rains Law Library has 11 professional staff members and contains more than 436,836 volumes and 6,628 periodicals. 683 seats are available in the library. When classes are in session, the library is open 106 hours per week.

WESTLAW and LEXIS-NEXIS are available, as are the World Wide Web, online bibliographic services, and CD-ROM players. Special law collections include foreign and state depositories; foreign collections of European, Latin American and Pacific Rim nations; complete US legislative history (1970-present); complete collection of UN documents; CBS News O.J. Simpson archive.

First-Year Program Class size in the average section is 77; 100% of the first-year courses are taught by full-time faculty.

Upper-Level Program Among the electives are:

Administrative Law
Advocacy
Business and Corporate Law
Constitutional Law
Consumer Law
Criminal Law
Disability Law
Education Law
★ Entertainment Law
Environmental Law
Family Law
Government/Regulation
Health Care/Human Services
Indian/Tribal Law
Intellectual Property
International/Comparative Law
Jurisprudence

Labor Law
Land Use Law/Natural Resources
Law and Society
Lawyering Skills
Legal History/Philosophy
Litigation
Maritime Law
Media Law
★ Mediation
Personal Injury
Probate Law
Property/Real Estate
★ Public Interest
Securities
Tax Law
(★ indicates an area of special strength)

Clinical Courses Students receive degree credit for clinical courses. (Clinical practicum is not required.) Among the clinical areas offered are:

Children and the Law
Civil Litigation
Civil Rights
Corporate Law
Criminal Defense
Criminal Prosecution
Domestic Violence
Elderly Advocacy
Entertainment Law
Environmental Law
Family Practice
General Practice
Government Litigation
Health
Immigration
Intellectual Property
International Law
Juvenile Law
Land Rights/Natural Resource
Landlord/Tenant
Mediation
Poverty/Welfare Law
Public Interest
Tax Law

23% of the students participate in internship programs. International exchange programs available.

DEAN'S STATEMENT . . .

Each of you has your own reasons for going to law school. Some of you may want the challenge of being an advocate for others. Others may wish to use the law as an instrument for social betterment. Some others among you may wish to pursue a career that will allow you to branch out into business, the arts, or even education. A final group of you may simply want a challenging job that will provide a good living for you and your family.

No matter what your reason, you should take a close and careful look at Loyola Law School. Put simply, Loyola Law School is an outstanding law school. From its opening day in 1920, Loyola has been an integral part of the history and life of southern California. Anyone who has lived in California, anyone who has been touched by the California sun and invigorated by its geographical and ethnic diversity, knows that the future belongs to California.

If you wish to be challenged by a superb faculty and by a group of alumni who influence the history of southern California and the United States daily, come to Loyola. If you wish to help vindicate the rights of the disadvantaged, come to Loyola to participate in our legal clinics and in our mandatory public service program. If you wish to go to law school simply to keep your options open, then come to Loyola to follow the path of many of our alumni who, after graduation, have gone into politics, the entertainment industry, and business.

Yesterday, today, and tomorrow, Loyola is an outstanding law school. Look carefully—if you do, you will find that many wonderful opportunities await you here on our campus.

—*Gerald T. McLaughlin, Dean*

HISTORY, CAMPUS, AND LOCATION

Loyola Law School is located in the heart of Los Angeles, one of the country's most important centers of commerce, industry, and culture. Los Angeles offers endless opportunities for law students and lawyers alike. As the capital of the Pacific Rim community, the headquarters of the entertainment industry, the home of numerous major college and professional sports teams, the birthplace of the Internet, and the largest federal government center outside of Washington, D.C., the possibilities for those pursuing professional education in Los Angeles are truly exciting.

Law students at Loyola enjoy state-of-the-art facilities on an award-winning modern campus. The campus is situated near the downtown business center, which includes the federal, state, and local courts; many of the world's largest law firms; numerous government and public service agencies; and various cultural and arts organizations. Both spacious and well maintained, the campus includes nine buildings, a basketball court, and beautiful landscaped lawns. One of the largest law school campuses in the country, Loyola provides its students with an ideal environment for studying the law.

Loyola Law School, a division of Loyola Marymount University, is accredited by the American Bar Association and a member of the Association of American Law Schools.

SPECIAL QUALITIES OF THE SCHOOL

The faculty members of Loyola Law School are nationally and internationally renowned scholars who publish numerous scholarly legal articles, books, and treatises that influence the direction of the legal profession. Yet, so committed are they to the intellectual development of their students that they maintain an open door to encourage free and continuous interaction. Loyola also offers a broad curriculum with specialized courses in the areas of business, constitutional, criminal, international, entertain-

ment, and environmental law; intellectual property; public interest; social policy; taxation; and trial advocacy. Loyola's dedicated faculty members and excellent curriculum and externship opportunities combine to form an educational program that produces many of the most well-trained and highly successful attorneys in the nation.

TECHNOLOGY ON CAMPUS

Loyola has a long-standing reputation for innovation in legal education. The Law School Web site features an easy online admissions application. Applicants and law students can also check the status of their application and their grades through an automated telephone voice-response system. In addition, the library also offers numerous electronic databases, a CD-ROM collection, four computer labs, computer-assisted legal research (WESTLAW, LEXIS), and Computer Assisted Legal Instruction (CALI). The Trial Advocacy Center features audiovisual recording and editing equipment. Plans for the near future include additional computer labs, Web-based course registration, and a new state-of-the-art moot court room and auditorium.

SCHOLARSHIPS AND LOANS

Loyola awards a significant number of merit-based scholarships to entering students each year. In addition, continuing students are awarded scholarships based on their academic performance. The scholarship awards range from half tuition to full tuition and fees plus a stipend. The Public Interest Scholars Program is one of the most innovative programs of its kind and is specially designed for law students who are committed to practicing in the field of public interest.

STUDENT ACTIVITIES AND OPPORTUNITIES

Law Review Loyola students publish three prominent scholarly law journals—the *Law Review*, the *Entertainment*

Law Journal, and the *International and Comparative Law Journal*. The staff members and boards of editors are selected based on their legal research, writing skills, academic performance, and leadership. Students receive academic units for their work.

Moot Court Throughout the past few years, teams of Loyola students have won several major national and regional competitions, including the National Hispanic Bar Association Moot Court Competition, Frederick Douglass Moot Court Competition, National Trial Advocacy Competition, and NITA Tournament of Champions. Students are selected for moot court teams through intramural competition.

Special Opportunities Loyola offers many special opportunities for its students, including summer study-abroad programs in San Jose, Costa Rica, and Bologna, Italy. The programs offer courses in global human rights, international environmental law, and international business law. An entertainment law practicum is also offered and gives students an opportunity to receive hands-on experience in the entertainment industry while earning credit toward a degree. Much like an externship, the practicum includes a field placement and a required classroom component. Sample placements include Paramount Pictures, Rhino Records, and the Directors Guild of America. There is also a pro bono graduation requirement. Every Loyola student is given a chance to help someone (or a group) while learning some of the practical lawyering skills they will need after graduation. All students are required to complete 40 hours of supervised, uncompensated, legally related public service work prior to graduation. Loyola also offers an externship program, which offers off-campus placement coordinated by the Law School, which affords students the opportunity to experience the day-to-day operation of various legal institutions. More than 300 students take advantage of these experiences each year, which include placements with the District Attorney, Public Defender, SEC, and the U.S. Department of Justice as well as public interest law firms.

The Law School and the College of Business Administration offer a dual-degree program (J.D./M.B.A.) in business and law. Graduates of the program receive both the Juris Doctor degree and the Master of Business Administration.

Special Certificate Programs A Graduate Certificate in International Business is available from the International Master of Business Administration program.

Opportunities for Members of Minority Groups and Women Loyola offers one of the country's largest and most diverse student populations. Faculty members find the diversity of the student body both stimulating and essential to the development of their educational experience. Numerous student organizations have been formed to support a wide variety of interests, including practice and professional specialties, political affiliations, public service, religious activities, issues for students of color, and women's issues.

BAR PASSAGE, CAREER SERVICES, AND PLACEMENT

First-time passage rate for graduates taking the July 1997 California Bar Exam was 84 percent. The five-year average for first-time bar passage in California is 87 percent.

The Office of Career Services offers individual counseling appointments and group workshops on the legal job search, resume preparation, and interviewing skills. The Office of Career Services also maintains a library of job listings and employer information, hosts and participates in several annual career specialties programs, and conducts on-campus and off-site interviewing programs. Nine months after graduation, 86 percent of the 1997 graduates surveyed have reported working in the following professional fields.

Legal Field	Percentage of Graduates	Average Salary
Academic	4%	n/a
Business	23%	$52,000
Government	7%	$42,000
Judicial Clerkships	3%	$37,950
Private Practice	61%	$75,000
Public Interest	3%	$32,000
Other	n/a	n/a

CORRESPONDENCE AND INFORMATION

Admissions Office
Loyola Law School
919 South Albany Street
Los Angeles, California 90015
Telephone: 213-736-1180
Fax: 213-736-6523
E-mail: admissions@lls.edu
World Wide Web: http://www.lls.edu

PEPPERDINE UNIVERSITY
SCHOOL OF LAW

Malibu, California

INFORMATION CONTACT

Dr. Richardson Lynn, Interim Dean
24255 Pacific Coast Highway
Malibu, CA 90263

Phone: 310-456-4611   Fax: 310-456-4266
Web site: http://www.pepperdine.edu/

LAW STUDENT PROFILE [1997–98]

FULL-TIME   Enrollment: 653
Women: 45%   Men: 55%

PART-TIME   Enrollment: 32
Women: 59%   Men: 41%

RACIAL or ETHNIC COMPOSITION
African American, 4%; Asian/Pacific Islander, 7%; Hispanic, 4%; Native American, 1%; International, 2%

APPLICANTS and ADMITTEES
Number applied: 2,281
Admitted: 1,057
Percentage accepted: 46%
Seats available: 230
Average LSAT score: 157
Average GPA: 3.3

Pepperdine University School of Law is a private institution that organizes classes on a semester calendar system. The campus is situated in a suburban setting. Founded in 1970, first ABA approved in 1972, and an AALS member, Pepperdine University School of Law offers JD, JD/MBA, JD/MDR, and MDR degrees.

Faculty consists of 38 full-time and 22 part-time members in 1997–98. 6 full-time faculty members and 8 part-time faculty members are women. 100% of all faculty members have a JD; 18% have advanced law degrees. Of all faculty members, 7% are Asian/Pacific Islander, 3.5% are African American, 3.5% are Hispanic, 86% are white.

Application Information *Required:* LSAT, LSDAS, application form, application fee of $50, baccalaureate degree, 2 letters of recommendation, personal statement, college transcripts.

Costs The 1997–98 tuition is $22,830 full-time; $845 per unit part-time.

Financial Aid Loans, merit-based grants/scholarships, need-based grants/scholarships, and federal work-study loans are available. The average student debt at graduation is $79,500. To apply for financial assistance, students must complete the Free Application for Federal Student Aid, institutional forms,

AT a GLANCE

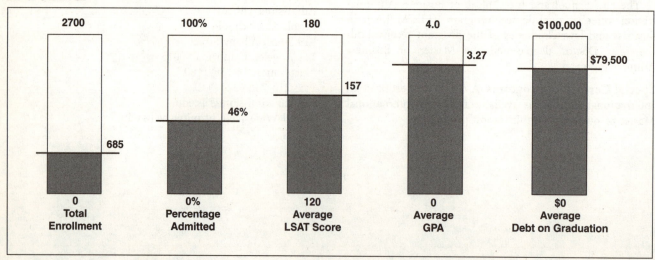

Degree Options

Degree	Total Credits Required	Length of Program
JD–Doctor of Laws	88	3 yrs, full-time only [day]
JD/MBA–Juris Doctor/Master of Business Administration–Joint-degree Program	130	4 yrs, full-time only [day]
JD/MDR–Juris Doctor/Master of Dispute Resolution–Joint-degree Program		full-time only [day]
MDR–Master of Dispute Resolution	32	1 yr, full-time or part-time [day, weekend, summer]

scholarship specific applications, and tax returns. Financial aid contact: Janet Lockhart, Director of Financial Aid, 24255 Pacific Coast Highway, Malibu, CA 90263. Phone: 310-456-4633. Fax: 310-456-4266. Completed financial aid forms should be received by May 1.

Law School Library Jerene Appleby Harnish Law Library has 5 professional staff members and contains more than 264,673 volumes and 1,350 periodicals. 500 seats are available in the library. When classes are in session, the library is open 109 hours per week.

WESTLAW and LEXIS-NEXIS are available, as are the World Wide Web, online bibliographic services, and CD-ROM players. 52 computer workstations are available to students in the library.

First-Year Program Class size in the average section is 76; 100% of the first-year courses are taught by full-time faculty.

Upper-Level Program Class size in the average section is 60. Among the electives are:

  Administrative Law
  Advocacy
★ Business and Corporate Law
★ Dispute Resolution

★ Entertainment Law
  Environmental Law
  Family Law
  Intellectual Property
  International/Comparative Law
  Labor Law
  Land Use Law/Natural Resources
  Lawyering Skills
  Litigation
★ Mediation
  Probate Law
  Public Interest
★ Securities
★ Tax Law
(★ *indicates an area of special strength*)

Clinical Courses Students receive degree credit for clinical courses. (Clinical practicum is not required.) Among the clinical areas offered are:

  Criminal Defense
  Criminal Prosecution
  International Law
  Judicial Clerkship
  Juvenile Law
  Mediation
  Public Interest

Internships are available. International exchange programs permit students to visit United Kingdom.

SANTA CLARA UNIVERSITY
SCHOOL OF LAW

Santa Clara, California

INFORMATION CONTACT

Mack Player, Dean
500 El Camino Real
Santa Clara, CA 95053

Phone: 408-554-4361   Fax: 408-554-7897
Web site: http://www.scu.edu/law/

LAW STUDENT PROFILE [1997–98]

FULL-TIME   Enrollment: 865
Women: 48%   Men: 52%

PART-TIME   Enrollment: 62
Women: 40%   Men: 60%

RACIAL or ETHNIC COMPOSITION
African American, 4%; Asian/Pacific Islander, 17%; Hispanic, 7%; Native American, 1%; International, 3%

APPLICANTS and ADMITTEES
Number applied: 2,676
Admitted: 1,353
Percentage accepted: 51%
Seats available: 298
Average LSAT score: 156
Average GPA: 3.2

Santa Clara University School of Law is a private institution that organizes classes on a semester calendar system. The campus is situated in an urban setting. Founded in 1912, first ABA approved in 1937, and an AALS member, Santa Clara University School of Law offers JD and JD/MBA degrees.

Faculty consists of 35 full-time and 11 part-time members in 1997–98. 13 full-time faculty members and 4 part-time faculty members are women. 97% of all faculty members have a JD; 30.3% have advanced law degrees. Of all faculty members, 6% are Asian/Pacific Islander, 12% are African American, 3% are Hispanic, 76% are white, 3% are international.

Application Information *Required:* LSAT, LSDAS, application form, application fee of $40, baccalaureate degree, college transcripts. *Recommended:* recommendations, personal statement, essay. *Application deadline* for fall term is March 1.

Financial Aid Fellowships, graduate assistantships, loans, loan repayment assistance program (LRAP), merit-based grants/scholarships, need-based grants/scholarships, and federal work-study loans are available. The average student debt at graduation is $55,500. To apply for financial assistance, students must complete the Free Application for Federal Student Aid, institutional forms, and scholarship

AT a GLANCE

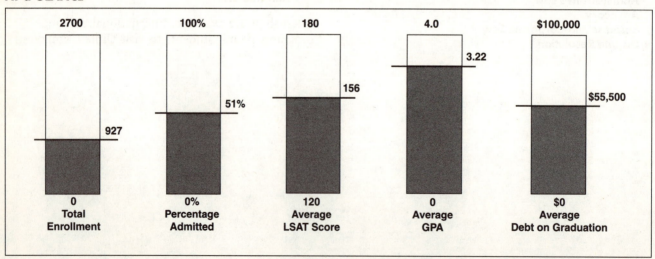

Degree Options

Degree	Total Credits Required	Length of Program
JD–Doctor of Laws	86	3–4 yrs, full-time or part-time [day, evening, summer]
JD/MBA–Juris Doctor/Master of Business Administration–Combined-degree Program		3.5–4 yrs, full-time only [day, evening, summer]

specific applications. Financial aid contact: Nora Lee, Financial Aid Counselor, Santa Clara University School of Law, Santa Clara, CA 95053. Phone: 408-554-5048. Fax: 408-554-7897. E-mail: lawadmission@mailer.scu.edu. Completed financial aid forms should be received by February 1.

Law School Library Heafey Law Library has 8 professional staff members and contains more than 267,545 volumes and 3,454 periodicals. 448 seats are available in the library. When classes are in session, the library is open 105 hours per week.

WESTLAW and LEXIS-NEXIS are available, as are the World Wide Web, online bibliographic services, and CD-ROM players. 38 computer workstations are available to students in the library.

First-Year Program Class size in the average section is 80; 100% of the first-year courses are taught by full-time faculty.

Upper-Level Program Among the electives are:

Administrative Law
★ Advocacy
★ Business and Corporate Law
Consumer Law
Education Law
Environmental Law
Family Law
Government/Regulation
Health Care/Human Services
Indian/Tribal Law
★ Intellectual Property

★ International/Comparative Law
Jurisprudence
Labor Law
Land Use Law/Natural Resources
★ Lawyering Skills
Legal History/Philosophy
★ Litigation
Maritime Law
Media Law
Mediation
Probate Law
★ Public Interest
Securities
Tax Law
(★ indicates an area of special strength)

Clinical Courses Students receive degree credit for clinical courses. (Clinical practicum is not required.) Among the clinical areas offered are:

Civil Litigation
Criminal Defense
Environmental Law
Immigration
Intellectual Property
Public Interest

15% of the students participate in internship programs. International exchange programs permit students to visit China; France; Hong Kong; Hungary; Korea, Republic of; Malaysia; Japan; Singapore; Switzerland; Thailand; United Kingdom; and Viet Nam.

SOUTHWESTERN UNIVERSITY SCHOOL OF LAW

Los Angeles, California

INFORMATION CONTACT

Leigh H. Taylor, Dean
675 South Westmoreland Avenue
Los Angeles, CA 90005-3992

Phone: 213-738-6710
E-mail: admissions@swlaw.edu
Web site: http://www.swlaw.edu/

LAW STUDENT PROFILE [1997–98]

FULL-TIME Enrollment: 703
Women: 51%   Men: 49%

PART-TIME Enrollment: 326
Women: 48%   Men: 52%

RACIAL or ETHNIC COMPOSITION
African American, 6%; Asian/Pacific Islander, 18%; Hispanic, 10%; Native American, 1%; International, 1%

APPLICANTS and ADMITTEES
Seats available: 328

Southwestern University School of Law is a private nonprofit institution that organizes classes on a semester calendar system. The campus is situated in an urban setting. Founded in 1911, first ABA approved in 1970, and an AALS member, Southwestern University School of Law offers a JD degree.

Faculty consists of 49 full-time and 45 part-time members in 1997–98. 16 full-time faculty members and 9 part-time faculty members are women.

Application Information *Required:* LSAT, LSDAS, application form, baccalaureate degree, application fee of $50. *Recommended:* personal statement and 3 letters of recommendation. *Application deadline* for fall term is June 30.

Financial Aid Fellowships, merit-based grants/scholarships, need-based grants/scholarships, and federal work-study loans are available. To apply for financial assistance, students must complete the Free Application for Federal Student Aid and Need Access diskette. Financial aid contact: Office of Financial Aid, Room 102, 675 South Westmoreland Avenue, Los Angeles, CA 90005-3992. E-mail: finaid@swlaw.edu. Completed financial aid forms should be received by June 1.

Law School Library has 10 professional staff members and contains more than 381,889 volumes

AT a GLANCE

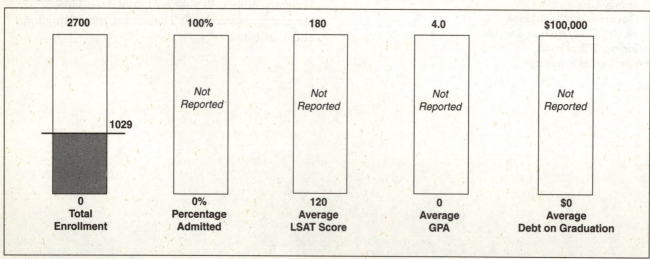

Degree Options		
Degree	Total Credits Required	Length of Program
JD–Juris Doctor	87	3–4 yrs, full-time or part-time [day, evening]

and 4,984 periodicals. 610 seats are available in the library. When classes are in session, the library is open 103 hours per week.

WESTLAW and LEXIS-NEXIS are available, as is the World Wide Web. 80 computer workstations are available to students in the library.

First-Year Program Class size in the average section is 89.

Upper-Level Program Among the electives are:

Accounting
Administrative Law
Advocacy
Bankruptcy
Business and Corporate Law
Civil Procedure
Conflict of Laws
Constitutional Law
Consumer Law
Criminal Law
Entertainment Law
Environmental Law
Evidence
Family Law
Government/Regulation
Health Care/Human Services
Immigration
Indian/Tribal Law
Insurance
Intellectual Property
International/Comparative Law
Jurisprudence

Labor Law
Land Use Law/Natural Resources
Lawyering Skills
Legal History/Philosophy
Maritime Law
Media Law
Mediation
Property/Real Estate
Race and Law
Securities
Sports Law
Tax Law

Clinical Courses Among the clinical areas offered are:

Civil Litigation
Civil Rights
Criminal Defense
Criminal Prosecution
Elderly Advocacy
Entertainment Law
Family Practice
General Practice
Government Litigation
Health
Intellectual Property
Judicial Clerkship
Juvenile Law
Public Interest
Tax Law

International exchange programs permit students to visit Argentina; Canada; and Mexico.

STANFORD UNIVERSITY
LAW SCHOOL

Stanford, California

INFORMATION CONTACT

Paul A. Brest, Dean
559 Nathan Abbott Way
Stanford, CA 94305-8610

Phone: 650-723-4455
Web site: http://lawschool.stanford.edu/

LAW STUDENT PROFILE [1997–98]

FULL-TIME   Enrollment: 565
Women: 42%   Men: 58%

PART-TIME   Enrollment: 32
Women: 38%   Men: 63%

RACIAL or ETHNIC COMPOSITION
African American, 8%; Asian/Pacific Islander, 8%; Hispanic, 11%; Native American, 2%; International, 7%

APPLICANTS and ADMITTEES
Number applied: 4,127
Admitted: 521
Percentage accepted: 13%
Seats available: 177
Average LSAT score: 167
Average GPA: 3.8

Stanford University Law School is a private institution that organizes classes on a semester calendar system. The campus is situated in a suburban setting. Founded in 1908, first ABA approved in 1923, and an AALS member, Stanford University Law School offers JD, JD/MBA, JSD, JSM, and MLSt degrees.

Faculty consists of 41 full-time members in 1997–98. 8 full-time faculty members are women.

Application Information *Required:* LSAT, LSDAS, application form, application fee of $65, baccalaureate degree, 2 letters of recommendation, personal statement. *Recommended:* resume. *Application deadline* for fall term is March 1. Students are required to have their own computers.

Financial Aid In 1997–98, 43% of all students received some form of financial aid. 191 fellowships, 55 research assistantships, totaling $502,512; 11 teaching assistantships, totaling $119,515, were awarded. Fellowships, graduate assistantships, loans, loan repayment assistance program (LRAP), need-based grants/scholarships, and federal work-study loans are also available. The average student debt at graduation is $70,000. To apply for financial assistance, students must complete the Free Application for Federal Student Aid, institutional forms, and Need Access diskette. Financial aid contact:

AT a GLANCE

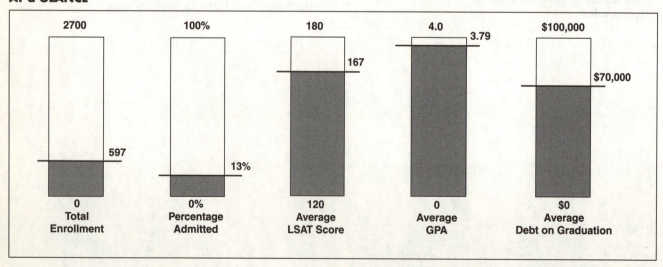

Total Enrollment	Percentage Admitted	Average LSAT Score	Average GPA	Average Debt on Graduation
2700 / 597 / 0	100% / 13% / 0%	180 / 167 / 120	4.0 / 3.79 / 0	$100,000 / $70,000 / $0

Degree Options

Degree	Total Credits Required	Length of Program
JD–Doctor of Laws	86	3 yrs, full-time only [day]
JD/MBA–Juris Doctor/Master of Business Administration–Dual-degree Program	110	4 yrs, full-time only [day]
JSD–Doctor of Juridical Science		full-time only [day]
JSM–Master of the Science of Law		1 yr, full-time only [day]
MLSt–Master of Legal Studies	30	1 yr, full-time only

Ruth Burciaga, Assistant Director of Financial Aid, 559 Nathan Abbot Way, Stanford, CA 94305. Phone: 650-723-9247. Completed financial aid forms should be received by March 15.

Law School Library Robert Crown Law Library has 7 professional staff members and contains more than 458,973 volumes and 7,112 periodicals. 555 seats are available in the library. When classes are in session, the library is open 96 hours per week.

WESTLAW and LEXIS-NEXIS are available, as are the World Wide Web, online bibliographic services, and CD-ROM players. 35 computer workstations are available to students in the library.

First-Year Program Class size in the average section is 60; 60% of the first-year courses are taught by full-time faculty.

Upper-Level Program Among the electives are:

Administrative Law
Advocacy
Business and Corporate Law
Consumer Law
Education Law
Entertainment Law
Environmental Law
Family Law
Government/Regulation
Health Care/Human Services
Indian/Tribal Law
Intellectual Property
International/Comparative Law
Jurisprudence
Labor Law
Land Use Law/Natural Resources
Lawyering Skills
Legal History/Philosophy
Litigation
Media Law
Mediation
Probate Law
Public Interest
Securities
Tax Law

Clinical Courses Students receive degree credit for clinical courses. (Clinical practicum is not required.) Among the clinical areas offered are:

Civil Rights
Education
Environmental Law
Family Practice
International Law
Public Interest

5% of the students participate in internship programs.

THOMAS JEFFERSON SCHOOL OF LAW

San Diego, California

INFORMATION CONTACT

Kenneth L. Vandevelde, Dean
2121 San Diego Avenue
San Diego, CA 92110-2905

Phone: 619-297-9700   Fax: 619-294-4713
        Ext. 1404
E-mail: jkeller@tjsl.edu
Web site: http://www.jeffersonlaw.edu/

LAW STUDENT PROFILE [1997–98]

FULL-TIME   Enrollment: 297
Women: 38%   Men: 62%

PART-TIME   Enrollment: 281
Women: 37%   Men: 63%

RACIAL or ETHNIC COMPOSITION
African American, 4%; Asian/Pacific Islander, 7%; Hispanic, 10%; Native American, 1%; International, 1%

APPLICANTS and ADMITTEES
Number applied: 1,045
Admitted: 846
Percentage accepted: 81%
Seats available: 200
Median LSAT score: 147
Average GPA: 2.7

Thomas Jefferson School of Law is a private nonprofit institution that organizes classes on a semester calendar system. The campus is situated in an urban setting. Founded in 1969, first ABA approved in 1996, Thomas Jefferson School of Law offers a JD degree.

Faculty consists of 20 full-time and 28 part-time members in 1997–98. 11 full-time faculty members and 6 part-time faculty members are women. 100% of all faculty members have a JD; 12% have advanced law degrees. Of all faculty members, 3% are Asian/Pacific Islander, 7% are African American, 90% are white.

Application Information *Required:* LSAT, LSDAS, application form, application fee of $35, minimum 2.0 GPA, personal statement, college transcripts. *Recommended:* baccalaureate degree and 2 letters of recommendation. *Application deadline* for fall term is August 26.

Financial Aid In 1997–98, 100% of all students received some form of financial aid. 16 research assistantships, 18 teaching assistantships were awarded. Loans, merit-based grants/scholarships, and federal work-study loans are also available. To apply for financial assistance, students must complete the Free Application for Federal Student Aid and institutional forms. Financial aid contact: Miriam Safir, Director of Financial Assistance, 2121

AT a GLANCE

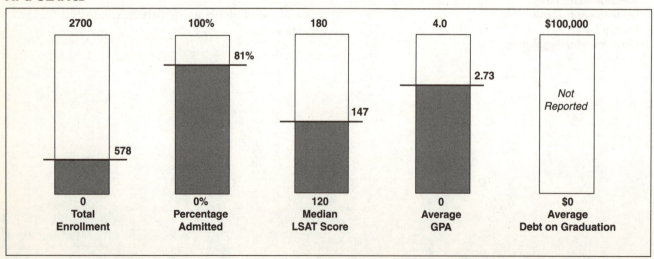

Degree Options

Degree	Total Credits Required	Length of Program
JD–Doctor of Laws	88	3–4 yrs, full-time or part-time [day, evening, summer]

San Diego Avenue, San Diego, CA 92110. Phone: 619-297-9700 or toll-free 800-936-7529. Fax: 619-294-4713. E-mail: miriams@tjsl.edu. Completed financial aid forms should be received by April 23.

Law School Library Thomas Jefferson School of Law Library has 8 professional staff members and contains more than 84,199 volumes and 1,091 periodicals. 284 seats are available in the library. When classes are in session, the library is open 95 hours per week.

WESTLAW and LEXIS-NEXIS are available, as are the World Wide Web, online bibliographic services, and CD-ROM players. 35 computer workstations are available to students in the library. Special law collections include The Thomas Jefferson Collection.

First-Year Program Class size in the average section is 33.

Upper-Level Program Among the electives are:

Administrative Law
★ Advocacy
Business and Corporate Law
Consumer Law
Entertainment Law
★ Environmental Law
Family Law
Government/Regulation
Health Care/Human Services
Indian/Tribal Law
★ Intellectual Property
★ International/Comparative Law
Jurisprudence
Labor Law
Land Use Law/Natural Resources
★ Lawyering Skills
Legal History/Philosophy
★ Litigation
Maritime Law
Media Law
Mediation
Probate Law
Public Interest
Securities
Tax Law
(★ indicates an area of special strength)

Clinical Courses Students receive degree credit for clinical courses. (Clinical practicum is not required.) Among the clinical areas offered are:

Civil Litigation
Civil Rights
Criminal Defense
Criminal Prosecution
Environmental Law
Government Litigation
Immigration
Juvenile Law
Land Rights/Natural Resource
Mediation

Internships are available.

UNIVERSITY OF CALIFORNIA, BERKELEY
BOALT HALL SCHOOL OF LAW

Berkeley, California

INFORMATION CONTACT

Herma Hill Kay, Dean
221 Boalt Hall
Berkeley, CA 94720

Phone: 510-642-6483   Fax: 510-643-6171
E-mail: admissions@boalt.berkeley.edu
Web site: http://www.law.berkeley.edu/

LAW STUDENT PROFILE [1997–98]

FULL-TIME   Enrollment: 852
Women: 51%   Men: 49%

RACIAL or ETHNIC COMPOSITION
African American, 5%; Asian/Pacific Islander, 13%; Hispanic, 9%; Native American, 1%; International, 3%

APPLICANTS and ADMITTEES
Number applied: 4,171
Admitted: 860
Percentage accepted: 21%
Seats available: 270
Average LSAT score: 167
Average GPA: 3.7

University of California, Berkeley Boalt Hall School of Law is a public institution that organizes classes on a semester calendar system. The campus is situated in an urban setting. Founded in 1894, first ABA approved in 1923, and an AALS member, University of California, Berkeley Boalt Hall School of Law offers JD, JD/MA, JD/MBA, JD/MCRP, JD/MJ, JD/MPPo, JD/MSW, JD/PhD, JSD, LLM, MA, and PhD degrees.

Faculty consists of 48 full-time and 82 part-time members in 1997–98. 16 full-time faculty members and 22 part-time faculty members are women. 94% of all faculty members have a JD degree. Of all faculty members, 3% are Asian/Pacific Islander, 3% are African American, 2% are Hispanic, 92% are white.

Application Information *Required:* LSAT, LSDAS, application form, application fee of $40, baccalaureate degree, personal statement, college transcripts. *Recommended:* recommendations and resume. *Application deadline* for fall term is February 1.

Costs The 1997–98 tuition is $0 for state residents. Tuition is $9384 for nonresidents. Fees: $10,815.

Financial Aid In 1997–98, 76% of all students received some form of financial aid. 13 fellowships, totaling $111,761; 36 research assistantships, totaling $259,732; 10 teaching assistantships, totaling $84,115, were awarded. Fellowships, graduate assistantships, loans, loan repayment assistance

AT a GLANCE

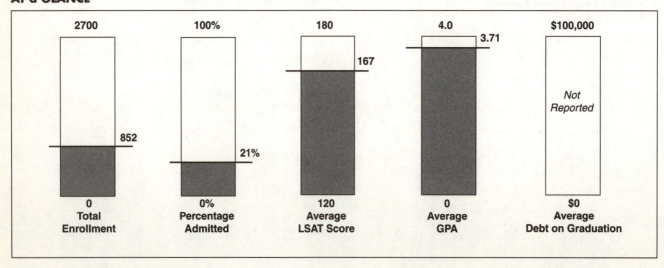

	Total Enrollment	Percentage Admitted	Average LSAT Score	Average GPA	Average Debt on Graduation
Top	2700	100%	180	4.0	$100,000
Value	852	21%	167	3.71	Not Reported
Bottom	0	0%	120	0	$0

Degree Options

Degree	Total Credits Required	Length of Program
JD–Juris Doctor	85	3 yrs, full-time only [day]
JD/MA–Juris Doctor/Master of Arts–Asian Studies, Economics, International and Area Studies, Jurisprudence and Social Policy, School of Information Management and Systems		4 yrs
JD/MBA–Juris Doctor/Master of Business Administration, JD/MCRP–Juris Doctor/Master of Community and Regional Planning, JD/MJ–Juris Doctor/Master of Journalism, JD/MPPo–Juris Doctor/Master of Public Policy		
JD/MSW–Juris Doctor/Master of Social Work–Social Welfare		4 yrs
JD/PhD–Juris Doctor/Doctor of Philosophy–Economics, History, Jurisprudence and Social Policy		7 yrs
JSD–Doctor of Juridical Science		2 yrs, full-time only [day]
LLM–Master of Laws	20	1 yr, full-time only [day]
MA–Master of Arts–Jurisprudence and Social Policy		4 yrs, full-time only [day]
PhD–Doctor of Philosophy–Jurisprudence and Social Policy		6 yrs, full-time only [day]

program (LRAP), merit-based grants/scholarships, need-based grants/scholarships, and federal work-study loans are also available. To apply for financial assistance, students must complete the Free Application for Federal Student Aid and institutional forms. Financial aid contact: The Boalt Hall Financial Aid Office, Boalt Hall 5, Berkeley, CA 94720. Phone: 510-642-1563. Fax: 510-643-6171. E-mail: financial_aid@boalt.berkeley.edu. Completed financial aid forms should be received by March 2.

Law School Library Garret W. McEnerney Law Library has 15 professional staff members and contains more than 601,123 volumes and 7,401 periodicals. 401 seats are available in the library. When classes are in session, the library is open 94 hours per week.

WESTLAW and LEXIS-NEXIS are available, as are the World Wide Web, online bibliographic services, and CD-ROM players. 96 computer workstations are available to students in the library. Special law collections include Robbins Collection of ecclesiastical, civil, comparative, and international law.

First-Year Program Class size in the average section is 60; 83% of the first-year courses are taught by full-time faculty.

Upper-Level Program Class size in the average section is 34. Among the electives are:

Administrative Law
Advocacy
Business and Corporate Law
★ Discrimination
Education Law
Entertainment Law
★ Environmental Law
Family Law

Government/Regulation
Health Care/Human Services
★ Indian/Tribal Law
★ Intellectual Property
★ International/Comparative Law
Jurisprudence
Labor Law
Land Use Law/Natural Resources
Lawyering Skills
Legal History/Philosophy
Litigation
Maritime Law
Media Law
Mediation
Probate Law
Public Interest
Securities
Sports Law
Tax Law
★ Technology Law
Telecommunications Law
Trusts and Estates
(★ indicates an area of special strength)

Clinical Courses Students receive degree credit for clinical courses. (Clinical practicum is not required.) Among the clinical areas offered are:

Disability Law
Domestic Violence
Environmental Law
Human Rights
Immigration
Indian/Tribal Law
International Law
Juvenile Law
Public Interest

12% of the students participate in internship programs. International exchange programs available.

UNIVERSITY OF CALIFORNIA, DAVIS
SCHOOL OF LAW

Davis, California

INFORMATION CONTACT

Bruce Wolk, Dean
400 Mrak Hall Drive
Davis, CA 95616-5201

Phone: 530-752-0243   Fax: 530-752-7279
E-mail: lawadmissions@ucdavis.edu
Web site: http://kinghall.ucdavis.edu/

LAW STUDENT PROFILE [1997–98]

FULL-TIME   Enrollment: 491
Women: 51%   Men: 49%

RACIAL or ETHNIC COMPOSITION
African American, 3%; Asian/Pacific Islander, 14%; Hispanic, 8%; Native American, 2%; International, 4%

APPLICANTS and ADMITTEES
Number applied: 2,095
Admitted: 805
Percentage accepted: 38%
Seats available: 172
Average LSAT score: 160
Median GPA: 3.5

University of California, Davis School of Law is a public institution that organizes classes on a semester calendar system. The campus is situated in a suburban setting. Founded in 1965, first ABA approved in 1968, and an AALS member, University of California, Davis School of Law offers JD, JD/MA, JD/MBA, JD/MS, and LLM degrees.

Faculty consists of 32 full-time and 23 part-time members in 1997–98. 11 full-time faculty members and 8 part-time faculty members are women. 100% of all faculty members have a JD; 3% have advanced law degrees. Of all faculty members, 5% are Asian/Pacific Islander, 5% are African American, 8% are Hispanic, 80.4% are white, 1.6% are international.

Application Information *Required:* LSAT, LSDAS, application form, application fee of $40, baccalaureate degree, 2 letters of recommendation, personal statement, college transcripts. *Application deadline* for fall term is February 1.

Costs The 1997–98 tuition is $0 for state residents. Tuition is $9384 for nonresidents. Fees: $10,859.

Financial Aid In 1997–98, 84% of all students received some form of financial aid. Loans, loan repayment assistance program (LRAP), need-based grants/scholarships, and federal work-study loans are

AT a GLANCE

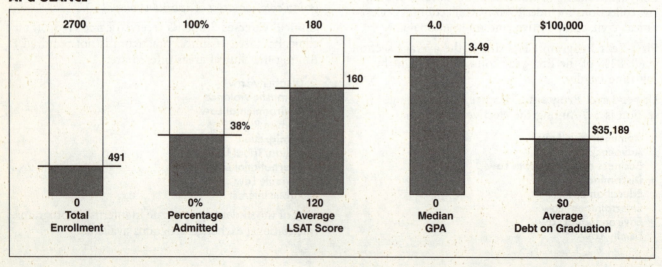

Degree Options

Degree	Total Credits Required	Length of Program
JD–Doctor of Laws	88	3 yrs, full-time only [day]
JD/MA–Juris Doctor/Master of Arts–Dual-degree Program	110	3.5–4 yrs, full-time only [day]
JD/MBA–Juris Doctor/Master of Business Administration–Dual-degree Program	110	3.5–4 yrs, full-time only [day]
JD/MS–Juris Doctor/Master of Science–Dual-degree Program	110	3.5–4 yrs, full-time only [day]
LLM–Master of Laws	20	1 yr, full-time only [day]

also available. The average student debt at graduation is $35,189. To apply for financial assistance, students must complete the Free Application for Federal Student Aid and scholarship specific applications. Financial aid contact: Cyndie Alvarez Necoechea, Financial Aid Assistant, Financial Aid Office, 400 Mrak Hall Drive, Davis, CA 95616-5201. Phone: 530-752-6573. Fax: 530-752-7279. E-mail: lawfinaid@ucdavis.cdu. Completed financial aid forms should be received by March 2.

Law School Library UC Davis Law Library has 6 professional staff members and contains more than 272,370 volumes and 5,219 periodicals. 375 seats are available in the library. When classes are in session, the library is open 78 hours per week.

WESTLAW and LEXIS-NEXIS are available, as are the World Wide Web, online bibliographic services, and CD-ROM players. 39 computer workstations are available to students in the library. Special law collections include Federal and California government documents, environmental law, intellectual property, immigration, international law.

First-Year Program Class size in the average section is 72; 84% of the first-year courses are taught by full-time faculty.

Upper-Level Program Class size in the average section is 25. Among the electives are:

Administrative Law
★ Advocacy
Business and Corporate Law
★ Civil Rights
Consumer Law
★ Employment Law
Entertainment Law
★ Environmental Law
★ Family Law
Government/Regulation

Health Care/Human Services
★ Immigration
Indian/Tribal Law
Intellectual Property
International/Comparative Law
★ Judicial
Jurisprudence
★ Labor Law
Land Use Law/Natural Resources
★ Lawyering Skills
Legal History/Philosophy
★ Litigation
Media Law
Mediation
★ Prisoners' Rights
Probate Law
Professional Responsibility
★ Public Interest
Securities
★ Tax Law
(★ indicates an area of special strength)

Clinical Courses Students receive degree credit for clinical courses. (Clinical practicum is not required.) Among the clinical areas offered are:

Civil Rights
Criminal Defense
Criminal Prosecution
Employment Law
Environmental Law
Family Practice
Immigration
Judicial
Legislation
Mediation
Public Interest
Tax Law

20% of the students participate in internship programs.

UNIVERSITY OF CALIFORNIA, HASTINGS COLLEGE OF THE LAW

San Francisco, California

INFORMATION CONTACT

Mary Kay Kane, Dean
200 McAllister Street
San Francisco, CA 94102-4978

Phone: 415-565-4600   Fax: 415-565-4863
Web site: http://www.uchastings.edu/

LAW STUDENT PROFILE [1997–98]

FULL-TIME   Enrollment: 1,156
Women: 48%   Men: 52%

RACIAL or ETHNIC COMPOSITION

African American, 4%; Asian/Pacific Islander, 17%; Hispanic, 7%; Native American, 1%; International, 0%

APPLICANTS and ADMITTEES

Number applied: 3,605
Admitted: 1,278
Percentage accepted: 35%
Seats available: 311
Average LSAT score: 162
Average GPA: 3.3

University of California, Hastings College of the Law is a private nonprofit institution that organizes classes on a semester calendar system. The campus is situated in an urban setting. Founded in 1878, first ABA approved in 1939, and an AALS member, University of California, Hastings College of the Law offers a JD degree.

Faculty consists of 46 full-time and 73 part-time members in 1997–98. 13 full-time faculty members and 31 part-time faculty members are women. 100% of all faculty members have a JD degree. Of all faculty members, 11.9% are Asian/Pacific Islander, 9.5% are African American, 3.6% are Hispanic, 75% are white.

Application Information *Required:* LSAT, LSDAS, application form, application fee of $40, baccalaureate degree, personal statement. *Recommended:* recommendations and resume. *Application deadline* for fall term is February 16.

Financial Aid In 1997–98, 87% of all students received some form of financial aid. Loans, loan repayment assistance program (LRAP), merit-based grants/scholarships, need-based grants/scholarships, and federal work-study loans are also available. The average student debt at graduation is $42,000. To apply for financial assistance, students must

AT a GLANCE

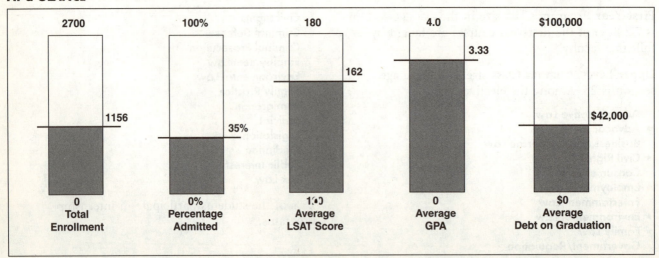

Degree Options

Degree	Total Credits Required	Length of Program
JD–Doctor of Laws	86	3 yrs, full-time only

complete the Free Application for Federal Student Aid and institutional forms. Financial aid contact: Linda Bisesi, Director of Financial Aid, 200 McAllister Street, San Francisco, CA 94102. Phone: 415-565-4624. Fax: 415-565-4863. Completed financial aid forms should be received by February 16.

Law School Library Hastings Law Library has 11 professional staff members and contains more than 597,499 volumes and 8,350 periodicals. 652 seats are available in the library. When classes are in session, the library is open 102 hours per week. c.14/DAY

WESTLAW and LEXIS-NEXIS are available, as are the World Wide Web, online bibliographic services, and CD-ROM players. 40 computer workstations are available to students in the library. Special law collections include Federal and California depositories.

First-Year Program Class size in the average section is 80; 99% of the first-year courses are taught by full-time faculty.

Upper-Level Program Class size in the average section is 60. Among the electives are:

Administrative Law
Advocacy
Business and Corporate Law
Consumer Law
Entertainment Law
Environmental Law
Family Law
Government/Regulation
Health Care/Human Services

Indian/Tribal Law
Intellectual Property
★ International/Comparative Law
Jurisprudence
Labor Law
Land Use Law/Natural Resources
Lawyering Skills
Legal History/Philosophy
Litigation
Maritime Law
Media Law
Mediation
Probate Law
★ Public Interest
Securities
★ Tax Law
(★ indicates an area of special strength)

Clinical Courses Students receive degree credit for clinical courses. (Clinical practicum is not required.) Among the clinical areas offered are:

Civil Litigation
Criminal Defense
Criminal Prosecution
Education
Environmental Law
Immigration
Judicial Externship
Juvenile Law
Local Government
Public Interest

60% of the students participate in internship programs. International exchange programs permit students to visit Canada and Netherlands.

UNIVERSITY OF CALIFORNIA, LOS ANGELES
SCHOOL OF LAW

Los Angeles, California

INFORMATION CONTACT
Dr. Susan Westerberg-Prager, Dean
405 Hilgard Avenue
Los Angeles, CA 90024

Phone: 310-825-4841
Web site: http://www.ucla.edu/

LAW STUDENT PROFILE [1997–98]

FULL-TIME   Enrollment: 984
Women: 48%   Men: 52%

RACIAL or ETHNIC COMPOSITION
African American, 5%; Asian/Pacific Islander, 18%; Hispanic, 11%; Native American, 1%; International, 1%

APPLICANTS and ADMITTEES
Number applied: 4,139
Admitted: 1,051
Percentage accepted: 25%
Seats available: 381
Average LSAT score: 162
Average GPA: 3.6

University of California, Los Angeles School of Law is a public institution that organizes classes on a semester calendar system. The campus is situated in an urban setting. Founded in 1947, first ABA approved in 1950, and an AALS member, University of California, Los Angeles School of Law offers JD, JD/MA, JD/MBA, and LLM degrees.

Application Information *Required:* LSAT, LSDAS, application form, application fee of $40, baccalaureate degree, recommendations, personal statement, college transcripts. *Application deadline* for fall term is January 15.

Financial Aid In 1997–98, 85% of all students received some form of financial aid. Fellowships, loans, loan repayment assistance program (LRAP), merit-based grants/scholarships, need-based grants/scholarships, and federal work-study loans are also available. The average student debt at graduation is $45,243. To apply for financial assistance, students must complete the Free Application for Federal Student Aid, institutional forms, and Need Access electronic applications for need-based grants. Financial aid contact: Veronica Wilson, Director of Financial Aid, Box 951476, Los Angeles, CA

AT a GLANCE

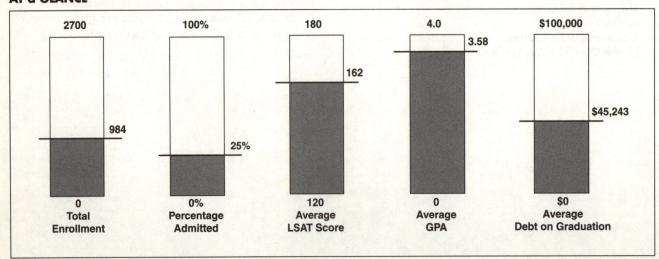

Degree Options

Degree	Total Credits Required	Length of Program
JD–Doctor of Laws	87	3 yrs, full-time only [day]
JD/MA–Juris Doctor/Master of Arts–Urban Planning Dual-degree Program		4 yrs, full-time only
JD/MA–Juris Doctor/Master of Arts–American Indian Studies Dual-degree Program		4 yrs, full-time only
JD/MA–Juris Doctor/Master of Arts–Public Policy Dual-degree Program		4 yrs, full-time only [day]
JD/MA–Juris Doctor/Master of Arts–Social Welfare Dual-degree Program		4 yrs, full-time only [day]
JD/MBA–Juris Doctor/Master of Business Administration–Dual-degree Program		4 yrs, full-time only [day]
LLM–Master of Laws	20	1 yr, full-time only

90095-1476. Phone: 310-825-2459. Completed financial aid forms should be received by March 1.

Law School Library Hugh and Hazel Darling Law Library has 10 professional staff members and contains more than 475,000 volumes and 7,050 periodicals. 780 seats are available in the library. When classes are in session, the library is open 98 hours per week.

WESTLAW and LEXIS-NEXIS are available, as are the World Wide Web, online bibliographic services, and CD-ROM players. 65 computer workstations are available to students in the library. Special law collections include Aviation Law.

First-Year Program Class size in the average section is 80; 95% of the first-year courses are taught by full-time faculty.

Upper-Level Program Among the electives are:

Administrative Law
Advocacy
Animal Rights Law
★ Business and Corporate Law
Education Law
Entertainment Law
★ Environmental Law
Family Law
Government/Regulation
Health Care/Human Services
Indian/Tribal Law
Intellectual Property
★ International/Comparative Law
Jurisprudence
Labor Law
Land Use Law/Natural Resources
Lawyering Skills
Legal History/Philosophy
Litigation
Media Law
Mediation
Probate Law
★ Public Interest
Securities
Tax Law
(★ *indicates an area of special strength*)

Clinical Courses Students receive degree credit for clinical courses. (Clinical practicum is required.) Among the clinical areas offered are:

Civil Litigation
Criminal Defense
Elderly Advocacy
Environmental Law
Family Practice
General Practice
Juvenile Law
Land Rights/Natural Resource
Mediation
Public Interest

8% of the students participate in internship programs.

UNIVERSITY OF SAN DIEGO
SCHOOL OF LAW

San Diego, California

INFORMATION CONTACT
Kristine Strachan, Dean
5998 Alcala Park
San Diego, CA 92110

Phone: 619-260-4527   Fax: 619-260-2218
Web site: http://www.acusd.edu/

LAW STUDENT PROFILE [1997–98]

FULL-TIME   Enrollment: 781
Women: 41%   Men: 59%

PART-TIME   Enrollment: 350
Women: 41%   Men: 59%

RACIAL or ETHNIC COMPOSITION
African American, 2%; Asian/Pacific Islander, 12%; Hispanic, 6%; Native American, 2%; International, 4%

APPLICANTS and ADMITTEES
Number applied: 2,786
Admitted: 1,281
Percentage accepted: 46%
Seats available: 320
Average LSAT score: 160
Average GPA: 3.1

University of San Diego School of Law is a private institution that organizes classes on a semester calendar system. The campus is situated in an urban setting. Founded in 1954, first ABA approved in 1961, and an AALS member, University of San Diego School of Law offers JD and LLM degrees.

Faculty consists of 50 full-time and 34 part-time members in 1997–98. 16 full-time faculty members and 13 part-time faculty members are women. 100% of all faculty members have a JD degree. Of all faculty members, 1% are Asian/Pacific Islander, 4% are African American, 7% are Hispanic, 88% are white.

Application Information *Required:* LSAT, LSDAS, application form, application fee of $40, baccalaureate degree, minimum 2.0 GPA, personal statement, college transcripts. *Recommended:* resume. *Application deadline* for fall term is March 1.

Costs The 1997–98 tuition is $20,980 full-time; $710 per unit part-time. Fees: $50 full-time; $40 part-time.

Financial Aid Loans, loan repayment assistance program (LRAP), merit-based grants/scholarships, need-based grants/scholarships, and federal work-study loans are available. The average student debt at graduation is $65,000. To apply for financial

AT a GLANCE

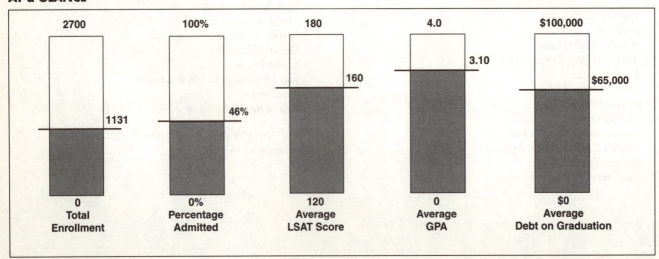

Degree Options

Degree	Total Credits Required	Length of Program
JD–Juris Doctor	85	3–4 yrs, full-time or part-time [day, evening]
LLM–Master of Laws–Comparative Law for Foreign Attorneys	25	1 yr, full-time or part-time [day, evening]
LLM–Master of Laws	24	1 yr, full-time or part-time [day, evening]
LLM–Master of Laws–International Law	24	1 yr, full-time or part-time [day, evening]
LLM–Master of Laws–Taxation	24	1 yr, full-time or part-time [day, evening]

assistance, students must complete the Free Application for Federal Student Aid and institutional forms. Financial aid contact: Carl J. Eging, Director of Admissions and Financial Aid, 5998 Alcala Park, San Diego, CA 92110. Phone: 619-260-4570. Fax: 619-260-2218. E-mail: jdinfo@agusd.edu. Completed financial aid forms should be received by March 1.

Law School Library Legal Research Center has 10 professional staff members and contains more than 432,000 volumes and 5,450 periodicals. 600 seats are available in the library. When classes are in session, the library is open 108 hours per week.

WESTLAW and LEXIS-NEXIS are available, as are the World Wide Web, online bibliographic services, and CD-ROM players. 40 computer workstations are available to students in the library. Special law collections include Taxation, Mexican Law.

First-Year Program Class size in the average section is 80; 100% of the first-year courses are taught by full-time faculty.

Upper-Level Program Class size in the average section is 30. Among the electives are:

Administrative Law
Advocacy
Business and Corporate Law
Entertainment Law
★ Environmental Law
Family Law
Government/Regulation
Health Care/Human Services
Indian/Tribal Law
Intellectual Property
★ International/Comparative Law
Jurisprudence
Labor Law
★ Land Use Law/Natural Resources
Lawyering Skills
Legal History/Philosophy
Litigation
Maritime Law
Media Law
Mediation
Probate Law
★ Public Interest
Securities
★ Tax Law
(★ indicates an area of special strength)

Clinical Courses Students receive degree credit for clinical courses. (Clinical practicum is not required.) Among the clinical areas offered are:

Children and the Law
Civil Litigation
Criminal Defense
Criminal Law
Criminal Prosecution
Environmental Law
General Practice
Immigration
Land Rights/Natural Resource
Mental Health and Law
Public Interest

10% of the students participate in internship programs.

UNIVERSITY OF SAN FRANCISCO
SCHOOL OF LAW

San Francisco, California

INFORMATION CONTACT

Jay Folberg, Dean
2100 Fulton Street
San Francisco, CA 94117-1080

Phone: 415-422-6304   Fax: 415-422-6433
Web site: http://www.usfca.edu/law/

LAW STUDENT PROFILE [1997–98]

FULL-TIME	Enrollment: 534
Women: 54%	Men: 46%
PART-TIME	Enrollment: 127
Women: 46%	Men: 54%

RACIAL or ETHNIC COMPOSITION
African American, 3%; Asian/Pacific Islander, 15%; Hispanic, 7%; Native American, 1%; International, 1%

APPLICANTS and ADMITTEES
Number applied: 2,459
Admitted: 1,190
Percentage accepted: 48%
Seats available: 218
Median LSAT score: 156
Median GPA: 3.1

University of San Francisco School of Law is a private institution that organizes classes on a semester calendar system. The campus is situated in an urban setting. Founded in 1912, first ABA approved in 1933, and an AALS member, University of San Francisco School of Law offers JD, JD/MBA, and LLM degrees.

Faculty consists of 27 full-time and 34 part-time members in 1997–98. 7 full-time faculty members and 9 part-time faculty members are women.

Application Information *Required:* LSAT, LSDAS, application form, application fee of $40, baccalaureate degree, 2 letters of recommendation, personal statement, college transcripts. *Application deadline* for fall term is April 1.

Financial Aid In 1997–98, 84% of all students received some form of financial aid. Fellowships, loans, loan repayment assistance program (LRAP), merit-based grants/scholarships, need-based grants/scholarships, and federal work-study loans are also available. The average student debt at graduation is $70,000. To apply for financial assistance, students must complete the Free Application for Federal Student Aid. Financial aid contact: Gabriela De la Vega, Financial Aid Counselor, USF School of Law, San Francisco, CA 94117-1080. Phone: 415-422-6210. Fax: 415-422-6433. E-mail:

AT a GLANCE

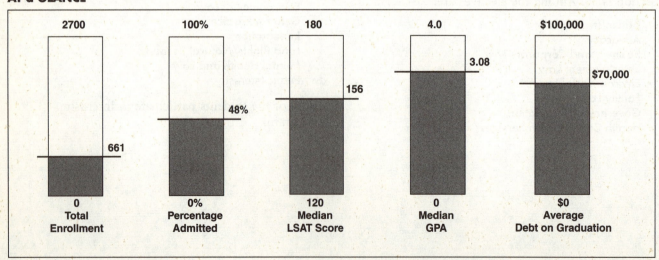

Degree Options

Degree	Total Credits Required	Length of Program
JD–Doctor of Laws	86	3–4 yrs, full-time or part-time [day, evening, summer]
JD/MBA–Juris Doctor/Master of Business Administration–Concurrent Program	114	4 yrs, full-time only [day, evening, summer]
LLM–Master of Laws–Foreign Lawyers in International Transactions and Comparative Law	25	1–2 yrs, full-time or part-time

delavegag@usfca.edu. Completed financial aid forms should be received by March 2.

Law School Library University of San Francisco School of Law Library has 6 professional staff members and contains more than 281,939 volumes and 2,488 periodicals. 293 seats are available in the library. When classes are in session, the library is open 100 hours per week.

WESTLAW and LEXIS-NEXIS are available, as are the World Wide Web, online bibliographic services, and CD-ROM players. 34 computer workstations are available to students in the library. Special law collections include California law.

First-Year Program Class size in the average section is 80; 100% of the first-year courses are taught by full-time faculty.

Upper-Level Program Class size in the average section is 28. Among the electives are:

   Administrative Law
   Advocacy
   Business and Corporate Law
   Consumer Law
 ★ Criminal Law
 ★ Dispute Resolution
   Entertainment Law
   Environmental Law
   Family Law

   Government/Regulation
   Indian/Tribal Law
 ★ Intellectual Property
 ★ International/Comparative Law
   Labor Law
   Law and Democracy
   Lawyering Skills
   Litigation
   Maritime Law
   Media Law
   Mediation
   Probate Law
 ★ Public Interest
   Securities
   Tax Law
(★ *indicates an area of special strength*)

Clinical Courses Students receive degree credit for clinical courses. (Clinical practicum is not required.) Among the clinical areas offered are:

   Civil Litigation
   Criminal Defense
   Investigation
   Mediation

11% of the students participate in internship programs. International exchange programs permit students to visit Czech Republic; Indonesia; and Ireland.

UNIVERSITY OF SOUTHERN CALIFORNIA
LAW SCHOOL

Los Angeles, California

LAW STUDENT PROFILE [1997–98]

FULL-TIME   Enrollment: 601
Women: 45%   Men: 55%

RACIAL or ETHNIC COMPOSITION
African American, 12%; Asian/Pacific Islander, 13%;
Hispanic, 15%; Native American, 0.3%; International, 0%

APPLICANTS and ADMITTEES
Seats available: 205
Average LSAT score: 164
Average GPA: 3.5

University of Southern California Law School is a private institution that organizes classes on a semester calendar system. The campus is situated in an urban setting. Founded in 1900, first ABA approved in 1923, and an AALS member, University of Southern California Law School offers JD, JD/MA, JD/MBA, JD/MPAd, JD/MPPo, JD/MS, JD/MSW, JD/MTAX, and JD/PhD degrees.

Application Information *Required:* LSAT, LSDAS, application form, application fee of $60, baccalaureate degree, 2 letters of recommendation, personal statement, college transcripts. *Recommended:* resume.

Costs The 1997–98 tuition is $24,638 full-time; $952 per unit part-time. Fees: $414.

Financial Aid 295 fellowships, 8 teaching assistantships were awarded. 105 other awards were given. Fellowships, graduate assistantships, loans, loan repayment assistance program (LRAP), merit-based grants/scholarships, need-based grants/scholarships, and federal work-study loans are also available. The average student debt at graduation is $60,000. To apply for financial assistance, students must complete the Free Application for Federal Student Aid, institutional forms, and photocopy of tax return. Financial aid contact: Mary Bingham, Director of Financial Aid, University Park, Los Angeles, CA 90089-0071. Phone: 213-740-7331. Fax:

AT a GLANCE

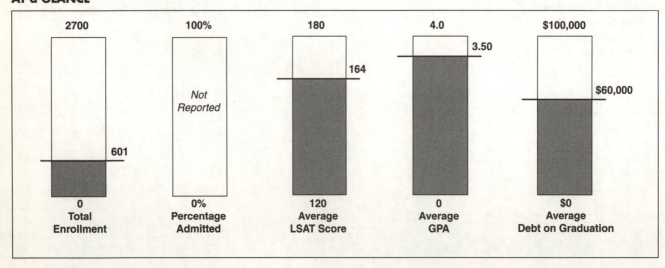

2700	100%	180	4.0	$100,000
	Not Reported	164	3.50	$60,000
601				
0	0%	120	0	$0
Total Enrollment	Percentage Admitted	Average LSAT Score	Average GPA	Average Debt on Graduation

Degree Options

Degree	Total Credits Required	Length of Program
JD–Doctor of Laws	88	3 yrs, full-time only [day]
JD–Juris Doctor–Graduate Certificate–Gender Studies		3 yrs, full-time only [day]
JD/MA–Juris Doctor/Master of Arts–(Economics, Communication, Religion, Philosophy)	89–91	3 yrs, full-time only [day]
JD/MA–Juris Doctor/Master of Arts–(International Relations) Dual Degree	95	3.5 yrs, full-time only [day]
JD/MBA–Juris Doctor/Master of Business Administration–Dual Degree	122	4 yrs, full-time only [day]
JD/MPAd–Juris Doctor/Master of Public Administration–Dual Degree	97	3.5 yrs, full-time only [day]
JD/MPPo–Juris Doctor/Master of Public Policy–Dual Degree	112	4 yrs, full-time only [day]
JD/MS–Juris Doctor/Master of Science–(Gerontology) Dual Degree	110	4 yrs, full-time only [day]
JD/MSW–Juris Doctor/Master of Social Work–Dual Degree	117	4 yrs, full-time only [day]
JD/MTAX–Juris Doctor/Master of Taxation–Business Tax Dual-degree	118	4 yrs [day]
JD/PhD–Juris Doctor/Doctor of Philosophy–California Institute of Technology		full-time only [day]

213-740-5502. E-mail: mbingham@law.usc.edu. Completed financial aid forms should be received by February 15.

Law School Library Asa V. Call Law Library has 10 professional staff members and contains more than 352,143 volumes and 1,950 periodicals. 294 seats are available in the library. When classes are in session, the library is open 101 hours per week.

WESTLAW and LEXIS-NEXIS are available, as are the World Wide Web, online bibliographic services, and CD-ROM players. 88 computer workstations are available to students in the library. Special law collections include Client (self-help) Library.

First-Year Program Class size in the average section is 70; 100% of the first-year courses are taught by full-time faculty.

Upper-Level Program Class size in the average section is 40. Among the electives are:

Accounting
Administrative Law
★ Advocacy
★ Business and Corporate Law
Civil Rights
Discrimination
Dispute Resolution
★ Entertainment Law
Environmental Law
★ Family Law
Government/Regulation
★ Health Care/Human Services

Indian/Tribal Law
★ Intellectual Property
★ International/Comparative Law
Jurisprudence
★ Labor Law
Land Use Law/Natural Resources
Law and Economics
Lawyering Skills
★ Legal History/Philosophy
★ Litigation
Maritime Law
★ Media Law
★ Mediation
Probate Law
★ Public Interest
Securities
★ Tax Law
(★ indicates an area of special strength)

Clinical Courses Students receive degree credit for clinical courses. (Clinical practicum is not required.) Among the clinical areas offered are:

Civil Litigation
Civil Rights
Corporate Law
Criminal Defense
General Practice
Health
Juvenile Law
Law and Economics
Mediation
Public Interest

25% of the students participate in internship programs.

UNIVERSITY OF THE PACIFIC
MCGEORGE SCHOOL OF LAW

Stockton, California

INFORMATION CONTACT

Gerald M. Caplan, Dean
3200 Fifth Avenue
Sacramento, CA 95817

Phone: 916-739-7151   Fax: 916-739-7134
E-mail: admissionsmcgeorge@uop.edu
Web site: http://www.mcgeorge.edu/

LAW STUDENT PROFILE [1997–98]

FULL-TIME   Enrollment: 817
Women: 47%   Men: 53%

PART-TIME   Enrollment: 322
Women: 48%   Men: 52%

RACIAL or ETHNIC COMPOSITION
African American, 3%; Asian/Pacific Islander, 12%; Hispanic, 7%; Native American, 2%

APPLICANTS and ADMITTEES
Number applied: 1,811
Admitted: 1,240
Percentage accepted: 68%
Seats available: 370
Median LSAT score: 152
Median GPA: 3.0

University of the Pacific McGeorge School of Law is a private institution that organizes classes on a semester calendar system. The campus is situated in an urban setting. Founded in 1924, first ABA approved in 1969, and an AALS member, University of the Pacific McGeorge School of Law offers JD, JD/MBA, JD/MPPA, and LLM degrees.

Faculty consists of 46 full-time and 34 part-time members in 1997–98. 13 full-time faculty members and 6 part-time faculty members are women. 100% of all faculty members have a JD; 16% have advanced law degrees. Of all faculty members, 1% are Native American, 1% are Asian/Pacific Islander, 3% are African American, 1% are Hispanic, 93% are white.

Application Information *Required:* LSAT, LSDAS, application form, application fee of $40, baccalaureate degree, personal statement, college transcripts. *Recommended:* recommendations. *Application deadline* for fall term is May 1.

Costs The 1997–98 tuition is $20,762 full-time; $13,324 part-time.

Financial Aid 420 awards were given. Loans, loan repayment assistance program (LRAP), merit-based grants/scholarships, need-based grants/scholarships, and federal work-study loans are also available. The

AT a GLANCE

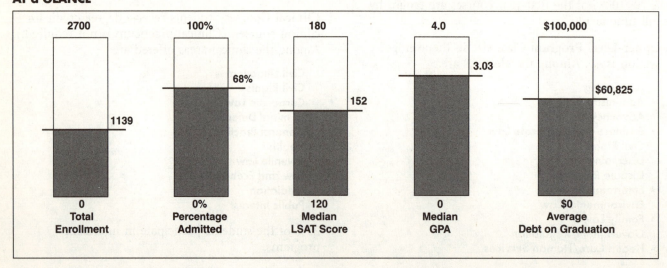

Degree Options

Degree	Total Credits Required	Length of Program
JD–Doctor of Laws	88	3–4 yrs, full-time or part-time [day, evening, summer]
JD/MBA–Juris Doctor/Master of Business Administration–Dual-degree Program	112	4–5 yrs, full-time or part-time [day, evening, summer]
JD/MPPA–Juris Doctor/Master of Public Policy and Administration–Dual-degree Program	112	4–5 yrs, full-time or part-time [day, evening, summer]
LLM–Master of Laws–Transnational Business Practice	24	1 yr, full-time only [day]

average student debt at graduation is $60,825. To apply for financial assistance, students must complete the Free Application for Federal Student Aid and institutional forms. Financial aid contact: Financial Aid Office, 3200 Fifth Avenue, Sacramento, CA 95817. Phone: 916-739-7158. Fax: 916-739-7134. E-mail: admissionsmcgeorge@uop.edu.

Law School Library Gordon D. Schaber Law Library has 8 professional staff members and contains more than 430,207 volumes and 4,509 periodicals. 605 seats are available in the library. When classes are in session, the library is open 110 hours per week.

WESTLAW and LEXIS-NEXIS are available, as are the World Wide Web, online bibliographic services, and CD-ROM players. 73 computer workstations are available to students in the library. Special law collections include Tax and International Law; California; California and US documents depository.

First-Year Program Class size in the average section is 100; 100% of the first-year courses are taught by full-time faculty.

Upper-Level Program Among the electives are:

- ★ Administrative Law
- ★ Advocacy
- ★ Business and Corporate Law
- Constitutional Law
- Consumer Law
- ★ Criminal Law
- Education
- Employment Law
- Entertainment Law
- ★ Environmental Law
- ★ Family Law
- ★ Government/Regulation
- Health Care/Human Services
- Intellectual Property
- ★ International/Comparative Law
- Jurisprudence
- Juvenile Law
- Labor Law
- ★ Land Use Law/Natural Resources
- ★ Lawyering Skills
- Legal History/Philosophy
- ★ Litigation
- Maritime Law
- Media Law
- Mediation
- Probate Law
- Public Interest
- Securities
- ★ Tax Law

(★ *indicates an area of special strength*)

Clinical Courses Students receive degree credit for clinical courses. (Clinical practicum is not required.) Among the clinical areas offered are:

- Civil Litigation
- Civil Rights
- Corporate Law
- Criminal Defense
- Criminal Prosecution
- Education
- Elderly Advocacy
- Environmental Law
- Family Practice
- General Practice
- Government Litigation
- Health
- Juvenile Law
- Land Rights/Natural Resource
- Mediation
- Public Interest
- Tax Law

90% of the students participate in internship programs.

WESTERN STATE UNIVERSITY COLLEGE OF LAW

Fullerton, California

INFORMATION CONTACT
Dennis R. Honabach, Dean
1111 North State College Boulevard
Fullerton, CA 92831-3014

Phone: 714-738-1000
Ext. 2900
E-mail: adm@wsulaw.edu
Web site: http://www.wsulaw.edu/

LAW STUDENT PROFILE [1997–98]

FULL-TIME   Enrollment: 253
Women: 42%   Men: 58%

PART-TIME   Enrollment: 641
Women: 44%   Men: 56%

RACIAL or ETHNIC COMPOSITION
African American, 7%; Asian/Pacific Islander, 14%; Hispanic, 12%; Native American, 1%

APPLICANTS and ADMITTEES
Number applied: 288
Admitted: 170
Percentage accepted: 59%
Seats available: 126
Average LSAT score: 146
Average GPA: 2.9

Western State University College of Law is a private nonprofit institution that organizes classes on a semester calendar system. The campus is situated in an urban setting. Founded in 1966, first ABA approved in 1998, Western State University College of Law offers a JD degree.

Faculty consists of 29 full-time and 42 part-time members in 1997–98. 11 full-time faculty members and 6 part-time faculty members are women.

Application Information *Required:* LSAT, LSDAS, application form, application fee of $50, 2 letters of recommendation, personal statement, college transcripts.

Financial Aid In 1997–98, 85% of all students received some form of financial aid. Loans, merit-based grants/scholarships, need-based grants/scholarships, and federal work-study loans are also available. The average student debt at graduation is $48,192. To apply for financial assistance, students must complete the Free Application for Federal Student Aid. Financial aid contact: Financial Assistance Office, 1111 North State College Boulevard, Fullerton, CA 92831-3014. Phone: 714-738-1000 Ext. 2350.

Law School Library Western State University Law Library has 12 professional staff members and

AT a GLANCE

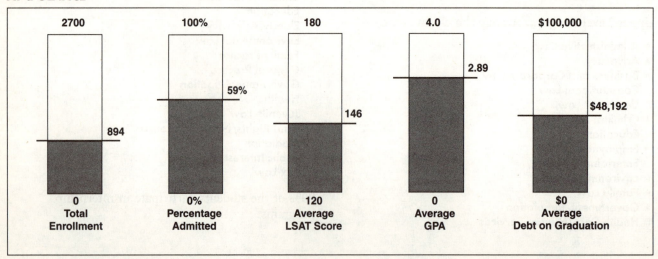

Degree Options		
Degree	Total Credits Required	Length of Program
JD–Juris Doctor	88	3–4 yrs, full-time or part-time [day, evening]

contains more than 147,000 volumes. 340 seats are available in the library. When classes are in session, the library is open 108 hours per week.

LEXIS-NEXIS is available, as are the World Wide Web and CD-ROM players.

First-Year Program Class size in the average section is 37; 100% of the first-year courses are taught by full-time faculty.

Upper-Level Program Class size in the average section is 32. Among the electives are:

Administrative Law
Business and Corporate Law
Consumer Law
Environmental Law
Family Law
Health Care/Human Services
Intellectual Property

Jurisprudence
Lawyering Skills
Legal History/Philosophy
Litigation
Mediation
Probate Law
Tax Law

Clinical Courses Among the clinical areas offered are:

Appellate Litigation
Civil Litigation
Criminal Defense
Criminal Prosecution
Family Practice
General Practice

Internships are available.

DEAN'S STATEMENT . . .

The decision to enter law school is exciting, exhilarating, and intimidating. Let me share with you some of the strengths of Western State, the ABA's newest law school. Western State is a private institution with a top-notch faculty drawn by our strong sense of campus community and the unparalleled natural beauty of southern California. We pride ourselves on our small class sizes and the tremendous amount of personal attention our students receive. The close-knit relationships that develop among faculty and students are key to the success of our students. Because we recognize that the transition from undergraduate school to law school is challenging, we offer additional learning resources outside regular course work. Our Academic Success and Enrichment Program provides a cadre of dedicated, inspired tutors who will work with you one-on-one or in small groups. Within the student body itself you will find a strong network of peer support.

Another of our strengths is our innovative, hands-on practical curriculum that emphasizes the effective combination of legal theory and professional skills. Every good law school will equip you with the ability to "think like a lawyer." The difference at Western State is that we are also committed to preparing you to function as a lawyer the day you complete our program. We tailor specific courses to assist you in bridging the gap between classroom learning and real-world practice. You will also have the opportunity to participate in one of our three externship programs, where you will work side-by-side with district attorneys, public defenders, prominent jurists, or private practitioners who are experts in their fields.

We offer a full-time program and a part-time program. In each program students work with the same faculty, take the same courses, and have the same opportunities to participate fully in the life of the law school community.

The next few years will be an exciting period of growth for Western State. We hope you choose to join us and share the excitement.

—Dennis R. Honbach, Dean

HISTORY, CAMPUS, AND LOCATION

Western State is in Orange County, California, listed as the most livable community in the U.S. by a recent Places Rated survey. World-class beaches, mountain ski resorts, and dramatic desert panoramas are within an hour of the campus. Cultural and recreational opportunities abound. The campus is located within the university district of Fullerton, a small gem of a city noted for excellence of its five institutes of higher education and the charm of its "old California" downtown. The history of Western State spans four decades. The law school's growth has paralleled the evolution of Orange County, a region whose vitality is continually fed by the influx of businesses and people from around the nation and the world. The growing number of small start-up companies, the resurgence of the real estate industry, and the vitality of the country's ethnic diversity are key factors in creating opportunities for new law graduates.

SPECIAL QUALITIES OF THE SCHOOL

Western State's cutting-edge curriculum integrates abstract legal concepts with real-world scenarios, making learning law directly relevant to students' lives. The law school's professional skills training helps students develop the combination of analytical ability and finely honed instincts that makes the difference between becoming a great attorney or merely a good one.

The law school has graduated more than 8,800 alumni who have distinguished themselves as lawmakers, jurists, prosecutors, public defenders, and highly respected private practitioners in every legal specialty from aviation law to elder law. Opportunities for students to find supportive legal mentors or to volunteer for rewarding public service

assignments in a variety of government and nonprofit environments abound because of the alumni's strong presence here and the school's long-standing relationship with the community.

TECHNOLOGY ON CAMPUS

With the opening of a state-of-the-art library last September, Western State's students and faculty now have direct access to highly advanced, technologically sophisticated research materials. Students can plug in their laptops anywhere in the library and access electronic legal resources right at their seats. Professors have that same option thanks to "smart podiums" in new classrooms. A thirty-one–station computer lab in the library provides users access to tutorial programs, a fifty-six–bay CD-ROM tower, and the Internet, as well as the legal database services. Law students also have the chance to interact with virtual judges on multimedia computers.

SCHOLARSHIPS AND LOANS

Most students finance their education through low-interest federal loans. Students are also eligible for scholarships based on their performance on the Law School Admission Test (LSAT). First-year scholarships range from $5000 to total tuition expense for full-time students and from $3750 to total part-time tuition expense for part-time students. For upper-level students, Trustees' Scholarships are awarded to those with cumulative GPAs that put them in the top 30 percent. Other specialty scholarships are also available.

STUDENT ACTIVITIES AND OPPORTUNITIES

Law Review One of the most prestigious venues for law students to showcase their abilities and to refine their research, writing, analytical, and editing skills is by serving on the Western State University Law Review.

Moot Court Western State has incorporated moot court into the third course of a 10-unit professional skills sequence in which students learn how to interview a client and develop the facts of a case as they learn the skills of critical thinking, legal writing, and legal research. The third course, advocacy, has students apply these skills in a variety of settings. Students conduct an arbitration and negotiate a settlement. The semester culminates in the Ferguson Moot Court Competition, in which students write an appellate brief and argue orally before a panel of judges.

Extracurricular Activities Active student organizations include students with similar law specialty interests, as well as students interested in literature and Christian ethics as they relate to law. Several minority student organizations address the issues and concerns of those who are members of ethnic and racial minorities. Many students engage in public service work through Western State's voluntary public service program. Through their efforts, students make an impact on the world around them. They volunteer at government agencies, legal service organizations, charitable organizations, and private law firms that conduct pro bono cases. The Delta Theta Phi law fraternity and the Student Bar Association sponsor several annual charitable events for underprivileged children.

Special Opportunities Students may translate their training into real-world experience by participating in externships with appellate judges, trial judges, district attorneys, public defenders, and lawyers in private practice. Students in Western's three externship programs spend 15 to 40 hours a week working directly with a supervising attorney or judge. This one-on-one partnership gives the extern a crucial insider's perspective into the law as it is actually practiced. Externs do far more than merely observe. By making decisions that affect real people, they gain confidence quickly.

Opportunities for Members of Minority Groups and Women More than 30 percent of the law school's students come from ethnic and minority backgrounds underrepresented in the legal profession. About 44 percent of the student body is women. Western State's minority student leaders champion causes and address concerns of importance to the entire student body. Among the seventeen student groups active on campus are several that provide forums for their members to discuss the issues facing women and minorities in law school. These include the Asian-Pacific American Law Student, Black Law Student, Latino Law Student, and Women's Law Associations.

BAR PASSAGE, CAREER SERVICES, AND PLACEMENT

First-time bar passage rate was 53.7 percent for the February 1997 California Bar and 50 percent for the July 1997 California Bar Examination.

Western State's Career Services Offices provides new graduates and alumni with attorney, law clerk, and alternative career placement counseling; campus interviews; workshops and seminars; library and computer resources; and career-related brochures and monthly publications. Eighty percent of 1996–97 graduates found legal employment within six months of graduation.

Legal Field	Percentage of Graduates	Average Salary
Academic	3%	$44,900
Business	22%	$59,300
Government	9%	$45,200
Judicial Clerkship	1%	$50,000
Private Practice	60%	$46,200
Public Interest	4%	$31,700
Other	1%	$49,000

CORRESPONDENCE AND INFORMATION

Admissions Office
Western State University College of Law
1111 North State College Boulevard
Fullerton, California 92831-3014
Telephone: 714-738-1000
Fax: 714-526-1062
E-mail: www.adm@wsulaw.edu

WHITTIER COLLEGE
SCHOOL OF LAW

Whittier, California

LAW STUDENT PROFILE [1997–98]

FULL-TIME   Enrollment: 369
Women: 51%   Men: 49%

PART-TIME   Enrollment: 266
Women: 47%   Men: 53%

RACIAL or ETHNIC COMPOSITION
African American, 6%; Asian/Pacific Islander, 15%; Hispanic, 16%; Native American, 1%

APPLICANTS and ADMITTEES
Number applied: 1,743
Admitted: 1,103
Percentage accepted: 63%
Seats available: 230
Average LSAT score: 151
Average GPA: 2.9

Whittier College School of Law is a private institution that organizes classes on a semester calendar system. The campus is situated in a suburban setting. Founded in 1975, first ABA approved in 1978, and an AALS member, Whittier College School of Law offers a JD degree.

Faculty consists of 28 full-time and 12 part-time members in 1997–98. 12 full-time faculty members and 1 part-time faculty members are women. 100% of all faculty members have a JD; 15% have advanced law degrees. Of all faculty members, 1.7% are Asian/Pacific Islander, 3.4% are African American, 1.7% are Hispanic, 93.2% are white.

Application Information *Required:* LSAT, LSDAS, application form, application fee of $50, personal statement, writing sample, college transcripts. *Recommended:* baccalaureate degree, recommendations, resume. *Application deadline* for fall term is March 15.

Financial Aid In 1997–98, 90% of all students received some form of financial aid. 11 research assistantships, 44 teaching assistantships were awarded. Fellowships, graduate assistantships, loans, merit-based grants/scholarships, need-based grants/scholarships, and federal work-study loans are also available. The average student debt at graduation is $70,000. To apply for financial assistance,

AT a GLANCE

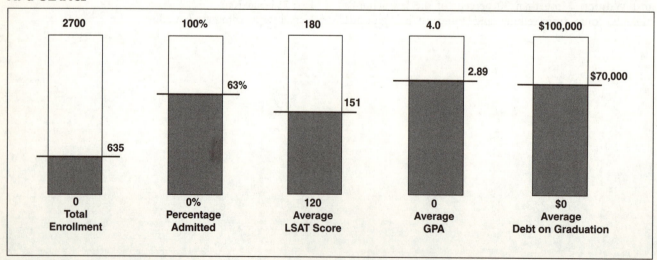

Degree Options

Degree	Total Credits Required	Length of Program
JD–Doctor of Laws	87	3–4 yrs, full-time or part-time [day, evening]

students must complete the Free Application for Federal Student Aid. Financial aid contact: Julie McAllister, Director of Financial Aid, 3333 Harbor Boulevard, Costa Mesa, CA 92626. Phone: 714-444-4141. Fax: 714-444-0855. E-mail: jmallister@law.whittier.edu. Completed financial aid forms should be received by June 1.

Law School Library has 7 professional staff members and contains more than 297,614 volumes and 4,952 periodicals. 315 seats are available in the library. When classes are in session, the library is open 102 hours per week.

WESTLAW and LEXIS-NEXIS are available, as are the World Wide Web, online bibliographic services, and CD-ROM players. 68 computer workstations are available to students in the library.

First-Year Program Class size in the average section is 85; 100% of the first-year courses are taught by full-time faculty.

Upper-Level Program Class size in the average section is 25. Among the electives are:

Advocacy

Business and Corporate Law
★ Children's Rights
Consumer Law
Entertainment Law
Environmental Law
Family Law
Government/Regulation
★ Health Care/Human Services
Indian/Tribal Law
★ Intellectual Property
International/Comparative Law
Labor Law
Land Use Law/Natural Resources
Lawyering Skills
Litigation
Maritime Law
Mediation
Probate Law
Public Interest
Securities
Tax Law

(★ indicates an area of special strength)

70% of the students participate in internship programs. International exchange program available.

UNIVERSITY OF COLORADO AT BOULDER
SCHOOL OF LAW

Boulder, Colorado

INFORMATION CONTACT

Harold H. Bruff, Dean
Fleming Law Building
Campus Box 401
Boulder, CO 80309-0401

Phone: 303-492-8047   Fax: 303-492-1200
E-mail: lawadmin@colorado.edu
Web site: http://www.colorado.edu/Law/

LAW STUDENT PROFILE [1997–98]

FULL-TIME   Enrollment: 507
Women: 49%   Men: 51%

RACIAL or ETHNIC COMPOSITION
African American, 4%; Asian/Pacific Islander, 4%; Hispanic, 7%; Native American, 3%

APPLICANTS and ADMITTEES
Number applied: 1,806
Admitted: 644
Percentage accepted: 36%
Seats available: 165
Average LSAT score: 161
Average GPA: 3.5

University of Colorado at Boulder School of Law is a public institution that organizes classes on a semester calendar system. The campus is situated in an urban setting. Founded in 1892, first ABA approved in 1923, and an AALS member, University of Colorado at Boulder School of Law offers JD, JD/MBA, and JD/MPAd degrees.

Faculty consists of 32 full-time members in 1997–98. 6 full-time faculty members are women. 100% of all faculty members have a JD; 1% have advanced law degrees. Of all faculty members, 1% are Native American, 1% are Asian/Pacific Islander, 4% are African American, 6% are Hispanic, 88% are white.

Application Information *Required:* LSAT, LSDAS, application form, application fee of $45, baccalaureate degree, 1 recommendation, personal statement, college transcripts. *Application deadline* for fall term is February 15.

Costs The 1997–98 tuition is $4760 full-time for state residents; $792 per semester (minimum) part-time for state residents. Tuition is $16,434 full-time for nonresidents; $2739 per semester (minimum) part-time for nonresidents. Fees: $667 full-time; $130 per semester (minimum) part-time.

AT a GLANCE

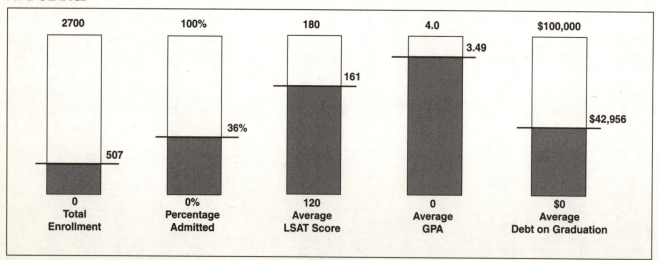

Degree Options		
Degree	**Total Credits Required**	**Length of Program**
JD–Juris Doctor	89	3 yrs, full-time only [day, summer]
JD/MBA–Juris Doctor/Master of Business Administration		4 yrs, full-time only [day]
JD/MPAd–Juris Doctor/Master of Public Administration		4 yrs, full-time only [day]

Financial Aid Fellowships, graduate assistantships, loans, merit-based grants/scholarships, need-based grants/scholarships, and federal work-study loans are available. The average student debt at graduation is $42,956. To apply for financial assistance, students must complete the Free Application for Federal Student Aid. Financial aid contact: Jamy Couson, Financial Aid Counselor, Fleming Law Building, Campus Box 403, Boulder, CO 80309-0403. Phone: 303-492-0647. Fax: 303-492-1200. E-mail: coulson_j@gems.colorado.edu. Completed financial aid forms should be received by March 1.

Law School Library University of Colorado Law Library has 7 professional staff members and contains more than 365,800 volumes and 3,660 periodicals. 333 seats are available in the library. When classes are in session, the library is open 109 hours per week.

WESTLAW and LEXIS-NEXIS are available, as are the World Wide Web, online bibliographic services, and CD-ROM players. 46 computer workstations are available to students in the library. Special law collections include American Indian/Native American Law, water law.

First-Year Program Class size in the average section is 46; 100% of the first-year courses are taught by full-time faculty.

Upper-Level Program Class size in the average section is 25. Among the electives are:

Administrative Law

Advocacy
★ Business and Corporate Law
Consumer Law
Education Law
★ Environmental Law
Family Law
Health Care/Human Services
Indian/Tribal Law
Intellectual Property
International/Comparative Law
Jurisprudence
Labor Law
★ Land Use Law/Natural Resources
Lawyering Skills
Litigation
Media Law
Mediation
Probate Law
Securities
★ Tax Law
(★ indicates an area of special strength)

Clinical Courses Students receive degree credit for clinical courses. (Clinical practicum is not required.) Among the clinical areas offered are:

Civil Litigation
Criminal Defense
Family Practice
Health
Immigration
Indian/Tribal Law

Internships are available.

UNIVERSITY OF DENVER
COLLEGE OF LAW

Denver, Colorado

INFORMATION CONTACT
Robert Yegge, Interim Dean
7039 East 18th Avenue
Denver, CO 80220

Phone: 303-871-6000   Fax: 303-871-6100
Web site: http://www.law.du.edu/

LAW STUDENT PROFILE [1997–98]

TOTAL ENROLLMENT   1188

RACIAL or ETHNIC COMPOSITION
African American, 2%; Asian/Pacific Islander, 4%; Hispanic, 4%; Native American, 1%; International, 1%

APPLICANTS and ADMITTEES
Number applied: 2,256
Admitted: 1,288
Percentage accepted: 57%
Seats available: 340
Average LSAT score: 155
Average GPA: 3.2

University of Denver College of Law is a private institution that organizes classes on a semester calendar system. Founded in 1892, first ABA approved in 1928, and an AALS member, University of Denver College of Law offers JD, JD/MS, LLM, and MS degrees.

Faculty consists of 40 full-time members in 1997–98. 10 full-time faculty members are women. 96% of all faculty members have a JD; 13.4% have advanced law degrees.

Application Information *Required:* LSAT, LSDAS, application form, application fee of $45, baccalaureate degree, minimum 2.0 GPA, personal statement, college transcripts. *Application deadline* for fall term is May 1.

Costs The 1997–98 tuition is $622 per credit hour.

Financial Aid In 1997–98, 87% of all students received some form of financial aid. 165 other awards, totaling $846,319, were given. Graduate assistantships, loans, merit-based grants/scholarships, need-based grants/scholarships, and federal work-study loans are also available. The average student debt at graduation is $55,000. To apply for financial assistance, students must complete the Free Application for Federal Student Aid. Financial aid contact: Donna Ellis, Director of Financial Aid, 7039 East

AT a GLANCE

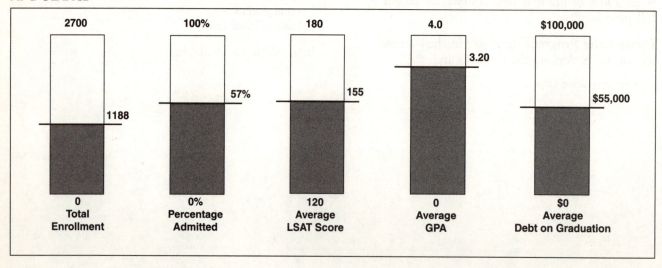

Degree Options

Degree	Total Credits Required	Length of Program
JD–Doctor of Laws	90	4–5 yrs, full-time or part-time [day, evening, summer]
JD/MS–Juris Doctor/Master of Science–Natural Resources Law and Policy	24	1 yr, full-time or part-time
LLM–Master of Laws–American and Comparative Laws	24	1 yr, full-time only [day]
LLM–Master of Laws–Taxation	30	1 yr, full-time or part-time [evening]
LLM–Master of Laws–Natural Resource Law Graduate Program	24	1 yr, full-time or part-time [day, evening]
MS–Master of Science–Master of Science in Legal Administration		1.5 yrs, full-time or part-time [day, evening]
Certificate–Certificate of Studies in Natural Resources Law and Policy	12	.5 yrs, full-time or part-time

18th Avenue, Denver, CO 80220. Phone: 303-871-6136. Fax: 303-871-6100. E-mail: dellis@adm.law.du.edu. Completed financial aid forms should be received by February 15.

Law School Library Westminster Law Library has 10 professional staff members and contains more than 314,155 volumes and 3,100 periodicals. 624 seats are available in the library. When classes are in session, the library is open 107 hours per week.

WESTLAW and LEXIS-NEXIS are available, as is the World Wide Web. 60 computer workstations are available to students in the library. Special law collections include government document selective depository, Hughs Rare Book Room.

First-Year Program Class size in the average section is 87; 100% of the first-year courses are taught by full-time faculty.

Upper-Level Program Class size in the average section is 40. Among the electives are:

Administrative Law
★ Advocacy
★ Business and Corporate Law
★ Environmental Law
Family Law
Government/Regulation
Health Care/Human Services
Indian/Tribal Law
Intellectual Property
★ International/Comparative Law
Jurisprudence
Labor Law
★ Land Use Law/Natural Resources
★ Lawyering Skills
Legal History/Philosophy
Litigation
Media Law
Mediation
Probate Law
★ Public Interest
Securities
Tax Law
(★ indicates an area of special strength)

Clinical Courses Students receive degree credit for clinical courses. (Clinical practicum is not required.) Among the clinical areas offered are:

Civil Litigation
Criminal Defense
Environmental Law
Family Practice
Land Rights/Natural Resource
Public Interest

30% of the students participate in internship programs.

DEAN'S STATEMENT . . .

The greatest strengths of the University of Denver College of Law are our students and faculty members. Among our approximately 1,000 students, many select Denver because of our outstanding international law, natural resources law, and public interest law programs, including our twelve annual Chancellor Scholars who receive full tuition waivers and provide community leadership in public interest law. Denver also has a productive and an energetic faculty. Our distinguished senior faculty members have earned national reputations in their fields. Thirteen of our 40 faculty members were hired since 1988. Remarkably, 10 of these 13 newer faculty members are members of minority groups and/or women. Across the board, the faculty prides itself on its commitment to innovative teaching and scholarship.

Denver's College of Law also enjoys unique opportunities for interdisciplinary scholarship. Denver was the original home of the Law and Society Association, whose first president and administrators will serve on our faculty, a faculty that continues to play a significant role in the association. The school's Hughes Research and Development Fund Committee, which is composed of nationally prominent scholars, provides regular financial support and substantive guidance for the faculty's interdisciplinary research. In addition, the school's long-recognized program in international law reaps the benefits of collaborative work with scholars throughout the University, which emphasizes internationalization in every department. Similarly, our outstanding natural resources program interacts with other natural resources professionals through our joint programs with Rocky Mountain Land Institute and the Colorado School of Mines. Our recently established Earthlaw Clinic has garnered considerable attention for its innovative representation of conservation and other community groups, including being the first to use the enforcement provision of NAFTA to protect the environment in the United States. We now offer LL.M. degrees in both our natural resources and international law programs. Finally, our programs in graduate tax, legal administration, preventative law, public interest law, and transportation law provide further opportunities for interdisciplinary study.

—*Nell Jessup Newton, Dean*

HISTORY, CAMPUS, AND LOCATION

The University of Denver College of Law was founded in 1892. From the outset the College was an educational pioneer—the initial class included men and women. The College has offered both full-time and part-time divisions since 1895. The College of Law received accreditation from the American Bar Association in 1928 and became a member of the Association of American Law Schools (AALS) in 1929. The College concentrated on its regional academic mission until Robert Yegge was named dean in 1965. Under the leadership of Dean Yegge, the faculty tripled in size. New programs were established to increase the access of members of minority groups to legal education, including the creation of a Ford Foundation summer preparatory program for Hispanic students that became the model for CLEO. In 1978, Daniel Hoffman was appointed Dean. Under his leadership, the College moved to its current location, a 33-acre campus in a residential area about 7 miles from downtown Denver.

SPECIAL QUALITIES OF THE SCHOOL

The College has maintained an outstanding set of clinical opportunities for its students. The first-year course in lawyering process, a variety of hands-on clinical offerings, extensive opportunities for internships, and a good deal of in-class practical training are all part of the College's focus on clinical and practical training. Another feature at the College is the Master of Science in Legal Administration that seeks to prepare students to occupy leadership positions in the administration of law firms and court systems. The College has endowments valued at more than

$22 million. A portion of the interest income from these endowments is used for student scholarships and in support of faculty scholarship, the library, and capital improvements for the school.

TECHNOLOGY ON CAMPUS

The College of Law offers students access to the campus network via sixty PC workstations divided among three computer labs and forty network ports in the library for their personal laptops. Home access is offered via the main campus network or a competitively priced Internet service provider (ISP). All classrooms have a network connection to allow professors access to resources for in-class activities. The following network resources are available to students: word processing (Word, WordPerfect); Personal Information Manager for e-mail, calendar, and contacts (Outlook); online legal research services (LEXIS, WESTLAW); Internet (Internet Explorer, Netscape); and instructional resources (CALI, Matthew Bender Authority, Law Desk Expertise, BNA's Environment Library, and EPA Shadow Law Manual).

SCHOLARSHIPS AND LOANS

Eighty percent of the student population borrows a combination of federal and private loans to fund their law school education. Merit and need-based scholarships are offered to new students and remain with the student throughout law school. In addition, new students may apply for a Chancellor's Scholarship, which provides full tuition for those pursuing the practice of public interest law. Continuing students may receive named and endowed scholarships based on their achievement during law school. Approximately 27 percent of the students receive some scholarship assistance.

STUDENT ACTIVITIES AND OPPORTUNITIES

Law Review There are six student publications at the College of Law. Three of these are officially recognized journals. *Denver University Law Review* has 80 members, the *Denver Journal of International Law and Public Policy* has 60, and the *Transportation Law Journal* has 25. Additionally, the *Water Court Reporter* has 15–25 student members, and the editorial board of the *Student Writ* comprises 6 students. Each journal has a selection process for students who wish to participate. Students may receive academic credit for service on editorial boards.

Moot Court At least 150 students participate in moot court competitions as organizers, witnesses, or competitors. The Moot Court Board organizes and runs the moot court program, including the six intraschool competitions: Negotiations, Client Counseling, Hoffman Cup Trial, Jessup Cup International, Natural Resources, and Barrister's Cup Appellate.

Extracurricular Activities The College of Law has more than forty student law organizations to accommodate a variety of interests, including human rights, business law, criminal law, disability law, immigration law, motorcycle law, sports and entertainment law, and public interest law.

Special Opportunities In the Student Law Office, the in-house clinic, 100 students represent 800 clients every year. In Earthlaw, students work in a clinical setting to protect the environment. The Child Advocacy Clinic provides 8 students with a yearlong clinical experience representing abused and neglected children. Student interns may work with practicing attorneys in a wide range of field placements. Interviewing and counseling, trial advocacy, and appellate advocacy competitions are also available.

Opportunities for Members of Minority Groups and Women These include the Asian Pacific American Law Students Association, the Black Law Students' Association, the Hispanic Law Students' Association, the Jewish Law Students' Association, the Native American Law Students' Association, the Women's Law Caucus, and AWARE (Accepting Women as Recognized Equals).

Special Certificate Programs The College offers three LL.M. programs for education beyond a J.D. degree—taxation, American and comparative law, and international natural resources and environmental law.

BAR PASSAGE, CAREER SERVICES, AND PLACEMENT

The total bar passage rate for the College of Law for 1997–98 was 72.87 percent. The total percent for first-time takers was 79.37 percent, and for those who had previously failed, the total was 13.06 percent.

The Career Services Office (CSO) provides services to assist students and graduates in their employment search. Career counselors help students draft effective resumes and cover letters, define career goals, identify networking contacts, and set up mock interviews. Job postings, fall recruiting programs, and career fairs offer students diverse opportunities to locate positions. A majority of students work in clinics or as law clerks or interns while in law school, reflecting the CSO's philosophy that practical experience is invaluable preparation for postgraduate employment. Seventy-nine percent of students were employed within six months of graduation; 93 percent within nine months.

Legal Field	Percentage of Graduates	Average Starting Salary
Academic	1.2%	n/a
Business	16.6%	$44,000
Government	13.0%	$33,900
Judicial Clerkship	9.5%	$32,000
Private Practice	53.8%	$38,250
Public Interest	1.8%	n/a
Other	4.1%	n/a

CORRESPONDENCE AND INFORMATION

Admissions Office
University of Denver College of Law
7039 East 18th Avenue
Denver, Colorado 80220
Telephone: 303-871-6135
Fax: 303-871-6100
E-mail: ctomlin@mail.law.du.edu
World Wide Web: http://www.law.du.edu

QUINNIPIAC COLLEGE
SCHOOL OF LAW

Hamden, Connecticut

LAW STUDENT PROFILE [1997–98]

FULL-TIME   Enrollment: 542
Women: 37%   Men: 63%

PART-TIME   Enrollment: 239
Women: 41%   Men: 59%

RACIAL or ETHNIC COMPOSITION
African American, 5%; Asian/Pacific Islander, 2%; Hispanic, 3%; Native American, 1%; International, 1%

APPLICANTS and ADMITTEES
Number applied: 1,965
Admitted: 1,085
Percentage accepted: 55%
Seats available: 225
Average LSAT score: 148
Average GPA: 2.8

Quinnipiac College School of Law is a private institution that organizes classes on a semester calendar system. The campus is situated in a suburban setting. Founded in 1974, first ABA approved in 1979, and an AALS member, Quinnipiac College School of Law offers JD, JD/MBA, and JD/MHA degrees.

Faculty consists of 45 full-time and 34 part-time members in 1997–98. 17 full-time faculty members and 8 part-time faculty members are women. 100% of all faculty members have a JD; 25% have advanced law degrees. Of all faculty members, 2.6% are Asian/Pacific Islander, 10.6% are African American, 86.8% are white.

Application Information *Required:* LSAT, LSDAS, application form, application fee of $40, baccalaureate degree, personal statement, college transcripts. *Recommended:* 2 letters of recommendation, essay, resume.

Financial Aid In 1997–98, 85% of all students received some form of financial aid. Graduate assistantships, loans, merit-based grants/scholarships, need-based grants/scholarships, and federal work-study loans are also available. The average student debt at graduation is $70,000. To apply for financial assistance, students must complete the Free Application for Federal Student Aid and institutional forms.

AT a GLANCE

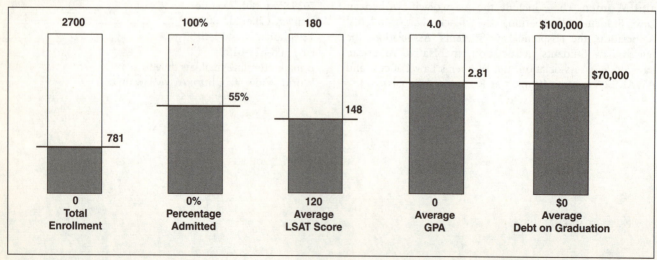

Degree Options

Degree	Total Credits Required	Length of Program
JD–Doctor of Laws	86	3–4 yrs, full-time or part-time [day, evening, summer]
JD/MBA–Juris Doctor/Master of Business Administration–Joint-degree Program	107	3.5–4 yrs, full-time or part-time [day, evening, summer]
JD/MHA–Juris Doctor/Master of Health Administration–Joint-degree Program	107	3.5–4 yrs, full-time or part-time [day, evening, summer]

Financial aid contact: Anne Traverso, Director of Financial Aid, 275 Mt. Carmel Avenue, Hamden, CT 06518. Phone: 203-287-3405. Fax: 203-287-3339. E-mail: lawfinaid@quinnipiac.edu. Completed financial aid forms should be received by May 1.

Law School Library has 7 professional staff members and contains more than 308,759 volumes and 3,054 periodicals. 400 seats are available in the library. When classes are in session, the library is open 96 hours per week.

WESTLAW and LEXIS-NEXIS are available, as are the World Wide Web, online bibliographic services, and CD-ROM players. 72 computer workstations are available to students in the library. Special law collections include federal tax materials, Connecticut statutes, laws, and historical documents.

First-Year Program Class size in the average section is 75; 100% of the first-year courses are taught by full-time faculty.

Upper-Level Program Class size in the average section is 35. Among the electives are:

Administrative Law
★ Advocacy
★ Business and Corporate Law
Consumer Law
Education Law
Environmental Law
★ Family Law
Government/Regulation

★ Health Care/Human Services
Indian/Tribal Law
Intellectual Property
★ International/Comparative Law
Jurisprudence
Labor Law
Land Use Law/Natural Resources
★ Lawyering Skills
Legal History/Philosophy
★ Litigation
Maritime Law
Media Law
Mediation
Probate Law
Public Interest
Securities
★ Tax Law
(★ indicates an area of special strength)

Clinical Courses Students receive degree credit for clinical courses. (Clinical practicum is not required.) Among the clinical areas offered are:

Appellate Litigation
Civil Litigation
Criminal Defense
Criminal Prosecution
Family Practice
General Practice
Health
Tax Law

50% of the students participate in internship programs.

UNIVERSITY OF CONNECTICUT
SCHOOL OF LAW

Storrs, Connecticut

INFORMATION CONTACT
Ellen Keane Rutt, Assistant Dean, Admissions and
Student Affairs
55 Elizabeth Street
Hartford, CT 06105

Phone: 860-570-5100
Web site: http://www.law.uconn.edu/

LAW STUDENT PROFILE [1997–98]

FULL-TIME   Enrollment: 462
Women: 47%   Men: 53%

PART-TIME   Enrollment: 170
Women: 48%   Men: 52%

APPLICANTS and ADMITTEES
Seats available: 149
Median LSAT score: 158
Median GPA: 3.3

University of Connecticut School of Law is a
public institution that organizes classes on a
semester calendar system. The campus is situated in
a suburban setting. First ABA approved in 1933, and
an AALS member, University of Connecticut School
of Law offers JD, JD/MA, JD/MBA, JD/MLS,
JD/MPA, JD/MPH, JD/MSW, and LLM degrees.

Application Information *Required:* LSAT, LSDAS,
application form, application fee of $30, baccalaure-
ate degree, 2 letters of recommendation, essay,
resume. *Application deadline* for fall term is
March 1.

Financial Aid In 1997–98, 71% of all students
received some form of financial aid. Fellowships,
merit-based grants/scholarships, need-based
grants/scholarships, and federal work-study loans are
also available. To apply for financial assistance,
students must complete the Free Application for
Federal Student Aid and institutional forms.
Financial aid contact: University of Connecticut
School of Law, Student Finance Office, 55 Elizabeth
Street, Hartford, CT 06105. Phone: 860-570-5147.
Completed financial aid forms should be received by
March 1.

Law School Library has 15 professional staff
members and contains more than 458,434 volumes
and 6,342 periodicals. 388 seats are available in the

AT a GLANCE

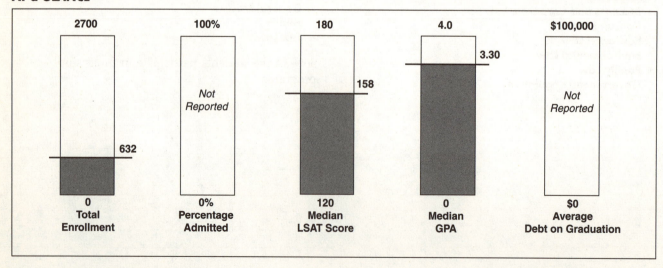

Degree Options

Degree	Total Credits Required	Length of Program
JD–Juris Doctor	86	
JD/MA–Juris Doctor/Master of Arts–Public Policy		
JD/MBA–Juris Doctor/Master of Business Administration		
JD/MLS–Juris Doctor/Master of Library Science		
JD/MPA–Juris Doctor/Master of Professional Accountancy		
JD/MPH–Juris Doctor/Master of Public Health		
JD/MSW–Juris Doctor/Master of Social Work		
LLM–Master of Laws–US Legal Studies		

library. When classes are in session, the library is open 92 hours per week.

WESTLAW and LEXIS-NEXIS are available, as are the World Wide Web and CD-ROM players. 46 computer workstations are available to students in the library.

First-Year Program Class size in the average section is 63.

Clinical Courses Students receive degree credit for clinical courses. (Clinical practicum is not required.) Among the clinical areas offered are:

Civil Litigation
Civil Rights
Criminal Defense
General Practice
Government Litigation
Health
Juvenile Law
Land Rights/Natural Resource
Mediation
Public Interest
Tax Law

Internships are available. International exchange programs permit students to visit France; Puerto Rico; and United Kingdom.

YALE UNIVERSITY
YALE LAW SCHOOL

New Haven, Connecticut

INFORMATION CONTACT
Anthony T. Kronman, Dean
127 Wall Stret
New Haven, CT 06520

Phone: 203-432-1660   Fax: 203-432-8147
E-mail: admissions@mail.law.yale.edu
Web site: http://www.yale.edu/lawweb/lawschool/
ylsfd.htm

LAW STUDENT PROFILE [1997–98]

FULL-TIME   Enrollment: 619
Women: 43%   Men: 57%

APPLICANTS and ADMITTEES
Number applied: 3,575
Admitted: 306
Percentage accepted: 9%
Seats available: 188
Median LSAT score: 172
Median GPA: 3.9

Yale University Yale Law School is a private institution that organizes classes on a semester calendar system. The campus is situated in an urban setting. Founded in 1824, first ABA approved in 1923, and an AALS member, Yale University Yale Law School offers JD, JD/MA, JD/MM, JSD, and LLM degrees.

Faculty consists of 68 full-time and 25 part-time members in 1997–98. 14 full-time faculty members and 7 part-time faculty members are women.

Application Information *Required:* LSAT, LSDAS, application form, application fee of $65, baccalaureate degree, 2 letters of recommendation, personal statement, writing sample. *Application deadline* for fall term is February 15.

Financial Aid Need-based grants/scholarships are available. To apply for financial assistance, students must complete the Free Application for Federal Student Aid and Need Access diskette. Financial aid contact: Zina Shaffer, Registrar and Director of Financial Aid, Office of Financial Aid, 451 College Street, New Haven, CT 06511. Phone: 203-432-1688. Fax: 203-432-8147. Completed financial aid forms should be received by March 15.

Law School Library Lillian Goldman Law Library has 18 professional staff members and contains

AT a GLANCE

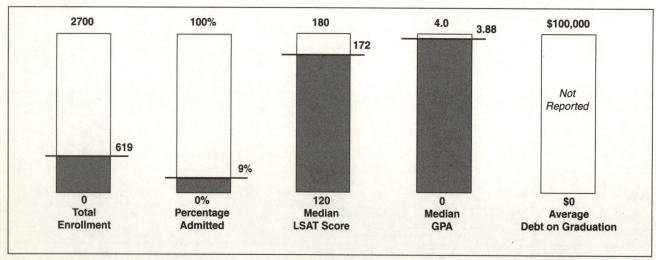

Degree Options

Degree	Total Credits Required	Length of Program
JD–Doctor of Laws	82	3 yrs, full-time only
JD/MA–Juris Doctor/Master of Arts–Joint-degree Program		4 yrs
JD/MM–Juris Doctor/Master of Management–Joint-degree Program		4 yrs, full-time only
JSD–Doctor of Juridical Science		
LLM–Master of Laws	106	4 yrs, full-time only

more than 978,538 volumes and 9,358 periodicals. 250 seats are available in the library. When classes are in session, the library is open 168 hours per week.

WESTLAW and LEXIS-NEXIS are available, as are the World Wide Web, online bibliographic services, and CD-ROM players. Special law collections include law and the social sciences, foreign and international law, rare books in English legal history.

First-Year Program Class size in the average section is 85.

Upper-Level Program Among the electives are:

Administrative Law
Advocacy
Business and Corporate Law
Consumer Law
Education Law
Entertainment Law
Environmental Law
Family Law
Government/Regulation
Health Care/Human Services
Indian/Tribal Law
Intellectual Property
International/Comparative Law
Jurisprudence

Labor Law
Land Use Law/Natural Resources
Lawyering Skills
Legal History/Philosophy
Litigation
Maritime Law
Media Law
Mediation
Probate Law
Public Interest
Securities
Tax Law

Clinical Courses Students receive degree credit for clinical courses. (Clinical practicum is not required.) Among the clinical areas offered are:

Civil Litigation
Civil Rights
Education
Elderly Advocacy
Environmental Law
General Practice
Health
Human Rights
Immigration
Juvenile Law
Nonprofit Organizations
Public Interest

WIDENER UNIVERSITY
SCHOOL OF LAW

Wilmington, Delaware

INFORMATION CONTACT

Dr. Arthur Frakt, Dean
4601 Concord Pike
PO Box 7474
Wilmington, DE 19803-0474

Phone: 302-477-2100   Fax: 302-477-2282
E-mail: barbara.l.ayars@law.widener.ed
Web site: http://www.widener.edu/law/law.html

LAW STUDENT PROFILE [1997–98]

FULL-TIME   Enrollment: 1,064
Women: 45%   Men: 55%

PART-TIME   Enrollment: 644
Women: 40%   Men: 60%

RACIAL or ETHNIC COMPOSITION
African American, 3%; Asian/Pacific Islander, 2%; Hispanic, 1%; Nataive American, 0.4%

APPLICANTS and ADMITTEES
Number applied: 1,064
Admitted: 1,423
Percentage accepted: 72%
Seats available: 386
Median LSAT score: 149
Median GPA: 3.0

Widener University School of Law is a private institution that organizes classes on a semester calendar system. The campus is situated in a suburban setting. Founded in 1971, first ABA approved in 1989, and an AALS member, Widener University School of Law offers a JD degree.

Faculty consists of 81 full-time and 83 part-time members in 1997–98. 34 full-time faculty members and 24 part-time faculty members are women. 100% of all faculty members have a JD; 26% have advanced law degrees. Of all faculty members, 7% are African American, 93% are white.

Application Information *Required:* LSAT, LSDAS, application form, application fee of $60, baccalaureate degree, college transcripts. *Recommended:* recommendations and personal statement. *Application deadline* for fall term is May 15.

Financial Aid Loans, loan repayment assistance program (LRAP), merit-based grants/scholarships, need-based grants/scholarships, and federal work-study loans are available. The average student debt at graduation is $55,276. To apply for financial assistance, students must complete the Free Application for Federal Student Aid and institutional forms. Financial aid contact: Anthony Doyle, Assistant Dean for Financial Aid, 4601 Concord Pike, PO Box 7474, Wilmington, DE 19803-0474. Phone: 302-477-

AT a GLANCE

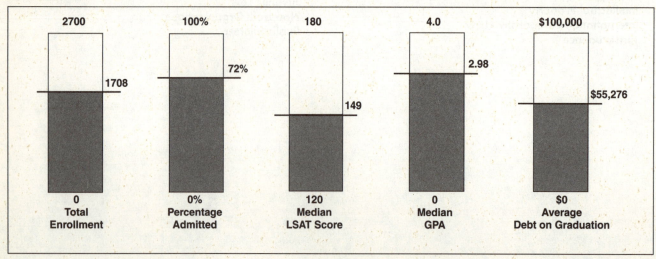

Total Enrollment	Percentage Admitted	Median LSAT Score	Median GPA	Average Debt on Graduation
2700	100%	180	4.0	$100,000
1708	72%	149	2.98	$55,276
0	0%	120	0	$0

Degree Options

Degree	Total Credits Required	Length of Program
JD–Juris Doctor	87	3–4 yrs, full-time or part-time [day, evening, summer]
JD/MBA–Juris Doctor/Master of Business Administration–Dual-degree Program	105	3–5 yrs, full-time or part-time [day, evening, summer]
JD/PsyD–Juris Doctor/Doctor of Psychology—Dual-degree Program	172	6 yrs, full-time only [day, evening, summer]
LLM–Master of Laws–Corporate Law and Finance	24	1 yr, full-time or part-time [day, evening, summer]
LLM–Master of Laws–Health Law	24	1 yr, full-time or part-time [day, evening, summer]

2272. Fax: 302-477-2224. Completed financial aid forms should be received by February 15.

Law School Library Widener University School of Law Legal Information Center has 10 professional staff members and contains more than 395,595 volumes and 1,805 periodicals. 461 seats are available in the library. When classes are in session, the library is open 107 hours per week.

WESTLAW and LEXIS-NEXIS are available, as are the World Wide Web, online bibliographic services, and CD-ROM players. 50 computer workstations are available to students in the library. Special law collections include Corporate Law, Health Law, U.S. Selective Depository for government documents.

First-Year Program Class size in the average section is 70; 100% of the first-year courses are taught by full-time faculty.

Upper-Level Program Class size in the average section is 50. Among the electives are:

Administrative Law
★ Advocacy
Business and Corporate Law
★ Children's Advocacy
★ Civil Law
Consumer Law
★ Criminal Law
★ Environmental Law

★ Family Law
Government/Regulation
★ Health Care/Human Services
Intellectual Property
International/Comparative Law
★ Judicial Externship
Jurisprudence
Labor Law
Land Use Law/Natural Resources
Lawyering Skills
Litigation
Maritime Law
Mediation
Probate Law
Public Interest
Securities
Tax Law
(★ indicates an area of special strength)

Clinical Courses Students receive degree credit for clinical courses. (Clinical practicum is not required.) Among the clinical areas offered are:

Civil Litigation
Criminal Defense
Criminal Prosecution
Environmental Law
General Practice
Juvenile Law

27% of the students participate in internship programs.

AMERICAN UNIVERSITY
WASHINGTON COLLEGE OF LAW

Washington, District of Columbia

INFORMATION CONTACT

Claudio Grossman, Dean
4801 Massachusetts Avenue, NW, Suite 366
Washington, DC 20016

Phone: 202-274-4004   Fax: 202-274-4130
Web site: http://www.wcl.american.edu/

LAW STUDENT PROFILE [1997–98]

FULL-TIME   Enrollment: 926
Women: 62%   Men: 38%

PART-TIME   Enrollment: 448
Women: 45%   Men: 55%

RACIAL or ETHNIC COMPOSITION
African American, 7%; Asian/Pacific Islander, 9%; Hispanic, 5%; Native American, 1%; International, 13%

APPLICANTS and ADMITTEES
Number applied: 4,796
Admitted: 2,126
Percentage accepted: 44%
Seats available: 370
Average LSAT score: 157
Average GPA: 3.3

American University Washington College of Law is a private institution that organizes classes on a semester calendar system. The campus is situated in an urban setting. Founded in 1896, first ABA approved in 1940, and an AALS member, American University Washington College of Law offers JD, JD/MA, JD/MBA, JD/MS, and LLM degrees.

Faculty consists of 51 full-time and 95 part-time members in 1997–98. 17 full-time faculty members and 27 part-time faculty members are women. 95% of all faculty members have a JD; 19% have advanced law degrees. Of all faculty members, .5% are Native American, 1% are Asian/Pacific Islander, 4.5% are African American, 1% are Hispanic, 93% are white.

Application Information *Required:* LSAT, LSDAS, application form, application fee of $55, baccalaureate degree, college transcripts. *Recommended:* 2 letters of recommendation, personal statement, resume.

Costs The 1997–98 tuition is $22,590 full-time; $837 per credit part-time. Fees: $382 full-time; $242 part-time.

Financial Aid Graduate assistantships, loans, loan repayment assistance program (LRAP), need-based grants/scholarships, and federal work-study loans are available. The average student debt at graduation is $66,000. To apply for financial assistance, students

AT a GLANCE

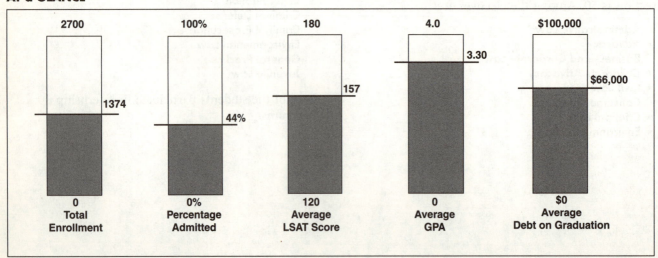

2700	100%	180	4.0	$100,000
1374	44%	157	3.30	$66,000
0	0%	120	0	$0
Total Enrollment	Percentage Admitted	Average LSAT Score	Average GPA	Average Debt on Graduation

Degree Options

Degree	Total Credits Required	Length of Program
JD–Doctor of Laws	86	3–4 yrs, full-time or part-time [day, evening, summer]
JD/MA–Juris Doctor/Master of Arts–Dual-degree Program in Law and International Affairs	101	3.5–4 yrs, full-time or part-time [day, evening, summer]
JD/MBA–Juris Doctor/Master of Business Administration–Dual-degree Program in Law and Business Administration	112	3.5–4 yrs, full-time or part-time [day, evening, summer]
JD/MS–Juris Doctor/Master of Science–Dual-degree Program–Law and Justice	107	3.5–4 yrs, full-time or part-time [day, evening, summer]
LLM–Master of Laws–International Legal Studies, Law and Government	24	1–1.5 yrs, full-time or part-time [day, evening, summer]

must complete the Free Application for Federal Student Aid and Need Access diskette. Financial aid contact: Barbara Williams, Director, 4801 Massachusetts Avenue, NW, Washington, DC 20016. Phone: 202-274-4040. Fax: 202-274-4130. E-mail: bwilli@wcl.american.edu. Completed financial aid forms should be received by February 15.

Law School Library Washington College of Law Library has 10 professional staff members and contains more than 412,309 volumes and 5,773 periodicals. 623 seats are available in the library. When classes are in session, the library is open 119 hours per week.

WESTLAW and LEXIS-NEXIS are available, as are the World Wide Web, online bibliographic services, and CD-ROM players. 52 computer workstations are available to students in the library. Special law collections include United States Archive, Baxter Collection in International Law, European Union Depository, Goodman Collection of Rare and Semi-rare Law Books, The National Bankruptcy Review Commission Archive.

First-Year Program Class size in the average section is 95; 90% of the first-year courses are taught by full-time faculty.

Upper-Level Program Among the electives are:

Administrative Law
Advocacy
★ Business and Corporate Law
Consumer Law
Criminal Law
Education Law
Entertainment Law
★ Environmental Law
Family Law

★ Gender and the Law
★ Government/Regulation
Health Care/Human Services
★ Human Rights
Indian/Tribal Law
Intellectual Property
★ International Environmental Law
★ International/Comparative Law
Jurisprudence
Labor Law
Land Use Law/Natural Resources
★ Lawyering Skills
Legal History/Philosophy
Litigation
Maritime Law
Media Law
Mediation
Probate Law
Public Interest
Securities
Tax Law

(★ indicates an area of special strength)

Clinical Courses Students receive degree credit for clinical courses. (Clinical practicum is not required.) Among the clinical areas offered are:

Appellate Litigation
Civil Litigation
Criminal Defense
Criminal Prosecution
Domestic Violence
Economic Development
General Practice
Immigration
International Law
Landlord/Tenant
Public Interest
Tax Law
Women and the Law

Internships are available. International exchange programs available.

THE CATHOLIC UNIVERSITY OF AMERICA
COLUMBUS SCHOOL OF LAW

Washington, District of Columbia

INFORMATION CONTACT
Bernard Dobranski, Dean
Cardinal Station Post Office
Washington, DC 20064

Phone: 202-319-5144   Fax: 202-319-4498
E-mail: braxton@law.cua.edu
Web site: http://law.edu/

LAW STUDENT PROFILE [1997–98]

FULL-TIME	Enrollment: 659
Women: 50%	Men: 50%
PART-TIME	Enrollment: 282
Women: 43%	Men: 57%

RACIAL or ETHNIC COMPOSITION
African American, 11%; Asian/Pacific Islander, 4%; Hispanic, 2%; International, 1%

APPLICANTS and ADMITTEES
Number applied: 2,161
Admitted: 1,080
Percentage accepted: 50%
Seats available: 300
Average LSAT score: 155
Average GPA: 3.2

The Catholic University of America Columbus School of Law is a private institution that organizes classes on a semester calendar system. The campus is situated in an urban setting. Founded in 1898, first ABA approved in 1925, and an AALS member, The Catholic University of America Columbus School of Law offers a JD degree.

Faculty consists of 50 full-time and 80 part-time members in 1997–98. 15 full-time faculty members and 19 part-time faculty members are women. 100% of all faculty members have a JD; 20% have advanced law degrees. Of all faculty members, 10% are African American, 2% are Hispanic, 83% are white, 5% are international.

Application Information *Required:* LSAT, LSDAS, application form, application fee of $55, baccalaureate degree, 2 letters of recommendation, college transcripts. *Recommended:* personal statement and resume. *Application deadline* for fall term is March 1.

Financial Aid Fellowships, loans, merit-based grants/scholarships, need-based grants/scholarships, and federal work-study loans are available. The average student debt at graduation is $75,000. To apply for financial assistance, students must complete the Free Application for Federal Student Aid and institutional forms. Financial aid contact:

AT a GLANCE

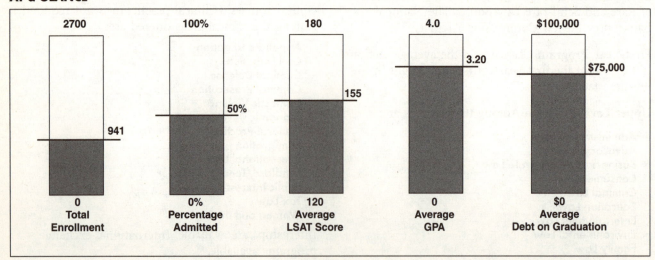

	Total Enrollment	Percentage Admitted	Average LSAT Score	Average GPA	Average Debt on Graduation
top	2700	100%	180	4.0	$100,000
value	941	50%	155	3.20	$75,000
bottom	0	0%	120	0	$0

Degree Options

Degree	Total Credits Required	Length of Program
JD–Juris Doctor	86	3–4 yrs, full-time or part-time [day, evening]

Gretchen Bonfardine, Director of Financial Aid, CUA-CSL, Cardinal Station, Washington, DC 20064. Phone: 202-319-5143. Fax: 202-319-4498. E-mail: bonfardine@law.edu. Completed financial aid forms should be received by March 1.

Law School Library Kathryn Dufour Law Library has 8 professional staff members and contains more than 275,000 volumes and 5,378 periodicals. 502 seats are available in the library. When classes are in session, the library is open 120 hours per week.

WESTLAW and LEXIS-NEXIS are available, as are the World Wide Web, online bibliographic services, and CD-ROM players. 40 computer workstations are available to students in the library.

First-Year Program Class size in the average section is 50; 100% of the first-year courses are taught by full-time faculty.

Upper-Level Program Class size in the average section is 50. Among the electives are:

* ★ Administrative Law
* ★ Advocacy
* ★ Business and Corporate Law
* Consumer Law
* Education Law
* Entertainment Law
* Environmental Law
* Family Law
* ★ Government/Regulation
* Health Care/Human Services

* Indian/Tribal Law
* Intellectual Property
* ★ International/Comparative Law
* Jurisprudence
* Labor Law
* Land Use Law/Natural Resources
* ★ Lawyering Skills
* ★ Legal History/Philosophy
* ★ Litigation
* Maritime Law
* Media Law
* Mediation
* Probate Law
* Public Interest
* ★ Securities

(★ indicates an area of special strength)

Clinical Courses Students receive degree credit for clinical courses. (Clinical practicum is not required.) Among the clinical areas offered are:

* Civil Litigation
* Criminal Defense
* Criminal Prosecution
* Elderly Advocacy
* General Practice
* Government Litigation
* Juvenile Law

20% of the students participate in internship programs. International exchange programs permit students to visit Poland.

GEORGETOWN UNIVERSITY
LAW CENTER

Washington, District of Columbia

LAW STUDENT PROFILE [1997–98]

FULL-TIME	Enrollment: 2,212
Women: 45%	Men: 55%
PART-TIME	Enrollment: 487
Women: 41%	Men: 59%

RACIAL or ETHNIC COMPOSITION
African American, 9%; Asian/Pacific Islander, 8%; Hispanic, 5%; Native American, 1%; International, 6%

APPLICANTS and ADMITTEES
Seats available: 634
Median LSAT score: 166
Median GPA: 3.5

Georgetown University Law Center is a private institution that organizes classes on a semester calendar system. The campus is situated in an urban setting. First ABA approved in 1924, and an AALS member, Georgetown University Law Center offers JD, JD/MA, JD/MBA, JD/MPH, JD/MS, JD/PhD, and LLM degrees.

Faculty consists of 92 full-time and 28 part-time members in 1997–98. 30 full-time faculty members and 4 part-time faculty members are women.

Application Information *Required:* LSAT, application form, application fee of $65, baccalaureate degree, recommendations, LSDAS. *Application deadline* for fall term is February 1.

Costs The 1997–98 tuition is $24,530 full-time; $855 per credit part-time. Fees: $99 (one-time charge).

Financial Aid In 1997–98, 55% of all students received some form of financial aid. 25 fellowships, totaling $39,000, were awarded. Loans, need-based grants/scholarships, and federal work-study loans are also available. To apply for financial assistance, students must complete the Free Application for Federal Student Aid and Need Access diskette. Financial aid contact: Georgetown University Law Center, Financial Aid Office, 600 New Jersey Avenue, NW, Washington, DC 20001. Phone: 202-662-9210. E-mail: finaid@law.

AT a GLANCE

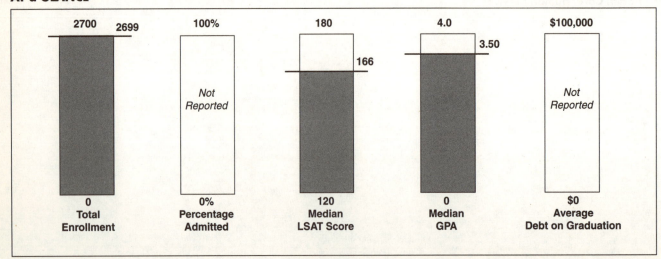

Degree Options

Degree	Total Credits Required	Length of Program
JD–Juris Doctor		full-time or part-time [day, evening, summer]
JD/MA–Juris Doctor/Master of Arts–Philosophy, Government Joint-degree Programs	98	
JD/MBA–Juris Doctor/Master of Business Administration–Joint-degree Program	122	4 yrs, full-time only [day]
JD/MPH–Juris Doctor/Master of Public Health–Joint-degree Program		4 yrs, full-time only [day]
JD/MS–Juris Doctor/Master of Science–Foreign Service Joint-degree Program	113	4 yrs, full-time only [day]
JD/PhD–Juris Doctor/Doctor of Philosophy–Government Joint-degree Program	110–119	
LLM–Master of Laws–Taxation, Securities and Financial Regulation, Labor and Employment Law, International and Comparative Law	24	1–3 yrs, full-time or part-time [day, evening]
LLM–Master of Laws–Common Law Studies	20	1–3 yrs, full-time only [day, summer]

georgetown.edu. Completed financial aid forms should be received by March 1.

Law School Library E. B. Williams Law Library has 22 professional staff members and contains more than 892,428 volumes and 12,430 periodicals. 1,260 seats are available in the library. When classes are in session, the library is open 107 hours per week.

WESTLAW and LEXIS-NEXIS are available, as are the World Wide Web and CD-ROM players. Special law collections include International and Foreign Law Collection.

First-Year Program Class size in the average section is 125.

Upper-Level Program Among the electives are:

Accounting
Administrative Law
Advocacy
Aviation Law
Bankruptcy
Business and Corporate Law
Canon Law
Church-State
Civil Procedure
Civil Rights
Conflict of Laws
Constitutional Law
Criminal Procedure
Entertainment Law
Environmental Law
Evidence
Family Law
Government/Regulation
Health Care/Human Services

Immigration
Insurance
Intellectual Property
International/Comparative Law
Jurisprudence
Labor Law
Land Use Law/Natural Resources
Lawyering Skills
Legal History/Philosophy
Litigation
Maritime Law
Media Law
Mediation
Probate Law
Public Interest
Securities
Sports Law
Tax Law
Water Law

Clinical Courses Among the clinical areas offered are:

Appellate Litigation
Civil Litigation
Civil Rights
Criminal Defense
Environmental Law
Fair Housing
Family Practice
General Practice
Government Litigation
Health
Immigration
Juvenile Law
Legislation
Public Interest

Internships are available.

THE GEORGE WASHINGTON UNIVERSITY
LAW SCHOOL

Washington, District of Columbia

INFORMATION CONTACT
Michael Young, Dean
2000 H Street, NW
Washington, DC 20052

Phone: 202-994-6288   Fax: 202-994-5157
Web site: http://www.law.gwu.edu/

LAW STUDENT PROFILE [1997–98]

FULL-TIME   Enrollment: 1,384
Women: 44%   Men: 56%

PART-TIME   Enrollment: 363
Women: 38%   Men: 62%

RACIAL or ETHNIC COMPOSITION
African American, 11%; Asian/Pacific Islander, 8%; Hispanic, 6%; Native American, 1%; International, 2%

APPLICANTS and ADMITTEES
Number applied: 7,011
Seats available: 436
Average LSAT score: 162
Average GPA: 3.4

The George Washington University Law School is a private institution that organizes classes on a semester calendar system. The campus is situated in an urban setting. Founded in 1865, first ABA approved in 1925, and an AALS member, The George Washington University Law School offers JD, JD/MA, JD/MBA, JD/MPAd, JD/MPH, JSD, LLM, and LLM/MPH degrees.

Faculty consists of 65 full-time and 184 part-time members in 1997–98. 17 full-time faculty members and 57 part-time faculty members are women. 100% of all faculty members have a JD; 18% have advanced law degrees. Of all faculty members, 2% are Asian/Pacific Islander, 5.5% are African American, 1.5% are Hispanic, 91% are white.

Application Information *Required:* LSAT, LSDAS, application form, application fee of $55, baccalaureate degree, personal statement, writing sample, college transcripts. *Recommended:* recommendations and resume. *Application deadline* for fall term is March 1.

Financial Aid In 1997–98, 35% of all students received some form of financial aid. Graduate assistantships, loans, loan repayment assistance program (LRAP), merit-based grants/scholarships, need-based grants/scholarships, and federal work-study loans are also available. The average student debt at graduation is $68,500. To apply for financial assistance, students must complete the Free Application for Federal Student Aid, institutional forms,

AT a GLANCE

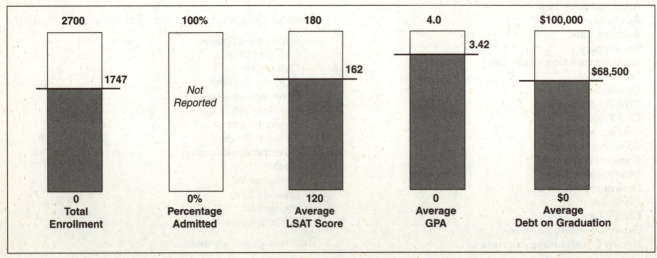

Total Enrollment	Percentage Admitted	Average LSAT Score	Average GPA	Average Debt on Graduation
2700	100%	180	4.0	$100,000
1747	Not Reported	162	3.42	$68,500
0	0%	120	0	$0

Degree Options

Degree	Total Credits Required	Length of Program
JD–Doctor of Laws	84	3–4 yrs, full-time or part-time [day, evening, summer]
JD/MA–Juris Doctor/Master of Arts–Majors include: Int'l Affairs; Science, Technology & Public Policy; Security Policy Studies; East Asian Studies; Latin American Studies; Russian & East European Studies; European Studies; Int'l Development Studies; Int'l Trade & Investment Policy; History	96	4 yrs, full-time or part-time [day, evening, summer]
JD/MBA–Juris Doctor/Master of Business Administration, JD/MPAd–Juris Doctor/Master of Public Administration, JD/MPH–Juris Doctor/Master of Public Health–Joint Degrees	96	4 yrs, full-time or part-time [day, evening, summer]
JSD–Doctor of Juridical Science	8	3 yrs, full-time or part-time [day, evening, summer]
LLM–Master of Laws	24	1–2 yrs, full-time or part-time [day, evening, summer]
LLM/MPH–Master of Laws/Master in Public Health–Joint-degree Program		4 yrs, full-time or part-time [day, evening, summer]

and CSS PROFILE form. Financial aid contact: Nancy LaMotta, Financial Aid Director, 2003 G Street, N.W., Room 102, Washington, DC 20052. Phone: 202-994-6592. Fax: 202-994-5157. Completed financial aid forms should be received by March 1.

Law School Library Jacob Burns Law Library has 16 professional staff members and contains more than 500,013 volumes and 5,031 periodicals. 797 seats are available in the library. When classes are in session, the library is open 110 hours per week.

WESTLAW and LEXIS-NEXIS are available, as are the World Wide Web, online bibliographic services, and CD-ROM players. 80 computer workstations are available to students in the library. Special law collections include Intellectual Property, Environmental Law, International Law.

First-Year Program Class size in the average section is 90; 100% of the first-year courses are taught by full-time faculty.

Upper-Level Program Class size in the average section is 36. Among the electives are:

* ★ Administrative Law
* ★ Advocacy
* ★ Business and Corporate Law
* ★ Consumer Law
* Education Law
* Entertainment Law
* ★ Environmental Law
* ★ Family Law
* ★ Government Procurement
* ★ Government/Regulation
* ★ Health Care/Human Services
* ★ Immigration

* Indian/Tribal Law
* ★ Intellectual Property
* ★ International/Comparative Law
* Jurisprudence
* Labor Law
* Land Use Law/Natural Resources
* ★ Lawyering Skills
* ★ Legal History/Philosophy
* ★ Litigation
* Maritime Law
* Media Law
* ★ Mediation
* ★ Prisoners' Rights
* Probate Law
* ★ Public Interest
* Securities
* Tax Law

(★ indicates an area of special strength)

Clinical Courses Students receive degree credit for clinical courses. (Clinical practicum is required.) Among the clinical areas offered are:

* Civil Litigation
* Corporate Law
* Criminal Defense
* Elderly Advocacy
* Environmental Law
* Family Practice
* General Practice
* Government Litigation
* Health
* Immigration
* Juvenile Law
* Mediation
* Public Interest

42% of the students participate in internship programs.

HOWARD UNIVERSITY
SCHOOL OF LAW

Washington, District of Columbia

INFORMATION CONTACT
Alice Gresham Bullock, Dean
2900 Van Ness Street, NW
Holy Cross Hall, Room 200
Washington, DC 20008

Phone: 202-806-8000   Fax: 202-806-8162
Web site: http://www.law.howard.edu/

LAW STUDENT PROFILE [1997–98]

FULL-TIME   Enrollment: 434
Women: 53%   Men: 47%

RACIAL or ETHNIC COMPOSITION
African American, 83%; Asian/Pacific Islander, 3%; Hispanic, 3%; Nataive American, 0.2%; International, 3%

Howard University School of Law is a private institution that organizes classes on a semester calendar system. The campus is situated in an urban setting. Founded in 1869, first ABA approved in 1931, and an AALS member, Howard University School of Law offers JD, JD/MBA, and LLM degrees.

Faculty consists of 28 full-time and 13 part-time members in 1997–98. 9 full-time faculty members and 5 part-time faculty members are women. 100% of all faculty members have a JD; 8% have advanced law degrees. Of all faculty members, 4% are Asian/Pacific Islander, 76% are African American, 20% are white.

Application Information *Required:* LSAT, LSDAS, application form, application fee of $60, baccalaureate degree, minimum 3.0 GPA, 2 letters of recommendation, personal statement, college transcripts. *Application deadline* for fall term is April 30.

Financial Aid In 1997–98, 83% of all students received some form of financial aid. 228 other awards were given. Loans, merit-based grants/scholarships, need-based grants/scholarships, and federal work-study loans are also available. The average student debt at graduation is $45,000. To apply for financial assistance, students must complete the Free Application for Federal Student Aid, institutional forms, and Financial Aid Tran-

AT a GLANCE

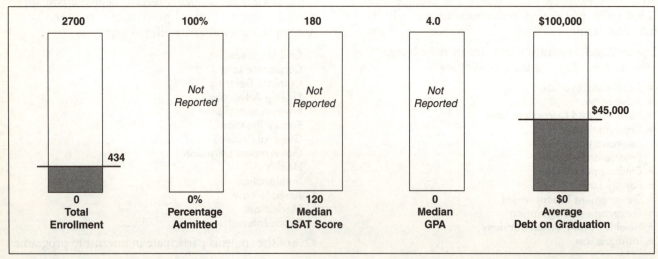

Degree Options

Degree	Total Credits Required	Length of Program
JD–Juris Doctor	88	3 yrs, full-time only [day]
JD/MBA–Juris Doctor/Master of Business Administration		4–5 yrs, full-time only
LLM–Master of Laws	24	1 yr, full-time only [day]

scripts, Need Access diskette. Financial aid contact: James Marks, Financial Aid Officer, 2900 Van Ness Street, NW, Washington, DC 20008. Phone: 202-806-8005. Fax: 202-806-8162. Completed financial aid forms should be received by April 30.

Law School Library Allen Mercer Daniel Law Library has 9 professional staff members and contains more than 280,000 volumes and 3,000 periodicals. 173 seats are available in the library. When classes are in session, the library is open 93 hours per week.

WESTLAW and LEXIS-NEXIS are available. 37 computer workstations are available to students in the library. Special law collections include South Africa laws, the Phineas Indritz Papers.

First-Year Program Class size in the average section is 50; 100% of the first-year courses are taught by full-time faculty.

Upper-Level Program Class size in the average section is 35. Among the electives are:

Administrative Law
Advocacy
Business and Corporate Law
Church-State
Civil Rights
Consumer Law
Election Law
Entertainment Law

Environmental Law
Family Law
Government/Regulation
Intellectual Property
International/Comparative Law
Jurisprudence
Labor Law
Land Use Law/Natural Resources
Law and Medicine
Lawyering Skills
Legal History/Philosophy
Litigation
Media Law
Mediation
Municipal Law
Probate Law
Public Ethics
Public Interest
Securities

Clinical Courses Students receive degree credit for clinical courses. (Clinical practicum is not required.) Among the clinical areas offered are:

Civil Litigation
Criminal Defense
Elderly Advocacy
Immigration
Small Business Counseling

10% of the students participate in internship programs.

UNIVERSITY OF THE DISTRICT OF COLUMBIA
SCHOOL OF LAW

Washington, District of Columbia

LAW STUDENT PROFILE [1997–98]

FULL-TIME   Enrollment: 172
Women, 53%;   Men, 47%;

RACIAL or ETHNIC COMPOSITION
African American, 62%; Asian/Pacific Islander, 6%; Hispanic,
5%; Native American, 1%

APPLICANTS and ADMITTEES
Number applied: 330
Admitted: 143
Percentage accepted: 43%
Seats available: 100
Average LSAT score: 147
Average GPA: 2.8

**University of the District of Columbia School of
Law** is a public institution. The campus is situated
in an urban setting. Founded in 1988, first ABA
approved in 1991, University of the District of
Columbia School of Law offers a JD degree.

Faculty consists of 20 full-time and 9 part-time
members in 1997–98. 10 full-time faculty members
and 3 part-time faculty members are women. 100%
of all faculty members have a JD; 10% have
advanced law degrees. Of all faculty members, 30%
are African American, 70% are white.

Application Information *Required:* LSAT, LSDAS,
application form, application fee of $35, baccalaure-
ate degree, 2 letters of recommendation, essay,
minimum 2.3 GPA. *Recommended:* personal
statement. *Application deadline* for fall term is
April 1. Students are required to have their own
computers.

Costs The 1997–98 tuition is $7000 for District
residents. Tuition is $14,000 for nonresidents. Fees:
$135.

Financial Aid In 1997–98, 97% of all students
received some form of financial aid. Loans, merit-
based grants/scholarships, need-based grants/

AT a GLANCE

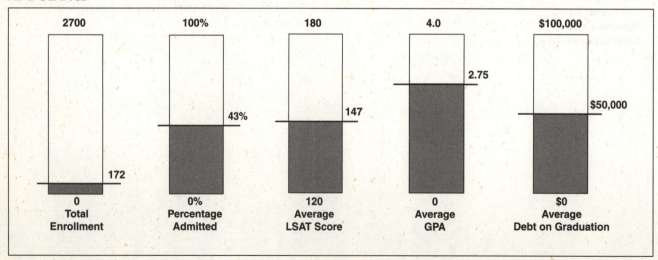

Degree Options		
Degree	**Total Credits Required**	**Length of Program**
JD–Doctor of Laws	90	3 yrs, full-time only [day]

scholarships, and federal work-study loans are also available. The average student debt at graduation is $50,000. To apply for financial assistance, students must complete the Free Application for Federal Student Aid, scholarship specific applications, and Need Access diskette. Financial aid contact: Anne El Shazli, Financial Aid Officer, 4200 Connecticut Avenue, NW, Washington, DC 20008. Phone: 202-274-7337. Fax: 202-274-5583. Completed financial aid forms should be received by May 1.

Law School Library UDC School of Law Library has 4 professional staff members and contains more than 172,104 volumes and 2,486 periodicals. 105 seats are available in the library. When classes are in session, the library is open 104 hours per week.

WESTLAW and LEXIS-NEXIS are available, as are the World Wide Web, online bibliographic services, and CD-ROM players. 10 computer workstations are available to students in the library.

First-Year Program Class size in the average section is 50; 100% of the first-year courses are taught by full-time faculty.

Upper-Level Program Class size in the average section is 25. Among the electives are:

  Administrative Law
★ Advocacy
★ AIDS and the Law
  Business and Corporate Law
★ Consumer Law
  Education Law

  Environmental Law
  Family Law
★ Government/Regulation
  Health Care/Human Services
★ Housing Law
  International/Comparative Law
  Jurisprudence
★ Juvenile Law
  Labor Law
★ Lawyering Skills
★ Legislation
★ Litigation
★ Public Benefits
★ Public Interest
  Race and Law
  Securities

(★ *indicates an area of special strength*)

Clinical Courses Students receive degree credit for clinical courses. 14 credit hours of clinical practicum are required. Among the clinical areas offered are:

  AIDS and the Law
  Civil Litigation
  Consumer Law
  Education
  Family Practice
  Housing Law
  Juvenile Law
  Legislation
  Public Benefits

10% of the students participate in internship programs.

FLORIDA STATE UNIVERSITY
COLLEGE OF LAW

Tallahassee, Florida

INFORMATION CONTACT
Paul A. Lebel, Dean
425 West Jefferson Street
Tallahassee, FL 32306-1601

Phone: 850-644-3400   Fax: 850-644-5487
E-mail: admissions@law.fsu.edu
Web site: http://www.law.fsu.edu/

LAW STUDENT PROFILE [1997–98]

FULL-TIME   Enrollment: 638
Women: 43%   Men: 57%

PART-TIME   Enrollment: 2
Women: 50%   Men: 50%

RACIAL or ETHNIC COMPOSITION
African American, 12%; Asian/Pacific Islander, 2%; Hispanic,
10%; Native American, 1%; International, 1%

APPLICANTS and ADMITTEES
Number applied: 1,896
Admitted: 643
Percentage accepted: 34%
Seats available: 220
Average LSAT score: 156
Average GPA: 3.3

Florida State University College of Law is a public institution that organizes classes on a semester calendar system. The campus is situated in an urban setting. Founded in 1966, first ABA approved in 1970, and an AALS member, Florida State University College of Law offers JD, JD/MBA, JD/MEc, JD/MPAd, JD/MPIA, JD/MSW, and JD/MURP degrees.

Faculty consists of 43 full-time and 12 part-time members in 1997–98. 15 full-time faculty members and 4 part-time faculty members are women. 100% of all faculty members have a JD; 11% have advanced law degrees. Of all faculty members, 1% are Native American, 9% are African American, 3% are Hispanic, 87% are white.

Application Information *Required:* LSAT, LSDAS, application form, application fee of $20, baccalaureate degree, 2 letters of recommendation, personal statement, college transcripts. *Application deadline for fall term is February 15.*

Financial Aid In 1997–98, 23% of all students received some form of financial aid. 148 fellowships, totaling $742,581; 35 research assistantships, totaling $100,800; 16 teaching assistantships, totaling $30,720, were awarded. Fellowships, graduate assistantships, loans, merit-based grants/scholarships, and need-based grants/scholarships are also avail-

AT a GLANCE

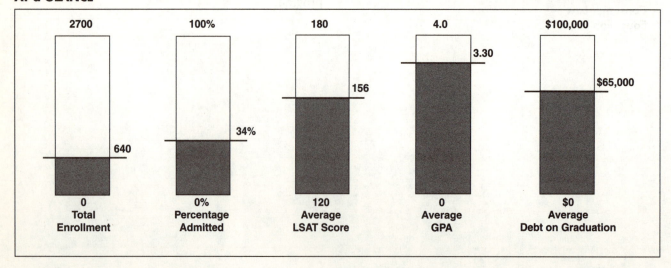

Degree Options

Degree	Total Credits Required	Length of Program
JD–Juris Doctor–Law	88	3 yrs, full-time only [day]
JD/MBA–Juris Doctor/Master of Business Administration–Joint-degree Program	107	4 yrs, full-time only [day]
JD/MEc–Juris Doctor/Master of Economics–Joint-degree Program	104	4 yrs, full-time only
JD/MPAd–Juris Doctor/Master of Public Administration–Joint-degree Program	112	4 yrs, full-time only [day]
JD/MPIA–Juris Doctor/Master of Public and International Affairs–Joint-degree Program	104	4 yrs, full-time only [day]
JD/MSW–Juris Doctor/Master of Social Work–Joint-degree Program	133	4 yrs, full-time only [day]
JD/MURP–Juris Doctor/Masters of Urban and Regional Planning–Joint-degree Program	111	4 yrs, full-time only [day]

able. The average student debt at graduation is $65,000. To apply for financial assistance, students must complete the Free Application for Federal Student Aid and scholarship specific applications. Financial aid contact: JoAnne Clark, Coordinator for Law Student Financial Aid, Office of Financial Aid, University Center A4423, Tallahassee, FL 32306-2430. Phone: 850-644-5716. Fax: 850-644-5487. E-mail: jclark@admin.fsu.edu. Completed financial aid forms should be received by April 1.

Law School Library FSU College of Law Library has 9 professional staff members and contains more than 394,144 volumes and 5,711 periodicals. 429 seats are available in the library. When classes are in session, the library is open 93 hours per week.

WESTLAW and LEXIS-NEXIS are available, as are the World Wide Web, online bibliographic services, and CD-ROM players. 50 computer workstations are available to students in the library. Special law collections include Commonwealth Caribbean Law Materials.

First-Year Program Class size in the average section is 70; 100% of the first-year courses are taught by full-time faculty.

Upper-Level Program Class size in the average section is 28. Among the electives are:

Administrative Law
★ Advocacy
Business and Corporate Law
Consumer Law
Education Law
Entertainment Law
★ Environmental Law
Family Law
Health Care/Human Services
Intellectual Property
★ International/Comparative Law
Jurisprudence
Labor Law
Land Use Law/Natural Resources
Legal History/Philosophy
Litigation
Maritime Law
Media Law
Mediation
Securities
Tax Law

(★ indicates an area of special strength)

Clinical Courses Students receive degree credit for clinical courses. (Clinical practicum is not required.) Among the clinical areas offered are:

Civil Litigation
Civil Rights
Criminal Defense
Domestic Violence
Education
Family Practice
Juvenile Law
Public Interest

60% of the students participate in internship programs. International exchange programs permit students to visit Barbados; Czech Republic; Netherlands; and United Kingdom.

NOVA SOUTHEASTERN UNIVERSITY
SHEPARD BROAD LAW CENTER

Fort Lauderdale, Florida

INFORMATION CONTACT

Joseph D. Harbaugh, Dean
3305 College Avenue
Ft. Lauderdale, FL 33314

Phone: 954-262-6101   Fax: 954-262-3844
E-mail: sanguinin@nsu.law.nova.edu
Web site: http://www.nsulaw.nova.edu/

LAW STUDENT PROFILE [1997–98]

FULL-TIME   Enrollment: 780
Women: 41%   Men: 59%

PART-TIME   Enrollment: 140
Women: 41%   Men: 59%

RACIAL or ETHNIC COMPOSITION

African American, 6%; Asian/Pacific Islander, 1%; Hispanic, 11%; Nataive American, 0.4%; International, 2%

APPLICANTS and ADMITTEES

Number applied: 1,448
Admitted: 797
Percentage accepted: 55%
Seats available: 320
Average LSAT score: 147
Average GPA: 2.9

Nova Southeastern University Shepard Broad Law Center is a private institution that organizes classes on a semester calendar system. The campus is situated in a suburban setting. Founded in 1974, first ABA approved in 1975, and an AALS member, Nova Southeastern University Shepard Broad Law Center offers JD, JD/MBA, JD/MS, and JD/MUP degrees.

Faculty consists of 43 full-time and 45 part-time members in 1997–98. 15 full-time faculty members and 12 part-time faculty members are women. 100% of all faculty members have a JD; 50% have advanced law degrees. Of all faculty members, 2.5% are Asian/Pacific Islander, 5% are African American, 10% are Hispanic, 82.5% are white.

Application Information *Required:* LSAT, LSDAS, application form, application fee of $50, baccalaureate degree, personal statement, essay, college transcripts. *Application deadline* for fall term is March 1. Students are required to have their own computers.

Costs The 1997–98 tuition is $19,710 full-time; $14,780 part-time.

Financial Aid In 1997–98, 22% of all students received some form of financial aid. 182 fellowships, 40 research assistantships, 13 teaching assistantships

AT a GLANCE

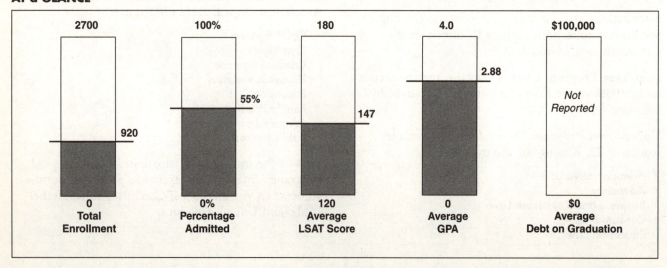

Total Enrollment	Percentage Admitted	Average LSAT Score	Average GPA	Average Debt on Graduation
2700	100%	180	4.0	$100,000
920	55%	147	2.88	Not Reported
0	0%	120	0	$0

Degree Options

Degree	Total Credits Required	Length of Program
JD–Doctor of Laws	90	3–4 yrs, full-time or part-time [day, evening]
JD/MBA–Juris Doctor/Master of Business Administration–Dual Degree		4–5 yrs, full-time only [day, evening, weekend]
JD/MS–Juris Doctor/Master of Science–Psychology Dual Degree		4–5 yrs, full-time only [day, evening, weekend]
JD/MS–Juris Doctor/Master of Science–Dispute Resolution Dual-degree		4–5 yrs, full-time only [day, evening, weekend]
JD/MUP–Juris Doctor/Masters of Urban Planning–Dual Degree		4–5 yrs, full-time only [day, evening, weekend]

were awarded. 35 other awards were given. Completed financial aid forms should be received by April 1.

Law School Library Law Library and Technology Center has 11 professional staff members and contains more than 294,698 volumes. 559 seats are available in the library. When classes are in session, the library is open 105 hours per week.

WESTLAW and LEXIS-NEXIS are available, as are the World Wide Web, online bibliographic services, and CD-ROM players. 56 computer workstations are available to students in the library. Special law collections include UN Depository, depository for state and federal documents.

First-Year Program Class size in the average section is 62; 100% of the first-year courses are taught by full-time faculty.

Upper-Level Program Class size in the average section is 30. Among the electives are:

Administrative Law
★ Advocacy
★ Business and Corporate Law
Consumer Law
Education Law
Entertainment Law
★ Environmental Law
★ Family Law
Government/Regulation

Health Care/Human Services
Intellectual Property
★ International/Comparative Law
Jurisprudence
Labor Law
★ Land Use Law/Natural Resources
★ Lawyering Skills
Legal History/Philosophy
★ Litigation
Maritime Law
Media Law
★ Mediation
Probate Law
★ Public Interest
Securities
Tax Law
(★ indicates an area of special strength)

Clinical Courses Students receive degree credit for clinical courses. (Clinical practicum is not required.) Among the clinical areas offered are:

Civil Litigation
Corporate Law
Criminal Defense
Criminal Prosecution
Environmental Law
Family Practice
International Law
Mediation
Public Interest

Internships are available.

ST. THOMAS UNIVERSITY
SCHOOL OF LAW

Miami, Florida

LAW STUDENT PROFILE [1997–98]

FULL-TIME   Enrollment: 531
Women: 39%   Men: 61%

RACIAL or ETHNIC COMPOSITION

African American, 11%; Asian/Pacific Islander, 2%; Hispanic, 21%

APPLICANTS and ADMITTEES

Seats available: 191
Average LSAT score: 150
Average GPA: 2.8

St. Thomas University School of Law is a public institution that organizes classes on a semester calendar system. The campus is situated in an urban setting. Founded in 1984, first ABA approved in 1995, St. Thomas University School of Law offers a JD degree.

Faculty consists of 23 full-time and 34 part-time members in 1997–98. 100% of all faculty members have a JD; 30% have advanced law degrees. Of all faculty members, 20% are African American, 10% are Hispanic, 70% are white.

Application Information *Required:* LSAT, LSDAS, application form, application fee of $40, baccalaureate degree, recommendations, personal statement, college transcripts. *Application deadline* for fall term is July 1.

Costs The 1997–98 tuition is $19,144. Fees: $830.

Financial Aid Fellowships, graduate assistantships, loans, merit-based grants/scholarships, and federal work-study loans are available. The average student debt at graduation is $79,500. To apply for financial assistance, students must complete the Free Application for Federal Student Aid and institutional forms. Financial aid contact: Andres Marrero, Financial Aid Counselor, 16400 NW 32 Avenue, Miami, FL 33054. Phone: 305-628-6547. Fax: 305-623-2397. E-mail:

AT a GLANCE

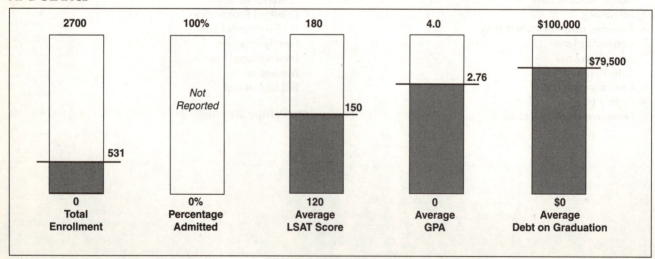

Degree Options		
Degree	**Total Credits Required**	**Length of Program**
JD–Doctor of Laws	90	3 yrs, full-time only [day, summer]

amarrero@stu.edu. Completed financial aid forms should be received by May 1.

Law School Library St. Thomas University School of Law Library has 6 professional staff members and contains more than 276,621 volumes and 1,050 periodicals. 308 seats are available in the library. When classes are in session, the library is open 105 hours per week.

WESTLAW and LEXIS-NEXIS are available, as are the World Wide Web and online bibliographic services. 50 computer workstations are available to students in the library. Special law collections include Native Americans, Canon Law, Supreme Court Records and Briefs 1897–present.

First-Year Program Class size in the average section is 61; 100% of the first-year courses are taught by full-time faculty.

Upper-Level Program Class size in the average section is 35. Among the electives are:

Administrative Law
Advocacy
Banking and Financial Aid
Bankruptcy
Business and Corporate Law
Consumer Law
Employment Law
Entertainment Law
Environmental Law
Family Law
Federal Courts
Government/Regulation
Health Care/Human Services
Intellectual Property
International/Comparative Law
Jurisprudence
Juvenile Law
Labor Law
Land Use Law/Natural Resources
Lawyering Skills
Legal History/Philosophy
Litigation
Maritime Law
Media Law
Mediation
Probate Law
Product Liability
Securities
Tax Law

Clinical Courses Students receive degree credit for clinical courses. (Clinical practicum is not required.) Among the clinical areas offered are:

Civil Litigation
Criminal Defense
Criminal Prosecution
Family Practice
Immigration

14% of the students participate in internship programs.

STETSON UNIVERSITY
COLLEGE OF LAW

DeLand, Florida

INFORMATION CONTACT
Lizabeth A. Moody, Dean
1401 61st Street South
St. Petersburg, FL 33707

Phone: 813-562-7809   Fax: 727-347-3738
E-mail: lawadmit@hermes.law.stetson.ed
Web site: http://www.law.stetson.edu/

LAW STUDENT PROFILE [1997–98]

FULL-TIME   Enrollment: 629
Women: 52%   Men: 48%

PART-TIME   Enrollment: 16
Women: 63%   Men: 38%

RACIAL or ETHNIC COMPOSITION
African American, 7%; Asian/Pacific Islander, 2%; Hispanic, 9%; Native American, 1%

APPLICANTS and ADMITTEES
Seats available: 120
Average LSAT score: 154
Average GPA: 3.3

Stetson University College of Law is a private institution that organizes classes on a semester calendar system. The campus is situated in a suburban setting. Founded in 1900, first ABA approved in 1930, and an AALS member, Stetson University College of Law offers JD, JD/MBA, and LLM degrees.

Faculty consists of 36 full-time and 42 part-time members in 1997–98. 12 full-time faculty members and 6 part-time faculty members are women. 100% of all faculty members have a JD; 45% have advanced law degrees. Of all faculty members, 1% are Native American, 4% are African American, 4% are Hispanic, 91% are white.

Application Information *Required:* LSAT, LSDAS, application form, application fee of $50, baccalaureate degree, personal statement, college transcripts. *Recommended:* resume. *Application deadline* for fall term is March 1. Students are required to have their own computers.

Costs The 1997–98 tuition is $19,750. Fees: $135.

Financial Aid 39 research assistantships, 39 teaching assistantships were awarded. 157 other awards were given. Fellowships, graduate assistantships, loans, merit-based grants/scholarships, and need-based grants/scholarships are also available. The average

AT a GLANCE

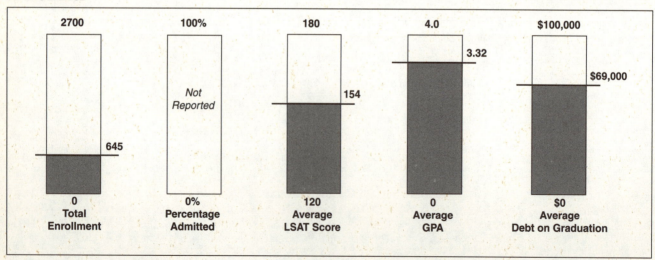

Degree Options

Degree	Total Credits Required	Length of Program
JD–Doctor of Laws	88	3 yrs, full-time only [day]
JD/MBA–Juris Doctor/Master of Business Administration–Joint-degree Program	94	3–4 yrs, full-time only [day]
LLM–Master of Laws–International Law and Business	30	1 yr, full-time or part-time [day, summer]

student debt at graduation is $69,000. To apply for financial assistance, students must complete the Free Application for Federal Student Aid, institutional forms, and tax returns (for need based financial aid applicants). Financial aid contact: Kathy Schiedel, Assistant Director of Financial Aid, 1401 61st Street South, St. Petersburg, FL 33707. Phone: 727-562-7813. Fax: 727-347-3738. Completed financial aid forms should be received by April 1.

Law School Library has 8 professional staff members and contains more than 350,000 volumes and 5,100 periodicals. 400 seats are available in the library. When classes are in session, the library is open 111 hours per week.

WESTLAW and LEXIS-NEXIS are available, as are the World Wide Web, online bibliographic services, and CD-ROM players. 61 computer workstations are available to students in the library.

First-Year Program Class size in the average section is 58; 100% of the first-year courses are taught by full-time faculty.

Upper-Level Program Class size in the average section is 25. Among the electives are:

* ★ Advocacy
* Business and Corporate Law
* Civil Litigation
* Entertainment Law
* ★ Environmental Law
* Family Law

* Government/Regulation
* Health Care/Human Services
* Intellectual Property
* ★ International/Comparative Law
* Jurisprudence
* ★ Labor Law
* ★ Land Use Law/Natural Resources
* ★ Lawyering Skills
* ★ Litigation
* Maritime Law
* ★ Mediation
* Probate Law
* ★ Public Interest
* Securities
* Tax Law

(★ *indicates an area of special strength*)

Clinical Courses Students receive degree credit for clinical courses. (Clinical practicum is not required.) Among the clinical areas offered are:

* Civil Litigation
* Criminal Defense
* Criminal Prosecution
* Elderly Advocacy
* Employment Law
* Environmental Law
* Government Litigation
* Land Rights/Natural Resource
* Mediation

20% of the students participate in internship programs.

DEAN'S STATEMENT . . .

Stetson University College of Law, founded in 1900, is Florida's first law school. For almost a century, it has been training outstanding lawyers, those who are ethical and competent professionals, ever mindful that law is both a learned and a public profession. The law school seeks the most highly qualified graduates from the nation's colleges and universities while recognizing special responsibilities to minorities, women, persons with disabilities, and those who approach law as a second career. Legal training prepares our graduates to serve ably in many callings, including practitioners, judges, bankers, developers, philanthropists, business executives, academics, and many others.

Stetson offers a program of legal education designed for all times. Its curriculum combines the traditional with the cutting edge. Here, students, assisted by faculty members who genuinely care about their success, learn how to try a case, the ins and outs of the global practice of law, the uses of technology, and what environmental law is all about. Students may participate in a wide range of activities. They may compete on award-winning trial teams, do hands-on work as interns, and assist those who need, but cannot afford, legal services.

Our classrooms, courtrooms, and living and recreational facilities make the law school an inviting place. Stetson is a beautiful place to live and study. The Tampa Bay area provides a great climate as well as the advantages of an urban environment.

—Lizabeth Moody, Dean

HISTORY, CAMPUS, AND LOCATION

Founded as a private law school in 1900, Stetson is Florida's first law school. For more than half a century, the College of Law was located on Stetson University's main campus in DeLand, Florida. In 1954, the College was relocated to a 21-acre campus in St. Petersburg. The original buildings, patterned after a medieval Spanish village clustered around a plaza of fountains and palm trees, were a resort hotel. Additional structures echo the Spanish architecture. The campus is centrally located in the dynamic Tampa Bay area, one of the nation's largest metropolitan areas.

SPECIAL QUALITIES OF THE SCHOOL

Since 1994, Stetson University College of Law has been recognized nationally as the best law school for the study of trial advocacy. Students receive intensive training in trial skills and participate actively in mock trial competitions. With dozens of state, regional, and national trial team championships to its credit, Stetson truly is a leading law school in training trial attorneys. In 1994, Stetson became the only law school in the United States ever to win all five national-level law school trial competitions in one academic year. In 1998, Stetson's academic standing is being enhanced tremendously by the opening of its state-of-the-art Law Library.

TECHNOLOGY ON CAMPUS

All incoming students are required to have a laptop computer. Each student is assigned an e-mail address. The new Law Library houses a cutting-edge library that contains more than 350,000 volumes, well above the median size for academic law libraries in the United States. The Law Library's resources are enriched by subscriptions to LEXIS-NEXIS, WESTLAW, and other electronic information systems. The 134 study carrels are wired for access to the Internet and the advanced legal research systems. There are thirty-four computer workstations available in the Law Library.

SCHOLARSHIPS AND LOANS

Most student aid is in the form of government- and privately sponsored loans. The school also offers merit scholarships that are awarded to entering students with exceptional credentials without regard to financial need. Stetson grants are awarded on the basis of need. Minority students who are Florida residents are eligible to apply for the Minority Participation in Legal Education (MPLE) scholarship, funded by the state of Florida.

STUDENT ACTIVITIES AND OPPORTUNITIES

Law Review *Stetson Law Review*, the school's only academic journal, is published four times a year. Students in the top 5 percent of their class are invited to join, and other students can gain admission through participation in a ten-day writing competition that is held twice a year. Currently, the *Law Review* has 14 members on the editorial board and 38 staff members. All members are involved full-time with law review, earning academic credit for each semester of service.

Moot Court Moot Court is an elective activity. Approximately 30 students participate each semester. The Moot Court Board competes in interscholastic competitions throughout the year and throughout the United States. Members are selected each fall through a tryout competition. A student may also gain admission through excellent performance in Research and Writing II. Each student who wants to try out must write a brief based on a hypothetical fact pattern. Then, each student presents an oral argument on the issues to a panel of local attorneys and faculty members. Members earn 1 academic credit each semester.

Extracurricular Activities The Student Bar Association includes ten committees. Student memberships are available in three local bar associations. In addition, there are specialty and minority student bar associations. There are one legal fraternity and one honorary fraternity. Religious groups, a business society, an online law forum, and political groups are available. Schoolwide social events are held regularly. Students may participate in local Inns of Court as well as the College's annual Inns of Court Banquet, which features renowned lecturers.

Special Opportunities The legal clinics include Civil Government Law, Civil Poverty Law, Elderlaw, Employment Discrimination, Labor Law, Prosecution, and Public Defender Clinics. State and federal judicial internships are available. Several students have interned at the Florida Supreme Court. There are space law internships available with the Spaceport Authority. Students must perform 20 at least hours of pro bono work.

Opportunities for Members of Minority Groups and Women All students may participate in all extracurricular and clinical programs, law reviews, and student organizations. A strong local specialty organization, the George Edgecomb Bar Association, hosts events with Stetson students. There is a chapter of the Florida Association of Women Lawyers at Stetson (FAWLS).

Special Certificate Programs The J.D./M.B.A. program, administered by the School of Business Administration at Stetson University in DeLand, is designed to broaden career opportunities in the fields of business and law. The program is ideal for those already in management positions who wish to prepare for a career shift into management. The program has successfully served the new graduate and the person returning to academic work from a career. All foundation course work for the M.B.A. program must be satisfied. The M.B.A. courses are offered at both the St. Petersburg and DeLand campuses.

The one-year Master of Laws (LL.M.) program in international law and business is designed to prepare graduates for international law practice or related professions. Professionalism, leadership, and business skills are emphasized in addition to training in the law. Special assistance is available for students interested in a law teaching career. The LL.M. class is a mix of U.S. and international lawyers and is kept small to ensure that each student may maximize his or her potential. In addition to course work on Stetson's Florida campus, students also may choose from a variety of interesting summer internship opportunities in law firms, corporations, or government agencies in other countries around the world. A prestigious International Advisory Council assists the College in providing placement advice to students seeking professional positions after graduation.

BAR PASSAGE, CAREER SERVICES, AND PLACEMENT

The first-time bar passage rate for 1996–97 graduates was 91 percent.

The Office of Career Services brings many legal organizations to campus each year to interview second- and third-year students. The office posts hundreds of employment opportunities for associate positions and part-time and summer clerkships throughout the year. Conversely, potential employers are also regularly provided data about job applicants. Stetson also participates in regional job fairs, where a diverse pool of employers grants on-the-spot interviews. Ninety-one percent of 1996–97 graduates are working full-time in the following legal professional fields.

Legal Field	Percentage of Graduates	Average Starting Salary
Academic	1%	n/a
Business	10%	$38,000
Government	20%	$32,000
Judicial Clerkship	14%	$34,000
Private Practice	51%	$40,000
Public Interest	4%	$30,000
Other	n/a	n/a

CORRESPONDENCE AND INFORMATION

Office of Admissions
College of Law
Stetson University
1401 61st Street South
St. Petersburg, Florida 33707
Telephone: 727-562-7802
Fax: 727-343-0136
E-mail: lawadmit@hermes.law.stetson.edu
World Wide Web: http://www.law.stetson.edu

UNIVERSITY OF FLORIDA
COLLEGE OF LAW

Gainesville, Florida

INFORMATION CONTACT
Richard A. Matasar, Dean
Box 112620
Gainesville, FL 32611

Phone: 352-392-9238   Fax: 352-392-8727
E-mail: patrick@law.ufl.edu
Web site: http://www.ufl.edu/

LAW STUDENT PROFILE [1997–98]
FULL-TIME   Enrollment: 1,245

PART-TIME   Enrollment: 46

APPLICANTS and ADMITTEES
Number applied: 2,094
Admitted: 109
Percentage accepted: 5%
Seats available: 200
Median LSAT score: 159
Median GPA: 3.6

University of Florida College of Law is a public institution that organizes classes on a semester calendar system. Founded in 1909, first ABA approved in 1925, and an AALS member, University of Florida College of Law offers JD and LLM degrees.

Application Information *Required:* LSAT, LSDAS, application form, application fee of $20, baccalaureate degree, college transcripts. *Recommended:* 3 letters of recommendation, personal statement, essay, resume.

Costs The 1997–98 tuition is $154 per credit hour for state residents. Tuition is $512 per credit hour for nonresidents.

Financial Aid In 1997–98, 2% of all students received some form of financial aid. 2 fellowships, 30 research assistantships were awarded. Fellowships, graduate assistantships, loans, merit-based grants/scholarships, need-based grants/scholarships, and federal work-study loans are also available. The average student debt at graduation is $33,000. To apply for financial assistance, students must complete the Free Application for Federal Student Aid. Financial aid contact: Patricia Varnes, Financial Aid Administrator, PO Box 117620, Gainesville, FL 32611. Phone: 352-392-0421. Fax: 352-392-8727. E-mail: trish-varnes@sfa.ufl.edu.

AT a GLANCE

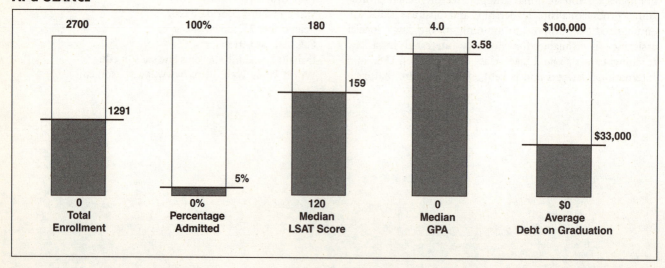

Degree Options

Degree	Total Credits Required	Length of Program
JD–Juris Doctor	88	3 yrs, full-time only [day, summer]
LLM–Master of Laws–Taxation	26	1 yr, full-time or part-time [day, summer]
LLM–Master of Laws–Comparative Law	30	1 yr, full-time only [day, summer]

Law School Library Legal Information Center has 11 professional staff members and contains more than 568,762 volumes and 6,317 periodicals. 474 seats are available in the library. When classes are in session, the library is open 103 hours per week.

WESTLAW and LEXIS-NEXIS are available, as are the World Wide Web, online bibliographic services, and CD-ROM players. 97 computer workstations are available to students in the library. Special law collections include British Commonwealth, Slavery.

First-Year Program Class size in the average section is 100; 100% of the first-year courses are taught by full-time faculty.

Upper-Level Program Class size in the average section is 75. Among the electives are:

Administrative Law
★ Advocacy
Business and Corporate Law
★ Criminal Procedure
Entertainment Law
★ Environmental Law
★ Family Law
Government/Regulation
Health Care/Human Services
Immigration
★ Intellectual Property
★ International/Comparative Law

Jurisprudence
Labor Law
★ Land Use Law/Natural Resources
Lawyering Skills
Legal Writing
★ Litigation
Maritime Law
Media Law
★ Mediation
Probate Law
Public Interest
★ Race and Race Relations
Securities
★ Tax Law
(★ indicates an area of special strength)

Clinical Courses Students receive degree credit for clinical courses. (Clinical practicum is not required.) Among the clinical areas offered are:

Civil Litigation
Criminal Defense
Criminal Prosecution
Family Practice
Juvenile Law
Mediation

4% of the students participate in internship programs. International exchange programs permit students to visit France; Germany; and Netherlands.

UNIVERSITY OF MIAMI
SCHOOL OF LAW

Coral Gables, Florida

LAW STUDENT PROFILE [1997–98]

FULL-TIME   Enrollment: 1,236
Women: 43%   Men: 57%

PART-TIME   Enrollment: 320
Women: 44%   Men: 56%

RACIAL or ETHNIC COMPOSITION
African American, 8%; Asian/Pacific Islander, 3%; Hispanic, 17%; Nataive American, 0.5%; International, 8%

APPLICANTS and ADMITTEES
Number applied: 2,501
Admitted: 1,586
Percentage accepted: 63%
Seats available: 482
Average LSAT score: 154
Average GPA: 3.2

University of Miami School of Law is a private institution that organizes classes on a semester calendar system. The campus is situated in a suburban setting. Founded in 1926, first ABA approved in 1941, and an AALS member, University of Miami School of Law offers JD, JD/MBA, JD/MPH, and JD/MS degrees.

Faculty consists of 50 full-time and 156 part-time members in 1997–98. 12 full-time faculty members and 33 part-time faculty members are women. 100% of all faculty members have a JD degree. Of all faculty members, 1.9% are Asian/Pacific Islander, 7.5% are African American, 5.7% are Hispanic, 84.9% are white.

Application Information *Required:* LSAT, LSDAS, application form, application fee of $45, baccalaureate degree, 2 letters of recommendation. *Recommended:* personal statement and resume. *Application deadline* for fall term is March 8.

Costs The 1997–98 tuition is $21,530 full-time; $897 per credit hour part-time.

Financial Aid In 1997–98, 84% of all students received some form of financial aid. Loans, merit-based grants/scholarships, and federal work-study loans are also available. The average student debt at graduation is $68,000. To apply for financial

AT a GLANCE

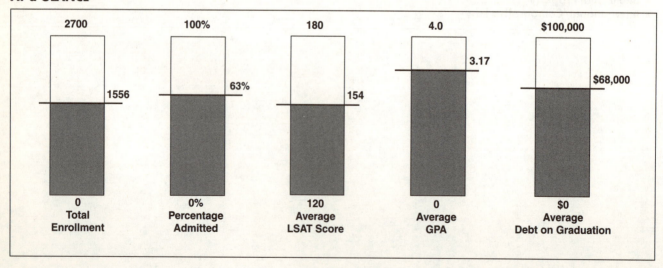

Degree Options

Degree	Total Credits Required	Length of Program
JD–Doctor of Laws	88	3–4 yrs, full-time or part-time [day, evening, summer]
JD/MBA–Juris Doctor/Master of Business Administration–Joint-degree Program	112	3.5–4 yrs, full-time only [day, summer]
JD/MPH–Juris Doctor/Master of Public Health–Joint-degree Program	115	4 yrs, full-time only
JD/MS–Juris Doctor/Master of Science–Joint-degree Program Marine Science	106	3.5–4 yrs, full-time only [day, summer]

assistance, students must complete the Free Application for Federal Student Aid and scholarship specific applications. Financial aid contact: Financial Aid Office, PO Box 248087, Coral Gables, FL 33124. Phone: 305-284-3115. Fax: 305-284-3084. E-mail: finaid@law.miami.edu. Completed financial aid forms should be received by March 1.

Law School Library University of Miami Law Library has 13 professional staff members and contains more than 460,000 volumes and 1,925 periodicals. 663 seats are available in the library. When classes are in session, the library is open 119 hours per week.

WESTLAW and LEXIS-NEXIS are available, as are the World Wide Web, online bibliographic services, and CD-ROM players. 110 computer workstations are available to students in the library. Special law collections include Foreign Law, taxation, estate planning, labor law, ocean law, environmental law, Latin American/Caribbean Law, Everglades Collection.

First-Year Program Class size in the average section is 90; 100% of the first-year courses are taught by full-time faculty.

Upper-Level Program Among the electives are:

Administrative Law
★ Advocacy
★ Business and Corporate Law
Entertainment Law
Environmental Law
Family Law
Health Care/Human Services
Intellectual Property

★ International/Comparative Law
Jurisprudence
Labor Law
Land Use Law/Natural Resources
★ Lawyering Skills
Legal History/Philosophy
★ Litigation
★ Maritime Law
Media Law
Probate Law
Securities
★ Tax Law
(★ indicates an area of special strength)

Clinical Courses Students receive degree credit for clinical courses. (Clinical practicum is not required.) Among the clinical areas offered are:

Civil Litigation
Civil Rights
Corporate Law
Criminal Defense
Criminal Prosecution
Elderly Advocacy
Environmental Law
Family Practice
General Practice
Government Litigation
Immigration
Juvenile Law
Mediation
Public Interest
Tax Law

56% of the students participate in internship programs. International exchange programs permit students to visit Spain and United Kingdom.

EMORY UNIVERSITY
SCHOOL OF LAW

Atlanta, Georgia

INFORMATION CONTACT

Howard O. Hunter, Dean
Gambrell Hall
1301 Clifton Avenue
Atlanta, GA 30322-2770

Phone: 404-727-6895   Fax: 404-727-6820
E-mail: lcadray@law.emory.edu
Web site: http://www.emory.edu/

LAW STUDENT PROFILE [1997–98]

FULL-TIME   Enrollment: 638
Women: 46%   Men: 54%

PART-TIME   Enrollment: 5
Women: 60%   Men: 40%

RACIAL or ETHNIC COMPOSITION

African American, 10%; Asian/Pacific Islander, 5%; Hispanic, 7%; Nataive American, 0.3%; International, 1%

APPLICANTS and ADMITTEES

Number applied: 2,757
Admitted: 1,049
Percentage accepted: 38%
Seats available: 207
Average LSAT score: 161
Average GPA: 3.5

Emory University School of Law is a private institution that organizes classes on a semester calendar system. The campus is situated in a suburban setting. Founded in 1916, first ABA approved in 1923, and an AALS member, Emory University School of Law offers JD, JD/MBA, JD/MDiv, JD/MPH, and JD/MTS degrees.

Faculty consists of 41 full-time and 55 part-time members in 1997–98. 9 full-time faculty members and 16 part-time faculty members are women. 100% of all faculty members have a JD; 34% have advanced law degrees. Of all faculty members, 5.2% are African American, 94.8% are white.

Application Information *Required:* LSAT, LSDAS, application form, application fee of $50, baccalaureate degree, 2 letters of recommendation, personal statement, college transcripts. *Application deadline* for fall term is March 1.

Costs The 1997–98 tuition is $23,175.

Financial Aid In 1997–98, 78% of all students received some form of financial aid. 12 fellowships were awarded. Fellowships, loans, merit-based grants/scholarships, need-based grants/scholarships, and federal work study loans are also available. The average student debt at graduation is $48,000. To apply for financial assistance, students must

AT a GLANCE

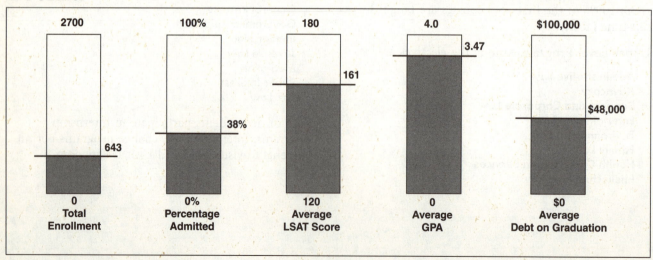

Degree Options

Degree	Total Credits Required	Length of Program
JD–Doctor of Law	88	3 yrs, full-time only [day]
JD/MBA–Juris Doctor/Master of Business Administration–Joint Degree	125	4 yrs, full-time only [day]
JD/MDiv–Juris Doctor/Master of Divinity–Joint Degree	147	5 yrs, full-time only [day]
JD/MPH–Juris Doctor/Master of Public Health–Joint Degree		4 yrs, full-time only [day]
JD/MTS–Juris Doctor/Master of Theological Studies–Joint Degree	116	4 yrs, full-time only [day]

complete the Free Application for Federal Student Aid, institutional forms, and scholarship specific applications. Financial aid contact: Mary McAbee, Assistant Director for Admission, 1301 Clifton Road, Atlanta, GA 30322-2770. Phone: 404-727-6802. Fax: 404-727-6820. E-mail: mmcabee@law.emory.edu. Completed financial aid forms should be received by March 1.

Law School Library Hugh F. MacMillan Law Library has 8 professional staff members and contains more than 332,803 volumes and 4,952 periodicals. 451 seats are available in the library. When classes are in session, the library is open 114 hours per week.

WESTLAW and LEXIS-NEXIS are available, as are the World Wide Web, online bibliographic services, and CD-ROM players. 50 computer workstations are available to students in the library. Special law collections include European Union Depository.

First-Year Program Class size in the average section is 60; 100% of the first-year courses are taught by full-time faculty.

Upper-Level Program Class size in the average section is 50. Among the electives are:

Administrative Law
Advocacy
Business and Corporate Law
★ Capital Punishment
Entertainment Law
★ Environmental Law
Family Law
Government/Regulation
Health Care/Human Services

Intellectual Property
International/Comparative Law
Jurisprudence
Labor Law
Land Use Law/Natural Resources
Lawyering Skills
Legal History/Philosophy
★ Litigation
Maritime Law
Mediation
Probate Law
★ Public Interest
Securities
Tax Law
(★ *indicates an area of special strength*)

Clinical Courses Students receive degree credit for clinical courses. (Clinical practicum is not required.) Among the clinical areas offered are:

Civil Litigation
Civil Rights
Corporate Law
Criminal Defense
Criminal Prosecution
Environmental Law
General Practice
Government Litigation
Health
Immigration
Intellectual Property
Juvenile Law
Mediation
Public Interest
Tax Law

52% of the students participate in internship programs. International exchange programs permit students to visit Hungary and Poland.

GEORGIA STATE UNIVERSITY
COLLEGE OF LAW

Atlanta, Georgia

INFORMATION CONTACT
Dr. Janice C. Griffith, Dean
PO Box 4037
Atlanta, GA 30302-4037

Phone: 404-651-2035   Fax: 404-651-1244
E-mail: lawcry@gsusgi2.gsu.edu
Web site: http://law.gsu.edu/

LAW STUDENT PROFILE [1997–98]

FULL-TIME   Enrollment: 392
Women: 48%   Men: 52%

PART-TIME   Enrollment: 249
Women: 51%   Men: 49%

RACIAL or ETHNIC COMPOSITION
African American, 15%; Asian/Pacific Islander, 5%; Hispanic, 2%; Nataive American, 0.2%; International, 1%

APPLICANTS and ADMITTEES
Number applied: 1,872
Admitted: 464
Percentage accepted: 25%
Seats available: 200
Average LSAT score: 157
Average GPA: 3.3

Georgia State University College of Law is a public institution that organizes classes on a semester calendar system. The campus is situated in an urban setting. Founded in 1982, first ABA approved in 1984, and an AALS member, Georgia State University College of Law offers JD, JD/MBA, and JD/MPAd degrees.

Faculty consists of 40 full-time and 28 part-time members in 1997–98. 17 full-time faculty members and 9 part-time faculty members are women. 100% of all faculty members have a JD; 14% have advanced law degrees. Of all faculty members, 1% are Native American, 1% are Asian/Pacific Islander, 16% are African American, 82% are white.

Application Information *Required:* LSAT, LSDAS, application form, application fee of $30, baccalaureate degree, 2 letters of recommendation, personal statement, college transcripts. *Application deadline* for fall term is March 15.

Costs The 1997–98 tuition is $3132 for state residents. Tuition is $12,528 for nonresidents. Fees: $275.

Financial Aid In 1997–98, 57% of all students received some form of financial aid. 66 research assistantships, totaling $63,500; 12 teaching assistantships, totaling $12,000, were awarded. Graduate

AT a GLANCE

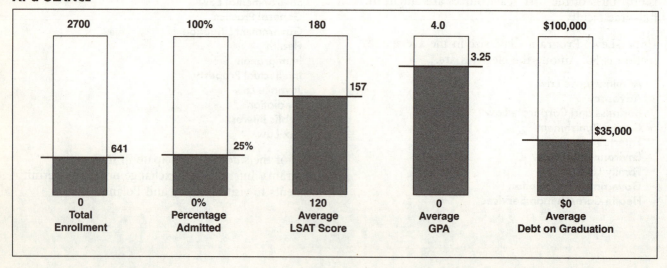

Degree Options

Degree	Total Credits Required	Length of Program
JD–Doctor of Law	90	3–4.5 yrs, full-time or part-time [day, evening, summer]
JD/MBA–Juris Doctor/Master of Business Administration–Dual-degree Program		4–6 yrs, full-time or part-time [day, evening, summer]
JD/MPAd–Juris Doctor/Master of Public Administration–Dual-degree Program		4–6 yrs, full-time or part-time [day, evening, summer]

assistantships, loans, merit-based grants/scholarships, need-based grants/scholarships, and federal work-study loans are also available. The average student debt at graduation is $35,000. To apply for financial assistance, students must complete the Free Application for Federal Student Aid. Financial aid contact: Benita Mathews, Financial Aid Counselor, P.O. Box 4040, Atlanta, GA 30302-4040. Phone: 404-651-2675. Fax: 404-651-1244. E-mail: fiabms@langate.gsu.edu. Completed financial aid forms should be received by April 1.

Law School Library Georgia State University College of Law Library has 6 professional staff members and contains more than 137,564 volumes and 3,548 periodicals. 335 seats are available in the library. When classes are in session, the library is open 105 hours per week.

WESTLAW and LEXIS-NEXIS are available, as are the World Wide Web, online bibliographic services, and CD-ROM players. 20 computer workstations are available to students in the library. Special law collections include tax law, labor law, health law, and international law.

First-Year Program Class size in the average section is 65; 100% of the first-year courses are taught by full-time faculty.

Upper-Level Program Class size in the average section is 30. Among the electives are:

Administrative Law
Advocacy
Business and Corporate Law
Consumer Law
★ Dispute Resolution
Education Law
Entertainment Law
Environmental Law

Family Law
Government/Regulation
Health Care/Human Services
Intellectual Property
International/Comparative Law
Jurisprudence
Labor Law
Land Use Law/Natural Resources
★ Lawyering Skills
Legal History/Philosophy
★ Litigation
Maritime Law
Media Law
★ Mediation
Probate Law
Public Interest
Securities
★ Tax Law
(★ *indicates an area of special strength*)

Clinical Courses Students receive degree credit for clinical courses. (Clinical practicum is not required.) Among the clinical areas offered are:

Civil Rights
Criminal Defense
Criminal Prosecution
Elderly Advocacy
Environmental Law
Family Practice
Health
Immigration
Judicial Clerkship
Juvenile Law
Labor Law
Land Rights/Natural Resource
Mediation
Tax Law

International exchange programs permit students to visit Austria.

MERCER UNIVERSITY
WALTER F. GEORGE SCHOOL OF LAW

Macon, Georgia

INFORMATION CONTACT

R. Lawrence Dessem, Dean
1021 Georgia Avenue
Macon, GA 31207

Phone: 912-752-2602   Fax: 912-752-2989
Web site: http://www.law.mercer.edu/

LAW STUDENT PROFILE [1997–98]

FULL-TIME   Enrollment: 405
Women: 40%   Men: 60%

RACIAL or ETHNIC COMPOSITION
African American, 6%; Asian/Pacific Islander, 2%; Hispanic, 2%; Nataive American, 0.5%; International, 0%

APPLICANTS and ADMITTEES
Number applied: 1,071
Admitted: 483
Percentage accepted: 45%
Seats available: 151
Average LSAT score: 154
Average GPA: 3.1

Mercer University Walter F. George School of Law is a private institution that organizes classes on a semester calendar system. The campus is situated in a suburban setting. Founded in 1873, first ABA approved in 1925, and an AALS member, Mercer University Walter F. George School of Law offers JD and JD/MBA degrees.

Faculty consists of 28 full-time and 24 part-time members in 1997–98. 6 full-time faculty members and 7 part-time faculty members are women. 100% of all faculty members have a JD; 15% have advanced law degrees. Of all faculty members, 6% are African American, 94% are white.

Application Information *Required:* LSAT, LSDAS, application form, application fee of $45, baccalaureate degree, 2 letters of recommendation, personal statement, college transcripts. *Recommended:* writing sample and resume. *Application deadline* for fall term is March 15.

Costs The 1997–98 tuition is $18,590 full-time; $8995 part-time.

Financial Aid In 1997–98, 87% of all students received some form of financial aid. 1 fellowship, totaling $4000, was awarded. 97 other awards, totaling $927,131, were given. Fellowships, loans, merit-based grants/scholarships, and federal

AT a GLANCE

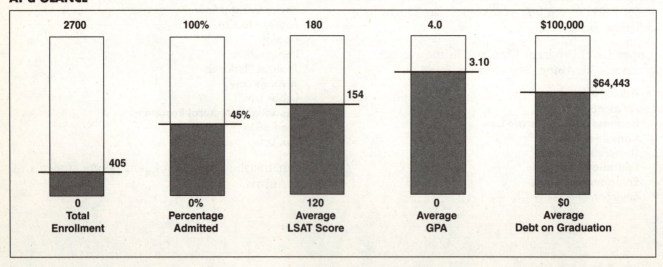

Degree Options

Degree	Total Credits Required	Length of Program
JD–Doctor of Laws	90	3 yrs, full-time only
JD/MBA–Juris Doctor/Master of Business Administration–Joint-degree Program	109	6 yrs, full-time only

work-study loans are also available. The average student debt at graduation is $64,443. To apply for financial assistance, students must complete the Free Application for Federal Student Aid, institutional forms, and financial aid transcripts. Financial aid contact: Marilyn E. Sutton, Director of Financial Aid/Associate Director of Admissions, 1021 Georgia Avenue, Macon, GA 31201. Phone: 912-752-2429. Fax: 912-752-2989. E-mail: sutton_me@mercer.edu. Completed financial aid forms should be received by April 1.

Law School Library Furman Smith Law Library has 6 professional staff members and contains more than 280,000 volumes and 2,770 periodicals. 326 seats are available in the library. When classes are in session, the library is open 75 hours per week.

WESTLAW and LEXIS-NEXIS are available, as are the World Wide Web, online bibliographic services, and CD-ROM players. 60 computer workstations are available to students in the library. Special law collections include law school archives.

First-Year Program Class size in the average section is 70; 100% of the first-year courses are taught by full-time faculty.

Upper-Level Program Class size in the average section is 50. Among the electives are:

Administrative Law
Advocacy
Business and Corporate Law
Consumer Law
Entertainment Law
Environmental Law
Family Law
Government/Regulation
Health Care/Human Services
Intellectual Property
International/Comparative Law
Jurisprudence
Labor Law
Land Use Law/Natural Resources
Lawyering Skills
Legal History/Philosophy
Litigation
Media Law
Mediation
Probate Law
Public Interest
Securities
Tax Law

UNIVERSITY OF GEORGIA
SCHOOL OF LAW

Athens, Georgia

INFORMATION CONTACT

David E. Shipley, Dean
Athens, GA 30602

Phone: 706-542-7140   Fax: 706-542-5556
Web site: http://www.lawsch.uga.edu/

LAW STUDENT PROFILE [1997–98]

APPLICANTS and ADMITTEES
Seats available: 229
Median LSAT score: 162
Median GPA: 3.5

University of Georgia School of Law is a public institution that organizes classes on a semester calendar system. The campus is situated in an urban setting. Founded in 1859, first ABA approved in 1930, and an AALS member, University of Georgia School of Law offers JD, JD/MA, JD/MBA, JD/MPA, and LLM degrees.

Application Information *Required:* LSAT, LSDAS, application form, application fee of $30, baccalaureate degree, 2 letters of recommendation, essay. *Application deadline* for fall term is March 1.

Financial Aid Loans, merit-based grants/scholarships, need-based grants/scholarships, and federal work-study loans are available. To apply for financial assistance, students must complete the Free Application for Federal Student Aid and institutional forms. Financial aid contact: University of Georgia, Office of Financial Aid, Academic Building, Athens, GA 30602-6114. Phone: 706-542-6147. Fax: 706-542-5556. Completed financial aid forms should be received by January 31.

Law School Library University of Georgia School of Law Law Library has 9 professional staff members and contains more than 459,513 volumes and 6,782 periodicals. 421 seats are available in the library. When classes are in session, the library is open 115 hours per week.

AT a GLANCE

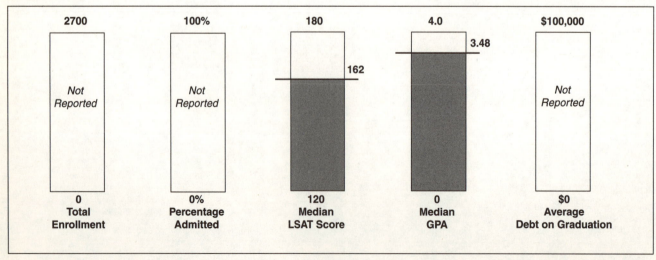

Degree Options

Degree	Total Credits Required	Length of Program
JD–Juris Doctor	88	3 yrs, full-time only
JD/MA–Juris Doctor/Master of Arts–Joint-degree Program		
JD/MA–Juris Doctor/Master of Arts–Historic Preservation		4 yrs
JD/MBA–Juris Doctor/Master of Business Administration		4 yrs
JD/MPA–Juris Doctor/Master of Professional Accountancy		
LLM–Master of Laws	27	1 yr, full-time only

WESTLAW and LEXIS-NEXIS are available, as is the World Wide Web.

First-Year Program Class size in the average section is 78.

Upper-Level Program Among the electives are:

Administrative Law
Advocacy
Banking and Financial Aid
Bankruptcy
Business and Corporate Law
Constitutional Law
Criminal Procedure
Entertainment Law
Environmental Law
Family Law
Government/Regulation
Health Care/Human Services
Immigration
Intellectual Property
International/Comparative Law
Jurisprudence
Labor Law
Land Use Law/Natural Resources
Lawyering Skills
Legal History/Philosophy
Litigation
Maritime Law
Mediation
Probate Law
Property/Real Estate
Public Interest
Securities
Sports Law
Tax Law
Trusts and Estates

Clinical Courses Students receive degree credit for clinical courses. Among the clinical areas offered are:

Civil Litigation
Criminal Defense
Criminal Prosecution
Elderly Advocacy
Family Practice
General Practice
Juvenile Law
Public Interest

Internships are available. International exchange programs permit students to visit Argentina; Belgium; France; Germany; and United Kingdom.

UNIVERSITY OF HAWAII AT MANOA
WILLIAM S. RICHARDSON SCHOOL OF LAW

Honolulu, Hawaii

INFORMATION CONTACT
Lawrence C. Foster, Dean
2515 Dole Street
Honolulu, HI 96822

Phone: 808-956-6363   Fax: 808-956-6402
E-mail: lawadm@hawaii.edu
Web site: http://www.hawaii.edu/catalog/law.html

LAW STUDENT PROFILE [1997–98]

FULL-TIME   Enrollment: 238
Women: 52%   Men: 48%

RACIAL or ETHNIC COMPOSITION
African American, 1%; Asian/Pacific Islander, 47%; Hispanic, 1%; International, 8%

APPLICANTS and ADMITTEES
Number applied: 431
Admitted: 157
Percentage accepted: 36%
Seats available: 77

University of Hawaii at Manoa William S. Richardson School of Law is a public institution that organizes classes on a semester calendar system. The campus is situated in an urban setting. Founded in 1973, first ABA approved in 1974, and an AALS member, University of Hawaii at Manoa William S. Richardson School of Law offers JD, JD/MA, JD/MBA, and JD/MURP degrees.

Faculty consists of 18 full-time and 28 part-time members in 1997–98. 8 full-time faculty members and 7 part-time faculty members are women.

Application Information *Required:* LSAT, LSDAS, application fee of $30, baccalaureate degree, 2 letters of recommendation. *Application deadline* for fall term is March 1.

Costs The 1997–98 tuition is $8016 for state residents. Tuition is $14,112 for nonresidents.

Financial Aid In 1997–98, 55% of all students received some form of financial aid. 22 research assistantships were awarded. To apply for financial assistance, students must complete the Free Application for Federal Student Aid. Financial aid contact: Financial Aid Services, University of Hawaii at Manoa, Student Services Center, 2600 Campus Road, Honolulu, HI 96822. Phone: 808-956-7251.

AT a GLANCE

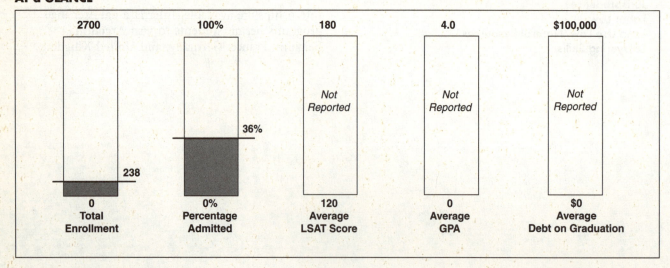

2700	100%	180	4.0	$100,000
		Not Reported	Not Reported	Not Reported
	36%			
238				
0	0%	120	0	$0
Total Enrollment	Percentage Admitted	Average LSAT Score	Average GPA	Average Debt on Graduation

Degree Options

Degree	Total Credits Required	Length of Program
JD–Juris Doctor	89	3 yrs, full-time only
JD/MA–Juris Doctor/Master of Arts–Asian Studies Joint-degree Program		
JD/MBA–Juris Doctor/Master of Business Administration–Joint-degree Program		
JD/MURP–Juris Doctor/Masters of Urban and Regional Planning–Joint-degree Program		

Fax: 808-956-6402. Completed financial aid forms should be received by March 1.

Law School Library has 5 professional staff members and contains more than 248,829 volumes and 2,736 periodicals. 392 seats are available in the library. When classes are in session, the library is open 74 hours per week.

WESTLAW and LEXIS-NEXIS are available.

First-Year Program Class size in the average section is 69.

Upper-Level Program Among the electives are:

Accounting
Administrative Law
Business and Corporate Law
Civil Rights
Conflict of Laws
Constitutional Law
Consumer Law
Criminal Law
Elder Law
Environmental Law
Evidence
Family Law
Health Care/Human Services
Immigration
Insurance
Intellectual Property

International/Comparative Law
Jurisprudence
Labor Law
Land Use Law/Natural Resources
Lawyering Skills
Legal History/Philosophy
Litigation
Maritime Law
Mediation
Native Hawaiian Rights
Probate Law
Property/Real Estate
Race and Law
Tax Law

Clinical Courses Among the clinical areas offered are:

Criminal Defense
Criminal Prosecution
Elderly Advocacy
Estate Planning
Family Practice
Japanese Law
Mediation
Ocean and Coastal Law
Wildlife Law

Internships are available. International exchange program available.

UNIVERSITY OF IDAHO
COLLEGE OF LAW

Moscow, Idaho

INFORMATION CONTACT

Dr. John A. Miller, Dean
Moscow, ID 83844-4977

Phone: 208-885-6208   Fax: 208-885-7609
Web site: http://www.uidaho.edu/law/

LAW STUDENT PROFILE [1997–98]

FULL-TIME   Enrollment: 275
Women: 34%   Men: 66%

PART-TIME   Enrollment: 16
Women: 50%   Men: 50%

RACIAL or ETHNIC COMPOSITION
African American, 3%; Asian/Pacific Islander, 3%; Native
American, 1%

APPLICANTS and ADMITTEES
Seats available: 128
Average LSAT score: 152
Average GPA: 3.2

University of Idaho College of Law is a public institution that organizes classes on a semester calendar system. The campus is situated in a small-town setting. Founded in 1909, first ABA approved in 1925, and an AALS member, University of Idaho College of Law offers a JD degree.

Faculty consists of 14 full-time members in 1997–98. 3 full-time faculty members are women. 100% of all faculty members have a JD; 6% have advanced law degrees. Of all faculty members, 100% are white.

Application Information *Required:* LSAT, LSDAS, application form, application fee of $30, college transcripts. *Recommended:* baccalaureate degree, recommendations, personal statement. *Application deadline* for fall term is February 1.

Financial Aid Loans, merit-based grants/scholarships, need-based grants/scholarships, and federal work-study loans are available. The average student debt at graduation is $15,000. To apply for financial assistance, students must complete the Free Application for Federal Student Aid and institutional forms. Financial aid contact: Shawna Lindquist, Student Financial Aid, University of Idaho, Moscow, ID 83844-4291. Phone: 208-885-6312. Fax: 208-885-7609. E-mail: finaid@uidaho.edu. Completed

AT a GLANCE

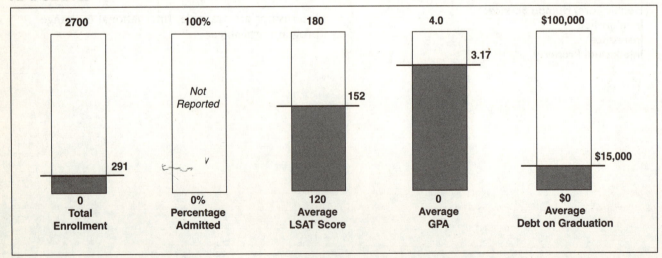

Degree Options

Degree	Total Credits Required	Length of Program
JD–Juris Doctor	88	3 yrs, full-time only [day]

financial aid forms should be received by February 15.

Law School Library University of Idaho Law Library has 4 professional staff members and contains more than 174,395 volumes and 2,758 periodicals. 369 seats are available in the library. When classes are in session, the library is open 96 hours per week.

WESTLAW and LEXIS-NEXIS are available, as are the World Wide Web, online bibliographic services, and CD-ROM players. 31 computer workstations are available to students in the library. Special law collections include Idaho Supreme Court records and briefs.

First-Year Program Class size in the average section is 60; 100% of the first-year courses are taught by full-time faculty.

Upper-Level Program Class size in the average section is 55. Among the electives are:

Administrative Law
Advocacy
★ Business and Corporate Law
★ Environmental Law
Family Law
Government/Regulation
Indian/Tribal Law
Intellectual Property
International/Comparative Law
Jurisprudence
Labor Law
Land Rights/Natural Resource
★ Lawyering Skills
Legal History/Philosophy
Litigation
Mediation
Probate Law
Securities
Tax Law
(★ *indicates an area of special strength*)

Clinical Courses Students receive degree credit for clinical courses. (Clinical practicum is not required.) Among the clinical areas offered are:

Civil Litigation
Civil Rights
Corporate Law
Criminal Defense
Elderly Advocacy
Environmental Law
Family Practice
General Practice
Government Litigation
Health
Indian/Tribal Law
Intellectual Property
Juvenile Law
Land Rights/Natural Resource
Mediation
Public Interest
Tax Law

20% of the students participate in internship programs. International exchange programs permit students to visit United Kingdom.

DEAN'S STATEMENT . . .

Iinvite you to consider the University of Idaho, where we provide a high-quality legal education in the beautiful inland Northwest. Our campus combines the collegial and intimate feeling of a dignified small college, encircled by natural splendor, with the technological and social advantages of a major state university. Our faculty members have been hand-picked over many years to provide you with excellent instruction and mentoring. Our building is a comfortable, well-designed, fully networked facility. It has all the appropriate amenities, including computer labs, distance learning facilities, recreational space, and dining facilities. Our entering class usually numbers slightly more than 100, providing you with plenty of opportunities to get to know your teachers and your classmates. At Idaho, you will make friendships that will last for the rest of your life while earning an honored degree that has potent market impact.

The University of Idaho's low tuition and the relatively modest cost of living in Moscow mean that our graduates can begin their careers on a firm financial footing. This low tuition, combined with the quality of education and services we provide, makes the University of Idaho College of Law one of the best bargains in legal education in the United States.

For ninety years, Idaho has produced high-quality lawyers who have gone on to make a positive difference in the world they inhabit. Numbered among our thousands of graduates are leading lawyers, businesspeople, judges, and other public servants. Our curriculum is well balanced and offers you the opportunity to succeed in a variety of settings after graduation. I invite you to visit our campus, our university, and our community. The Admissions Office will be happy to assist you in scheduling a visit. I look forward to seeing you.

—*John A. Miller, Dean*

HISTORY, CAMPUS, AND LOCATION

The University of Idaho is located in the northern Idaho town of Moscow, a friendly walking and biking community of 20,000. Ties between this family-oriented community and the University are strong and mutually supportive. Located approximately 80 miles from Spokane, Washington, Moscow is the centerpiece of the Palouse, an area of rolling wheat-covered hills and forested mountains. The school's small size and informal atmosphere provide a supportive collegial environment for the study of law.

The University's uncommon setting, only 8 miles from Washington State University in Pullman, offers numerous cultural, academic, employment, research, athletic, and social opportunities. A free bus service operates between the two universities, and a biking/walking path connects Moscow and Pullman.

During the year, Moscow is home to an annual springtime Renaissance Fair and summer outdoor concerts, and in February the University hosts the Lionel Hampton Jazz Festival. From early spring through late fall, Moscow's Farmers' Market is alive with music, arts, crafts, and vegetable and fruit vendors. Recreational opportunities abound, and nearby rivers and mountains offer hiking, white-water rafting, skiing, mountain biking, snowboarding, hunting, and fishing adventures.

Established in 1909, the University of Idaho College of Law has been accredited by the American Bar Association since 1925. It is the only law school in Idaho and has more than 3,000 living alumni.

SPECIAL QUALITIES OF THE SCHOOL

While the University of Idaho College of Law has a strong basic curriculum, there is particular depth in the areas of environmental and natural resources law, business, and professional and litigation skills.

The curriculum and location, with access to the vast wilderness areas of Idaho, create a natural place to study environmental law. The business curriculum is varied, and the faculty has extensive commercial law experience gained in large national firms. Extensive clinical offerings and externship opportunities allow students to gain practical experience through both actual and simulated trial practice and mediation opportunities.

To complement the broad range of curriculum topics, the Bellwood Lecture Series, funded by an endowment of more than $1 million, brings nationally known speakers on a variety of legal topics to the College each year.

TECHNOLOGY ON CAMPUS

The College of Law is dedicated to providing the audiovisual, computer, and other technological advances that impact the practice of law. Currently under construction is an interactive video classroom that will connect the College with the Idaho Law Center in Boise, Idaho. The courtroom and all classrooms are networked, and the College is moving steadily toward its goal to provide 100 percent network access at all carrel locations. Portable audiovisual equipment, such as a large-screen computer/video projector, camcorders, closed-circuit television, and computers, are readily available. Computers are maintained and upgraded by an in-house technology team, and student labs provide assistants to answer both software- and hardware-related questions.

SCHOLARSHIPS AND LOANS

In addition to assistance that is available to qualified students in the form of grants, loans, and work-study, the College of Law awards a number of scholarships to incoming students. Recipients are selected on the basis of academic ability, need, and professional promise. Highly qualified applicants are eligible for scholarships equal to the entire cost of tuition for residents and the difference between resident and nonresident tuition for nonresidents.

STUDENT ACTIVITIES AND OPPORTUNITIES

Law Review Published three times a year, the *Idaho Law Review* provides scholarly discussion of timely legal issues. Membership on the board is a distinct honor that allows students to hone their writing and editing skills. The *Law Review* also sponsors annual symposia to bring regional and national experts together to address topics of current interest.

Moot Court All first-year students compete in an appellate moot court argument under the guidance and direction of the faculty. From a voluntary intramural moot court competition, a student Board of Advocates selects winning teams to participate in a number of national forensic competitions, including National Moot Court.

Extracurricular Activities More than twenty student organizations provide students with diverse opportunities to enhance personal interests and to participate in social and educational activities. Organizations include student divisions of the American Bar Association, the Idaho Trial Lawyer's Association, and the Idaho Women's Caucus. Several organizations are dedicated to particular types of law, such as environmental law, international law, public interest law, and sports law. Student fraternities include Phi Alpha Delta, Phi Delta Phi, and Delta Theta Phi. There is also a student spouse organization to provide support and to enhance participation between students and their families.

Special Opportunities The College of Law operates three clinics: a General Clinic that represents clients in civil and criminal cases; an Appellate Clinic that represents clients before the Ninth Circuit Court of Appeals, the Idaho Supreme Court, and the Idaho Court of Appeals; and a Native American Defender Clinic, where students function as public defenders for the Nez Perce tribe.

Opportunities for Members of Minority Groups and Women Idaho celebrates the proud Native American heritage of the region. To enhance this relationship, students in the Native American Defender Clinic travel to the nearby Nez Perce Indian Reservation to serve as public defenders in criminal cases. This clinic, one of the few in the country to offer representation to Native Americans, provides firsthand experience in comparative law, sensitizes students to new ways of legal thinking, and exposes students to tribal law. A course in Indian law examines treaties, tribal sovereignty and self-government, hunting and fishing rights, and the historical development of federal Indian policy.

Special Certificate Programs Students may receive 6 credit hours of graduate-level courses from outside the College of Law. Up to 10 credit hours may be earned by students who participate in the Public Service Externship Program, with employers such as the Idaho Attorney General, the United States Attorney for Idaho, federal and state appellate courts, or other public interest organizations. Students spend a semester under the supervision of prominent attorneys and judges on pending cases. This program, a valuable asset for first- and second-year students, provides practical work experiences not offered through regular employment channels and offers unique insights into the legal process.

BAR PASSAGE, CAREER SERVICES, AND PLACEMENT

Eighty-three percent of Idaho graduates passed the Idaho state bar examination in 1996. In 1997, the Idaho passage rate was 72 percent.

Career Services arranges on-campus interviews and other appearances by employers and alumni. Students receive information to help define and focus their career goals and job searches. Employment position opportunities are compiled and posted for both permanent employment and contract work opportunities. The office maintains employer files and directories to assist students in networking with alumni and prospective employers.

Idaho graduates are quite successful in securing full-time legal postgraduate employment. Ninety-five percent of the 1996–97 graduates were employed within six months of graduation.

Legal Field	Percentage of Graduates	Average Starting Salary
Academic	1%	n/a
Business	10%	$56,000
Government	15%	$35,000
Judicial Clerkship	30%	$34,700
Private Practice	42%	$34,500
Public Interest	1%	n/a
Other	n/a	n/a

CORRESPONDENCE AND INFORMATION

Admissions
College of Law
University of Idaho
Moscow, Idaho 83844-2321
Telephone: 208-885-6423
Fax: 208-885-7609
E-mail: tamaram@uidaho.edu
World Wide Web: http://www.uidaho.edu/law

DEPAUL UNIVERSITY
COLLEGE OF LAW

Chicago, Illinois

INFORMATION CONTACT

Teree E. Foster, Dean
25 East Jackson Boulevard
Chicago, IL 60604-2287

Phone: 312-362-8701   Fax: 312-632-5448
E-mail: dshea@wppost.depaul.edu
Web site: http://www.law.depaul.edu/

LAW STUDENT PROFILE [1997–98]

FULL-TIME   Enrollment: 799
Women: 50%   Men: 50%

PART-TIME   Enrollment: 363
Women: 47%   Men: 53%

RACIAL or ETHNIC COMPOSITION
African American, 5%; Asian/Pacific Islander, 4%; Hispanic, 5%; Nataive American, 0.3%; International, 1%

APPLICANTS and ADMITTEES
Number applied: 2,077
Admitted: 1,444
Percentage accepted: 70%
Seats available: 335
Average LSAT score: 154
Average GPA: 3.2

DePaul University College of Law is a private institution that organizes classes on a semester calendar system. The campus is situated in an urban setting. Founded in 1912, first ABA approved in 1925, and an AALS member, DePaul University College of Law offers JD, JD/MBA, and LLM degrees.

Faculty consists of 39 full-time and 90 part-time members in 1997–98. 12 full-time faculty members and 27 part-time faculty members are women. 100% of all faculty members have a JD; 40% have advanced law degrees. Of all faculty members, 2% are Native American, 2% are Asian/Pacific Islander, 4% are African American, 4% are Hispanic, 88% are white.

Application Information *Required:* LSAT, LSDAS, application form, application fee of $40, baccalaureate degree, 1 recommendation, personal statement, essay, writing sample, college transcripts. *Recommended:* interview and resume. *Application deadline* for fall term is April 1.

Financial Aid In 1997–98, 54% of all students received some form of financial aid. 154 other awards, totaling $903,500, were given. Loans, merit-based grants/scholarships, need-based grants/scholarships, and federal work-study loans are also available. The average student debt at gradua-

AT a GLANCE

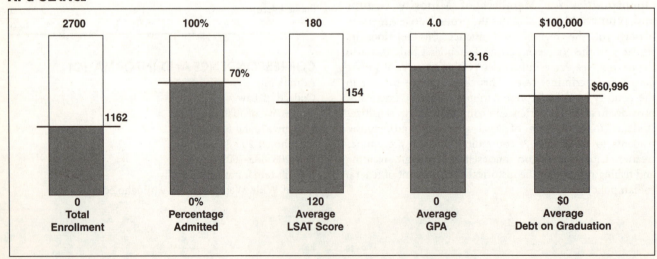

Total Enrollment	Percentage Admitted	Average LSAT Score	Average GPA	Average Debt on Graduation
2700	100%	180	4.0	$100,000
1162	70%	154	3.16	$60,996
0	0%	120	0	$0

Degree Options

Degree	Total Credits Required	Length of Program
JD–Doctor of Laws	86	3–4 yrs, full-time or part-time [day, evening, summer]
JD/MBA–Juris Doctor/Master of Business Administration–Joint Program	120	4–5 yrs, full-time or part-time [day, evening, summer]
LLM–Master of Laws–Taxation	24	1–5 yrs, full-time or part-time [day, evening, summer]
LLM–Master of Laws–Health	24	1–5 yrs, full-time or part-time [day, evening, summer]

tion is $60,996. To apply for financial assistance, students must complete the Free Application for Federal Student Aid, institutional forms, and scholarship specific applications. Financial aid contact: John Corrigan, Assistant Director of Financial Aid, 1 East Jackson Boulevard, Suite 9000, Chicago, IL 60604. Phone: 312-362-5755. Fax: 312-632-5448. E-mail: jcorriga@wppost.depaul.edu. Completed financial aid forms should be received by April 21.

Law School Library DePaul University Law Library has 10 professional staff members and contains more than 333,791 volumes and 4,648 periodicals. 465 seats are available in the library. When classes are in session, the library is open 95 hours per week.

WESTLAW and LEXIS-NEXIS are available, as are the World Wide Web, online bibliographic services, and CD-ROM players. 42 computer workstations are available to students in the library. Special law collections include Tax Law, Health Law, International Human Rights Law.

First-Year Program Class size in the average section is 83; 100% of the first-year courses are taught by full-time faculty.

Upper-Level Program Class size in the average section is 50. Among the electives are:

Administrative Law
★ Advocacy
★ Business and Corporate Law
  Consumer Law
★ Entertainment Law
  Environmental Law
  Family Law
  Government/Regulation
★ Health Care/Human Services
★ Intellectual Property
★ International/Comparative Law
  Jurisprudence
  Labor Law
  Land Use Law/Natural Resources
★ Lawyering Skills
  Legal History/Philosophy
★ Litigation
★ Media Law
★ Mediation
  Probate Law
★ Public Interest
★ Securities
★ Tax Law
(★ indicates an area of special strength)

Clinical Courses Students receive degree credit for clinical courses. (Clinical practicum is not required.) Among the clinical areas offered are:

Community Development
Criminal Defense
Immigration
Mediation

40% of the students participate in internship programs. International exchange programs permit students to visit Ireland.

ILLINOIS INSTITUTE OF TECHNOLOGY
CHICAGO-KENT COLLEGE OF LAW

Chicago, Illinois

INFORMATION CONTACT

Mr. Henry H. Perritt Jr., Dean
565 West Adams Street
Chicago, IL 60661-3691

Phone: 312-906-5010   Fax: 312-906-5280
E-mail: admitq@kentlaw.edu
Web site: http://www.kentlaw.edu/

LAW STUDENT PROFILE [1997–98]

FULL-TIME   Enrollment: 883
Women: 49%   Men: 51%

PART-TIME   Enrollment: 387
Women: 44%   Men: 56%

RACIAL or ETHNIC COMPOSITION

African American, 4%; Asian/Pacific Islander, 8%; Hispanic, 4%; Nataive American, 0.4%; International, 0%

APPLICANTS and ADMITTEES

Number applied: 1,864
Admitted: 1,200
Percentage accepted: 64%
Seats available: 402

Illinois Institute of Technology Chicago-Kent College of Law is a private institution that organizes classes on a semester calendar system. The campus is situated in an urban setting. Founded in 1888, first ABA approved in 1936, and an AALS member, Illinois Institute of Technology Chicago-Kent College of Law offers JD, JD/LLM, JD/MBA, JD/MPAd, JD/MS, and LLM degrees.

Faculty consists of 65 full-time and 125 part-time members in 1997–98. 24 full-time faculty members and 24 part-time faculty members are women.

Application Information *Required:* application fee of $45, LSAT, LSDAS, baccalaureate degree, 2 letters of recommendation, personal statement. *Application deadline* for fall term is April 1.

Costs The 1997–98 tuition is $20,680 full-time; $14,915 part-time. Fees: $40 per semester (minimum).

Financial Aid In 1997–98, 75% of all students received some form of financial aid. 109 research assistantships, 29 teaching assistantships were awarded. 422 other awards were given. Merit-based grants/scholarships and need-based grants/scholarships are also available. To apply for financial assistance, students must complete the Free Application for Federal Student Aid. Financial aid contact:

AT a GLANCE

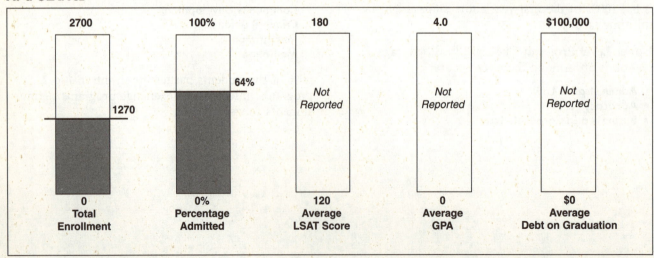

	Total Enrollment	Percentage Admitted	Average LSAT Score	Average GPA	Average Debt on Graduation
Max	2700	100%	180	4.0	$100,000
Value	1270	64%	Not Reported	Not Reported	Not Reported
Min	0	0%	120	0	$0

Degree Options

Degree	Total Credits Required	Length of Program
JD–Juris Doctor	84	
JD/LLM–Juris Doctor/Master of Laws–Financial Services		
JD/LLM–Juris Doctor/Master of Laws–Taxation	24	
JD/MBA–Juris Doctor/Master of Business Administration		
JD/MPAd–Juris Doctor/Master of Public Administration		
JD/MS–Juris Doctor/Master of Science–Financial Markets	24	
JD/MS–Juris Doctor/Master of Science–Environmental Management		
LLM–Master of Laws–International and Comparative Law		1 yr

Joline B. Weidner Director, Office of Financial Aid, 565 West Adams Street, Chicago, IL 60661-3691. Phone: 302-906-5180. Fax: 312-906-5280. E-mail: finaid@kentlaw.edu. Complctcd financial aid forms should be received by April 15.

Law School Library has 8 professional staff members and contains more than 535,375 volumes and 132,780 periodicals. 686 seats are available in the library. When classes are in session, the library is open 104 hours per week.

WESTLAW and LEXIS-NEXIS arc available, as are the World Wide Web, online bibliographic services, and CD-ROM players. Special law collections include International relations, intellectual property, labor law, environmental/energy law.

First-Year Program Class size in the average section is 100.

Upper-Level Program Among the electives are:

Business and Corporate Law
Civil Procedure
Constitutional Law
Criminal Law
Education Law
Energy Law
Environmental Law
Estate Planning
Family Law
Financial Services
Health Care/Human Services
Intellectual Property
International/Comparative Law
Jurisprudence
★ **Labor Law**
Legal History/Philosophy
Litigation
Personal Injury
Property/Real Estate
Public Interest
Tax Law
(★ *indicates an area of special strength*)

Clinical Courses Students receive degree credit for clinical courses. Among the clinical areas offered are:

Child Abuse
Civil Litigation
Civil Rights
Corporate Law
Criminal Defense
Criminal Prosecution
Elderly Advocacy
Environmental Law
General Practice
Government Litigation
Health
Immigration
Intellectual Property
Juvenile Law
Landlord/Tenant
Mediation
Public Interest
Tax Law

Internships are available.

JOHN MARSHALL LAW SCHOOL

Chicago, Illinois

INFORMATION CONTACT

Robert Gilbert Johnson, Dean
315 South Plymouth Court
Chicago, IL 60604-3968

Phone: 312-427-2737   Fax: 312-427-5134
E-mail: 6alonzo@jmls.edu
Web site: http://www.jmls.edu/

LAW STUDENT PROFILE [1997–98]

FULL-TIME   Enrollment: 786
Women: 44%   Men: 56%

PART-TIME   Enrollment: 486
Women: 38%   Men: 62%

RACIAL or ETHNIC COMPOSITION

African American, 6%; Asian/Pacific Islander, 5%; Hispanic, 5%; Native American, 5%; International, 2%

APPLICANTS and ADMITTEES

Number applied: 1,503
Admitted: 945
Percentage accepted: 63%
Seats available: 240
Average LSAT score: 149
Average GPA: 3.0

John Marshall Law School is a private nonprofit institution that organizes classes on a semester calendar system. The campus is situated in an urban setting. Founded in 1899, first ABA approved in 1951, and an AALS member, John Marshall Law School offers JD and LLM degrees.

Faculty consists of 52 full-time and 230 part-time members in 1997–98. 14 full-time faculty members and 43 part-time faculty members are women. 100% of all faculty members have a JD; 6% have advanced law degrees.

Application Information *Required:* LSAT, LSDAS, application form, application fee of $50, baccalaureate degree, personal statement, college transcripts. *Recommended:* recommendations and resume. *Application deadline* for fall term is March 1.

Financial Aid In 1997–98, 74% of all students received some form of financial aid. Loans, merit-based grants/scholarships, and need-based grants/scholarships are also available. The average student debt at graduation is $61,683. To apply for financial assistance, students must complete the Free Application for Federal Student Aid. Financial aid contact: Susan Sweeny, Financial Aid Officer, 315 South Plymouth Court, Chicago, IL 60604. Phone: 800-537-4280. Fax: 312-427-5134. E-mail: 6sweeny@jmls.edu.

AT a GLANCE

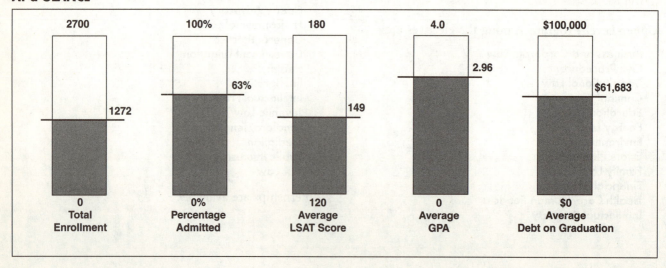

2700	100%	180	4.0	$100,000
1272	63%	149	2.96	$61,683
0	0%	120	0	$0
Total Enrollment	Percentage Admitted	Average LSAT Score	Average GPA	Average Debt on Graduation

Degree Options

Degree	Total Credits Required	Length of Program
JD–Juris Doctor	90	3–4 yrs, full-time or part-time [day, evening, summer]
LLM–Master of Laws–Intellectual Property	24	1.5–2 yrs, full-time or part-time [evening, summer]
LLM–Master of Laws–Taxation	24	1.5–2 yrs, full-time or part-time [evening, summer]
LLM–Master of Laws–Real Estate	24	1.5–2 yrs, full-time or part-time [evening, summer]
LLM–Master of Laws–Comparative Law	24	1.5–2 yrs, full-time or part-time [evening, summer]
LLM–Master of Laws–Information/Technology Law	24	1.5–2 yrs, full-time or part-time [evening, summer]
LLM–Master of Laws–International Business and Trade	24	1.5–2 yrs, full-time or part-time [evening, summer]

Law School Library The John Marshall Law School Library has 10 professional staff members and contains more than 359,009 volumes and 815 periodicals. 624 seats are available in the library. When classes are in session, the library is open 100 hours per week.

WESTLAW and LEXIS-NEXIS are available, as are the World Wide Web, online bibliographic services, and CD-ROM players. 50 computer workstations are available to students in the library. Special law collections include International Human Rights, Animal Rights, Intellectual Rights, Taxation.

First-Year Program Class size in the average section is 60; 90% of the first-year courses are taught by full-time faculty.

Upper-Level Program Class size in the average section is 50. Among the electives are:

Administrative Law
★ Advocacy
Business and Corporate Law
Consumer Law
Entertainment Law
Environmental Law

Family Law
Government/Regulation
★ Intellectual Property
★ International/Comparative Law
Labor Law
Land Use Law/Natural Resources
★ Lawyering Skills
Legal History/Philosophy
★ Litigation
Maritime Law
Media Law
Mediation
Probate Law
Public Interest
Securities
★ Tax Law
(★ indicates an area of special strength)

Clinical Courses Students receive degree credit for clinical courses. (Clinical practicum is not required.) Among the clinical areas offered are:

Civil Litigation
Fair Housing
Immigration

DEAN'S STATEMENT . . .

Beginning in 1998–99, the John Marshall Law School celebrates its 100th anniversary. From the small group of lawyers who founded the Law School in 1899 to the dedicated academic and administrative professionals who ensure the operation of the Law School today, people have always made the difference at John Marshall. They have been the embodiment of our centennial slogan, A Legacy of Opportunity, A Lifetime of Achievement.

The John Marshall Law School provides one of the most comprehensive and aggressive professional skills training curricula in the country, including trial and appellate advocacy, alternative dispute resolution, client counseling, negotiations, and legal drafting. Students and faculty also benefit from state-of-the-art computer technology both in the library and in our modern computer classroom.

Our seven Centers for Excellence serve as an academic foundation for our students' successes. Their specialized curriculums are among the most comprehensive in the country, and the number of advanced degrees offered rank second in the nation. In addition to our six LL.M. programs—employee benefits, information technology law, intellectual property law, international business and trade law, real estate law, and tax law—John Marshall offers its students a joint J.D./LL.M., J.D./M.B.A., J.D./M.P.A., and J.D./M.A. International students may elect to earn an LL.M. in comparative legal studies.

Our faculty of 52 professors/scholars and our adjunct faculty of 215 judges and practicing lawyers instruct and mentor students to provide them with the tools necessary to become competent, ethical practitioners with a broad range of interests.

Our location in the heart of Chicago's legal, financial, and commercial districts offers students a vibrant, cosmopolitan setting for legal study. The federal courthouse is across the street, and the nation's largest circuit court—that of Cook County—is just a few blocks away, as are many government offices. This proximity offers students enhanced learning experiences. So pay us a visit. I am sure you will be impressed.

—Dean Robert Gilbert Johnston

HISTORY, CAMPUS, AND LOCATION

Throughout its history, the John Marshall Law School has upheld a tradition of diversity, innovation, and opportunity and has consistently provided an education that combines an understanding of the theory, the philosophy, and the practice of law. Founded in 1899, the John Marshall Law School today is proud to be recognized as a dynamic independent law school, promoting excellence in all aspects of legal education.

When John Marshall first opened its doors nearly 100 years ago, its student body numbered only 3. Ninety-nine years later, the Law School has an enrollment in excess of 1,300 students from more than thirty states and thirteen other countries.

Cultural and ethnic diversity have been characteristic of the John Marshall Law School student body from the very beginning. John Marshall was founded as a not-for-profit corporation by a small group of distinguished lawyers who believed in the noble principle that admission to the Law School should not be determined by arbitrary and discriminatory factors such as racial origin or religious affiliation.

John Marshall's three-building campus is in the heart of Chicago's legal and financial district. Located across the street from the Dirksen and Kluczynski Federal Buildings, John Marshall is within a few blocks of the Circuit Court of Cook County and the LaSalle Street law firms, enhancing students' efforts to secure employment—during law school and after graduation.

SPECIAL QUALITIES OF THE SCHOOL

John Marshall's Centers for Excellence offer students the opportunity to engage in penetrating study and practical training in specialized areas of the law, including advocacy and dispute resolution, fair housing, information technology and privacy law, intellectual property law, international and comparative studies, real estate law, and tax law and employee benefits.

Special facilities include a moot courtroom complex with videotape recording and editing facilities and a jury deliberation room, a state-of-the-art computer classroom with twenty workstations, new faculty offices, a ninety-seat tiered lecture hall, two 45-seat classrooms, and a full-service conference facility seating more than 150.

John Marshall's library provides a collection of some 350,000 volumes, in addition to a 10,000-volume faculty library to promote scholarly research. John Marshall's library also provides students with access to cutting-edge computer research and reference services.

TECHNOLOGY ON CAMPUS

As the first law school in Chicago to teach legal research by computer, the John Marshall Law School is dedicated to the technological advances demanded by successful students. In addition to a computerized classroom, library study carrels wired for laptop computers, and an online library catalog, the Law School offers access to LEXIS-NEXIS, WESTLAW, CALI, Dialog, INFOTRAC, and OCLC. Every student has access to the Law School's network of software, including word processing, spreadsheets, e-mail, and Internet access. Through this technology, students and professors communicate via e-mail and often conduct routine classroom activity through the School's advanced computer technology.

SCHOLARSHIPS AND LOANS

A variety of financial aid programs, including loans, scholarships, grants, and need-based aid, are available to John Marshall students. Merit scholarships and grants are awarded to entering students on the basis of academic achievement, undergraduate course work, and LSAT scores.

STUDENT ACTIVITIES AND OPPORTUNITIES

Law Review The Law School's two journals—the *John Marshall Law Review* and the *Journal of Computer and Information Law*—are staffed and edited by more than 100 students. Admission to both journals is based upon academic standing and a write-on competition.

Moot Court John Marshall is represented by more than 60 students in more than thirty moot court and mock trial competitions annually. Their ninety-seven awards over the last five years, including a World Championship in 1995, highlight the talent of the student body.

Extracurricular Activities The Student Bar Association heads the long list of student organizations. These thirty or more groups engage in social awareness, community service, legal issues discussions, and social activities. They reflect the diversity of the student body and offer a glimpse at the opportunities available to John Marshall students. The highlight of the social year is the annual Barrister's Ball. In celebration of the Law School's centennial, the dance will be held at the Field Museum, an exciting atmosphere only John Marshall could provide.

Special Opportunities John Marshall provides its students the opportunity to gain an understanding of the basic competencies expected of attorneys. In addition to the many courses that help meet this commitment, the Law School has established a clinical legal education program, an academic program for which credit may be received. The program has two divisions—the Fair Housing Legal Clinic and the general externship program.

Opportunities for Members of Minority Groups and Women John Marshall has a long history of diversity. The current first-year class is composed of 52 percent women and 21 percent members of minority groups. Students participate in the Black Law Students Association, the Asian Law Students Association, the Women's Law Caucus, and the Hispanic Law Students Association, which earned the 1997–98 Student Organization Merit Award.

BAR PASSAGE, CAREER SERVICES, AND PLACEMENT

In 1996–97, 79 percent of the John Marshall graduates passed the bar exam on their first attempt. Most graduates take the Illinois bar exam.

Through individual counseling sessions and workshops, the Career Services Offices provides students and alumni with the skills they need for successful job searches throughout their legal careers. The office sponsors panels on various areas of law practice and assists students in applying for judicial clerkships. The large and supportive alumni base helps provide students with mentors and other contacts that can help them establish a network within the legal community. John Marshall graduates eagerly volunteer their time and experience to help current students make the transition from law student to lawyer. Of the 1996–97 graduates, 89 percent found full-time legal employment within six months of graduation.

Legal Field	Percentage of Graduates	Average Starting Salary
Academic	1.4%	n/a
Business	14.1%	$48,250
Government	15.5%	$35,200
Judicial Clerkship	4.2%	$38,750
Private Practice	60.1%	$48,250
Public Interest	0.5%	n/a
Other	4.2%	n/a

CORRESPONDENCE AND INFORMATION

The John Marshall Law School
315 South Plymouth Court
Chicago, Illinois 60604
Telephone: 800-537-4280 (toll-free)
Fax: 312-427-8307
E-mail: admission@jmls.edu
World Wide Web: http://www.jmls.edu

LOYOLA UNIVERSITY CHICAGO
SCHOOL OF LAW

Chicago, Illinois

LAW STUDENT PROFILE [1997–98]

FULL-TIME Enrollment: 556
Women: 56%   Men: 44%

PART-TIME Enrollment: 195
Women: 48%   Men: 52%

RACIAL or ETHNIC COMPOSITION
African American, 6%; Asian/Pacific Islander, 7%; Hispanic, 3%; Nataive American, 0.4%; International, 3%

APPLICANTS and ADMITTEES
Number applied: 2,329
Admitted: 959
Percentage accepted: 41%
Seats available: 162
Median LSAT score: 159
Median GPA: 3.3

Loyola University Chicago School of Law is a private institution that organizes classes on a semester calendar system. The campus is situated in an urban setting. First ABA approved in 1925, and an AALS member, Loyola University Chicago School of Law offers JD, JD/MA, JD/MBA, JD/MS, JD/MSW, JSD, LLM, and MJ degrees.

Faculty consists of 26 full-time and 72 part-time members in 1997–98. 5 full-time faculty members and 29 part-time faculty members are women.

Application Information *Required:* LSAT, LSDAS, application form, application fee of $45, baccalaureate degree, 2 letters of recommendation, personal statement. *Recommended:* resume. *Application deadline* for fall term is April 1.

Costs The 1997–98 tuition is $22,000 full-time; $16,500 part-time.

Financial Aid In 1997–98, 77% of all students received some form of financial aid. Fellowships, graduate assistantships, merit-based grants/scholarships, need-based grants/scholarships, and federal work-study loans are also available. To apply for financial assistance, students must complete the Free Application for Federal Student Aid and Need Access diskette. Financial aid contact: School of Law Admission and Financial Aid Office, 1 East Pearson

AT a GLANCE

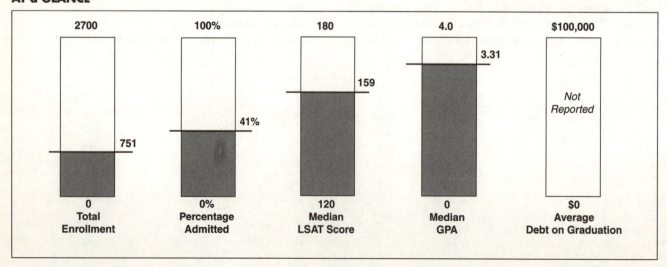

Degree Options

Degree	Total Credits Required	Length of Program
JD–Juris Doctor	86	
JD/MA–Juris Doctor/Master of Arts–Political Science		
JD/MBA–Juris Doctor/Master of Business Administration		
JD/MS–Juris Doctor/Master of Science–Institute of Human Resources and Industrial Relations		
JD/MSW–Juris Doctor/Master of Social Work		
JSD–Doctor of Juridical Science–Health Law and Policy		
LLM–Master of Laws–Health Law		
LLM–Master of Laws–Child and Family Law		
LLM–Master of Laws–Corporate Law		
LLM–Master of Laws–International Business Law		
MJ–Master of Jurisprudence–Corporate Law		
MJ–Master of Jurisprudence–Child and Family Law		
MJ–Master of Jurisprudence–Health Law		

Street, Chicago, IL 60611. Phone: 312-915-7170. E-mail: law-admissions@luc.edu. Completed financial aid forms should be received by March 1.

Law School Library has 7 professional staff members and contains more than 324,021 volumes and 3,499 periodicals. 380 seats are available in the library. When classes are in session, the library is open 90 hours per week.

WESTLAW and LEXIS-NEXIS are available. Special law collections include Health law.

First-Year Program Class size in the average section is 55.

Clinical Courses Among the clinical areas offered are:

Civil Litigation
Disability Law
Family Practice
General Practice
Juvenile Law
Landlord/Tenant
Tax Law
Unemployment Compensation

Internships are available. International exchange programs permit students to visit Italy and United Kingdom.

NORTHERN ILLINOIS UNIVERSITY
COLLEGE OF LAW

De Kalb, Illinois

INFORMATION CONTACT
LeRoy Pernell, Dean
DeKalb, IL 60115

Phone: 815-753-1067   Fax: 815-753-4501
Web site: http://www.niu.edu/

LAW STUDENT PROFILE [1997–98]

FULL-TIME   Enrollment: 273
Women: 37%   Men: 63%

PART-TIME   Enrollment: 7
Women: 29%   Men: 71%

RACIAL or ETHNIC COMPOSITION
African American, 8%; Asian/Pacific Islander, 7%; Hispanic, 5%; Native American, 1%; International, 0%

APPLICANTS and ADMITTEES
Seats available: 105
Average LSAT score: 155
Average GPA: 3.0

Northern Illinois University College of Law is a public institution that organizes classes on a semester calendar system. The campus is situated in a small-town setting. Founded in 1974, first ABA approved in 1978, and an AALS member, Northern Illinois University College of Law offers JD and JD/MBA degrees.

Faculty consists of 19 full-time members in 1997–98. 6 full-time faculty members are women. 100% of all faculty members have a JD; 42% have advanced law degrees. Of all faculty members, 5% are Asian/Pacific Islander, 20% are African American, 5% are Hispanic, 70% are white.

Application Information *Required:* LSAT, LSDAS, application form, application fee of $40, baccalaureate degree, 2 letters of recommendation, personal statement, college transcripts. *Application deadline for fall term is June 1.*

Financial Aid 14 awards were given. Graduate assistantships, loans, merit-based grants/scholarships, need-based grants/scholarships, and federal work-study loans are also available. The average student debt at graduation is $13,250. To apply for financial assistance, students must complete the Free Application for Federal Student Aid, institutional forms, and NIU Financial Aid Application. Financial aid contact: Judith L. Malen, Director of Admissions

AT a GLANCE

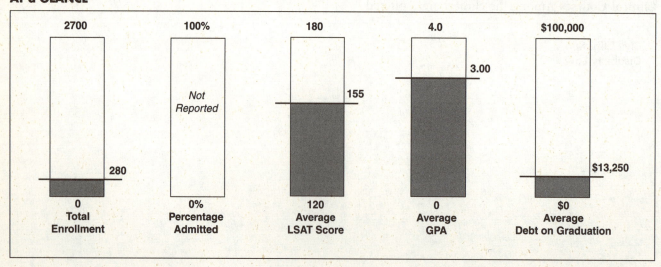

Degree Options

Degree	Total Credits Required	Length of Program
JD–Doctor of Laws	90	3 yrs, full-time only [day]
JD/MBA–Juris Doctor/Master of Business Administration–Dual-degree Program	120	4 yrs, full-time only [day]

and Financial Aid, De Kalb, IL 60115. Phone: 815-753-9487. Fax: 815-753-4501. E-mail: jmalen@niu.edu.

Law School Library David C. Shapiro Memorial Law Library has 5 professional staff members and contains more than 201,875 volumes and 3,112 periodicals. 210 seats are available in the library. When classes are in session, the library is open 97 hours per week.

WESTLAW and LEXIS-NEXIS are available, as are the World Wide Web, online bibliographic services, and CD-ROM players. 26 computer workstations are available to students in the library.

First-Year Program Class size in the average section is 44; 100% of the first-year courses are taught by full-time faculty.

Upper-Level Program Class size in the average section is 25. Among the electives are:

    Administrative Law
    Advocacy
  ★ Business and Corporate Law
    Consumer Law
    Education Law
    Entertainment Law
    Environmental Law
    Family Law
    Government/Regulation
    Health Care/Human Services
    Intellectual Property
    International/Comparative Law
    Jurisprudence
    Labor Law
    Land Use Law/Natural Resources
  ★ Lawyering Skills
    Legal History/Philosophy
    Litigation
    Maritime Law
    Media Law
  ★ Mediation
    Probate Law
  ★ Public Interest
    Securities
    Tax Law
(★ *indicates an area of special strength*)

Clinical Courses Students receive degree credit for clinical courses. (Clinical practicum is not required.) Among the clinical areas offered are:

    Civil Litigation
    Criminal Defense
    Criminal Prosecution
    Elderly Advocacy
    Family Practice
    Juvenile Law

25% of the students participate in internship programs.

NORTHWESTERN UNIVERSITY
SCHOOL OF LAW

Evanston, Illinois

INFORMATION CONTACT
David VanZandt, Dean
357 East Chicago Avenue
Chicago, IL 60611

Phone: 312-503-8460   Fax: 312-503-0178
E-mail: nulawadm@harold.law.nwu.edu
Web site: http://www.law1.nwu.edu/

LAW STUDENT PROFILE [1997–98]

FULL-TIME   Enrollment: 678
Women: 42%   Men: 58%

RACIAL or ETHNIC COMPOSITION
African American, 7%; Asian/Pacific Islander, 7%; Hispanic, 6%; Native American, 1%; International, 8%

APPLICANTS and ADMITTEES
Number applied: 3,537
Admitted: 749
Percentage accepted: 21%
Seats available: 205
Average LSAT score: 165
Average GPA: 3.5

Northwestern University School of Law is a private institution that organizes classes on a semester calendar system. The campus is situated in an urban setting. Founded in 1859, first ABA approved in 1923, and an AALS member, Northwestern University School of Law offers JD, JD/MM, JD/PhD, and LLM degrees.

Faculty consists of 56 full-time and 134 part-time members in 1997–98. 16 full-time faculty members and 31 part-time faculty members are women. 100% of all faculty members have a JD degree. Of all faculty members, 2% are Asian/Pacific Islander, 7% are African American, 93% are white.

Application Information *Required:* LSAT, LSDAS, application form, application fee of $80, baccalaureate degree, 2 letters of recommendation, personal statement, college transcripts, resume. *Recommended:* interview. *Application deadline* for fall term is February 16. Students are required to have their own computers.

Costs The 1997–98 tuition is $23,974.

Financial Aid In 1997–98, 61% of all students received some form of financial aid. Loans, loan repayment assistance program (LRAP), merit-based grants/scholarships, and need-based grants/scholarships are also available. The average student debt at

AT a GLANCE

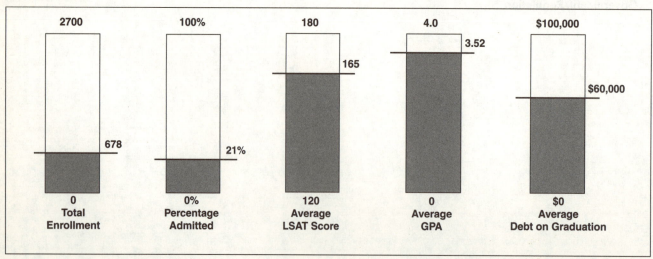

Degree Options

Degree	Total Credits Required	Length of Program
JD–Doctor of Laws	86	3 yrs, full-time only [day]
JD/MM–Juris Doctor/Master of Management–Dual-degree Program		4 yrs, full-time only [day]
JD/PhD–Juris Doctor/Doctor of Philosophy–Dual-degree Program		6 yrs, full-time only [day]
LLM–Master of Laws	20	1 yr [day]

graduation is $60,000. To apply for financial assistance, students must complete the Free Application for Federal Student Aid, institutional forms, and parental and student tax returns. Financial aid contact: Don Rebstock, Assistant Dean of Admissions and Financial Aid, 357 East Chicago Avenue, Chicago, IL 60611. Phone: 312-503-0179. Fax: 312-503-0178. E-mail: d-rebstock@nwu.edu. Completed financial aid forms should be received by March 17.

Law School Library Northwestern University School of Law Library has 13 professional staff members and contains more than 634,272 volumes and 8,257 periodicals. 718 seats are available in the library. When classes are in session, the library is open 105 hours per week.

WESTLAW and LEXIS-NEXIS are available, as is the World Wide Web. 69 computer workstations are available to students in the library. Special law collections include the United States Supreme Court papers of Justice Arthur J. Goldberg, the Anglo-American Collection.

First-Year Program Class size in the average section is 75; 100% of the first-year courses are taught by full-time faculty.

Upper-Level Program Class size in the average section is 29. Among the electives are:

Administrative Law
★ Advocacy
★ Business and Corporate Law
Consumer Law
Education Law
Entertainment Law
Environmental Law
Family Law
Government/Regulation
Health Care/Human Services
Indian/Tribal Law
Intellectual Property
★ International/Comparative Law
Jurisprudence
Labor Law
Land Use Law/Natural Resources
Lawyering Skills
Legal History/Philosophy
★ Litigation
Maritime Law
Media Law
Mediation
Probate Law
Public Interest
Securities
Tax Law
(★ *indicates an area of special strength*)

Clinical Courses Students receive degree credit for clinical courses. (Clinical practicum is not required.) Among the clinical areas offered are:

Civil Litigation
Civil Rights
Corporate Law
Criminal Defense
Criminal Prosecution
Family Practice
Immigration
International Law
Juvenile Law
Public Interest

Internships are available. International exchange programs permit students to visit Australia; Belgium; Israel; and Netherlands.

SOUTHERN ILLINOIS UNIVERSITY AT CARBONDALE
SCHOOL OF LAW

Carbondale, Illinois

INFORMATION CONTACT
Thomas F. Guernsey, Dean
Lesar Law Building
Carbondale, IL 62901-6804

Phone: 618-536-7711   Fax: 618-453-8769
Web site: http://www.siu.edu/~lawsch/

LAW STUDENT PROFILE [1997–98]

FULL-TIME   Enrollment: 365
Women: 39%   Men: 61%

PART-TIME   Enrollment: 4
Women: 25%   Men: 75%

RACIAL or ETHNIC COMPOSITION
African American, 5%; Asian/Pacific Islander, 7%; Hispanic, 3%; Native American, 1%

APPLICANTS and ADMITTEES
Number applied: 681
Admitted: 389
Percentage accepted: 57%
Seats available: 130
Average LSAT score: 153
Average GPA: 3.1

Southern Illinois University at Carbondale School of Law is a public institution that organizes classes on a semester calendar system. The campus is situated in a small-town setting. Founded in 1973, first ABA approved in 1980, and an AALS member, Southern Illinois University at Carbondale School of Law offers JD, JD/MBA, JD/MD, JD/MPA, JD/MPAd, and JD/MSW degrees.

Faculty consists of 30 full-time and 8 part-time members in 1997–98. 12 full-time faculty members and 2 part-time faculty members are women. 97% of all faculty members have a JD; 27% have advanced law degrees. Of all faculty members, 3% are Asian/Pacific Islander, 3% are African American, 6% are Hispanic, 88% are white.

Application Information *Required:* LSAT, LSDAS, application form, application fee of $25, baccalaureate degree, 1 recommendation, personal statement. *Application deadline* for fall term is March 1.

Costs The 1997–98 tuition is $4620 for state residents. Tuition is $13,860 for nonresidents. Fees: $1034.

Financial Aid In 1997–98, 81% of all students received some form of financial aid. Loans, merit-

AT a GLANCE

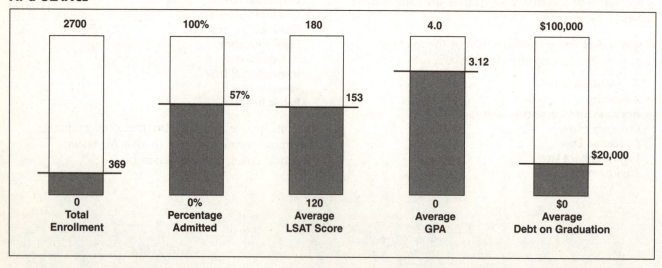

Degree Options

Degree	Total Credits Required	Length of Program
JD–Doctor of Laws	90	3 yrs, full-time only [day]
JD/MBA–Juris Doctor/Master of Business Administration–Dual-degree Program	120	4 yrs, full-time only [day]
JD/MD–Juris Doctor/Doctor of Medicine–Dual-degree Program		6 yrs, full-time only [day]
JD/MPA–Juris Doctor/Master of Professional Accountancy–Dual-degree Program	120	4 yrs, full-time only [day]
JD/MPAd–Juris Doctor/Master of Public Administration–Dual-degree Program		4 yrs, full-time only [day]
JD/MSW–Juris Doctor/Master of Social Work–Dual-degree Program		full-time only [day]

based grants/scholarships, need-based grants/scholarships, and federal work-study loans are also available. The average student debt at graduation is $20,000. To apply for financial assistance, students must complete the Free Application for Federal Student Aid. Financial aid contact: Financial Aid Office, Woody Hall, B Wing, 3rd Floor, Mailcode 4702, Carbondale, IL 62901-4702. Phone: 618-453-4334 or toll-free 800-739-9187. Fax: 618-453-8769.

Law School Library Southern Illinois University School of Law Library has 7 professional staff members and contains more than 330,000 volumes and 4,800 periodicals. 407 seats are available in the library.

WESTLAW and LEXIS-NEXIS are available, as are the World Wide Web, online bibliographic services, and CD-ROM players. 30 computer workstations are available to students in the library.

First-Year Program Class size in the average section is 62; 100% of the first-year courses are taught by full-time faculty.

Upper-Level Program Class size in the average section is 27. Among the electives are:

Administrative Law
Advocacy
Business and Corporate Law
Commercial Law
Education Law

★ **Environmental Law**
  Family Law
  Federal Courts
★ **Health Care/Human Services**
  Intellectual Property
  International/Comparative Law
  Jurisprudence
  Labor Law
★ **Land Use Law/Natural Resources**
  Lawyering Skills
  Legal History/Philosophy
  Litigation
  Mediation
  Probate Law
★ **Property/Real Estate**
  Public Interest
  Securities
  Tax Law
(★ *indicates an area of special strength*)

Clinical Courses Students receive degree credit for clinical courses. (Clinical practicum is not required.) Among the clinical areas offered are:

Civil Litigation
Criminal Defense
Criminal Prosecution
Elderly Advocacy
Legal Externship
Mediation
Public Interest

UNIVERSITY OF CHICAGO
LAW SCHOOL

Chicago, Illinois

INFORMATION CONTACT
Douglas Baird, Dean
1111 East 60th Street
Chicago, IL 60637

Phone: 773-702-9494
Web site: http://www.law.uchicago.edu/

LAW STUDENT PROFILE [1997–98]

FULL-TIME   Enrollment: 584
Women: 41%   Men: 59%

RACIAL or ETHNIC COMPOSITION
African American, 7%; Asian/Pacific Islander, 10%; Hispanic, 5%; Nataive American, 0.2%; International, 7%

APPLICANTS and ADMITTEES
Seats available: 175
Median LSAT score: 170
Median GPA: 3.8

University of Chicago Law School is a private institution that organizes classes on a semester calendar system. The campus is situated in an urban setting. Founded in 1902, first ABA approved in 1923, and an AALS member, University of Chicago Law School offers DCL, JD, JD/MA, JD/MBA, JD/PhD, JSD, LLM, and MCL degrees.

Application Information *Required:* LSAT, LSDAS, application form, application fee of $60, baccalaureate degree, 2 letters of recommendation. *Application deadline* for fall term is February 1.

Financial Aid Merit-based grants/scholarships and need-based grants/scholarships are available. To apply for financial assistance, students must complete the Free Application for Federal Student Aid and Need Access diskette. Completed financial aid forms should be received by March 15.

Law School Library the D'Angelo Law Library has 8 professional staff members and contains more than 619,753 volumes and 7,708 periodicals. 445 seats are available in the library. When classes are in session, the library is open 90 hours per week.

First-Year Program Class size in the average section is 88.

Upper-Level Program Among the electives are:

AT a GLANCE

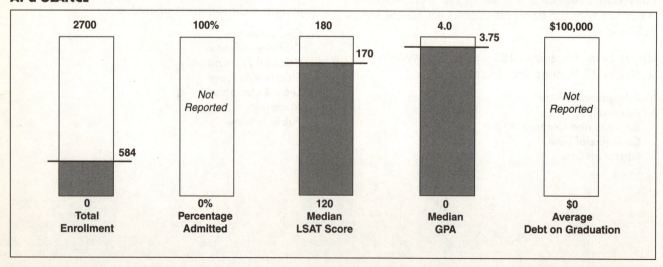

Degree Options

Degree	Total Credits Required	Length of Program
DCL–Doctor of Comparative Law		
JD–Juris Doctor	105	3 yrs, full-time only
JD/MA–Juris Doctor/Master of Arts–History Joint Degree		
JD/MA–Juris Doctor/Master of Arts–Economics Joint Degree		
JD/MBA–Juris Doctor/Master of Business Administration–Joint Degree		4 yrs
JD/PhD–Juris Doctor/Doctor of Philosophy–History Joint Degree		
JD/PhD–Juris Doctor/Doctor of Philosophy–Economics Joint Degree		
JSD–Doctor of Juridical Science		
LLM–Master of Laws	27	1 yr, full-time only
MCL–Master of Comparative Law	27	1 yr, full-time only

Administrative Law
Advocacy
Bankruptcy
Business and Corporate Law
Constitutional Law
Education Law
Environmental Law
Family Law
Feminist Jurisprudence
Government/Regulation
Health Care/Human Services
Intellectual Property
International/Comparative Law
Jurisprudence
Labor Law
Land Use Law/Natural Resources
Lawyering Skills
Legal History/Philosophy

Litigation
Maritime Law
Mediation
Public Interest
Securities
Tax Law
Trusts and Estates

Clinical Courses Among the clinical areas offered are:

Civil Rights
Criminal Defense
Health
Juvenile Law

UNIVERSITY OF ILLINOIS AT URBANA–CHAMPAIGN
COLLEGE OF LAW

Urbana, Illinois

INFORMATION CONTACT

Thomas M. Mengler, Dean
504 East Pennsylvania Avenue
Champaign, IL 61820

Phone: 217-333-9857   Fax: 217-244-1478
Web site: http://www.law.uiuc.edu/

LAW STUDENT PROFILE [1997–98]

FULL-TIME   Enrollment: 651
Women: 40%   Men: 60%

RACIAL or ETHNIC COMPOSITION
African American, 11%; Asian/Pacific Islander, 6%; Hispanic, 4%; International, 4%

APPLICANTS and ADMITTEES
Number applied: 1,951
Admitted: 534
Percentage accepted: 27%
Seats available: 200
Average LSAT score: 161
Average GPA: 3.5

University of Illinois at Urbana–Champaign College of Law is a public institution that organizes classes on a semester calendar system. The campus is situated in a small-town setting. Founded in 1897, first ABA approved in 1923, and an AALS member, University of Illinois at Urbana–Champaign College of Law offers JD, JD/DVM, JD/MA, JD/MBA, JD/MD, JD/MED, JD/MS, JD/MUP, and JD/PhD degrees.

Faculty consists of 32 full-time and 39 part-time members in 1997–98. 8 full-time faculty members and 10 part-time faculty members are women. 97% of all faculty members have a JD degree. Of all faculty members, 3% are Asian/Pacific Islander, 9% are African American, 6% are Hispanic, 82% are white.

Application Information *Required:* LSAT, LSDAS, application form, application fee of $40, baccalaureate degree, 2 letters of recommendation, personal statement, college transcripts, resume. *Application deadline* for fall term is March 15. Students are required to have their own computers.

Costs The 1997–98 tuition is $7234 full-time for state residents; $1206 per semester (minimum) part-time for state residents. Tuition is $17,608 full-time for nonresidents; $2835 per semester (minimum) part-time for nonresidents. Fees: $1053 full-time; $401 per semester (minimum) part-time.

AT a GLANCE

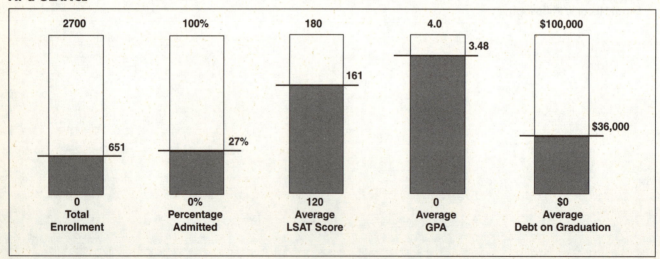

Degree Options

Degree	Total Credits Required	Length of Program
JD–Juris Doctor	90	3 yrs, full-time only [day]
JD/DVM–Juris Doctor/Doctor of Veterinary Medicine		6 yrs, full-time only [day]
JD/MA–Juris Doctor/Master of Arts–Labor and Industrial Relations Joint-degree Program	98	3.5 yrs, full-time only [day]
JD/MBA–Juris Doctor/Master of Business Administration–Joint-degree Program	119	4 yrs, full-time only [day]
JD/MD–Juris Doctor/Doctor of Medicine–Joint-degree	210	6 yrs, full-time only [day]
JD/MED–Juris Doctor/Master of Education–Joint-degree Program	96	3.5 yrs, full-time only [day]
JD/MS–Juris Doctor/Master of Science–Journalism Joint-degree Program	93	3–4 yrs, full-time only [day]
JD/MUP–Juris Doctor/Masters of Urban Planning–Joint-degree Program	104	4 yrs, full-time only [day]
JD/PhD–Juris Doctor/Doctor of Philosophy–Education Joint-degree Program	114	5–6 yrs, full-time only [day]

Financial Aid 4 research assistantships were awarded. Loans, merit-based grants/scholarships, need-based grants/scholarships, and federal work-study loans are also available. The average student debt at graduation is $36,000. To apply for financial assistance, students must complete the Free Application for Federal Student Aid, institutional forms, and scholarship specific applications. Financial aid contact: Ann Killian Perry, Assistant Dean for Student Affairs and Financial Aid, 504 East Pennsylvania Avenue, Champaign, IL 61820. Phone: 217-333-1097. Fax: 217-244-1478. E-mail: akperry@law.uiuc.edu.

Law School Library Albert E. Jenner, Jr. Memorial Law Library has 5 professional staff members and contains more than 677,635 volumes and 8,190 periodicals. 429 seats are available in the library. When classes are in session, the library is open 100 hours per week.

WESTLAW and LEXIS-NEXIS are available, as are the World Wide Web, online bibliographic services, and CD-ROM players. 93 computer workstations are available to students in the library.

First-Year Program Class size in the average section is 70; 80% of the first-year courses are taught by full-time faculty.

Upper-Level Program Among the electives are:

Administrative Law
★ Advocacy
★ Business and Corporate Law
Consumer Law
Education Law
★ Environmental Law
★ Family Law
Government/Regulation
Health Care/Human Services
Indian/Tribal Law
★ Intellectual Property
★ International/Comparative Law
Jurisprudence
★ Labor Law
Land Use Law/Natural Resources
★ Lawyering Skills
Legal History/Philosophy
★ Litigation
Media Law
Mediation
★ Probate Law
★ Public Interest
★ Securities
★ Tax Law
(★ *indicates an area of special strength*)

Clinical Courses Students receive degree credit for clinical courses. (Clinical practicum is not required.) Among the clinical areas offered are:

Civil Litigation
Corporate Law
Criminal Defense
Environmental Law
Family Practice
Government Litigation
Public Interest
Tax Law

INDIANA UNIVERSITY BLOOMINGTON
INDIANA UNIVERSITY SCHOOL OF LAW-BLOOMINGTON

Bloomington, Indiana

INFORMATION CONTACT

Alfred C. Aman Jr., Dean
211 South Indiana Avenue
Bloomington, IN 47405

Phone: 812-855-7995   Fax: 812-855-0555
E-mail: patclark@law.indiana.edu
Web site: http://www.law.indiana.edu/

LAW STUDENT PROFILE [1997–98]

FULL-TIME   Enrollment: 637
Women: 42%   Men: 58%

PART-TIME   Enrollment: 33
Women: 48%   Men: 52%

RACIAL or ETHNIC COMPOSITION

African American, 8%; Asian/Pacific Islander, 4%; Hispanic,
4%; Nataive American, 0.2%; International, 7%

APPLICANTS and ADMITTEES

Seats available: 200
Average LSAT score: 160
Average GPA: 3.4

Indiana University Bloomington Indiana University School of Law-Bloomington is a public institution that organizes classes on a semester calendar system. The campus is situated in a small-town setting. Founded in 1842, first ABA approved in 1937, and an AALS member, Indiana University Bloomington Indiana University School of Law-Bloomington offers JD, JD/MBA, JD/MES, JD/MLS, JD/MPA, JD/MPAf, JD/MS/MA, JSD, LLM, MCL, and PhD degrees.

Faculty consists of 20 full-time members in 1997–98. 2 full-time faculty members are women. 99.9% of all faculty members have a JD; 11% have advanced law degrees. Of all faculty members, 6% are African American, 94% are white.

Application Information *Required:* LSAT, LSDAS, application form, application fee of $35, baccalaureate degree, college transcripts. *Recommended:* 3 letters of recommendation and personal statement. *Application deadline* for fall term is March 1. Students are required to have their own computers.

Costs The 1997–98 tuition is $217 per credit hour for state residents. Tuition is $556 per credit hour for nonresidents. Fees: $343.

Financial Aid Fellowships, graduate assistantships, loans, merit-based grants/scholarships, need-based grants/scholarships, and federal work-study loans are available. The average student debt at graduation is $40,000. To apply for financial assistance, students must complete the Free Application for Federal Student Aid, institutional forms, and internal applica-

AT a GLANCE

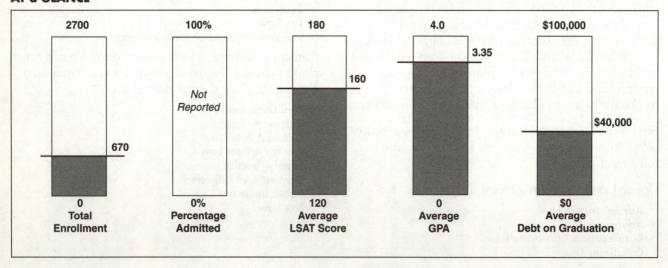

Degree Options

Degree	Total Credits Required	Length of Program
JD–Juris Doctor	86	3 yrs, full-time only [day, summer]
JD–Juris Doctor–Business Minor, Women's Studies Minor	86–92	3 yrs, full-time only [day, summer]
JD/MBA–Juris Doctor/Master of Business Administration–Dual-degree Program	119	4 yrs, full-time only [day, summer]
JD/MES–Juris Doctor/Master of Environmental Studies, JD/MPAf–Juris Doctor/Master of Public Affairs–Dual-degree Programs	113	4 yrs, full-time only [day, summer]
JD/MLS–Juris Doctor/Master of Library Science–JD/MPA–Juris Doctor/Master of Professional Accountancy–Dual-degree Programs	107–110	4 yrs, full-time only [day, summer]
JD/MS/MA–Juris Doctor/Master of Science or Master of Arts–Telecommunications Dual-degree Program	104	4 yrs, full-time only [day, summer]
JSD–Doctor of Juridical Science	30	1 yr, full-time only [day, summer]
LLM–Master of Laws	30	1 yr, full-time only [day, summer]
MCL–Master of Comparative Law	24	1 yr, full-time only [day, summer]
PhD–Doctor of Philosophy–Law and Social Science		[day, summer]

tion. Financial aid contact: Frank Motley, Assistant Dean for Admissions, Indiana University School of Law, 211 South Indiana Avenue, Bloomington, IN 47405. Phone: 812-855-4765. Fax: 812-855-0555. E-mail: frankmotley@law.indiana.edu. Completed financial aid forms should be received by March 1.

Law School Library Indiana University School of Law - Bloomington Law Library has 9 professional staff members and contains more than 603,808 volumes and 7,584 periodicals. 723 seats are available in the library. When classes are in session, the library is open 115 hours per week.

WESTLAW and LEXIS-NEXIS are available, as are the World Wide Web, online bibliographic services, and CD-ROM players. 86 computer workstations are available to students in the library. Special law collections include depository for records and briefs of the U.S. Supreme Court, Seventh Circuit Court of Appeals, and Indiana Supreme and Appellate Courts.

First-Year Program Class size in the average section is 70; 100% of the first-year courses are taught by full-time faculty.

Upper-Level Program Class size in the average section is 50. Among the electives are:

Administrative Law
★ Advocacy
★ Business and Corporate Law
Consumer Law
Education Law
Entertainment Law
★ Environmental Law
Family Law
★ Global Legal Studies
Government/Regulation
Health Care/Human Services
Indian/Tribal Law
★ Information and Communications
Intellectual Property
★ International/Comparative Law
Jurisprudence
Labor Law
Land Use Law/Natural Resources
★ Law and Society
Lawyering Skills
Legal History/Philosophy
★ Legal Writing
Litigation
Maritime Law
Media Law
Mediation
Probate Law
Public Interest
Securities
Tax Law

(★ *indicates an area of special strength*)

Clinical Courses Students receive degree credit for clinical courses. (Clinical practicum is not required.) Among the clinical areas offered are:

Civil Litigation
Criminal Defense
Criminal Prosecution
Environmental Law
Family Practice
General Practice
Government Litigation
Juvenile Law
Land Rights/Natural Resource
Mediation
Public Interest

20% of the students participate in internship programs. International exchange programs available.

INDIANA UNIVERSITY–PURDUE UNIVERSITY INDIANAPOLIS
INDIANA UNIVERSITY SCHOOL OF LAW-INDIANAPOLIS

Indianapolis, Indiana

INFORMATION CONTACT

Norman Lefstein, Dean
735 West New York Street
Indianapolis, IN 46202-5194

Phone: 317-274-2581   Fax: 317-274-3955
E-mail: amespada@iupui.edu
Web site: http://www.iulaw.indy.indiana.edu/

LAW STUDENT PROFILE [1997–98]

FULL-TIME   Enrollment: 563
Women: 46%   Men: 54%

PART-TIME   Enrollment: 294
Women: 47%   Men: 53%

RACIAL or ETHNIC COMPOSITION

African American, 7%; Asian/Pacific Islander, 2%; Hispanic, 2%; Nataive American, 0.5%; International, 2%

APPLICANTS and ADMITTEES

Number applied: 945
Admitted: 504
Percentage accepted: 53%
Seats available: 270
Average LSAT score: 156
Average GPA: 3.2

Indiana University–Purdue University Indianapolis Indiana University School of Law-Indianapolis is a public institution that organizes classes on a semester calendar system. The campus is situated in an urban setting. Founded in 1895, first ABA approved in 1936, and an AALS member, Indiana University–Purdue University Indianapolis Indiana University School of Law-Indianapolis offers JD, JD/MBA, JD/MHA, and JD/MPAf degrees.

Faculty consists of 45 full-time and 25 part-time members in 1997–98. 13 full-time faculty members and 7 part-time faculty members are women. 100% of all faculty members have a JD; 17% have advanced law degrees. Of all faculty members, 1% are Asian/Pacific Islander, 4% are African American, 95% are white.

Application Information *Required:* LSAT, LSDAS, application form, application fee of $35, baccalaureate degree, personal statement, college transcripts. *Recommended:* 2 letters of recommendation. *Application deadline* for fall term is March 1.

Financial Aid Fellowships, loans, merit-based grants/scholarships, need-based grants/scholarships, and federal work-study loans are available. The average student debt at graduation is $49,000. To

AT a GLANCE

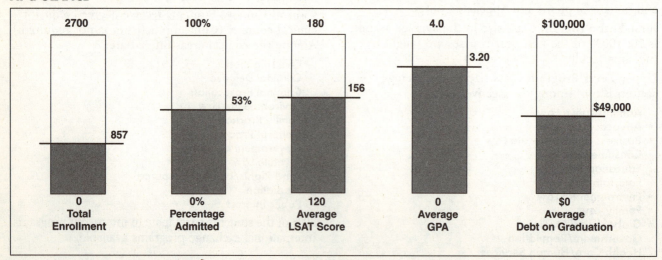

2700	100%	180	4.0	$100,000
			3.20	
	53%	156		
857				$49,000
0	0%	120	0	$0
Total Enrollment	**Percentage Admitted**	**Average LSAT Score**	**Average GPA**	**Average Debt on Graduation**

Degree Options

Degree	Total Credits Required	Length of Program
JD–Juris Doctor	90	3–4 yrs, full-time or part-time [day, evening, summer]
JD/MBA–Juris Doctor/Master of Business Administration	119	4–5 yrs, full-time or part-time [day, evening, summer]
JD/MHA–Juris Doctor/Master of Health Administration	130	4–5 yrs, full-time or part-time [day, evening, summer]
JD/MPAf–Juris Doctor/Master of Public Affairs	118	4–5 yrs, full-time or part-time [day, evening, summer]

apply for financial assistance, students must complete the Free Application for Federal Student Aid, institutional forms, and scholarship specific applications. Financial aid contact: Jim Schutter, Assistant Director Graduate Programs, 425 University Boulevard, CA103, Indianapolis, IN 46202-5145. Phone: 317-278-GRAD. Fax: 317-274-3955. E-mail: finaid5@iupui.edu.

Law School Library Indiana University School of Law - Indianapolis law library has 8 professional staff members and contains more than 475,000 volumes and 6,881 periodicals. 452 seats are available in the library. When classes are in session, the library is open 101 hours per week.

WESTLAW and LEXIS-NEXIS are available, as are the World Wide Web, online bibliographic services, and CD-ROM players. 23 computer workstations are available to students in the library. Special law collections include selective U.S. depository, United Nations depository, European community legal publications.

First-Year Program Class size in the average section is 85; 100% of the first-year courses are taught by full-time faculty.

Upper-Level Program Class size in the average section is 40. Among the electives are:

Administrative Law
Advocacy
Business and Corporate Law
Consumer Law
Education Law
Entertainment Law
Environmental Law
Family Law
Government/Regulation
★ Health Care/Human Services
Intellectual Property
International/Comparative Law
Jurisprudence
Labor Law
Land Use Law/Natural Resources
Law and Economics
★ Lawyering Skills
Legal History/Philosophy
Litigation
Media Law
Mediation
Probate Law
Property/Real Estate
Securities
Tax Law
(★ *indicates an area of special strength*)

Clinical Courses Students receive degree credit for clinical courses. (Clinical practicum is not required.) Among the clinical areas offered are:

Civil Litigation
Criminal Defense
Elderly Advocacy
Family Practice
General Practice
Health
Juvenile Law
Public Interest

12% of the students participate in internship programs. International exchange programs permit students to visit France.

UNIVERSITY OF NOTRE DAME
LAW SCHOOL

Notre Dame, Indiana

INFORMATION CONTACT
Dr. David T. Link, Dean
Notre Dame, IN 46556

Phone: 219-631-7015   Fax: 219-631-6371
E-mail: law.bulletin.1@nd.edu
Web site: http://www.nd.edu/~ndlaw/

LAW STUDENT PROFILE [1997–98]
FULL-TIME   Enrollment: 550
Women: 37%   Men: 63%

RACIAL or ETHNIC COMPOSITION
African American, 3%; Asian/Pacific Islander, 6%; Hispanic, 7%; Native American, 2%; International, 4%

APPLICANTS and ADMITTEES
Seats available: 180
Average LSAT score: 163
Average GPA: 3.4

University of Notre Dame Law School is a private institution that organizes classes on a semester calendar system. The campus is situated in a suburban setting. Founded in 1869, first ABA approved in 1925, and an AALS member, University of Notre Dame Law School offers JD, JD/MBA, JSD, and LLM degrees.

Faculty consists of 39 full-time and 34 part-time members in 1997–98. 10 full-time faculty members and 7 part-time faculty members are women. 94% of all faculty members have a JD; 12% have advanced law degrees. Of all faculty members, 4% are African American, 2% are Hispanic, 94% are white.

Application Information *Required:* LSAT, LSDAS, application form, application fee of $65, baccalaureate degree, 2 letters of recommendation, personal statement, college transcripts. *Recommended:* resume. *Application deadline* for fall term is March 1.

Financial Aid 200 fellowships, 20 research assistantships, 10 teaching assistantships were awarded. Fellowships, graduate assistantships, loans, merit-based grants/scholarships, need-based grants/scholarships, and federal work-study loans are also available. To apply for financial assistance, students must complete the Free Application for Federal Student Aid and institutional forms. Financial aid

AT a GLANCE

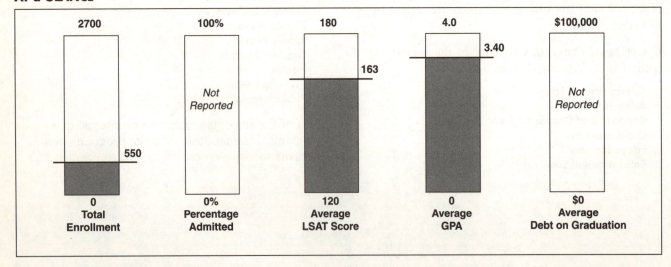

Degree Options

Degree	Total Credits Required	Length of Program
JD–Doctor of Laws	90	3 yrs, full-time only [day]
JD/MBA–Juris Doctor/Master of Business Administration–Dual-degree Program	122	4 yrs, full-time only [day]
JSD–Doctor of Juridical Science–Civil and Human Rights		full-time or part-time
LLM–Master of Laws–Civil and Human Rights	24	1 yr, full-time only
LLM–Master of Laws–International and Comparative Law	24	1 yr, full-time only

contact: Anne C. Hamilton, Director of Admissions, PO Box 959, Notre Dame, IN 46556-0959. Phone: 219-631-6626. Fax: 219-631-6371. E-mail: law.bulletin.1@nd.edu. Completed financial aid forms should be received by March 1.

Law School Library Kresge Law Library has 10 professional staff members and contains more than 454,082 volumes and 5,276 periodicals. 509 seats are available in the library. When classes are in session, the library is open 168 hours per week.

WESTLAW and LEXIS-NEXIS are available, as are the World Wide Web, online bibliographic services, and CD-ROM players. 40 computer workstations are available to students in the library.

First-Year Program Class size in the average section is 62; 100% of the first-year courses are taught by full-time faculty.

Upper-Level Program Class size in the average section is 23. Among the electives are:

Administrative Law
★ Advocacy
★ Business and Corporate Law
Consumer Law
Education Law
Environmental Law
Family Law
Health Care/Human Services
Intellectual Property
International/Comparative Law
★ Jurisprudence
Labor Law
Land Use Law/Natural Resources
★ Lawyering Skills
Legal History/Philosophy
Litigation
Maritime Law
Mediation
Securities
Tax Law

(★ *indicates an area of special strength*)

Clinical Courses Students receive degree credit for clinical courses. (Clinical practicum is not required.) Among the clinical areas offered are:

Civil Litigation
Criminal Defense
Elderly Advocacy
Family Practice
Immigration
Mediation
Public Interest

Internships are available.

VALPARAISO UNIVERSITY
SCHOOL OF LAW

Valparaiso, Indiana

INFORMATION CONTACT

Ivan E. Bodensteiner, Dean
Weseman Hall
Valparaiso, IN 46383

Phone: 219-465-7834   Fax: 219-465-7872
E-mail: heike.spahn@valpo.edu
Web site: http://www.valpo.edu/law/

LAW STUDENT PROFILE [1997–98]

FULL-TIME   Enrollment: 369
Women: 46%   Men: 54%

PART-TIME   Enrollment: 38
Women: 50%   Men: 50%

RACIAL or ETHNIC COMPOSITION

African American, 11%; Asian/Pacific Islander, 2%; Hispanic, 4%; Native American, 1%; International, 1%

APPLICANTS and ADMITTEES

Number applied: 674
Admitted: 401
Percentage accepted: 59%
Seats available: 140
Average LSAT score: 151
Average GPA: 3.1

Valparaiso University School of Law is a private institution that organizes classes on a semester calendar system. The campus is situated in a small-town setting. Founded in 1879, first ABA approved in 1929, and an AALS member, Valparaiso University School of Law offers JD and LLM degrees.

Faculty consists of 25 full-time and 37 part-time members in 1997–98. 7 full-time faculty members and 13 part-time faculty members are women. 100% of all faculty members have a JD; 20% have advanced law degrees. Of all faculty members, 8% are African American, 92% are white.

Application Information *Required:* LSAT, LSDAS, application form, application fee of $30, baccalaureate degree, personal statement, essay. *Recommended:* recommendations and resume. *Application deadline* for fall term is April 15.

Costs The 1997–98 tuition is $17,100 full-time; $660 per credit hour part-time. Fees: $480 full-time; $250 part-time.

Financial Aid In 1997–98, 88% of all students received some form of financial aid. Loans, loan repayment assistance program (LRAP), merit-based grants/scholarships, need-based grants/scholarships, and federal work-study loans are also available. The

AT a GLANCE

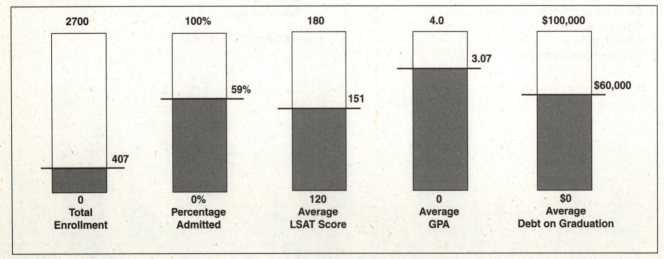

Degree Options

Degree	Total Credits Required	Length of Program
JD–Juris Doctor	90	3–5 yrs, full-time or part-time [day]
LLM–Master of Laws	24	1–2 yrs, full-time or part-time [day]

average student debt at graduation is $60,000. To apply for financial assistance, students must complete the Free Application for Federal Student Aid. Financial aid contact: Kim Jenkins, Financial Aid Counselor, Wesemann Hall, Valparaiso, IN 46383. Phone: 219-465-7818. Fax: 219-465-7872. E-mail: kjenkins@zeus.valpo.edu. Completed financial aid forms should be received by May 1.

Law School Library School of Law Library has 6 professional staff members and contains more than 265,289 volumes and 2,989 periodicals. 347 seats are available in the library. When classes are in session, the library is open 110 hours per week.

WESTLAW and LEXIS-NEXIS are available, as are the World Wide Web, online bibliographic services, and CD-ROM players. 39 computer workstations are available to students in the library. Special law collections include Indiana Supreme Court and Indiana Court of Appeals briefs.

First-Year Program Class size in the average section is 55; 100% of the first-year courses are taught by full-time faculty.

Upper-Level Program Class size in the average section is 35. Among the electives are:

Administrative Law
Advocacy
Business and Corporate Law
Elder Law
Entertainment Law

★ Environmental Law
Family Law
Government/Regulation
Health Care/Human Services
Intellectual Property
★ International/Comparative Law
Jurisprudence
★ Labor Law
Land Use Law/Natural Resources
Lawyering Skills
Legal History/Philosophy
Litigation
Maritime Law
Media Law
★ Mediation
Probate Law
Public Interest
Securities
Tax Law
(★ *indicates an area of special strength*)

Clinical Courses Students receive degree credit for clinical courses. (Clinical practicum is not required.) Among the clinical areas offered are:

Civil Litigation
Criminal Defense
Environmental Law
Juvenile Law
Mediation
Public Interest

Internships are available. International exchange programs permit students to visit United Kingdom.

DRAKE UNIVERSITY
LAW SCHOOL

Des Moines, Iowa

INFORMATION CONTACT
C. Peter Goplerud III, Dean
Cartwright Hall, 2507 University Avenue
Des Moines, IA 50311-4505

Phone: 515-271-2824   Fax: 515-271-1990
E-mail: lawadmit@drake.edu
Web site: http://www.drake.edu/

LAW STUDENT PROFILE [1997–98]

FULL-TIME   Enrollment: 399
Women: 43%   Men: 57%

PART-TIME   Enrollment: 8
Women: 25%   Men: 75%

RACIAL or ETHNIC COMPOSITION
African American, 3%; Asian/Pacific Islander, 2%; Hispanic, 3%; Native American, 1%; International, 1%

APPLICANTS and ADMITTEES
Number applied: 888
Admitted: 395
Percentage accepted: 44%
Seats available: 125
Average LSAT score: 153
Average GPA: 3.2

Drake University Law School is a private institution that organizes classes on a semester calendar system. The campus is situated in an urban setting. Founded in 1865, first ABA approved in 1923, and an AALS member, Drake University Law School offers JD, JD/MA, JD/MBA, JD/MPAd, JD/MS, JD/MSW, and JD/PharmD degrees.

Faculty consists of 26 full-time and 47 part-time members in 1997–98. 5 full-time faculty members and 21 part-time faculty members are women. 100% of all faculty members have a JD; 9.6% have advanced law degrees. Of all faculty members, 5.5% are African American, 1.3% are Hispanic, 93.2% are white.

Application Information *Required:* LSAT, LSDAS, application form, application fee of $35, baccalaureate degree, personal statement, college transcripts. *Recommended:* recommendations and resume. *Application deadline* for fall term is March 1.

Costs The 1997–98 tuition is $16,950 full-time; $565 per hour part-time.

Financial Aid In 1997–98, 92% of all students received some form of financial aid. 24 research assistantships, 7 teaching assistantships were awarded. 10 other awards were given. Fellowships, graduate assistantships, loans, loan repayment

AT a GLANCE

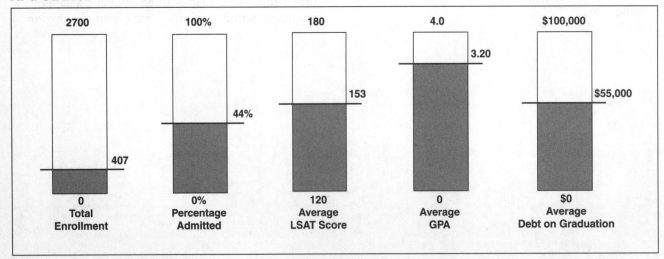

Degree Options

Degree	Total Credits Required	Length of Program
JD–Juris Doctor	90	3 yrs, full-time or part-time [day, evening, summer]
JD/MA–Juris Doctor/Master of Arts–Mass Communication, Political Science		full-time only [day, evening, summer]
JD/MBA–Juris Doctor/Master of Business Administration–Joint-degree Program		full-time only [day, evening, summer]
JD/MPAd–Juris Doctor/Master of Public Administration–Joint-degree Program		full-time only [day, evening, summer]
JD/MS–Juris Doctor/Master of Science–Agricultural Economics Joint-degree Program		full-time only [day, evening, summer]
JD/MSW–Juris Doctor/Master of Social Work–Joint-degree Program		full-time only [day, evening, summer]
JD/PharmD–Juris Doctor/Doctor of Pharmacy–Joint-degree Program		full-time only [day, evening, summer]

assistance program (LRAP), merit-based grants/ scholarships, need-based grants/scholarships, and federal work-study loans are also available. The average student debt at graduation is $55,000. To apply for financial assistance, students must complete the Free Application for Federal Student Aid, institutional forms, and scholarship specific applications. Financial aid contact: Kara Blanchard, Director of Admission and Financial Aid, 2507 University Avenue, Des Moines, IA 50311. Phone: 800-44-DRAKE Ext. 2782 or toll-free 800-44DRAKE Ext. 2782. Fax: 515-271-1990. E-mail: lawadmit@drake.edu. Completed financial aid forms should be received by March 1.

Law School Library Drake University Law Library has 4 professional staff members and contains more than 265,170 volumes and 3,066 periodicals. 705 seats are available in the library. When classes are in session, the library is open 109 hours per week.

WESTLAW and LEXIS-NEXIS are available, as are the World Wide Web, online bibliographic services, and CD-ROM players. 80 computer workstations are available to students in the library. Special law collections include Agricultural Law, Iowa Law, Constitutional Law.

First-Year Program Class size in the average section is 65; 100% of the first-year courses are taught by full-time faculty.

Upper-Level Program Class size in the average section is 16. Among the electives are:

Administrative Law

Advocacy
★ **Agricultural Law**
Business and Corporate Law
★ **Constitutional Law**
Consumer Law
Education Law
Environmental Law
Family Law
★ **Government/Regulation**
Health Care/Human Services
Intellectual Property
★ **International/Comparative Law**
Jurisprudence
Labor Law
Land Use Law/Natural Resources
Lawyering Skills
Legal History/Philosophy
Litigation
Media Law
Mediation
Probate Law
Securities
Tax Law
(★ *indicates an area of special strength*)

Clinical Courses Students receive degree credit for clinical courses. (Clinical practicum is not required.) Among the clinical areas offered are:

Civil Litigation
Criminal Defense
Criminal Prosecution
General Practice

80% of the students participate in internship programs.

THE UNIVERSITY OF IOWA
COLLEGE OF LAW

Iowa City, Iowa

INFORMATION CONTACT

N. William Hines, Dean
Boyd Law Building
Iowa City, IA 52442

Phone: 319-335-9034   Fax: 319-335-9019
E-mail: law-admissions@uiowa.edu
Web site: http://www.uiowa.edu/

LAW STUDENT PROFILE [1997–98]

FULL-TIME   Enrollment: 657
Women: 42%   Men: 58%

RACIAL or ETHNIC COMPOSITION
African American, 7%; Asian/Pacific Islander, 5%; Hispanic, 5%; Native American, 2%

APPLICANTS and ADMITTEES
Number applied: 1,118
Admitted: 451
Percentage accepted: 40%
Seats available: 225
Average LSAT score: 159
Average GPA: 3.5

The University of Iowa College of Law is a public institution that organizes classes on a semester calendar system. The campus is situated in a small-town setting. Founded in 1865, first ABA approved in 1923, and an AALS member, The University of Iowa College of Law offers JD, JD/MA, JD/MBA, JD/MSW, JD/PhD, and LLM degrees.

Faculty consists of 51 full-time and 22 part-time members in 1997–98. 15 full-time faculty members and 10 part-time faculty members are women. 98% of all faculty members have a JD; 34% have advanced law degrees. Of all faculty members, 2% are Native American, 2% are Asian/Pacific Islander, 8% are African American, 2% are Hispanic, 86% are white.

Application Information *Required:* LSAT, LSDAS, application form, application fee of $20, baccalaureate degree, personal statement, essay, college transcripts. *Recommended:* recommendations. *Application deadline* for fall term is March 1.

Costs The 1997–98 tuition is $6240 for state residents. Tuition is $16,156 for nonresidents. Fees: $285.

Financial Aid In 1997–98, 93% of all students received some form of financial aid. 30 fellowships, 163 research assistantships were awarded. Fellow-

AT a GLANCE

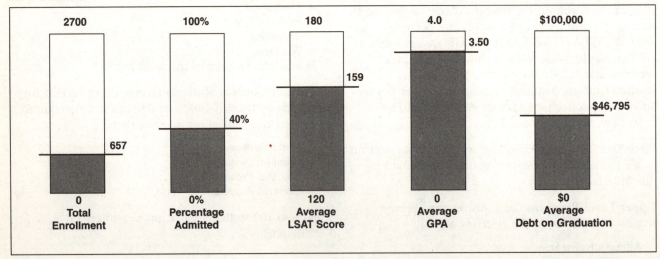

Degree Options

Degree	Total Credits Required	Length of Program
JD–Juris Doctor	90	3 yrs, full-time only [day]
JD/MA–Juris Doctor/Master of Arts		full-time only
JD/MBA–Juris Doctor/Master of Business Administration	123	4 yrs, full-time only [day]
JD/MSW–Juris Doctor/Master of Social Work	126	full-time only
JD/PhD–Juris Doctor/Doctor of Philosophy		
LLM–Master of Laws	24	1 yr, full-time only [day]

ships, graduate assistantships, loans, loan repayment assistance program (LRAP), merit-based grants/scholarships, need-based grants/scholarships, and federal work-study loans are also available. The average student debt at graduation is $46,795. To apply for financial assistance, students must complete the Free Application for Federal Student Aid, institutional forms, and federal tax return (student only). Financial aid contact: Admissions and Financial Aid Staff, College of Law, 276 Boyd Law Building, Iowa City, IA 52242. Phone: 319-335-9095. Fax: 319-335-9019.

Law School Library University of Iowa Law Library has 14 professional staff members and contains more than 864,882 volumes and 8,261 periodicals. 672 seats are available in the library. When classes are in session, the library is open 104 hours per week.

WESTLAW and LEXIS-NEXIS are available, as are the World Wide Web, online bibliographic services, and CD-ROM players. 57 computer workstations are available to students in the library. Special law collections include UN collection, records and briefs, NAACP papers.

First-Year Program Class size in the average section is 60; 100% of the first-year courses are taught by full-time faculty.

Upper-Level Program Among the electives are:

Administrative Law
Advocacy
★ Business and Corporate Law
Consumer Law
★ Disability Law
Education Law
Entertainment Law

Environmental Law
Family Law
Government/Regulation
★ Health Care/Human Services
★ Indian/Tribal Law
★ Intellectual Property
★ International/Comparative Law
Jurisprudence
Labor Law
Land Use Law/Natural Resources
★ Lawyering Skills
★ Legal History/Philosophy
Litigation
★ Media Law
★ Mediation
Probate Law
Public Interest
Securities
Tax Law
(★ indicates an area of special strength)

Clinical Courses Students receive degree credit for clinical courses. (Clinical practicum is not required.) Among the clinical areas offered are:

AIDS and the Law
Civil Litigation
Civil Rights
Employment Law
Health
Immigration
Intellectual Property
International Law
Mediation
Post-conviction Relief
Public Interest

15% of the students participate in internship programs.

UNIVERSITY OF KANSAS
SCHOOL OF LAW

Lawrence, Kansas

INFORMATION CONTACT
Michael H. Hoeflich, Dean
Green Hall
Lawrence, KS 66045

Phone: 785-864-4550   Fax: 785-864-5054
E-mail: lindeman@law.wpo.ukans.edu
Web site: http://www.law.ukans.edu/

LAW STUDENT PROFILE [1997–98]

FULL-TIME   Enrollment: 533
Women: 39%   Men: 61%

RACIAL or ETHNIC COMPOSITION
African American, 3%; Asian/Pacific Islander, 1%; Hispanic, 4%; Native American, 2%; International, 1%

APPLICANTS and ADMITTEES
Number applied: 813
Admitted: 403
Percentage accepted: 50%
Seats available: 180
Average LSAT score: 156
Median GPA: 3.4

University of Kansas School of Law is a public institution that organizes classes on a semester calendar system. The campus is situated in a small-town setting. Founded in 1878, first ABA approved in 1923, and an AALS member, University of Kansas School of Law offers JD, JD/MA, JD/MBA, JD/MHA, JD/MPAd, JD/MSW, and JD/MUP degrees.

Faculty consists of 36 full-time and 14 part-time members in 1997–98. 10 full-time faculty members and 5 part-time faculty members are women. 100% of all faculty members have a JD; 2.7% have advanced law degrees. Of all faculty members, 2.7% are Native American, 5.5% are African American, 5.5% are Hispanic, 86.3% are white.

Application Information *Required:* LSAT, LSDAS, application form, application fee of $40, baccalaureate degree, 1 recommendation, personal statement, writing sample, college transcripts. *Application deadline* for fall term is March 15.

Costs The 1997–98 tuition is $3100 for state residents. Tuition is $10,191 for nonresidents. Fees: $2598.

Financial Aid In 1997–98, 80% of all students received some form of financial aid. Graduate assistantships, loans, merit-based grants/scholarships,

AT a GLANCE

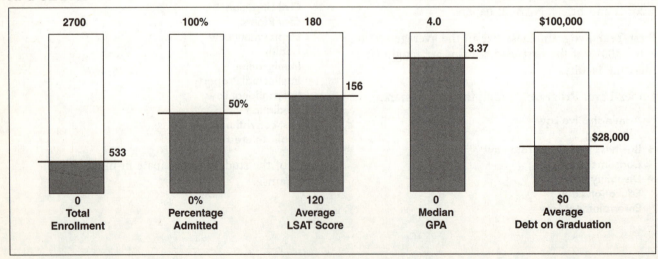

Degree Options

Degree	Total Credits Required	Length of Program
JD–Juris Doctor	90	3 yrs, full-time only [day, summer]
JD/MA–Juris Doctor/Master of Arts–Economics Joint-degree Program	120	3 yrs, full-time only [day, summer]
JD/MA–Juris Doctor/Master of Arts–Philosophy Joint-degree Program	102	3 yrs, full-time only [day, summer]
JD/MBA–Juris Doctor/Master of Business Administration–Joint-degree Program	118	4 yrs, full-time only [day, summer]
JD/MHA–Juris Doctor/Master of Health Administration–Joint-degree Program	127	4 yrs, full-time only [day, summer]
JD/MPAd–Juris Doctor/Master of Public Administration–Joint-degree Program	115	4 yrs, full-time only [day, summer]
JD/MSW–Juris Doctor/Master of Social Work–Joint-degree Program	131	4 yrs, full-time only [day, summer]
JD/MUP–Juris Doctor/Masters of Urban Planning–Joint-degree Program	115	4 yrs, full-time only [day, summer]

need-based grants/scholarships, and federal work-study loans are also available. The average student debt at graduation is $28,000. To apply for financial assistance, students must complete the Free Application for Federal Student Aid. Financial aid contact: Diane Lindeman, Director of Admissions, University of Kansas School of Law, Lawrence, KS 66045. Phone: 785-864-4378. Fax: 785-864-5054. E-mail: admit@law.wpo.ukans.edu. Completed financial aid forms should be received by March 1.

Law School Library University of Kansas School of Law Library has 5 professional staff members and contains more than 331,393 volumes and 4,345 periodicals. 276 seats are available in the library. When classes are in session, the library is open 103 hours per week.

WESTLAW and LEXIS-NEXIS are available, as are the World Wide Web, online bibliographic services, and CD-ROM players. 50 computer workstations are available to students in the library. Special law collections include Kansas State Law, Indian Law.

First-Year Program Class size in the average section is 90; 100% of the first-year courses are taught by full-time faculty.

Upper-Level Program Class size in the average section is 28. Among the electives are:

Administrative Law
Advocacy
Business and Corporate Law
Consumer Law
Education Law
Environmental Law
Family Law
Government/Regulation
Health Care/Human Services
★ **Indian/Tribal Law**
Intellectual Property
International/Comparative Law
Jurisprudence
Labor Law
Land Use Law/Natural Resources
Lawyering Skills
Legal History/Philosophy
Litigation
★ **Media Law**
Mediation
Probate Law
Public Interest
Securities
Tax Law

(★ indicates an area of special strength)

Clinical Courses Students receive degree credit for clinical courses. (Clinical practicum is not required.) Among the clinical areas offered are:

Civil Litigation
Criminal Defense
Criminal Prosecution
Elderly Advocacy
Family Practice
General Practice
Judicial Clerkship
Legislation
Public Interest
Public Policy

Internships are available.

WASHBURN UNIVERSITY OF TOPEKA
SCHOOL OF LAW

Topeka, Kansas

INFORMATION CONTACT

James M. Concannon, Dean
1700 College
Topeka, KS 66621

Phone: 785-231-1010   Fax: 785-232-8087
    Ext. 1662
E-mail: zzkerr@washburn.edu
Web site: http://www.washburn.law/

LAW STUDENT PROFILE [1997–98]

FULL-TIME   Enrollment: 441
Women: 44%   Men: 56%

RACIAL or ETHNIC COMPOSITION
African American, 4%; Asian/Pacific Islander, 3%; Hispanic, 4%; Native American, 1%; International, 3%

APPLICANTS and ADMITTEES
Number applied: 649
Admitted: 389
Percentage accepted: 60%
Seats available: 148
Median LSAT score: 151
Average GPA: 3.2

Washburn University of Topeka School of Law is a public institution that organizes classes on a semester calendar system. The campus is situated in an urban setting. Founded in 1903, first ABA approved in 1923, and an AALS member, Washburn University of Topeka School of Law offers JD, JD/MBA, and JD/MCJ degrees.

Faculty consists of 27 full-time and 31 part-time members in 1997–98. 9 full-time faculty members and 7 part-time faculty members are women. 100% of all faculty members have a JD; 42% have advanced law degrees. Of all faculty members, 7.4% are Asian/Pacific Islander, 11.1% are African American, 7.4% are Hispanic, 74.1% are white.

Application Information *Required:* LSAT, LSDAS, application form, application fee of $30, baccalaureate degree, 1 recommendation, personal statement, college transcripts, resume. *Application deadline* for fall term is March 15.

Financial Aid In 1997–98, 90% of all students received some form of financial aid. 15 research assistantships, totaling $70,000; 7 teaching assistantships, totaling $14,000, were awarded. 146 other awards, totaling $468,730, were given. Graduate assistantships, loans, merit-based grants/scholarships, need-based grants/scholarships, and federal work-study loans are also available. The average student

AT a GLANCE

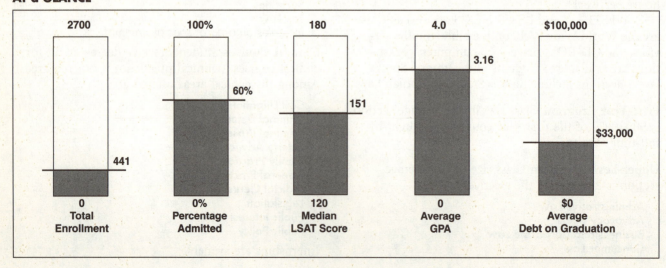

Degree Options

Degree	Total Credits Required	Length of Program
JD–Juris Doctor	90	3–4 yrs, full-time or part-time [day, summer]
JD/MBA–Juris Doctor/Master of Business Administration	111	3.5–5 yrs, full-time or part-time [day, evening, weekend, summer]
JD/MCJ–Juris Doctor/Master of Criminal Justice	108	3.5–5 yrs, full-time or part-time [day, evening, weekend, summer]

debt at graduation is $33,000. To apply for financial assistance, students must complete the Free Application for Federal Student Aid, institutional forms, scholarship specific applications, and CSS PROFILE form. Financial aid contact: Janell Harris, Assistant Director, Financial Aid, 1700 College, Topeka, KS 66621. Phone: 785-231-1151. Fax: 785-232-8087. E-mail: zzharr@washburn.edu. Completed financial aid forms should be received by March 1.

Law School Library Washburn University School of Law Library has 11 professional staff members and contains more than 303,423 volumes and 3,737 periodicals. 346 seats are available in the library. When classes are in session, the library is open 99 hours per week.

WESTLAW and LEXIS-NEXIS are available, as are the World Wide Web, online bibliographic services, and CD-ROM players. 74 computer workstations are available to students in the library. Special law collections include US Government Documents, Kansas Government Documents, Wolf Creek Collection (Nuclear Regulatory Commission Depository).

First-Year Program Class size in the average section is 70; 100% of the first-year courses are taught by full-time faculty.

Upper-Level Program Class size in the average section is 42. Among the electives are:

    Administrative Law
★   Advocacy
★   Agricultural Law
    Business and Corporate Law
★   Consumer Law
    Education Law
    Entertainment Law
★   Environmental Law

★   Family Law
    Government/Regulation
    Health Care/Human Services
    Indian/Tribal Law
    Intellectual Property
    International/Comparative Law
    Jurisprudence
    Labor Law
★   Land Use Law/Natural Resources
★   Lawyering Skills
    Legal History/Philosophy
★   Litigation
    Maritime Law
    Media Law
★   Mediation
★   Mental Health and Law
    Probate Law
★   Public Interest
    Securities
★   Tax Law
(★ *indicates an area of special strength*)

Clinical Courses Students receive degree credit for clinical courses. (Clinical practicum is not required.) Among the clinical areas offered are:

    Civil Litigation
    Civil Rights
    Criminal Defense
    Criminal Prosecution
    Elderly Advocacy
    Family Practice
    General Practice
    Health
    Juvenile Law
    Mediation
    Public Interest
    Tax Law

20% of the students participate in internship programs.

NORTHERN KENTUCKY UNIVERSITY
SALMON P. CHASE COLLEGE OF LAW

Highland Heights, Kentucky

INFORMATION CONTACT

Prof. David Short, Dean
Nunn Hall
Highland Heights, KY 41099

Phone: 606-572-6406   Fax: 606-572-6081
Web site: http://www.nku.edu/~chase/

LAW STUDENT PROFILE [1997–98]

FULL-TIME   Enrollment: 202
Women: 34%   Men: 66%

PART-TIME   Enrollment: 199
Women: 38%   Men: 62%

RACIAL or ETHNIC COMPOSITION
African American, 5%; Asian/Pacific Islander, 0.3%; Hispanic, 1%; Nataive American, 0.3%

APPLICANTS and ADMITTEES
Number applied: 699
Admitted: 272
Percentage accepted: 39%
Seats available: 117
Average LSAT score: 155
Average GPA: 3.2

Northern Kentucky University Salmon P. Chase College of Law is a public institution that organizes classes on a semester calendar system. The campus is situated in a suburban setting. Founded in 1893, first ABA approved in 1954, and an AALS member, Northern Kentucky University Salmon P. Chase College of Law offers JD and JD/MBA degrees.

Faculty consists of 24 full-time members in 1997–98. 7 full-time faculty members are women. 100% of all faculty members have a JD; 10% have advanced law degrees. Of all faculty members, 7.25% are African American, 92.75% are white.

Application Information *Required:* LSAT, LSDAS, application form, application fee of $30, baccalaureate degree, recommendations, personal statement, essay, writing sample. *Application deadline* for fall term is May 1.

Costs The 1997–98 tuition is $5390 full-time for state residents; $227 per semester hour part-time for state residents. Tuition is $14,000 full-time for nonresidents; $585 per semester hour part-time for nonresidents.

Financial Aid 2 research assistantships were awarded. 80 other awards were given. Graduate

AT a GLANCE

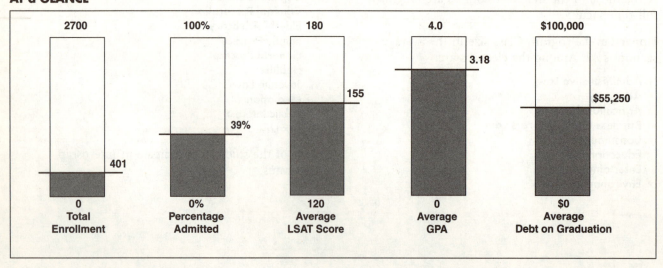

Degree Options

Degree	Total Credits Required	Length of Program
JD–Doctor of Laws	90	3–4 yrs, full-time or part-time [day, evening, summer]
JD/MBA–Juris Doctor/Master of Business Administration–Dual-degree Program	110	4–5 yrs, full-time or part-time [day, evening, summer]

assistantships, loans, merit-based grants/scholarships, need-based grants/scholarships, and federal work-study loans are also available. The average student debt at graduation is $55,250. To apply for financial assistance, students must complete the Free Application for Federal Student Aid. Financial aid contact: Office of Student Financial Assistance, AC 416, Highland Heights, KY 41099. Phone: 606-572-5134. Fax: 606-572-6081. Completed financial aid forms should be received by April 1.

Law School Library Salmon P. Chase College of Law Library has 7 professional staff members and contains more than 245,777 volumes and 1,945 periodicals. 200 seats are available in the library. When classes are in session, the library is open 100 hours per week.

WESTLAW and LEXIS-NEXIS are available, as are the World Wide Web, online bibliographic services, and CD-ROM players. 27 computer workstations are available to students in the library. Special law collections include Siebenthaler Rare Book Collection.

First-Year Program Class size in the average section is 60; 100% of the first-year courses are taught by full-time faculty.

Upper-Level Program Class size in the average section is 25. Among the electives are:

    Administrative Law
★ Advocacy
    Business and Corporate Law
    Consumer Law

    Education Law
    Entertainment Law
★ Environmental Law
    Family Law
    Government/Regulation
    Health Care/Human Services
    Intellectual Property
    International/Comparative Law
    Jurisprudence
★ Juvenile Law
    Labor Law
    Land Use Law/Natural Resources
★ Lawyering Skills
    Legal History/Philosophy
    Litigation
★ Local Government
    Media Law
    Mediation
    Probate Law
    Public Interest
    Securities
    Tax Law
(★ indicates an area of special strength)

Clinical Courses Students receive degree credit for clinical courses. (Clinical practicum is not required.) Among the clinical areas offered are:

    Judicial
    Juvenile Law
    Local Government
    Public Interest
    Tax Law

DEAN'S STATEMENT . . .

Thank you for considering attending the Salmon P. Chase College of Law. Chase was founded in 1893 as an evening law school. Its mission was to offer an exceptional legal education to students with limited means. In time, Chase became known as "the lawyers' school" because the faculty consisted predominately of practicing attorneys.

Chase continues to earn the reputation as "the lawyers' school" by providing our students with an excellent legal education enhanced by frequent contact with members of the practicing bar. The Chase faculty is distinguished by a real-world approach to the study of law and a genuine love of teaching. Many of our faculty members have left thriving practices to become educators. A number of our professors have traveled and taught extensively in the Far East, Great Britain, and the former Soviet Union. Additionally, our faculty includes published authorities in environmental and natural resources law, Ohio and Kentucky corporations law, Kentucky real estate law, civil rights litigation, defamation and privacy law, and domestic relations. An adjunct faculty composed of respected practicing attorneys and distinguished members of the judiciary complements our full-time faculty.

Affordable tuition and a convenient location just 7 miles from downtown Cincinnati also make Chase College of Law an excellent choice for legal education. We offer both a full-time day program and a part-time evening program. Chase is accredited by the American Bar Association and is a member of the Association of American Law Schools.

I encourage you to learn more about Chase. Please contact our Admissions Office if you have questions or would like to visit. Best wishes as you embark on your legal career.

—David C. Short, Dean

HISTORY, CAMPUS, AND LOCATION

The College of Law is named for Salmon P. Chase, who served as Governor of Ohio, was the U.S. Secretary of the Treasury, and was appointed Chief Justice of the United States Supreme Court by President Abraham Lincoln. The Chase Room on the fifth floor of Nunn Hall contains portraits, photographs, original documents, and possessions of the School's namesake.

Although Chase was founded in Ohio, Chase today is part of Northern Kentucky University (NKU), a learner-centered metropolitan university located in Highland Heights, Kentucky, just minutes from Cincinnati, Ohio. NKU serves approximately 11,500 undergraduate, graduate, and law students. The modern campus is housed on 250 acres of rolling countryside and has earned recognition for being handicapped accessible. The area offers many cultural and recreational opportunities for students, such as theaters, concerts, restaurants, art galleries, museums, professional sporting events, parks, outdoor festivals, and fireworks displays. Both on-campus and off-campus housing is available.

To put the location in a geographical perspective, Chase is 12 miles from the Northern Kentucky/Greater Cincinnati Airport; 79 miles from Lexington, Kentucky; 93 miles from Louisville, Kentucky; 60 miles from Dayton, Ohio; 115 miles from Columbus, Ohio; and 114 miles from Indianapolis, Indiana.

SPECIAL QUALITIES OF THE SCHOOL

The Chase College Foundation, a private, nonprofit organization, provides ongoing funding to enhance educational opportunities at Chase through a $2.2-million endowment. Additionally, the Northern Kentucky University Foundation manages endowment assets for the benefit of Chase College of Law in the amount of $2,033,284. The Chase Alumni Club provides additional support.

TECHNOLOGY ON CAMPUS

The Legal Information Technology Lab in the Chase Law Library has twenty stations equipped with state-of-the-art personal computers. The lab also has a high-quality projection system that enables the LIT lab to be used as an electronic classroom. Students have access to both LEXIS and WESTLAW legal research databases. Chase students also have Internet and e-mail access. Smart classrooms have been incorporated into two lecture halls and the Moot Court Room.

SCHOLARSHIPS AND LOANS

Both privately funded and institutional scholarships are available. Most scholarships are based on merit or a combination of merit and need. Scholarship amounts vary. Applicants are not required to complete a separate scholarship application to be considered for merit-based scholarships. Applicants must complete the FAFSA in order to be considered for scholarships based on merit and need. The NKU Office of Student Financial Assistance advises students regarding financial aid programs and the application process.

STUDENT ACTIVITIES AND OPPORTUNITIES

Law Review Chase students serve on the *Northern Kentucky Law Review* staff as writers, editors, proofreaders, and subciters. A position on the editorial board is one of the highest honors a student can attain. Chase has been chosen to serve as the host school for the 1999 annual meeting of the National Conference of Law Reviews (NCLR). The NCLR is an organization composed of approximately 120 law reviews. The group meets annually to discuss practical and general issues regarding law review publications. The *Northern Kentucky Law Review* will serve on the Executive Committee of the NCLR for the next three years.

Moot Court Chase offers an active moot court program. Participation is available for those students with a demonstrated ability and interest in moot court. The Moot Court Board conducts two intramural competitions annually, administers the National Environmental Law Moot Court Competition, and selects students to attend various competitions throughout the country.

Extracurricular Activities Chase students have numerous opportunities for personal and professional development through a wide variety of extracurricular activities such as community service, professional organizations, student government, minority student groups, political groups, religious groups, and recreational activities.

Special Opportunities The Local Government Law Center provides students with clinical experience and educational opportunities that pertain to local government law. Chase students have the opportunity to work in the area of juvenile law through opportunities available from the Children's Law Center, Inc. The Ohio Valley Environment and Natural Resources Law Institute enhances the environmental law curriculum. Students interested in taxation may participate in the Volunteer Income Tax Assistance Program, which helps low-income, elderly, and disabled taxpayers. The Academic Development Program enhances first-year student study, learning, and exam-taking skills.

Opportunities for Members of Minority Groups and Women In addition to all other student programs and activities, opportunities exist for members of minority groups and women, including the Black Law Students Association (BLSA) and Women's Law Caucus. Chase also works closely with the Black Lawyers' Association of Cincinnati (BLAC) and the Cincinnati Bar Roundtable to provide mentoring and summer clerkship opportunities for minority students.

Special Certificate Programs The J.D./M.B.A. Program is an attractive option for individuals who wish to practice law and/or business in an increasingly dynamic and complex environment. Courses in the College of Law serve as electives for the M.B.A. degree; M.B.A. courses serve as electives for the law degree. Thus, the number of hours required to obtain both degrees through the combined program is less than the number of hours required to complete each degree independent of the other. Upon satisfactory completion of the requirements of the program, a student is awarded both a J.D. degree and an M.B.A. degree.

BAR PASSAGE, CAREER SERVICES, AND PLACEMENT

The most common states in which Chase graduates sit for the bar exam are Kentucky and Ohio. The most recent bar results for the first-time test-takers in Kentucky are 83 percent and in Ohio, 79 percent. The Chase Career Development Office assists students in career planning and development of job-seeking skills. The office sponsors seminars on a variety of career issues. The office recently sponsored a presentation by Kimm Alayne Walton, author of *Guerilla Tactics for Getting the Legal Job of Your Dreams* and columnist for the *National Law Journal*.

Chase graduates generally find employment in solo practice; small, medium, and large law firms; corporations and businesses; government; judicial clerkships; public interest and public service work; and education. The average starting salary for the 1997 graduating class was $37,000.

Legal Field	Percentage of Graduates	Average Salary
Academic	2%	n/a
Business	20%	$47,100
Government	22%	$28,944
Judicial Clerkship	5%	$24,233
Private Practice	48%	$36,292
Public Interest	n/a	n/a
Other	3%	$31,000

CORRESPONDENCE AND INFORMATION

Office of Admissions
Salmon P. Chase College of Law
Northern Kentucky University
529 Nunn Hall
Highland Heights, Kentucky 41099
Telephone: 606-572-6476
Fax: 606-572-6081

UNIVERSITY OF KENTUCKY
COLLEGE OF LAW

Lexington, Kentucky

INFORMATION CONTACT
David E. Shipley, Dean
Lexington, KY 40506-0048

Phone: 606-257-1678   Fax: 606-323-1061
E-mail: dbakert@pop.uky.edu
Web site: http://www.uky.edu/Law/

LAW STUDENT PROFILE [1997–98]

FULL-TIME   Enrollment: 421
Women: 37%   Men: 63%

RACIAL or ETHNIC COMPOSITION
African American, 5%; Asian/Pacific Islander, 1%;
International, 0%

APPLICANTS and ADMITTEES
Number applied: 750
Admitted: 318
Percentage accepted: 42%
Seats available: 142
Average LSAT score: 158
Average GPA: 3.4

University of Kentucky College of Law is a public institution that organizes classes on a semester calendar system. The campus is situated in a suburban setting. Founded in 1908, first ABA approved in 1925, and an AALS member, University of Kentucky College of Law offers JD, JD/MBA, and JD/MPAd degrees.

Faculty consists of 28 full-time and 22 part-time members in 1997–98. 8 full-time faculty members and 8 part-time faculty members are women. 100% of all faculty members have a JD; 26% have advanced law degrees. Of all faculty members, 7.5% are African American, 92.5% are white.

Application Information *Required:* LSAT, LSDAS, application form, application fee of $25, baccalaureate degree, personal statement. *Application deadline* for fall term is March 1.

Costs The 1997–98 tuition is $4956 for state residents. Tuition is $12,796 for nonresidents.

Financial Aid In 1997–98, 71% of all students received some form of financial aid. 105 other awards were given. Loans, merit-based grants/scholarships, need-based grants/scholarships, and federal work-study loans are also available. The average student debt at graduation is $36,000. To apply for financial assistance, students must

AT a GLANCE

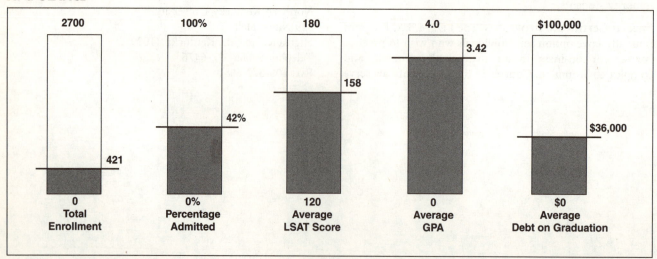

Degree Options

Degree	Total Credits Required	Length of Program
JD–Juris Doctor	90	2.5–3 yrs, full-time only [day, summer]
JD/MBA–Juris Doctor/Master of Business Administration–Dual-degree Program	111	3.5–4 yrs, full-time only [day, summer]
JD/MPAd–Juris Doctor/Master of Public Administration–Dual-degree Program	111	3.5–4 yrs, full-time only [day, summer]

complete the Free Application for Federal Student Aid and scholarship specific applications. Financial aid contact: UK Student Financial Aid, 128 Funkhouser Building, University of Kentucky, Lexington, KY 40506-0054. Phone: 606-257-3172. Fax: 606-323-1061. Completed financial aid forms should be received by April 1.

Law School Library Alvin E. Evans Law Library has 8 professional staff members and contains more than 385,250 volumes and 3,926 periodicals. 279 seats are available in the library. When classes are in session, the library is open 106 hours per week.

WESTLAW and LEXIS-NEXIS are available, as are the World Wide Web, online bibliographic services, and CD-ROM players. 92 computer workstations are available to students in the library.

First-Year Program Class size in the average section is 60; 100% of the first-year courses are taught by full-time faculty.

Upper-Level Program Class size in the average section is 40. Among the electives are:

Administrative Law
Advocacy
Business and Corporate Law
Consumer Law
Environmental Law
Family Law
Government/Regulation
Health Care/Human Services
Intellectual Property
International/Comparative Law
Jurisprudence
Labor Law
Land Use Law/Natural Resources
Legal History/Philosophy
Litigation
Mediation
Probate Law
Public Interest
Securities
Tax Law

Clinical Courses Students receive degree credit for clinical courses. (Clinical practicum is not required.) Among the clinical areas offered are:

Criminal Prosecution
Elderly Advocacy
Environmental Law
Judicial Clerkship
Mediation
Prisoners' Rights

40% of the students participate in internship programs.

UNIVERSITY OF LOUISVILLE
LOUIS D. BRANDEIS SCHOOL OF LAW

Louisville, Kentucky

INFORMATION CONTACT
Donald L. Burnett Jr., Dean
Wilson W. Wyatt Hall
Louisville, KY 40292

Phone: 502-852-6879   Fax: 502-852-0862
E-mail: gjjack01@ulkyvm.louisville.edu
Web site: http://www.louisville.edu/brandeislaw/

LAW STUDENT PROFILE [1997–98]
FULL-TIME   Enrollment: 459
Women: 43%   Men: 57%

RACIAL or ETHNIC COMPOSITION
African American, 4%; Asian/Pacific Islander, 2%; Hispanic, 1%; Nataive American, 0.2%; International, 0%

APPLICANTS and ADMITTEES
Seats available: 125
Average LSAT score: 157
Average GPA: 3.2

University of Louisville Louis D. Brandeis School of Law is a public institution that organizes classes on a semester calendar system. The campus is situated in an urban setting. Founded in 1846, first ABA approved in 1933, and an AALS member, University of Louisville Louis D. Brandeis School of Law offers JD, JD/MBA, and JD/MDiv degrees.

Faculty consists of 25 full-time and 6 part-time members in 1997–98. 7 full-time faculty members and 1 part-time faculty members are women. 100% of all faculty members have a JD; 30% have advanced law degrees. Of all faculty members, 5% are African American, 2% are Hispanic, 93% are white.

Application Information *Required:* LSAT, LSDAS, application form, application fee of $30, baccalaureate degree. *Recommended:* recommendations and personal statement. *Application deadline* for fall term is February 15.

Costs The 1997–98 tuition is $5330 for state residents. Tuition is $13,940 for nonresidents.

Financial Aid In 1997–98, 24% of all students received some form of financial aid. Fellowships, loans, merit-based grants/scholarships, and federal work-study loans are also available. The average student debt at graduation is $40,000. To apply for

AT a GLANCE

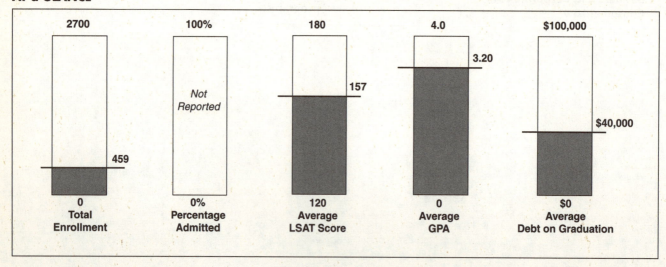

Degree Options

Degree	Total Credits Required	Length of Program
JD–Juris Doctor	90	3–4 yrs, full-time or part-time [day, evening]
JD/MBA–Juris Doctor/Master of Business Administration–Joint Degree	108	4–6 yrs, full-time or part-time [day, evening]
JD/MDiv–Juris Doctor/Master of Divinity–Joint Degree		4.5–6 yrs, full-time only [day]

financial assistance, students must complete the Free Application for Federal Student Aid. Financial aid contact: Jerie Torbeck, Assistant Dean, Brandeis School of Law, University of Louisville, Louisville, KY 40292. Phone: 502-852-6096. Fax: 502-852-0862. E-mail: jltorb01@homer.louisville.edu.

Law School Library University of Louisville Law Library has 4 professional staff members and contains more than 281,633 volumes and 5,048 periodicals. 391 seats are available in the library. When classes are in session, the library is open 88 hours per week.

WESTLAW and LEXIS-NEXIS are available, as are the World Wide Web, online bibliographic services, and CD-ROM players. 38 computer workstations are available to students in the library. Special law collections include the papers of Justice Louis D. Brandeis and of Justice John Marshall Harlan.

First-Year Program Class size in the average section is 45; 100% of the first-year courses are taught by full-time faculty.

Upper-Level Program Class size in the average section is 35. Among the electives are:

Administrative Law
Advocacy
Business and Corporate Law
Consumer Law
★ Education Law
Entertainment Law
Environmental Law
★ Family Law
Government/Regulation
★ Health Care/Human Services
Indian/Tribal Law
Intellectual Property
International/Comparative Law
Jurisprudence
★ Labor Law
Land Use Law/Natural Resources
Lawyering Skills
Legal History/Philosophy
Litigation
Maritime Law
Media Law
Mediation
Probate Law
Public Interest
Securities
Tax Law

(★ *indicates an area of special strength*)

100% of the students participate in internship programs. International exchange programs permit students to visit Australia; China; Finland; France; Germany; Japan; South Africa; and United Kingdom.

LOUISIANA STATE UNIVERSITY AND AGRICULTURAL AND MECHANICAL COLLEGE
PAUL M. HEBERT LAW CENTER

Baton Rouge, Louisiana

INFORMATION CONTACT
Howard W. L'Enfant, Chancellor
210 Law Center
Baton Rouge, LA 70803

Phone: 504-388-8491
Web site: http://www.lsu.edu/guests/lsulaw/
index.html

LAW STUDENT PROFILE [1997–98]

FULL-TIME   Enrollment: 624
Women: 45%   Men: 55%

RACIAL or ETHNIC COMPOSITION
African American, 9%; Asian/Pacific Islander, 0.5%; Hispanic,
1%; Nataive American, 0.5%; International, 2%

APPLICANTS and ADMITTEES
Number applied: 986
Admitted: 531
Percentage accepted: 54%
Seats available: 235

Louisiana State University and Agricultural and Mechanical College Paul M. Hebert Law Center is a public institution that organizes classes on a semester calendar system. The campus is situated in an urban setting. Founded in 1907, first ABA approved in 1926, and an AALS member, Louisiana State University and Agricultural and Mechanical College Paul M. Hebert Law Center offers JD, JD/MPAd, LLM, and MCl degrees.

Faculty consists of 33 full-time and 10 part-time members in 1997–98.

Application Information *Required:* LSAT, LSDAS, application form, application fee of $25, baccalaureate degree. *Application deadline* for fall term is February 1.

Financial Aid Merit-based grants/scholarships and need-based grants/scholarships are available. To apply for financial assistance, students must complete the Free Application for Federal Student Aid. Financial aid contact: Louisiana State University, Office of Student Aid and Scholarships, 202 Himes Hall, Baton Rouge, LA 70803-3701. Phone:

AT a GLANCE

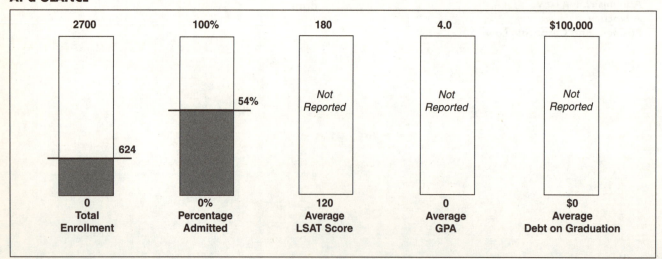

Degree Options

Degree	Total Credits Required	Length of Program
JD–Juris Doctor	97	3–4 yrs
JD/MPAd–Juris Doctor/Master of Public Administration–Joint-degree Program		3 yrs, full-time only
LLM–Master of Laws	24	1 yr, full-time only
MCl–Master of Civil Law		

504-388-3103. Completed financial aid forms should be received by April 16.

Law School Library Louisiana State University Law Library has 18 professional staff members and contains more than 568,350 volumes and 2,928 periodicals. 464 seats are available in the library. When classes are in session, the library is open 99 hours per week.

WESTLAW and LEXIS-NEXIS are available, as are the World Wide Web and online bibliographic services. Special law collections include US government documents depository, Louisiana state documents depository, records and briefs of Louisiana Supreme Court and Courts of Appeals.

First-Year Program Class size in the average section is 60.

Upper-Level Program Among the electives are:

Administrative Law
Advocacy
Banking and Financial Aid
Business and Corporate Law
Constitutional Law
Consumer Law
Environmental Law
Family Law
French Law
Government/Regulation
Insurance
Intellectual Property
International/Comparative Law
Jurisprudence
Labor Law
Land Use Law/Natural Resources
Lawyering Skills
Legal History/Philosophy
Litigation
Media Law
Mediation
Mineral Rights
Probate Law
Securities

International exchange programs permit students to visit France.

LOYOLA UNIVERSITY NEW ORLEANS
SCHOOL OF LAW

New Orleans, Louisiana

INFORMATION CONTACT
John Makdisi Jr., Dean
7214 St. Charles Avenue
New Orleans, LA 70118

Phone: 504-861-5550   Fax: 504-861-5729
Web site: http://www.loyno.edu/

LAW STUDENT PROFILE [1997–98]

FULL-TIME   Enrollment: 400
Women: 47%   Men: 53%

PART-TIME   Enrollment: 282
Women: 47%   Men: 53%

RACIAL or ETHNIC COMPOSITION
African American, 5%; Asian/Pacific Islander, 2%; Hispanic,
4%; Nataive American, 0.3%; International, 48%

APPLICANTS and ADMITTEES
Number applied: 1,311
Admitted: 706
Percentage accepted: 54%
Seats available: 230
Average LSAT score: 152
Average GPA: 3.0

Loyola University New Orleans School of Law is a
private institution that organizes classes on a
semester calendar system. The campus is situated in
an urban setting. Founded in 1914, first ABA
approved in 1931, and an AALS member, Loyola
University New Orleans School of Law offers JD,
JD/MA, JD/MBA, JD/MCRP, and JD/MPAd degrees.

Faculty consists of 30 full-time and 18 part-time
members in 1997–98. 10 full-time faculty members
and 2 part-time faculty members are women. 100%
of all faculty members have a JD; 25% have
advanced law degrees. Of all faculty members, 7%
are African American, 4% are Hispanic, 89% are
white.

Application Information *Required:* LSAT, LSDAS,
application form, application fee of $20, college
transcripts. *Recommended:* recommendations,
personal statement, resume. *Application deadline* for
fall term is August 20.

Costs The 1997–98 tuition is $18,330 full-time; $611
per credit hour part-time. Fees: $556 full-time; $164
part-time.

Financial Aid In 1997–98, 87% of all students
received some form of financial aid. Graduate
assistantships, loans, loan repayment assistance
program (LRAP), merit-based grants/scholarships,

AT a GLANCE

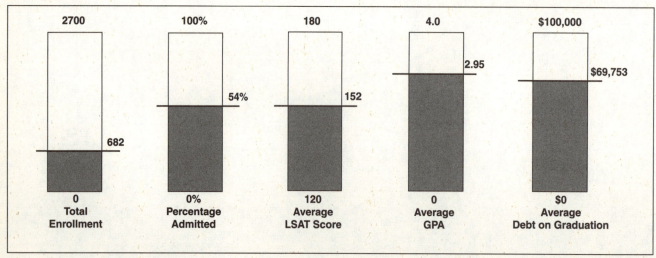

	Total Enrollment	Percentage Admitted	Average LSAT Score	Average GPA	Average Debt on Graduation
Top	2700	100%	180	4.0	$100,000
Value	682	54%	152	2.95	$69,753
Bottom	0	0%	120	0	$0

Degree Options

Degree	Total Credits Required	Length of Program
JD–Doctor of Laws	90	3–4 yrs, full-time or part-time [day, evening]
JD/MA–Juris Doctor/Master of Arts–Religious Studies Dual-degree Program	108	3.5–5 yrs, full-time or part-time [day, evening]
JD/MA–Juris Doctor/Master of Arts–Mass Communication Dual-degree Program	102	3.5–5 yrs, full-time or part-time [day, evening]
JD/MBA–Juris Doctor/Master of Business Administration–Dual-degree Program	102	3.5–5 yrs, full-time or part-time [day]
JD/MCRP–Juris Doctor/Master of Community and Regional Planning–Joint-degree Program	117	4–5 yrs, full-time or part-time [day, evening]
JD/MPAd–Juris Doctor/Master of Public Administration–Joint-degree Program	114	4–5 yrs, full-time or part-time [day, evening]

need-based grants/scholarships, and federal work-study loans are also available. The average student debt at graduation is $69,753. To apply for financial assistance, students must complete the Free Application for Federal Student Aid. Financial aid contact: Edward P. Seybold Jr., Director of Financial Aid, 6363 St. Charles Avenue, New Orleans, LA 70118. Phone: 504-865-3231. Fax: 504-861-5729. Completed financial aid forms should be received by May 1.

Law School Library Loyola Law Library has 8 professional staff members and contains more than 265,089 volumes and 2,543 periodicals. 525 seats are available in the library. When classes are in session, the library is open 104 hours per week.

WESTLAW and LEXIS-NEXIS are available, as is the World Wide Web. 36 computer workstations are available to students in the library.

First-Year Program Class size in the average section is 73; 100% of the first-year courses are taught by full-time faculty.

Upper-Level Program Among the electives are:

Advocacy
Business and Corporate Law
★ Civil Law
★ Common Law
Education Law
Entertainment Law
Environmental Law
Family Law
Intellectual Property
★ International/Comparative Law
Jurisprudence
Labor Law
★ Lawyering Skills
Legal History/Philosophy
Litigation
Maritime Law
Mediation
Probate Law
Public Interest
Securities
Tax Law

(★ *indicates an area of special strength*)

Clinical Courses Students receive degree credit for clinical courses. (Clinical practicum is not required.) Among the clinical areas offered are:

Civil Litigation
Criminal Defense
Criminal Prosecution
Immigration

10% of the students participate in internship programs.

SOUTHERN UNIVERSITY AND AGRICULTURAL AND MECHANICAL COLLEGE
SOUTHERN UNIVERSITY LAW CENTER

Baton Rouge, Louisiana

> **INFORMATION CONTACT**
> Bhishma K. Agnihotri, Chancellor
> PO Box 9294
> Baton Rouge, LA 70813
>
> Phone: 504-771-2552   Fax: 225-771-2474

LAW STUDENT PROFILE [1997–98]

FULL-TIME   Enrollment: 326
Women: 45%   Men: 55%

RACIAL or ETHNIC COMPOSITION
African American, 64%; Asian/Pacific Islander, 0.3%

APPLICANTS and ADMITTEES
Number applied: 700
Admitted: 186
Percentage accepted: 27%
Seats available: 125
Average LSAT score: 146
Average GPA: 2.7

Southern University and Agricultural and Mechanical College Southern University Law Center is a public institution that organizes classes on a semester calendar system. The campus is situated in an urban setting. Founded in 1947, first ABA approved in 1953, Southern University and Agricultural and Mechanical College Southern University Law Center offers a JD degree.

Faculty consists of 27 full-time and 10 part-time members in 1997–98. 11 full-time faculty members and 2 part-time faculty members are women. 100% of all faculty members have a JD; 16% have advanced law degrees. Of all faculty members, 3% are Asian/Pacific Islander, 59% are African American, 38% are white.

Application Information *Required:* LSAT, LSDAS, application form, baccalaureate degree, 2 letters of recommendation, college transcripts. *Application deadline* for fall term is March 31.

Costs The 1997–98 tuition is $3128 for state residents. Tuition is $7728 for nonresidents.

AT a GLANCE

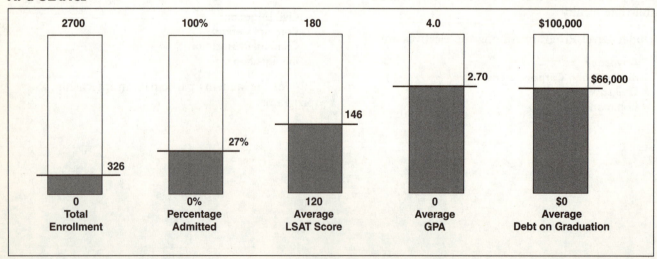

Degree Options

Degree	Total Credits Required	Length of Program
JD–Juris Doctor	96	3 yrs, full-time only [day]

Financial Aid In 1997–98, 78% of all students received some form of financial aid. 29 research assistantships, 20 teaching assistantships were awarded. 57 other awards were given. Graduate assistantships, loans, loan repayment assistance program (LRAP), merit-based grants/scholarships, need-based grants/scholarships, and federal work-study loans are also available. The average student debt at graduation is $66,000. To apply for financial assistance, students must complete the Free Application for Federal Student Aid, institutional forms, and scholarship specific applications. Financial aid contact: Benjamin Lewis, Director of Financial Aid, PO Box 9294, Baton Rouge, LA 70813. Phone: 225-771-2141 or toll-free 800-537-1135. Fax: 225-771-2474. Completed financial aid forms should be received by April 15.

Law School Library Southern University Law Library has 7 professional staff members and contains more than 388,614 volumes and 4,357 periodicals. 284 seats are available in the library. When classes are in session, the library is open 94 hours per week.

WESTLAW and LEXIS-NEXIS are available. 52 computer workstations are available to students in the library. Special law collections include Civil law, civil rights, human rights.

First-Year Program Class size in the average section is 42; 100% of the first-year courses are taught by full-time faculty.

Upper-Level Program Class size in the average section is 40. Among the electives are:

Administrative Law
Advocacy
Business and Corporate Law
Environmental Law
Family Law
Intellectual Property
International/Comparative Law
Labor Law
Lawyering Skills
Public Interest
Securities
Tax Law

Clinical Courses Students receive degree credit for clinical courses. (Clinical practicum is not required.) Among the clinical areas offered are:

Criminal Defense
Family Practice
Juvenile Law

10% of the students participate in internship programs.

TULANE UNIVERSITY
SCHOOL OF LAW

New Orleans, Louisiana

INFORMATION CONTACT

Edward Sherman, Dean
Weinmann Hall
6329 Freret Street
New Orleans, LA 70118

Phone: 504-865-5938   Fax: 504-865-6710
Web site: http://www.law.tulane.edu/

LAW STUDENT PROFILE [1997-98]

FULL-TIME   Enrollment: 1,042
Women: 47%   Men: 53%

PART-TIME   Enrollment: 14
Women: 50%   Men: 50%

RACIAL or ETHNIC COMPOSITION

African American, 8%; Asian/Pacific Islander, 5%; Hispanic, 5%; Native American, 1%; International, 8%

APPLICANTS and ADMITTEES

Number applied: 2,461
Admitted: 1,417
Percentage accepted: 58%
Seats available: 315
Average LSAT score: 159
Average GPA: 3.3

Tulane University School of Law is a private institution that organizes classes on a semester calendar system. The campus is situated in an urban setting. Founded in 1847, first ABA approved in 1925, and an AALS member, Tulane University School of Law offers JD and LLM degrees.

Faculty consists of 54 full-time and 105 part-time members in 1997–98. 12 full-time faculty members and 18 part-time faculty members are women. 100% of all faculty members have a JD degree.

Application Information *Required:* LSAT, LSDAS, application form, application fee of $50, personal statement, college transcripts. *Recommended:* baccalaureate degree. *Application deadline* for fall term is March 15.

Financial Aid In 1997–98, 83% of all students received some form of financial aid. 3 fellowships were awarded. Loans, loan repayment assistance program (LRAP), merit-based grants/scholarships, need-based grants/scholarships, and federal work-study loans are also available. The average student debt at graduation is $75,000. To apply for financial assistance, students must complete the Free Application for Federal Student Aid and institutional forms. Financial aid contact: Ms. Georgia Whiddon, Associate Director of Financial Aid, Weinmann Hall, New Orleans, LA 70118. Phone: 504-865-5931. Fax:

AT a GLANCE

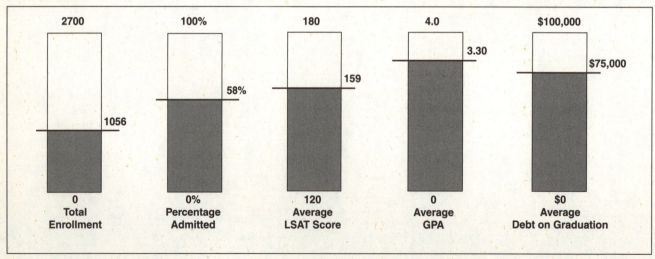

Degree Options

Degree	Total Credits Required	Length of Program
JD–Juris Doctor	88	3 yrs, full-time only [day]
LLM–Master of Laws	24	1 yr, full-time only [day]
LLM–Master of Laws–Admiralty	24	1–2 yrs, full-time or part-time [day, evening]
LLM–Master of Laws–Energy and Environment	24	1–2 yrs, full-time or part-time [day, evening]
LLM–Master of Laws–International and Comparative Law	24	1 yr, full-time only [day]

504-865-6710. E-mail: admissions@law.tulane.edu. Completed financial aid forms should be received by February 15.

Law School Library Tulane Law School Library has 19 professional staff members and contains more than 500,000 volumes and 5,517 periodicals. 587 seats are available in the library. When classes are in session, the library is open 112 hours per week.

WESTLAW and LEXIS-NEXIS are available, as are the World Wide Web, online bibliographic services, and CD-ROM players. 70 computer workstations are available to students in the library. Special law collections include canon law, civil law, maritime law.

First-Year Program Class size in the average section is 80; 100% of the first-year courses are taught by full-time faculty.

Upper-Level Program Class size in the average section is 30. Among the electives are:

Administrative Law
★ Advocacy
★ Business and Corporate Law
Consumer Law
Entertainment Law
★ Environmental Law
Family Law
Government/Regulation
Health Care/Human Services
★ Intellectual Property
★ International/Comparative Law
Jurisprudence
Labor Law
Land Use Law/Natural Resources
Lawyering Skills
Legal History/Philosophy
Litigation
★ Maritime Law
Media Law
Mediation
★ Public Interest
Securities
Tax Law
(★ indicates an area of special strength)

Clinical Courses Students receive degree credit for clinical courses. (Clinical practicum is not required.) Among the clinical areas offered are:

Appellate Litigation
Civil Litigation
Civil Rights
Criminal Defense
Elderly Advocacy
Environmental Law
Family Practice
Immigration
Juvenile Law
Public Interest

5% of the students participate in internship programs. International exchange programs permit students to visit France; Germany; and New Zealand.

UNIVERSITY OF SOUTHERN MAINE
UNIVERSITY OF MAINE SCHOOL OF LAW

Portland, Maine

INFORMATION CONTACT
Donald Zillman, Dean
246 Deering Avenue
Portland, ME 04102

Phone: 207-780-4344   Fax: 207-780-4239
E-mail: gauditz@usm.maine.edu
Web site: http://www.law.usm.maine.edu/

LAW STUDENT PROFILE [1997–98]

FULL-TIME   Enrollment: 294
Women: 42%   Men: 58%

RACIAL or ETHNIC COMPOSITION
African American, 2%; Asian/Pacific Islander, 2%; Hispanic, 1%; Native American, 1%; International, 2%

APPLICANTS and ADMITTEES
Number applied: 569
Admitted: 288
Percentage accepted: 51%
Seats available: 95
Average LSAT score: 155
Average GPA: 3.2

University of Southern Maine University of Maine School of Law is a public institution that organizes classes on a semester calendar system. The campus is situated in an urban setting. Founded in 1962, first ABA approved in 1962, and an AALS member, University of Southern Maine University of Maine School of Law offers a JD degree.

Faculty consists of 16 full-time members in 1997–98. 5 full-time faculty members are women. 100% of all faculty members have a JD degree. Of all faculty members, 100% are white.

Application Information *Required:* LSDAS, LSAT, application form, application fee of $25, baccalaureate degree, 1 recommendation, personal statement. *Application deadline* for fall term is February 15.

Costs The 1997–98 tuition is $9360 full-time for state residents; $300 per credit hour part-time for state residents. Tuition is $14,040 (minimum) full-time for nonresidents; $450 per credit hour (minimum) part-time for nonresidents. Fees: $404 full-time; $103 per semester (minimum) part-time.

Financial Aid In 1997–98, 82% of all students received some form of financial aid. Loans, merit-based grants/scholarships, need-based grants/scholarships, and federal work-study loans are also available. The average student debt at graduation is

AT a GLANCE

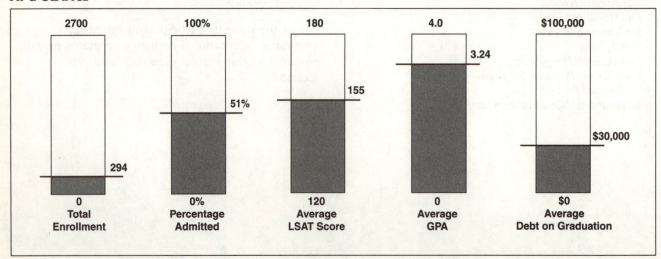

Degree Options		
Degree	Total Credits Required	Length of Program
JD–Juris Doctor	89	3–4 yrs, full-time or part-time [day, summer]

$30,000. To apply for financial assistance, students must complete the Free Application for Federal Student Aid. Financial aid contact: Barabara Gauditz, Assistant Dean, 246 Deering Avenue, Portland, ME 04102. Phone: 207-780-4345. Fax: 207-780-4239. E-mail: gauditz@usm.maine.edu. Completed financial aid forms should be received by February 1.

Law School Library Donald L. Garbrecht Law Library has 6 professional staff members and contains more than 300,000 volumes and 3,605 periodicals. 172 seats are available in the library. When classes are in session, the library is open 99 hours per week.

WESTLAW and LEXIS-NEXIS are available, as are the World Wide Web, online bibliographic services, and CD-ROM players. 14 computer workstations are available to students in the library. Special law collections include Canadian, Commonwealth, European Union.

First-Year Program Class size in the average section is 95; 100% of the first-year courses are taught by full-time faculty.

Upper-Level Program Class size in the average section is 35. Among the electives are:

Administrative Law
Advocacy
Business and Corporate Law
Commercial Law
Constitutional Law
Consumer Law
Criminal Procedure

Education Law
Environmental Law
Family Law
Government/Regulation
Health Care/Human Services
Intellectual Property
International/Comparative Law
Jurisprudence
Labor Law
Land Use Law/Natural Resources
Lawyering Skills
Legal History/Philosophy
Litigation
Maritime Law
Mediation
Ocean and Coastal Law
Probate Law
Public Interest
Securities
Tax Law

Clinical Courses Students receive degree credit for clinical courses. (Clinical practicum is not required.) Among the clinical areas offered are:

Civil Litigation
Criminal Defense
Environmental Law
Estate Planning
Family Practice
General Practice
Juvenile Law
Public Interest

International exchange programs permit students to visit Canada; France; Ireland; and United Kingdom.

UNIVERSITY OF BALTIMORE
SCHOOL OF LAW

Baltimore, Maryland

LAW STUDENT PROFILE [1997–98]

FULL-TIME   Enrollment: 659
Women: 51%   Men: 49%

PART-TIME   Enrollment: 344
Women: 46%   Men: 54%

RACIAL or ETHNIC COMPOSITION
African American, 13%; Asian/Pacific Islander, 4%; Hispanic, 2%; Native American, 1%

APPLICANTS and ADMITTEES
Number applied: 1,684
Admitted: 902
Percentage accepted: 54%
Seats available: 310
Median LSAT score: 151
Average GPA: 3.0

University of Baltimore School of Law is a public institution that organizes classes on a semester calendar system. The campus is situated in an urban setting. Founded in 1925, first ABA approved in 1972, and an AALS member, University of Baltimore School of Law offers JD, JD/LLM, JD/MBA, JD/MPAd, JD/MS, and JD/PhD degrees.

Faculty consists of 41 full-time and 60 part-time members in 1997–98. 16 full-time faculty members and 17 part-time faculty members are women. 100% of all faculty members have a JD degree. Of all faculty members, 6% are African American.

Application Information *Required:* LSAT, LSDAS, application form, application fee of $35, baccalaureate degree, 2 letters of recommendation, personal statement, college transcripts, resume. *Application deadline* for fall term is April 1.

Costs The 1997–98 tuition is $8376 full-time for state residents; $349 per credit part-time for state residents. Tuition is $14,136 full-time for nonresidents; $589 per credit part-time for nonresidents. Fees: $550 full-time; $208 per semester (minimum) part-time.

Financial Aid In 1997–98, 65% of all students received some form of financial aid. 27 teaching assistantships were awarded. Loans, merit-based

AT a GLANCE

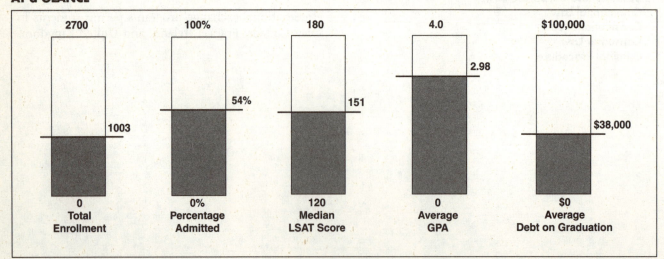

Degree Options

Degree	Total Credits Required	Length of Program
JD–Doctor of Laws	90	3–4 yrs, full-time or part-time [day, evening, summer]
JD/LLM–Juris Doctor/Master of Laws–Dual Program in Taxation	105	4–5 yrs, full-time or part-time [day, evening, summer]
JD/MBA–Juris Doctor/Master of Business Administration–Dual-degree Program	110	4–5 yrs, full-time or part-time [day, evening, summer]
JD/MPAd–Juris Doctor/Master of Public Administration–Dual Program	110	4–5 yrs, full-time or part-time [day, evening, summer]
JD/MS–Juris Doctor/Master of Science–Dual Program in Criminal Justice	110	4–5 yrs, full-time or part-time [day, evening, weekend, summer]
JD/PhD–Juris Doctor/Doctor of Philosophy–Dual Program in Policy Science	110	4–6 yrs, full-time or part-time [day, evening, summer]

grants/scholarships, need-based grants/scholarships, and federal work-study loans are also available. The average student debt at graduation is $38,000. To apply for financial assistance, students must complete the Free Application for Federal Student Aid, institutional forms, scholarship specific applications, and loan papers. Financial aid contact: Anna Breland, Director of Financial Aid, 1420 North Charles Street, Baltimore, MD 21201. Phone: 410-837-4763. Fax: 410-837-4450. E-mail: abreland@ubmail.ubalt.edu. Completed financial aid forms should be received by April 1.

Law School Library has 7 professional staff members and contains more than 287,125 volumes and 3,306 periodicals. 314 seats are available in the library. When classes are in session, the library is open 110 hours per week.

WESTLAW and LEXIS-NEXIS are available, as is the World Wide Web. 75 computer workstations are available to students in the library.

First-Year Program Class size in the average section is 75; 100% of the first-year courses are taught by full-time faculty.

Upper-Level Program Class size in the average section is 40. Among the electives are:

Administrative Law
★ Advocacy
★ Business and Corporate Law
Consumer Law
★ Criminal Law

Entertainment Law
★ Environmental Law
★ Estate Planning
★ Family Law
Government/Regulation
Health Care/Human Services
★ Intellectual Property
★ International/Comparative Law
Jurisprudence
Labor Law
Land Use Law/Natural Resources
★ Lawyering Skills
★ Legal History/Philosophy
Litigation
Maritime Law
Media Law
Mediation
★ Property/Real Estate
★ Public Interest
Securities
★ Tax Law
(★ *indicates an area of special strength*)

Clinical Courses Students receive degree credit for clinical courses. (Clinical practicum is not required.) Among the clinical areas offered are:

Civil Litigation
Community Development
Criminal Defense
Family Practice

Internships are available. International exchange programs permit students to visit United Kingdom.

UNIVERSITY OF MARYLAND
SCHOOL OF LAW

Baltimore, Maryland

INFORMATION CONTACT
Donald G. Gifford, Dean
500 West Baltimore Street
Baltimore, MD 21201

Phone: 410-706-7214   Fax: 410-706-4045

LAW STUDENT PROFILE [1997–98]

FULL-TIME   Enrollment: 598
Women: 52%   Men: 48%

PART-TIME   Enrollment: 258
Women: 46%   Men: 54%

RACIAL or ETHNIC COMPOSITION
African American, 14%; Asian/Pacific Islander, 10%;
Hispanic, 3%; Nataive American, 0.4%; International, 1%

APPLICANTS and ADMITTEES
Number applied: 2,534
Admitted: 964
Percentage accepted: 38%
Seats available: 274
Average LSAT score: 156
Average GPA: 3.4

University of Maryland School of Law is a public institution that organizes classes on a semester calendar system. The campus is situated in an urban setting. Founded in 1816, first ABA approved in 1930, and an AALS member, University of Maryland School of Law offers JD, JD/MA, JD/MBA, JD/MSW, and JD/PhD degrees.

Faculty consists of 45 full-time and 34 part-time members in 1997–98. 17 full-time faculty members and 10 part-time faculty members are women. Of all faculty members, 1.25% are Asian/Pacific Islander, 8.75% are African American, 90% are white.

Application Information *Required:* LSAT, LSDAS, application form, application fee of $50, college transcripts. *Recommended:* baccalaureate degree, recommendations, personal statement, essay, resume. *Application deadline* for fall term is March 1.

Financial Aid In 1997–98, 75% of all students received some form of financial aid. Loans, loan repayment assistance program (LRAP), need-based grants/scholarships, and federal work-study loans are also available. The average student debt at graduation is $45,092. To apply for financial assistance, students must complete the Free Application for Federal Student Aid. Financial aid contact: Mary S. Vansickle, Director of Financial Aid, 624 West

AT a GLANCE

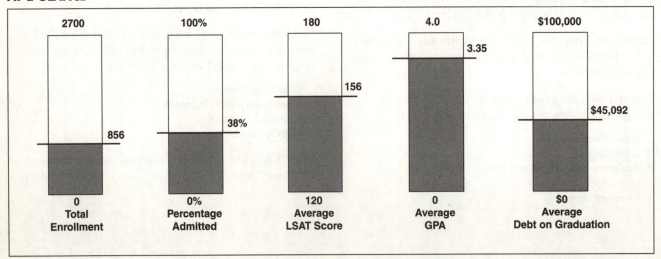

Degree Options

Degree	Total Credits Required	Length of Program
JD–Doctor of Laws	85	3–4 yrs, full-time or part-time [day, evening, summer]
JD/MA–Juris Doctor/Master of Arts–Criminal Justice Dual-degree	96	4–5 yrs, full-time or part-time [day, evening, summer]
JD/MA–Juris Doctor/Master of Arts–Liberal Education Dual Degree	112	4–5 yrs, full-time or part-time [day, evening, summer]
JD/MA–Juris Doctor/Master of Arts–Public Management Dual Degree	115	4–5 yrs, full-time or part-time [day, evening, summer]
JD/MBA–Juris Doctor/Master of Business Administration–Dual Degree	112	4–5 yrs, full-time or part-time [day, evening, summer]
JD/MSW–Juris Doctor/Master of Social Work–Dual Degree	131	4–5 yrs, full-time or part-time [day, evening, summer]
JD/PhD–Juris Doctor/Doctor of Philosophy–Dual Degree		5–6 yrs, full-time or part-time [day, evening, summer]

Lombard Street, Baltimore, MD 21201. Phone: 410-706-7347. Fax: 410-706-4045. E-mail: mvansick@umabnet.ab.umd.edu. Completed financial aid forms should be received by April 15.

Law School Library Thurgood Marshall Law Library has 9 professional staff members and contains more than 364,212 volumes and 4,127 periodicals. 372 seats are available in the library. When classes are in session, the library is open 98 hours per week.

WESTLAW and LEXIS-NEXIS are available, as is online bibliographic services. 51 computer workstations are available to students in the library.

First-Year Program Class size in the average section is 75; 100% of the first-year courses are taught by full-time faculty.

Upper-Level Program Among the electives are:

Administrative Law
★ Advocacy
★ Business and Corporate Law
Consumer Law
Education Law
★ Environmental Law
★ Family Law
Government/Regulation
★ Health Care/Human Services
★ Intellectual Property
★ International/Comparative Law
★ Jurisprudence
Labor Law
Land Use Law/Natural Resources
★ Lawyering Skills
★ Legal History/Philosophy

★ Litigation
★ Mediation
Probate Law
★ Public Interest
Securities
Tax Law
(★ indicates an area of special strength)

Clinical Courses Students receive degree credit for clinical courses. 8 credit hours of clinical practicum are required. Among the clinical areas offered are:

Civil Litigation
Civil Rights
Corporate Law
Criminal Defense
Criminal Prosecution
Education
Elderly Advocacy
Environmental Law
Family Practice
General Practice
Government Litigation
Health
Immigration
Intellectual Property
International Law
Juvenile Law
Mediation
Public Interest
Tax Law

25% of the students participate in internship programs. International exchange programs permit students to visit South Africa and United Kingdom.

DEAN'S STATEMENT . . .

The law is not a static concept. It evolves. It is transformed. Yet, at its core, there are fundamentals that remain impervious to the currents of change. This creative tension between new insights and foundation principles is what invests the law with its nobility and viability.

In much the same way, the legal education we offer here at the University of Maryland School of Law is a traditional and transforming process. It finds expression in the transition our students make from learning first principles in the law to front-line experiences in the actual practice of law. Our legal studies program is comprehensive in scope, affording our students the opportunity to sample a wide range of subjects or focus on a particular field of interest.

In emerging fields of the law, our students move from a background in the fundamentals to explore and resolve complex legal issues related to the environment, health, business and intellectual property, international, and other arenas.

The law school brings together students of different backgrounds and intellectual interests, ethnic and racial roots, ages, and genders to form a community where individuals are valued for what they do, not for who they are. From this diverse atmosphere, our students enter the larger society with reverence for the purpose and power of the law.

We expect our graduates to hold fast to the precepts that speak to justice and fairness; to be steadfast in serving the community with integrity and commitment. In our legal education program, we foster professional leadership with a public calling.

However the School of Law is perceived, it is our faculty whose scholarship determines its deserved reputation, whose teaching elevates the interests and aspirations of our students, whose supervision of experiential programs brings it down to earth, whose attitude creates a collegial and friendly atmosphere for learning, and whose presence establishes its distinctive personality and character. Above all, it is our faculty whose zest for teaching and zeal for the law is instrumental in transforming our students from eager novitiates to effective legal advocates.

—*Donald G. Gifford, Dean and Professor of Law*

HISTORY, CAMPUS, AND LOCATION

In 1816, David Hoffman was appointed the School's first professor of law. Regular instruction began in 1824, but was suspended approximately ten years later when Hoffman departed for Europe. The law school was revived in 1869, and in 1870, regular instruction resumed.

The law school has held American Bar Association approval since 1930 and Association of American Law Schools membership since 1931. A chapter of Order of the Coif, the national law honor society, was established at the school in 1938.

The School of Law is a constituent member of the graduate and professional community of the University of Maryland, Baltimore. Located in the heart of Baltimore, the law school shares a campus with the Schools of Dentistry, Medicine, Nursing, Pharmacy, and Social Work and the Graduate School.

The law school is within easy walking distance of Oriole Park at Camden Yards for American League Baseball and the Ravens Stadium for National Football League play. A short distance away is Baltimore's famed inner harbor with restaurants and shops, the National Aquarium, Maryland Science Center, museums, ethnic festivals, and boating facilities.

SPECIAL QUALITIES OF THE SCHOOL

Through a series of core courses exploring fundamental principles of legal doctrine, students are taught the skills of legal reasoning, analysis, argumentating, research and writing, and judgment making. What gives the School's legal education its energy and vitality is the array of clinics, externships, and fellowships that connect legal theory with practice. One of the most highly regarded in the nation, the School's experiential program comprises as many as 18 full-time faculty members who supervise the work of student attorneys. Students' practice experiences are combined with weekly seminars sessions in which faculty and students discuss legal and ethical issues, integrating theory and practice.

TECHNOLOGY ON CAMPUS

The School maintains a fully equipped computer laboratory—the Technology Assisted Learning (TAL) Center—with IBM compatible Pentium PCs. Each PC provides access to the WESTLAW and LEXIS research databases, word processing, outlining and thought processing software, legal instruction, and essential legal utilities. At the TAL Center, students may take advantage of current technology, and faculty members may experiment with innovative course materials.

SCHOLARSHIPS AND LOANS

The law school's financial aid program is designed to help students who have academic potential and limited financial resources by meeting 100 percent of need with a combination of financial aid resources, including grants/scholarships, loans, and/or work-study. By filing one application (the FAFSA), students are considered for all of these sources of funds. The typical financial aid award package consists of approximately 20 percent grant/scholarship and 80 percent loan and/or employment. This ratio may vary, depending on need, availability of funds, and residency.

STUDENT ACTIVITIES AND OPPORTUNITIES

Law Review Publications, which are managed and edited by students, with opportunity for credit, include the *Business Lawyer, Maryland Law Review, Journal of Health Care Law & Policy*, and *Maryland Journal of International Law and Trade*.

Moot Court In addition to the required course on Introduction to Appellate Advocacy in the first year, optional moot court competitions provide opportunities to refine students' skills in legal research, persuasive writing, and oral advocacy. The best advocates are eligible for membership on the Moot Court Board.

Students represent the law school in a variety of nationwide competitions, including international law, health law, environmental law, criminal law, and international law.

Extracurricular Activities The Student Bar Association (SBA), the official student government organization, is affiliated with the Law Student Division of the American Bar Association. The SBA sponsors community programs, social functions, and lectures by members of the bench and the bar and supports more than forty student professional, social, and cultural organizations.

Special Opportunities Maryland is one of very few law schools that requires full-time day students to take a course that provides an introduction to client representation and the needs of the poor and other underrepresented people and communities. These legal theory and practice courses are designed for the experience in practice to inform the theory in the classroom and vice versa. These courses become the basis for advanced client representation, under close supervision by faculty, in the nationally recognized clinical program. Additionally, the School's location in the Baltimore/Washington region provides opportunity for extensive externship experience, working in the legal community under the close supervision of recognized expert practitioners in a wide variety of substantive and professional positions.

Opportunities for Members of Minority Groups and Women The law school community is rich in diversity, with both students and faculty reflecting the composition of the larger society. For many years, the student body has been 50 percent women and approximately 30 percent students of color. The average age of entering students is typically 25 in the day division and 30 in the evening division. The entering class of 260 normally includes graduates of more than 130 undergraduate schools, 20 percent of whom have earned graduate degrees. Students come from states throughout the country and several other countries. With this diversity, the School has fostered a sense of community; cooperation is a strong ethic among students, who share knowledge and work together in groups. The student-faculty ratio of 14:1 translates into many small and middle-size classes, which creates an intimacy among students and faculty that is good for learning.

Special Certificate Programs Juris Doctor studies become interdisciplinary through the opportunity for dual-degree graduate programs in applied and professional ethics, business administration, community planning, criminal justice, liberal education, policy sciences, public management, and social work. Within the J.D. program, special concentration opportunities are available in environmental law and health-care law.

BAR PASSAGE, CAREER SERVICES, AND PLACEMENT

The most recent Maryland bar passage rate for first-time takers from the School of Law was 75 percent compared to 71 percent for all first-time takers.

The School helps prepare students for initiation as professionals, providing opportunities to make contact with prospective employers.

Of the 1997 graduating class, almost 94 percent reported employment within six months after graduation.

Legal Field	Percentage of Graduates	Average Salary
Academic	1%	$52,500
Business	19%	$55,067
Government	18%	$44,464
Judicial Clerkships	17%	$32,531
Private Practice	38%	$49,364
Public Interest	2%	$44,167
Other	5%	n/a

CORRESPONDENCE AND INFORMATION

Admissions Office
University of Maryland School of Law
500 West Baltimore Street
Baltimore, Maryland 21201
Telephone: 410-706-3492
Fax: 410-706-4045
E-mail: admissions@law.umaryland.edu

BOSTON COLLEGE
LAW SCHOOL

Chestnut Hill, Massachusetts

> **INFORMATION CONTACT**
>
> Aviam Soifer, Dean
> 885 Centre Street
> Newton Centre, MA 02459
>
> Phone: 617-552-4340
> Web site: http://www.bc.edu/lawschool/

LAW STUDENT PROFILE [1997–98]

FULL-TIME   Enrollment: 829
Women: 51%   Men: 49%

RACIAL or ETHNIC COMPOSITION
African American, 8%; Asian/Pacific Islander, 7%; Hispanic, 5%; Nataive American, 0.1%; International, 1%

APPLICANTS and ADMITTEES
Number applied: 4,158
Admitted: 1,133
Percentage accepted: 27%
Seats available: 289
Median LSAT score: 164
Median GPA: 3.5

Boston College Law School is a private institution that organizes classes on a semester calendar system. The campus is situated in an urban setting. Founded in 1929, first ABA approved in 1932, and an AALS member, Boston College Law School offers JD, JD/MBA, JD/MED, and JD/MSW degrees.

Faculty consists of 54 full-time and 53 part-time members in 1997–98. 19 full-time faculty members and 9 part-time faculty members are women. 100% of all faculty members have a JD; 20% have advanced law degrees. Of all faculty members, 5.7% are Asian/Pacific Islander, 7.5% are African American, 1.9% are Hispanic, 84.9% are white.

Application Information *Required:* LSAT, LSDAS, application form, application fee of $65, baccalaureate degree, 2 letters of recommendation, personal statement. *Application deadline* for fall term is March 1.

Costs The 1997–98 tuition is $23,420. Fees: $60.

Financial Aid In 1997–98, 40% of all students received some form of financial aid. Loans, loan repayment assistance program (LRAP), merit-based grants/scholarships, need-based grants/scholarships, and federal work study loans are also available. The average student debt at graduation is $62,000. To apply for financial assistance, students must

AT a GLANCE

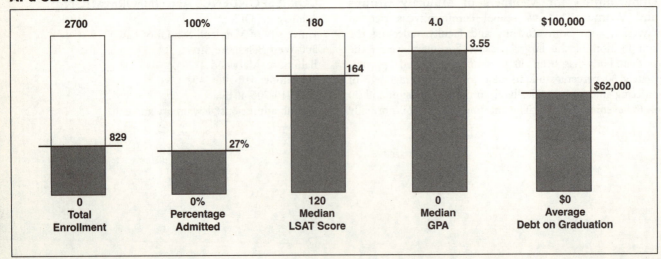

Degree Options

Degree	Total Credits Required	Length of Program
JD–Juris Doctor	85	3 yrs
JD/MBA–Juris Doctor/Master of Business Administration		4 yrs
JD/MED–Juris Doctor/Master of Education		
JD/MSW–Juris Doctor/Master of Social Work		4 yrs

complete the Free Application for Federal Student Aid and Need Access diskette or College Scholarship Service Profile form, federal income tax forms. Financial aid contact: Boston College Law School, Financial Aid Office, 120 Lyons Hall, Chestnut Hill, MA 02167. Phone: 800-294-0294. Completed financial aid forms should be received by March 1.

Law School Library Boston College Law Library has 10 professional staff members and contains more than 371,611 volumes and 6,133 periodicals. 617 seats are available in the library. When classes are in session, the library is open 106 hours per week.

WESTLAW and LEXIS-NEXIS are available, as are the World Wide Web and CD-ROM players. Special law collections include US Government Documents Collection.

First-Year Program Class size in the average section is 90; 100% of the first-year courses are taught by full-time faculty.

Upper-Level Program Class size in the average section is 40. Among the electives are:

  Administrative Law
★ Advocacy
★ Business and Corporate Law
  Consumer Law
  Education Law
  Entertainment Law
  Environmental Law
★ Family Law

  Government/Regulation
  Health Care/Human Services
  Intellectual Property
★ International/Comparative Law
  Jurisprudence
★ Juvenile Law
  Labor Law
  Land Use Law/Natural Resources
★ Lawyering Skills
  Legal History/Philosophy
★ Litigation
  Mediation
★ Public Interest
★ Securities
  Tax Law
(★ *indicates an area of special strength*)

Clinical Courses Students receive degree credit for clinical courses. (Clinical practicum is not required.) Among the clinical areas offered are:

  Civil Litigation
  Criminal Defense
  Criminal Prosecution
  Elderly Advocacy
  Family Practice
  General Practice
  Government Litigation
  Immigration
  Juvenile Law
  Women and the Law

Internships are available. International exchange programs permit students to visit United Kingdom.

BOSTON UNIVERSITY
SCHOOL OF LAW

Boston, Massachusetts

INFORMATION CONTACT

Ronald A. Cass, Dean
765 Commonwealth Avenue
Boston, MA 02215

Phone: 617-353-3112   Fax: 617-353-7400
E-mail: bulawadm@bu.edu
Web site: http://www.bu.edu/law/

LAW STUDENT PROFILE [1997–98]

FULL-TIME   Enrollment: 1,103
Women: 45%   Men: 55%
PART-TIME   Enrollment: 154
Women: 44%   Men: 56%

RACIAL or ETHNIC COMPOSITION

African American, 3%; Asian/Pacific Islander, 8%; Hispanic,
4%; Native American, 1%; International, 5%

APPLICANTS and ADMITTEES

Number applied: 4,103
Admitted: 1,651
Percentage accepted: 40%
Seats available: 320
Average LSAT score: 161
Average GPA: 3.3

Boston University School of Law is a private institution
that organizes classes on a semester calendar system. The
campus is situated in an urban setting. Founded in 1872,
first ABA approved in 1925, and an AALS member, Boston University School of Law offers JD, JD/MA, JD/
MBA, JD/MPH, JD/MS, and LLM degrees.

Faculty consists of 60 full-time and 75 part-time members in 1997–98. 20 full-time faculty members and 21
part-time faculty members are women. 96.3% of all
faculty members have a JD; 12.26% have advanced law
degrees. Of all faculty members, .9% are Asian/Pacific
Islander, 6.6% are African American, 3.8% are Hispanic, 88.7% are white.

Application Information *Required:* LSAT, application
form, application fee of $50, baccalaureate degree, 3 letters
of recommendation, personal statement, college transcripts,
resume. *Application deadline* for fall term is March 1.

Financial Aid In 1997–98, 64% of all students received
some form of financial aid. 3 fellowships, totaling
$87,759, were awarded. 488 other awards were given.
Loans, loan repayment assistance program (LRAP),
merit-based grants/scholarships, need-based grants/
scholarships, and federal work-study loans are also
available. The average student debt at graduation is
$66,800. To apply for financial assistance, students
must complete the Free Application for Federal Student Aid, institutional forms, and CSS PROFILE form.
Financial aid contact: Barbara J. Selmo, Director of
Admissions and Financial Aid, Boston University
School of Law, 765 Commonwealth Avenue, Boston,
MA 02215. Phone: 617-353-3100. Fax: 617-353-7400.
E-mail: bulawadm@bu.edu. Completed financial aid
forms should be received by April 1.

AT a GLANCE

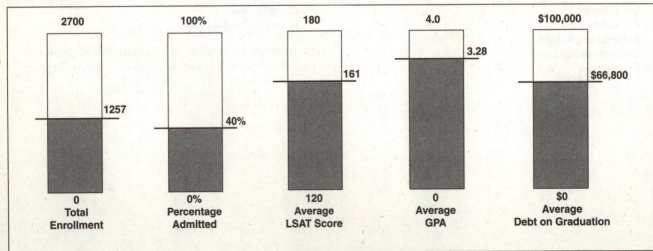

Degree Options

Degree	Total Credits Required	Length of Program
JD–Doctor of Laws	84	3 yrs, full-time only [day]
JD/MA–Juris Doctor/Master of Arts–Program in Law and International Relations, Program in law and Preservation Studies	94–95	3.5–4 yrs, full-time or part-time [day, evening, summer]
JD/MBA–Juris Doctor/Master of Business Administration–Program in Law and Health Care Management	102	4 yrs, full-time or part-time [day, evening, summer]
JD/MBA–Juris Doctor/Master of Business Administration–Program in Law and Management	94	4 yrs, full-time or part-time [day, evening]
JD/MPH–Juris Doctor/Master of Public Health–Program in Law and Public Health	132	3.5–4 yrs, full-time or part-time [day, evening, summer]
JD/MS–Juris Doctor/Master of Science–Program in Law and Mass Communication	93	3.5–4 yrs, full-time or part-time [day, evening, summer]
LLM–Master of Laws–Graduate Tax Program, Graduate Program in Banking Law Studies/American and International	20–24	1–3 yrs, full-time or part-time [evening]
LLM–Master of Laws–American Law	24	1 yr, full-time only [day]

Law School Library Pappas Law Library has 11 professional staff members and contains more than 557,300 volumes and 6,472 periodicals. 797 seats are available in the library. When classes are in session, the library is open 102 hours per week.

WESTLAW and LEXIS-NEXIS are available, as are the World Wide Web, online bibliographic services, and CD-ROM players. 65 computer workstations are available to students in the library. Special law collections include International Law, Financial Services, Tax, and Health Law.

First-Year Program Class size in the average section is 80; 100% of the first-year courses are taught by full-time faculty.

Upper-Level Program Class size in the average section is 37. Among the electives are:

Administrative Law
Advocacy
Antitrust Law
★ Banking and Financial Aid
★ Business and Corporate Law
Conflict of Laws
Constitutional Law
Consumer Law
Criminal Procedure
Entertainment Law
★ Environmental Law
Evidence
Family Law
Government/Regulation
★ Health Care/Human Services
★ Intellectual Property
★ International/Comparative Law
★ Jewish Law
Jurisdiction
Jurisprudence

Juvenile Law
Labor Law
Land Use Law/Natural Resources
★ Law and Disability
★ Law and Technology
Lawyering Skills
Legal History/Philosophy
★ Litigation
Media Law
Mediation
Professional Responsibility
Securities
Tax Law

(★ indicates an area of special strength)

Clinical Courses Students receive degree credit for clinical courses. (Clinical practicum is not required.) Among the clinical areas offered are:

Civil Litigation
Corporate Law
Criminal Defense
Criminal Prosecution
Elderly Advocacy
Family Practice
General Practice
Government Litigation
Health
Housing Law
Immigration
Judicial Internship
Juvenile Law
Legal Externship
Legislative Services
Mediation
Public Interest
Tax Law

13% of the students participate in internship programs. International exchange programs available.

HARVARD UNIVERSITY
LAW SCHOOL

Cambridge, Massachusetts

INFORMATION CONTACT
Robert Clark, Dean
1563 Massachusetts Avenue
Cambridge, MA 02138

Phone: 617-495-4601   Fax: 617-495-1110
Web site: http://www.law.harvard.edu/

LAW STUDENT PROFILE [1997–98]

FULL-TIME   Enrollment: 1,902

APPLICANTS and ADMITTEES
Seats available: 556
Median LSAT score: 169
Median GPA: 3.8

Harvard University Law School is a private institution that organizes classes on a semester calendar system. The campus is situated in an urban setting. Founded in 1817, first ABA approved in 1923, and an AALS member, Harvard University Law School offers JD, JD/MBA, JSD, and LLM degrees.

Application Information *Required:* LSAT, LSDAS, application form, application fee of $65, baccalaureate degree, 2 letters of recommendation, personal statement, essay.

Financial Aid In 1997–98, 65% of all students received some form of financial aid. Fellowships, graduate assistantships, loans, loan repayment assistance program (LRAP), need-based grants/scholarships, and federal work-study loans are also available. The average student debt at graduation is $64,092. To apply for financial assistance, students must complete the Free Application for Federal Student Aid, institutional forms, and CSS PROFILE form, Need Access diskette. Financial aid contact: Elizabeth Turnquist, Director of Financial Aid, 1563 Massachusetts Avenue, Cambridge, MA 02138. Phone: 617-495-4607. Fax: 617-495-1110.

Law School Library Langdell Library has 40 professional staff members and contains more than 1.9 million volumes and 14,560 periodicals. 300

AT a GLANCE

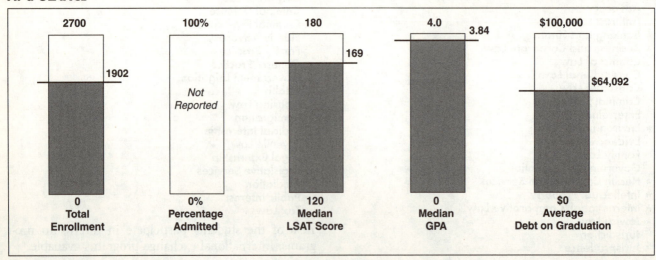

Degree Options

Degree	Total Credits Required	Length of Program
JD–Doctor of Laws	80	3 yrs, full-time only [day]
JD/MBA–Juris Doctor/Master of Business Administration		4 yrs, full-time only [day]
JSD–Doctor of Juridical Science	8	4 yrs, full-time only [day]
LLM–Master of Laws	18	1 yr, full-time only [day]

seats are available in the library. When classes are in session, the library is open 99 hours per week.

WESTLAW and LEXIS-NEXIS are available, as are the World Wide Web, online bibliographic services, and CD-ROM players. 221 computer workstations are available to students in the library. Special law collections include Anglo-American collection, special collections, Foreign and International law collection.

First-Year Program Class size in the average section is 138; 91% of the first-year courses are taught by full-time faculty.

Upper-Level Program Among the electives are:

Administrative Law
Advocacy
★ Asian Legal Systems
★ Business and Corporate Law
Consumer Law
Entertainment Law
Environmental Law
Family Law
Gender and Sexuality
Government/Regulation
Health Care/Human Services
Indian/Tribal Law
Intellectual Property
★ International/Comparative Law
★ Internet Law
★ Islamic Law
Jurisprudence
Labor Law
Land Use Law/Natural Resources

Lawyering Skills
Legal History/Philosophy
Litigation
Media Law
★ Mediation
★ Negotiation
Probate Law
★ Public Interest
★ Race and Law
Securities
★ Tax Law
(★ indicates an area of special strength)

Clinical Courses Students receive degree credit for clinical courses. (Clinical practicum is not required.) Among the clinical areas offered are:

Civil Litigation
Civil Rights
Corporate Law
Criminal Defense
Criminal Prosecution
Elderly Advocacy
Family Practice
General Practice
Government Litigation
Health
Immigration
Juvenile Law
Mediation
Public Interest
Tax Law

20% of the students participate in internship programs.

NEW ENGLAND SCHOOL OF LAW

Boston, Massachusetts

INFORMATION CONTACT

John F. O'Brien, Dean
154 Stuart Street
Boston, MA 02116-5687

Phone: 617-451-0010   Fax: 617-422-7333
E-mail: admit@admin.nesl.edu
Web site: http://www.nesl.edu/

LAW STUDENT PROFILE [1997–98]

FULL-TIME   Enrollment: 549
Women: 50%   Men: 50%
PART-TIME   Enrollment: 392
Women: 46%   Men: 54%

RACIAL or ETHNIC COMPOSITION

African American, 5%; Asian/Pacific Islander, 5%; Hispanic, 5%; Native American, 1%; International, 1%

APPLICANTS and ADMITTEES

Number applied: 2,218
Admitted: 1,513
Percentage accepted: 68%
Seats available: 285

New England School of Law is a private nonprofit institution that organizes classes on a semester calendar system. The campus is situated in an urban setting. First ABA approved in 1969, and an AALS member, New England School of Law offers a JD degree.

Faculty consists of 38 full-time and 49 part-time members in 1997–98. 8 full-time faculty members and 12 part-time faculty members are women. 100% of all faculty members have a JD; 17% have advanced law degrees. Of all faculty members, 1% are Native American, 1% are Asian/Pacific Islander, 3% are African American, 1% are Hispanic, 94% are white.

Application Information *Required:* LSAT, LSDAS, application form, application fee of $50, baccalaureate degree, minimum 2.0 GPA, 2 letters of recommendation, writing sample, college transcripts. *Recommended:* personal statement. *Application deadline* for fall term is June 1.

Financial Aid In 1997–98, 82% of all students received some form of financial aid. Loans, merit-based grants/scholarships, need-based grants/scholarships, and federal work-study loans are also available. The average student debt at graduation is $50,600. To apply for financial assistance, students must complete the Free Application for Federal Student Aid and institutional forms. Financial aid

AT a GLANCE

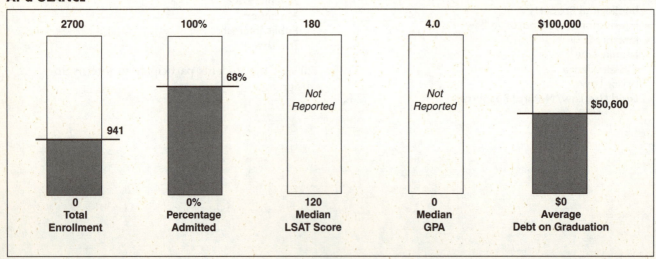

Degree Options		
Degree	**Total Credits Required**	**Length of Program**
JD–Juris Doctor–Law Program	84	3–4 yrs, full-time or part-time

contact: Doug Leman, Director of Financial Aid, 154 Stuart Street, Boston, MA 02116. Phone: 617-422-7232. Fax: 617-422-7333. E-mail: dleman@admin.nesl.edu. Completed financial aid forms should be received by April 15.

Law School Library New England School of Law Library has 9 professional staff members and contains more than 290,000 volumes and 3,023 periodicals. 392 seats are available in the library. When classes are in session, the library is open 101 hours per week.

WESTLAW and LEXIS-NEXIS are available, as are the World Wide Web, online bibliographic services, and CD-ROM players. 47 computer workstations are available to students in the library. Special law collections include Women and the Law, Massachusetts Law.

First-Year Program Class size in the average section is 88; 100% of the first-year courses are taught by full-time faculty.

Upper-Level Program Class size in the average section is 47. Among the electives are:

Administrative Law
★ Advocacy
★ Business and Corporate Law
Consumer Law
Education Law
Entertainment Law
★ Environmental Law
Family Law
Government/Regulation
Health Care/Human Services

Indian/Tribal Law
★ Intellectual Property
★ International/Comparative Law
Jurisprudence
Labor Law
★ Land Use Law/Natural Resources
Lawyering Skills
Legal History/Philosophy
★ Litigation
Maritime Law
Media Law
Mediation
★ Probate Law
★ Public Interest
Securities
★ Tax Law
(★ *indicates an area of special strength*)

Clinical Courses Students receive degree credit for clinical courses. (Clinical practicum is not required.) Among the clinical areas offered are:

Civil Litigation
Criminal Defense
Criminal Prosecution
Environmental Law
Family Practice
General Practice
Government Litigation
Health
Immigration
Land Rights/Natural Resource
Tax Law

25% of the students participate in internship programs.

NORTHEASTERN UNIVERSITY
SCHOOL OF LAW

Boston, Massachusetts

LAW STUDENT PROFILE [1997–98]

FULL-TIME   Enrollment: 577
Women: 67%   Men: 33%

RACIAL or ETHNIC COMPOSITION
African American, 10%; Asian/Pacific Islander, 10%;
Hispanic, 7%; Nataive American, 0.3%; International, 1%

APPLICANTS and ADMITTEES
Number applied: 2,167
Admitted: 773
Percentage accepted: 36%
Seats available: 175
Median LSAT score: 155
Median GPA: 3.3

Northeastern University School of Law is a private institution that organizes classes on a semester calendar system. The campus is situated in an urban setting. Founded in 1898, first ABA approved in 1969, and an AALS member, Northeastern University School of Law offers JD, JD/MBA, and JD/MS/MBA degrees.

Faculty consists of 29 full-time and 42 part-time members in 1997–98. 13 full-time faculty members and 14 part-time faculty members are women. 98% of all faculty members have a JD degree. Of all faculty members, 4% are Asian/Pacific Islander, 12.5% are African American, 4% are Hispanic, 79.5% are white.

Application Information *Required:* LSAT, LSDAS, application form, application fee of $55, baccalaureate degree, recommendations, personal statement, college transcripts, resume. *Recommended:* essay and interview. *Application deadline* for fall term is March 1.

Costs The 1997–98 tuition is $22,500.

Financial Aid In 1997–98, 83% of all students received some form of financial aid. 15 research assistantships, 11 teaching assistantships were awarded. Loans, merit-based grants/scholarships, need-based grants/scholarships, and federal work-

AT a GLANCE

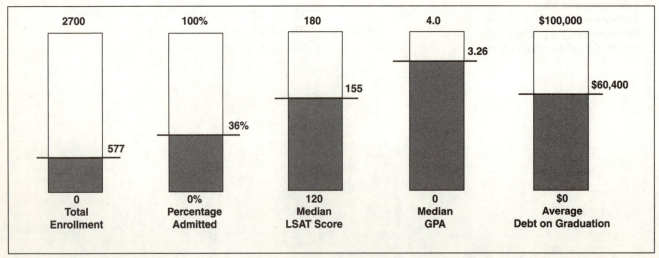

Total Enrollment	Percentage Admitted	Median LSAT Score	Median GPA	Average Debt on Graduation
577	36%	155	3.26	$60,400

Degree Options

Degree	Total Credits Required	Length of Program
JD–Doctor of Laws	99	3 yrs, full-time only [day, summer]
JD/MBA–Juris Doctor/Master of Business Administration–Concurrent Degree Program	168	3.75 yrs, full-time only [day, summer]
JD/MS/MBA–Juris Doctor/Master of Science/Master of Business Administration–Concurrent Degree Program	181	3.5 yrs, full-time only [day, summer]

study loans are also available. The average student debt at graduation is $60,400. To apply for financial assistance, students must complete the Free Application for Federal Student Aid and institutional forms. Financial aid contact: Paul D. Bauer, Assistant Dean and Director of Admissions, 400 Huntington Avenue, Boston, MA 02115. Phone: 617-373-2395. Fax: 617-373-8793. E-mail: pbauer@nunet.neu.edu. Completed financial aid forms should be received by March 1.

Law School Library The Berkowitz Law Library has 8 professional staff members and contains more than 277,010 volumes and 2,778 periodicals. 388 seats are available in the library. When classes are in session, the library is open 95 hours per week.

WESTLAW and LEXIS-NEXIS are available, as are the World Wide Web, online bibliographic services, and CD-ROM players. 85 computer workstations are available to students in the library. Special law collections include Pappas Public Interest Law Collection.

First-Year Program Class size in the average section is 68; 82% of the first-year courses are taught by full-time faculty.

Upper-Level Program Class size in the average section is 27. Among the electives are:

Administrative Law
★ Advocacy
★ Business and Corporate Law
★ Constitutional Law
★ Criminal Law
★ Diversity in the Legal Profession

★ Domestic Violence
Entertainment Law
★ Environmental Law
★ Family Law
Government/Regulation
Health Care/Human Services
Intellectual Property
★ International/Comparative Law
Jurisprudence
★ Labor Law
Land Use Law/Natural Resources
★ Lawyering Skills
Legal History/Philosophy
★ Litigation
Media Law
★ Mediation
★ Poverty/Welfare Law
Probate Law
★ Public Interest
Securities
Tax Law
★ Urban Economic Development
(★ *indicates an area of special strength*)

Clinical Courses Students receive degree credit for clinical courses. (Clinical practicum is not required.) Among the clinical areas offered are:

Certiorari Criminal Appeals
Criminal Defense
Domestic Violence
Poverty/Welfare Law
Prisoners' Rights
Tobacco Control

100% of the students participate in internship programs.

SUFFOLK UNIVERSITY
LAW SCHOOL

Boston, Massachusetts

LAW STUDENT PROFILE [1997–98]

FULL-TIME   Enrollment: 1,001
Women: 52%   Men: 48%

PART-TIME   Enrollment: 742
Women: 46%   Men: 54%

RACIAL or ETHNIC COMPOSITION
African American, 4%; Asian/Pacific Islander, 3%; Hispanic, 3%; Nataive American, 0.3%; International, 1%

APPLICANTS and ADMITTEES
Seats available: 510
Average LSAT score: 153
Average GPA: 3.1

Suffolk University Law School is a private institution that organizes classes on a semester calendar system. The campus is situated in an urban setting. Founded in 1906, first ABA approved in 1953, and an AALS member, Suffolk University Law School offers JD, JD/MBA, JD/MPAd, and JD/MS degrees.

Application Information *Required:* LSAT, LSDAS, application form, application fee of $50, baccalaureate degree, 1 recommendation, personal statement, college transcripts. *Recommended:* minimum 3.0 GPA and resume. *Application deadline* for fall term is March 1.

Financial Aid Fellowships, loans, loan repayment assistance program (LRAP), merit-based grants/scholarships, need-based grants/scholarships, and federal work-study loans are available. The average student debt at graduation is $58,000. To apply for financial assistance, students must complete the Free Application for Federal Student Aid, institutional forms, and Profile form. Financial aid contact: Kathy Gay, Director of Financial Aid, 41 Temple Street, Boston, MA 02114. Phone: 617-573-8147. Fax: 617-573-8706. E-mail: kgay@admin.suffolk.edu. Completed financial aid forms should be received by March 1.

Law School Library Mugar Library, Pallot Library has 10 professional staff members and contains

AT a GLANCE

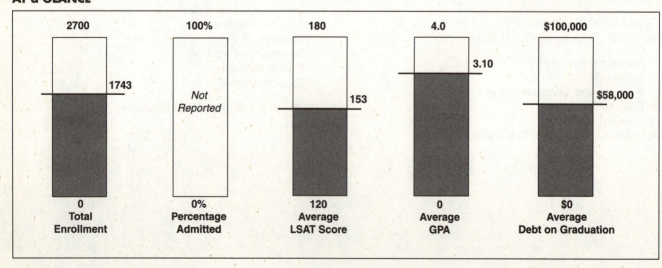

Degree Options

Degree	Total Credits Required	Length of Program
JD–Doctor of Laws	90	3–4 yrs, full-time or part-time [day, evening, summer]
JD/MBA–Juris Doctor/Master of Business Administration–Dual-degree Program	110	4–5 yrs, full-time only [day]
JD/MPAd–Juris Doctor/Master of Public Administration	120	4 yrs, full-time only [day]
JD/MS–Juris Doctor/Master of Science–International Economics	110	4–5 yrs, full-time or part-time [day, evening]
JD/MS–Juris Doctor/Master of Science–Finance	117	4 yrs, full-time only [day]

more than 300,000 volumes and 5,300 periodicals. 743 seats are available in the library. When classes are in session, the library is open 95 hours per week.

WESTLAW and LEXIS-NEXIS are available, as are the World Wide Web, online bibliographic services, and CD-ROM players. 50 computer workstations are available to students in the library. Special law collections include regional depository for United States documents.

First-Year Program Class size in the average section is 91; 100% of the first-year courses are taught by full-time faculty.

Upper-Level Program Among the electives are:

Administrative Law
★ Advocacy
Business and Corporate Law
Consumer Law
Education Law
Entertainment Law
Environmental Law
★ Family Law
★ Government/Regulation
★ Health Care/Human Services
Indian/Tribal Law
★ Intellectual Property
★ International/Comparative Law
Jurisprudence
Labor Law
Land Use Law/Natural Resources
★ Lawyering Skills

Legal History/Philosophy
★ Litigation
Maritime Law
Media Law
Mediation
Probate Law
★ Public Interest
★ Securities
★ Tax Law
(★ indicates an area of special strength)

Clinical Courses (Clinical practicum is not required.) Among the clinical areas offered are:

AIDS and the Law
Civil Litigation
Civil Rights
Criminal Defense
Criminal Prosecution
Employment Law
Family Practice
General Practice
Government Litigation
Health
Immigration
Intellectual Property
International Law
Juvenile Law
Public Interest

99% of the students participate in internship programs. International exchange program available.

WESTERN NEW ENGLAND COLLEGE
SCHOOL OF LAW

Springfield, Massachusetts

INFORMATION CONTACT
Donald J. Dunn, Interim Dean
1215 Wilbraham Road
Springfield, MA 01119

Phone: 413-782-1412   Fax: 413-796-2067

LAW STUDENT PROFILE [1997–98]

FULL-TIME   Enrollment: 379
Women: 48%   Men: 52%

PART-TIME   Enrollment: 255
Women: 49%   Men: 51%

APPLICANTS and ADMITTEES
Number applied: 1,406
Admitted: 881
Percentage accepted: 63%
Seats available: 202
Average LSAT score: 148
Average GPA: 3.0

Western New England College School of Law is a private institution that organizes classes on a semester calendar system. The campus is situated in a suburban setting. Founded in 1919, first ABA approved in 1978, and an AALS member, Western New England College School of Law offers JD and JD/MRP degrees.

Faculty consists of 19 full-time and 37 part-time members in 1997–98. 6 full-time faculty members and 15 part-time faculty members are women. 100% of all faculty members have a JD; 26% have advanced law degrees. Of all faculty members, 7.4% are Asian/Pacific Islander, 3.7% are African American, 88.9% are white.

Application Information *Required:* LSAT, LSDAS, application form, application fee of $45, baccalaureate degree, 2 letters of recommendation, college transcripts. *Recommended:* interview. *Application deadline* for fall term is March 15.

Financial Aid Loans, merit-based grants/scholarships, need-based grants/scholarships, and federal work-study loans are available. The average student debt at graduation is $50,263. To apply for financial assistance, students must complete the Free Application for Federal Student Aid and institutional forms.

AT a GLANCE

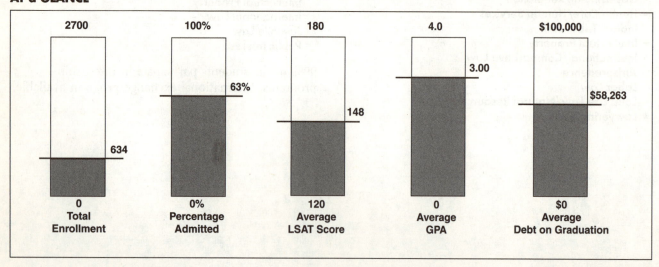

Degree Options

Degree	Total Credits Required	Length of Program
JD–Doctor of Laws	88	3–4.5 yrs, full-time or part-time [day]
JD/MRP–Juris Doctor/Master of Regional Planning– Combined-degree Program	124	4 yrs, full-time only [day]

Financial aid contact: Sandra Belanger, Financial Aid Specialist, 1215 Wilbraham Road, Student Administrative Services, Springfield, MA 01119. Phone: 413-796-2080. Fax: 413-796-2067. Completed financial aid forms should be received by April 1.

Law School Library Western New England College School of Law Library has 6 professional staff members and contains more than 338,029 volumes and 4,513 periodicals. 397 seats are available in the library. When classes are in session, the library is open 103 hours per week.

WESTLAW and LEXIS-NEXIS are available, as are the World Wide Web, online bibliographic services, and CD-ROM players. 35 computer workstations are available to students in the library. Special law collections include Federal Government document depository, law and popular fiction (print and video).

First-Year Program Class size in the average section is 67; 100% of the first-year courses are taught by full-time faculty.

Upper-Level Program Class size in the average section is 30. Among the electives are:

Administrative Law
Advocacy
Bankruptcy
Business and Corporate Law
★ Consumer Law
★ Criminal Procedure
★ Disability Law
★ Discrimination
Education Law
Employment Law
Entertainment Law
Environmental Law
Family Law
Government/Regulation
Health Care/Human Services
Intellectual Property
International/Comparative Law
Interviewing and Counseling
Jurisprudence
Labor Law
Land Use Law/Natural Resources
Lawyering Skills
Legal History/Philosophy
★ Litigation
Media Law
Mediation
Probate Law
★ Public Interest
Securities
Tax Law
(★ *indicates an area of special strength*)

Clinical Courses Students receive degree credit for clinical courses. (Clinical practicum is not required.) Among the clinical areas offered are:

Civil Litigation
Civil Rights
Consumer Law
Criminal Prosecution
Disability Law
Legal Services
Public Interest

8% of the students participate in internship programs.

DEAN'S STATEMENT . . .

I like to think of myself as representing the old and the new, someone who has seen, and is seeing, change among the midst of stability. I joined the faculty as law librarian in 1973 when we began our full-time law programs and, although the deanship is new to me, administration is old hat. My role as dean is to keep our positive momentum going into the twenty-first century.

Over the years I have had the pleasure of watching our law school grow and mature in adulthood, and yet still see an institution filled with the vibrancy and enthusiasm of youth. It's a wonderful mix.

Western New England has many outstanding attributes, but the quality of our faculty members overshadows all others. They bring a rich diversity of experiences with them and strive to provide their students with a broad, practical legal education in a relaxed setting. Ours is a community where everyone—students, faculty, administration—participate together to enrich each other's lives. To truly appreciate what we have to offer, you have to be here. But don't take my word on it. In a recent national survey of law students, our law school ranked third in overall student satisfaction.

The enthusiasm of our faculty is contagious. It is shared by students, administrators, librarians, and staff. All offices and operations at the School of Law are service oriented. Making your experience here rewarding is indeed a collaborative effort.

Springfield and its environs have much to offer as well. The city is near the ocean, ski slopes, the beautiful Berkshire Hills, and the capitals of three states. In fact, all states in New England and New York City are within a 3-hour drive. If you get the opportunity, visit us. You will be pleased with what you find.

—*Donald Dunn, Dean*

HISTORY, CAMPUS, AND LOCATION

Founded in 1919, Western New England College is the only law school in western Massachusetts. Originally affiliated with Northeastern University, Western New England College became independent in 1951. A member of the Association of American Law Schools (AALS), the School of Law is private and has been accredited by the American Bar Association (ABA) since 1978.

Students are drawn to Western New England College by a combination of location—Springfield is a peaceful small city with a low cost of living—and flexibility—the law school offers both part-time day and evening programs in addition to its full-time program and supplements its traditional classroom curriculum with several small clinical programs.

Western New England's dedication to the practical aspects of lawyering is evidenced by the fact that every one of its 60 full- and part-time faculty members has experience practicing law. The faculty and administration seek to foster a collaborative atmosphere that is virtually devoid of the cutthroat competitiveness that is elsewhere the rule.

Springfield is a city of approximately 157,000 residents, 19 percent of whom are African American and 17 percent of whom are Hispanic. Springfield offers distinguished museums, a symphony orchestra, major recreational activities, and the Basketball Hall of Fame. Along with the cultural opportunities available in Springfield, the nearby five colleges—Amherst, Hampshire, Mt. Holyoke, Smith, and the University of Massachusetts—contribute to the recreational and cultural activities in the Pioneer Valley.

SPECIAL QUALITIES OF THE SCHOOL

A student-faculty ratio of 18:1 and a variety of social events combine to form an intimate, stimulating environment in which to study the law. Throughout the semester there are Dean's Teas, which provide an opportunity for students and faculty to get together and learn about what is happening at the law school. "WNEC Week," a series of receptions hosted by alumni, occurs during Spring Break. These receptions are an invaluable opportunity for current students to network with alumni.

Every spring there is an intercollege basketball tournament hosted by the law school. A number of law schools field men's and women's teams and make their way to the Alumni Healthful Living Center, Western New England College's state-of-the-art athletic facility.

TECHNOLOGY ON CAMPUS

There are thirty-five computer workstations available in the law school library. Twenty-one of these are IBM and Macintosh machines. The other fourteen machines are either WESTLAW or LEXIS-NEXIS stations. There is ready access from the library to the World Wide Web. Each student is issued an Internet e-mail account, which can be accessed from the library or from student residences through the School's Local Area Network. Several classrooms are wired for computer use. The moot courtroom is wired for audio and video recording and features a large-screen monitor for playback.

SCHOLARSHIPS AND LOANS

Most student aid is in the form of government-sponsored and privately sponsored loans. In a typical year, more than 20 percent of incoming students receive scholarship support. Award amounts generally range from $3000 to $12,000. Several full tuition scholarships are also awarded. Most awards are based on merit, though some scholarships are designed to assist students who have overcome hardships. Among the named scholarships are the O'Connell, O'Connor, Sheehan, and Sullivan Scholarships.

STUDENT ACTIVITIES AND OPPORTUNITIES

Law Review The School publishes the *Western New England Law Review* twice per year. Selection to the *Law Review* for the majority of members is based on academic standing, while a smaller number of students are selected based on their performance in Lawyering Process, the first-year legal research and writing course. Thirty-three full- and part-time students participated in the publication in 1997–98.

Moot Court Participation in moot court competition is elective and allows the participant to practice and refine legal writing and advocacy skills. The Law School participates in intercollegiate competitions, including the National Moot Court Competition, the ABA National Trial Competition, the ABA Negotiation Moot Court Competition, the Securities Law Moot Court Competition, and the Jessup International Moot Court Competition. Recent moot court teams have placed as high as fifth nationally.

Extracurricular Activities Students sit on faculty committees such as the Admissions Committee and the Academic Standards Committee, and two students attend regular faculty meetings as voting members. Student organizations include the Multi-Cultural Law Student Association, the Women's Law Association, the Environmental Law Coalition, the Jewish Law Students Association, the Phi Alpha Delta legal fraternity, the Lesbian/Gay/Bisexual Alliance, the Christian Law Student Association, the newspaper (*Lex Brevis*), the yearbook, and the Law Rugby Club.

Special Opportunities Many students participate in the clinical offerings at the School of Law. Clinics allow students to work with actual clients under the supervision of faculty and members of the legal community. The School of Law offers five clinical programs, including the Consumer Protection, Criminal Law, Disabilities Law, Discrimination Law, and Legal Service Clinics. Clinical internships are also available. Such internships allow students to work in the office of an attorney, judge, or magistrate to acquire substantive legal knowledge and practical skills.

In conjunction with the University of Massachusetts Amherst, the School of Law offers a combined Juris Doctor/Master of Regional Planning (J.D./M.R.P.) degree program. The regional planning degree provides students the opportunity to study how regions develop and grow from economic and environmental standpoints. Combining the two degrees is invaluable, especially for those interested in environmental law issues.

Opportunities for Members of Minority Groups and Women Members of minority groups and women participate fully in all extracurricular and clinical programs, law reviews, and student organizations. In recent years, the law school has hosted a Northeastern People of Color Legal Scholarship Conference and a student-organized Students of Color Scholarship Conference.

The School of Law believes strongly that its student body should mirror society and, as such, actively encourages the application of qualified women and minority students.

BAR PASSAGE, CAREER SERVICES, AND PLACEMENT

Western New England students pass the various state bar examinations at or above the state averages in the vast majority of cases. Most students sit for the bar exam in Massachusetts, Connecticut, or New York. The School of Law's Career Services Office provides support to law students and alumni in their professionalization, starting in the first year with resume workshops. The Career Services Office maintains a database of employer contacts, clerkships, and job listings. The Office of Alumni Relations also plays an important role in the professionalization of students.

Legal Field	Percentage of Graduates	Average Starting Salary
Academic	2.2%	n/a
Business	25.9%	n/a
Government	20.5%	n/a
Judicial Clerkship	9.2%	n/a
Private Practice	38.9%	n/a
Public Interest	1.6%	n/a
Other	1.7%	n/a

CORRESPONDENCE AND INFORMATION

Office of Admissions
Western New England College School of Law
1215 Wilbraham Road
Springfield, Massachusetts 01119
Telephone: 800-782-6665 (toll-free)
Fax: 413-796-2067
E-mail: lawadmis@wnec.edu

DETROIT COLLEGE OF LAW AT MICHIGAN STATE UNIVERSITY

East Lansing, Michigan

INFORMATION CONTACT

Jeremy T. Harrison, Dean
364 Law College Building
East Lansing, MI 48824-1300

Phone: 517-432-6804   Fax: 517-432-6801
E-mail: heatleya@pilot.msu.edu
Web site: http://www.dcl.edu/

LAW STUDENT PROFILE [1997–98]

FULL-TIME   Enrollment: 517
Women: 40%   Men: 60%

PART-TIME   Enrollment: 231
Women: 39%   Men: 61%

RACIAL or ETHNIC COMPOSITION
African American, 8%; Asian/Pacific Islander, 1%; Hispanic, 2%; Native American, 1%; International, 4%

APPLICANTS and ADMITTEES
Number applied: 756
Admitted: 463
Percentage accepted: 61%
Seats available: 241
Average LSAT score: 152.29
Average GPA: 3.1

Detroit College of Law at Michigan State University is a private nonprofit institution that organizes classes on a semester calendar system. The campus is situated in a suburban setting. Founded in 1891, first ABA approved in 1941, and an AALS member, Detroit College of Law at Michigan State University offers JD, JD/MBA, and JD/MPAd degrees.

Faculty consists of 23 full-time and 31 part-time members in 1997–98. 9 full-time faculty members and 3 part-time faculty members are women. 100% of all faculty members have a JD; 29% have advanced law degrees. Of all faculty members, 1% are African American, 1% are Hispanic, 98% are white.

Application Information *Required:* LSAT, LSDAS, application form, application fee of $50, baccalaureate degree, personal statement, essay, writing sample, college transcripts. *Recommended:* recommendations and interview. *Application deadline* for fall term is April 15.

Financial Aid 53 awards were given. Loans, merit-based grants/scholarships, need-based grants/scholarships, and federal work-study loans are also available. The average student debt at graduation is $39,566. To apply for financial assistance, students must complete the Free Application for

AT a GLANCE

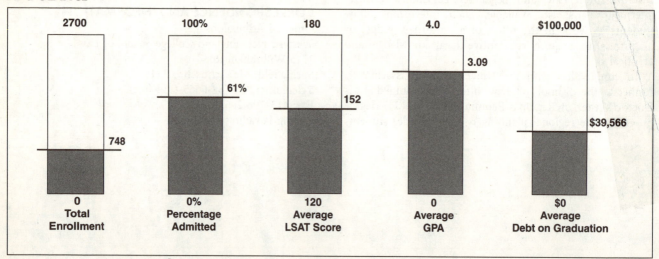

Degree Options

Degree	Total Credits Required	Length of Program
JD–Doctor of Laws	89	3–4 yrs, full-time or part-time [day, evening]
JD/MBA–Juris Doctor/Master of Business Administration–Dual-degree Program	115	4–5 yrs, full-time or part-time [day, evening]
JD/MPAd–Juris Doctor/Master of Public Administration–Dual-degree Program	127	4–5 yrs, full-time or part-time [day, evening]

Federal Student Aid and scholarship specific applications. Financial aid contact: Andrea Heatley, Director of Admissions and Financial Aid, 301 Law College Building, East Lansing, MI 48824. Phone: 517-432-6810. Fax: 517-432-6801. E-mail: heatleya@pilot.msu.edu. Completed financial aid forms should be received by April 15.

Law School Library The Detroit College of Law at Michigan State University Law Library has 6 professional staff members and contains more than 230,215 volumes and 2,920 periodicals. 455 seats are available in the library. When classes are in session, the library is open 110 hours per week.

WESTLAW and LEXIS-NEXIS are available, as are the World Wide Web, online bibliographic services, and CD-ROM players. 49 computer workstations are available to students in the library.

First-Year Program Class size in the average section is 70; 100% of the first-year courses are taught by full-time faculty.

Upper-Level Program Class size in the average section is 20. Among the electives are:

Administrative Law
Advocacy

Business and Corporate Law
Consumer Law
Education Law
Entertainment Law
Environmental Law
Family Law
Government/Regulation
Health Care/Human Services
Indian/Tribal Law
Intellectual Property
★ International/Comparative Law
Jurisprudence
Labor Law
Land Use Law/Natural Resources
Lawyering Skills
Legal History/Philosophy
Litigation
Maritime Law
Media Law
Mediation
Probate Law
Public Interest
Securities
★ Tax Law
(★ indicates an area of special strength)

40% of the students participate in internship programs.

THOMAS M. COOLEY LAW SCHOOL

Lansing, Michigan

INFORMATION CONTACT
Don LeDuc, Dean
217 South Capitol Ave, PO Box 13038
Lansing, MI 48901-3038

Phone: 517-371-5140
Web site: http://www.cooley.edu/

LAW STUDENT PROFILE [1997–98]

FULL-TIME   Enrollment: 228
Women: 39%   Men: 61%

PART-TIME   Enrollment: 1,345
Women: 39%   Men: 61%

RACIAL or ETHNIC COMPOSITION
African American, 8%; Asian/Pacific Islander, 4%; Hispanic, 3%; Native American, 1%; International, 2%

APPLICANTS and ADMITTEES
Number applied: 2,118
Admitted: 1,610
Percentage accepted: 76%
Seats available: 732

Thomas M. Cooley Law School is a private nonprofit institution. First ABA approved in 1975, Thomas M. Cooley Law School offers a JD degree.

Faculty consists of 61 full-time members in 1997–98. 17 full-time faculty members are women.

Application Information *Required:* LSAT, LSDAS, application form, application fee of $50.

Financial Aid In 1997–98, 84% of all students received some form of financial aid. Merit-based grants/scholarships, need-based grants/scholarships, and federal work-study loans are also available. To apply for financial assistance, students must complete the Free Application for Federal Student Aid. Financial aid contact: Thomas M. Cooley Law School, Financial Aid Office, 507 South Grand Avenue, PO Box 13038, Lansing, MI 13038. Phone: 517-371-5140 Ext. 420.

Law School Library has 11 professional staff members and contains more than 361,885 volumes and 5,259 periodicals. 530 seats are available in the library. When classes are in session, the library is open 117 hours per week.

WESTLAW and LEXIS-NEXIS are available, as are the World Wide Web and online bibliographic services. Special law collections include selected United States government document depository.

AT a GLANCE

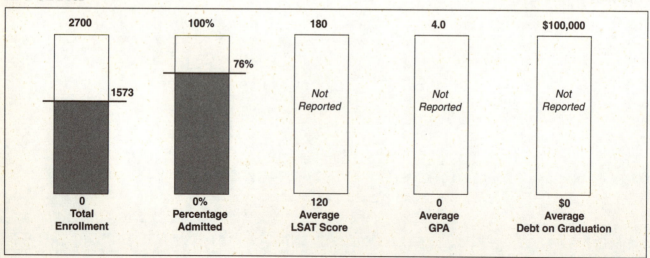

Degree Options		
Degree	Total Credits Required	Length of Program
JD–Juris Doctor	90	2–4 yrs, full-time or part-time [day, evening, weekend, summer]

First-Year Program Class size in the average section is 71.

Clinical Courses Among the clinical areas offered are:

Civil Litigation
Criminal Defense
Criminal Prosecution

Elderly Advocacy
Family Practice
General Practice
Health
Nonprofit Organizations

Internships are available. International exchange programs permit students to visit Australia.

UNIVERSITY OF DETROIT MERCY
SCHOOL OF LAW

Detroit, Michigan

INFORMATION CONTACT
Bernard Dobranski, Dean
651 East Jefferson Avenue
Detroit, MI 48226

Phone: 313-596-0200   Fax: 313-596-0280
Web site: http://www.udmercy.edu/

LAW STUDENT PROFILE [1997–98]

FULL-TIME   Enrollment: 685
Women: 48%   Men: 52%

PART-TIME   Enrollment: 114
Women: 41%   Men: 59%

RACIAL or ETHNIC COMPOSITION
African American, 12%; Asian/Pacific Islander, 3%; Hispanic, 1%; Nataive American, 0.4%; International, 5%

APPLICANTS and ADMITTEES
Seats available: 200
Average LSAT score: 148
Average GPA: 3.0

University of Detroit Mercy School of Law is a private institution that organizes classes on a semester calendar system. The campus is situated in an urban setting. Founded in 1912, first ABA approved in 1933, and an AALS member, University of Detroit Mercy School of Law offers JD and JD/MBA degrees.

Faculty consists of 27 full-time members in 1997–98. 4 full-time faculty members are women. 100% of all faculty members have a JD degree.

Application Information *Required:* LSAT, LSDAS, application form, application fee of $50, baccalaureate degree, 2 letters of recommendation, personal statement, college transcripts. *Recommended:* writing sample. *Application deadline* for fall term is April 15.

Financial Aid Loans, merit-based grants/scholarships, and federal work-study loans are available. The average student debt at graduation is $55,500. To apply for financial assistance, students must complete the Free Application for Federal Student Aid, institutional forms, and scholarship-specific applications for private scholarships only; not needed for finanical aid application. Financial aid contact: Denise M. Daniel, Financial Aid Coordinator School of Law, 651 East Jefferson Avenue, Detroit, MI 48226. Phone: 313-596-0214. Fax: 313-596-0280. E-mail: udmlawfa@udmercy.edu.

AT a GLANCE

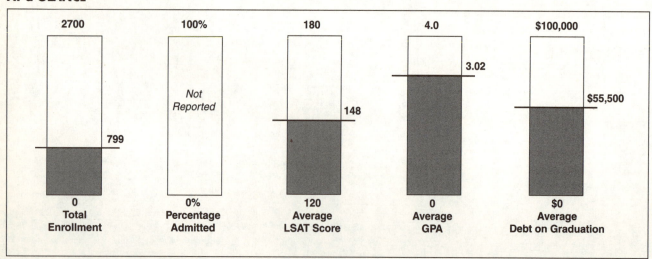

Degree Options

Degree	Total Credits Required	Length of Program
JD–Doctor of Laws	90	3–4 yrs, full-time or part-time [day, evening, summer]
JD/MBA–Juris Doctor/Master of Business Administration–Dual-degree Program	110	4–5 yrs, full-time only [day, evening, summer]

Law School Library University of Detroit Mercy School of Law Library has 5 professional staff members and contains more than 300,000 volumes and 3,495 periodicals. 406 seats are available in the library. When classes are in session, the library is open 92 hours per week.

WESTLAW and LEXIS-NEXIS are available, as are the World Wide Web, online bibliographic services, and CD-ROM players. 42 computer workstations are available to students in the library. Special law collections include Canadian, Labor, Tax.

First-Year Program Class size in the average section is 55; 100% of the first-year courses are taught by full-time faculty.

Upper-Level Program Class size in the average section is 25. Among the electives are:

Business and Corporate Law
Entertainment Law
Environmental Law
Health Care/Human Services

★ **Intellectual Property**
★ **International/Comparative Law**
  Labor Law
★ **Lawyering Skills**
  Litigation
  Tax Law
(★ *indicates an area of special strength*)

Clinical Courses Students receive degree credit for clinical courses. (Clinical practicum is not required.) Among the clinical areas offered are:

Civil Rights
Criminal Defense
Criminal Prosecution
Elderly Advocacy
Environmental Law
Government Litigation
Immigration
International Law
Tax Law

Internships are available. International exchange programs permit students to visit France.

UNIVERSITY OF MICHIGAN
LAW SCHOOL

Ann Arbor, Michigan

INFORMATION CONTACT
Jeffrey S. Lehman, Dean
625 South State Street
Ann Arbor, MI 48109-1215

Phone: 734-764-1358   Fax: 734-764-8309
Web site: http://www.umich.edu/

LAW STUDENT PROFILE [1997–98]

APPLICANTS and ADMITTEES
Seats available: 339
Average LSAT score: 167
Average GPA: 3.5

University of Michigan Law School is a public institution that organizes classes on a semester calendar system. The campus is situated in an urban setting. Founded in 1859, first ABA approved in 1923, and an AALS member, University of Michigan Law School offers JD, JD/MA, JD/MBA, JD/MHA, JD/MPPo, JD/MS, JD/PhD, LLM, MCL, and SJD degrees.

Application Information *Required:* LSAT, LSDAS, application form, application fee of $70, baccalaureate degree, 1 recommendation, personal statement, college transcripts. *Recommended:* essay, writing sample, resume.

Costs The 1997–98 tuition is $17,726 full-time for state residents; $3085 per semester (minimum) part-time for state residents. Tuition is $23,696 full-time for nonresidents; $3762 per semester (minimum) part-time for nonresidents. Fees: $185.

Financial Aid Graduate assistantships, loans, loan repayment assistance program (LRAP), merit-based grants/scholarships, need-based grants/scholarships, and federal work-study loans are available. To apply for financial assistance, students must complete the Free Application for Federal Student Aid, institutional forms, scholarship specific applications, and Need access diskette, tax returns. Financial aid contact: Katherine Gottschalk, Director of Financial Aid, 308 Hutchins Hall, Ann Arbor, MI 48109-1215. Phone: 734-764-5289. Fax: 734-764-8309. E-mail: lawfinaid@umich.edu.

AT a GLANCE

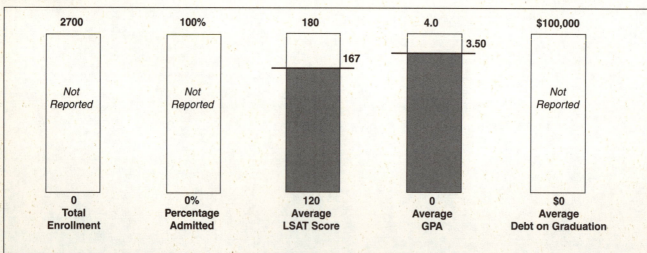

Degree Options

Degree	Total Credits Required	Length of Program
JD–Doctor of Laws	83	3 yrs, full-time only [day, summer]
JD/MA–Juris Doctor/Master of Arts–Law and World Politics, Russian and East European Studies, Modern Middle Eastern and North African Studies Joint-degree Programs		3.5 yrs, full-time only [day, summer]
JD/MBA–Juris Doctor/Master of Business Administration, JD/MHA–Juris Doctor/Master of Health Administration, JD/MPPo–Juris Doctor/Master of Public Policy, JD/MS–Juris Doctor/Master of Science–Natural Resources Joint-degree Programs		4 yrs, full-time only [day, summer]
JD/PhD–Juris Doctor/Doctor of Philosophy–Joint-degree Program in Economics		5 yrs, full-time only [day, summer]
LLM–Master of Laws–International Law, International Economic Law	24	1 yr, full-time only [day, summer]
MCL–Master of Comparative Law	20	1 yr, full-time only
SJD–Doctor of Juridical Science	24	1 yr, full-time only

Law School Library University of Michigan Law School Library has 10 professional staff members and contains more than 811,774 volumes and 9,835 periodicals. 843 seats are available in the library. When classes are in session, the library is open 122 hours per week.

WESTLAW and LEXIS-NEXIS are available, as are the World Wide Web, online bibliographic services, and CD-ROM players. Special law collections include European Economic Community documents, selected United States government documents, Roman Law, international law, comparative law, trial records, biographies, and legal biographies.

First-Year Program Class size in the average section is 80; 100% of the first-year courses are taught by full-time faculty.

Upper-Level Program Class size in the average section is 50. Among the electives are:

Administrative Law
Advocacy
Blood Feuds
Business and Corporate Law
Consumer Law
Democratic Theory
Education Law
Entertainment Law
Ethics
Family Law
Government/Regulation
Health Care/Human Services
Indian/Tribal Law
Insurance
Intellectual Property
International/Comparative Law
Japanese Law
Jurisprudence
Labor Law
Land Use Law/Natural Resources
Lawyering Skills
Legal History/Philosophy
Litigation
Maritime Law
Media Law
Medicine
Probate Law
Public Interest
Securities
Tax Law

Clinical Courses Students receive degree credit for clinical courses. (Clinical practicum is not required.) Among the clinical areas offered are:

Appellate Litigation
Civil Litigation
Civil Rights
Criminal Defense
Criminal Prosecution
Domestic Violence
Economic Development
Environmental Law
Family Practice
General Practice
Housing Law
Immigration
Juvenile Law
Land Rights/Natural Resource
Mediation
Poverty/Welfare Law
Public Interest

Internships are available. International exchange programs available.

WAYNE STATE UNIVERSITY
LAW SCHOOL

Detroit, Michigan

INFORMATION CONTACT

James K. Robinson, Dean
468 Ferry Mall
Detroit, MI 48202

Phone: 313-577-3933   Fax: 317-577-2620
E-mail: jfriedl@cms.cc.wayne.edu
Web site: http://www.law.wayne.edu/

LAW STUDENT PROFILE [1997–98]

FULL-TIME   Enrollment: 693
Women: 46%   Men: 54%

PART-TIME   Enrollment: 149
Women: 39%   Men: 61%

RACIAL or ETHNIC COMPOSITION
African American, 11%; Asian/Pacific Islander, 0.5%;
Hispanic, 2%; Native American, 2%

APPLICANTS and ADMITTEES
Number applied: 1,102
Admitted: 602
Percentage accepted: 55%
Seats available: 260
Average LSAT score: 154
Average GPA: 3.3

Wayne State University Law School is a public
institution that organizes classes on a semester
calendar system. The campus is situated in an urban
setting. Founded in 1927, first ABA approved in
1936, and an AALS member, Wayne State University
Law School offers JD, JD/MA, JD/MBA, and LLM
degrees.

Application Information *Required:* LSAT, LSDAS,
application form, application fee of $20, baccalaure-
ate degree, recommendations, personal statement,
college transcripts. *Application deadline* for fall term
is April 15.

Costs The 1997–98 tuition is $237 per credit hour
for state residents. Tuition is $508 per credit hour
for nonresidents. Fees: $498 full-time; $114 per
semester (minimum) part-time.

Financial Aid Loans, merit-based grants/scholar-
ships, need-based grants/scholarships, and federal
work-study loans are available. The average student
debt at graduation is $27,000. To apply for financial
assistance, students must complete the Free Application for Federal Student Aid and institutional forms.
Financial aid contact: Ms. Chiquita McKenzie,
Assistant Director, 468 Ferry Mall, Room 191, Law
Library Annex, Detroit, MI 48202. Phone: 313-577-
5142. Fax: 317-577-2620. E-mail:
c.mckenzie@wayne.edu.

AT a GLANCE

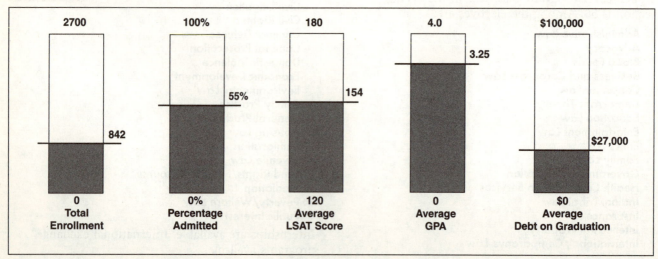

Degree Options

Degree	Total Credits Required	Length of Program
JD–Doctor of Laws	86	3–6 yrs, full-time or part-time [day, evening, summer]
JD/MA–Juris Doctor/Master of Arts–History Dual-degree Program	121	3–6 yrs, full-time or part-time [day, evening, summer]
JD/MA–Juris Doctor/Master of Arts–Political Science Dual-degree Program	122	3–6 yrs, full-time or part-time [day, evening, summer]
JD/MBA–Juris Doctor/Master of Business Administration–Dual-degree Program	122	3–6 yrs, full-time or part-time [day, evening, summer]
LLM–Master of Laws–Corporate and Finance Law	26	1–6 yrs, full-time or part-time [day, evening]
LLM–Master of Laws–Labor Law	26	1–6 yrs, full-time or part-time [day, evening]
LLM–Master of Laws–Taxation	26	1–6 yrs, full-time or part-time [day, evening]

Law School Library Arthur Neef Law Library has 5 professional staff members and contains more than 549,755 volumes and 4,840 periodicals. 506 seats are available in the library. When classes are in session, the library is open 97 hours per week.

WESTLAW and LEXIS-NEXIS are available, as are the World Wide Web, online bibliographic services, and CD-ROM players. 35 computer workstations are available to students in the library. Special law collections include Michigan Probate Opinions, Michigan Environmental Law Collection, Michigan Supreme Court Records and Briefs.

First-Year Program Class size in the average section is 90; 100% of the first-year courses are taught by full-time faculty.

Upper-Level Program Class size in the average section is 40. Among the electives are:

- Administrative Law
- Advocacy
- Business and Corporate Law
- Education Law
- Entertainment Law
- Environmental Law
- Family Law
- Government/Regulation
- Health Care/Human Services
- Intellectual Property
- International/Comparative Law
- Jurisprudence
- Labor Law
- Land Use Law/Natural Resources
- Lawyering Skills

- Legal History/Philosophy
- Litigation
- Media Law
- Mediation
- Probate Law
- Securities
- Tax Law

Clinical Courses Students receive degree credit for clinical courses. (Clinical practicum is not required.) Among the clinical areas offered are:

- Civil Litigation
- Civil Rights
- Corporate Law
- Criminal Defense
- Criminal Prosecution
- Elderly Advocacy
- Environmental Law
- Family Practice
- General Practice
- Government Litigation
- Health
- Immigration
- Intellectual Property
- International Law
- Juvenile Law
- Land Rights/Natural Resource
- Mediation
- Public Interest
- Tax Law

10% of the students participate in internship programs. International exchange programs permit students to visit Netherlands and United Kingdom.

HISTORY, CAMPUS, AND LOCATION

The Law School was established by a group of public-spirited lawyers in cooperation with the Detroit Board of Education as part of the Colleges of the City of Detroit in 1927. The Law School, with the other colleges, grew and flourished. They were subsequently renamed Wayne University. In 1956, the University joined the University of Michigan and Michigan State University as one of Michigan's three major public universities and was renamed Wayne State University. Wayne State University is located in the heart of the University/Cultural Center area about 4 miles from downtown Detroit. Within a few blocks of the Law School are the Detroit Public Library, the Detroit Institute of Arts, the International Institute, the Detroit Historical Museum, the Detroit Science Center, and the Museum of African-American History. South of the main campus area are the Detroit Medical Center and the Wayne State University Medical School. State and federal courts and offices are concentrated in the downtown area.

SPECIAL QUALITIES OF THE SCHOOL

The Law School's faculty is actively involved in scholarly research. Professors at Wayne State University Law School make significant contributions to the understanding of issues in environmental law, taxation, criminal procedure, constitutional law, urban law, and many other fields. Their books and articles contribute to the depth and quality of classroom teaching. It is the interaction of teaching and research that creates an especially stimulating environment for the law student. The Law School community takes great pride in its diversity. The full-time faculty includes individuals experienced in local, state, and federal government; others who have served as judicial clerks for federal judges; a number with backgrounds in private practice; and others who are well-known public interest advocates. They combine excellent academic credentials with practical experience.

TECHNOLOGY ON CAMPUS

The Law Library houses a thirty-station computer laboratory for use by Wayne State law students. The laboratory includes both Power Macs and personal computers that provide access to LEXIS-NEXIS, WESTLAW, CALI (Computer Assisted Legal Instruction), LUIS (Library User Information System), Telnet, e-mail, the Internet, and Microsoft Office 97. Law students receive training on LEXIS-NEXIS and WESTLAW and may access them from computers in the lab or from home via modem and the Internet.

SCHOLARSHIPS AND LOANS

There are six financial aid programs: Board of Governors' Grant (maximum of $1600 for continuing full-time students and $2600 for first-year full-time students), Perkins Loan (maximum of $2000), College Work Study (maximum of $3500, not available to first-year students), Stafford/Unsubsidized Stafford Loan (maximum of $18,500), and Law Access Private Loan (maximum cost of education). All awards are capped at the cost of education. All students must complete the Free Application for Federal Student Aid (FAFSA) or Renewal Form each year. The FAFSA or Renewal Form must reach the Federal Processor before April 30 for grant consideration. Students must also complete the Wayne State University Law School Financial Aid Application. The estimated fall 1998 cost of education is $22,058 for first-year full-time Michigan residents and $29,798 for nonresidents. These costs include tuition, room/board, books, transportation, and miscellaneous expenses.

STUDENT ACTIVITIES AND OPPORTUNITIES

Law Review The *Wayne Law Review*, published since 1954, is the Law School's official scholarly journal. Three of the four annual issues include articles of general academic and professional interest authored by practicing attorneys and law professors, as well as comments written by *Law Review* members. A fourth issue is an annual survey of developments in Michigan law and is widely read by members of the Michigan legal community.

Moot Court Wayne State's Moot Court program is a widely recognized and well-respected program. The program, directed by a 6-member executive board, is open to upperclass students selected on the basis of their first-year grades or through a petitioning process in which students present an oral argument on a topic selected by the Moot Court board.

Extracurricular Activities More than twenty student organizations add greatly to the quality of life at the Law School. Student organizations sponsor speakers and debates on topics of current interest or on topics in such specialized areas of law as international or intellectual property law. Several groups combine to put on programs such as the annual Alternative Legal Careers Day with practitioners from various areas of public interest law. Other organizations jointly sponsor clothing drives for the needy or get together to volunteer at an area soup kitchen, and the members of one organization help Detroit school children with homework.

Special Opportunities The Law School offers numerous courses, internships, and student academic programs that give students a unique opportunity to acquire skills important to the practice of law. Students are encouraged to take advantage of the special opportunities available in the Detroit metropolitan area for internships with judges, prosecutors' and defenders' offices, and public interest law practices. Courses such as Pretrial Advocacy and Trial Advocacy teach students how to prepare for and conduct a trial. Participation in the Free Legal Aid Clinic allows students, under attorney supervision, to assist actual clients, including representing them in court. Students may join the Student Trial Advocacy Program, which is devoted to enhancing students' trial advocacy skills or the Moot Court program. The Law School, in cooperation with other units in the University, offers several joint-degree programs, including a joint J.D./M.B.A. program and a J.D./M.A. in alternative dispute resolution. Students may also obtain an M.A. from the history or political science departments in the College of Liberal Arts. The Law School also sponsors a student exchange program with Utrecht University in the Netherlands, which allows 1 or 2 students per semester to study at the other school. Additionally, the Law School and the University of Warwick in England have an exchange program that involves a student from each school visiting the other for a period of six weeks during the summer. Each year, a Wayne student is selected for the Freeman Fellowship to support study during a summer session at the Hague Academy of International Law. The Wayne State University Center for Legal Studies provides the University and the wider community it serves with a forum for communication, collaboration, and research on legal issues. The Center promotes combined graduate degree programs in law and related fields and encourages interdisciplinary study by law students and others.

Opportunities for Members of Minority Groups and Women The Law School has several active student organizations dedicated to members of minority groups and women, including the Black Law Student Association, the Gay/Lesbian Law Caucus, and the Women's Law Caucus.

BAR PASSAGE, CAREER SERVICES, AND PLACEMENT

A majority of our graduates take the Michigan bar examination. In the July 1997 examination, the overall pass rate was 94 percent. Ninety-five percent of the first-time takers were successful on that exam. In February 1998, 94 percent of the first-time takers were successful, while 36 percent of individuals retaking the exam were successful. The Career Services Office publicizes employment opportunities from hundreds of employers on its 24-hour telephone job hot line, updated weekly, and in its two publications, the *Student Newsletter and Job Bulletin*, published weekly, and the *Alumni Newsletter and Job Bulletin*, published monthly. The percentage of last year's graduates entering each specific legal field and the average starting salary are listed below.

Legal Field	Percentage of Graduates	Average Starting Salary
Academic	2.3%	$42,095
Business	18.6%	$42,095
Government	15.0%	$42,095
Judicial Clerkship	6.9%	$42,095
Private Practice	53.5%	$42,095
Public Interest	2.9%	$42,095
Other	0.8%	$42,095

CORRESPONDENCE AND INFORMATION

Assistant Dean Linda Fowler Sims
Wayne State Law School
468 Ferry Mall
Detroit, Michigan 48202
Telephone: 313-577-3937
Fax: 313-577-6000
E-mail: lfsims@wayne.edu
World Wide Web: http://www.law.wayne.edu

HAMLINE UNIVERSITY
SCHOOL OF LAW

St. Paul, Minnesota

INFORMATION CONTACT
Raymond R. Krause, Dean
1536 Hewitt Avenue
St. Paul, MN 55104

Phone: 651-523-2968   Fax: 612-523-2435
Web site: http://www.hamline.edu/

LAW STUDENT PROFILE [1997–98]

FULL-TIME   Enrollment: 450
Women: 50%   Men: 50%

PART-TIME   Enrollment: 49
Women: 43%   Men: 57%

RACIAL or ETHNIC COMPOSITION
African American, 5%; Asian/Pacific Islander, 3%; Hispanic, 1%; Native American, 1%; International, 2%

APPLICANTS and ADMITTEES
Number applied: 993
Admitted: 522
Percentage accepted: 53%
Seats available: 142
Median LSAT score: 153
Median GPA: 3.2

Hamline University School of Law is a private institution that organizes classes on a semester calendar system. The campus is situated in an urban setting. Founded in 1972, first ABA approved in 1975, and an AALS member, Hamline University School of Law offers JD, JD/AMBA, JD/MAPA, JD/MBA, and LLM degrees.

Faculty consists of 32 full-time and 70 part-time members in 1997–98. 14 full-time faculty members and 22 part-time faculty members are women. 98.9% of all faculty members have a JD; 9.3% have advanced law degrees. Of all faculty members, 2.1% are Native American, 1% are Asian/Pacific Islander, 1% are African American, 2.1% are Hispanic, 92.8% are white, 1% are international.

Application Information *Required:* LSAT, LSDAS, application form, application fee of $50, baccalaureate degree, personal statement, college transcripts. *Recommended:* recommendations and resume. *Application deadline* for fall term is May 15. Students are required to have their own computers.

Costs The 1997–98 tuition is $16,500 full-time; $8200 part-time.

Financial Aid 201 awards were given. Fellowships, loans, merit-based grants/scholarships, need-based grants/scholarships, and federal work-study loans are

AT a GLANCE

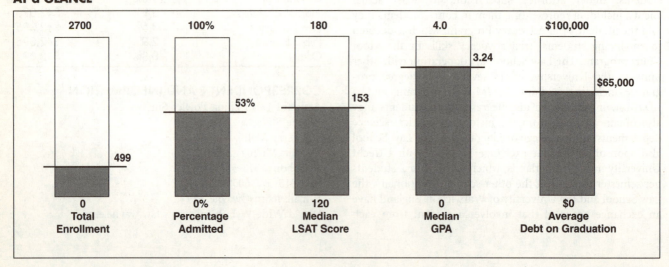

Degree Options

Degree	Total Credits Required	Length of Program
JD–Doctor of Laws	88	3–6 yrs, full-time or part-time [day, summer]
JD/AMBA–Juris Doctor/Master of Business Administration with Accounting Major–Joint-degree Program	129	4 yrs, full-time only [day, summer]
JD/MAPA–Juris Doctor/Master of Arts in Public Administration–Dual-degree Program	109	4 yrs, full-time or part-time [day, evening, weekend, summer]
JD/MBA–Juris Doctor/Master of Business Administration–Dual-degree Program	106	4–6 yrs, full-time or part-time [day, evening, weekend, summer]
LLM–Master of Laws–for Foreign Lawyers	29	1 yr, full-time only [day]

also available. The average student debt at graduation is $65,000. To apply for financial assistance, students must complete the Free Application for Federal Student Aid, institutional forms, and tax return. Financial aid contact: Lynette M. Wahl, Associate Director of Financial Aid, 1536 Hewitt Avenue, Saint Paul, MN 55104-1284. Phone: 612-523-2280. Fax: 612-523-2435. E-mail: lwahl@gw.hamline.edu.

Law School Library Hamline University Law Library has 6 professional staff members and contains more than 230,000 volumes and 960 periodicals. 365 seats are available in the library. When classes are in session, the library is open 107 hours per week.

WESTLAW and LEXIS-NEXIS are available, as are the World Wide Web, online bibliographic services, and CD-ROM players. 30 computer workstations are available to students in the library.

First-Year Program Class size in the average section is 48; 100% of the first-year courses are taught by full-time faculty.

Upper-Level Program Among the electives are:

Administrative Law
Advocacy
★ Business and Corporate Law
★ Children and the Law
★ Consumer Law
Education Law
Entertainment Law
Environmental Law

Family Practice
★ Government/Regulation
Health Care/Human Services
Indian/Tribal Law
Intellectual Property
★ International/Comparative Law
Jurisprudence
★ Labor Law
Land Use Law/Natural Resources
Lawyering Skills
Legal History/Philosophy
Litigation
★ Maritime Law
Media Law
★ Mediation
Probate Law
Public Interest
Securities
Tax Law
(★ *indicates an area of special strength*)

Clinical Courses Students receive degree credit for clinical courses. (Clinical practicum is not required.) Among the clinical areas offered are:

Corporate Law
Education
Family Practice
General Practice
Juvenile Law
Legal Assistance to Minnesota Prisoners (LAMP)
Mediation

7% of the students participate in internship programs. International exchange programs permit students to visit Norway.

UNIVERSITY OF MINNESOTA, TWIN CITIES CAMPUS
LAW SCHOOL

Minneapolis, Minnesota

INFORMATION CONTACT

E. Thomas Sullivan, Dean
229 19th Avenue South
Minneapolis, MN 55455

Phone: 612-625-1000
Web site: http://www.law.umn.edu/

LAW STUDENT PROFILE [1997–98]

FULL-TIME   Enrollment: 801
Women: 42%   Men: 58%

RACIAL or ETHNIC COMPOSITION
African American, 3%; Asian/Pacific Islander, 8%; Hispanic, 4%; Native American, 1%; International, 6%

APPLICANTS and ADMITTEES
Number applied: 1,513
Admitted: 644
Percentage accepted: 43%
Seats available: 241

University of Minnesota, Twin Cities Campus Law School is a public institution that organizes classes on a semester calendar system. The campus is situated in an urban setting. Founded in 1888, first ABA approved in 1923, and an AALS member, University of Minnesota, Twin Cities Campus Law School offers JD, JD/MA, JD/MBA, JD/MPP, and LLM degrees.

Faculty consists of 42 full-time and 83 part-time members in 1997–98. 15 full-time faculty members and 29 part-time faculty members are women.

Application Information *Required:* LSAT, LSDAS, application form, application fee of $40, baccalaureate degree, 2 letters of recommendation, personal statement. *Application deadline* for fall term is March 1. Students are required to have their own computers.

Costs The 1997–98 tuition is $9000 for state residents. Tuition is $15,300 for nonresidents. Fees: $662.

Financial Aid In 1997–98, 96% of all students received some form of financial aid. Loans, merit-based grants/scholarships, need-based grants/scholarships, and federal work-study loans are also

AT a GLANCE

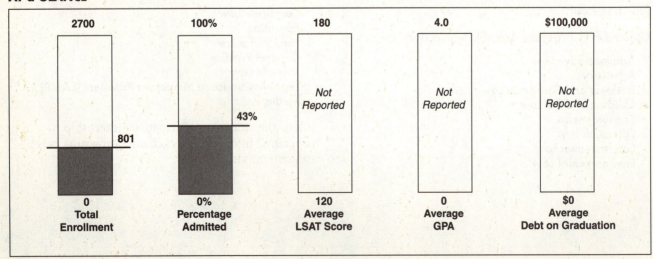

2700	100%	180	4.0	$100,000
		Not Reported	Not Reported	Not Reported
801	43%			
0	0%	120	0	$0
Total Enrollment	**Percentage Admitted**	**Average LSAT Score**	**Average GPA**	**Average Debt on Graduation**

Degree Options

Degree	Total Credits Required	Length of Program
JD–Juris Doctor	88	3 yrs, full-time only
JD/MA–Juris Doctor/Master of Arts–Joint-degree Program		4 yrs
JD/MBA–Juris Doctor/Master of Business Administration–Joint-degree Program		4 yrs
JD/MPP–Juris Doctor/Master of Public Planning–Joint-degree Program		4 yrs
LLM–Master of Laws–American Studies for Graduates of Foreign Law Schools	24	1 yr, full-time only

available. To apply for financial assistance, students must complete the Free Application for Federal Student Aid and financial aid transcript, CLEO. Financial aid contact: Office of Scholarship and Financial Aid, University of Minnesota Law School, 229 19 Avenue South, 210 Fraser Hall, Minneapolis, MN 55455. Phone: 612-625-5005. Completed financial aid forms should be received by March 15.

Law School Library has 12 professional staff members and contains more than 830,290 volumes and 9,661 periodicals. 934 seats are available in the library. When classes are in session, the library is open 81 hours per week.

WESTLAW and LEXIS-NEXIS are available, as are the World Wide Web and CD-ROM players.

First-Year Program Class size in the average section is 108.

Upper-Level Program Among the electives are:

Advocacy
Agricultural Law
Bankruptcy
Business and Corporate Law
Children's Advocacy
Chinese Law
Civil Procedure
Civil Rights
Constitutional Law
Education Law
Environmental Law
Estate Planning
Family Law

Government/Regulation
Health Care/Human Services
Indian/Tribal Law
International/Comparative Law
Jurisprudence
Labor Law
Land Use Law/Natural Resources
Lawyering Skills
Legal History/Philosophy
Legislation
Litigation
Probate Law
Property/Real Estate
Public Interest
Sports Law
Tax Law

Clinical Courses Among the clinical areas offered are:

Bankruptcy
Civil Litigation
Criminal Defense
Criminal Prosecution
Family Practice
General Practice
Immigration
Indian/Tribal Law
Prisoners' Rights
Public Interest
Tax Law

Internships are available. International exchange programs permit students to visit France; Germany; Ireland; Mexico; and Sweden.

WILLIAM MITCHELL COLLEGE OF LAW

St. Paul, Minnesota

INFORMATION CONTACT

Harry J. Haynsworth, President and Dean
875 Summit Avenue
St. Paul, MN 55105-3076

Phone: 612-290-6310   Fax: 612-290-6414
E-mail: admissions@wmitchell.edu
Web site: http://www.wmitchell.edu/

LAW STUDENT PROFILE [1997–98]

FULL-TIME   Enrollment: 508
Women: 48%   Men: 52%

PART-TIME   Enrollment: 545
Women: 45%   Men: 55%

RACIAL or ETHNIC COMPOSITION

African American, 4%; Asian/Pacific Islander, 4%; Hispanic,
1%; Native American, 1%; International, 1%

APPLICANTS and ADMITTEES

Number applied: 937
Admitted: 694
Percentage accepted: 74%
Seats available: 335
Median LSAT score: 152
Median GPA: 3.2

William Mitchell College of Law is a private
nonprofit institution that organizes classes on a
semester calendar system. The campus is situated in
an urban setting. Founded in 1900, first ABA
approved in 1938, and an AALS member, William
Mitchell College of Law offers JD and LLM degrees.

Faculty consists of 31 full-time and 86 part-time
members in 1997–98. 8 full-time faculty members
and 19 part-time faculty members are women. 100%
of all faculty members have a JD degree.

Application Information *Required:* LSAT, LSDAS,
application form, application fee of $45, baccalaure-
ate degree, 2 letters of recommendation, personal
statement, college transcripts, resume. *Application
deadline* for fall term is July 1.

Financial Aid In 1997–98, 88% of all students
received some form of financial aid. Loans, loan
repayment assistance program (LRAP), merit-based
grants/scholarships, need-based grants/scholarships,
and federal work-study loans are also available. The
average student debt at graduation is $56,136. To
apply for financial assistance, students must
complete the Free Application for Federal Student
Aid and institutional forms. Financial aid contact:
Debra Velasco, Assistant Director, Financial Aid, 875
Summit Avenue, St. Paul, MN 55105. Phone:
612-290-6403. Fax: 612-290-6414. E-mail:

AT a GLANCE

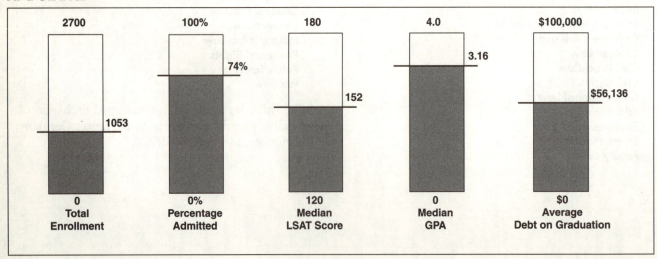

Degree Options

Degree	Total Credits Required	Length of Program
JD–Doctor of Laws	86	3–4 yrs, full-time or part-time [day, evening, summer]
LLM–Master of Laws–Master of Laws (program will only be offered through Fall, 1999)	22	2 yrs, part-time only [evening, summer]

dvelasco@wmitchell.edu. Completed financial aid forms should be received by March 15.

Law School Library Warren E. Burger Library has 9 professional staff members and contains more than 277,036 volumes and 4,317 periodicals. 672 seats are available in the library. When classes are in session, the library is open 106 hours per week.

WESTLAW and LEXIS-NEXIS are available, as are the World Wide Web, online bibliographic services, and CD-ROM players. 73 computer workstations are available to students in the library.

First-Year Program Class size in the average section is 72; 100% of the first-year courses are taught by full-time faculty.

Upper-Level Program Class size in the average section is 35. Among the electives are:

- ★ Administrative Law
- ★ Advocacy
- ★ Business and Corporate Law
  Education Law
  Entertainment Law
  Environmental Law
  Family Law
  Government/Regulation
  Health Care/Human Services
  Indian/Tribal Law

- ★ Intellectual Property
  International/Comparative Law
  Jurisprudence
  Labor Law
  Land Use Law/Natural Resources
  Lawyering Skills
  Legal History/Philosophy
- ★ Litigation
  Maritime Law
- ★ Mediation
  Probate Law
  Securities
- ★ Tax Law

(★ *indicates an area of special strength*)

Clinical Courses Students receive degree credit for clinical courses. (Clinical practicum is not required.) Among the clinical areas offered are:

Civil Litigation
Civil Rights
Corporate Law
Criminal Defense
Criminal Prosecution
Government Litigation
Immigration
International Law
Tax Law

Internships are available.

MISSISSIPPI COLLEGE
SCHOOL OF LAW

Clinton, Mississippi

INFORMATION CONTACT

J. Richard Hurt, Dean
151 East Griffith Street
Jackson, MS 39201

Phone: 601-925-7104   Fax: 601-925-7117
E-mail: pevans@mc.edu
Web site: http://www.mc.edu/

LAW STUDENT PROFILE [1997–98]

FULL-TIME   Enrollment: 418
Women: 38%   Men: 62%

RACIAL or ETHNIC COMPOSITION
African American, 8%; Asian/Pacific Islander, 2%; Hispanic, 0.5%; Native American, 1%

APPLICANTS and ADMITTEES
Number applied: 699
Admitted: 483
Percentage accepted: 69%
Seats available: 145
Average LSAT score: 150
Average GPA: 3.0

Mississippi College School of Law is a private institution that organizes classes on a semester calendar system. The campus is situated in an urban setting. Founded in 1975, first ABA approved in 1980, and an AALS member, Mississippi College School of Law offers JD and JD/MBA degrees.

Faculty consists of 16 full-time and 19 part-time members in 1997–98. 6 full-time faculty members and 1 part-time faculty members are women. 100% of all faculty members have a JD; 35% have advanced law degrees. Of all faculty members, 6% are African American, 94% are white.

Application Information *Required:* LSAT, LSDAS, application form, application fee of $25, baccalaureate degree, personal statement, college transcripts. *Recommended:* recommendations. *Application deadline* for fall term is May 1.

Costs The 1997–98 tuition is $14,291. Fees: $162.

Financial Aid In 1997–98, 85% of all students received some form of financial aid. 98 other awards, totaling $766,028, were given. Loans, merit-based grants/scholarships, and federal work-study loans are also available. The average student debt at graduation is $67,000. To apply for financial assistance, students must complete the Free Application for Federal Student Aid and school's law

AT a GLANCE

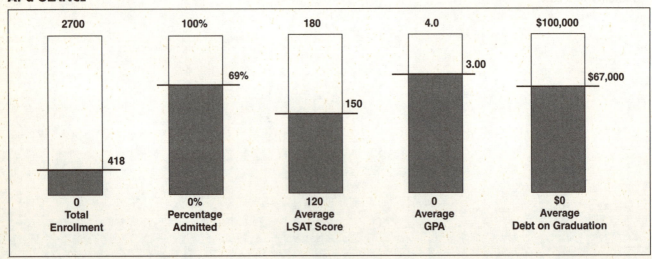

Degree Options

Degree	Total Credits Required	Length of Program
JD–Juris Doctor	88	3 yrs, full-time only [day]
JD/MBA–Juris Doctor/Master of Business Administration	103	3.5 yrs, full-time only [day]

financial aid application. Financial aid contact: Cathy Nash, Director of Financial Aid, 151 East Griffith Street, Jackson, MS 39201. Phone: 601-925-7110. Fax: 601-925-7117. E-mail: cnash@mc.edu. Completed financial aid forms should be received by May 1.

Law School Library has 6 professional staff members and contains more than 253,000 volumes and 3,438 periodicals. 275 seats are available in the library. When classes are in session, the library is open 80 hours per week.

WESTLAW and LEXIS-NEXIS are available, as is the World Wide Web. 28 computer workstations are available to students in the library.

First-Year Program Class size in the average section is 75; 100% of the first-year courses are taught by full-time faculty.

Upper-Level Program Class size in the average section is 50.

Internships are available.

Mississippi ∎

UNIVERSITY OF MISSISSIPPI
SCHOOL OF LAW

University, Mississippi

LAW STUDENT PROFILE [1997–98]

FULL-TIME Enrollment: 493
Women: 41%   Men: 59%

PART-TIME Enrollment: 4
Women: 25%   Men: 75%

RACIAL or ETHNIC COMPOSITION
African American, 10%; Asian/Pacific Islander, 1%; Hispanic, 1%; Native American, 1%

APPLICANTS and ADMITTEES
Seats available: 170
Average LSAT score: 153
Average GPA: 3.3

University of Mississippi School of Law is a public institution that organizes classes on a semester calendar system. The campus is situated in a small-town setting. Founded in 1854, first ABA approved in 1930, and an AALS member, University of Mississippi School of Law offers JD and JD/MBA degrees.

Faculty consists of 23 full-time members in 1997–98. 5 full-time faculty members are women. 100% of all faculty members have a JD; 38% have advanced law degrees. Of all faculty members, 4% are Native American, 12% are African American, 84% are white.

Application Information *Required:* LSAT, LSDAS, application form, application fee of $25, baccalaureate degree, college transcripts. *Recommended:* recommendations and personal statement. *Application deadline* for fall term is March 1.

Costs The 1997–98 tuition is $3581 full-time for state residents; $179 per hour part-time for state residents. Tuition is $7503 full-time for nonresidents; $375 per hour part-time for nonresidents.

Financial Aid Fellowships, loans, merit-based grants/scholarships, need-based grants/scholarships, and federal work-study loans are available. The average student debt at graduation is $35,000. To

AT a GLANCE

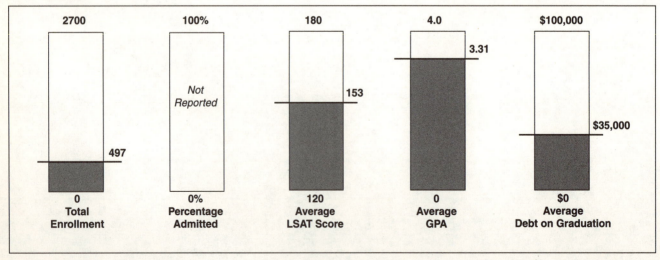

Degree Options

Degree	Total Credits Required	Length of Program
JD–Doctor of Laws	90	3 yrs, full-time only [day, summer]
JD/MBA–Juris Doctor/Master of Business Administration–Concurrent Degree Program	133	4–5 yrs, full-time only [day, summer]

apply for financial assistance, students must complete the Free Application for Federal Student Aid. Financial aid contact: Mr. Larry Ridgeway, Director, 25 Old Chemistry, University, MS 38677. Phone: 601-232-7175. Fax: 601-232-5313. E-mail: lridgeway@olemiss.edu. Completed financial aid forms should be received by March 1.

Law School Library University of Mississippi Law Library has 6 professional staff members and contains more than 143,831 volumes and 2,891 periodicals. 332 seats are available in the library. When classes are in session, the library is open 107 hours per week.

WESTLAW and LEXIS-NEXIS are available, as are the World Wide Web, online bibliographic services, and CD-ROM players. 40 computer workstations are available to students in the library.

First-Year Program Class size in the average section is 55; 100% of the first-year courses are taught by full-time faculty.

Upper-Level Program Class size in the average section is 37. Among the electives are:

Administrative Law
Advocacy

Business and Corporate Law
Entertainment Law
Environmental Law
Family Law
Intellectual Property
International/Comparative Law
Jurisprudence
Labor Law
Land Use Law/Natural Resources
Lawyering Skills
Legal History/Philosophy
Litigation
Maritime Law
Mediation
Probate Law
Securities
Tax Law

Clinical Courses Students receive degree credit for clinical courses. (Clinical practicum is not required.) Among the clinical areas offered are:

Criminal Defense
Criminal Prosecution
Juvenile Law

16% of the students participate in internship programs.

SAINT LOUIS UNIVERSITY
SCHOOL OF LAW

St. Louis, Missouri

INFORMATION CONTACT

John B. Attanasio, Dean
3700 Lindell Boulevard
St. Louis, MO 63108

Phone: 314-977-2760   Fax: 314-977-3333
Web site: http://www.slu.edu/

LAW STUDENT PROFILE [1997–98]

FULL-TIME   Enrollment: 563
Women: 47%   Men: 53%

PART-TIME   Enrollment: 261
Women: 37%   Men: 63%

RACIAL or ETHNIC COMPOSITION
African American, 9%; Asian/Pacific Islander, 4%; Hispanic, 2%; Nataive American, 0.5%; International, 1%

APPLICANTS and ADMITTEES
Number applied: 1,067
Admitted: 675
Percentage accepted: 63%
Seats available: 247
Average LSAT score: 153
Median GPA: 3.3

Saint Louis University School of Law is a private institution that organizes classes on a semester calendar system. The campus is situated in an urban setting. Founded in 1818, first ABA approved in 1924, and an AALS member, Saint Louis University School of Law offers JD, JD/MA, JD/MBA, JD/MHA, JD/MPAd, JD/MPH, and LLM degrees.

Faculty consists of 34 full-time and 37 part-time members in 1997–98. 8 full-time faculty members and 4 part-time faculty members are women. 100% of all faculty members have a JD; 30% have advanced law degrees. Of all faculty members, 6.5% are African American, 87% are white, 6.5% are international.

Application Information *Required:* LSAT, LSDAS, application form, application fee of $40, baccalaureate degree, 2 letters of recommendation. *Recommended:* personal statement, college transcripts, resume. *Application deadline* for fall term is March 1.

Costs The 1997–98 tuition is $19,170 full-time; $14,360 part-time.

Financial Aid In 1997–98, 81% of all students received some form of financial aid. Fellowships, loans, merit-based grants/scholarships, and federal work-study loans are also available. To apply for financial assistance, students must complete the Free

AT a GLANCE

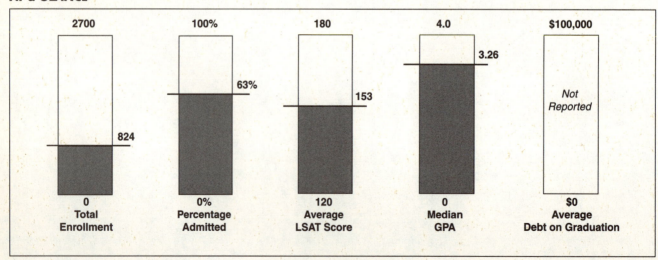

Degree Options

Degree	Total Credits Required	Length of Program
JD–Doctor of Laws	88	3–5 yrs, full-time or part-time [day, evening]
JD/MA–Juris Doctor/Master of Arts–Urban Affairs Joint Degree	103	3.5–4 yrs, full-time only [day, evening]
JD/MBA–Juris Doctor/Master of Business Administration–Joint Degree		4 yrs, full-time or part-time [day, evening]
JD/MHA–Juris Doctor/Master of Health Administration–Joint Degree		4 yrs, full-time or part-time [day, evening]
JD/MPAd–Juris Doctor/Master of Public Administration–Joint Degree	103	3.5–4 yrs, full-time only [day, evening]
JD/MPH–Juris Doctor/Master of Public Health–Joint Degree		4 yrs, full-time only [day, evening]
LLM–Master of Laws–Health Law	24	1–2 yrs, full-time or part-time [day, evening]
LLM–Master of Laws–Foreign Lawyers	24	1–2 yrs, full-time or part-time [day]

Application for Federal Student Aid and scholarship specific applications. Financial aid contact: Michael J. Kolnik, Assistant Director, Admissions, 3700 Lindell Boulevard, St. Louis, MO 63108. Phone: 314-977-2800. Fax: 314-977-3333. Completed financial aid forms should be received by April 1.

Law School Library St. Louis University Law School Library has 9 professional staff members and contains more than 530,000 volumes and 6,253 periodicals. 404 seats are available in the library. When classes are in session, the library is open 104 hours per week.

WESTLAW and LEXIS-NEXIS are available, as are the World Wide Web, online bibliographic services, and CD-ROM players. 70 computer workstations are available to students in the library. Special law collections include Constitutional Law, Smurfit Irish Law Center, Polish Law, Missouri and Illinois Law, Law Journals, Health Law, Employment Law, Leonor K. Sullivan papers.

First-Year Program Class size in the average section is 85; 100% of the first-year courses are taught by full-time faculty.

Upper-Level Program Class size in the average section is 40. Among the electives are:

Administrative Law
Advocacy
Business and Corporate Law
Commercial Law
Consumer Law
Criminal Law
Education Law
Environmental Law
Family Law
Government/Regulation
★ **Health Care/Human Services**
Intellectual Property
★ **International/Comparative Law**
Jurisprudence
★ **Labor Law**
Land Use Law/Natural Resources
Lawyering Skills
Legal History/Philosophy
Litigation
Maritime Law
Media Law
Mediation
Probate Law
Public Interest
Securities
Tax Law
(★ *indicates an area of special strength*)

Clinical Courses Students receive degree credit for clinical courses. (Clinical practicum is not required.) Among the clinical areas offered are:

Civil Litigation
Civil Rights
Corporate Law
Criminal Defense
Elderly Advocacy
Health
Housing Law
Juvenile Law
Mediation
Public Interest

15% of the students participate in internship programs.

UNIVERSITY OF MISSOURI–COLUMBIA
SCHOOL OF LAW

Columbia, Missouri

INFORMATION CONTACT
Timothy J. Heinsz, Dean
Hulston Hall
Columbia, MO 65211

Phone: 573-882-3246   Fax: 573-882-4984
E-mail: gregory@law.missouri.edu
Web site: http://www.missouri.edu/

LAW STUDENT PROFILE [1997–98]

FULL-TIME   Enrollment: 538
Women: 38%   Men: 62%

RACIAL or ETHNIC COMPOSITION
African American, 4%; Asian/Pacific Islander, 2%; Hispanic, 2%; Native American, 1%

APPLICANTS and ADMITTEES
Number applied: 727
Admitted: 413
Percentage accepted: 57%
Seats available: 180
Average LSAT score: 155
Average GPA: 3.3

University of Missouri–Columbia School of Law is a public institution that organizes classes on a semester calendar system. The campus is situated in a small-town setting. Founded in 1872, first ABA approved in 1923, and an AALS member, University of Missouri–Columbia School of Law offers JD, JD/MBA, and JD/MPAd degrees.

Faculty consists of 33 full-time and 7 part-time members in 1997–98. 100% of all faculty members have a JD degree. Of all faculty members, 8% are African American, 92% are white.

Application Information *Required:* LSAT, LSDAS, application form, application fee of $40, baccalaureate degree, college transcripts. *Application deadline* for fall term is August 24.

Financial Aid In 1997–98, 89% of all students received some form of financial aid. Fellowships, graduate assistantships, loans, merit-based grants/scholarships, need-based grants/scholarships, and federal work-study loans are also available. The average student debt at graduation is $39,000. To apply for financial assistance, students must complete the Free Application for Federal Student Aid and scholarship specific applications. Financial aid contact: Russell Thye, Financial Aid Officer, 103 Hulston Hall, Columbia, MO 65211. Phone:

AT a GLANCE

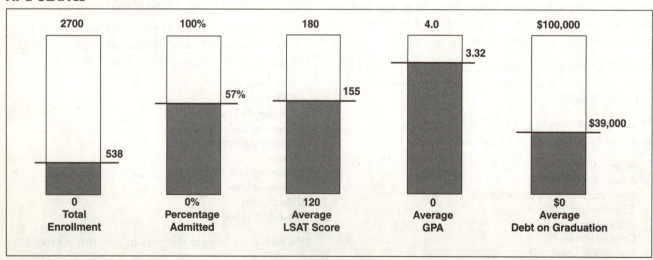

Degree Options

Degree	Total Credits Required	Length of Program
JD–Doctor of Law	89	3 yrs, full-time only [day, summer]
JD/MBA–Juris Doctor/Master of Business Administration–Dual Degree	119	4 yrs, full-time only [day, summer]
JD/MPAd–Juris Doctor/Master of Public Administration–Dual Degree	113	4 yrs, full-time only [day, summer]

573-882-1383. Fax: 573-882-4984. E-mail: thye@law.missouri.edu.

Law School Library University of Missouri-Columbia School of Law Library has 7 professional staff members and contains more than 311,976 volumes. 376 seats are available in the library. When classes are in session, the library is open 89 hours per week.

WESTLAW and LEXIS-NEXIS are available, as are the World Wide Web, online bibliographic services, and CD-ROM players. 31 computer workstations are available to students in the library. Special law collections include John O. Lawson Library of Criminal Law and Criminology.

First-Year Program Class size in the average section is 65.

Upper-Level Program Among the electives are:

Administrative Law
Advocacy
Business and Corporate Law
★ Criminal Prosecution
★ Dispute Resolution
★ Domestic Violence
Education Law
Environmental Law

Family Law
Government/Regulation
Health Care/Human Services
Intellectual Property
International/Comparative Law
Jurisprudence
Labor Law
Land Use Law/Natural Resources
Lawyering Skills
Legal History/Philosophy
Litigation
Media Law
★ Mediation
Probate Law
Securities
Tax Law
(★ indicates an area of special strength)

Clinical Courses Students receive degree credit for clinical courses. (Clinical practicum is not required.) Among the clinical areas offered are:

Criminal Prosecution
Domestic Violence
Mediation

20% of the students participate in internship programs. International exchange programs permit students to visit United Kingdom.

UNIVERSITY OF MISSOURI–KANSAS CITY
SCHOOL OF LAW

Kansas City, Missouri

INFORMATION CONTACT
Dr. Burnele Powell, Dean
5100 Rockhill Road
Kansa City, MO 64110

Phone: 816-235-1672   Fax: 816-235-5276
Web site: http://www.law.umkc.edu/

LAW STUDENT PROFILE [1997–98]

FULL-TIME   Enrollment: 487
Women: 45%   Men: 55%

PART-TIME   Enrollment: 44
Women: 45%   Men: 55%

RACIAL or ETHNIC COMPOSITION
African American, 4%; Asian/Pacific Islander, 2%; Hispanic, 3%; Native American, 2%; International, 0%

APPLICANTS and ADMITTEES
Number applied: 766
Admitted: 491
Percentage accepted: 64%
Seats available: 160
Average LSAT score: 154
Average GPA: 3.2

University of Missouri–Kansas City School of Law is a public institution that organizes classes on a semester calendar system. The campus is situated in an urban setting. Founded in 1895, first ABA approved in 1936, and an AALS member, University of Missouri–Kansas City School of Law offers JD, JD/LLM, JD/MBA, and LLM degrees.

Faculty consists of 26 full-time and 35 part-time members in 1997–98. 8 full-time faculty members and 5 part-time faculty members are women. 100% of all faculty members have a JD; 34% have advanced law degrees. Of all faculty members, 6% are African American, 94% are white.

Application Information *Required:* LSAT, LSDAS, application form, application fee of $25, baccalaureate degree, 2 letters of recommendation, personal statement, college transcripts. *Application deadline* for fall term is April 1.

Costs The 1997–98 tuition is $8274 for state residents. Tuition is $16,548 for nonresidents. Fees: $326.

Financial Aid In 1997–98, 74% of all students received some form of financial aid. Graduate assistantships, loans, merit-based grants/scholarships, need-based grants/scholarships, and federal work-study loans are also available. To apply for financial

AT a GLANCE

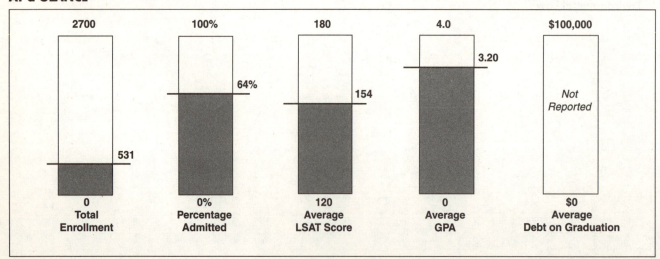

	Total Enrollment	Percentage Admitted	Average LSAT Score	Average GPA	Average Debt on Graduation
Top	2700	100%	180	4.0	$100,000
Value	531	64%	154	3.20	Not Reported
Bottom	0	0%	120	0	$0

Degree Options

Degree	Total Credits Required	Length of Program
JD–Doctor of Laws	91	3 yrs, full-time or part-time [day]
JD/LLM–Juris Doctor/Master of Laws–Taxation Combined-Cegree Program	105	3.5 yrs, full-time or part-time [day, evening]
JD/MBA–Juris Doctor/Master of Business Administration–Dual-degree Program	109	3–4 yrs, full-time or part-time [day, evening]
LLM–Master of Laws–General and Taxation	24	1 yr, full-time or part-time [day, evening]

assistance, students must complete the Free Application for Federal Student Aid and scholarship specific applications. Financial aid contact: Jean Klosterman, Director of Admissions, 5100 Rockhill Road, Kansas City, MO 64110. Phone: 816-235-1644. Fax: 816-235-5276. E-mail: klosterj@smtpgate.umkc.edu.

Law School Library Leon E. Bloch Law Library has 5 professional staff members and contains more than 263,989 volumes and 3,847 periodicals. 310 seats are available in the library. When classes are in session, the library is open 92 hours per week.

WESTLAW and LEXIS-NEXIS are available, as are the World Wide Web, online bibliographic services, and CD-ROM players. 45 computer workstations are available to students in the library.

First-Year Program Class size in the average section is 56; 100% of the first-year courses are taught by full-time faculty.

Upper-Level Program Among the electives are:

Administrative Law
Advocacy
Business and Corporate Law
Consumer Law
Education Law
Entertainment Law
Environmental Law
Family Law
Government/Regulation
Health Care/Human Services
Indian/Tribal Law
Intellectual Property
International/Comparative Law
Jurisprudence
Labor Law
Land Use Law/Natural Resources
Lawyering Skills
Legal History/Philosophy
Litigation
Mediation
Probate Law
Public Interest
Securities
Tax Law

Clinical Courses Students receive degree credit for clinical courses. (Clinical practicum is not required.) The clinical area offered includes:

Tax Law

Internships are available.

WASHINGTON UNIVERSITY IN ST. LOUIS
SCHOOL OF LAW

St. Louis, Missouri

INFORMATION CONTACT

Dorsey D. Ellis Jr., Dean
1 Brookings Drive
Campus Box 1120
St. Louis, MO 63130

Phone: 314-935-6400   Fax: 314-935-6959
E-mail: admiss@wulaw.wustl.edu
Web site: http://www.ls.wustl.edu/

LAW STUDENT PROFILE [1997–98]

FULL-TIME   Enrollment: 647
Women: 39%   Men: 61%

PART-TIME   Enrollment: 18
Women: 28%   Men: 72%

RACIAL or ETHNIC COMPOSITION

African American, 9%; Asian/Pacific Islander, 7%; Hispanic, 1%; Native American, 1%; International, 1%

APPLICANTS and ADMITTEES

Number applied: 1,357
Admitted: 758
Percentage accepted: 56%
Seats available: 197
Average LSAT score: 160
Average GPA: 3.4

Washington University in St. Louis School of Law is a private institution that organizes classes on a semester calendar system. The campus is situated in a suburban setting. First ABA approved in 1923, and an AALS member, Washington University in St. Louis School of Law offers JD, JD/MA, JD/MBA, JD/MHA, JD/MS, JD/MSW, JSD, and LLM degrees.

Faculty consists of 44 full-time and 68 part-time members in 1997–98. 16 full-time faculty members and 15 part-time faculty members are women. 100% of all faculty members have a JD; 15% have advanced law degrees.

Application Information *Required:* LSAT, LSDAS, application form, application fee of $50, baccalaureate degree, personal statement, college transcripts. *Recommended:* 2 letters of recommendation and resume. *Application deadline* for fall term is March 1.

Costs The 1997–98 tuition is $23,080.

Financial Aid Fellowships, loans, merit-based grants/scholarships, and federal work-study loans are available. To apply for financial assistance, students must complete the Free Application for Federal Student Aid and institutional forms. Financial aid contact: Jo Ann Eckrich, Director of Financial Aid, One Brookings Drive, Campus Box 1120, St. Louis,

AT a GLANCE

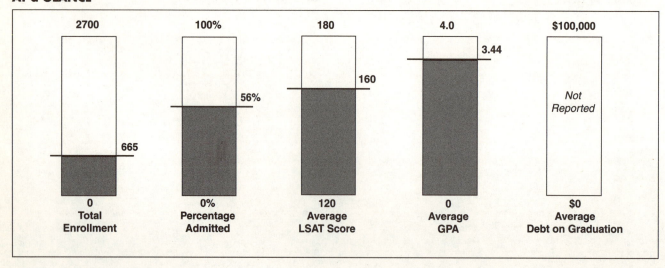

Degree Options

Degree	Total Credits Required	Length of Program
JD–Doctor of Laws	85	3 yrs, full-time only [day]
JD/MA–Juris Doctor/Master of Arts–East Asian Studies		
JD/MA–Juris Doctor/Master of Arts–Economics		
JD/MA–Juris Doctor/Master of Arts–Political Science		
JD/MA–Juris Doctor/Master of Arts–European Studies		
JD/MBA–Juris Doctor/Master of Business Administration–Joint-degree Program		
JD/MHA–Juris Doctor/Master of Health Administration–Health Administration		
JD/MS–Juris Doctor/Master of Science–Engineering and Policy		
JD/MSW–Juris Doctor/Master of Social Work–Social Work		
JSD–Doctor of Juridical Science–Graduate Research Degree		
LLM–Master of Laws–Taxation	24	4 yrs, full-time or part-time [day]
LLM–Master of Laws–International Students		

MO 63130. Phone: 314-935-4605. Fax: 314-935-6959. E-mail: eckrich@wulaw.wustl.edu. Completed financial aid forms should be received by March 1.

Law School Library Washington University Law Library has 7 professional staff members and contains more than 563,291 volumes and 6,488 periodicals. 517 seats are available in the library. When classes are in session, the library is open 120 hours per week.

WESTLAW and LEXIS-NEXIS are available, as are the World Wide Web, online bibliographic services, and CD-ROM players. 38 computer workstations are available to students in the library. Special law collections include U.S. Depository Program, Rare Book Collection, Bryce Collection.

First-Year Program Class size in the average section is 60; 100% of the first-year courses are taught by full-time faculty.

Upper-Level Program Class size in the average section is 25. Among the electives are:

Administrative Law
Advocacy
Business and Corporate Law
Consumer Law
Entertainment Law
Environmental Law
Family Law
Government/Regulation
Health Care/Human Services
Intellectual Property
International/Comparative Law
Jurisprudence
Labor Law
Land Use Law/Natural Resources
★ Lawyering Skills
Legal History/Philosophy
Litigation
Mediation
Probate Law
Public Interest
Securities
Tax Law
(★ indicates an area of special strength)

Clinical Courses Students receive degree credit for clinical courses. (Clinical practicum is not required.) Among the clinical areas offered are:

Capital Defense
Civil Litigation
Congressional Clinic
Criminal Defense
Criminal Prosecution
Employment Law
Federal Administrative Agency Clinic
Judicial Clerkship
Public Interest

Internships are available.

THE UNIVERSITY OF MONTANA–MISSOULA
SCHOOL OF LAW

Missoula, Montana

LAW STUDENT PROFILE [1997–98]

FULL-TIME　　Enrollment: 235
Women: 43%　　Men: 57%

RACIAL or ETHNIC COMPOSITION
African American, 1%; Asian/Pacific Islander, 0.4%; Hispanic, 2%; Native American, 3%; International, 1%

APPLICANTS and ADMITTEES
Number applied: 413
Admitted: 221
Percentage accepted: 54%
Seats available: 75
Average LSAT score: 156
Average GPA: 3.3

The University of Montana–Missoula School of Law is a public institution that organizes classes on a semester calendar system. The campus is situated in a small-town setting. Founded in 1911, first ABA approved in 1923, and an AALS member, The University of Montana–Missoula School of Law offers JD, JD/MPAd, and JD/MS degrees.

Faculty consists of 15 full-time and 15 part-time members in 1997–98. 6 full-time faculty members and 2 part-time faculty members are women. 100% of all faculty members have a JD; 22% have advanced law degrees. Of all faculty members, 4% are Native American, 96% are white.

Application Information *Required:* LSAT, LSDAS, application form, application fee of $60, baccalaureate degree, 3 letters of recommendation, personal statement, college transcripts. *Application deadline* for fall term is March 1.

Costs The 1997–98 tuition is $6622 for state residents. Tuition is $11,993 for nonresidents.

Financial Aid In 1997–98, 76% of all students received some form of financial aid. 22 research assistantships, 16 teaching assistantships, totaling $39,137, were awarded. Graduate assistantships,

AT a GLANCE

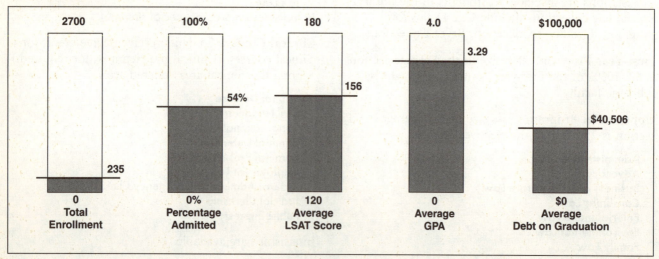

Degree Options

Degree	Total Credits Required	Length of Program
JD–Juris Doctor	90	3 yrs, full-time only [day, evening, weekend, summer]
JD/MPAd–Juris Doctor/Master of Public Administration–Joint-degree Program	120	4 yrs, full-time only [day, evening, weekend, summer]
JD/MS–Juris Doctor/Master of Science–Joint-degree Program in Environmental Studies	120	4 yrs, full-time only [day, evening, weekend, summer]

loans, merit-based grants/scholarships, need-based grants/scholarships, and federal work-study loans are also available. The average student debt at graduation is $40,506. To apply for financial assistance, students must complete the Free Application for Federal Student Aid. Financial aid contact: Elizabeth Oleson, Administrative Officer, Law School, Missoula, MT 59812. Phone: 406-243-2694. E-mail: olegou@selway.umt.edu. Completed financial aid forms should be received by March 1.

Law School Library Jameson Law Library has 3 professional staff members and contains more than 90,608 volumes and 1,710 periodicals. 212 seats are available in the library. When classes are in session, the library is open 93 hours per week.

WESTLAW and LEXIS-NEXIS are available, as are the World Wide Web, online bibliographic services, and CD-ROM players. 44 computer workstations are available to students in the library.

First-Year Program Class size in the average section is 75; 100% of the first-year courses are taught by full-time faculty.

Upper-Level Program Class size in the average section is 28. Among the electives are:

Administrative Law
Advocacy
Business and Corporate Law
Consumer Law
Education Law

★ Environmental Law
Family Law
Government/Regulation
★ Indian/Tribal Law
Intellectual Property
International/Comparative Law
Labor Law
★ Land Use Law/Natural Resources
Lawyering Skills
Legal History/Philosophy
Litigation
Mediation
Probate Law
Securities
Tax Law
(★ indicates an area of special strength)

Clinical Courses Students receive degree credit for clinical courses. 4 credit hours of clinical practicum are required. Among the clinical areas offered are:

Civil Litigation
Criminal Defense
Criminal Prosecution
Disability Law
Education
Environmental Law
Indian/Tribal Law
Judicial Clerkship
Land Rights/Natural Resource
Mediation

CREIGHTON UNIVERSITY
SCHOOL OF LAW

Omaha, Nebraska

INFORMATION CONTACT

Lawrence Raful, Dean
2500 California Plaza
Omaha, NE 68178

Phone: 402-280-2874   Fax: 402-280-2244
Web site: http://www.creighton.edu/CULAW/

LAW STUDENT PROFILE [1997–98]

FULL-TIME   Enrollment: 432
Women: 41%   Men: 59%

PART-TIME   Enrollment: 17
Women: 41%   Men: 59%

RACIAL or ETHNIC COMPOSITION
African American, 1%; Asian/Pacific Islander, 1%; Hispanic, 2%; Nataive American, 0.4%

APPLICANTS and ADMITTEES
Number applied: 692
Admitted: 514
Percentage accepted: 74%
Seats available: 150
Median LSAT score: 149
Median GPA: 3.0

Creighton University School of Law is a private institution that organizes classes on a semester calendar system. The campus is situated in an urban setting. Founded in 1904, first ABA approved in 1924, and an AALS member, Creighton University School of Law offers JD and JD/MBA degrees.

Faculty consists of 24 full-time and 34 part-time members in 1997–98. 100% of all faculty members have a JD; 16% have advanced law degrees. Of all faculty members, 1.7% are African American, 98.3% are white.

Application Information *Required:* LSAT, LSDAS, application form, application fee of $40, baccalaureate degree, 2 letters of recommendation, personal statement, college transcripts. *Application deadline* for fall term is May 1.

Costs The 1997–98 tuition is $15,684 full-time; $525 per credit hour part-time. Fees: $536 full-time; $28 per semester part-time.

Financial Aid In 1997–98, 84% of all students received some form of financial aid. Loans and merit-based grants/scholarships are also available. The average student debt at graduation is $58,000. To apply for financial assistance, students must complete the Free Application for Federal Student Aid and scholarship specific applications. Financial

AT a GLANCE

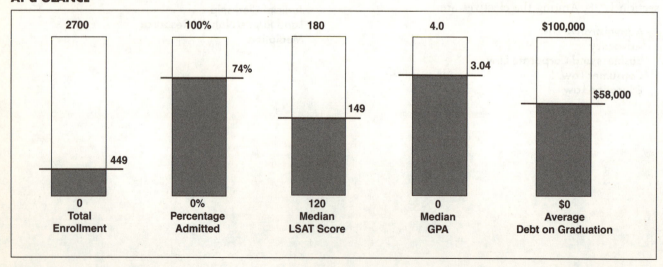

Total Enrollment	Percentage Admitted	Median LSAT Score	Median GPA	Average Debt on Graduation
2700	100%	180	4.0	$100,000
449	74%	149	3.04	$58,000
0	0%	120	0	$0

Degree Options

Degree	Total Credits Required	Length of Program
JD–Doctor of Laws	94	3–6 yrs, full-time or part-time [day, summer]
JD/MBA–Juris Doctor/Master of Business Administration–Combined-degree Program	110	3–6 yrs, full-time or part-time [day, evening, summer]

aid contact: Dean Obenauer, Associate Director of Financial Aid for Graduate / Professional Students, 2500 California Plaza, Omaha, NE 68178. Phone: 402-280-2731. Fax: 402-280-2244. E-mail: obenauer@creighton.edu. Completed financial aid forms should be received by July 1.

Law School Library Klutznick Law Library has 6 professional staff members and contains more than 238,467 volumes and 3,966 periodicals. 241 seats are available in the library. When classes are in session, the library is open 104 hours per week.

WESTLAW and LEXIS-NEXIS are available, as are the World Wide Web, online bibliographic services, and CD-ROM players. 49 computer workstations are available to students in the library.

First-Year Program Class size in the average section is 55; 100% of the first-year courses are taught by full-time faculty.

Upper-Level Program Class size in the average section is 30. Among the electives are:

Administrative Law
Advocacy
★ Business and Corporate Law
★ Civil Litigation
Consumer Law
★ Criminal Law
Education Law
Environmental Law
★ Estate Planning
Family Law
★ General Practice
Health Care/Human Services
Intellectual Property
★ International/Comparative Law

Jurisprudence
★ Labor Law
★ Land Use Law/Natural Resources
Lawyering Skills
Legal History/Philosophy
Litigation
Mediation
★ Probate Law
Public Interest
Securities
★ Tax Law
★ Trial Advocacy
(★ indicates an area of special strength)

Clinical Courses Students receive degree credit for clinical courses. (Clinical practicum is not required.) Among the clinical areas offered are:

Civil Litigation
Civil Rights
Corporate Law
Criminal Defense
Criminal Prosecution
Education
Elderly Advocacy
Environmental Law
Family Law
General Practice
Government Litigation
Health
Intellectual Property
Juvenile Law
Land Rights/Natural Resource
Mediation
Public Interest
Tax Law

35% of the students participate in internship programs.

UNIVERSITY OF NEBRASKA–LINCOLN
COLLEGE OF LAW

Lincoln, Nebraska

LAW STUDENT PROFILE [1997–98]

FULL-TIME   Enrollment: 373
Women: 43%   Men: 57%

PART-TIME   Enrollment: 4
Women: 100%

RACIAL or ETHNIC COMPOSITION
African American, 3%; Asian/Pacific Islander, 3%; Hispanic, 2%; Native American, 1%; International, 1%

APPLICANTS and ADMITTEES
Number applied: 682
Admitted: 351
Percentage accepted: 51%
Seats available: 140
Average LSAT score: 154
Average GPA: 3.5

University of Nebraska–Lincoln College of Law is a public institution that organizes classes on a semester calendar system. The campus is situated in a suburban setting. Founded in 1888, first ABA approved in 1921, and an AALS member, University of Nebraska–Lincoln College of Law offers JD/MA, JD/MBA, JD/MCRP, JD/MPA, JD/Maitrise en Driot, and JD/PhD degrees.

Faculty consists of 14 full-time and 1 part-time members in 1997–98. 1 full-time faculty member is a woman. 100% of all faculty members have a JD; 21% have advanced law degrees. Of all faculty members, 7.4% are African American, 92.6% are white.

Application Information *Required:* LSAT, LSDAS, application form, application fee of $25, baccalaureate degree, personal statement, writing sample, college transcripts. *Recommended:* 2 letters of recommendation.

Financial Aid Loans, merit-based grants/scholarships, need-based grants/scholarships, and federal work-study loans are available. The average student debt at graduation is $25,000. To apply for financial assistance, students must complete the Free Application for Federal Student Aid and need-based grant application. Financial aid contact: Glenda Pierce, Assistant Dean, PO Box 830902, Lincoln, NE 68516.

AT a GLANCE

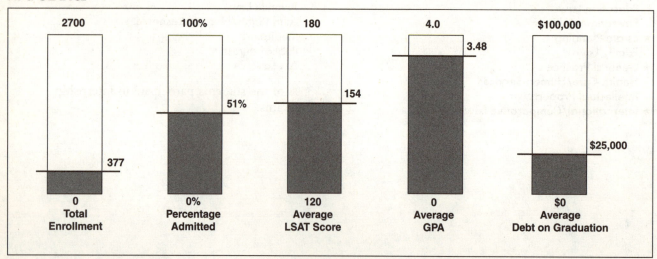

Degree Options

Degree	Total Credits Required	Length of Program
JD/MA–Juris Doctor/Master of Arts–Joint-degree Program in Law and Psychology	132	4 yrs, full-time only [day, summer]
JD/MA–Juris Doctor/Master of Arts–Joint-degree Program in Law and Economics	114	4 yrs, full-time only [day, summer]
JD/MA–Juris Doctor/Master of Arts–Joint-degree Program in Law and International Affairs	114	4 yrs, full-time only [day, summer]
JD/MA–Juris Doctor/Master of Arts–Joint-degree Program in Law and Political Science	108	4 yrs, full-time only [day, summer]
JD/MBA–Juris Doctor/Master of Business Administration–Joint-degree Program in Law and Business	120	4 yrs, full-time only [day, summer]
JD/MCRP–Juris Doctor/Master of Community and Regional Planning–Joint-degree in Law and Community/Regional Planning	117	4 yrs, full-time only [day, summer]
JD/MPA–Juris Doctor/Master of Professional Accountancy–Joint-degree Program in Law and Accounting	126	4 yrs, full-time only [day, summer]
JD/Maitrise en Driot–Juris Doctor	96	3 yrs, full-time only [day, summer]
JD/PhD–Juris Doctor/Doctor of Philosophy–Joint-degree Program in Law and Psychology	186	6 yrs, full-time only [day, summer]
JD/PhD–Juris Doctor/Doctor of Philosophy–Dual-degree Program for Law and Education	129	5 yrs, full-time only [day, summer]

Phone: 402-472-2161. Fax: 402-472-5185. E-mail: gpierce@unlinfo.unl.edu.

Law School Library Marvin and Virginia Schmid Law Library has 6 professional staff members and contains more than 341,071 volumes and 2,858 periodicals. 339 seats are available in the library. When classes are in session, the library is open 108 hours per week.

WESTLAW and LEXIS-NEXIS are available, as are the World Wide Web, online bibliographic services, and CD-ROM players. 27 computer workstations are available to students in the library. Special law collections include tax.

First-Year Program Class size in the average section is 70; 100% of the first-year courses are taught by full-time faculty.

Upper-Level Program Class size in the average section is 27. Among the electives are:

Administrative Law
★ Advocacy
Business and Corporate Law
Environmental Law
Family Law

Health Care/Human Services
Indian/Tribal Law
Intellectual Property
International/Comparative Law
Jurisprudence
Labor Law
Land Use Law/Natural Resources
Lawyering Skills
Legal History/Philosophy
★ Litigation
Media Law
Mediation
Probate Law
Public Interest
Securities
Tax Law
(★ *indicates an area of special strength*)

Clinical Courses Students receive degree credit for clinical courses. (Clinical practicum is not required.) Among the clinical areas offered are:

Civil Litigation
Criminal Prosecution
Domestic Violence

FRANKLIN PIERCE LAW CENTER

Concord, New Hampshire

INFORMATION CONTACT
James E. Duggan, Interim Dean
2 White Street
Concord, NH 03301-4197

Phone: 603-228-1541   Fax: 603-228-1074
Web site: http://www.fplc.edu/

LAW STUDENT PROFILE [1997–98]

FULL-TIME   Enrollment: 403
Women: 37%   Men: 63%

PART-TIME   Enrollment: 4
Women: 75%   Men: 25%

RACIAL or ETHNIC COMPOSITION
African American, 1%; Asian/Pacific Islander, 4%; Hispanic, 2%; Nataive American, 0.5%; International, 10%

APPLICANTS and ADMITTEES
Number applied: 1,134
Admitted: 533
Percentage accepted: 47%
Seats available: 137
Average LSAT score: 152
Average GPA: 2.9

Franklin Pierce Law Center is a private nonprofit institution that organizes classes on a semester calendar system. The campus is situated in an urban setting. Founded in 1973, first ABA approved in 1980, Franklin Pierce Law Center offers JD, LLM, and MIP degrees.

Faculty consists of 19 full-time and 56 part-time members in 1997–98. 5 full-time faculty members and 13 part-time faculty members are women. 100% of all faculty members have a JD degree. Of all faculty members, 90% are white, 10% are international.

Application Information *Required:* LSAT, LSDAS, application form, application fee of $45, baccalaureate degree, personal statement, resume. *Recommended:* 2 letters of recommendation. *Application deadline* for fall term is May 1.

Financial Aid 49 teaching assistantships, totaling $57,756, were awarded. Loans, loan repayment assistance program (LRAP), merit-based grants/scholarships, need-based grants/scholarships, and federal work-study loans are also available. The average student debt at graduation is $63,342. To apply for financial assistance, students must complete the Free Application for Federal Student Aid and institutional forms. Financial aid contact: Clinton A. Hanson Jr., Director of Financial Aid, 2 White Street, Concord, NH 03301. Phone: 603-228-

AT a GLANCE

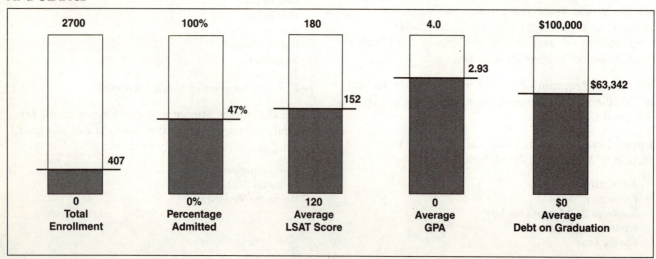

Degree Options

Degree	Total Credits Required	Length of Program
JD–Doctor of Laws	84	3 yrs, full-time or part-time [day]
LLM–Master of Laws–Intellectual Property	24	1 yr, full-time or part-time [day]
MIP–Master of Intellectual Property–Master of Intellectual Property	30	1 yr, full-time or part-time [day]

1541 Ext. 1104. Fax: 603-228-1074. E-mail: chanson@fplc.edu. Completed financial aid forms should be received by April 1.

Law School Library Franklin Pierce Law Center has 5 professional staff members and contains more than 205,960 volumes and 1,044 periodicals. 231 seats are available in the library. When classes are in session, the library is open 104 hours per week.

WESTLAW and LEXIS-NEXIS are available, as are the World Wide Web, online bibliographic services, and CD-ROM players. 49 computer workstations are available to students in the library. Special law collections include intellectual property law.

First-Year Program Class size in the average section is 135; 100% of the first-year courses are taught by full-time faculty.

Upper-Level Program Class size in the average section is 26. Among the electives are:

Administrative Law
★ Advocacy
★ Business and Corporate Law
★ Education Law
Entertainment Law
Environmental Law
★ Family Law

Government/Regulation
★ Health Care/Human Services
★ Intellectual Property
International/Comparative Law
Land Use Law/Natural Resources
Lawyering Skills
★ Litigation
Media Law
★ Mediation
Property/Real Estate
★ Public Interest
★ Tax Law
(★ indicates an area of special strength)

Clinical Courses Students receive degree credit for clinical courses. (Clinical practicum is not required.) Among the clinical areas offered are:

Children's Advocacy
Civil Litigation
Criminal Defense
Family Practice
Intellectual Property
Juvenile Law
Mediation
Nonprofit Organizations
Public Interest

20% of the students participate in internship programs.

RUTGERS, THE STATE UNIVERSITY OF NEW JERSEY, CAMDEN
SCHOOL OF LAW

Camden, New Jersey

INFORMATION CONTACT

Jay Feinman, Acting Dean
217 North Fifth Street
Camden, NJ 08102

Phone: 609-225-6191   Fax: 609-225-6537
Web site: http://www-camlaw.rutgers.edu/

LAW STUDENT PROFILE [1997–98]

FULL-TIME Enrollment: 549
Women: 48%   Men: 52%

PART-TIME Enrollment: 162
Women: 38%   Men: 62%

RACIAL or ETHNIC COMPOSITION
African American, 9%; Asian/Pacific Islander, 5%; Hispanic,
4%; Nataive American, 0.1%; International, 2%

APPLICANTS and ADMITTEES
Number applied: 1,503
Admitted: 754
Percentage accepted: 50%
Seats available: 236
Average LSAT score: 153
Average GPA: 3.2

Rutgers, The State University of New Jersey, Camden School of Law is a public institution that organizes classes on a semester calendar system. The campus is situated in an urban setting. Founded in 1926, first ABA approved in 1951, and an AALS member, Rutgers, The State University of New Jersey, Camden School of Law offers JD, JD/MBA, JD/MCRP, JD/MD, JD/MPAd, JD/MS, and JD/MSW degrees.

Faculty consists of 39 full-time and 47 part-time members in 1997–98. 12 full-time faculty members and 6 part-time faculty members are women. 99% of all faculty members have a JD; 20% have advanced law degrees. Of all faculty members, 1% are Asian/Pacific Islander, 4% are African American, 1% are Hispanic, 94% are white.

Application Information *Required:* LSAT, LSDAS, application form, application fee of $40, baccalaureate degree, recommendations, personal statement, college transcripts. *Recommended:* minimum 3.2 GPA. *Application deadline* for fall term is March 1.

Costs The 1997–98 tuition is $9682 full-time for state residents; $401 per credit part-time for state residents. Tuition is $14,206 full-time for nonresidents; $591 per credit part-time for nonresidents. Fees: $1099 full-time; $212 per semester (minimum) part-time.

Financial Aid In 1997–98, 83% of all students received some form of financial aid. Loans, merit-

AT a GLANCE

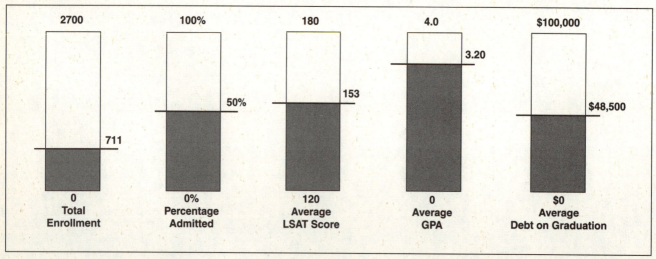

Total Enrollment	Percentage Admitted	Average LSAT Score	Average GPA	Average Debt on Graduation
2700	100%	180	4.0	$100,000
711	50%	153	3.20	$48,500
0	0%	120	0	$0

Degree Options

Degree	Total Credits Required	Length of Program
JD–Doctor of Laws	84	3–4 yrs, full-time or part-time [day, evening, summer]
JD/MBA–Juris Doctor/Master of Business Administration–Dual-degree Program, Dual-degree Program Graduate School of Management - Newark	120–121	3.5–4 yrs, full-time or part-time [day, evening, summer]
JD/MCRP–Juris Doctor/Master of Community and Regional Planning–Dual-degree Program		4 yrs
JD/MD–Juris Doctor/Doctor of Medicine–Dual-degree Program Camden		6 yrs, full-time only [day, evening, summer]
JD/MPAd–Juris Doctor/Master of Public Administration–Dual-degree Program, Dual-degree Program Health Care Management	102	3.5 yrs, full-time or part-time [day, evening, summer]
JD/MS–Juris Doctor/Master of Science–Dual-degree Program Public Policy	102	3.5 yrs, full-time only [day, evening]
JD/MSW–Juris Doctor/Master of Social Work–Dual-degree Program	120	4 yrs, full-time or part-time [day, evening, summer]

based grants/scholarships, need-based grants/scholarships, and federal work-study loans are also available. The average student debt at graduation is $48,500. To apply for financial assistance, students must complete the Free Application for Federal Student Aid. Financial aid contact: Richard Woodland, Director of Financial Aid, Office of Financial Aid, Rutgers State University of New Jersey, 401 Cooper Street, Camden, NJ 08102. Phone: 609-225-6103 or toll-free 800-466-7561. Fax: 609-225-6537. E-mail: wood@crab.rutgers.edu.

Law School Library Rutgers University School of Law Library - Camden has 7 professional staff members and contains more than 399,018 volumes and 1,390 periodicals. 402 seats are available in the library. When classes are in session, the library is open 100 hours per week.

WESTLAW and LEXIS-NEXIS are available, as are the World Wide Web, online bibliographic services, and CD-ROM players. 50 computer workstations are available to students in the library. Special law collections include Ginsburgs collection - collection of Soviet legal materials.

First-Year Program 100% of the first-year courses are taught by full-time faculty.

Upper-Level Program Class size in the average section is 43. Among the electives are:

Administrative Law

★ Advocacy
★ Business and Corporate Law
★ Commercial Law
★ Constitutional Law
★ Environmental Law
★ Family Law
★ Government/Regulation
★ Health Care/Human Services
Indian/Tribal Law
Intellectual Property
★ International/Comparative Law
Jurisprudence
Labor Law
Land Use Law/Natural Resources
★ Lawyering Skills
Legal History/Philosophy
★ Litigation
Maritime Law
Mediation
Probate Law
Public Interest
Securities
Sports Law
Tax Law
(★ indicates an area of special strength)

Clinical Courses Students receive degree credit for clinical courses. (Clinical practicum is not required.) Among the clinical areas offered are:

Civil Litigation
Education
Small Business Counseling

Internships are available.

DEAN'S STATEMENT . . .

Chartered in 1766 by George III of Great Britain as the Queen's College, today Rutgers, the State University of New Jersey, is one of the oldest and largest state higher educational systems in the nation. Building on the University's distinguished past, Rutgers School of Law at Camden is emerging as one of the finest public law schools in the nation. As the law school prepares for the celebration of its seventy-fifth anniversary in 2001, we invite you to join our dynamic institution.

Rutgers School of Law at Camden is a place where the highest standards of legal scholarship accompany the deepest commitment to the law. We will challenge you at every turn. As a member of a community steeped in this tradition of excellence, I welcome your interest in our school.

—Dean Rayman Solomon

HISTORY, CAMPUS, AND LOCATION

Rutgers School of Law at Camden is part of Rutgers, the State University of New Jersey, one of the nation's oldest and most esteemed universities. Chartered in 1766, Rutgers University is the eighth-oldest institution of higher education in the nation. The law school at Camden was founded in 1926 by Arthur E. Armitage Sr. A member of the Association of American Law Schools (AALS) and approved by the American Bar Association (ABA), the law school is known for excellence in scholarship and rigor in the training of new lawyers.

The law school offers a safe, attractive urban campus located on 25 tree-lined acres. The recently renovated main law school building houses research facilities, seminar and reading rooms, student lounges, a study area, a cafeteria, classrooms, and faculty and administration offices. Law students have access to the other facilities on campus, including the gymnasium with squash and tennis courts and a swimming pool, a fine arts building, a theater, a campus center and dining hall, the Walt Whitman International Poetry Center, and the Paul Robeson Library. The campus is part of the ongoing development of the Camden waterfront. The Blockbuster-Sony Music Entertainment Center, the New Jersey State Aquarium, and new federal and state courthouses are located adjacent to or within a few blocks of the law school.

Just minutes from the Liberty Bell and Independence Hall in Philadelphia, this urban campus is just 1 hour from the famous New Jersey shore and its miles of beaches and Atlantic City. In just under 2 hours students can venture to New York City, Baltimore, Annapolis, Bucks County, and the Pine Barrens. Washington, D.C., can be reached in just 3 hours.

SPECIAL QUALITIES OF THE SCHOOL

Emerging as one of the top public law schools in the nation, Rutgers University School of Law at Camden is known for its eminent faculty and prestigious alumni. Faculty members are ranked among the most accomplished producers of scholarly articles in eminent journals, and their scholarship has been cited by numerous courts, including the United States Supreme Court and the New Jersey Supreme Court. Faculty members also serve as consultants and reporters for the American Bar Association, the American Law Institute, and federal and state commissions and are counsel in important public interest litigation.

An overwhelming number of students choose the School because of its national reputation, geographic location, and reasonable tuition. The law school is deeply committed to the enrichment of the law school community and educational experiences created by a diverse student body. Students are drawn from 230 undergraduate institutions, twenty-seven states, and eight other countries. Approximately 20 percent of the total enrollment are students of color, and more than 46 percent are women. Although admission is highly competitive, the admissions office does consider each applicant's file individually, and special qualities may occasionally overcome lower numbers.

TECHNOLOGY ON CAMPUS

The law school is a leader in the use of computers. Four computer labs, e-mail accounts, Internet connections, and online research, including individual WESTLAW and LEXIS-NEXIS accounts, online nutshells, hornbooks, and restatements, are available to students. Students residing on campus have direct Internet access from their apartments. Professors utilize Web sites for their courses, thus creating an exciting opportunity for students to raise issues, ask questions, and exchange ideas about the substantive course materials outside the classroom.

SCHOLARSHIPS AND LOANS

Rutgers is a direct student loan university. As such, a vast majority of our students receive aid in the form of government-sponsored loans. The law school also awards numerous merit-based scholarships, including prestigious Dean's Merit Scholarships and the William G. Bischoff Scholarship without regard to financial need. These awards are the highest forms of recognizing academic achievements.

STUDENT ACTIVITIES AND OPPORTUNITIES

Law Review The *Rutgers Law Journal* is a professional publication devoted to critical discussions of current legal problems. One issue of the journal each year is devoted to a survey of state constitutional law. Invitations for staff positions are extended to a limited number of first-year students on the basis of their academic achievement in the first year of law school and a writing competition. Other students may compete for *Rutgers Law Journal* membership through subsequent open writing competitions. Approximately 60 students participate in the publication.

Moot Court All first-year students are required to take moot court. A highlight of the upper-level curriculum is the Judge James A. Hunter III Advanced Moot Court program. Most second-year students participate in this competition to represent the School in the National Moot Court Competition. Students also compete in many other national competitions, including Jessup International Moot Court, Gibbons National Criminal Procedure Moot Court, National Black Law Students Association Frederick Douglass Moot Court, National Latino Law Students Association Moot Court, and the Environmental Moot Court.

Extracurricular Activities Law students participate in a wide range of activities that enhance their academic experience. Student organizations are numerous and include the Student Bar Association and Women's Law Caucus, along with associations for every major interest group and most nationalities. Student activity offices and a student lounge are located adjacent to the main law school building. Rutgers students also participate in intramural sports programs for men and women.

Special Opportunities An outstanding externship program offers third-year students an opportunity to gain academic credit while working in federal and state judicial chambers, public agencies, and public interest organizations, including the United States Court of Appeals for the Third Circuit, U.S. District Courts, the U.S. Attorney's office, legal services and public defender offices, and the Internal Revenue Service. Other third-year students participate in the Civil Practice Clinic, a live-client clinic housed in the law school that represents elderly and disabled clients, as well as children and their families who seek free education and related services. The law school supports an active pro bono program that provides opportunities for students to represent clients in a wide range of pro bono activities, including domestic violence, mediation, bankruptcy, legal education, and income tax assistance. Law students also have the opportunity to serve in prestigious judicial clerkships. Rutgers places more than twice the national average and ranks third in the nation in placing its graduates in these highly desirable federal and state clerkships.

Opportunities for Members of Minority Groups and Women With a national reputation for academic excellence, the law school is committed to increasing diversity within the legal profession. Its African-American, Asian, Hispanic, and women graduates are practicing law throughout the United States as federal and state judges, as

corporate counsel, in prestigious large and small firms, in corporations, in government agencies, and in legal service organizations. The diverse student body is reflected in the law school's community. Women and members of minority groups may participate in numerous student organizations, such as the Women's Law Caucus, the Domestic Violence Project, the Black Law Students Association (BLSA), the Hispanic Law Student Association (ALIANZA), and the Asian/Pacific American Law Students Association (APALSA). BLSA also participates in a law-related education and mentoring pro bono project in the Camden City public schools. From the moment students arrive on campus, the law school provides academic support by assigning academic advisers to each student. A student may also be invited to participate in the Academic Support Program or to tutor other students. Special scholarships, such as the C. Clyde Ferguson Scholarship, also encourage women and minorities to excel in the study of law.

BAR PASSAGE, CAREER SERVICES, AND PLACEMENT
Bar passage rates for Rutgers-Camden graduates typically exceed state averages. For July 1997, Rutgers-Camden graduates had a first-time bar passage rate of 78.4 percent, compared to an overall pass rate of only 72.6 percent in New Jersey. The most popular states in which the bar exams were taken were New York (14 percent), New Jersey (80 percent), and Pennsylvania (60 percent).

Located at the base of the Benjamin Franklin Bridge leading to Philadelphia, Rutgers-Camden sits in the fifth-largest legal job market in the country. All major Philadelphia, New Jersey, and Delaware firms recruit from Rutgers, as do prestigious firms from New York City, California, and Washington, D.C. As a direct result of the quality of legal education at Rutgers, more than 95 percent of last year's class is working in the following fields.

Legal Field	Percentage of Graduates	Average Starting Salary
Academic	1%	n/a
Business	13%	$54,000
Government	9%	$40,400
Judicial Clerkships	38%	$31,600
Private Practice	37%	$50,200
Public Interest	2%	$45,000
Other	n/a	n/a

CORRESPONDENCE AND INFORMATION
Admissions Office
Rutgers School of Law at Camden
406 Penn Street, Third Floor
Camden, New Jersey 08102
Telephone: 800-466-7561 (toll-free)
Fax: 609-225-6537
E-mail: admissions@camlaw.rutgers.edu

RUTGERS, THE STATE UNIVERSITY OF NEW JERSEY, NEWARK
SCHOOL OF LAW

Newark, New Jersey

INFORMATION CONTACT

Eric Neisser, Acting Dean
15 Washington Street
University Heights
Newark, NJ 07102

Phone: 973-353-5551   Fax: 973-353-1248
Web site:
http://info.rutgers.edu/RUSLN/rulnindx.html

LAW STUDENT PROFILE [1997–98]

FULL-TIME   Enrollment: 511
Women: 49%   Men: 51%

PART-TIME   Enrollment: 222
Women: 39%   Men: 61%

RACIAL or ETHNIC COMPOSITION
African American, 13%; Asian/Pacific Islander, 7%; Hispanic, 10%; International, 5%

APPLICANTS and ADMITTEES
Number applied: 2,327
Admitted: 758
Percentage accepted: 33%
Seats available: 209

Rutgers, The State University of New Jersey, Newark School of Law is a public institution that organizes classes on a semester calendar system. The campus is situated in an urban setting. First ABA approved in 1941, and an AALS member, Rutgers, The State University of New Jersey, Newark School of Law offers JD, JD/MA, JD/MBA, and JD/MCRP degrees.

Faculty consists of 44 full-time and 39 part-time members in 1997–98. 14 full-time faculty members and 9 part-time faculty members are women.

Application Information *Required:* LSAT, LSDAS, application form, application fee of $50, baccalaureate degree, 1 recommendation, personal statement. *Application deadline* for fall term is March 15.

Financial Aid In 1997–98, 80% of all students received some form of financial aid. 4 fellowships, 15 research assistantships, 16 teaching assistantships were awarded. Fellowships, merit-based grants/scholarships, need-based grants/scholarships, and federal work-study loans are also available. To apply for financial assistance, students must complete the Free Application for Federal Student Aid and institutional forms. Financial aid contact: Rutgers, The State University of New Jersey, Financial Aid

AT a GLANCE

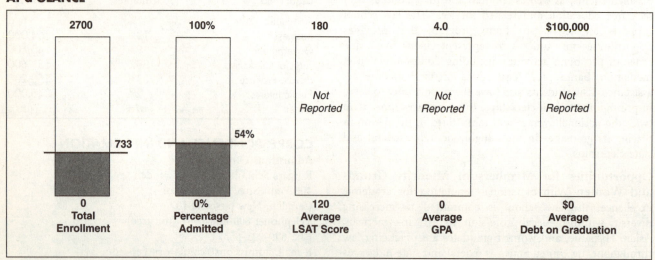

2700	100%	180	4.0	$100,000
733	54%	Not Reported	Not Reported	Not Reported
0	0%	120	0	$0
Total Enrollment	**Percentage Admitted**	**Average LSAT Score**	**Average GPA**	**Average Debt on Graduation**

Degree Options

Degree	Total Credits Required	Length of Program
JD–Juris Doctor–Joint-degree Program Political Science	84	3–4 yrs, full-time or part-time
JD/MA–Juris Doctor/Master of Arts–Joint-degree Program Criminal Science		
JD/MBA–Juris Doctor/Master of Business Administration–Joint-degree Program		
JD/MCRP–Juris Doctor/Master of Community and Regional Planning–Joint-degree Program		

Office, School of Law - Newark, University Heights, 15 Washington Street, Newark, NJ 07102-3192. Phone: 973-353-5644. Fax: 973-353-1248. Completed financial aid forms should be received by March 1.

Law School Library The Justice Henry E. Ackerson Law Library has 10 professional staff members and contains more than 412,542 volumes and 3,073 periodicals. 397 seats are available in the library. When classes are in session, the library is open 107 hours per week.

WESTLAW and LEXIS-NEXIS are available, as is the World Wide Web.

First-Year Program Class size in the average section is 80.

Upper-Level Program Among the electives are:

Administrative Law
Advertising Law
Bankruptcy
★ Business and Corporate Law
★ Civil Rights
★ Commercial Law
Conflict of Laws
★ Constitutional Law
★ Criminal Procedure
Employment Law
Entertainment Law
★ Environmental Law
Evidence
★ Family Law
★ Health Care/Human Services
Immigration
★ Intellectual Property
International/Comparative Law

★ Jurisprudence
Labor Law
Land Use Law/Natural Resources
Lawyering Skills
Legal History/Philosophy
Legislation
Litigation
Media Law
★ Mediation
Probate Law
Property/Real Estate
Public Interest
Race and Law
★ Securities
Tax Law
Trusts and Estates
(★ indicates an area of special strength)

Clinical Courses Among the clinical areas offered are:

Animal Rights Law
Civil Litigation
Civil Rights
Education
Elderly Advocacy
Environmental Law
Family Practice
General Practice
Immigration
Public Interest
Special Education Law
Tax Law
Women's Rights

Internships are available.

SETON HALL UNIVERSITY
SCHOOL OF LAW

South Orange, New Jersey

LAW STUDENT PROFILE [1997–98]

FULL-TIME   Enrollment: 917
Women: 44%   Men: 56%

PART-TIME   Enrollment: 335
Women: 42%   Men: 58%

RACIAL or ETHNIC COMPOSITION
African American, 5%; Asian/Pacific Islander, 5%; Hispanic, 5%; Nataive American, 0.4%

APPLICANTS and ADMITTEES
Number applied: 2,402
Admitted: 1,134
Percentage accepted: 47%
Seats available: 385
Median LSAT score: 155
Average GPA: 3.2

Seton Hall University School of Law is a private institution that organizes classes on a semester calendar system. The campus is situated in an urban setting. Founded in 1951, first ABA approved in 1951, and an AALS member, Seton Hall University School of Law offers JD, JD/MBA, and LLM degrees.

Faculty consists of 44 full-time and 88 part-time members in 1997–98. 15 full-time faculty members and 18 part-time faculty members are women.

Application Information *Required:* LSAT, LSDAS, application form, application fee of $50, baccalaureate degree, 2 letters of recommendation, personal statement. *Application deadline* for fall term is April 1.

Costs The 1997–98 tuition is $20,940 full-time; $698 per credit part-time. Fees: $190 full-time; $90 part-time.

Financial Aid In 1997–98, 84% of all students received some form of financial aid. 70 research assistantships were awarded. Graduate assistantships, merit-based grants/scholarships, and need-based grants/scholarships are also available. To apply for financial assistance, students must complete the Free Application for Federal Student Aid, institutional forms, and Seton Hall Law School Financial Aid application, federal income tax return of student

AT a GLANCE

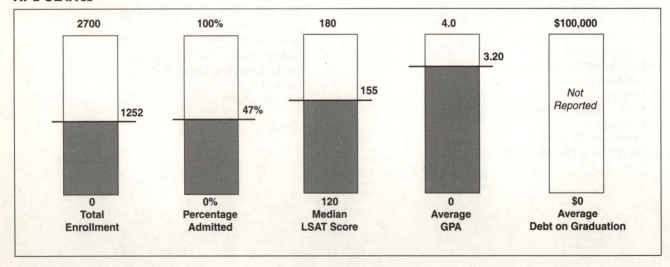

Degree Options

Degree	Total Credits Required	Length of Program
JD–Juris Doctor	85	3–4 yrs, full-time or part-time [day, evening]
JD/MBA–Juris Doctor/Master of Business Administration–Dual-degree Program	110	4 yrs, full-time only
LLM–Master of Laws–Health Law	24	2 yrs

and parents for year prior to application, Financial Aid transcript. Financial aid contact: Seton Hall University School of Law, Office of Financial Resource Management, 1 Newark Center, Newark, NJ 07102-5210. or toll-free 888-415-7271. Completed financial aid forms should be received by April 15.

Law School Library Peter W. Rodino, Jr. Law Library has 10 professional staff members and contains more than 374,067 volumes and 3,320 periodicals. 600 seats are available in the library. When classes are in session, the library is open 98 hours per week.

WESTLAW and LEXIS-NEXIS are available. Special law collections include Government (Federal and State) Documents, the Rodino Collection, Rare Book collection.

First-Year Program Class size in the average section is 80.

Upper-Level Program Among the electives are:

Accounting
Administrative Law
Advocacy
Bankruptcy
Business and Corporate Law
Commercial Law
Consumer Law
Criminal Procedure
Entertainment Law
Environmental Law
Family Law
Government/Regulation
Health Care/Human Services
Insurance
Intellectual Property
International/Comparative Law
Jurisprudence
Labor Law
Land Use Law/Natural Resources
Lawyering Skills
Legal History/Philosophy
Litigation
Media Law
Mediation
Probate Law
Public Interest
Securities
Tax Law

Clinical Courses Students receive degree credit for clinical courses. (Clinical practicum is not required.) Among the clinical areas offered are:

Administrative Law
Bankruptcy
Civil Litigation
Criminal Defense
Family Practice
General Practice
Health
Immigration
Juvenile Law

Internships are available. International exchange programs permit students to visit Egypt and Italy.

DEAN'S STATEMENT . . .

In the institutional life of every law school there is a defining moment. For Seton Hall, it has been our coming of age as a law school of the highest quality. In national rankings, our status and standing in legal education achieved the highest marks, and we have been judged by our peers to be among the best. Those welcome and worthy judgments mirror the growing pride and regard that our own community has for the law school.

After all, if we have earned the respect of those who know the law school the best, and we have, then I am certain that our highly favorable ratings by outside observers are wholly justified. What distinguishes our law school, in my opinion, is the rigor we demand in our courses of study combined with the respect we have for our students. We educate our students to be ethical in pursuing the law, faithful to legal principles, steeped in knowledge of the law, dedicated to client interests, and committed to the public good. We provide this rigorous education in an environment that is sensitive, caring, respectful, and nurturing.

When our students graduate, at last count, 94.7 percent found employment in the legal field within six months after graduation, well above the national average of 89.2 percent. Historically, Seton Hall ranked second nationally in placing 43 percent of its graduates in judicial clerkships.

Our School of Law not only benefits from state-of-the-art facilities at our Newark campus, including sophisticated computer systems, but also benefits from the services and resources of Seton Hall University, a major academic center of which we are a constituent member. In Newark, Seton Hall is situated in the heart of the city's most impressive renaissance area, with a nearby performing arts center, concert stages, museums, educational institutions, restaurants, and shopping, and a neighboring legal, financial, and government community. From where we stand, we have a commanding view of our future.

—*Dean Ronald J. Riccio*

HISTORY, CAMPUS, AND LOCATION

Founded in 1951, Seton Hall is the only private law school in the state of New Jersey. The law school is housed in a state-of-the-art facility in downtown Newark. Growing regional and national reputation is reflected in the *Princeton Review*, which ranked the law school first in the nation for placement in judicial clerkships, and in a 1994 *National Jurist* poll of 18,000 law students, which ranked the School second in the nation for overall student satisfaction.

The law school's location benefits the career interests of students. One Newark Center, where the law school is located, and the Newark Legal Center across the street are home to many of the hundreds of large and small firms in Newark. These same law firms serve as major sources of employment after graduation. Several blocks away are a variety of state and federal government offices, including the new federal courthouse and Essex County courthouse, all invaluable sources of part-time clerkships and exciting internships for law students and for full-time posts clerking for judges or working with prosecutors and public defenders.

SPECIAL QUALITIES OF THE SCHOOL

The University's high standards are evidenced in numerous ways, including its outstanding faculty of master teachers who are actively engaged in the professional and educational development of students and of celebrated scholars whose publications are highly regarded in legal circles.

The law school building has a design that engenders a comfortable and challenging interaction between students and faculty.

TECHNOLOGY ON CAMPUS

An online computer system in the library allows students to search and access information quickly and easily, both from library terminals and from home computers. In the computer laboratory, more than fifty terminals are designated for student use.

The campus computer system supplies bibliographies, keyword search, and even some full text online through access to LEXIS and WESTLAW national database services and the latest audiovisual equipment.

The Rodino Library computer network is connected to a local area network, linked to the new Walsh Library on the University's main campus in South Orange, and, ultimately, to other law school and university libraries nationwide through the Internet.

SCHOLARSHIPS AND LOANS

Seton Hall University School of Law offers programs of financial assistance to students based on financial need and merit. In the 1997–98 academic year, the School of Law awarded more than $21 million in financial aid; 85 percent of Seton Hall law students receive financial assistance. Need-based scholarships are available to eligible day division and evening division students. In determining an applicant's need, the student's income and assets are taken into consideration. Entering students are encouraged to apply early because funds are limited and awarded on a rolling basis.

STUDENT ACTIVITIES AND OPPORTUNITIES

Law Review Seton Hall law students serve as editors and managers of four distinctive law journals. Academic credit is given to the student editors and staff of these journals.

Seton Hall Law Review is a quarterly publication that features articles written by judges, scholars, public officials, and lawyers on major legal issues as well as student commentary and information on recent legal developments. The *Law Review* is among the most cited in the federal judiciary. *Constitutional Law Journal* is a semiannual publication that includes articles on important constitutional issues at the federal and state levels written by judges, lawyers, and professors. *Sports Law Journal* is the only law school journal in the country devoted to the legal aspects of amateur and professional sports. *Seton Hall Legislative Journal* examines legislation and the legislative process with articles by lawyers, judges, law professors, legislators, legislative analysts, and students.

Moot Court Seton Hall's most recent victory was in the prestigious 235-team National Moot Court Competition, where Seton Hall finished third in the country and won an award for the second-best brief in the nation. Its climb to national prominence is reflected in Seton Hall's 1995–96 moot court record. The law school had a second-place finish and best brief award at a national criminal procedure competition. It also recorded a first-place finish in the northeast regional competition of the Frederick Douglas Moot Court Competition and a sweep of the Federal Bar Association's inaugural Thurgood Marshall Moot Court Competition. Overall, Seton Hall received six best brief awards and five best oralist awards.

Extracurricular Activities Student organizations flourish at Seton Hall University School of Law. Many are related to specific areas of practice; others related to student governance and student representation on faculty standing committees. International law fraternities have chapters here. Several organizations, including the St. Thomas More Society, are committed to community service. Many other groups represent a wide range of professional interests, religious commitments, and cultural identities found among an enormously diverse student population.

Special Opportunities Seton Hall students earn academic credit by working with client problems in the capacity of practicing attorneys. The representation in the clinics includes interviewing and counseling clients, drafting and filing pleadings, preparing pretrial motions, conducting discovery, participating in trial in appropriate state and federal courts, engaging in negotiation and/or dispute resolution, and preparing appeals. Clinical programs are open to upper-division students and usually require a commitment of 12 hours a week over one or two semesters. Operating under the supervision of staff attorneys, the following are the clinical experiences available to Seton Hall students: consumer law clinic, disability law clinic, housing law clinic, immigration law clinic, inmate advocacy clinic, and juvenile justice clinic.

Opportunities for Members of Minority Groups and Women Applicants for admission to the law school who are recognized as educationally disadvantaged may be invited to the Monsignor Thomas Fahy Legal Education Opportunities (LEO) Institute. Established in 1977, LEO is named for Monsignor Thomas Fahy, the late president of Seton Hall University, who worked to increase opportunities for advanced education for all members of the community. LEO candidates participate in a full-time eight-week summer program during which the participants complete a regular first-year core course and a program in legal analysis and writing. The work completed by LEO students constitutes one of the criteria considered in making a final evaluation of their application for admission to the law school.

Special Certificate Programs Seton Hall Law School and the University's W. Paul Stillman School of Business jointly sponsor an M.B.A./J.D. program that grants students a law degree and a graduate degree in business.

The Seton Hall Law School Health Law and Policy Program (HeLPP) offers an expansive and rigorous graduate education experience (M.S.J. and LL.M. program in health law) to those preparing to confront the health-care challenges of the next century. HeLPP's faculty members offer an expertise in health law unmatched in the tristate region. They have substantial practice experience representing institutional providers and third-party payers, health-care consumers, and the government. *U.S. News & World Report* has ranked HeLPP among the top ten health law programs in the nation.

BAR PASSAGE, CAREER SERVICES, AND PLACEMENT

Year after year, the vast majority of graduating students have exciting employment opportunities awaiting them. Within six months after graduation, 94.7 percent of Seton Hall's most recent graduates are employed, higher than the 89.2 percent national average.

Legal Field	Percentage of Graduates	Average Starting Salary
Academic	2.0%	n/a
Business	23.4%	$53,654
Government	7.2%	$34,272
Judicial Clerkships	33.0%	$31,979
Private Practice	35.8%	$50,745
Public Interest	2.0%	n/a
Other	2.0%	n/a

CORRESPONDENCE AND INFORMATION

School of Law
Seton Hall University
One Newark Center
Newark, New Jersey 07102
Telephone: 973-642-8747
Fax: 973-642-8876
E-mail: admitme@shu.edu
World Wide Web: http://www.shu.edu/law

UNIVERSITY OF NEW MEXICO
SCHOOL OF LAW

Albuquerque, New Mexico

INFORMATION CONTACT
Robert J. Desiderio, Dean
1117 Stanford NE
Albuquerque, NM 87131-1431

Phone: 505-277-4700   Fax: 505-277-0068
E-mail: mitchell@libra.unm.edu
Web site:
http://www.unm.edu/~unmlaw/lawsch.html

LAW STUDENT PROFILE [1997–98]

FULL-TIME   Enrollment: 341
Women: 51%   Men: 49%

RACIAL or ETHNIC COMPOSITION
African American, 3%; Asian/Pacific Islander, 2%; Hispanic, 27%; Native American, 7%

APPLICANTS and ADMITTEES
Number applied: 732
Admitted: 251
Percentage accepted: 34%
Seats available: 115

University of New Mexico School of Law is a public institution that organizes classes on a semester calendar system. The campus is situated in an urban setting. Founded in 1947, first ABA approved in 1948, and an AALS member, University of New Mexico School of Law offers JD, JD/MA, JD/MAPA, and JD/MBA degrees.

Faculty consists of 34 full-time and 27 part-time members in 1997–98. 15 full-time faculty members and 13 part-time faculty members are women.

Application Information *Required:* LSAT, LSDAS, application form, application fee of $40, baccalaureate degree, 1 recommendation, personal statement. *Application deadline* for fall term is February 15.

Costs The 1997–98 tuition is $3952 for state residents. Tuition is $13,306 for nonresidents. Fees: $32.

Financial Aid Loans, need-based grants/scholarships, and federal work-study loans are available. To apply for financial assistance, students must complete the Free Application for Federal Student Aid. Financial aid contact: University of New Mexico, Office of Student Financial Aid, Albuquerque, NM 87131-1431. Phone: 505-277-4169. Fax: 505-277-0068. Completed financial aid forms should be received by March 1.

AT a GLANCE

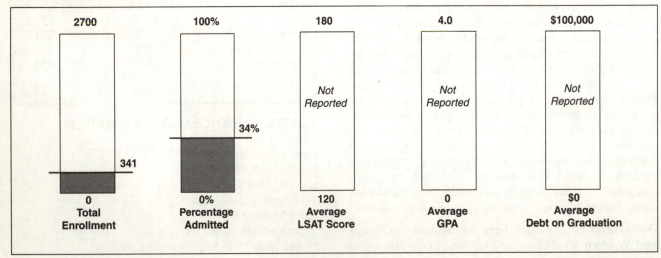

Degree Options

Degree	Total Credits Required	Length of Program
JD–Juris Doctor	86	3–4.5 yrs, full-time only [day]
JD/MA–Juris Doctor/Master of Arts–Latin American Studies	107	4 yrs
JD/MAPA–Juris Doctor/Master of Arts in Public Administration–Master of Arts in Public Administration		
JD/MBA–Juris Doctor/Master of Business Administration		

Law School Library UNM Law Library has 4 professional staff members and contains more than 346,000 volumes and 3,168 periodicals. 100 seats are available in the library. When classes are in session, the library is open 105 hours per week.

WESTLAW and LEXIS-NEXIS are available, as is the World Wide Web. Special law collections include New Mexico Appellate Briefs and Records, American Indian Law, Land Grants, Natural Resources Law, Mexican and Latin American Law.

First-Year Program Class size in the average section is 54.

Upper-Level Program Among the electives are:

★ Environmental Law
★ Health Care/Human Services
★ Indian/Tribal Law
(★ indicates an area of special strength)

Clinical Courses Students receive degree credit for clinical courses. 6 credit hours of clinical practicum are required. Among the clinical areas offered are:

Client Representation
Community Advocacy
Criminal Prosecution
District Attorney Clinic
General Practice
Indian/Tribal Law

Internships are available. International exchange programs permit students to visit Australia; Canada; and Mexico.

ALBANY LAW SCHOOL OF UNION UNIVERSITY

Albany, New York

INFORMATION CONTACT

Thomas H. Sponsler, Dean
80 New Scotland Avenue
Albany, NY 12208-3494

Phone: 518-445-2321   Fax: 518-445-2315
E-mail: admissions@mail.als.edu
Web site: http://www.als.edu/

LAW STUDENT PROFILE [1997–98]

FULL-TIME   Enrollment: 690
Women: 52%   Men: 48%

PART-TIME   Enrollment: 42
Women: 67%   Men: 33%

RACIAL or ETHNIC COMPOSITION

African American, 6%; Asian/Pacific Islander, 5%; Hispanic, 4%; Native American, 1%; International, 1%

APPLICANTS and ADMITTEES

Number applied: 1,200
Admitted: 849
Percentage accepted: 71%
Seats available: 240
Average LSAT score: 150
Average GPA: 3.1

Albany Law School of Union University is a private nonprofit institution that organizes classes on a semester calendar system. The campus is situated in an urban setting. Founded in 1851, first ABA approved in 1930, and an AALS member, Albany Law School of Union University offers JD, JD/MBA, and JD/MPAd degrees.

Faculty consists of 45 full-time and 39 part-time members in 1997–98. 21 full-time faculty members and 9 part-time faculty members are women. 100% of all faculty members have a JD; 27% have advanced law degrees. Of all faculty members, 5% are Asian/Pacific Islander, 8% are African American, 87% are white.

Application Information *Required:* LSAT, LSDAS, application form, application fee of $50, 2 letters of recommendation. *Recommended:* baccalaureate degree, personal statement, resume. *Application deadline* for fall term is March 15.

Financial Aid 33 research assistantships, totaling $50,000, were awarded. 321 other awards were given. Fellowships, loans, merit-based grants/scholarships, need-based grants/scholarships, and federal work-study loans are also available. The average student debt at graduation is $64,500. To apply for financial assistance, students must

AT a GLANCE

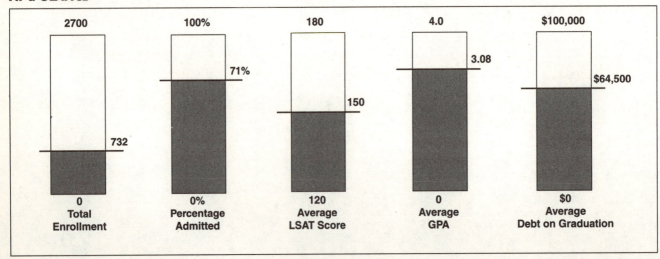

Degree Options

Degree	Total Credits Required	Length of Program
JD–Doctor of Laws	87	3–4.5 yrs, full-time or part-time [day, summer]
JD/MBA–Juris Doctor/Master of Business Administration–Joint Degree		3.5–4.5 yrs, full-time or part-time [day, summer]
JD/MPAd–Juris Doctor/Master of Public Administration–Joint Degree		3.5–4.5 yrs, full-time or part-time [day, summer]

complete the Free Application for Federal Student Aid, institutional forms, and federal tax return. Financial aid contact: Dawn M. Chamberlaine, Assistant Dean Admissions and Financial Aid, 80 New Scotland Avenue, Albany, NY 12208. Phone: 518-445-2357. Fax: 518-445-2315. E-mail: finaid@mail.als.edu. Completed financial aid forms should be received by April 15.

Law School Library Schaffer Law Library has 7 professional staff members and contains more than 529,567 volumes and 1,437 periodicals. 482 seats are available in the library. When classes are in session, the library is open 104 hours per week.

WESTLAW and LEXIS-NEXIS are available, as are the World Wide Web, online bibliographic services, and CD-ROM players. 43 computer workstations are available to students in the library. Special law collections include videotapes of NY Court of Appeals oral arguments.

First-Year Program Class size in the average section is 80; 100% of the first-year courses are taught by full-time faculty.

Upper-Level Program Class size in the average section is 40. Among the electives are:

★ **Administrative Law**
★ **Advocacy**
★ **Business and Corporate Law**
  Consumer Law
  Education Law

★ **Environmental Law**
★ **Family Law**
★ **Government/Regulation**
★ **Health Care/Human Services**
★ **Intellectual Property**
★ **International/Comparative Law**
  Jurisprudence
★ **Labor Law**
  Land Use Law/Natural Resources
★ **Lawyering Skills**
  Legal History/Philosophy
★ **Litigation**
  Mediation
★ **Probate Law**
  Public Interest
  Securities
★ **Tax Law**
(★ *indicates an area of special strength)*

Clinical Courses Students receive degree credit for clinical courses. (Clinical practicum is not required.) Among the clinical areas offered are:

Civil Litigation
Domestic Violence
Education
Family Practice
General Practice
Government Litigation
Health

46% of the students participate in internship programs.

BROOKLYN LAW SCHOOL

Brooklyn, New York

INFORMATION CONTACT

Joan G. Wexler, Dean
250 Joralemon Street
Brooklyn, NY 11201-3798

Phone: 718-780-7900   Fax: 718-780-0393
E-mail: admitq@brooklaw.edu
Web site: http://www.brooklaw.edu/

LAW STUDENT PROFILE [1997–98]

FULL-TIME   Enrollment: 936
Women: 47%   Men: 53%

PART-TIME   Enrollment: 534
Women: 45%   Men: 55%

RACIAL or ETHNIC COMPOSITION

African American, 5%; Asian/Pacific Islander, 7%; Hispanic, 5%; Nataive American, 0.2%; International, 0%

APPLICANTS and ADMITTEES

Number applied: 2,826
Admitted: 1,396
Percentage accepted: 49%
Seats available: 275
Median LSAT score: 157
Average GPA: 3.3

Brooklyn Law School is a private nonprofit institution that organizes classes on a semester calendar system. The campus is situated in an urban setting. Founded in 1901, first ABA approved in 1937, and an AALS member, Brooklyn Law School offers JD, JD/MBA, JD/MPAd, JD/MS, and JD/MUP degrees.

Faculty consists of 63 full-time and 85 part-time members in 1997–98. 25 full-time faculty members and 29 part-time faculty members are women. 99% of all faculty members have a JD; 10% have advanced law degrees. Of all faculty members, .7% are Asian/Pacific Islander, 3% are African American, 2% are Hispanic, 94.3% are white.

Application Information *Required:* LSAT, LSDAS, application form, application fee of $60, baccalaureate degree, personal statement, college transcripts. *Recommended:* recommendations, essay, writing sample, resume. *Application deadline* for fall term is February 1.

Financial Aid In 1997–98, 92% of all students received some form of financial aid. 29 fellowships, totaling $125,000; 60 research assistantships, totaling $145,000, were awarded. Fellowships, graduate assistantships, loans, loan repayment assistance program (LRAP), merit-based grants/scholarships, need-based grants/scholarships, and federal work-study loans are also available. The average student

AT a GLANCE

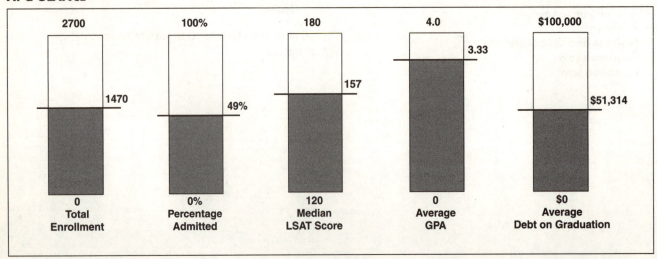

Degree Options

Degree	Total Credits Required	Length of Program
JD–Doctor of Laws	86	3–4 yrs, full-time or part-time [day, evening, summer]
JD/MBA–Juris Doctor/Master of Business Administration–Dual-degree Program	122	4–5 yrs, full-time or part-time [day, evening, summer]
JD/MPAd–Juris Doctor/Master of Public Administration–Dual-degree Program	110	4–5 yrs, full-time or part-time [day, evening, summer]
JD/MS–Juris Doctor/Master of Science–City Regional Planning Dual-degree Program	125	4–5 yrs, full-time or part-time [day, evening, summer]
JD/MS–Juris Doctor/Master of Science–Library Science Dual-degree Program	104	4–5 yrs, full-time or part-time [day, evening, summer]
JD/MUP–Juris Doctor/Masters of Urban Planning–Dual-degree Program	121	4–5 yrs, full-time or part-time [day, evening, summer]

debt at graduation is $51,314. To apply for financial assistance, students must complete the Free Application for Federal Student Aid, institutional forms, and Need Access diskette. Financial aid contact: Gerard N. Anderson, Director of Financial Aid, Brooklyn Law School, 250 Joralemon Street, Brooklyn, NY 11201. Phone: 718-780-7915. Fax: 718-780-0393. E-mail: ganders@brooklaw.edu. Completed financial aid forms should be received by April 15.

Law School Library Brooklyn Law School Library has 11 professional staff members and contains more than 465,022 volumes and 1,000 periodicals. 702 seats are available in the library. When classes are in session, the library is open 106 hours per week.

WESTLAW and LEXIS-NEXIS are available, as are the World Wide Web, online bibliographic services, and CD-ROM players. Special law collections include International Law.

First-Year Program Class size in the average section is 54; 75% of the first-year courses are taught by full-time faculty.

Upper-Level Program Class size in the average section is 33. Among the electives are:

Administrative Law
Advocacy
★ Business and Corporate Law
★ Consumer Law
Entertainment Law
Environmental Law
Family Law
★ Government/Regulation
Health Care/Human Services
★ Intellectual Property
★ International/Comparative Law
Jurisprudence
Labor Law
Land Use Law/Natural Resources
Lawyering Skills
Legal History/Philosophy
★ Litigation
Maritime Law
Media Law
★ Mediation
Probate Law
★ Public Interest
Securities
Tax Law
(★ indicates an area of special strength)

Clinical Courses Students receive degree credit for clinical courses. (Clinical practicum is not required.) Among the clinical areas offered are:

Civil Litigation
Criminal Defense
Criminal Prosecution
Elderly Advocacy
General Practice
Government Litigation
Immigration
Juvenile Law
Mediation
Public Interest

71% of the students participate in internship programs.

CITY UNIVERSITY OF NEW YORK SCHOOL OF LAW AT QUEENS COLLEGE

Flushing, New York

INFORMATION CONTACT

Kristin Booth Glen, Dean
65-21 Main Street
Flushing, NY 11367-1358

Phone: 718-340-4201
E-mail: perez@maclaw.law.cuny.edu

LAW STUDENT PROFILE [1997–98]

FULL-TIME   Enrollment: 461
Women: 60%   Men: 40%

PART-TIME   Enrollment: 6
Women: 83%   Men: 17%

RACIAL or ETHNIC COMPOSITION

African American, 16%; Asian/Pacific Islander, 12%;
Hispanic, 11%; Native American, 1%

APPLICANTS and ADMITTEES

Number applied: 1,441
Admitted: 543
Percentage accepted: 38%
Seats available: 160

City University of New York School of Law at Queens College is a private nonprofit institution. The campus is situated in an urban setting. First ABA approved in 1985, City University of New York School of Law at Queens College offers a JD degree.

Faculty consists of 42 full-time and 21 part-time members in 1997–98. 27 full-time faculty members and 12 part-time faculty members are women. 100% of all faculty members have a JD; 19% have advanced law degrees. Of all faculty members, 8% are Asian/Pacific Islander, 15.8% are African American, 8% are Hispanic, 68.2% are white.

Application Information *Required:* LSAT, LSDAS, application form, application fee of $40, baccalaureate degree, 2 letters of recommendation, personal statement, resume. *Application deadline* for fall term is March 15.

Financial Aid In 1997–98, 82% of all students received some form of financial aid. 14 fellowships, totaling $28,000, were awarded. Fellowships, graduate assistantships, loans, loan repayment assistance program (LRAP), need-based grants/scholarships, and federal work-study loans are also available. The average student debt at graduation is $39,000. To apply for financial assistance, students must complete the Free Application for Federal

AT a GLANCE

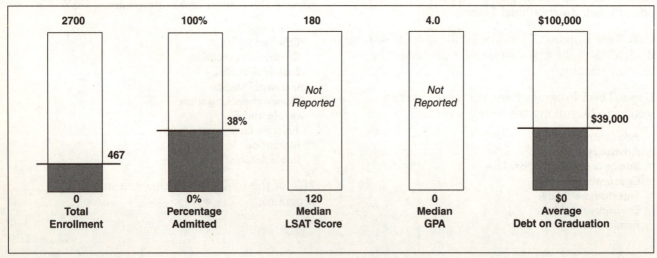

Degree Options		
Degree	**Total Credits Required**	**Length of Program**
JD–Juris Doctor	91	3 yrs, full-time only [day]

Student Aid and institutional forms. Financial aid contact: Angela M. Joseph, Director of Financial Aid, 65-21 Main Street, Flushing, NY 11367. Phone: 718-340-4284. E-mail: amj@maclaw.law.cuny.edu. Completed financial aid forms should be received by May 1.

Law School Library City University of New York School of Law Library has 9 professional staff members and contains more than 224,000 volumes and 2,619 periodicals. 397 seats are available in the library. When classes are in session, the library is open 57 hours per week.

WESTLAW and LEXIS-NEXIS are available, as are the World Wide Web, online bibliographic services, and CD-ROM players.

First-Year Program Class size in the average section is 48; 100% of the first-year courses are taught by full-time faculty.

Upper-Level Program Class size in the average section is 47. Among the electives are:

Administrative Law
Advocacy
Business and Corporate Law
Entertainment Law
Environmental Law
★ Family Law
First Amendment
★ Government/Regulation
Health Care/Human Services
★ Human Rights
Intellectual Property
★ International/Comparative Law
Jurisprudence
Juvenile Law
Labor Law
★ Lawyering Skills
Legal History/Philosophy
Litigation
★ Mediation
Probate Law
Property/Real Estate
★ Public Interest
Securities
Tax Law

(★ *indicates an area of special strength*)

Clinical Courses Students receive degree credit for clinical courses. 12 credit hours of clinical practicum are required. Among the clinical areas offered are:

Battered Women
Criminal Defense
Elderly Advocacy
Family Practice
General Practice
Immigration
International Law
Mediation
Public Benefits
Public Interest

33% of the students participate in internship programs.

COLUMBIA UNIVERSITY
SCHOOL OF LAW

New York, New York

INFORMATION CONTACT
David W. Leebron, Dean of Faculty of Law
435 West 116th Street
New York, NY 10027

Phone: 212-854-2675   Fax: 212-854-7946
Web site: http://www.columbia.edu/cu/law/

LAW STUDENT PROFILE [1997–98]

FULL-TIME   Enrollment: 1,105
Women: 45%   Men: 55%

RACIAL or ETHNIC COMPOSITION
African American, 12%; Asian/Pacific Islander, 13%;
Hispanic, 8%; Native American, 1%; International, 4%

APPLICANTS and ADMITTEES
Seats available: 358
Median LSAT score: 169
Median GPA: 3.6

Columbia University School of Law is a private institution that organizes classes on a semester calendar system. The campus is situated in an urban setting. First ABA approved in 1923, and an AALS member, Columbia University School of Law offers JD, JD/MA, JD/MBA, JD/MPAd, JD/MPAf, and JD/MS degrees.

Faculty consists of 71 full-time and 30 part-time members in 1997–98. 19 full-time faculty members and 3 part-time faculty members are women. 99% of all faculty members have a JD degree. Of all faculty members, 2% are Asian/Pacific Islander, 7% are African American, 2% are Hispanic, 87% are white, 2% are international.

Application Information *Required:* LSAT, LSDAS, application form, application fee of $65, 2 letters of recommendation, essay. *Application deadline* for fall term is February 15.

Costs The 1997–98 tuition is $26,570.

Financial Aid Loans, loan repayment assistance program (LRAP), and need-based grants/scholarships are available. The average student debt at graduation is $73,000. To apply for financial assistance, students must complete the Free Application for Federal Student Aid, institutional forms, and Need Access diskette, financial aid transcripts.

AT a GLANCE

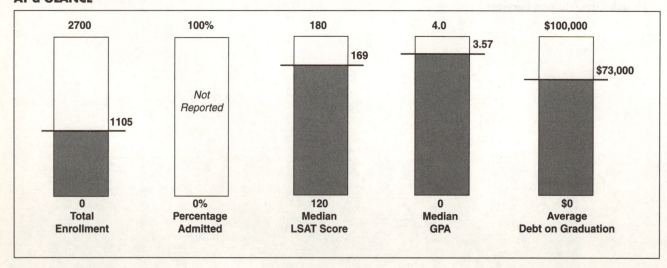

Degree Options

Degree	Total Credits Required	Length of Program
JD–Juris Doctor	83	3 yrs, full-time only [day]
JD/MA–Juris Doctor/Master of Arts–Anthropology, Economics, History, Policy Science, Psychology, or Sociology Joint Degree		7 yrs, full-time only [day]
JD/MBA–Juris Doctor/Master of Business Administration–Joint Degree		3–4 yrs, full-time only [day]
JD/MPAd–Juris Doctor/Master of Public Administration–Joint-degree Public Administration		4 yrs, full-time only [day]
JD/MPAf–Juris Doctor/Master of Public Affairs–Joint-degree Public Affairs		4 yrs, full-time only [day]
JD/MS–Juris Doctor/Master of Science–Joint Degree Journalism		3.5 yrs, full-time only [day]
JD/MS–Juris Doctor/Master of Science–Joint-degree Social Work		4 yrs, full-time only [day]
JD/MS–Juris Doctor/Master of Science–Joint-degree Urban Planning		4 yrs, full-time only [day]

Financial aid contact: Office of Financial Aid, Columbia Law School, Box A4, 435 West 116th Street, New York, NY 10027. Phone: 212-854-7730. Fax: 212-854-7946. Completed financial aid forms should be received by March 1.

Law School Library Arthur W. Diamond Law Library has 19 professional staff members and contains more than 964,628 volumes and 6,055 periodicals. 417 seats are available in the library. When classes are in session, the library is open 102 hours per week.

WESTLAW and LEXIS-NEXIS are available. 80 computer workstations are available to students in the library. Special law collections include Rare book collection, Canon law, Roman law, War crimes trials, Imperial Russian law, rare manuscripts.

First-Year Program 100% of the first-year courses are taught by full-time faculty.

Upper-Level Program Among the electives are:

Administrative Law
★ Business and Corporate Law
★ Commercial Law
★ Constitutional Law
Consumer Law
★ Criminal Law
Education Law
★ Employment Law
★ Entertainment Law
★ Environmental Law
★ Family Law
Government/Regulation

★ Health Care/Human Services
★ Human Rights
★ Intellectual Property
★ International/Comparative Law
Jurisprudence
★ Labor Law
Land Use Law/Natural Resources
★ Law and Economics
Lawyering Skills
★ Legal History/Philosophy
★ Litigation
Maritime Law
Media Law
Mediation
Probate Law
★ Property/Real Estate
★ Public Interest
★ Securities
★ Tax Law
★ Trusts and Estates
(★ indicates an area of special strength)

Clinical Courses Students receive degree credit for clinical courses. (Clinical practicum is not required.) Among the clinical areas offered are:

Corporate Law
Fair Housing
Family Practice
General Practice
Intellectual Property
Mediation
Nonprofit Organizations
Prisoners' Rights
Public Interest

5% of the students participate in internship programs. International exchange programs available.

CORNELL UNIVERSITY
PROFESSIONAL FIELD OF THE LAW SCHOOL

Ithaca, New York

INFORMATION CONTACT
Russell K. Osgood, Dean
Myron Taylor Hall
Ithaca, NY 14853-4901

Phone: 607-255-3527
Web site: http://www.lawschool.cornell.edu/

LAW STUDENT PROFILE [1997–98]

FULL-TIME   Enrollment: 536
Women: 42%   Men: 58%

RACIAL or ETHNIC COMPOSITION
African American, 7%; Asian/Pacific Islander, 12%; Hispanic, 6%; Native American, 3%; International, 4%

APPLICANTS and ADMITTEES
Seats available: 180
Average LSAT score: 165
Average GPA: 3.6

Cornell University Professional Field of the Law School is a private institution that organizes classes on a semester calendar system. The campus is situated in a small-town setting. Founded in 1887, first ABA approved in 1923, and an AALS member, Cornell University Professional Field of the Law School offers JD, JD/LLM, JD/MA, JD/MBA, JD/MCRP, JD/MILR, JD/MPAd, JD/Maitrise en Driot, JD/PhD, and LLM degrees.

Faculty consists of 43 full-time and 9 part-time members in 1997–98. 14 full-time faculty members are women. 100% of all faculty members have a JD degree.

Application Information *Required:* LSAT, LSDAS, application form, application fee of $65, baccalaureate degree, 2 letters of recommendation, personal statement, college transcripts. *Recommended:* resume. *Application deadline* for fall term is February 1.

Financial Aid Loans, loan repayment assistance program (LRAP), merit-based grants/scholarships, need-based grants/scholarships, and federal work-study loans are available. The average student debt at graduation is $55,000. To apply for financial assistance, students must complete the Free Application for Federal Student Aid and Need Access diskette. Financial aid contact: Jane Deathe, Division

AT a GLANCE

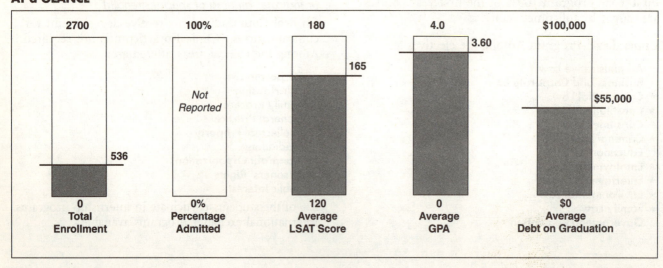

Degree Options

Degree	Total Credits Required	Length of Program
JD–Juris Doctor		3 yrs, full-time only [day]
JD/LLM–Juris Doctor/Master of Laws–International Legal Studies		3 yrs, full-time only [day]
JD/MA–Juris Doctor/Master of Arts		full-time only
JD/MBA–Juris Doctor/Master of Business Administration		4 yrs, full-time only [day]
JD/MCRP–Juris Doctor/Master of Community and Regional Planning		4 yrs, full-time only
JD/MILR–Juris Doctor/Master of in Industrial and Labor Relations		full-time only
JD/MPAd–Juris Doctor/Master of Public Administration		4 yrs, full-time only [day]
JD/Maitrise en Driot–Juris Doctor–American and French Law Degrees		4 yrs, full-time only [day]
JD/PhD–Juris Doctor/Doctor of Philosophy		full-time only
LLM–Master of Laws		1 yr, full-time only [day]

of Financial Aid, Myron Taylor Hall, Ithaca, NY 14853-4901. Phone: 607-255-5141.

Law School Library Cornell Law Library has 8 professional staff members and contains more than 585,501 volumes and 6,000 periodicals. 409 seats are available in the library. When classes are in session, the library is open 85 hours per week.

WESTLAW and LEXIS-NEXIS are available, as are the World Wide Web, online bibliographic services, and CD-ROM players. 50 computer workstations are available to students in the library. Special law collections include Bennett Collection, trials collection, foreign law collection.

First-Year Program Class size in the average section is 80; 100% of the first-year courses are taught by full-time faculty.

Upper-Level Program Among the electives are:

Administrative Law
★ Advocacy
★ Business and Corporate Law
★ Constitutional Law
Consumer Law
Education Law
Entertainment Law
Environmental Law
★ Family Law
★ Government/Regulation
Health Care/Human Services

Indian/Tribal Law
Intellectual Property
★ International/Comparative Law
Jurisprudence
Labor Law
Land Use Law/Natural Resources
★ Lawyering Skills
Legal History/Philosophy
Litigation
Media Law
Mediation
Probate Law
★ Public Interest
Securities
Tax Law
(★ indicates an area of special strength)

Clinical Courses Students receive degree credit for clinical courses. (Clinical practicum is not required.) Among the clinical areas offered are:

Civil Litigation
Civil Rights
Elderly Advocacy
General Practice
Government Litigation
Juvenile Law
Public Interest

Internships are available. International exchange programs permit students to visit Australia; France; and Germany.

FORDHAM UNIVERSITY
SCHOOL OF LAW

New York, New York

INFORMATION CONTACT

John Feerick, Dean
140 West 62nd Street
New York, NY 10023

Phone: 212-636-6875   Fax: 212-636-6899
Web site: http://corky.fordham.edu/law/admiss/

LAW STUDENT PROFILE [1997–98]

FULL-TIME   Enrollment: 1,043
Women: 43%   Men: 57%

PART-TIME   Enrollment: 361
Women: 45%   Men: 55%

APPLICANTS and ADMITTEES
Number applied: 4,100
Admitted: 1,252
Percentage accepted: 31%
Seats available: 442
Average LSAT score: 162
Average GPA: 3.4

Fordham University School of Law is a private institution that organizes classes on a semester calendar system. The campus is situated in an urban setting. Founded in 1905, first ABA approved in 1936, and an AALS member, Fordham University School of Law offers JD, JD/MBA, and JD/MSW degrees.

Faculty consists of 57 full-time and 93 part-time members in 1997–98. 17 full-time faculty members and 26 part-time faculty members are women. 100% of all faculty members have a JD; 35% have advanced law degrees. Of all faculty members, 1% are Asian/Pacific Islander, 4% are African American, 3% are Hispanic, 91% are white.

Application Information *Required:* LSAT, LSDAS, application form, application fee of $60, baccalaure-ate degree, personal statement, essay, college transcripts. *Application deadline* for fall term is March 1.

Financial Aid In 1997–98, 41% of all students received some form of financial aid. Loans, loan repayment assistance program (LRAP), merit-based grants/scholarships, and need-based grants/scholar-ships are also available. The average student debt at graduation is $77,900. To apply for financial assistance, students must complete the Free Applica-tion for Federal Student Aid and CSS PROFILE

AT a GLANCE

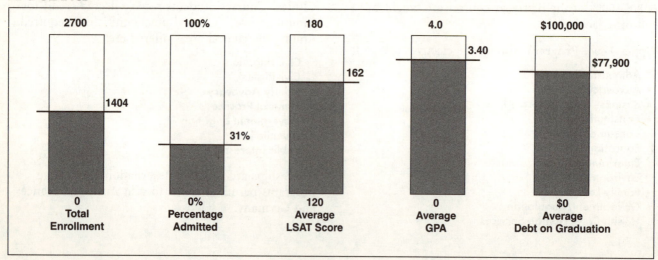

Degree Options

Degree	Total Credits Required	Length of Program
JD–Doctor of Laws	83	3–4 yrs, full-time or part-time [day, evening]
JD/MBA–Juris Doctor/Master of Business Administration–Joint Program	115	3.5–6.5 yrs, full-time or part-time [day, evening]
JD/MSW–Juris Doctor/Master of Social Work–Joint Program	133	4–5 yrs, full-time or part-time [day, evening]

form. Financial aid contact: Fordham Law School Financial Aid Office, 140 West 62nd Street, New York, NY 10023. Phone: 212-636-6815. Fax: 212-636-6899. Completed financial aid forms should be received by February 28.

Law School Library Leo T. Kissam Memorial Library has 13 professional staff members and contains more than 506,609 volumes and 3,721 periodicals. 465 seats are available in the library. When classes are in session, the library is open 122 hours per week.

WESTLAW and LEXIS-NEXIS are available, as are the World Wide Web, online bibliographic services, and CD-ROM players. 45 computer workstations are available to students in the library. Special law collections include European Community Law.

First-Year Program Class size in the average section is 77.

Upper-Level Program Class size in the average section is 40. Among the electives are:

Advocacy
Business and Corporate Law
Consumer Law
Education Law
Entertainment Law
Environmental Law
European Community Law
Family Law
Government/Regulation
Health Care/Human Services
Intellectual Property

International/Comparative Law
Jurisprudence
Labor Law
Land Use Law/Natural Resources
Lawyering Skills
Legal History/Philosophy
Litigation
Maritime Law
Media Law
Mediation
Probate Law
Public Interest
Securities
Tax Law

Clinical Courses Students receive degree credit for clinical courses. (Clinical practicum is not required.) Among the clinical areas offered are:

Civil Litigation
Civil Rights
Criminal Defense
Criminal Prosecution
Education
Elderly Advocacy
Environmental Law
Family Practice
General Practice
Government Litigation
Health
Juvenile Law
Mediation
Public Interest
Securities Law Arbitration
Welfare Rights

HOFSTRA UNIVERSITY
SCHOOL OF LAW

Hempstead, New York

INFORMATION CONTACT
Dr. Stuart Rabinowitz, Dean
121 Hofstra University
Hempstead, NY 11549

Phone: 516-463-5854   Fax: 516-463-6091
E-mail: lawaee@hofstra.edu
Web site: http://www.hofstra.edu/

LAW STUDENT PROFILE [1997–98]
FULL-TIME   Enrollment: 819
Women: 46%   Men: 54%

RACIAL or ETHNIC COMPOSITION
African American, 6%; Asian/Pacific Islander, 5%; Hispanic, 6%

APPLICANTS and ADMITTEES
Number applied: 1,689
Admitted: 823
Percentage accepted: 49%
Seats available: 290
Average LSAT score: 155
Average GPA: 3.3

Hofstra University School of Law is a private institution that organizes classes on a semester calendar system. The campus is situated in a suburban setting. Founded in 1971, first ABA approved in 1973, and an AALS member, Hofstra University School of Law offers JD and JD/MBA degrees.

Faculty consists of 35 full-time and 37 part-time members in 1997–98. 9 full-time faculty members and 5 part-time faculty members are women. 100% of all faculty members have a JD; 25% have advanced law degrees. Of all faculty members, 7% are African American, 2% are Hispanic, 91% are white.

Application Information *Required:* LSAT, LSDAS, application form, application fee of $60, baccalaureate degree, 1 recommendation, personal statement, college transcripts. *Recommended:* resume. *Application deadline* for fall term is April 15.

Financial Aid 447 fellowships were awarded. Loans, loan repayment assistance program (LRAP), merit-based grants/scholarships, need-based grants/scholarships, and federal work-study loans are also available. To apply for financial assistance, students must complete the Free Application for Federal Student Aid, institutional forms, and Need Access diskette, student and parent federal tax

---

AT a GLANCE

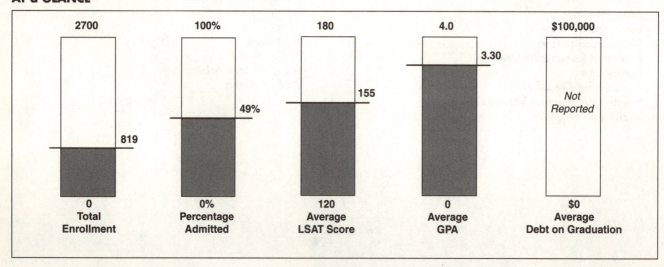

Degree Options

Degree	Total Credits Required	Length of Program
JD–Juris Doctor	87	3 yrs, full-time only [day]
JD/MBA–Juris Doctor/Master of Business Administration–Dual-degree Program	123	4 yrs, full-time only [day]

return. Financial aid contact: Nancy Modell, Assistant Dean, 121 Hofstra University, Hempstead, NY 11549-1210. Phone: 516-463-5929. Fax: 516-463-6091. E-mail: lawnzm@hofstra.edu. Completed financial aid forms should be received by May 15.

Law School Library Hofstra University School of Law Library has 12 professional staff members and contains more than 488,617 volumes and 5,476 periodicals. 595 seats are available in the library. When classes are in session, the library is open 98 hours per week.

WESTLAW and LEXIS-NEXIS are available, as are the World Wide Web, online bibliographic services, and CD-ROM players. 106 computer workstations are available to students in the library. Special law collections include records/briefs of US Supreme Court 1832 to date, records/briefs of New York Court of Appeals and Appellate Division of Supreme Court, federal depository materials, all UN documents 1976 to date, ABA archival collection 1878 to date.

First-Year Program Class size in the average section is 100; 100% of the first-year courses are taught by full-time faculty.

Upper-Level Program Class size in the average section is 40. Among the electives are:

Administrative Law

Advocacy
Business and Corporate Law
Dispute Resolution
Entertainment Law
Environmental Law
Family Law
Government/Regulation
Health Care/Human Services
Intellectual Property
International/Comparative Law
Jurisprudence
Labor Law
Lawyering Skills
Litigation
Mediation
Public Interest
Securities
Tax Law

Clinical Courses Students receive degree credit for clinical courses. (Clinical practicum is not required.) Among the clinical areas offered are:

Criminal Defense
Criminal Prosecution
General Practice
Public Interest

20% of the students participate in internship programs. International exchange programs permit students to visit France.

NEW YORK LAW SCHOOL

New York, New York

INFORMATION CONTACT

Harry H. Wellington, Dean
57 Worth Street
New York, NY 10013-2959

Phone: 212-431-2840   Fax: 212-966-1522
Web site: http://www.nyls.edu/

LAW STUDENT PROFILE [1997–98]

FULL-TIME   Enrollment: 880
Women: 47%   Men: 53%

PART-TIME   Enrollment: 488
Women: 45%   Men: 55%

RACIAL or ETHNIC COMPOSITION

African American, 8%; Asian/Pacific Islander, 6%; Hispanic, 7%; Nataive American, 0.4%; International, 1%

APPLICANTS and ADMITTEES

Number applied: 4,177
Admitted: 1,990
Percentage accepted: 48%
Seats available: 459
Average LSAT score: 154
Average GPA: 3.1

New York Law School is a private nonprofit institution that organizes classes on a semester calendar system. The campus is situated in an urban setting. Founded in 1891, first ABA approved in 1954, and an AALS member, New York Law School offers JD and JD/MBA degrees.

Faculty consists of 52 full-time and 82 part-time members in 1997–98. 16 full-time faculty members and 26 part-time faculty members are women. 100% of all faculty members have a JD; 18.6% have advanced law degrees. Of all faculty members, 1.5% are Asian/Pacific Islander, 4.5% are African American, 1.5% are Hispanic, 92.5% are white.

Application Information *Required:* LSAT, LSDAS, application form, application fee of $50, baccalaureate degree, college transcripts. *Recommended:* recommendations, personal statement, essay, writing sample. *Application deadline* for fall term is April 1.

Financial Aid 472 awards were given. Loans, merit-based grants/scholarships, need-based grants/scholarships, and federal work-study loans are also available. The average student debt at graduation is $47,000. To apply for financial assistance, students must complete the Free Application for Federal Student Aid and institutional forms. Financial aid contact: Eileen Doyle, Director of Financial Aid, New York Law School, 57 Worth Street, New York, NY 10013. Phone: 212-431-2828.

AT a GLANCE

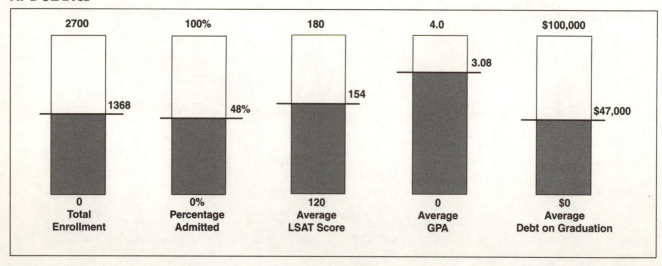

Degree Options

Degree	Total Credits Required	Length of Program
JD–Doctor of Laws	86	3–4 yrs, full-time or part-time [day, evening]
JD/MBA–Juris Doctor/Master of Business Administration–Joint-degree Program		full-time only [day]

Fax: 212-966-1522. Completed financial aid forms should be received by April 15.

Law School Library Mendik Library has 15 professional staff members and contains more than 435,198 volumes and 1,400 periodicals. 502 seats are available in the library. When classes are in session, the library is open 98 hours per week.

WESTLAW and LEXIS-NEXIS are available, as are the World Wide Web, online bibliographic services, and CD-ROM players. 110 computer workstations are available to students in the library.

First-Year Program Class size in the average section is 110; 100% of the first-year courses are taught by full-time faculty.

Upper-Level Program Class size in the average section is 50. Among the electives are:

- Administrative Law
- Advocacy
- Business and Corporate Law
- Consumer Law
- Education Law
- Entertainment Law
- Environmental Law
- Family Law

- ★ Government/Regulation
- Health Care/Human Services
- Intellectual Property
- ★ International/Comparative Law
- Jurisprudence
- Labor Law
- Land Use Law/Natural Resources
- ★ Lawyering Skills
- Legal History/Philosophy
- Litigation
- Maritime Law
- ★ Media Law
- Mediation
- Probate Law
- ★ Public Interest
- Securities
- Tax Law

(★ *indicates an area of special strength*)

Clinical Courses Students receive degree credit for clinical courses. (Clinical practicum is not required.) Among the clinical areas offered are:

- Civil Rights
- Judicial Externship

Internships are available.

NEW YORK UNIVERSITY
SCHOOL OF LAW

New York, New York

INFORMATION CONTACT

John Sexton, Dean
40 Washington Square South
Vanderbilt Hall
New York, NY 10012

Phone: 212-998-6000   Fax: 212-995-3156
Web site: http://www.law.nyu.edu/

LAW STUDENT PROFILE [1997–98]

FULL-TIME   Enrollment: 1,317
Women: 47%   Men: 53%

RACIAL or ETHNIC COMPOSITION
African American, 6%; Asian/Pacific Islander, 9%; Hispanic, 5%; Nataive American, 0.1%; International, 4%

APPLICANTS and ADMITTEES
Number applied: 6,185
Admitted: 1,493
Percentage accepted: 24%
Seats available: 400
Average LSAT score: 168
Average GPA: 3.7

New York University School of Law is a private institution that organizes classes on a semester calendar system. The campus is situated in an urban setting. Founded in 1835, first ABA approved in 1930, and an AALS member, New York University School of Law offers JD, JD/MA, JD/MBA, JD/MPAd, JD/MSW, JD/MUP, JSD, LLM, and MCJ degrees.

Faculty consists of 102 full-time and 123 part-time members in 1997–98. 37 full-time faculty members and 30 part-time faculty members are women. 93% of all faculty members have a JD; 22% have advanced law degrees.

Application Information *Required:* LSAT, LSDAS, application form, application fee of $65, baccalaureate degree, recommendations, personal statement, essay, writing sample, college transcripts. *Recommended:* resume. *Application deadline* for fall term is February 1.

Financial Aid In 1997–98, 85% of all students received some form of financial aid. Fellowships, graduate assistantships, loans, loan repayment assistance program (LRAP), merit-based grants/scholarships, need-based grants/scholarships, and federal work-study loans are also available. The average student debt at graduation is $70,000. To apply for financial assistance, students must complete the Free Application for Federal Student Aid and institutional forms. Financial aid contact: Stephen Brown, Director of Financial Aid, 110 West Third Street, New York, NY 10012. Phone: 212-998-

AT a GLANCE

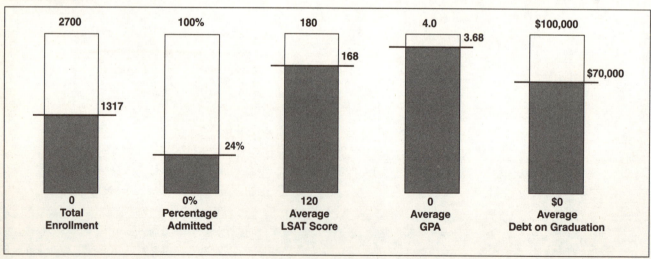

Degree Options

Degree	Total Credits Required	Length of Program
JD–Doctor of Laws	82	3 yrs, full-time only [day]
JD/MA–Juris Doctor/Master of Arts–Dual-degree Programs in Economics, French Studies, Law and Philosophy, Politics, Law and Society, Latin American and Caribbean Studies	94	3 yrs, full-time only
JD/MBA–Juris Doctor/Master of Business Administration–Dual-degree Program	131	4 yrs, full-time only [day]
JD/MPAd–Juris Doctor/Master of Public Administration–Dual-degree Programs w/Wagner School at NYU and Woodrow Wilson School of Public and International Affairs; JD/MUP–Juris Doctor/Masters of Urban Planning–Dual-degree Program	106–114	4 yrs, full-time only [day]
JD/MSW–Juris Doctor/Master of Social Work–Dual-degree Program	125	4 yrs, full-time only [day]
JSD–Doctor of Juridical Science	12	4–5 yrs, full-time only [day]
LLM–Master of Laws	24	1 yr, full-time or part-time [day, evening]
MCJ–Master of Comparative Jurisprudence–Master of Comparative Jurisprudence	24	1 yr, full-time only [day]

6050. Fax: 212-995-3156. E-mail: finaid.law@nyu.edu. Completed financial aid forms should be received by May 1.

Law School Library The Mills Memorial Library has 16 professional staff members and contains more than 963,754 volumes and 5,799 periodicals. 897 seats are available in the library. When classes are in session, the library is open 101 hours per week.

WESTLAW and LEXIS-NEXIS are available, as are the World Wide Web, online bibliographic services, and CD-ROM players. 1000 computer workstations are available to students in the library. Special law collections include Gruss, tax collection, intellectual property, commercial banking and trade law, public international law, private international law, foreign law, labor law, environmental law.

First-Year Program Class size in the average section is 100; 100% of the first-year courses are taught by full-time faculty.

Upper-Level Program Class size in the average section is 25. Among the electives are:

Administrative Law
★ Advocacy
★ Business and Corporate Law
Consumer Law
★ Criminal Law
Education Law
Entertainment Law
★ Environmental Law
★ Family Law
★ Government/Regulation
Health Care/Human Services
★ Intellectual Property
★ International/Comparative Law
Jurisprudence
★ Labor Law
Land Use Law/Natural Resources
★ Lawyering Skills
★ Legal History/Philosophy
★ Litigation
Maritime Law
Mediation
Probate Law
★ Public Interest
Securities
★ Tax Law
(★ indicates an area of special strength)

Clinical Courses Students receive degree credit for clinical courses. (Clinical practicum is not required.) Among the clinical areas offered are:

Civil Litigation
Civil Rights
Criminal Defense
Criminal Prosecution
Elderly Advocacy
Environmental Law
Family Practice
Government Litigation
Immigration
International Law
Juvenile Law
Land Rights/Natural Resource
Mediation
Public Interest

40% of the students participate in internship programs. International exchange programs available.

DEAN'S STATEMENT . . .

Legal education has changed dramatically in recent decades. The study of doctrine through the decisions of appellate courts has long been the staple of law school, but it is now generally recognized that this traditional method does not prepare students adequately to practice law. First, the law is not a closed system of rules but an instrument of social policy and moral values, so an interdisciplinary dimension is necessary. Second, the stage on which our leading lawyers act has expanded to include the entire world, so the law must be studied in a global context. Third, because law is a practice, students benefit greatly by confronting law and legal practice in the context of actual and simulated transactions and cases in progress; hence, the addition of a clinical dimension to the curriculum.

At the NYU School of Law, our goal has been to chart the future course for American legal education in each of these directions—to develop and refine programs of genuine excellence that encompass the strengths of the traditional curriculum while incorporating the interdisciplinary, global, and clinical dimensions. We are a work in progress, not a final product; but our success to date is remarkably encouraging. The breadth of advanced interdisciplinary work occurring at NYU School of Law is unmatched. Thus, for example, there is no law school in the world with NYU's philosophical sophistication; our faculty is on the cutting edge of work in law and economics, game theory, and rational choice theory; the School is an important center of research in legal history; and studies in law and society are flourishing. Our groundbreaking Global Law School Program has placed in residence on a permanent basis legal scholars and outstanding graduate students from every corner of the world; no other law school has implemented a program of this scope. In addition, NYU's clinical program's reputation as the premier program in clinical studies is seldom questioned and well deserved.

NYU is a law school with the extraordinary diversity, enterprise, and excellence that characterize New York City itself. We take pride in being a community of ideas, a community in which orthodoxy is challenged and invention is celebrated. We ask of our students that they share in and act on these commitments.

—John Sexton, Dean

HISTORY, CAMPUS, AND LOCATION

The School of Law is located at Washington Square in Greenwich Village, one of the most historic and best-preserved neighborhoods of New York City. Surrounding the School is an inexhaustible array of cultural and countercultural activity. As home to the United Nations and many of the world's major nongovernmental agencies, it is a hub of a global public law network. Leaders of the private and public bar regularly participate in classes at the law school, many as adjunct professors, and research and internship opportunities flow from these interactions. The intellectual life at the School is enriched as experts from around the world assemble at the School of Law for conferences on important and emerging issues.

SPECIAL QUALITIES OF THE SCHOOL

On any given day, NYU students may choose from a wide array of activities. Major events occur at the law school each week that would be the event of the year on other campuses. For example, students attended question-and-answer sessions with any of five sitting United States Supreme Court Justices, with justices from the highest courts of several other countries, or the Attorney General of the United States. In addition, they attended a cocktail party to celebrate the King and Queen of Spain or held conversations with the First Lady of the United States. They also participated in a panel discussion on legal services or one about amending the Federal Constitution. Campus life complements and extends the intellectual dialogue that begins in the more formal setting of the classroom.

TECHNOLOGY ON CAMPUS

The School of Law has invested heavily in state-of-the-art technology. It is fully wired with the latest equipment—in its faculty offices, student residences, classrooms (podiums and seats), library, and administrators' offices. The School's public computing network consists of public-use networked computers at more than 100 sites. These computers use a Windows 95 operating system, but a Macintosh operating system is also supported. On both platforms, there are word processing programs, a spreadsheet application, presentation software, LEXIS-NEXIS and WESTLAW legal research software, Internet browsers, and electronic mail. A CD-ROM LAN is accessible in various locations in the library (as well as in lounges around campus) to provide easy access to automated indices, and areas are set aside for students with laptop computers.

SCHOLARSHIPS AND LOANS

Both need-based and merit-based aid is available. Need-based aid is met first by money available from federal and private lending agencies. Grants are available to students with exceptional need. The Dean's Merit Scholarship, Root-Tilden-Kern, Soros, Sinsheimer, and An-Bryce Programs award merit scholarships based on such attributes as outstanding intellectual potential and demonstrated commitment to public service. Hauser Fellowships are available to outstanding international students. The School also has an array of generously funded fellowships. The Loan Repayment Assistance Program (LRAP) is designed to pay the costs of law school for graduates who pursue low-paying law-related careers.

STUDENT ACTIVITIES AND OPPORTUNITIES

Law Review One of the most important cocurricular aspects available at NYU School of Law is the opportunity to work on one of the nine student-edited journals, some of which are the leading journals in the field.

Moot Court The NYU Moot Court Board is a student-run honorary organization that combines legal scholarship with oral advocacy. Staff members are selected from the first-year class on the basis of a writing competition held in early spring. Each year, between 30 and 35 students are offered positions on the board.

Extracurricular Activities Many activities are available. For example, with funding from the School, students organize their own lecture series to bring faculty from around the country to present additional perspectives on the law. Students have also created outreach and community projects that enable students to put their nascent legal skills to work. There are daylong symposia on current legal issues, sessions with Supreme Court Justices, and workshops with judges and practitioners. Currently, there are about sixty-five student organizations, as well as athletic and social program opportunities.

Special Opportunities Throughout the year, the School of Law offers an array of exciting events. There is a set of distinguished lecture series. There are ten colloquiums, in which the distinction between teacher and student is abandoned in favor of joint pursuit of advanced study of the law and other disciplines. There are thirteen institutes and centers involving interaction among faculty members, leading judges and practitioners, and students in a conference, seminar, or course format. Many clinical opportunities are available, including the Public Interest Internship Program, which selects more than 130 first- and second-year students each year to receive grants from the School to pursue public interest work during the summer.

Opportunities for Members of Minority Groups and Women NYU has a historic commitment of seeking the best students from a broad range of backgrounds. For example, in 1890, NYU was one of a small handful of schools that offered legal education to women. In 1967, the National Black Allied Law Students Association (BALSA) was founded at NYU.

Special Certificate Programs In addition to the J.D., NYU offers the LL.M. (general, corporate law, labor and employment law, trade regulation, taxation, international taxation, and international legal studies), Master of Comparative Jurisprudence, and Doctor of Juridical Science degree programs. Joint-degree programs are offered with a master's or Ph.D. in economics, French studies, Latin American/Caribbean studies, legal history,

philosophy, and sociology. NYU also offers a joint degree (J.D./master's or J.D./Ph.D.) in its multidisciplinary Program in Law and Society. The J.D. may also be earned simultaneously with a master's degree in business administration, urban planning, public administration, social work, and public affairs (at Princeton's Woodrow Wilson School). The School of Law also offers a joint J.D./Master of Law (LL.M.) degree program in taxation.

BAR PASSAGE, CAREER SERVICES, AND PLACEMENT

Each year, NYU Law graduates pass the New York State Bar Examination at a rate of in excess of 90 percent. NYU students are assisted in their job search by the most extensive placement program in the country. NYU's Office of Career Counseling and Placement begins working with students in the fall of their first year. Together with the Public Interest Law Center, the office organizes panels and workshops on all aspects of job hunting, provides a videotaped simulated interview program, and offers individual counseling. Ninety-eight percent of the J.D. class of 1998 reported that they got their first or second choice of jobs.

On-campus interviews are scheduled on the basis of students' preference selections. During 1997–98, almost 600 private law firms, public interest organizations, government agencies, corporations, and public accounting firms visited the law school. The interviewers came from thirty-four states and six other countries; 57 percent were from outside New York and 49 percent from outside the tristate area. The placement office also arranges off-campus interview programs, and the law school hosts or participates with other schools in several placement programs that serve students with special interests or special needs.

Legal Field	Percentage of Graduates	Average Salary
Academic	1%	n/a
Business	1%	$88,200
Government	3%	$37,800
Judicial Clerkship	17%	$37,800
Private Practice	69%	$88,200
Public Interest	8%	$37,800
Other	1%	n/a

CORRESPONDENCE AND INFORMATION
New York University School of Law
110 West 3rd Street, 2nd floor
New York, New York 10012
Telephone: 212-998-6060
Fax: 212-995-4527
E-mail: law.jdadmissions@nyu.edu
World Wide Web: http://www.law.nyu.edu

PACE UNIVERSITY
SCHOOL OF LAW

New York, New York

LAW STUDENT PROFILE [1997–98]

FULL-TIME   Enrollment: 506
Women: 55%   Men: 45%

PART-TIME   Enrollment: 319
Women: 45%   Men: 55%

RACIAL or ETHNIC COMPOSITION
African American, 5%; Asian/Pacific Islander, 4%; Hispanic, 4%; Nataive American, 0.1%; International, 0%

APPLICANTS and ADMITTEES
Number applied: 2,638
Admitted: 971
Percentage accepted: 37%
Seats available: 264
Average LSAT score: 155
Average GPA: 3.1

Pace University School of Law is a private institution that organizes classes on a semester calendar system. The campus is situated in a suburban setting. Founded in 1976, first ABA approved in 1978, and an AALS member, Pace University School of Law offers JD, JD/MBA, JD/MPAd, JSD, and LLM degrees.

Faculty consists of 48 full-time and 60 part-time members in 1997–98. 100% of all faculty members have a JD; 27% have advanced law degrees. Of all faculty members, 8% are African American, 92% are white.

Application Information *Required:* LSAT, LSDAS, application form, application fee of $55, baccalaureate degree, 2 letters of recommendation, personal statement, college transcripts. *Recommended:* resume. *Application deadline* for fall term is March 15.

Costs The 1997–98 tuition is $21,750 full-time; $16,324 part-time. Fees: $80 full-time; $60 part-time.

Financial Aid Loans, merit-based grants/scholarships, need-based grants/scholarships, and federal work-study loans are available. The average student debt at graduation is $60,000. To apply for financial assistance, students must complete the Free Application for Federal Student Aid and institutional forms.

AT a GLANCE

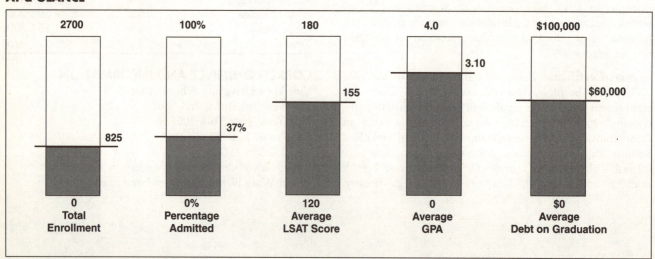

Degree Options

Degree	Total Credits Required	Length of Program
JD–Doctor of Laws	90	3–4 yrs, full-time or part-time [day, evening, summer]
JD/MBA–Juris Doctor/Master of Business Administration–Dual-degree Program	129	4–6 yrs, full-time or part-time [day, evening, summer]
JD/MPAd–Juris Doctor/Master of Public Administration–Dual-degree Program	116	4–6 yrs, full-time or part-time [day, evening, summer]
JSD–Doctor of Juridical Science	12	1 yr, full-time only [day, evening, summer]
LLM–Master of Laws–Environmental Science	24	1–2 yrs, full-time or part-time [day, evening, summer]

Financial aid contact: Angela M. D'Agostino, Assistant Dean / Director of Admissions, 78 North Broadway, White Plains, NY 10603. Phone: 914-422-4210. Fax: 914-422-4015. E-mail: adagostino@genesis.law.pace.edu.

Law School Library The Pace Law Library has 11 professional staff members and contains more than 325,000 volumes and 1,168 periodicals. 346 seats are available in the library. When classes are in session, the library is open 102 hours per week.

WESTLAW and LEXIS-NEXIS are available, as are the World Wide Web, online bibliographic services, and CD-ROM players. 88 computer workstations are available to students in the library. Special law collections include Environmental law, US Government Depository collection.

First-Year Program Class size in the average section is 80; 100% of the first-year courses are taught by full-time faculty.

Upper-Level Program Class size in the average section is 40. Among the electives are:

Administrative Law
Advocacy
Business and Corporate Law
Civil Procedure
Constitutional Law
Criminal Law
Criminal Procedure
Education Law
Entertainment Law
★ Environmental Law
Family Law
Government/Regulation

★ Health Care/Human Services
Intellectual Property
★ International/Comparative Law
Jurisprudence
Labor Law
★ Land Use Law/Natural Resources
Lawyering Skills
Legal History/Philosophy
Litigation
Maritime Law
Media Law
Mediation
Municipal Law
Property/Real Estate
Public Interest
Securities
Social Justice
Tax Law
Trusts and Estates

(★ indicates an area of special strength)

Clinical Courses Students receive degree credit for clinical courses. (Clinical practicum is not required.) Among the clinical areas offered are:

Appellate Litigation
Criminal Defense
Criminal Prosecution
Domestic Violence
Elderly Advocacy
Environmental Law
Health
Securities Law Arbitration

13% of the students participate in internship programs. International exchange programs permit students to visit Australia and United Kingdom.

DEAN'S STATEMENT . . .

Law is one of humanity's most ambitious works-in-progress. Law seeks to present a durable, yet flexible, framework for resolving disagreements peacefully and justly. Our goal at Pace University School of Law is to provide students with the knowledge, the skill, and the perspective to contribute to one of civilization's noblest pursuits: the practice of law.

We believe that we achieve that goal by combining an innovative curriculum, a superlative faculty, and a positive environment that is conducive to learning. The curriculum emphasizes a broad foundation in legal principles as they apply throughout the United States.

First-year courses introduce students to the major building blocks of substantive law and to learning the tools of the lawyer's craft. Our program stresses the importance of incisive legal analysis, clear writing, and effective oral communication through the vehicle of a substantive law course. Students develop skill in the traditional and the newest electronic methods of legal research. Upper-level courses, constructed around a core curriculum, offer a breadth of electives that permit students to sample virtually any area of law while providing the depth for concentration in a particular area. Pace offers certificate programs for specialization in environmental law, health law, and international law. It offers one of the largest Master of Laws in environmental law programs in the nation. The Doctor of Juridical Science program helps prepare legal scholars for teaching environmental law in the United States and abroad.

School of Law faculty members take pride in their teaching excellence, as well as in their commitment to legal scholarship and community service. In and out of the classroom, Pace faculty members' obvious commitment to students' learning sets the tone for a stimulating and rigorous, yet supportive, academic environment. All these efforts to produce an academically excellent and supportive school have been recognized nationally. Pace is consistently ranked among the top five law schools in the United States for its environmental law program, and the excellence of its writing program has often been cited. Recently, the *National Jurist* ranked us as one of the top schools for women.

—*Richard L. Ottinger, Dean*

HISTORY, CAMPUS, AND LOCATION

Pace University is a comprehensive, independent, urban, and suburban New York institution of higher education that offers a wide range of academic and professional programs at the graduate and undergraduate levels in the following six colleges and schools: the Dyson College of Arts and Sciences, the Lubin School of Business, the School of Computer Science and Information Systems, the School of Education, the School of Law, and the Lienhard School of Nursing. Pace University considers teaching and learning to be its highest principles. In recognizing that its educational leadership implies broadening obligations, the University has become increasingly attentive to the integration of scholarship and service with excellent teaching. Faculty members engage in theoretical and applied research, as well as other scholarly and professional activities. As part of the teaching role, faculty members often involve undergraduate as well as graduate students in research. Pace University's commitment to the individual needs of students is at the heart of its teaching mission. By offering access and opportunity to qualified men and women, Pace embraces persons of diverse talents, interests, experiences, and origins who have the will to learn and the desire to participate in university life. As a multicampus institution that provides programmatic richness at urban and suburban locations, Pace offers pluralistic, interdependent, collegial environments that foster individual growth, human dignity, civil discourse, and the free exchange of ideas. The White Plains campus on historic North Broadway is the home of the School of Law, which satisfies a community need as the only law school between New York City and Albany. White Plains, the county seat of Westchester County, is an attractive and lively city of about 50,000. Located in White Plains is a new United States Court House that provides a permanent location for the operations of the federal courts in Westchester County.

SPECIAL QUALITIES OF THE SCHOOL

The curriculum at Pace is devoted to preparing graduates to become able and ethical lawyers, to become employable, and to make a difference in improving society. Pace has a strong dedication to excellence in teaching and outstanding training in specialized areas where the need for skilled lawyers is greatest. The majority of classes have less than 25 students, which enables close faculty-student relationships. Deans, other administrators, and faculty members maintain an open-door policy for students. Students participate actively in formulating law school policy through the Student Bar Association and by serving on all faculty committees.

TECHNOLOGY ON CAMPUS

First-year students receive 2 to 3 hours of formal instruction in online research from the library staff and from other instructors. Additional instruction on advanced research techniques and on research in specialized areas of law is always available to groups of second- and third-year students on demand. The Law Library's many computer terminals give students free access to all the information in the LEXIS-NEXIS, WESTLAW, and Dialog databases; on the World Wide Web; and e-mail.

SCHOLARSHIPS AND LOANS

The School of Law assists students with financial need to the extent that funds are available. A comprehensive aid program has been developed that includes grants, employment, scholarships, and loans, which may be available on the basis of financial need, academic merit, educational costs, or credit considerations.

STUDENT ACTIVITIES AND OPPORTUNITIES

Law Review Pace law school publishes three law reviews, the *Pace Law Review*, the *Pace Environmental Law Review*, and the *Pace International Law Review*. Admission to the reviews is based upon academic standing and a writing competition. Approximately 50 students participate in each law review.

Moot Court A mandatory first-year moot court competition is part of the Criminal Law Analysis and Writing curriculum. The School of Law also competes in interscholastic moot court competitions and hosts the National Environmental Moot Court Competition, the largest environmental moot court competition in the country. Moot team members are selected by professors and chosen based on writing ability and oral presentation skills.

Extracurricular Activities Pace law school offers more than thirty organizations in which students can participate. Available activities include professional organizations, minority student groups, issue-centered organizations, political groups, social action groups, religious groups, a student bar association, and a student newspaper.

Special Opportunities Pace offers three types of clinical courses. Direct representation clinics are clinics in which students, permitted to practice under a Student Practice Order, take full responsibility for their own caseload under the direct supervision of a full-time faculty member. These include Appellate Litigation, Criminal Defense, Environmental Litigation, Health Law Clinic, Prosecution of Domestic Violence, Securities Arbitration, and Wills and Advance Medical Directives. Externship programs are clinical courses in which fieldwork is conducted under the supervision of practicing attorneys who are not full-time members of the faculty and include Criminal Justice Defense; Criminal Justice Prosecution; the Environmental Externship in Washington, D.C.; Environmental Law; Health Law; Judicial Clerkship; and Legal Services. Simulation courses simulate specific components of lawyering work and include Pretrial Civil Litigation and Trial Advocacy. The Social Justice Center, the Battered Women's Justice Center, the Land Use Law Center, and the Permanent Judicial Commission on Justice for Children all offer opportunities for Pace law students to assist in legal research and discovery, to draft motions, and to attend trials.

Opportunities for Members of Minority Groups and Women A special program for students who are members of minority groups is held annually during the fall semester. This program includes a guest speaker and discussion of the enrollment and placement experiences of alumni who are members of minority groups, current students, and faculty.

Special Certificate Programs Pace offers Certificates of Concentration in environmental law, in health law, and in international law. These certificates are awarded upon graduation to students who have successfully completed 12–15 credits with satisfactory grades. A Master of Laws (LL.M.) degree is offered for lawyers in the field of environmental law. Pace also offers a Doctor of Juridical Science (S.J.D.) in environmental law. This program prepares legal scholars for the teaching of environmental law in the United States or abroad.

BAR PASSAGE, CAREER SERVICES, AND PLACEMENT

The first-time bar passage rate for the 1997 graduates was 75 percent for New York State and 81 percent for the state of Connecticut. The Office of Career Development actively solicits job listings for part-time, summer, and permanent positions after graduation, as well as full-time jobs for evening students while they are in school, through various types of outreach activities. In addition to regularly contacting legal employers through mailings and surveys regarding immediate hiring needs, visits with law firms and other organizations are scheduled throughout the year in an effort to establish—or maintain—relationships that result in the receipt of additional job notices as they become available.

Legal Field	Percentage of Graduates	Average Starting Salary
Academic	0%	n/a
Business	17%	$65,035
Government	12%	$36,509
Judicial Clerkship	4%	$34,735
Private Practice	57%	$52,132
Public Interest	4%	$42,000
Other	5%	n/a

CORRESPONDENCE AND INFORMATION

Office of Admissions
School of Law
Pace University
78 North Broadway
White Plains, New York 10603
Telephone: 914-422-4210
Fax: 914-422-4010
E-mail: admissions@genesis.law.pace.edu
World Wide Web: http://www.law.pace.edu

ST. JOHN'S UNIVERSITY
SCHOOL OF LAW

Jamaica, New York

INFORMATION CONTACT

Prof. Brian Tamanaha, Acting Dean
8000 Utopia Parkway
Jamaica, NY 11439

Phone: 718-990-6600   Fax: 718-591-1855
Web site: http://www.stjohns.edu/law/

LAW STUDENT PROFILE [1997–98]

FULL-TIME   Enrollment: 771
Women: 42%   Men: 58%

PART-TIME   Enrollment: 289
Women: 31%   Men: 69%

RACIAL or ETHNIC COMPOSITION
African American, 7%; Asian/Pacific Islander, 8%; Hispanic, 9%; Nataive American, 0.5%; International, 1%

APPLICANTS and ADMITTEES
Number applied: 2,398
Admitted: 1,084
Percentage accepted: 45%
Seats available: 300
Average LSAT score: 156
Average GPA: 3.0

St. John's University School of Law is a private institution that organizes classes on a semester calendar system. The campus is situated in a suburban setting. Founded in 1925, first ABA approved in 1937, and an AALS member, St. John's University School of Law offers JD, JD/MA, and JD/MBA degrees.

Faculty consists of 50 full-time and 21 part-time members in 1997–98. 16 full-time faculty members and 3 part-time faculty members are women. 100% of all faculty members have a JD; 32.9% have advanced law degrees. Of all faculty members, 2% are Asian/Pacific Islander, 5.5% are African American, 5.5% are Hispanic, 87% are white.

Application Information *Required:* LSAT, LSDAS, application form, application fee of $50, baccalaureate degree, personal statement, college transcripts. *Application deadline* for fall term is March 1.

Costs The 1997–98 tuition is $22,000 full-time; $16,500 part-time. Fees: $150.

Financial Aid Merit-based grants/scholarships, need-based grants/scholarships, and federal work-study loans are available. The average student debt at graduation is $56,000. To apply for financial assistance, students must complete the Free Application for Federal Student Aid and TAP (if appli-

AT a GLANCE

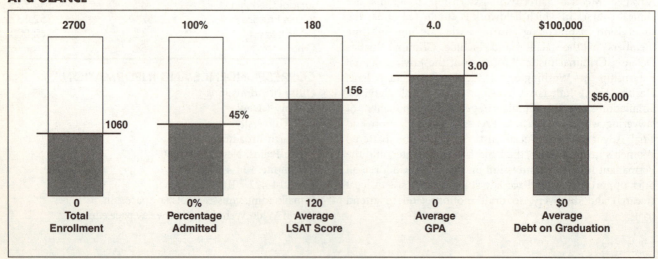

Degree Options

Degree	Total Credits Required	Length of Program
JD–Doctor of Laws	85	3–4 yrs, full-time or part-time [day, evening]
JD/MA–Juris Doctor/Master of Arts–Dual-degree Program	109	3 yrs, full-time only [day]
JD/MBA–Juris Doctor/Master of Business Administration–Dual-degree Program	115	3 yrs, full-time only [day]

cable). Financial aid contact: Ms. Karen Reddy, Assistant Director of Financial Aid, 8000 Utopia Parkway, Jamaica, NY 11439. Phone: 718-990-6403. Fax: 718-591-1855. E-mail: kreddy@stjohns.edu. Completed financial aid forms should be received by March 1.

Law School Library Rittenberg Law Library has 6 professional staff members and contains more than 413,778 volumes and 1,500 periodicals. 607 seats are available in the library. When classes are in session, the library is open 111 hours per week.

WESTLAW and LEXIS-NEXIS are available, as are the World Wide Web and online bibliographic services. 52 computer workstations are available to students in the library. Special law collections include United Nations Depository, Federal and New York State Depository.

First-Year Program Class size in the average section is 75; 100% of the first-year courses are taught by full-time faculty.

Upper-Level Program Class size in the average section is 41. Among the electives are:

Administrative Law
Advocacy
Business and Corporate Law
Consumer Law
Education Law
Entertainment Law

Environmental Law
Family Law
Government/Regulation
Health Care/Human Services
Indian/Tribal Law
Intellectual Property
International/Comparative Law
Jurisprudence
Labor Law
Land Use Law/Natural Resources
Lawyering Skills
Legal History/Philosophy
Litigation
Maritime Law
Media Law
Mediation
Probate Law
Public Interest
Securities
Tax Law

Clinical Courses Students receive degree credit for clinical courses. (Clinical practicum is not required.) Among the clinical areas offered are:

Civil Litigation
Criminal Defense
Elderly Advocacy
Judicial

23% of the students participate in internship programs.

STATE UNIVERSITY OF NEW YORK AT BUFFALO
SCHOOL OF LAW

Buffalo, New York

INFORMATION CONTACT

Barry B. Boyer, Dean
OBrian Hall
Buffalo, NY 14260

Phone: 716-645-2052
Web site: http://www.buffalo.edu/law/

LAW STUDENT PROFILE [1997–98]

FULL-TIME   Enrollment: 704
Women: 48%   Men: 52%

PART-TIME   Enrollment: 6
Women: 100%

RACIAL or ETHNIC COMPOSITION
African American, 6%; Asian/Pacific Islander, 4%; Hispanic, 5%; Native American, 1%; International, 1%

APPLICANTS and ADMITTEES
Number applied: 1,023
Admitted: 527
Percentage accepted: 52%
Seats available: 214
Median LSAT score: 155
Median GPA: 3.3

State University of New York at Buffalo School of Law is a public institution that organizes classes on a semester calendar system. The campus is situated in a suburban setting. Founded in 1887, first ABA approved in 1936, and an AALS member, State University of New York at Buffalo School of Law offers JD, JD/MBA, and JD/MSW degrees.

Faculty consists of 51 full-time and 35 part-time members in 1997–98. 20 full-time faculty members and 13 part-time faculty members are women.

Application Information *Required:* LSAT, LSDAS, application form, application fee of $50, baccalaureate degree, 2 letters of recommendation. *Application deadline* for fall term is February 1.

Financial Aid In 1997–98, 56% of all students received some form of financial aid. 91 fellowships, 37 research assistantships were awarded. 7 other awards, totaling $24,360, were given. Fellowships are also available. To apply for financial assistance, students must complete the Free Application for Federal Student Aid and financial aid transcripts, Tuition Assistance Program (TAP) application. Financial aid contact: University at Buffalo, Office of Financial Aid, Hayes C, 3435 Main Street, Buffalo, NY 14214-3016. Phone: 716-645-2907. E-mail:

AT a GLANCE

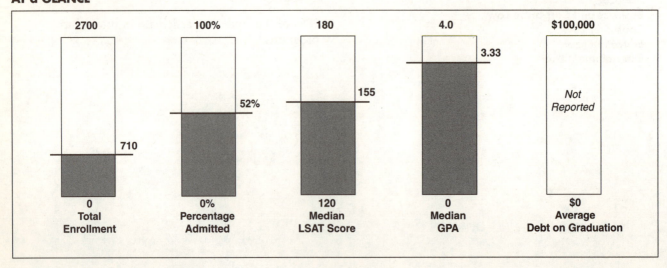

Degree Options

Degree	Total Credits Required	Length of Program
JD–Juris Doctor	87	3 yrs, full-time only [day]
JD/MBA–Juris Doctor/Master of Business Administration–Joint-degree Program in Management	123	4 yrs, full-time only
JD/MSW–Juris Doctor/Master of Social Work–Joint-degree Program		

dewaal@msmail.buffalo.edu. Completed financial aid forms should be received by March 1.

Law School Library The Charles B. Sears Law Library has 9 professional staff members and contains more than 506,447 volumes and 6,659 periodicals. 508 seats are available in the library. When classes are in session, the library is open 93 hours per week.

WESTLAW and LEXIS-NEXIS are available, as are the World Wide Web and CD-ROM players. 32 computer workstations are available to students in the library. Special law collections include The M. Robert Koren AV Center, the papers of John Lord O'Brian.

First-Year Program Class size in the average section is 110.

Upper-Level Program Among the electives are:

- ★ Administrative Law
- ★ Advocacy
  Bankruptcy
  Business and Corporate Law
  Commercial Law
- ★ Criminal Law

- ★ Environmental Law
- ★ Family Law
  Government/Regulation
  Health Care/Human Services
  Human Rights
  International/Comparative Law
  Labor Law
- ★ Lawyering Skills
- ★ Litigation
  Property/Real Estate
  Public Interest
  Securities
  Tax Law

(★ *indicates an area of special strength*)

Clinical Courses Among the clinical areas offered are:

  Criminal Defense
  Criminal Prosecution
  Education
  Elderly Advocacy
  Environmental Law
  Family Practice
  Public Interest

Internships are available.

SYRACUSE UNIVERSITY
COLLEGE OF LAW

Syracuse, New York

INFORMATION CONTACT

Daan Braveman, Dean
Syracuse, NY 13244-1030

Phone: 315-443-2524   Fax: 315-443-9568
E-mail: admissions@law.syr.edu
Web site: http://www.law.syr.cdu/

LAW STUDENT PROFILE [1997–98]

FULL-TIME   Enrollment: 716
Women: 45%   Men: 55%

PART-TIME   Enrollment: 24
Women: 33%   Men: 67%

RACIAL or ETHNIC COMPOSITION
African American, 7%; Asian/Pacific Islander, 8%; Hispanic, 5%; Nataive American, 0.1%; International, 3%

APPLICANTS and ADMITTEES
Number applied: 1,715
Seats available: 253
Average LSAT score: 151
Average GPA: 3.2

Syracuse University College of Law is a private institution that organizes classes on a semester calendar system. The campus is situated in an urban setting. Founded in 1895, first ABA approved in 1923, and an AALS member, Syracuse University College of Law offers JD, JD/MA, JD/MBA, JD/MFA, JD/MLS, JD/MPAd, JD/MS, JD/MSW, and JD/PhD degrees.

Faculty consists of 40 full-time and 43 part-time members in 1997–98. 19 full-time faculty members and 8 part-time faculty members are women. 97% of all faculty members have a JD; 41% have advanced law degrees. Of all faculty members, 2% are Native American, 7% are African American, 91% are white.

Application Information *Required:* LSAT, LSDAS, application form, application fee of $50, baccalaureate degree, 2 letters of recommendation, college transcripts. *Recommended:* personal statement and resume. *Application deadline* for fall term is April 1.

Costs The 1997–98 tuition is $21,860 full-time; $956 per credit hour part-time. Fees: $500 full-time; $189 part-time.

Financial Aid In 1997–98, 70% of all students received some form of financial aid. Fellowships, graduate assistantships, loans, merit-based grants/scholarships, need-based grants/scholarships, and federal work-study loans are also available. The average student debt at graduation is $60,000. To apply for financial assistance, students must complete the Free Application for Federal Student

AT a GLANCE

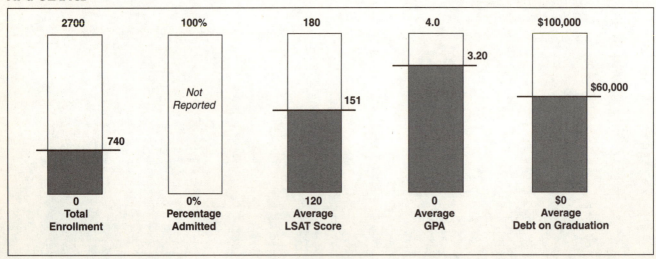

Degree Options

Degree	Total Credits Required	Length of Program
JD–Doctor of Laws	87	3–4 yrs, full-time or part-time [day]
JD/MA–Juris Doctor/Master of Arts–Economics, Education, Fine Arts/Art History, History, Political Science, International Relations		
JD/MBA–Juris Doctor/Master of Business Administration–Joint-degree Program		4 yrs, full-time only [day, summer]
JD/MFA–Juris Doctor/Master of Fine Arts–English/ Creative Writing		full-time only [day, summer]
JD/MLS–Juris Doctor/Master of Library Science	102	3 yrs, full-time only [day, summer]
JD/MPAd–Juris Doctor/Master of Public Administration	97	3.5 yrs, full-time only [day, summer]
JD/MS–Juris Doctor/Master of Science–Accounting		3–4 yrs, full-time only [day, summer]
JD/MS–Juris Doctor/Master of Science–Communications	102	3 yrs
JD/MS–Juris Doctor/Master of Science–Engineering and Computer Science, Environmental Science, Information Resources Management	102	3 yrs, full-time only [day, summer]
JD/MSW–Juris Doctor/Master of Social Work, JD/PhD–Juris Doctor/Doctor of Philosophy–History		full-time only [day, summer]

Aid, institutional forms, and income tax returns, W-2 forms. Financial aid contact: Melissa Ibanez, Associate Director of Financial Aid, Office of Admissions and Financial Aid, Suite 212, Syracuse, NY 13244-1030. Phone: 315-443-1963. Fax: 315-443-9568. Completed financial aid forms should be received by March 1.

Law School Library Barclay Law Library has 11 professional staff members and contains more than 368,251 volumes and 5,367 periodicals. 475 seats are available in the library. When classes are in session, the library is open 105 hours per week.

WESTLAW and LEXIS-NEXIS are available, as are the World Wide Web, online bibliographic services, and CD-ROM players. 91 computer workstations are available to students in the library. Special law collections include Human Rights, US Constitutional Law and its Legal History, Housing Law, Trial Practice Video Collection.

First-Year Program Class size in the average section is 90; 100% of the first-year courses are taught by full-time faculty.

Upper-Level Program Class size in the average section is 65. Among the electives are:

Administrative Law
★ Advocacy
★ Business and Corporate Law
Consumer Law
★ Criminal Law

Entertainment Law
Environmental Law
★ Family Law
Government/Regulation
★ Housing and Finance
Indian/Tribal Law
★ Intellectual Property
★ International/Comparative Law
Jurisprudence
Labor Law
Land Use Law/Natural Resources
★ Law and Economics
★ Law and Technology
★ Lawyering Skills
Legal History/Philosophy
★ Litigation
Media Law
Mediation
Probate Law
★ Public Interest
Securities
Tax Law

(★ indicates an area of special strength)

Clinical Courses Students receive degree credit for clinical courses. (Clinical practicum is not required.) Among the clinical areas offered are:

Criminal Defense
Family Practice
Housing and Finance
Public Interest

11% of the students participate in internship programs.

TOURO COLLEGE
JACOB D. FUCHSBERG LAW CENTER

New York, New York

LAW STUDENT PROFILE [1997–98]

TOTAL ENROLLMENT   776

APPLICANTS and ADMITTEES
Seats available: 230
Average LSAT score: 148
Average GPA: 3.0

Touro College Jacob D. Fuchsberg Law Center is a private institution that organizes classes on a semester calendar system. The campus is situated in a suburban setting. Founded in 1980, first ABA approved in 1983, and an AALS member, Touro College Jacob D. Fuchsberg Law Center offers JD, JD/MBA, JD/MPAd, JD/MS, LLM, and MPS degrees.

Faculty consists of 37 full-time and 14 part-time members in 1997–98. 100% of all faculty members have a JD; 35% have advanced law degrees. Of all faculty members, 7% are African American, 3% are Hispanic, 90% are white.

Application Information *Required:* LSAT, LSDAS, application form, application fee of $50, baccalaureate degree, personal statement, college transcripts. *Recommended:* resume. *Application deadline* for fall term is May 1.

Financial Aid Fellowships, loans, loan repayment assistance program (LRAP), merit-based grants/scholarships, need-based grants/scholarships, and federal work-study loans are available. The average student debt at graduation is $80,000. To apply for financial assistance, students must complete the Free Application for Federal Student Aid and institutional forms. Financial aid contact: Gail Drapala, Associate Director of Financial Aid, 300 Nassau Road, Huntington, NY 11743. Phone: 516-421-2244 Ext.

AT a GLANCE

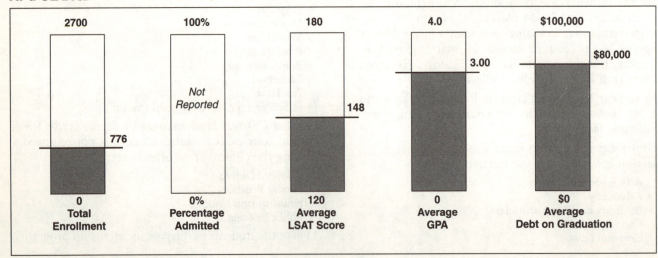

Degree Options

Degree	Total Credits Required	Length of Program
JD–Doctor of Laws	87	3–4 yrs, full-time or part-time [day, evening]
JD/MBA–Juris Doctor/Master of Business Administration–Dual-degree Program		4–5 yrs, full-time or part-time [day, evening]
JD/MPAd–Juris Doctor/Master of Public Administration–Health Law Dual-degree Program		4–5 yrs, full-time or part-time [day, evening]
JD/MS–Juris Doctor/Master of Science–Taxation Dual-degree Program		4–5 yrs, full-time or part-time [day, evening]
LLM–Master of Laws–American Legal Studies for Foreign Lawyers	27	1–1.5 yrs, full-time or part-time [day, evening]
MPS–Master of Professional Studies in Law	30	2–3 yrs, part-time only [day, evening]

322. Fax: 516-421-0271. E-mail: gaild@tourolaw.edu. Completed financial aid forms should be received by May 1.

Law School Library Touro College Jacob D. Fuchsberg Law Center Library has 7 professional staff members and contains more than 160,346 volumes and 2,025 periodicals. 395 seats are available in the library. When classes are in session, the library is open 86 hours per week.

WESTLAW and LEXIS-NEXIS are available, as are the World Wide Web, online bibliographic services, and CD-ROM players. 47 computer workstations are available to students in the library. Special law collections include Judiaca, the Scholar's Collection.

First-Year Program Class size in the average section is 55; 100% of the first-year courses are taught by full-time faculty.

Upper-Level Program Class size in the average section is 45. Among the electives are:

Administrative Law
Advocacy
Business and Corporate Law
Consumer Law
Education Law
Entertainment Law
Environmental Law
Family Law
Government/Regulation

Health Care/Human Services
Intellectual Property
★ **International/Comparative Law**
★ **Jurisprudence**
Labor Law
Land Use Law/Natural Resources
Lawyering Skills
Legal History/Philosophy
Litigation
Maritime Law
Mediation
Probate Law
★ **Public Interest**
Securities
Tax Law
(★ *indicates an area of special strength*)

Clinical Courses Students receive degree credit for clinical courses. (Clinical practicum is not required.) Among the clinical areas offered are:

Civil Litigation
Civil Rights
Criminal Defense
Criminal Prosecution
Elderly Advocacy
Family Practice
General Practice
Health
Immigration
Public Interest

Internships are available.

YESHIVA UNIVERSITY
BENJAMIN N. CARDOZO SCHOOL OF LAW

New York, New York

INFORMATION CONTACT
Paul Verkuil, Dean
55 Fifth Avenue
New York, NY 10003-4301

Phone: 212-790-0310   Fax: 212-790-0482
E-mail: robschwa@ymail.yu.edu
Web site: http://www.yu.edu/csl/law/

LAW STUDENT PROFILE [1997–98]

FULL-TIME   Enrollment: 916
Women: 47%   Men: 53%

RACIAL or ETHNIC COMPOSITION
African American, 6%; Asian/Pacific Islander, 8%; Hispanic, 5%; Nataive American, 0.3%; International, 3%

APPLICANTS and ADMITTEES
Number applied: 2,330
Admitted: 1,074
Percentage accepted: 46%
Seats available: 250
Median LSAT score: 157
Median GPA: 3.3

Yeshiva University Benjamin N. Cardozo School of Law is a private institution that organizes classes on a semester calendar system. The campus is situated in an urban setting. Founded in 1976, first ABA approved in 1978, and an AALS member, Yeshiva University Benjamin N. Cardozo School of Law offers JD and LLM degrees.

Faculty consists of 43 full-time and 89 part-time members in 1997–98. 13 full-time faculty members and 24 part-time faculty members are women. 98% of all faculty members have a JD; 13% have advanced law degrees. Of all faculty members, 7% are African American, 93% are white.

Application Information *Required:* LSAT, LSDAS, application form, application fee of $60, baccalaureate degree, 2 letters of recommendation, personal statement, essay, writing sample, college transcripts. *Recommended:* resume. *Application deadline* for fall term is April 1.

Costs The 1997–98 tuition is $21,760 full-time; $985 per credit part-time. Fees: $270.

Financial Aid In 1997–98, 59% of all students received some form of financial aid. 50 research assistantships were awarded. Loans, loan repayment assistance program (LRAP), merit-based grants/scholarships, need-based grants/scholarships, and

AT a GLANCE

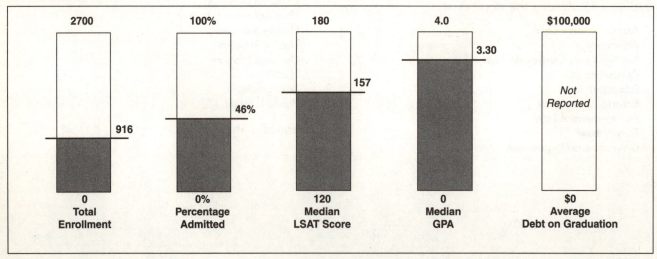

Degree Options

Degree	Total Credits Required	Length of Program
JD–Doctor of Laws	84	3 yrs, full-time only [day, summer]
LLM–Master of Laws–Intellectual Property Law	24	1 yr, full-time or part-time [day, evening]
LLM–Master of Laws	24	1 yr, full-time or part-time [day, evening]

federal work-study loans are also available. To apply for financial assistance, students must complete the Free Application for Federal Student Aid and Needs Access diskette. Financial aid contact: Tom Curtin, Assistant Director of Student Finance, 55 Fifth Avenue, New York, NY 10003. Phone: 212-790-0392. Fax: 212-790-0482. Completed financial aid forms should be received by April 15.

Law School Library Dr. Lillian and Dr. Rebecca Chutick Law Library has 7 professional staff members and contains more than 414,973 volumes and 1,640 periodicals. 500 seats are available in the library. When classes are in session, the library is open 88 hours per week.

WESTLAW and LEXIS-NEXIS are available, as are the World Wide Web, online bibliographic services, and CD-ROM players. 59 computer workstations are available to students in the library. Special law collections include Israeli and Jewish Law, Arts and Entertainment Law.

First-Year Program Class size in the average section is 75; 83% of the first-year courses are taught by full-time faculty.

Upper-Level Program Class size in the average section is 45. Among the electives are:

Administrative Law
★ Advocacy
★ Business and Corporate Law
Consumer Law
★ Criminal Law
Education Law
★ Entertainment Law
Environmental Law
★ Family Law

Government/Regulation
Health Care/Human Services
Indian/Tribal Law
★ Intellectual Property
★ International/Comparative Law
★ Jewish Law
★ Jurisprudence
Labor Law
Land Use Law/Natural Resources
★ Lawyering Skills
Legal History/Philosophy
★ Litigation
Maritime Law
★ Media Law
Mediation
Probate Law
★ Public Interest
Securities
Tax Law
(★ indicates an area of special strength)

Clinical Courses Students receive degree credit for clinical courses. (Clinical practicum is not required.) Among the clinical areas offered are:

Civil Litigation
Criminal Defense
Criminal Prosecution
Elderly Advocacy
Family Practice
Immigration
Intellectual Property
International Law
Mediation
Tax Law

Internships are available. International exchange programs permit students to visit Hungary and Israel.

CAMPBELL UNIVERSITY
NORMAN ADRIAN WIGGINS SCHOOL OF LAW

Buies Creek, North Carolina

INFORMATION CONTACT
Patrick K. Hetrick, Dean
PO Box 158
Buies Creek, NC 27506

Phone: 910-893-1750   Fax: 910-893-1780
E-mail: lanier@webster.campbell.edu
Web site: http://www.campbell.edu/

LAW STUDENT PROFILE [1997–98]

FULL-TIME   Enrollment: 333
Women: 46%   Men: 54%

RACIAL or ETHNIC COMPOSITION
African American, 3%; Asian/Pacific Islander, 2%; Hispanic, 1%; Native American, 1%; International, 0%

APPLICANTS and ADMITTEES
Number applied: 600
Admitted: 197
Percentage accepted: 33%
Seats available: 110
Average LSAT score: 156
Average GPA: 3.2

Campbell University Norman Adrian Wiggins School of Law is a private institution that organizes classes on a semester calendar system. The campus is situated in a rural setting. Founded in 1976, first ABA approved in 1979, Campbell University Norman Adrian Wiggins School of Law offers a JD degree.

Faculty consists of 17 full-time and 23 part-time members in 1997–98. 1 full-time faculty members and 6 part-time faculty members are women. 100% of all faculty members have a JD degree.

Application Information *Required:* LSAT, LSDAS, application form, application fee of $40, 2 letters of recommendation, personal statement, interview. *Recommended:* resume. *Application deadline* for fall term is March 31.

Costs The 1997–98 tuition is $16,500. Fees: $233.

Financial Aid 47 research assistantships, 6 teaching assistantships were awarded. 112 other awards were given. Loans and merit-based grants/scholarships are also available. The average student debt at graduation is $63,500. To apply for financial assistance, students must complete the Free Application for Federal Student Aid. Financial aid contact: Mrs. Peggy Mason, Director of Financial Aid, PO Box 158, Buies Creek, NC 27506. Phone: 910-893-1310.

AT a GLANCE

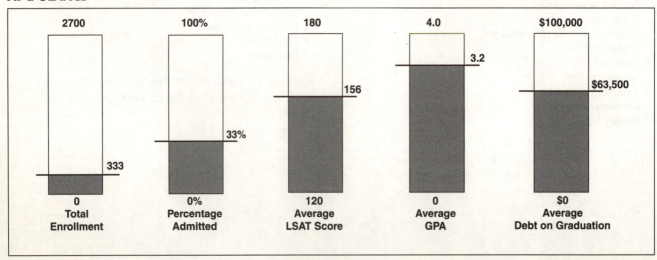

Degree Options

Degree	Total Credits Required	Length of Program
JD–Doctor of Laws	90	3 yrs, full-time only

Fax: 910-893-1780. Completed financial aid forms should be received by April 15.

Law School Library has 5 professional staff members and contains more than 162,450 volumes and 2,336 periodicals. 412 seats are available in the library. When classes are in session, the library is open 106 hours per week.

WESTLAW and LEXIS-NEXIS are available.

First-Year Program Class size in the average section is 110; 100% of the first-year courses are taught by full-time faculty.

Upper-Level Program Class size in the average section is 110. Among the electives are:

Administrative Law
Advocacy
Business and Corporate Law
Education
Environmental Law
Family Law
Health Care/Human Services
Intellectual Property
International/Comparative Law
Jurisprudence
Labor Law
Land Use Law/Natural Resources
Lawyering Skills
Legal History/Philosophy
Litigation
Maritime Law
Media Law
Securities
Tax Law

DUKE UNIVERSITY
SCHOOL OF LAW

Durham, North Carolina

LAW STUDENT PROFILE [1997–98]

FULL-TIME   Enrollment: 672
Women: 40%   Men: 60%

RACIAL or ETHNIC COMPOSITION
African American, 8%; Asian/Pacific Islander, 4%; Hispanic,
2%; Nataive American, 0.1%; International, 3%

APPLICANTS and ADMITTEES
Seats available: 200
Median LSAT score: 166
Median GPA: 3.6

Duke University School of Law is a private
institution that organizes classes on a semester
calendar system. The campus is situated in a
suburban setting. Founded in 1924, first ABA
approved in 1931, and an AALS member, Duke
University School of Law offers JD, JD/LLM,
JD/MA, JD/MBA, JD/MD, JD/MEM, JD/MPPo,
JD/MS, JD/MTS, and JD/PhD degrees.

Faculty consists of 35 full-time and 34 part-time
members in 1997–98. 10 full-time faculty members
and 15 part-time faculty members are women.

Application Information *Required:* LSAT, LSDAS,
application form, application fee of $65, baccalaure-
ate degree, 2 letters of recommendation, personal
statement, resume. *Recommended:* essay. *Application
deadline* for fall term is February 1. Students are
required to have their own computers.

Financial Aid In 1997–98, 68% of all students
received some form of financial aid. 353 other
awards were given. Loans, loan repayment assistance
program (LRAP), merit-based grants/scholarships,
need-based grants/scholarships, and federal work-
study loans are also available. The average student
debt at graduation is $44,745. To apply for financial
assistance, students must complete the Free Application for Federal Student Aid and institutional forms.
Financial aid contact: Kochie Richardson, Assistant

AT a GLANCE

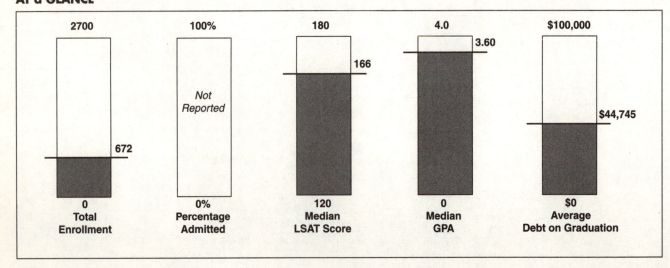

Degree Options

Degree	Total Credits Required	Length of Program
JD–Doctor of Laws	84	3 yrs, full-time only [day]
JD/LLM–Juris Doctor/Master of Laws–International and Comparative Law	104	3 yrs, full-time only [day]
JD/MA–Juris Doctor/Master of Arts–Cultural Anthropology, Economics, English, Forestry's Environmental Studies, History, Humanities, Philosophy, Political Science, Psychology, Public Policy Studies, Romance Studies		3 yrs, full-time only [day]
JD/MBA–Juris Doctor/Master of Business Administration		4 yrs, full-time only [day]
JD/MD–Juris Doctor/Doctor of Medicine		6 yrs, full-time only [day]
JD/MEM–Juris Doctor/Master of Environmental Management		4 yrs, full-time only [day]
JD/MPPo–Juris Doctor/Master of Public Policy		4 yrs, full-time only [day]
JD/MS–Juris Doctor/Master of Science–Mechanical Engineering		3 yrs, full-time only [day]
JD/MTS–Juris Doctor/Master of Theological Studies		4 yrs, full-time only [day]
JD/PhD–Juris Doctor/Doctor of Philosophy–English, Political Science, Literature, and others		7 yrs, full-time only [day]

Director of Financial Aid, Box 90363, Durham, NC 27708. Phone: 919-613-7026. Fax: 919-613-7231. E-mail: krichardson@law.duke.edu. Completed financial aid forms should be received by March 15.

Law School Library Duke Law School Library has 9 professional staff members and contains more than 509,776 volumes and 7,090 periodicals. 451 seats are available in the library. When classes are in session, the library is open 168 hours per week.

WESTLAW and LEXIS-NEXIS are available, as are the World Wide Web, online bibliographic services, and CD-ROM players. 347 computer workstations are available to students in the library. Special law collections include Christie Collection in Jurisprudence, Riddick Collection on Parliamentary Procedure, Cox Collection in Legal Fiction.

First-Year Program Class size in the average section is 85; 75% of the first-year courses are taught by full-time faculty.

Upper-Level Program Class size in the average section is 75. Among the electives are:

Administrative Law
Advocacy
Business and Corporate Law
Education Law
Entertainment Law
Environmental Law

Family Law
Government/Regulation
Health Care/Human Services
Intellectual Property
International/Comparative Law
Jurisprudence
Labor Law
Land Use Law/Natural Resources
Lawyering Skills
Legal History/Philosophy
Litigation
Maritime Law
Media Law
Mediation
Probate Law
Public Interest
Securities
Tax Law

Clinical Courses Students receive degree credit for clinical courses. (Clinical practicum is not required.) Among the clinical areas offered are:

AIDS and the Law
Capital Punishment
Civil Litigation
Criminal Defense
Criminal Prosecution
International Development
Public Interest

20% of the students participate in internship programs. International exchange programs available.

NORTH CAROLINA CENTRAL UNIVERSITY
SCHOOL OF LAW

Durham, North Carolina

INFORMATION CONTACT

Percy Luney, Dean
1512 South Alston Avenue
Durham, NC 27707

Phone: 919-560-6427   Fax: 919-560-6339
Web site: http://www.nccu.edu/

LAW STUDENT PROFILE [1997–98]

FULL-TIME   Enrollment: 379
Women: 55%   Men: 45%

PART-TIME   Enrollment: 3
Women: 33%   Men: 67%

RACIAL or ETHNIC COMPOSITION
African American, 48%; Asian/Pacific Islander, 1%; Hispanic,
1%; Native American, 2%

APPLICANTS and ADMITTEES
Number applied: 1,071
Admitted: 261
Percentage accepted: 24%
Seats available: 125
Average LSAT score: 151
Average GPA: 3.0

North Carolina Central University School of Law is a public institution that organizes classes on a semester calendar system. The campus is situated in an urban setting. Founded in 1939, first ABA approved in 1950, North Carolina Central University School of Law offers JD, JD/MBA, and JD/MLS degrees.

Faculty consists of 17 full-time and 10 part-time members in 1997–98. 9 full-time faculty members and 6 part-time faculty members are women. 100% of all faculty members have a JD; 14.28% have advanced law degrees. Of all faculty members, 47.62% are African American, 52.38% are white.

Application Information *Required:* LSAT, LSDAS, application form, application fee of $30, baccalaureate degree, 2 letters of recommendation, personal statement, college transcripts. *Recommended:* resume. *Application deadline* for fall term is April 15.

Costs The 1997–98 tuition is $2071 for state residents. Tuition is $10,997 for nonresidents.

Financial Aid Fellowships, loans, merit-based grants/scholarships, need-based grants/scholarships, and federal work-study loans are available. The average student debt at graduation is $25,500. To apply for financial assistance, students must complete the Free Application for Federal Student

AT a GLANCE

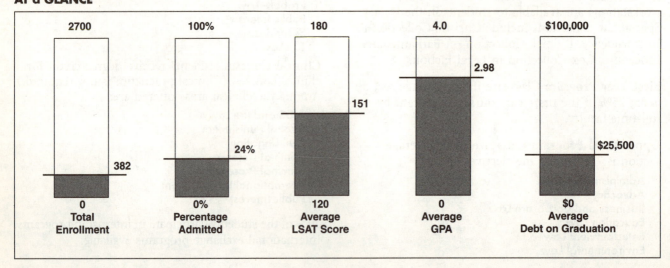

2700	100%	180	4.0	$100,000
			2.98	
		151		
	24%			$25,500
382				
0	0%	120	0	$0
Total Enrollment	Percentage Admitted	Average LSAT Score	Average GPA	Average Debt on Graduation

Degree Options

Degree	Total Credits Required	Length of Program
JD–Juris Doctor	88	3–4 yrs, full-time or part-time [day, evening, summer]
JD/MBA–Juris Doctor/Master of Business Administration–Dual-degree Program	121	4–5 yrs, full-time or part-time [day, evening, summer]
JD/MLS–Juris Doctor/Master of Library Science–Dual-degree Program	112	3–4 yrs, full-time or part-time

Aid, institutional forms, and scholarship specific applications. Financial aid contact: Ronald Steven Douglas, Assistant Dean, Day Program, 1512 South Alston Avenue, Durham, NC 27707. Phone: 919-560-6333. Fax: 919-560-6339. Completed financial aid forms should be received by May 1.

Law School Library North Carolina Central University School of Law Library has 6 professional staff members and contains more than 284,115 volumes and 3,075 periodicals. 334 seats are available in the library. When classes are in session, the library is open 97 hours per week.

WESTLAW and LEXIS-NEXIS are available, as are the World Wide Web, online bibliographic services, and CD-ROM players. 46 computer workstations are available to students in the library. Special law collections include The McKissick Collection (Civil Rights).

First-Year Program Class size in the average section is 56; 100% of the first-year courses are taught by full-time faculty.

Upper-Level Program Class size in the average section is 30. Among the electives are:

Administrative Law

Advocacy
Business and Corporate Law
Consumer Law
Education Law
Entertainment Law
Environmental Law
Family Law
Health Care/Human Services
Intellectual Property
International/Comparative Law
Labor Law
Litigation
Mediation
Probate Law
Public Interest
Tax Law

Clinical Courses Students receive degree credit for clinical courses. (Clinical practicum is not required.) Among the clinical areas offered are:

Child Protection Center
Civil Litigation
Criminal Defense
Land Rights/Natural Resource

THE UNIVERSITY OF NORTH CAROLINA AT CHAPEL HILL
SCHOOL OF LAW

Chapel Hill, North Carolina

INFORMATION CONTACT

Judith W. Wegner, Dean
Campus Box 3380
Van Hecke-Wettach Hall
Chapel Hill, NC 27599-3380

Phone: 919-962-4417   Fax: 919-962-1170
E-mail: law_admission@unc.edu
Web site: http://www.law.unc.edu/

LAW STUDENT PROFILE [1997–98]

FULL-TIME   Enrollment: 687
Women: 49%   Men: 51%

RACIAL or ETHNIC COMPOSITION
African American, 13%; Asian/Pacific Islander, 4%; Hispanic, 2%; Native American, 1%; International, 1%

APPLICANTS and ADMITTEES
Number applied: 1,720
Admitted: 582
Percentage accepted: 34%
Seats available: 235
Average LSAT score: 160
Average GPA: 3.5

The **University of North Carolina at Chapel Hill School of Law** is a public institution that organizes classes on a semester calendar system. The campus is situated in a small-town setting. Founded in 1843, first ABA approved in 1925, and an AALS member, The University of North Carolina at Chapel Hill School of Law offers JD, JD/MBA, JD/MCRP, JD/MPAd, JD/MPH, and JD/MSW degrees.

Faculty consists of 44 full-time and 35 part-time members in 1997–98. 17 full-time faculty members and 12 part-time faculty members are women. 100% of all faculty members have a JD degree. Of all faculty members, 6.8% are African American, 1% are Hispanic, 92.2% are white.

Application Information *Required:* LSAT, LSDAS, application form, application fee of $60, baccalaureate degree, 2 letters of recommendation, personal statement, essay, college transcripts, resume. *Application deadline* for fall term is February 1.

Costs The 1997–98 tuition is $1428 full-time for state residents; $357 per semester (minimum) part-time for state residents. Tuition is $13,290 full-time for nonresidents; $3323 per semester (minimum) part-time for nonresidents. Fees: $1453 full-time; $668 per semester (minimum) part-time.

AT a GLANCE

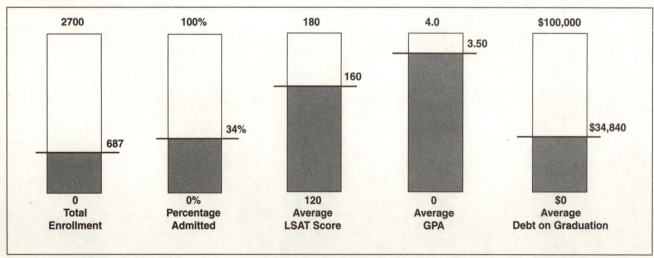

Degree Options

Degree	Total Credits Required	Length of Program
JD–Juris Doctor	86	3 yrs, full-time only [day, summer]
JD/MBA–Juris Doctor/Master of Business Administration	123	4 yrs, full-time only [day, summer]
JD/MCRP–Juris Doctor/Master of Community and Regional Planning	110	4 yrs, full-time only [day]
JD/MPAd–Juris Doctor/Master of Public Administration	128	4 yrs, full-time only [day, summer]
JD/MPH–Juris Doctor/Master of Public Health	116	4 yrs, full-time only
JD/MSW–Juris Doctor/Master of Social Work	124	4 yrs, full-time only [day, summer]

Financial Aid Fellowships, graduate assistantships, loans, loan repayment assistance program (LRAP), merit-based grants/scholarships, need-based grants/scholarships, and federal work-study loans are available. The average student debt at graduation is $34,840. To apply for financial assistance, students must complete the Free Application for Federal Student Aid. Financial aid contact: Bill Cox, Assistant Director, University of North Carolina Student Aid Office, CB#2300 Vance Hall, Chapel Hill, NC 27599-2300. Phone: 919-962-4163. Fax: 919-962-1170. Completed financial aid forms should be received by March 1.

Law School Library Kathrine R. Everett Law Library has 9 professional staff members and contains more than 447,320 volumes and 5,946 periodicals. 407 seats are available in the library. When classes are in session, the library is open 84 hours per week.

WESTLAW and LEXIS-NEXIS are available, as are the World Wide Web, online bibliographic services, and CD-ROM players. 48 computer workstations are available to students in the library.

First-Year Program Class size in the average section is 75; 95% of the first-year courses are taught by full-time faculty.

Upper-Level Program Class size in the average section is 75. Among the electives are:

Administrative Law
Advocacy
★ Business and Corporate Law
Consumer Law
Education Law
Environmental Law
Family Law
Government/Regulation
★ Health Care/Human Services
Intellectual Property
★ International/Comparative Law
Jurisprudence
Labor Law
★ Land Use Law/Natural Resources
Lawyering Skills
Legal History/Philosophy
Litigation
Mediation
Probate Law
★ Public Interest
Securities
Tax Law
(★ indicates an area of special strength)

Clinical Courses Students receive degree credit for clinical courses. (Clinical practicum is not required.) Among the clinical areas offered are:

Civil Litigation
Criminal Defense
General Practice
Juvenile Law
Public Interest

International exchange programs permit students to visit France; Mexico; Netherlands; and United Kingdom.

WAKE FOREST UNIVERSITY
SCHOOL OF LAW

Winston-Salem, North Carolina

INFORMATION CONTACT
Robert K. Walsh, Dean
PO Box 7206, Reynolda Station
Winston-Salem, NC 27109

Phone: 336-759-5434   Fax: 336-758-4632
E-mail: admissions@law.wfu.edu
Web site: http://www.law.wfu.edu/

LAW STUDENT PROFILE [1997–98]

FULL-TIME   Enrollment: 460
Women: 39%   Men: 61%

RACIAL or ETHNIC COMPOSITION
African American, 7%; Asian/Pacific Islander, 1%; Hispanic,
0.4% Nataive American, 0.4%; International, 0%

APPLICANTS and ADMITTEES
Number applied: 1,218
Admitted: 508
Percentage accepted: 42%
Seats available: 160
Average LSAT score: 160
Average GPA: 3.3

Wake Forest University School of Law is a private institution that organizes classes on a semester calendar system. The campus is situated in an urban setting. Founded in 1894, first ABA approved in 1937, and an AALS member, Wake Forest University School of Law offers JD, JD/MBA, and LLM degrees.

Faculty consists of 28 full-time and 38 part-time members in 1997–98. 100% of all faculty members have a JD degree.

Application Information *Required:* LSAT, LSDAS, application form, application fee of $60, baccalaureate degree, 1 recommendation, personal statement, essay, writing sample, college transcripts. *Recommended:* resume. *Application deadline* for fall term is March 15.

Costs The 1997–98 tuition is $20,450.

Financial Aid Merit-based grants/scholarships, need-based grants/scholarships, and federal work-study loans are available. The average student debt at graduation is $60,000. To apply for financial assistance, students must complete the Free Application for Federal Student Aid. Financial aid contact: Melanie E. Nutt, Director of Admissions and Financial Aid, PO Box 7206, Reynolda Station, Winston-Salem, NC 27109. Phone: 336-758-5437. Fax: 336-758-4632. E-mail: admissions@law.wfu.edu.

AT a GLANCE

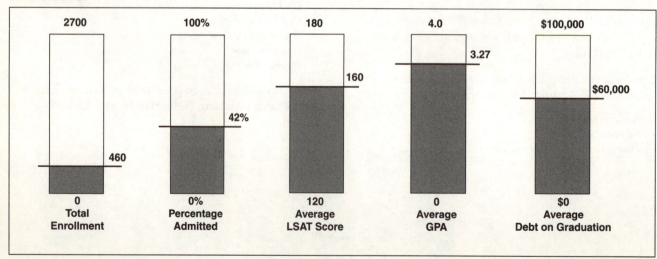

Degree Options

Degree	Total Credits Required	Length of Program
JD–Doctor of Laws	89	3–4 yrs, full-time only [day]
JD/MBA–Juris Doctor/Master of Business Administration–Dual-degree Program	110	4–5 yrs, full-time only [day]
LLM–Master of Laws–American Law	24	1 yr, full-time only [day]

Completed financial aid forms should be received by April 30.

Law School Library Worrell Professional Center for Law and Management has 6 professional staff members and contains more than 308,131 volumes and 5,140 periodicals. 552 seats are available in the library. When classes are in session, the library is open 109 hours per week.

WESTLAW and LEXIS-NEXIS are available, as are the World Wide Web, online bibliographic services, and CD-ROM players. 104 computer workstations are available to students in the library. Special law collections include Trial Practice, North Carolina Legal Publications.

First-Year Program Class size in the average section is 40; 100% of the first-year courses are taught by full-time faculty.

Upper-Level Program Among the electives are:

    Administrative Law
★ Advocacy
★ Business and Corporate Law
    Constitutional Law
    Consumer Law
    Family Law
    Government/Regulation
    Health Care/Human Services

    Intellectual Property
    International/Comparative Law
    Jurisprudence
    Labor Law
    Land Use Law/Natural Resources
    Lawyering Skills
    Legal History/Philosophy
★ Litigation
    Maritime Law
    Media Law
    Mediation
    Probate Law
    Securities
★ Tax Law
(★ indicates an area of special strength)

Clinical Courses Students receive degree credit for clinical courses. (Clinical practicum is not required.) Among the clinical areas offered are:

    Civil Litigation
    Criminal Defense
    Criminal Prosecution
    Elderly Advocacy
    General Practice
    Intellectual Property

55% of the students participate in internship programs. International exchange programs permit students to visit Italy and United Kingdom.

UNIVERSITY OF NORTH DAKOTA
SCHOOL OF LAW

Grand Forks, North Dakota

LAW STUDENT PROFILE [1997–98]

FULL-TIME   Enrollment: 192
Women: 39%   Men: 61%

RACIAL or ETHNIC COMPOSITION
African American, 1%; Asian/Pacific Islander, 1%; Hispanic,
1%; Native American, 3%; International, 4%

APPLICANTS and ADMITTEES
Number applied: 263
Admitted: 157
Percentage accepted: 60%
Seats available: 65
Median LSAT score: 152
Average GPA: 3.1

University of North Dakota School of Law is a
public institution that organizes classes on a
semester calendar system. The campus is situated in
an urban setting. Founded in 1899, first ABA
approved in 1923, and an AALS member, University
of North Dakota School of Law offers a JD degree.

Faculty consists of 14 full-time and 9 part-time
members in 1997–98. 5 full-time faculty members
and 3 part-time faculty members are women.

Application Information *Required:* LSAT, LSDAS,
application form, application fee of $35, baccalaure-
ate degree, recommendations. *Application deadline*
for fall term is April 1.

Costs The 1997–98 tuition is $3250 for state
residents. Tuition is $7896 for nonresidents.

Financial Aid Fellowships, loans, merit-based
grants/scholarships, need-based grants/scholarships,
and federal work-study loans are available. To apply
for financial assistance, students must complete the
Free Application for Federal Student Aid. Financial
aid contact: University of North Dakota Law School,
Financial Aid Office, PO Box 8371, Grand Forks,
ND 58202-8371. Phone: 701-777-3121.

Law School Library Thormodsgard Law Library has
2 professional staff members and contains more

AT a GLANCE

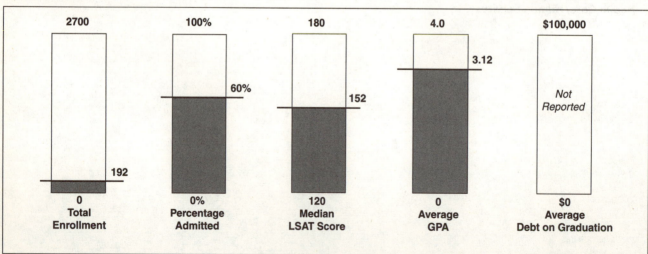

Degree Options

Degree	Total Credits Required	Length of Program
JD–Juris Doctor	90	full-time only

than 251,320 volumes and 2,710 periodicals. 279 seats are available in the library. When classes are in session, the library is open 106 hours per week.

WESTLAW and LEXIS-NEXIS are available, as is the World Wide Web. 17 computer workstations are available to students in the library.

First-Year Program Class size in the average section is 72.

Upper-Level Program Among the electives are:

Accounting
Administrative Law
Advocacy
Agricultural Law
Banking and Financial Aid
Business and Corporate Law
Commercial Law
Criminal Procedure
Environmental Law
Evidence
Family Law
Government/Regulation
Indian/Tribal Law
Insurance

Intellectual Property
International/Comparative Law
Labor Law
Land Use Law/Natural Resources
Lawyering Skills
Legal History/Philosophy
Legislation
Litigation
Probate Law
Tax Law
Trusts and Estates
Water Law

Clinical Courses Students receive degree credit for clinical courses. Among the clinical areas offered are:

Civil Litigation
Criminal Defense
Family Practice
General Practice
Indian/Tribal Law
Juvenile Law

Internships are available. International exchange programs permit students to visit Norway.

CAPITAL UNIVERSITY
LAW SCHOOL

Columbus, Ohio

INFORMATION CONTACT
Steven C. Bahls, Dean
303 East Broad Street
Columbus, OH 43215-3200

Phone: 614-236-6500   Fax: 614-236-6972
E-mail: law-admissions@capital.edu
Web site: http://www.law.cardinal.edu/

LAW STUDENT PROFILE [1997–98]

FULL-TIME   Enrollment: 458
Women: 47%   Men: 53%

PART-TIME   Enrollment: 369
Women: 42%   Men: 58%

RACIAL or ETHNIC COMPOSITION
African American, 7%; Asian/Pacific Islander, 1%; Hispanic, 2%; Nataive American, 0.2%; International, 1%

APPLICANTS and ADMITTEES
Number applied: 857
Admitted: 600
Percentage accepted: 70%
Seats available: 289
Average LSAT score: 150
Average GPA: 3.0

Capital University Law School is a private institution that organizes classes on a semester calendar system. The campus is situated in an urban setting. Founded in 1903, first ABA approved in 1950, and an AALS member, Capital University Law School offers JD, JD/LLM, JD/MBA, JD/MSA, JD/MSN, and LLM degrees.

Faculty consists of 30 full-time and 36 part-time members in 1997–98. 9 full-time faculty members and 5 part-time faculty members are women. 100% of all faculty members have a JD; 35.5% have advanced law degrees. Of all faculty members, 12.9% are African American, 87.1% are white.

Application Information *Required:* LSAT, LSDAS, application form, application fee of $35, baccalaureate degree, 2 letters of recommendation, personal statement, college transcripts. *Recommended:* essay. *Application deadline* for fall term is May 1.

Costs The 1997–98 tuition is $530 per credit hour. Fees: $200.

Financial Aid In 1997–98, 81% of all students received some form of financial aid. Graduate assistantships, loans, merit-based grants/scholarships, need-based grants/scholarships, and federal work-study loans are also available. The average student debt at graduation is $44,000. To apply for financial

AT a GLANCE

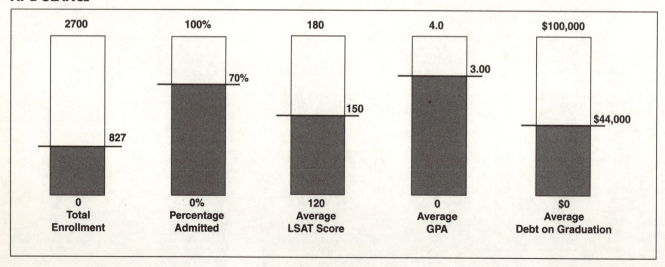

Degree Options

Degree	Total Credits Required	Length of Program
JD–Doctor of Laws	86	full-time or part-time [day, evening, summer]
JD/LLM–Juris Doctor/Master of Laws	98	3.5–4.5 yrs, full-time or part-time [day, evening, summer]
JD/MBA–Juris Doctor/Master of Business Administration	118	4–5 yrs, full-time or part-time [day, evening, summer]
JD/MSA–Juris Doctor/Master of Sports Administration		3.5–4.5 yrs, full-time or part-time [day, evening, summer]
JD/MSN–Juris Doctor/Master of Science in Nursing	101	4–5 yrs, full-time or part-time [day, evening, summer]
LLM–Master of Laws–Business and Taxation	24	1–2 yrs, full-time or part-time [day, evening, summer]

assistance, students must complete the Free Application for Federal Student Aid and institutional forms. Financial aid contact: Samantha Stalnaker, Assistant Director of Admissions and Financial Aid, 303 East Broad Street, Columbus, OH 43215-3200. Phone: 614-236-6350. Fax: 614-236-6972. E-mail: b.burk@law.capital.edu. Completed financial aid forms should be received by April 1.

Law School Library Capital University Law School Library has 5 professional staff members and contains more than 242,663 volumes and 1,306 periodicals. 480 seats are available in the library. When classes are in session, the library is open 93 hours per week.

WESTLAW and LEXIS-NEXIS are available, as are the World Wide Web, online bibliographic services, and CD-ROM players. 30 computer workstations are available to students in the library.

First-Year Program Class size in the average section is 85; 100% of the first-year courses are taught by full-time faculty.

Upper-Level Program Class size in the average section is 60. Among the electives are:

Administrative Law
Advocacy
★ Business and Corporate Law
Corporate Finance
★ Dispute Resolution

Environmental Law
Family Law
Government/Regulation
Health Care/Human Services
Indian/Tribal Law
Intellectual Property
International/Comparative Law
Jurisprudence
★ Labor Law
Land Use Law/Natural Resources
Lawyering Skills
Legal History/Philosophy
Litigation
★ Local Government
Media Law
★ Mediation
Probate Law
Securities
★ Tax Law
(★ indicates an area of special strength)

Clinical Courses Students receive degree credit for clinical courses. (Clinical practicum is not required.) Among the clinical areas offered are:

Civil Litigation
Criminal Defense
Mediation

20% of the students participate in internship programs. International exchange programs permit students to visit Canada; Germany; and United Kingdom.

CASE WESTERN RESERVE UNIVERSITY
SCHOOL OF LAW

Cleveland, Ohio

INFORMATION CONTACT
Gerald Korngold, Dean
11075 East Boulevard
Cleveland, OH 44106

Phone: 216-368-3283   Fax: 216-368-6144
E-mail: lawadmissions@po.cwru.edu
Web site: http://lawwww.cwru.edu/

LAW STUDENT PROFILE [1997–98]

FULL-TIME   Enrollment: 634
Women: 44%   Men: 56%

PART-TIME   Enrollment: 15
Women: 53%   Men: 47%

RACIAL or ETHNIC COMPOSITION
African American, 8%; Asian/Pacific Islander, 6%; Hispanic, 1%; Nataive American, 0.3%

APPLICANTS and ADMITTEES
Number applied: 1,292
Admitted: 825
Percentage accepted: 64%
Seats available: 201
Median LSAT score: 156
Median GPA: 3.3

Case Western Reserve University School of Law is a private institution that organizes classes on a semester calendar system. The campus is situated in an urban setting. Founded in 1892, first ABA approved in 1923, and an AALS member, Case Western Reserve University School of Law offers JD, JD/MA, JD/MBA, JD/MD, JD/MNO, JD/MSW, and LLM degrees.

Faculty consists of 41 full-time and 59 part-time members in 1997–98. 10 full-time faculty members and 13 part-time faculty members are women. 100% of all faculty members have a JD degree.

Application Information *Required:* LSAT, LSDAS, application form, application fee of $40, baccalaureate degree, personal statement, resume. *Recommended:* 3 letters of recommendation. *Application deadline* for fall term is April 1.

Costs The 1997–98 tuition is $20,500 full-time; $854 per credit hour part-time. Fees: $600.

Financial Aid In 1997–98, 86% of all students received some form of financial aid. 255 other awards were given. Graduate assistantships, loans, loan repayment assistance program (LRAP), merit-based grants/scholarships, and federal work-study loans are also available. The average student debt at graduation is $47,900. To apply for

AT a GLANCE

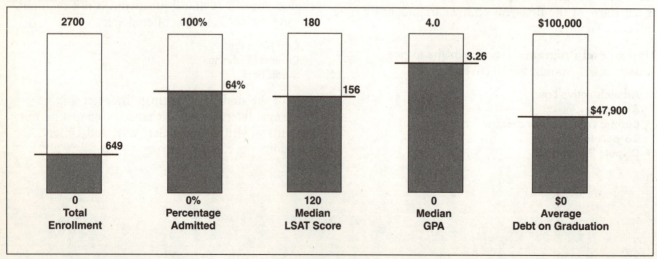

Degree Options

Degree	Total Credits Required	Length of Program
JD–Doctor of Laws	88	3 yrs, full-time only [day]
JD/MA–Juris Doctor/Master of Arts–Juris Doctor/ Master of Arts - Legal History		3–4 yrs, full-time only [day]
JD/MA–Juris Doctor/Master of Arts–Bioethics		full-time only [day]
JD/MBA–Juris Doctor/Master of Business Administration–Juris Doctor/Master of Business Administration - Management		4 yrs, full-time only [day]
JD/MD–Juris Doctor/Doctor of Medicine–Juris Doctor/ Medicine		6 yrs, full-time only [day, summer]
JD/MNO–Juris Doctor/Master of Nonprofit Organizations		
JD/MSW–Juris Doctor/Master of Social Work–Juris Doctor/Master of Social Services - Social Work		4 yrs, full-time only [day]
LLM–Master of Laws–US Legal Studies	24	1 yr, full-time only [day]
LLM–Master of Laws–Taxation		full-time or part-time [day, evening]

financial assistance, students must complete the Free Application for Federal Student Aid and institutional forms. Financial aid contact: Jay Ruffner, Student Finances Coordinator, 11075 East Boulevard, Cleveland, OH 44106. Phone: 877-889-4279 or toll-free 800-756-0036. Fax: 216-368-6144. E-mail: lawmoney@po.cwru.edu. Completed financial aid forms should be received by March 15.

Law School Library has 9 professional staff members and contains more than 351,576 volumes and 4,679 periodicals. 446 seats are available in the library. When classes are in session, the library is open 108 hours per week.

WESTLAW and LEXIS-NEXIS are available, as are the World Wide Web and CD-ROM players. Special law collections include British Collection, taxation, labor law, foreign investments, law-medicine, international law.

First-Year Program Class size in the average section is 72; 100% of the first-year courses are taught by full-time faculty.

Upper-Level Program Among the electives are:

Administrative Law
Advocacy
★ Business and Corporate Law
Consumer Law
Environmental Law
Family Law
Government/Regulation
★ Health
Health Care/Human Services
Intellectual Property
★ International/Comparative Law
Jurisprudence
Labor Law
Land Use Law/Natural Resources
★ Lawyering Skills
Legal History/Philosophy
★ Litigation
Media Law
Mediation
Probate Law
Public Interest
★ Securities
★ Tax Law
(★ indicates an area of special strength)

Clinical Courses Students receive degree credit for clinical courses. (Clinical practicum is not required.) Among the clinical areas offered are:

Civil Litigation
Criminal Defense
Criminal Prosecution
Family Practice
General Practice
Government Litigation
Health
Juvenile Law
Mediation

10% of the students participate in internship programs. International exchange programs permit students to visit Canada and Mexico.

CLEVELAND STATE UNIVERSITY
CLEVELAND-MARSHALL COLLEGE OF LAW

Cleveland, Ohio

INFORMATION CONTACT

Mr. Steven S. Steinglass, Dean
1801 Euclid Avenue
Cleveland, OH 44115

Phone: 216-687-2344   Fax: 216-687-6881
Web site: http://www.law.csuohio.edu/

LAW STUDENT PROFILE [1997–98]

FULL-TIME   Enrollment: 585
Women: 45%   Men: 55%

PART-TIME   Enrollment: 321
Women: 47%   Men: 53%

RACIAL or ETHNIC COMPOSITION
African American, 8%; Asian/Pacific Islander, 3%; Hispanic, 1%; Nataive American, 0.3%; International, 0%

APPLICANTS and ADMITTEES
Number applied: 1,330
Admitted: 765
Percentage accepted: 58%
Seats available: 288
Average LSAT score: 151
Average GPA: 3.1

Cleveland State University Cleveland-Marshall College of Law is a public institution that organizes classes on a semester calendar system. The campus is situated in an urban setting. Founded in 1897, first ABA approved in 1957, and an AALS member, Cleveland State University Cleveland-Marshall College of Law offers JD, JD/MBA, JD/MPAd, and JD/MUP degrees.

Faculty consists of 41 full-time members in 1997–98. 13 full-time faculty members are women. 98.6% of all faculty members have a JD; 14% have advanced law degrees. Of all faculty members, 1.3% are Asian/Pacific Islander, 6.8% are African American, 91.9% are white.

Application Information *Required:* LSAT, LSDAS, application form, application fee of $35, baccalaureate degree, 2 letters of recommendation, personal statement, writing sample, college transcripts. *Recommended:* resume. *Application deadline* for fall term is March 1.

Costs The 1997–98 tuition is $7391 full-time for state residents; $5685 part-time for state residents. Tuition is $14,782 full-time for nonresidents; $11,370 part-time for nonresidents. Fees: $61 full-time for state residents; $47 part-time for state residents. $122 full-time for nonresidents; $94 part-time for nonresidents.

AT a GLANCE

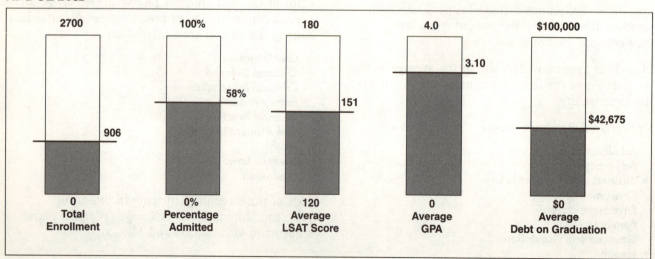

Degree Options

Degree	Total Credits Required	Length of Program
JD–Doctor of Laws	87	3–4 yrs, full-time or part-time [day, evening, summer]
JD/MBA–Juris Doctor/Master of Business Administration–Dual-degree Program	100	4–6 yrs, full-time or part-time [day, evening, summer]
JD/MPAd–Juris Doctor/Master of Public Administration–Dual Degree	111	4–6 yrs, full-time or part-time [day, evening, summer]
JD/MUP–Juris Doctor/Masters of Urban Planning–Dual Degree	119	4–6 yrs, full-time or part-time [day, evening, summer]

Financial Aid 59 research assistantships were awarded. Loans, merit-based grants/scholarships, need-based grants/scholarships, and federal work-study loans are also available. The average student debt at graduation is $42,675. To apply for financial assistance, students must complete the Free Application for Federal Student Aid, institutional forms, scholarship specific applications, and loan application. Financial aid contact: Catherine Buzanski, Financial Aid Administrator, Cleveland-Marshall College of Law, CSU, 1801 Euclid Avenue, Cleveland, OH 44115. Phone: 216-687-6887. Fax: 216-687-6881. E-mail: catherine.buzanski@law.csuohio.edu.

Law School Library Cleveland-Marshall College of Law Law Library has 15 professional staff members and contains more than 425,131 volumes and 2,249 periodicals. 483 seats are available in the library. When classes are in session, the library is open 95 hours per week.

WESTLAW and LEXIS-NEXIS are available, as are the World Wide Web, online bibliographic services, and CD-ROM players. 55 computer workstations are available to students in the library. Special law collections include Federal Government Depository.

First-Year Program Class size in the average section is 55; 100% of the first-year courses are taught by full-time faculty.

Upper-Level Program Class size in the average section is 40. Among the electives are:

Administrative Law
Advocacy
Business and Corporate Law
Entertainment Law
Environmental Law
Family Law
Health Care/Human Services
Indian/Tribal Law
Intellectual Property
International/Comparative Law
Jurisprudence
Labor Law
Land Use Law/Natural Resources
Lawyering Skills
Legal History/Philosophy
Litigation
Maritime Law
Mediation
Probate Law
Securities
Tax Law

Clinical Courses Students receive degree credit for clinical courses. (Clinical practicum is not required.) Among the clinical areas offered are:

Community Advocacy
Employment Law
Environmental Law
Fair Housing

5% of the students participate in internship programs.

OHIO NORTHERN UNIVERSITY
CLAUDE W. PETTIT COLLEGE OF LAW

Ada, Ohio

INFORMATION CONTACT
Victor L. Streib III, Dean
Ohio Northern University of Law
525 South Main Street
Ada, OH 45810-1599

Phone: 419-772-2205
Web site: http://www.law.onu.edu/

LAW STUDENT PROFILE [1997–98]

TOTAL ENROLLMENT   380

APPLICANTS and ADMITTEES
Seats available: 129
Average LSAT score: 147
Average GPA: 2.9

Ohio Northern University Claude W. Pettit College of Law is a private institution that organizes classes on a semester calendar system. The campus is situated in a small-town setting. Founded in 1885, first ABA approved in 1948, and an AALS member, Ohio Northern University Claude W. Pettit College of Law offers a JD degree.

Application Information *Required:* LSAT, LSDAS, application form, application fee of $40, baccalaureate degree, minimum 2.0 GPA, college transcripts. *Recommended:* recommendations, personal statement, resume.

Financial Aid Loans, merit-based grants/scholarships, need-based grants/scholarships, and federal work-study loans are available. The average student debt at graduation is $65,760. To apply for financial assistance, students must complete the Free Application for Federal Student Aid and institutional forms. Financial aid contact: Wendell Schick, Director of Financial Aid Services, Ohio Northern University, Ada, OH 45810-1599. Phone: 419-772-2272. E-mail: w-schick@onu.edu. Completed financial aid forms should be received by May 1.

Law School Library Taggart Law Library has 4 professional staff members and contains more than 260,000 volumes and 780 periodicals. 291 seats are

AT a GLANCE

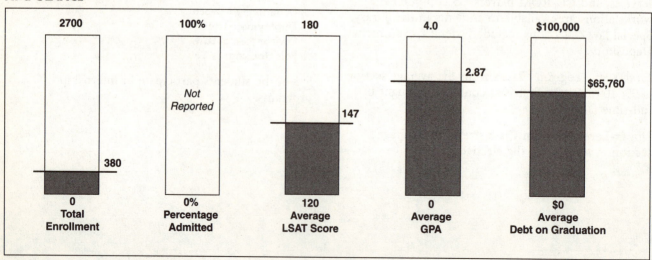

Degree Options

Degree	Total Credits Required	Length of Program
JD–Doctor of Laws	87	3 yrs, full-time only [day]

available in the library. When classes are in session, the library is open 108 hours per week.

WESTLAW and LEXIS-NEXIS are available, as are the World Wide Web and CD-ROM players. 26 computer workstations are available to students in the library. Special law collections include federal government depository.

First-Year Program Class size in the average section is 42; 100% of the first-year courses are taught by full-time faculty.

Upper-Level Program Class size in the average section is 30. Among the electives are:

Administrative Law
★ Advocacy
Business and Corporate Law
Consumer Law
Entertainment Law
Environmental Law
Family Law
Government/Regulation
Health Care/Human Services
Intellectual Property
International/Comparative Law
Jurisprudence
Labor Law
Land Use Law/Natural Resources
Lawyering Skills

Legal History/Philosophy
★ Litigation
Mediation
Probate Law
Public Interest
Securities
★ Tax Law
(★ indicates an area of special strength)

Clinical Courses Students receive degree credit for clinical courses. (Clinical practicum is not required.) Among the clinical areas offered are:

Civil Litigation
Civil Rights
Corporate Law
Criminal Defense
Criminal Prosecution
Elderly Advocacy
Environmental Law
Family Practice
Juvenile Law
Mediation
Public Interest
Tax Law

30% of the students participate in internship programs. International exchange programs permit students to visit Iceland and Ukraine.

THE OHIO STATE UNIVERSITY
COLLEGE OF LAW

Columbus, Ohio

INFORMATION CONTACT
Gregory H. Williams, Dean
55 West 12th Avenue
Columbus, OH 43210

Phone: 614-292-2631   Fax: 614-292-1383
Web site: http://www.osu.edu/law/

LAW STUDENT PROFILE [1997–98]

FULL-TIME   Enrollment: 668
Women: 44%   Men: 56%

PART-TIME   Enrollment: 4
Women: 50%   Men: 50%

RACIAL or ETHNIC COMPOSITION
African American, 8%; Asian/Pacific Islander, 6%; Hispanic, 3%; Nataive American, 0.1%; International, 0%

APPLICANTS and ADMITTEES
Number applied: 1,364
Admitted: 581
Percentage accepted: 43%
Seats available: 210
Median LSAT score: 157
Median GPA: 3.5

The Ohio State University College of Law is a public institution that organizes classes on a semester calendar system. The campus is situated in an urban setting. Founded in 1891, first ABA approved in 1923, and an AALS member, The Ohio State University College of Law offers JD, JD/MA, JD/MBA, JD/MHA, and JD/MPAd degrees.

Faculty consists of 40 full-time and 46 part-time members in 1997–98. 12 full-time faculty members and 16 part-time faculty members are women. 100% of all faculty members have a JD; 10% have advanced law degrees. Of all faculty members, 1% are Asian/Pacific Islander, 12% are African American, 3% are Hispanic, 84% are white.

Application Information *Required:* LSAT, LSDAS, application form, application fee of $30, baccalaureate degree, 2 letters of recommendation, personal statement, college transcripts. *Application deadline* for fall term is March 15.

Costs The 1997–98 tuition is $7692 for state residents. Tuition is $17,086 for nonresidents.

Financial Aid In 1997–98, 64% of all students received some form of financial aid. Fellowships, loans, loan repayment assistance program (LRAP), merit-based grants/scholarships, need-based grants/scholarships, and federal work-study loans are

AT a GLANCE

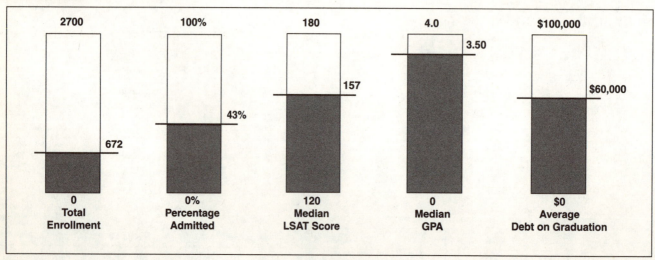

Degree Options

Degree	Total Credits Required	Length of Program
JD–Doctor of Laws	88	3 yrs, full-time only [day, summer]
JD/MA–Juris Doctor/Master of Arts–Dual-degree Program		full-time only [day]
JD/MBA–Juris Doctor/Master of Business Administration–Dual-degree Program		full-time only [day]
JD/MHA–Juris Doctor/Master of Health Administration–Dual-degree Program		full-time only [day]
JD/MPAd–Juris Doctor/Master of Public Administration–Dual-degree Program		full-time only [day]

also available. The average student debt at graduation is $60,000. To apply for financial assistance, students must complete the Free Application for Federal Student Aid. Financial aid contact: Linda Berry, Financial Aid Counselor, 55 West 12th Avenue, Columbus, OH 43210. Phone: 614-292-8807. Fax: 614-292-1383. E-mail: berry.78@osu.edu. Completed financial aid forms should be received by March 1.

Law School Library The Ohio State University College of Law Library has 9 professional staff members and contains more than 653,399 volumes and 6,974 periodicals. 660 seats are available in the library. When classes are in session, the library is open 107 hours per week.

WESTLAW and LEXIS-NEXIS are available, as are the World Wide Web, online bibliographic services, and CD-ROM players. 55 computer workstations are available to students in the library. Special law collections include dispute resolution, labor law, health care policy, foreign and international law.

First-Year Program Class size in the average section is 75; 100% of the first-year courses are taught by full-time faculty.

Upper-Level Program Class size in the average section is 39. Among the electives are:

Administrative Law
Advocacy
★ Arbitration
Business and Corporate Law
Consumer Law

★ Criminal Law
Education Law
Entertainment Law
Environmental Law
Family Law
Government/Regulation
Health Care/Human Services
Intellectual Property
★ International/Comparative Law
Jurisprudence
★ Juvenile Law
Labor Law
Land Use Law/Natural Resources
Lawyering Skills
Legal History/Philosophy
Litigation
Media Law
★ Mediation
★ Negotiation
Probate Law
Public Interest
Securities
Tax Law
(★ *indicates an area of special strength*)

Clinical Courses Students receive degree credit for clinical courses. (Clinical practicum is not required.) Among the clinical areas offered are:

Civil Litigation
Criminal Defense
Criminal Prosecution
Juvenile Law
Mediation

25% of the students participate in internship programs. International exchange program available.

THE UNIVERSITY OF AKRON
SCHOOL OF LAW

Akron, Ohio

INFORMATION CONTACT
Richard L. Aynes Jr., Dean
Akron, OH 44325-2901

Phone: 330-972-7331   Fax: 330-258-2343
Web site: http://www.uakron.edu//law/

LAW STUDENT PROFILE [1997–98]

FULL-TIME   Enrollment: 598
Women: 44%   Men: 56%

PART-TIME   Enrollment: 29
Women: 34%   Men: 66%

RACIAL or ETHNIC COMPOSITION
African American, 4%; Asian/Pacific Islander, 2%; Hispanic, 1%; Nataive American, 0.3%; International, 1%

APPLICANTS and ADMITTEES
Number applied: 1,170
Admitted: 595
Percentage accepted: 51%
Seats available: 200
Average LSAT score: 152
Average GPA: 3.1

The University of Akron School of Law is a public institution that organizes classes on a semester calendar system. The campus is situated in an urban setting. Founded in 1921, first ABA approved in 1961, and an AALS member, The University of Akron School of Law offers JD, JD/MBA, JD/MPAd, and JD/MTAX degrees.

Faculty consists of 25 full-time and 43 part-time members in 1997–98. 100% of all faculty members have a JD; 12% have advanced law degrees. Of all faculty members, 4% are Asian/Pacific Islander, 12% are African American, 84% are white.

Application Information *Required:* LSAT, LSDAS, application form, application fee of $35, baccalaureate degree, minimum 2.0 GPA, personal statement, essay, college transcripts. *Recommended:* recommendations.

Costs The 1997–98 tuition is $7769 full-time for state residents; $4872 part-time for state residents. Tuition is $13,217 full-time for nonresidents; $8277 part-time for nonresidents.

Financial Aid Graduate assistantships, loans, merit-based grants/scholarships, and need-based grants/scholarships are available. The average student debt at graduation is $37,000. To apply for financial assistance, students must complete the Free

AT a GLANCE

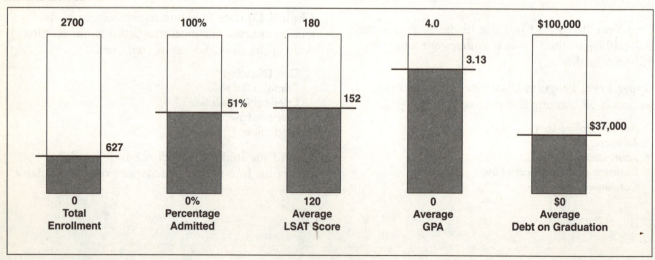

Degree Options

Degree	Total Credits Required	Length of Program
JD–Juris Doctor	88	3–4 yrs, full-time or part-time [day, evening, summer]
JD/MBA–Juris Doctor/Master of Business Administration–Dual-degree Program	103	3–4 yrs, full-time or part-time [day, evening, summer]
JD/MPAd–Juris Doctor/Master of Public Administration–Dual-degree Program	109	3–4 yrs, full-time or part-time [day, evening, summer]
JD/MTAX–Juris Doctor/Master of Taxation–Dual-degree Program	98	3–4 yrs, full-time or part-time [day, evening, summer]

Application for Federal Student Aid. Financial aid contact: Lauri S. File, Director of Admissions and Financial Aid, The University of Akron School of Law, Akron, OH 44325-2901. Phone: 330-972-7331 or toll-free 800-4-AKRONU. Fax: 330-258-2343. E-mail: lawadmissions@uakron.edu. Completed financial aid forms should be received by April 1.

Law School Library The University of Akron School of Law Library has 6 professional staff members and contains more than 256,603 volumes and 3,243 periodicals. 295 seats are available in the library. When classes are in session, the library is open 98 hours per week.

WESTLAW and LEXIS-NEXIS are available, as are the World Wide Web, online bibliographic services, and CD-ROM players. 40 computer workstations are available to students in the library. Special law collections include Intellectual Property.

First-Year Program Class size in the average section is 50; 95% of the first-year courses are taught by full-time faculty.

Upper-Level Program Class size in the average section is 25. Among the electives are:

Administrative Law
★ Advocacy
★ Business and Corporate Law
★ Constitutional Law
Consumer Law
Education Law
Entertainment Law

Environmental Law
Family Law
Government/Regulation
Health Care/Human Services
★ Intellectual Property
International/Comparative Law
Labor Law
Land Use Law/Natural Resources
Lawyering Skills
Legal History/Philosophy
★ Litigation
Maritime Law
Media Law
Mediation
Probate Law
Securities
★ Tax Law
(★ indicates an area of special strength)

Clinical Courses Students receive degree credit for clinical courses. (Clinical practicum is not required.) Among the clinical areas offered are:

Civil Litigation
Civil Rights
Criminal Defense
Criminal Prosecution
Family Practice
Juvenile Law
Mediation
Public Interest

33% of the students participate in internship programs.

UNIVERSITY OF CINCINNATI
COLLEGE OF LAW

Cincinnati, Ohio

INFORMATION CONTACT
Dr. Joseph Tomain, Dean
PO Box 210040
Cincinnati, OH 45221-0040

Phone: 513-556-0121   Fax: 513-556-2391
Web site: http://www.uc.edu/

LAW STUDENT PROFILE [1997–98]

APPLICANTS and ADMITTEES
Seats available: 125
Median LSAT score: 160
Median GPA: 3.4

University of Cincinnati College of Law is a public institution that organizes classes on a semester calendar system. The campus is situated in an urban setting. Founded in 1833, first ABA approved in 1923, and an AALS member, University of Cincinnati College of Law offers JD, JD/MA, JD/MBA, and JD/MCRP degrees.

Application Information *Required:* LSAT, LSDAS, application form, application fee of $35, baccalaureate degree, 2 letters of recommendation. *Recommended:* personal statement, essay, writing sample, college transcripts, resume. *Application deadline* for fall term is April 1.

Financial Aid Fellowships, loans, merit-based grants/scholarships, need-based grants/scholarships, and federal work-study loans are available. The average student debt at graduation is $42,000. To apply for financial assistance, students must complete the Free Application for Federal Student Aid and scholarship specific applications. Financial aid contact: Al Watson, Assistant Dean for Admission and Financial Aid, PO Box 210040, Cincinnati, OH 45221-0040. Phone: 513-556-6805. Fax: 513-556-2391. E-mail: admissions@law.uc.edu. Completed financial aid forms should be received by March 1.

AT a GLANCE

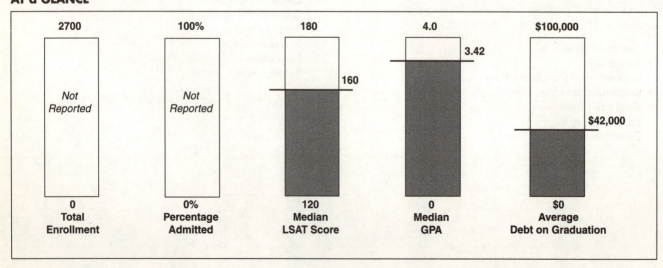

Degree Options

Degree	Total Credits Required	Length of Program
JD–Doctor of Laws	90	3 yrs, full-time only [day]
JD/MA–Juris Doctor/Master of Arts–Women's Studies Joint-degree Program		4 yrs, full-time only [day]
JD/MBA–Juris Doctor/Master of Business Administration–Dual Degree		4 yrs, full-time only [day]
JD/MCRP–Juris Doctor/Master of Community and Regional Planning–Joint-degree Program		4 yrs, full-time only [day]

Law School Library Marx Law Library has 7 professional staff members and contains more than 373,135 volumes and 716 periodicals. 401 seats are available in the library. When classes are in session, the library is open 107 hours per week.

WESTLAW and LEXIS-NEXIS are available, as are the World Wide Web, online bibliographic services, and CD-ROM players. 25 computer workstations are available to students in the library. Special law collections include human rights, city planning and land use planning.

First-Year Program Class size in the average section is 23; 100% of the first-year courses are taught by full-time faculty.

Upper-Level Program Among the electives are:

- Accounting
- Administrative Law
- Advocacy
- ★ Business and Corporate Law
- Consumer Law
- Education
- Entertainment Law
- Environmental Law
- Family Law
- Government/Regulation
- Health Care/Human Services
- ★ Human Rights
- ★ Intellectual Property
- International/Comparative Law
- Jurisprudence
- Labor Law
- Land Use Law/Natural Resources
- Lawyering Skills
- Legal History/Philosophy
- Litigation
- Maritime Law
- Media Law
- Mediation
- Probate Law
- Public Interest
- Securities
- Tax Law

(★ *indicates an area of special strength*)

40% of the students participate in internship programs.

UNIVERSITY OF DAYTON
SCHOOL OF LAW

Dayton, Ohio

INFORMATION CONTACT

Francis J. Conte, Dean
300 College Park
Dayton, OH 45469-2760

Phone: 937-229-3211   Fax: 937-229-2469
E-mail: lawinfo@udayton.edu
Web site: http://www.udayton.edu/~law/

LAW STUDENT PROFILE [1997–98]

FULL-TIME   Enrollment: 495
Women: 40%   Men: 60%

RACIAL or ETHNIC COMPOSITION

African American, 8%; Asian/Pacific Islander, 3%; Hispanic,
3%; Nataive American, 0.4%; International, 0%

APPLICANTS and ADMITTEES

Number applied: 1,350
Admitted: 830
Percentage accepted: 61%
Seats available: 178
Average LSAT score: 151
Average GPA: 3.2

University of Dayton School of Law is a private
institution that organizes classes on a semester
calendar system. The campus is situated in a
suburban setting. Founded in 1974, first ABA
approved in 1977, and an AALS member, University
of Dayton School of Law offers JD and JD/MBA
degrees.

Faculty consists of 26 full-time and 30 part-time
members in 1997–98. 9 full-time faculty members
and 4 part-time faculty members are women. 100%
of all faculty members have a JD; 45% have
advanced law degrees. Of all faculty members, 4%
are African American, 4% are Hispanic, 92% are
white.

Application Information *Required:* LSAT, LSDAS,
application form, application fee of $40, baccalaure-
ate degree, 2 letters of recommendation, college
transcripts. *Recommended:* personal statement, essay,
resume. *Application deadline* for fall term is May 1.
Students are required to have their own computers.

Financial Aid In 1997–98, 36% of all students
received some form of financial aid. Loans and
merit-based grants/scholarships are also available.
The average student debt at graduation is $57,000.
To apply for financial assistance, students must
complete the Free Application for Federal Student
Aid. Financial aid contact: Charles Roboski, Director

AT a GLANCE

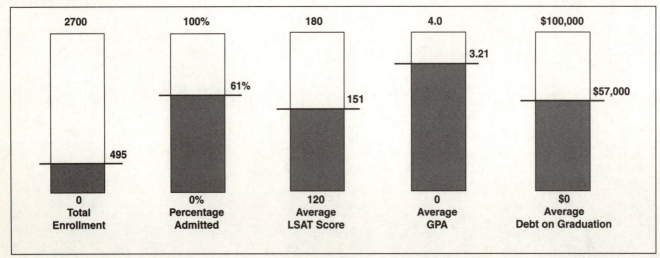

Degree Options

Degree	Total Credits Required	Length of Program
JD–Doctor of Laws	87	3 yrs, full-time only [day, summer]
JD/MBA–Juris Doctor/Master of Business Administration–Dual-degree Program	109	4–5 yrs [day, evening]

of Admission and Financial Aid, 300 College Park, Dayton, OH 45469-2760. Phone: 937-229-3555. Fax: 937-229-2469. E-mail: roboski@udayton.edu. Completed financial aid forms should be received by March 1.

Law School Library Zimmerman Law Library has 5 professional staff members and contains more than 258,941 volumes and 4,214 periodicals. 501 seats are available in the library. When classes are in session, the library is open 100 hours per week.

WESTLAW and LEXIS-NEXIS are available, as are the World Wide Web and CD-ROM players. 43 computer workstations are available to students in the library.

First-Year Program Class size in the average section is 83; 100% of the first-year courses are taught by full-time faculty.

Upper-Level Program Class size in the average section is 48. Among the electives are:

Administrative Law
★ Advocacy

Business and Corporate Law
★ Criminal Law
Environmental Law
Family Law
Health Care/Human Services
★ Intellectual Property
International/Comparative Law
Labor Law
Land Use Law/Natural Resources
★ Lawyering Skills
★ Litigation
Mediation
Probate Law
Public Interest
Securities
★ Tax Law
(★ indicates an area of special strength)

Clinical Courses Students receive degree credit for clinical courses. (Clinical practicum is not required.) The clinical area offered includes:

Civil Litigation

11% of the students participate in internship programs.

UNIVERSITY OF TOLEDO
COLLEGE OF LAW

Toledo, Ohio

INFORMATION CONTACT
Albert T. Quick, Dean
2801 West Bancroft Street
Toledo, OH 43606

Phone: 419-530-2379   Fax: 419-530-4526
E-mail: law0046@uoft01.utoledo.edu
Web site: http://www.utoledo.edu/law/

LAW STUDENT PROFILE [1997–98]

FULL-TIME   Enrollment: 457
Women: 42%   Men: 58%

PART-TIME   Enrollment: 165
Women: 45%   Men: 55%

RACIAL or ETHNIC COMPOSITION
African American, 5%; Asian/Pacific Islander, 1%; Hispanic, 2%; Native American, 1%; International, 0%

APPLICANTS and ADMITTEES
Number applied: 712
Admitted: 460
Percentage accepted: 65%
Seats available: 192
Average LSAT score: 152
Average GPA: 3.1

University of Toledo College of Law is a public institution that organizes classes on a semester calendar system. The campus is situated in a suburban setting. Founded in 1906, first ABA approved in 1939, and an AALS member, University of Toledo College of Law offers JD and JD/MBA degrees.

Faculty consists of 26 full-time and 23 part-time members in 1997–98. 7 full-time faculty members and 5 part-time faculty members are women. 100% of all faculty members have a JD; 50% have advanced law degrees. Of all faculty members, 2% are Asian/Pacific Islander, 2% are African American, 96% are white.

Application Information *Required:* LSAT, application form, application fee of $30, baccalaureate degree, minimum 2.0 GPA, 2 letters of recommendation, college transcripts. *Application deadline* for fall term is May 15.

Costs The 1997–98 tuition is $7350 full-time for state residents; $306 per hour part-time for state residents. Tuition is $14,168 full-time for nonresidents; $591 per hour part-time for nonresidents.

Financial Aid In 1997–98, 78% of all students received some form of financial aid. 17 research assistantships, 4 teaching assistantships were

AT a GLANCE

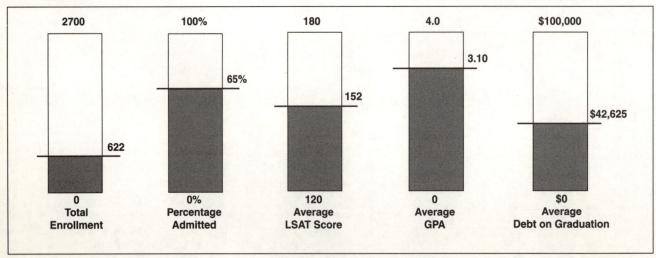

Degree Options

Degree	Total Credits Required	Length of Program
JD–Juris Doctor	89	3–4 yrs, full-time or part-time [day, evening, summer]
JD/MBA–Juris Doctor/Master of Business Administration–Joint Degree	107	3–3.5 yrs, full-time only [day, summer]

awarded. 169 other awards were given. Graduate assistantships, loans, merit-based grants/scholarships, need-based grants/scholarships, and federal work-study loans are also available. The average student debt at graduation is $42,625. To apply for financial assistance, students must complete the Free Application for Federal Student Aid. Financial aid contact: Beth Solo, Assistant Director, University of Toledo College of Law, Toledo, OH 43606. Phone: 419-530-7929. Fax: 419-530-4526. E-mail: bsolo@utnet.edu. Completed financial aid forms should be received by May 1.

Law School Library University of Toledo College of Law Library has 13 professional staff members and contains more than 306,000 volumes and 3,257 periodicals. 425 seats are available in the library. When classes are in session, the library is open 113 hours per week.

WESTLAW and LEXIS-NEXIS are available, as are the World Wide Web, online bibliographic services, and CD-ROM players. 40 computer workstations are available to students in the library. Special law collections include the Great Lakes law collection.

First-Year Program Class size in the average section is 50; 100% of the first-year courses are taught by full-time faculty.

Upper-Level Program Class size in the average section is 31. Among the electives are:

Administrative Law
★ Advocacy

★ Business and Corporate Law
Consumer Law
Education Law
Entertainment Law
★ Environmental Law
Family Law
Government/Regulation
★ Great Lakes Law
Health Care/Human Services
Indian/Tribal Law
★ Intellectual Property
★ International/Comparative Law
Jurisprudence
Labor Law
Land Use Law/Natural Resources
Lawyering Skills
Legal History/Philosophy
★ Litigation
Maritime Law
Mediation
Securities
★ Tax Law
(★ *indicates an area of special strength*)

Clinical Courses Students receive degree credit for clinical courses. (Clinical practicum is not required.) Among the clinical areas offered are:

Criminal Prosecution
General Practice
Juvenile Law
Mediation

6% of the students participate in internship programs. International exchange programs permit students to visit United Kingdom.

OKLAHOMA CITY UNIVERSITY
SCHOOL OF LAW

Oklahoma City, Oklahoma

INFORMATION CONTACT

Jay Conison, Interim Dean
2501 North Blackwelder
Oklahoma City, OK 73106

Phone: 405-521-5329   Fax: 405-521-5802
E-mail: gmercer@frodo.okcu.edu
Web site: http://www.okcu.edu/law/

LAW STUDENT PROFILE [1997–98]

FULL-TIME   Enrollment: 388
Women: 38%   Men: 62%

PART-TIME   Enrollment: 170
Women: 39%   Men: 61%

RACIAL or ETHNIC COMPOSITION
African American, 3%; Asian/Pacific Islander, 2%; Hispanic, 3%; Native American, 6%; International, 0%

APPLICANTS and ADMITTEES
Seats available: 200
Median LSAT score: 147
Median GPA: 2.9

Oklahoma City University School of Law is a private institution that organizes classes on a semester calendar system. The campus is situated in an urban setting. Founded in 1907, first ABA approved in 1964, Oklahoma City University School of Law offers JD and JD/MBA degrees.

Application Information *Required:* LSAT, LSDAS, application form, application fee of $35, baccalaureate degree, 2 letters of recommendation. *Application deadline* for fall term is June 1.

Costs The 1997–98 tuition is $504 per hour. Fees: $124.

Financial Aid Loans, merit-based grants/scholarships, and federal work-study loans are available. The average student debt at graduation is $45,000. To apply for financial assistance, students must complete the Free Application for Federal Student Aid and scholarship specific applications. Financial aid contact: Vicki Hendrickson, Director of Financial Aid, 2501 North Blackwelder, Oklahoma City, OK 73105. Phone: 405-521-5211. Fax: 405-521-5802. Completed financial aid forms should be received by August 1.

Law School Library has 8 professional staff members and contains more than 257,956 volumes and 3,940 periodicals. 364 seats are available in the

AT a GLANCE

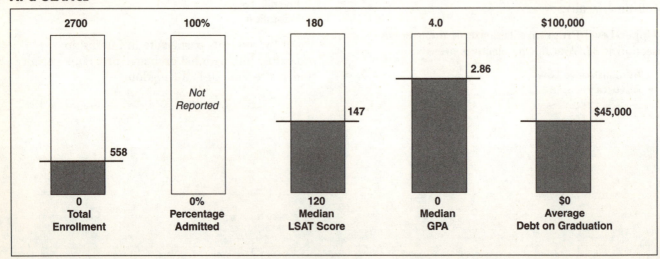

Degree Options

Degree	Total Credits Required	Length of Program
JD–Doctor of Laws	90	3–4 yrs, full-time or part-time [day, evening, summer]
JD/MBA–Juris Doctor/Master of Business Administration–Joint-degree Program	124	4 yrs, full-time only [day, summer]

library. When classes are in session, the library is open 102 hours per week.

WESTLAW and LEXIS-NEXIS are available, as are the World Wide Web, online bibliographic services, and CD-ROM players. 70 computer workstations are available to students in the library. Special law collections include Native American Collection.

First-Year Program Class size in the average section is 75; 100% of the first-year courses are taught by full-time faculty.

Upper-Level Program Class size in the average section is 35. Among the electives are:

Administrative Law
Advocacy
Business and Corporate Law
Consumer Law
Education Law
Elder Law
Entertainment Law
Environmental Law
Family Law
Government/Regulation
Health Care/Human Services

★ Indian/Tribal Law
Intellectual Property
International/Comparative Law
Jurisprudence
Labor Law
Land Use Law/Natural Resources
Lawyering Skills
Legal History/Philosophy
Litigation
★ Mediation
Probate Law
Public Interest
Securities
Tax Law

(★ *indicates an area of special strength*)

Clinical Courses Students receive degree credit for clinical courses. (Clinical practicum is not required.) Among the clinical areas offered are:

Criminal Defense
Criminal Prosecution
Government Litigation
Indian/Tribal Law
Mediation

Internships are available.

UNIVERSITY OF OKLAHOMA
COLLEGE OF LAW

Norman, Oklahoma

INFORMATION CONTACT

Dr. Andrew M. Coats, Dean
30 West Timberdell Road
Suite 200
Norman, OK 73019

Phone: 405-325-4699   Fax: 405-325-6282
Web site: http://www.law.ou.edu/

LAW STUDENT PROFILE [1997–98]

FULL-TIME   Enrollment: 544
Women: 41%   Men: 59%

PART-TIME   Enrollment: 7
Women: 57%   Men: 43%

RACIAL or ETHNIC COMPOSITION
African American, 3%; Asian/Pacific Islander, 3%; Hispanic, 4%; Native American, 5%; International, 0%

APPLICANTS and ADMITTEES
Number applied: 1,090
Admitted: 373
Percentage accepted: 34%
Seats available: 180
Average LSAT score: 152
Average GPA: 3.2

University of Oklahoma College of Law is a public institution that organizes classes on a semester calendar system. The campus is situated in a suburban setting. Founded in 1909, first ABA approved in 1923, and an AALS member, University of Oklahoma College of Law offers JD, JD/MBA, and JD/MS degrees.

Faculty consists of 35 full-time and 10 part-time members in 1997–98. 11 full-time faculty members and 5 part-time faculty members are women. 100% of all faculty members have a JD; 35% have advanced law degrees.

Application Information *Required:* LSAT, LSDAS, application form, application fee of $50, baccalaureate degree, personal statement, college transcripts. *Application deadline* for fall term is March 15.

Costs The 1997–98 tuition is $4140 full-time for state residents; $138 per credit hour part-time for state residents. Tuition is $12,924 full-time for nonresidents; $431 per credit hour part-time for nonresidents. Fees: $530 full-time; $53 per semester (minimum) part-time.

Financial Aid Graduate assistantships, loans, merit-based grants/scholarships, and need-based grants/scholarships are available. The average student debt at graduation is $39,000. To apply for

AT a GLANCE

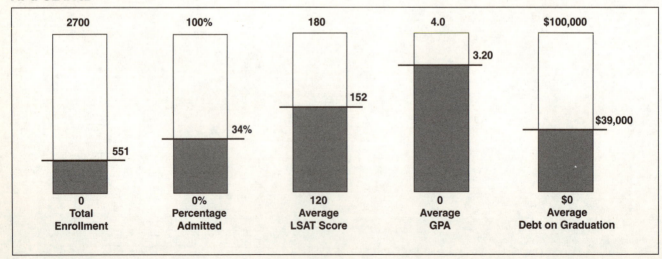

Degree Options

Degree	Total Credits Required	Length of Program
JD–Doctor of Laws	90	3–4 yrs, full-time only [day, summer]
JD/MBA–Juris Doctor/Master of Business Administration–Dual Degree		[day, summer]
JD/MS–Juris Doctor/Master of Science–Tailored Graduate Degree		4 yrs, full-time only [day, summer]

financial assistance, students must complete the Free Application for Federal Student Aid. Financial aid contact: Debbie Case, Registrar, 300 West Timberdell Road, Norman, OK 73019. Phone: 405-325-4726. Fax: 405-325-6282. E-mail: financialaid@ou.edu. Completed financial aid forms should be received by March 1.

Law School Library John N. Singletary Law Library has 7 professional staff members and contains more than 302,738 volumes and 3,977 periodicals. 375 seats are available in the library. When classes are in session, the library is open 99 hours per week.

WESTLAW and LEXIS-NEXIS are available, as are the World Wide Web, online bibliographic services, and CD-ROM players. 34 computer workstations are available to students in the library. Special law collections include Native Peoples.

First-Year Program Class size in the average section is 42; 100% of the first-year courses are taught by full-time faculty.

Upper-Level Program Class size in the average section is 30. Among the electives are:

  Administrative Law
★ Advocacy
  Business and Corporate Law
  Consumer Law
  Education Law
  Entertainment Law
  Environmental Law
  Family Law
  Government/Regulation
  Health Care/Human Services
★ Indian/Tribal Law
  Intellectual Property
  International/Comparative Law
  Jurisprudence
★ Land Use Law/Natural Resources
★ Lawyering Skills
  Legal History/Philosophy
★ Litigation
  Media Law
  Mediation
  Probate Law
  Public Interest
  Securities
  Tax Law
(★ *indicates an area of special strength*)

Clinical Courses Students receive degree credit for clinical courses. (Clinical practicum is not required.) Among the clinical areas offered are:

  Civil Litigation
  Criminal Defense
  Environmental Law
  General Practice

Internships are available. International exchange programs permit students to visit France.

UNIVERSITY OF TULSA
COLLEGE OF LAW

Tulsa, Oklahoma

INFORMATION CONTACT
Martin H. Belsky, Dean
3120 East 4th Place
Tulsa, OK 74008

Phone: 918-631-2400   Fax: 918-631-3630
E-mail: velda-staves@utulsa.edu
Web site: http://www.utulsa.edu/

LAW STUDENT PROFILE [1997–98]

FULL-TIME   Enrollment: 453
Women: 43%   Men: 57%

PART-TIME   Enrollment: 132
Women: 45%   Men: 55%

RACIAL or ETHNIC COMPOSITION
African American, 4%; Asian/Pacific Islander, 2%; Hispanic, 3%; Native American, 9%; International, 1%

APPLICANTS and ADMITTEES
Number applied: 747
Admitted: 585
Percentage accepted: 78%
Seats available: 190
Average LSAT score: 150
Average GPA: 3.0

University of Tulsa College of Law is a private institution that organizes classes on a semester calendar system. The campus is situated in a suburban setting. Founded in 1923, first ABA approved in 1953, and an AALS member, University of Tulsa College of Law offers JD, JD/MA, JD/MBA, and JD/MS degrees.

Faculty consists of 37 full-time and 31 part-time members in 1997–98. 14 full-time faculty members and 9 part-time faculty members are women. 100% of all faculty members have a JD; 33% have advanced law degrees. Of all faculty members, 2.8% are Native American, 2.8% are Asian/Pacific Islander, 2.8% are African American, 5.6% are Hispanic, 86% are white.

Application Information *Required:* LSAT, LSDAS, application form, application fee of $30, baccalaureate degree, college transcripts. *Recommended:* recommendations, personal statement, resume. *Application deadline* for fall term is August 19.

Financial Aid Graduate assistantships, loans, merit-based grants/scholarships, need-based grants/scholarships, and federal work-study loans are available. The average student debt at graduation is $71,664. To apply for financial assistance, students must complete the Free Application for Federal Student Aid, institutional forms, and scholarship

AT a GLANCE

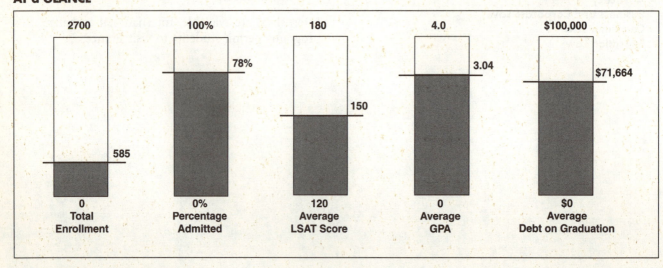

Degree Options

Degree	Total Credits Required	Length of Program
JD–Doctor of Laws	90	3–5 yrs, full-time or part-time [day, evening, weekend, summer]
JD/MA–Juris Doctor/Master of Arts–History	102	4–5 yrs, full-time only [day, evening, weekend, summer]
JD/MA–Juris Doctor/Master of Arts–Industrial Psychology	105	4–5 yrs, full-time only [day, evening, weekend, summer]
JD/MA–Juris Doctor/Master of Arts–Clinical Psychology	114	4–5 yrs, full-time only [day, evening, weekend, summer]
JD/MA–Juris Doctor/Master of Arts–English	105	4–5 yrs, full-time only [day, evening, weekend, summer]
JD/MA–Juris Doctor/Master of Arts–Taxation	102	4–5 yrs, full-time only [day, evening, weekend, summer]
JD/MBA–Juris Doctor/Master of Business Administration–Dual-degree Program	110	4–5 yrs, full-time only [day, evening, weekend, summer]
JD/MS–Juris Doctor/Master of Science–Biological Sciences	105	4–5 yrs, full-time only [day, evening, weekend, summer]
JD/MS–Juris Doctor/Master of Science–Geosciences	105	4–5 yrs, full-time only [day, evening, weekend, summer]

specific applications. Financial aid contact: Velda L. Staves, Director of Admissions, 3120 East 4th Place, Tulsa, OK 74104. Phone: 918-631-2709. Fax: 918-631-3630. E-mail: law_vls@centum.utulsa.edu. Completed financial aid forms should be received by March 1.

Law School Library The Taliaferro Savage Law Library has 8 professional staff members and contains more than 265,000 volumes and 3,743 periodicals. 497 seats are available in the library. When classes are in session, the library is open 120 hours per week.

WESTLAW and LEXIS-NEXIS are available, as are the World Wide Web, online bibliographic services, and CD-ROM players. 62 computer workstations are available to students in the library. Special law collections include Energy Law and Policy, Native American Law.

First-Year Program Class size in the average section is 60; 100% of the first-year courses are taught by full-time faculty.

Upper-Level Program Among the electives are:

Administrative Law
Advocacy
Business and Corporate Law
Consumer Law
★ Environmental Law
Family Law
★ Government/Regulation
★ Health Care/Human Services
★ Indian/Tribal Law
Intellectual Property
★ International/Comparative Law
Jurisprudence
Labor Law
★ Land Use Law/Natural Resources
Lawyering Skills
Legal History/Philosophy
Litigation
Mediation
Probate Law
★ Public Interest
Securities
Sports Law
Tax Law
(★ indicates an area of special strength)

Clinical Courses Students receive degree credit for clinical courses. (Clinical practicum is not required.) Among the clinical areas offered are:

Elderly Advocacy
General Practice
Health

25% of the students participate in internship programs. International exchange programs permit students to visit Argentina and United Kingdom.

LEWIS & CLARK COLLEGE
NORTHWESTERN SCHOOL OF LAW

Portland, Oregon

INFORMATION CONTACT

James L. Huffman, Dean
10015 SW Terwilliger Boulevard
Portland, OR 97219-7799

Phone: 503-768-6602
E-mail: spence@lclark.edu
Web site: http://www.lclark.edu/LAW/index.html

LAW STUDENT PROFILE [1997–98]

FULL-TIME   Enrollment: 464
Women: 44%   Men: 56%

PART-TIME   Enrollment: 163
Women: 50%   Men: 50%

RACIAL or ETHNIC COMPOSITION

African American, 2%; Asian/Pacific Islander, 8%; Hispanic, 4%; Native American, 1%; International, 3%

APPLICANTS and ADMITTEES

Number applied: 1,687
Admitted: 930
Percentage accepted: 55%
Seats available: 217

Lewis & Clark College Northwestern School of Law is a private institution that organizes classes on a semester calendar system. The campus is situated in an urban setting. First ABA approved in 1970, and an AALS member, Lewis & Clark College Northwestern School of Law offers JD and LLM degrees.

Faculty consists of 37 full-time and 40 part-time members in 1997–98. 11 full-time faculty members and 13 part-time faculty members are women.

Application Information *Required:* LSAT, LSDAS, application form, application fee of $50, 1 recommendation, essay. *Application deadline* for fall term is March 15.

Financial Aid 379 awards were given. Fellowships, loans, merit-based grants/scholarships, need-based grants/scholarships, and federal work-study loans are also available. To apply for financial assistance, students must complete the Free Application for Federal Student Aid and institutional forms. Financial aid contact: Marsha Webber, Assistant Director of Student Services for Law Students, 0615 S.W. Palatine Hill Road, Portland, OR 97219-7899. Phone: 503-768-7090. E-mail: mwebber@lclark.edu. Completed financial aid forms should be received by February 15.

AT a GLANCE

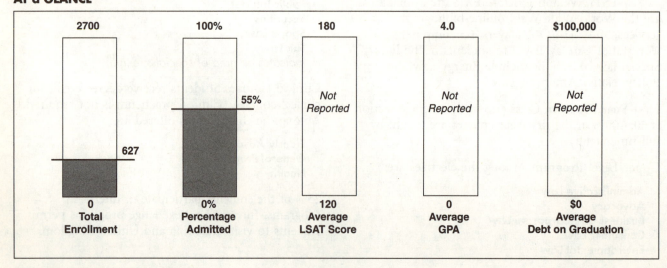

Degree Options

Degree	Total Credits Required	Length of Program
JD–Juris Doctor	86	3–4 yrs, full-time or part-time [day, evening]
LLM–Master of Laws–Environmental and Natural Resources	26	1–2 yrs

Law School Library Boley Law Library has 8 professional staff members and contains more than 429,167 volumes and 4,887 periodicals. 194 seats are available in the library. When classes are in session, the library is open 113 hours per week.

WESTLAW and LEXIS-NEXIS are available, as are CD-ROM players. 52 computer workstations are available to students in the library. Special law collections include the Pearl Environmental Law Library, the Johnson Public Land Law Collection.

First-Year Program Class size in the average section is 55.

Upper-Level Program Among the electives are:

Administrative Law
Advocacy
Agricultural Law
Animal Rights Law
Bankruptcy
Business and Corporate Law
Constitutional Law
Entertainment Law
Environmental Law
Family Law
Government/Regulation
Health Care/Human Services
Immigration
Indian/Tribal Law
Intellectual Property
International/Comparative Law
Jurisprudence
Labor Law
Land Use Law/Natural Resources
Lawyering Skills
Legal History/Philosophy
Litigation
Maritime Law
Mediation
Ocean and Coastal Law
Probate Law
Public Interest
Sports Law
Street Law
Tax Law

Clinical Courses Among the clinical areas offered are:

Civil Litigation
Criminal Defense
Family Practice
General Practice

Internships are available.

UNIVERSITY OF OREGON
SCHOOL OF LAW

Eugene, Oregon

INFORMATION CONTACT

Rennard Strickland, Dean
Eugene, OR 97403

Phone: 541-346-3852
E-mail: randisch@law.uoregon.edu
Web site: http://www.law.uoregon.edu/

LAW STUDENT PROFILE [1997–98]

FULL-TIME	Enrollment: 528
Women: 48%	Men: 52%
PART-TIME	Enrollment: 7
Women: 71%	Men: 29%

RACIAL or ETHNIC COMPOSITION
African American, 2%; Asian/Pacific Islander, 8%; Hispanic, 4%; Native American, 1%; International, 1%

APPLICANTS and ADMITTEES
Number applied: 1,046
Admitted: 602
Percentage accepted: 58%
Seats available: 194

University of Oregon School of Law is a public institution that organizes classes on a semester calendar system. Founded in 1884, first ABA approved in 1923, and an AALS member, University of Oregon School of Law offers JD, JD/MBA, and JD/MS degrees.

Faculty consists of 22 full-time and 11 part-time members in 1997–98. 9 full-time faculty members and 3 part-time faculty members are women.

Application Information *Required:* LSAT, LSDAS, application form, application fee of $50, baccalaureate degree. *Application deadline* for fall term is April 1. Students are required to have their own computers.

Costs The 1997–98 tuition is $10,236 for state residents. Tuition is $13,984 for nonresidents.

Financial Aid 27 teaching assistantships were awarded. Fellowships, merit-based grants/scholarships, and need-based grants/scholarships are also available. To apply for financial assistance, students must complete the Free Application for Federal Student Aid. Financial aid contact: University of Oregon School of Law, Student Financial Aid, 1278 University of Oregon, Eugene, OR 97403-1278. Phone: 800-760-6952. Completed financial aid forms should be received by February 1.

AT a GLANCE

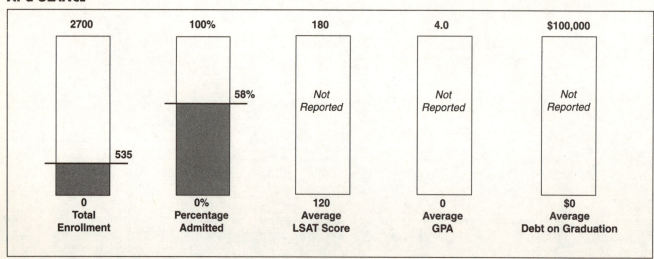

Degree Options

Degree	Total Credits Required	Length of Program
JD–Juris Doctor	85	full-time only [day]
JD/MBA–Juris Doctor/Master of Business Administration		4 yrs
JD/MS–Juris Doctor/Master of Science–Environmental Studies		

Law School Library University of Oregon Law Library has 6 professional staff members and contains more than 346,596 volumes and 3,314 periodicals. 227 seats are available in the library. When classes are in session, the library is open 110 hours per week.

WESTLAW and LEXIS-NEXIS are available. Special law collections include Ocean and Coastal Law collection.

First-Year Program Class size in the average section is 53.

Upper-Level Program Among the electives are:

Administrative Law
Advocacy
Business and Corporate Law
Commercial Law
Conflict of Laws
Constitutional Law
Criminal Procedure
Environmental Law
Family Law
Government/Regulation
Indian/Tribal Law
Insurance
International/Comparative Law
Jurisprudence
Labor Law
Land Use Law/Natural Resources
Legal History/Philosophy
Litigation
Maritime Law
Ocean and Coastal Law
Securities
Tax Law
Trusts and Estates

Clinical Courses Among the clinical areas offered are:

Civil Litigation
Criminal Defense
Criminal Prosecution
Elderly Advocacy
Environmental Law
Family Practice
General Practice
Government Litigation
Juvenile Law
Mediation

Internships are available.

WILLAMETTE UNIVERSITY
COLLEGE OF LAW

Salem, Oregon

INFORMATION CONTACT
Robert M. Ackerman, Dean
245 Winter Street, SE
Salem, OR 97301-3922

Phone: 503-370-6402   Fax: 503-370-6375
E-mail: lseno@willamette.edu
Web site: http://www.willamette.edu/

LAW STUDENT PROFILE [1997–98]

FULL-TIME   Enrollment: 398
Women: 47%   Men: 53%

PART-TIME   Enrollment: 5
Women: 60%   Men: 40%

RACIAL or ETHNIC COMPOSITION
African American, 2%; Asian/Pacific Islander, 5%; Hispanic, 2%; Native American, 1%; International, 2%

APPLICANTS and ADMITTEES
Number applied: 778
Admitted: 574
Percentage accepted: 74%
Seats available: 158
Average LSAT score: 154
Average GPA: 3.2

Willamette University College of Law is a private institution that organizes classes on a semester calendar system. The campus is situated in a small-town setting. Founded in 1883, first ABA approved in 1938, and an AALS member, Willamette University College of Law offers JD and JD/MM degrees.

Faculty consists of 27 full-time and 21 part-time members in 1997–98. 9 full-time faculty members and 9 part-time faculty members are women. 100% of all faculty members have a JD; 4% have advanced law degrees. Of all faculty members, 4% are African American, 96% are white.

Application Information *Required:* LSAT, LSDAS, application form, application fee of $50, baccalaureate degree, 2 letters of recommendation, personal statement, college transcripts. *Application deadline* for fall term is April 1.

Financial Aid In 1997–98, 34% of all students received some form of financial aid. Loans, loan repayment assistance program (LRAP), and merit-based grants/scholarships are also available. The average student debt at graduation is $52,900. To apply for financial assistance, students must complete the Free Application for Federal Student Aid. Financial aid contact: Zophia Miller, Assistant Director of Financial Aid, 900 State Street, Salem,

AT a GLANCE

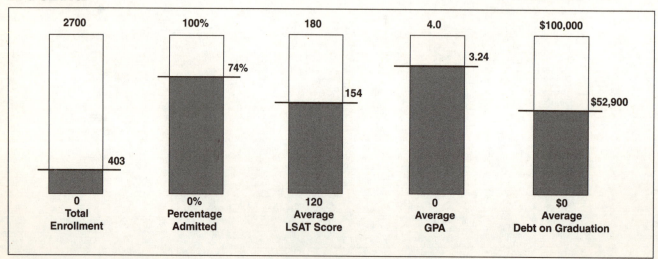

	Total Enrollment	Percentage Admitted	Average LSAT Score	Average GPA	Average Debt on Graduation
Top	2700	100%	180	4.0	$100,000
Value	403	74%	154	3.24	$52,900
Bottom	0	0%	120	0	$0

Degree Options

Degree	Total Credits Required	Length of Program
JD–Doctor of Laws	88	3 yrs, full-time or part-time
JD/MM–Juris Doctor/Master of Management–Joint-degree Program		4 yrs, full-time only [day]

OR 97301-3922. Phone: 503-370-6273. Fax: 503-370-6375. E-mail: zmiller@willamette.edu.

Law School Library J. W. Long Law Library has 6 professional staff members and contains more than 274,718 volumes and 1,800 periodicals. 398 seats are available in the library. When classes are in session, the library is open 113 hours per week.

WESTLAW and LEXIS-NEXIS are available, as are the World Wide Web, online bibliographic services, and CD-ROM players. 24 computer workstations are available to students in the library. Special law collections include Public International Law, Tax collection, Labor collection.

First-Year Program Class size in the average section is 90; 100% of the first-year courses are taught by full-time faculty.

Upper-Level Program Class size in the average section is 50. Among the electives are:

Administrative Law
Advocacy
Business and Corporate Law
Dispute Resolution
Education Law
Environmental Law

Family Law
Government/Regulation
Health Care/Human Services
Indian/Tribal Law
Intellectual Property
International/Comparative Law
Jurisprudence
Labor Law
Land Use Law/Natural Resources
Litigation
Maritime Law
Mediation
Probate Law
Securities
Tax Law

Clinical Courses Students receive degree credit for clinical courses. (Clinical practicum is not required.) Among the clinical areas offered are:

Family Practice
General Practice
Indian/Tribal Law
Public Interest

7% of the students participate in internship programs. International exchange programs permit students to visit Ecuador.

THE DICKINSON SCHOOL OF LAW OF THE PENNSYLVANIA STATE UNIVERSITY

Carlisle, Pennsylvania

INFORMATION CONTACT
Peter G. Glenn, Dean
150 South College Street
Carlisle, PA 17013-2899

Phone: 717-240-5000   Fax: 717-243-4366
E-mail: dsladmit@psu.edu
Web site: http://www.dsl.edu/

LAW STUDENT PROFILE [1997–98]

FULL-TIME   Enrollment: 515
Women: 40%   Men: 60%

PART-TIME   Enrollment: 4
Women: 100%

RACIAL or ETHNIC COMPOSITION
African American, 3%; Asian/Pacific Islander, 3%; Hispanic, 2%; Native American, 1%; International, 2%

APPLICANTS and ADMITTEES
Number applied: 1,054
Admitted: 560
Percentage accepted: 53%
Seats available: 176
Average LSAT score: 154
Average GPA: 3.2

The Dickinson School of Law of The Pennsylvania State University is a private nonprofit institution that organizes classes on a semester calendar system. The campus is situated in a small-town setting. Founded in 1834, first ABA approved in 1931, and an AALS member, The Dickinson School of Law of The Pennsylvania State University offers JD, JD/MBA, JD/ME, JD/MES, JD/MPAd, JD/MS, and LLM degrees.

Faculty consists of 28 full-time and 60 part-time members in 1997–98. 8 full-time faculty members and 10 part-time faculty members are women. 99% of all faculty members have a JD; 29% have advanced law degrees. Of all faculty members, 2.5% are Asian/Pacific Islander, 2.5% are African American, 95% are white.

Application Information *Required:* LSAT, LSDAS, application form, application fee of $50, baccalaureate degree, 2 letters of recommendation, personal statement, college transcripts, resume. *Application deadline* for fall term is March 1.

Financial Aid In 1997–98, 34% of all students received some form of financial aid. Loans, merit-based grants/scholarships, need-based grants/scholarships, and federal work-study loans are also available. The average student debt at graduation is

AT a GLANCE

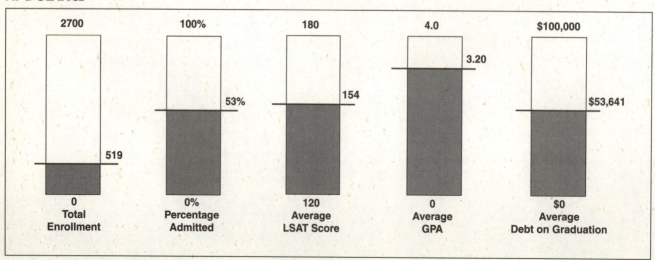

Degree Options

Degree	Total Credits Required	Length of Program
JD–Juris Doctor	88	3 yrs, full-time only [day]
JD/MBA–Juris Doctor/Master of Business Administration–Dual-degree Program	112	4 yrs, full-time only [day]
JD/ME–Juris Doctor/Master of Engineering–Dual-degree Program	98	4.5–5 yrs, full-time only [day, summer]
JD/MES–Juris Doctor/Master of Environmental Studies–Dual-degree Program–Pollution Control	94	4.5 yrs, full-time only [day, evening, summer]
JD/MPAd–Juris Doctor/Master of Public Administration–Dual-degree Program	106	4–5 yrs, full-time or part-time [day, evening, summer]
JD/MS–Juris Doctor/Master of Science–Dual-degree Program	98	4.5–5.5 yrs, full-time only [day, summer]
LLM–Master of Laws–Comparative Law	24	1 yr, full-time only [day]

$53,641. To apply for financial assistance, students must complete the Free Application for Federal Student Aid, institutional forms, scholarship specific applications, and Need Access diskette. Financial aid contact: Joyce E. James, Financial Aid Director, 150 South College Street, Carlisle, PA 17013. Phone: 717-240-5256. Fax: 717-243-4366. E-mail: jej8@psu.edu. Completed financial aid forms should be received by February 15.

Law School Library Sheely-Lee Law Library has 7 professional staff members and contains more than 393,000 volumes and 1,250 periodicals. 444 seats are available in the library. When classes are in session, the library is open 168 hours per week.

WESTLAW and LEXIS-NEXIS are available, as are the World Wide Web, online bibliographic services, and CD-ROM players. 45 computer workstations are available to students in the library. Special law collections include human rights.

First-Year Program Class size in the average section is 50; 100% of the first-year courses are taught by full-time faculty.

Upper-Level Program Class size in the average section is 30. Among the electives are:

Administrative Law
★ Advocacy
Business and Corporate Law
Consumer Law
★ Disability Law
Education Law
Elder Law
★ Entertainment Law
★ Environmental Law

★ Family Law
★ Government/Regulation
★ Health Care/Human Services
Indian/Tribal Law
Intellectual Property
★ International/Comparative Law
Jurisprudence
Labor Law
Land Use Law/Natural Resources
Lawyering Skills
Legal History/Philosophy
Litigation
Maritime Law
Media Law
Mediation
Probate Law
★ Public Interest
Securities
Tax Law
(★ indicates an area of special strength)

Clinical Courses Students receive degree credit for clinical courses. (Clinical practicum is not required.) Among the clinical areas offered are:

Criminal Defense
Criminal Prosecution
Education
Elderly Advocacy
Environmental Law
Family Practice
Government Litigation
Health
Land Rights/Natural Resource
Mediation
Public Interest

35% of the students participate in internship programs.

DUQUESNE UNIVERSITY
SCHOOL OF LAW

Pittsburgh, Pennsylvania

INFORMATION CONTACT
Nicholas P. Cafardi, Dean
900 Locust Street
Pittsburgh, PA 15282

Phone: 412-396-6280
E-mail: ricci@duq2.cc.duq.edu
Web site: http://www.duq.edu/law/

LAW STUDENT PROFILE [1997–98]

FULL-TIME   Enrollment: 337
Women: 45%   Men: 55%

PART-TIME   Enrollment: 330
Women: 42%   Men: 58%

RACIAL or ETHNIC COMPOSITION
African American, 4%; Asian/Pacific Islander, 0.3%; Hispanic, 1%; International, 0%

APPLICANTS and ADMITTEES
Seats available: 264
Median LSAT score: 155
Median GPA: 3.2

Duquesne University School of Law is a private institution that organizes classes on a semester calendar system. The campus is situated in an urban setting. Founded in 1911, first ABA approved in 1960, and an AALS member, Duquesne University School of Law offers JD, JD/MBA, JD/MDiv, and JD/MS degrees.

Faculty consists of 30 full-time and 45 part-time members in 1997–98. 9 full-time faculty members are women.

Application Information *Required:* LSAT, LSDAS, application form, application fee of $50, baccalaureate degree, 2 letters of recommendation. *Application deadline* for fall term is April 1.

Financial Aid In 1997–98, 40% of all students received some form of financial aid. Merit-based grants/scholarships, need-based grants/scholarships, and federal work-study loans are also available. To apply for financial assistance, students must complete the Free Application for Federal Student Aid. Financial aid contact: Duquesne University, Office of Financial Aid, Administration Building, Ground Floor, Pittsburgh, PA 15282. Phone: 412-396-6607. Completed financial aid forms should be received by May 31.

AT a GLANCE

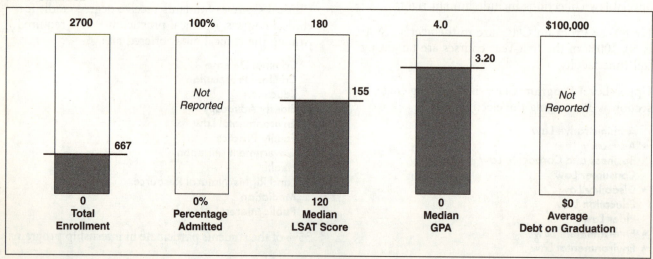

Degree Options

Degree	Total Credits Required	Length of Program
JD–Juris Doctor		3–5 yrs, full-time or part-time [day, evening]
JD/MBA–Juris Doctor/Master of Business Administration–Joint Degree		4 yrs [day]
JD/MDiv–Juris Doctor/Master of Divinity–Joint Degree		5 yrs, full-time only [day]
JD/MS–Juris Doctor/Master of Science–Environmental Science and Management Joint Degree		4 yrs, full-time only

Law School Library Duquesne University Law Library has 6 professional staff members and contains more than 218,158 volumes and 4,442 periodicals. 246 seats are available in the library. When classes are in session, the library is open 102 hours per week.

WESTLAW and LEXIS-NEXIS are available. Special law collections include Federal Depository for government documents collection, Microform collection.

First-Year Program Class size in the average section is 57.

Upper-Level Program Among the electives are:

Administrative Law
Advocacy
Bankruptcy
Business and Corporate Law
Constitutional Law
Consumer Law
Environmental Law
Evidence
Family Law
Government/Regulation
Health Care/Human Services
Immigration
Intellectual Property
International/Comparative Law
Jurisprudence
Labor Law
Land Use Law/Natural Resources
Lawyering Skills
Legal History/Philosophy
Litigation
Mediation
Probate Law
Securities
Tax Law

Clinical Courses Students receive degree credit for clinical courses. (Clinical practicum is not required.) Among the clinical areas offered are:

Civil Litigation
Civil Rights
Criminal Prosecution
Environmental Law
General Practice

Internships are available. International exchange programs permit students to visit China and Russian Federation.

TEMPLE UNIVERSITY
SCHOOL OF LAW

Philadelphia, Pennsylvania

INFORMATION CONTACT
Robert J. Reinstein, Dean
1719 North Broad Street
Philadelphia, PA 19122

Phone: 215-204-7863   Fax: 215-204-1185
E-mail: law@astro.ocis.temple.edu
Web site: http://www.temple.edu/lawschool/

LAW STUDENT PROFILE [1997–98]

FULL-TIME   Enrollment: 770
Women: 50%   Men: 50%

PART-TIME   Enrollment: 338
Women: 46%   Men: 54%

RACIAL or ETHNIC COMPOSITION
African American, 14%; Asian/Pacific Islander, 9%; Hispanic, 4%; Native American, 1%

APPLICANTS and ADMITTEES
Number applied: 2,712
Admitted: 1,064
Percentage accepted: 39%
Seats available: 370
Median LSAT score: 155
Median GPA: 3.2

Temple University School of Law is a public institution that organizes classes on a semester calendar system. The campus is situated in an urban setting. Founded in 1895, first ABA approved in 1933, and an AALS member, Temple University School of Law offers JD, JD/LLM, JD/MBA, and LLM degrees.

Faculty consists of 55 full-time and 171 part-time members in 1997–98. 17 full-time faculty members and 53 part-time faculty members are women. 100% of all faculty members have a JD; 31% have advanced law degrees. Of all faculty members, 3% are Asian/Pacific Islander, 8% are African American, 1% are Hispanic, 88% are white.

Application Information *Required:* LSAT, LSDAS, application form, application fee of $50, baccalaureate degree, minimum 2.4 GPA, personal statement, college transcripts. *Recommended:* recommendations and essay.

Financial Aid In 1997–98, 76% of all students received some form of financial aid. Loans, loan repayment assistance program (LRAP), merit-based grants/scholarships, need-based grants/scholarships, and federal work-study loans are also available. The average student debt at graduation is $48,935. To apply for financial assistance, students must complete the Free Application for Federal Student

AT a GLANCE

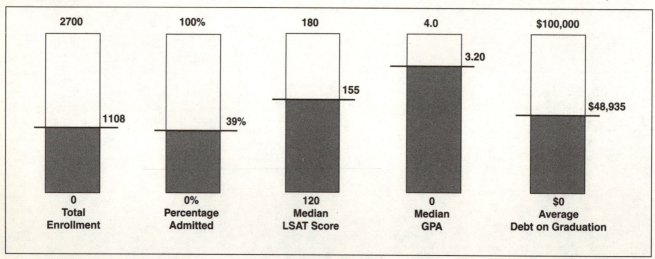

Degree Options

Degree	Total Credits Required	Length of Program
JD–Doctor of Laws	86	3–4 yrs, full-time or part-time [day, evening, summer]
JD/LLM–Juris Doctor/Master of Laws–Transnational Law	98	3.5–4.5 yrs, full-time or part-time [day, evening, summer]
JD/LLM–Juris Doctor/Master of Laws–Taxation	98	3.5–4.5 yrs, full-time or part-time [day, evening, summer]
JD/MBA–Juris Doctor/Master of Business Administration–Dual-degree Program	110	3–4 yrs, full-time or part-time [day, evening, summer]
LLM–Master of Laws–Trial Advocacy	24	1 yr, part-time only [evening, weekend, summer]

Aid and institutional forms. Financial aid contact: Johanne Johnston, Director of Financial Aid, 1719 North Broad Street, Philadelphia, PA 19122. Phone: 215-204-8943 or toll-free 800-560-1428. Fax: 215-204-1185. E-mail: jjohnsto@vm.temple.edu. Completed financial aid forms should be received by March 1.

Law School Library Charles Klein Law Library has 16 professional staff members and contains more than 481,649 volumes and 2,250 periodicals. 644 seats are available in the library. When classes are in session, the library is open 91 hours per week.

WESTLAW and LEXIS-NEXIS are available, as are the World Wide Web, online bibliographic services, and CD-ROM players. 126 computer workstations are available to students in the library. Special law collections include William Rawle collection of 17th, 18th, and 19th century law books.

First-Year Program Class size in the average section is 70; 90% of the first-year courses are taught by full-time faculty.

Upper-Level Program Class size in the average section is 23. Among the electives are:

  Administrative Law
★ Advocacy
★ Business and Corporate Law
  Consumer Law
  Education Law
  Entertainment Law
  Environmental Law
  Family Practice
  Government/Regulation

★ Health Care/Human Services
  Indian/Tribal Law
★ Intellectual Property
★ International/Comparative Law
  Jurisprudence
  Labor Law
  Land Use Law/Natural Resources
★ Lawyering Skills
  Legal History/Philosophy
★ Litigation
  Maritime Law
  Mediation
  Probate Law
★ Public Interest
  Securities
★ Tax Law
★ Technology Law
(★ indicates an area of special strength)

Clinical Courses Students receive degree credit for clinical courses. (Clinical practicum is not required.) Among the clinical areas offered are:

  Civil Litigation
  Corporate Law
  Criminal Defense
  Criminal Prosecution
  Elderly Advocacy
  Family Practice
  General Practice
  Health
  Immigration
  Mediation
  Public Interest
  Tax Law

International exchange programs permit students to visit Greece; Israel; Italy; and Japan.

UNIVERSITY OF PENNSYLVANIA
LAW SCHOOL

Philadelphia, Pennsylvania

INFORMATION CONTACT

Colin S. Diver, Dean
3400 Chestnut Street
Philadelphia, PA 19104

Phone: 215-898-7061   Fax: 215-573-2025
Web site: http://www.law.upenn.edu/

LAW STUDENT PROFILE [1997–98]

FULL-TIME   Enrollment: 788
Women: 41%   Men: 59%

PART-TIME   Enrollment: 16
Women: 38%   Men: 63%

RACIAL or ETHNIC COMPOSITION
African American, 8%; Asian/Pacific Islander, 7%; Hispanic, 7%; Nataive American, 0.4%; International, 13%

APPLICANTS and ADMITTEES
Number applied: 3,844
Admitted: 1,141
Percentage accepted: 30%
Seats available: 230
Average LSAT score: 166
Average GPA: 3.6

University of Pennsylvania Law School is a private institution that organizes classes on a semester calendar system. The campus is situated in an urban setting. Founded in 1790, first ABA approved in 1923, and an AALS member, University of Pennsylvania Law School offers JD, JD/BS, JD/MA, JD/MBA, JD/MSW, JD/MUP, JD/PhD, JSD, and LLM degrees.

Faculty consists of 43 full-time and 53 part-time members in 1997–98. 10 full-time faculty members and 17 part-time faculty members are women. 98% of all faculty members have a JD degree.

Application Information *Required:* LSAT, LSDAS, application form, application fee of $65, baccalaureate degree, 2 letters of recommendation, personal statement, college transcripts, resume. *Application deadline* for fall term is March 1.

Costs The 1997–98 tuition is $24,150. Fees: $1638.

Financial Aid In 1997–98, 40% of all students received some form of financial aid. Loans, loan repayment assistance program (LRAP), merit-based grants/scholarships, need-based grants/scholarships, and federal work-study loans are also available. The average student debt at graduation is $65,404. To apply for financial assistance, students must complete the Free Application for Federal Student Aid and institutional forms. Financial aid contact: Janice Austin, Assistant Dean of Admissions, 3400 Chestnut Street, Philadelphia, PA 19104. Phone: 215-898-7400. Fax: 215-573-2025. E-mail:

AT a GLANCE

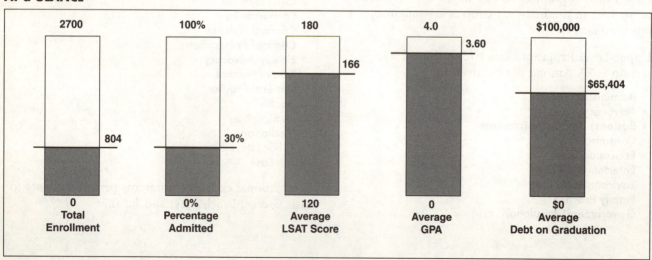

Degree Options

Degree	Total Credits Required	Length of Program
JD–Doctor of Laws	89	3 yrs, full-time only [day]
JD/BS–Juris Doctor/Bachelor of Science–Economics		6 yrs, full-time only [day]
JD/MA–Juris Doctor/Master of Arts–Islamic Studies Dual-degree		4 yrs, full-time only [day]
JD/MA–Juris Doctor/Master of Arts–Government Administration Dual Degree		4 yrs, full-time only
JD/MBA–Juris Doctor/Master of Business Administration–Dual Degree	134	4 yrs, full-time only [day]
JD/MSW–Juris Doctor/Master of Social Work–Dual Degree		4 yrs, full-time only [day]
JD/MUP–Juris Doctor/Masters of Urban Planning–Dual Degree		4 yrs, full-time only [day]
JD/PhD–Juris Doctor/Doctor of Philosophy–Economics, Public Policy, Philosophy Dual-degree		4–7 yrs, full-time only [day]
JSD–Doctor of Juridical Science		2–5 yrs, full-time only [day]
LLM–Master of Laws	20	1 yr, full-time only [day]
LLM–Master of Laws–Comparative Law	16	1 yr, full-time only [day]

admissions@oyez.law.upenn.edu. Completed financial aid forms should be received by March 1.

Law School Library Biddle Law Library has 15 professional staff members and contains more than 639,656 volumes and 7,311 periodicals. 550 seats are available in the library. When classes are in session, the library is open 111 hours per week.

WESTLAW and LEXIS-NEXIS are available, as are the World Wide Web, online bibliographic services, and CD-ROM players. 130 computer workstations are available to students in the library. Special law collections include Archives of the American Law Institute and of the National Conference of Commissioners on Uniform State Law, the papers of Judge David Bazelon.

First-Year Program Class size in the average section is 116; 92% of the first-year courses are taught by full-time faculty.

Upper-Level Program Class size in the average section is 70. Among the electives are:

Administrative Law
Advocacy
Business and Corporate Law
Consumer Law
Education Law
Entertainment Law
Environmental Law
Family Law
Government/Regulation
Health Care/Human Services
Intellectual Property
International/Comparative Law
Jurisprudence
Labor Law
Land Use Law/Natural Resources
Lawyering Skills
Legal History/Philosophy
Litigation
Media Law
Mediation
Probate Law
Public Interest
Securities
Tax Law

Clinical Courses Students receive degree credit for clinical courses. (Clinical practicum is not required.) Among the clinical areas offered are:

Civil Litigation
Civil Rights
Corporate Law
Criminal Defense
Criminal Prosecution
Elderly Advocacy
Family Practice
General Practice
Immigration
Juvenile Law
Mediation
Public Interest
Tax Law

1% of the students participate in internship programs.

DEAN'S STATEMENT . . .

The mission of the University of Pennsylvania Law School is to generate intellectual and human capital for the leadership of the legal profession in the twenty-first century through research and teaching. We foresee that in the coming century lawyers will be called upon to integrate the findings of an ever wider array of human knowledge, change specialties, and update substantive knowledge more frequently and rapidly, move readily across professional boundaries, and devote increasing energy to building, maintaining, and leading organizations. Leaders of the profession will require not only conventional doctrinal and institutional knowledge and skills in analytical reasoning, research, and written and oral communications, but also skills in integrations and synthesis of knowledge, strategic and tactical thinking, and the capacity of continuous self-criticism and self-education.

Two centuries after our founding, Penn Law School takes the lead by making the study of law central to the education of the new generation of leaders—the "interprofessional professionals" of the next century. Among elite, research-oriented American law schools, Penn has long been known for its strengths in such traditional doctrinal fields as administrative law, civil procedure, commercial law, criminal law, and labor law; its interdisciplinary research in fields such as economics, history, and philosophy; its contributions to law reform through its relationship with organizations like the American Law Institute and the National Constitutional Center; and its commitment to integrating theory and practice in such experiential learning contexts as clinical and public service programs. Creative and selective partnerships with those resources will enable Penn Law to re-create a national model for the study and teaching of leadership in law. I strongly encourage you to consider Penn Law as an institution to pursue your legal education.

—Colin S. Diver, Dean and Bernard G. Segal Professor of Law

HISTORY, CAMPUS, AND LOCATION

The University of Pennsylvania traces its roots to Benjamin Franklin's founding of the Academe and Charitable School of the Province of Pennsylvania in 1740. In 1790, the institution (reconstituted during the Revolutionary War as the College of Philadelphia) named as its first Professor of Law James Wilson (a signer of the Declaration of Independence, architect with James Madison of the Constitution, and one of the six original justices of the United States Supreme Court), who presented a series of lectures offering a wide-ranging comparative and critical analysis of legal systems past and present.

In 1900 the Law School moved into Lewis Hall at 34th and Chestnut Streets on the University campus. The Law School's location on the campus of a major research university is ideal because it combines the best of a small school environment with the resources of a large university. In many ways—academically, socially, philosophically, and professionally—Penn Law students benefit greatly from the dynamic communities that surround Penn Law, the University of Pennsylvania, University City, and Philadelphia. Students are fortunate in having easy access to all the amenities of a major metropolis at the School's doorstep.

Philadelphia's Center City is less than 2 miles from the University's campus on the west bank of the Schuylkill River, which provides law students with access to local, state, and federal judiciaries and government agencies; law firms; and public services organizations.

SPECIAL QUALITIES OF THE SCHOOL

The University of Pennsylvania Law School provides a hospitable and rigorous environment for learning. Each year it selects a small, able, and diverse class of approximately 240 individuals and combines an excellent student body with outstanding faculty members who have varied educational backgrounds and a wide spectrum of experience.

There is a certain quality of life at Penn Law that is not often found in law schools. These academically gifted individuals come together to tackle the rigorous curriculum, but do so in a way that is more collegial than is the norm in legal education. Students cooperate with each other, they share notes, and they help and support each other. Because there is no rank in class, a student competes against himself or herself rather than against other students.

TECHNOLOGY ON CAMPUS

The Law School maintains a Virtual Lab environment in which hundreds of network connections provide every student access to electronic resources within the library, classrooms, and University housing. Most commonly students use e-mail, Netnews, and the World Wide Web for classes and to keep informed of developments in the School and beyond. Students also use LEXIS, WESTLAW, CD-ROM databases, and the World Wide Web for legal research; word processing for class assignments; spreadsheets for classes with heavy quantitative content; and databases, provided by Career Planning and Services for employment searches.

SCHOLARSHIPS AND LOANS

It has long been the policy of the Law School that every admitted applicant who wishes to enroll should not be prevented from doing so by lack of funds. In recent years the necessary financial aid support has been provided by a combination of student and parental contributions, government guaranteed loans, grants, merit awards, and University loans, appropriate to the circumstances of each individual student.

STUDENT ACTIVITIES AND OPPORTUNITIES

Law Review The nation's oldest continuous law journal is the *University of Pennsylvania Law Review*. Other journals include the *Journal of Constitutional Law*, the *Journal of International Economic Law*, and the *Journal of Labor and Employment Law*. Admission to the reviews are based on academic standing and a writing competition. Approximately 90 students participate in the publications.

Moot Court Appellate Advocacy II is the Law School's second-year intramural moot court competition. The students research and write briefs and then present their case in one or perhaps two rounds of oral argument before a panel of students, faculty, and judges. In recent years, Penn students have participated in the National Moot Court Competition, the Merna B. Marshall Moot Court Competition, the Frederick B. Douglass Moot Court Competition, and the Jessup Cup Competition.

Extracurricular Activities Students at the Law School do not merely come to get an education and leave without giving something back to the school and the community. They actively participate in the daily operations of the Law School by serving on every standing committee. Student organizations provide opportunities for activities from intellectual and scholarly engagement to social and public service requirements.

Special Opportunities One of the hallmarks of Penn Law is the array of extraordinary interdisciplinary studies available at the University. Students can draw upon the vast resources of the University to pursue studies and joint degrees in many different disciplines, thus achieving a diverse and intensive education.

Since 1990, the Law School, in keeping with the ethical tenets of the legal profession to render public services, has adopted a public service requirement where all second- and third-year law students perform a total of 70 hours of law-related public service as a condition of graduation. Placements also increase the students' lawyering skills and expose them to new areas of the law. The Law School operates a state-of-the-art teaching law clinical program. Students have the opportunity to obtain valuable learning experiences for academic credit while at the same time providing much needed legal assistance to clients in the following clinics: the Civil Practice Clinic, the Mediation Clinic, the Small Business Clinic, and the Legislative Clinical Seminar.

Opportunities for Members of Minority Groups and Women Traditionally, the enrollment of minority students has been approximately 25 percent of each entering class. Members of minority groups actively participate in the entire life of the Law School. In addition to ethnic student organizations, the Women's Law Group, OWLS (Older, Wiser Law Students), and Lambda Law (gay and lesbian law student group) are examples of the opportunities for students to have vital roles in the law school community.

Special Certificate Programs There are two unique certificate programs: Certificate of Study in Public Policy and Management with the Wharton School and a Certificate in Women's Studies.

BAR PASSAGE, CAREER SERVICES, AND PLACEMENT

The majority of Penn Law students take the New York and Pennsylvania bar exams.

A wide range of programs to provide balance between practical, how-to sessions with broader programming that will expose students to the great wealth of opportunity and variety are available to the law graduate. Services include assistance to improve presentation skills with resume writing workshops and interviewing programs and, in the upperclass years, in-depth assistance for the clerkship application process.

In addition to the Career Services staff, expertise in conducting a successful job search is provided by hiring partners, recruiting coordinators, fellowships program directors, judges, law clerks, career planning experts, and particularly alumni.

Legal Field	Percentage of Graduates	Average Salary
Academic	1%	n/a
Business	7%	n/a
Government	4%	$37,700
Judicial Clerkship	16%	n/a
Private Practice	68%	$85,000
Public Interest	5%	$36,500
Other	n/a	n/a

CORRESPONDENCE AND INFORMATION

Law School
University of Pennsylvania
3400 Chestnut Street
Philadelphia, Pennsylvania 19104-6204
Telephone: 215-898-7400
Fax: 215-573-2025
E-mail: admissions@oyez.law.upenn.edu
World Wide Web: http://www.law.upenn.edu

UNIVERSITY OF PITTSBURGH
SCHOOL OF LAW

Pittsburgh, Pennsylvania

INFORMATION CONTACT
Dr. David Herring, Interim Dean
3900 Forbes Avenue
Pittsburgh, PA 15260

Phone: 412-648-1401   Fax: 412-648-2647
E-mail: miller@law.pitt.edu
Web site: http://www.pitt.edu/

LAW STUDENT PROFILE [1997–98]

FULL-TIME   Enrollment: 703
Women: 42%   Men: 58%

PART-TIME   Enrollment: 1
Women: 100%

RACIAL or ETHNIC COMPOSITION
African American, 6%; Asian/Pacific Islander, 2%; Hispanic, 2%; International, 2%

APPLICANTS and ADMITTEES
Number applied: 1,184
Admitted: 222
Percentage accepted: 19%
Seats available: 220
Average LSAT score: 155
Average GPA: 3.2

University of Pittsburgh School of Law is a public institution that organizes classes on a semester calendar system. The campus is situated in an urban setting. Founded in 1895, first ABA approved in 1923, and an AALS member, University of Pittsburgh School of Law offers JD, JD/MA, JD/MBA, JD/MPAd, JD/MPH, JD/MPIA, JD/MS, JD/MURP, and LLM degrees.

Faculty consists of 42 full-time and 20 part-time members in 1997–98. 18 full-time faculty members and 7 part-time faculty members are women. 91% of all faculty members have a JD; 25% have advanced law degrees. Of all faculty members, 7% are Asian/Pacific Islander, 4% are African American, 89% are white.

Application Information *Required:* LSAT, LSDAS, application form, application fee of $40, baccalaureate degree, personal statement, college transcripts. *Recommended:* recommendations.

Financial Aid Loans, loan repayment assistance program (LRAP), merit-based grants/scholarships, and need-based grants/scholarships are available. The average student debt at graduation is $55,000. To apply for financial assistance, students must complete the Free Application for Federal Student Aid, institutional forms, and scholarship specific applications. Financial aid contact: Fredi G. Miller,

AT a GLANCE

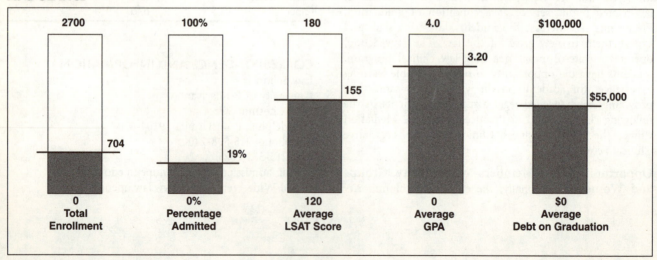

Total Enrollment	Percentage Admitted	Average LSAT Score	Average GPA	Average Debt on Graduation
2700 / 704 / 0	100% / 19% / 0%	180 / 155 / 120	4.0 / 3.20 / 0	$100,000 / $55,000 / $0

Degree Options

Degree	Total Credits Required	Length of Program
JD–Juris Doctor–Program	88	3 yrs, full-time only [day]
JD/MA–Juris Doctor/Master of Arts–Joint-degree in Medical Ethics	100	4 yrs, full-time only [day]
JD/MBA–Juris Doctor/Master of Business Administration–Joint Degree	115	3.5 yrs, full-time only [day]
JD/MPAd–Juris Doctor/Master of Public Administration–Joint Degree	115	4 yrs, full-time only [day]
JD/MPH–Juris Doctor/Master of Public Health–Joint Degree	118	4 yrs, full-time only [day]
JD/MPIA–Juris Doctor/Master of Public and International Affairs–Joint Degree	115	4 yrs, full-time only [day]
JD/MS–Juris Doctor/Master of Science–Joint-degree in Arts Management	118	4 yrs, full-time only [day]
JD/MS–Juris Doctor/Master of Science–Industrial Administration	118	4 yrs, full-time only [day]
JD/MURP–Juris Doctor/Masters of Urban and Regional Planning–Joint Degree	115	4 yrs, full-time only [day]
LLM–Master of Laws	24	1 yr, full-time only [day]

Assistant Dean for Admissions and Financial Aid, 3900 Forbes Avenue, Pittsburgh, PA 15260. Phone: 412-648-1400. Fax: 412-648-2647. E-mail: admissions@law.pitt.edu.

Law School Library Barco Law Library has 8 professional staff members and contains more than 364,397 volumes and 5,154 periodicals. 446 seats are available in the library. When classes are in session, the library is open 102 hours per week.

WESTLAW and LEXIS-NEXIS are available, as are the World Wide Web, online bibliographic services, and CD-ROM players. 43 computer workstations are available to students in the library. Special law collections include rare book collection.

First-Year Program Class size in the average section is 76; 100% of the first-year courses are taught by full-time faculty.

Upper-Level Program Class size in the average section is 36. Among the electives are:

Administrative Law
Advocacy
Business and Corporate Law
Commercial Law
Constitutional Law
Criminal Law
Education Law
★ **Elder Law**

Environmental Law
★ **Family Law**
★ **Health Care/Human Services**
Intellectual Property
★ **International/Comparative Law**
Jurisprudence
Labor Law
Land Use Law/Natural Resources
Lawyering Skills
Legal History/Philosophy
Litigation
Mediation
Personal Injury
Probate Law
Public Interest
Securities
Tax Law
(★ *indicates an area of special strength*)

Clinical Courses Students receive degree credit for clinical courses. (Clinical practicum is not required.) Among the clinical areas offered are:

Corporate Law
Disability Law
Elderly Advocacy
Health
Juvenile Law

38% of the students participate in internship programs.

VILLANOVA UNIVERSITY
SCHOOL OF LAW

Villanova, Pennsylvania

LAW STUDENT PROFILE [1997–98]

FULL-TIME   Enrollment: 697
Women: 46%   Men: 54%

PART-TIME   Enrollment: 80
Women: 35%   Men: 65%

RACIAL or ETHNIC COMPOSITION
African American, 5%; Asian/Pacific Islander, 6%; Hispanic, 3%; Native American, 1%; International, 0%

APPLICANTS and ADMITTEES
Number applied: 1,282
Admitted: 714
Percentage accepted: 56%
Seats available: 230
Average LSAT score: 158
Average GPA: 3.4

Villanova University School of Law is a private institution that organizes classes on a semester calendar system. The campus is situated in a suburban setting. Founded in 1953, first ABA approved in 1953, and an AALS member, Villanova University School of Law offers JD, JD/MBA, JD/PhD, and LLM degrees.

Faculty consists of 39 full-time and 68 part-time members in 1997–98. 10 full-time faculty members and 18 part-time faculty members are women. 100% of all faculty members have a JD; 29% have advanced law degrees. Of all faculty members, 1% are Native American, 1% are Asian/Pacific Islander, 4% are African American, 1% are Hispanic, 92% are white, 1% are international.

Application Information *Required:* LSAT, LSDAS, application form, application fee of $75, baccalaureate degree, college transcripts. *Recommended:* recommendations, personal statement, resume. *Application deadline* for fall term is March 1.

Financial Aid In 1997–98, 73% of all students received some form of financial aid. 107 research assistantships, totaling $250,000; 6 teaching assistantships, totaling $4800, were awarded. Fellowships, graduate assistantships, loans, merit-based grants/scholarships, need-based grants/scholarships, and federal work-study loans are also available. The

AT a GLANCE

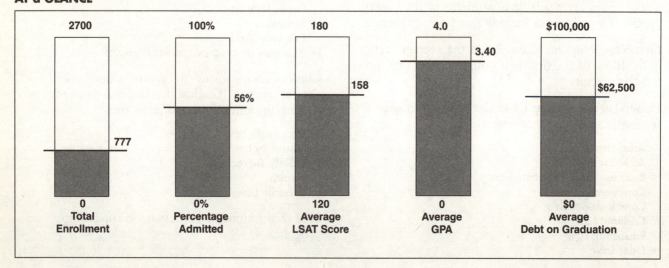

Degree Options

Degree	Total Credits Required	Length of Program
JD–Doctor of Laws	87	3 yrs, full-time only [day]
JD/MBA–Juris Doctor/Master of Business Administration	135	3–4 yrs, full-time only [day]
JD/PhD–Juris Doctor/Doctor of Philosophy–Clinical Psychology	199	6–7 yrs, full-time only [day]
LLM–Master of Laws–Taxation	24	1 yr, full-time or part-time [evening]

average student debt at graduation is $62,500. To apply for financial assistance, students must complete the Free Application for Federal Student Aid and institutional forms. Financial aid contact: Wendy Barron, Director of Financial Aid, 299 North Spring Mill Road, Villanova, PA 19087. Phone: 610-519-7015. Fax: 610-519-6291. E-mail: barron@law.vill.edu. Completed financial aid forms should be received by March 15.

Law School Library Arthur Clement Pulling Library has 8 professional staff members and contains more than 303,752 volumes and 3,369 periodicals. 368 seats are available in the library. When classes are in session, the library is open 168 hours per week.

WESTLAW and LEXIS-NEXIS are available, as are the World Wide Web, online bibliographic services, and CD-ROM players. 150 computer workstations are available to students in the library.

First-Year Program Class size in the average section is 117; 100% of the first-year courses are taught by full-time faculty.

Upper-Level Program Class size in the average section is 25.

Clinical Courses Students receive degree credit for clinical courses. (Clinical practicum is not required.) Among the clinical areas offered are:

Civil Litigation
Education
Elderly Advocacy
Juvenile Law
Public Interest
Tax Law

21% of the students participate in internship programs.

WIDENER UNIVERSITY
SCHOOL OF LAW

Chester, Pennsylvania

LAW STUDENT PROFILE [1997–98]

FULL-TIME   Enrollment: 1,064
Women: 45%   Men: 55%

PART-TIME   Enrollment: 644
Women: 40%   Men: 60%

RACIAL or ETHNIC COMPOSITION
African American, 3%; Asian/Pacific Islander, 2%; Hispanic, 1%; Nataive American, 0.4%

APPLICANTS and ADMITTEES
Number applied: 1,963
Admitted: 1,423
Percentage accepted: 72%
Seats available: 128
Median LSAT score: 151
Median GPA: 3.0

Widener University School of Law is a private institution that organizes classes on a semester calendar system. The campus is situated in a suburban setting. Founded in 1971, first ABA approved in 1989, and an AALS member, Widener University School of Law offers a JD degree.

Faculty consists of 81 full-time and 83 part-time members in 1997–98. 34 full-time faculty members and 24 part-time faculty members are women. 100% of all faculty members have a JD; 26% have advanced law degrees. Of all faculty members, 7% are African American, 93% are white.

Application Information *Required:* LSAT, LSDAS, application form, application fee of $60, baccalaureate degree, college transcripts. *Recommended:* recommendations and personal statement. *Application deadline* for fall term is May 15.

Financial Aid Loans, loan repayment assistance program (LRAP), merit-based grants/scholarships, need-based grants/scholarships, and federal work-study loans are available. The average student debt at graduation is $55,276. To apply for financial assistance, students must complete the Free Application for Federal Student Aid and institutional forms. Financial aid contact: Anthony Doyle, Assistant Dean for Financial Aid, 4601 Concord Pike, PO Box 7474, Wilmington, DE 19803-0474. Phone: 302-477-

AT a GLANCE

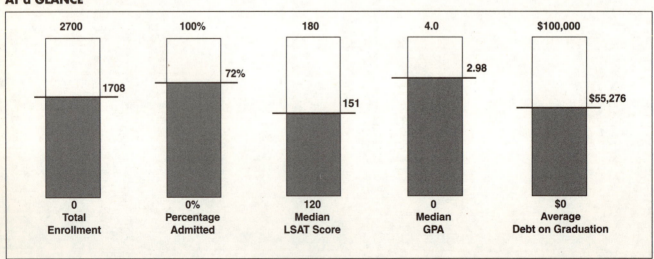

Degree Options

Degree	Total Credits Required	Length of Program
JD–Juris Doctor	87	3–4 yrs, full-time or part-time [day, evening, summer]

2272. Fax: 717-541-3999. Completed financial aid forms should be received by February 15.

Law School Library Widener University School of Law Legal Information Center has 5 professional staff members and contains more than 172,940 volumes and 875 periodicals. 461 seats are available in the library. When classes are in session, the library is open 104 hours per week.

WESTLAW and LEXIS-NEXIS are available, as are the World Wide Web, online bibliographic services, and CD-ROM players. 26 computer workstations are available to students in the library. Special law collections include Corporate Law, Health Law, U.S. Selective Depository for government documents.

First-Year Program Class size in the average section is 70; 100% of the first-year courses are taught by full-time faculty.

Upper-Level Program Class size in the average section is 50. Among the electives are:

    Administrative Law
★ Advocacy
    Business and Corporate Law
★ Civil Law
    Consumer Law
    Education Law

    Entertainment Law
★ Environmental Law
★ Family Law
    Government/Regulation
★ Health Care/Human Services
    Intellectual Property
    International/Comparative Law
★ Judicial Externship
    Jurisprudence
    Labor Law
    Land Use Law/Natural Resources
    Lawyering Skills
    Litigation
    Mediation
    Probate Law
    Public Interest
    Securities
    Tax Law
(★ indicates an area of special strength)

Clinical Courses Students receive degree credit for clinical courses. (Clinical practicum is not required.) Among the clinical areas offered are:

    Civil Litigation
    Environmental Law
    General Practice

27% of the students participate in internship programs.

ROGER WILLIAMS UNIVERSITY
SCHOOL OF LAW

Bristol, Rhode Island

INFORMATION CONTACT
John E. Ryan, Dean and Vice President
10 Metacom Avenue
Bristol, RI 02809

Phone: 401-254-4500   Fax: 401-254-4516
E-mail: mdu@rwulaw.rwu.edu
Web site: http://www.rwu.edu/law/

LAW STUDENT PROFILE [1997–98]

FULL-TIME   Enrollment: 246
Women: 44%   Men: 56%

PART-TIME   Enrollment: 202
Women: 39%   Men: 61%

RACIAL or ETHNIC COMPOSITION
African American, 4%; Asian/Pacific Islander, 1%; Hispanic, 3%

APPLICANTS and ADMITTEES
Number applied: 706
Admitted: 448
Percentage accepted: 63%
Seats available: 150
Median LSAT score: 151
Average GPA: 3.0

Roger Williams University School of Law is a private institution that organizes classes on a semester calendar system. The campus is situated in a small-town setting. Founded in 1992, first ABA approved in 1997, Roger Williams University School of Law offers JD, JD/MCRP, and JD/MMA degrees.

Faculty consists of 29 full-time and 27 part-time members in 1997–98. 10 full-time faculty members and 5 part-time faculty members are women. 97% of all faculty members have a JD; 30% have advanced law degrees. Of all faculty members, 3% are African American, 7% are Hispanic, 90% are white.

Application Information *Required:* LSAT, LSDAS, application form, application fee of $60, baccalaureate degree, personal statement, college transcripts. *Recommended:* 2 letters of recommendation. *Application deadline* for fall term is May 15.

Financial Aid In 1997–98, 86% of all students received some form of financial aid. 20 other awards, totaling $54,800, were given. Fellowships, loans, merit-based grants/scholarships, and need-based grants/scholarships are also available. The average student debt at graduation is $90,000. To apply for financial assistance, students must complete the Free Application for Federal Student Aid. Financial aid contact: Chris Earnshaw, Financial

AT a GLANCE

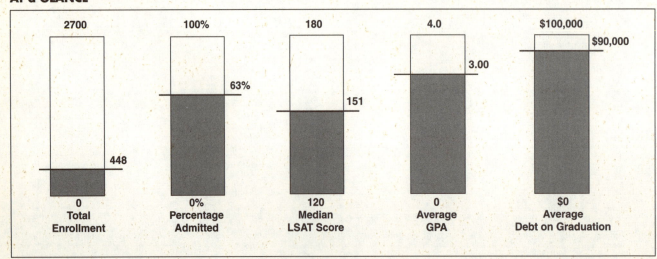

Degree Options

Degree	Total Credits Required	Length of Program
JD–Doctor of Laws	90	3–4 yrs, full-time or part-time [day, evening, weekend, summer]
JD/MCRP–Juris Doctor/Master of Community and Regional Planning–Joint-degree Program	125	4 yrs, full-time or part-time [day, evening, weekend, summer]
JD/MMA–Juris Doctor/Master of Marine Affairs–Joint-degree Program	105	3.5 yrs, full-time only [day, evening, weekend, summer]

Aid Counselor, 10 Metacom Avenue, Bristol, RI 02809. Phone: 401-254-4510. Fax: 401-254-4516. E-mail: cje@rwulaw.rwu.edu. Completed financial aid forms should be received by May 1.

Law School Library Law Library has 6 professional staff members and contains more than 219,629 volumes and 3,098 periodicals. 383 seats are available in the library. When classes are in session, the library is open 110 hours per week.

WESTLAW and LEXIS-NEXIS are available, as are the World Wide Web, online bibliographic services, and CD-ROM players. 56 computer workstations are available to students in the library.

First-Year Program Class size in the average section is 75; 100% of the first-year courses are taught by full-time faculty.

Upper-Level Program Class size in the average section is 40. Among the electives are:

Administrative Law
Advocacy
Business and Corporate Law
Consumer Law
Entertainment Law
★ Environmental Law

★ Family Law
Government/Regulation
Health Care/Human Services
Intellectual Property
International/Comparative Law
Jurisprudence
Labor Law
Land Use Law/Natural Resources
★ Lawyering Skills
Legal History/Philosophy
Litigation
★ Maritime Law
Mediation
Probate Law
Public Interest
Securities
Tax Law
(★ indicates an area of special strength)

Clinical Courses Students receive degree credit for clinical courses. (Clinical practicum is not required.) Among the clinical areas offered are:

Criminal Defense
Family Practice

Internships are available. International exchange programs permit students to visit United Kingdom.

UNIVERSITY OF SOUTH CAROLINA
SCHOOL OF LAW

Columbia, South Carolina

INFORMATION CONTACT

John Montgomery, Dean
Main and Grove Streets
Columbia, SC 29208

Phone: 803-777-6617
Web site: http://www.law.sc.edu/

LAW STUDENT PROFILE [1997–98]

FULL-TIME   Enrollment: 758
Women: 42%   Men: 58%

PART-TIME   Enrollment: 10
Women: 50%   Men: 50%

RACIAL or ETHNIC COMPOSITION
African American, 8%; Asian/Pacific Islander, 1%; Hispanic, 1%; Nataive American, 0.3%; International, 0%

APPLICANTS and ADMITTEES
Number applied: 1,740
Admitted: 440
Percentage accepted: 25%
Seats available: 243
Average LSAT score: 156
Average GPA: 3.2

University of South Carolina School of Law is a public institution that organizes classes on a semester calendar system. Founded in 1867, first ABA approved in 1925, and an AALS member, University of South Carolina School of Law offers JD, JD/MBA, JD/MCJ, JD/MEc, JD/MHR, JD/MPA, JD/MPAd, and JD/MS degrees.

Faculty consists of 45 full-time and 24 part-time members in 1997–98. 2 full-time faculty members and 1 part-time faculty members are women. 100% of all faculty members have a JD degree. Of all faculty members, 4% are African American, 96% are white.

Application Information *Required:* LSAT, LSDAS, application form, application fee of $25, 2 letters of recommendation, personal statement, baccalaureate degree. *Application deadline* for fall term is February 15.

Costs The 1997–98 tuition is $7228 full-time for state residents; $304 per credit hour part-time for state residents. Tuition is $14,986 full-time for nonresidents; $626 per credit hour part-time for nonresidents. Fees: $125 full-time; $37 per semester (minimum) part-time.

Financial Aid 15 fellowships were awarded. Graduate assistantships, loans, merit-based grants/

AT a GLANCE

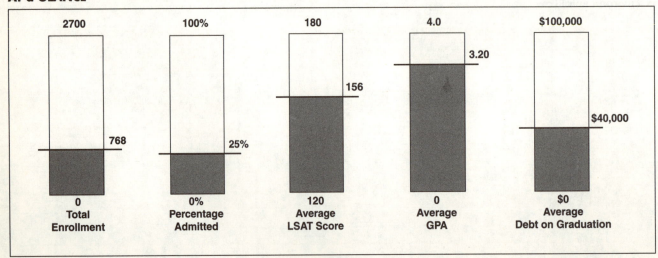

Degree Options

Degree	Total Credits Required	Length of Program
JD–Juris Doctor	90	3–4 yrs, full-time only
JD/MBA–Juris Doctor/Master of Business Administration		4 yrs, full-time only
JD/MCJ–Juris Doctor/Master of Criminal Justice–Joint-degree Program		4 yrs, full-time only
JD/MEc–Juris Doctor/Master of Economics–Joint-degree Program		4 yrs, full-time only
JD/MHR–Juris Doctor/Master of Human Resources		4 yrs, full-time only
JD/MPA–Juris Doctor/Master of Professional Accountancy–Joint-degree Program		4 yrs, full-time only
JD/MPAd–Juris Doctor/Master of Public Administration–Joint-degree Program		4 yrs, full-time only
JD/MS–Juris Doctor/Master of Science–Joint-degree Program International Business		4 yrs, full-time only

scholarships, and need-based grants/scholarships are also available. The average student debt at graduation is $40,000. To apply for financial assistance, students must complete the Free Application for Federal Student Aid and scholarship specific applications. Financial aid contact: John S. Benfield, Assistant Dean, 1714 College Street, Columbia, SC 29208. Phone: 803-777-6605. E-mail: uscfaid@sc.edu. Completed financial aid forms should be received by April 15.

Law School Library Coleman Karesh Law Library has 14 professional staff members and contains more than 412,406 volumes and 3,043 periodicals. 642 seats are available in the library. When classes are in session, the library is open 95 hours per week.

WESTLAW and LEXIS-NEXIS are available, as are the World Wide Web and CD-ROM players. 50 computer workstations are available to students in the library. Special law collections include South Carolina Legal History collection, rare books, microform collection.

First-Year Program Class size in the average section is 75; 100% of the first-year courses are taught by full-time faculty.

Upper-Level Program Class size in the average section is 85. Among the electives are:

Administrative Law
Advocacy

★ **Business and Corporate Law**
Education Law
Entertainment Law
Environmental Law
★ **Family Law**
Government/Regulation
Health Care/Human Services
Intellectual Property
International/Comparative Law
Jurisprudence
Labor Law
Land Use Law/Natural Resources
Lawyering Skills
Legal History/Philosophy
★ **Litigation**
Maritime Law
Media Law
Mediation
Probate Law
Public Interest
Securities
★ **Tax Law**
Unfair Trade Practices
(★ *indicates an area of special strength*)

Clinical Courses Among the clinical areas offered are:

Criminal Defense
Criminal Prosecution
Juvenile Law

Internships are available.

UNIVERSITY OF SOUTH DAKOTA
SCHOOL OF LAW

Vermillion, South Dakota

INFORMATION CONTACT

Barry R. Vickrey, Dean
414 East Clark Street
Vermillion, SD 57069-2390

Phone: 605-677-5443
E-mail: request@jurist.law.usd.edu
Web site: http://usd.edu/law/legal.html

LAW STUDENT PROFILE [1997–98]

FULL-TIME   Enrollment: 223
Women: 39%   Men: 61%

RACIAL or ETHNIC COMPOSITION
African American, 2%; Asian/Pacific Islander, 1%; Native American, 2%

APPLICANTS and ADMITTEES
Number applied: 321
Admitted: 172
Percentage accepted: 54%
Seats available: 182

University of South Dakota School of Law is a public institution that organizes classes on a semester calendar system. The campus is situated in a small-town setting. Founded in 1901, first ABA approved in 1923, and an AALS member, University of South Dakota School of Law offers JD, JD/MA, JD/MBA, JD/MPA, JD/MPAd, and JD/MS degrees.

Faculty consists of 15 full-time and 4 part-time members in 1997–98. 3 full-time faculty members and 1 part-time faculty members are women.

Application Information *Required:* LSAT, LSDAS, application form, application fee of $15, baccalaureate degree, 2 letters of recommendation, personal statement, college transcripts. *Application deadline* for fall term is March 1.

Financial Aid In 1997–98, 40% of all students received some form of financial aid. 17 research assistantships were awarded. Graduate assistantships, loans, and federal work-study loans are also available. To apply for financial assistance, students must complete the Free Application for Federal Student Aid. Financial aid contact: Office of Student Financial Aid, University of South Dakota, 414 East Clark, Vermillion, SD 57069-2390. Phone: 605-677-5446.

AT a GLANCE

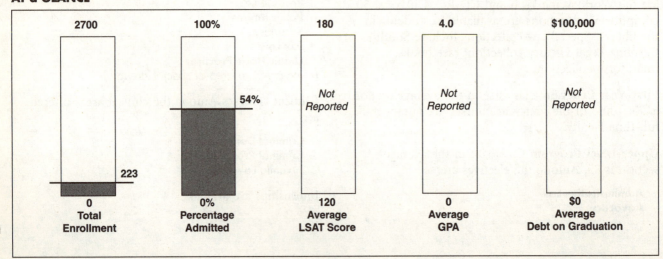

Degree Options

Degree	Total Credits Required	Length of Program
JD–Juris Doctor	90	3 yrs
JD/MA–Juris Doctor/Master of Arts–Joint-degree in Education Administration (non-certificated)		
JD/MA–Juris Doctor/Master of Arts–Joint-degree in English		
JD/MA–Juris Doctor/Master of Arts–Joint-degree in History		
JD/MA–Juris Doctor/Master of Arts–Joint-degree in Political Science		
JD/MA–Juris Doctor/Master of Arts–Joint-degree in Psychology (non-certificated)		
JD/MBA–Juris Doctor/Master of Business Administration–Joint Degree		
JD/MPA–Juris Doctor/Master of Professional Accountancy–Joint Degree		
JD/MPAd–Juris Doctor/Master of Public Administration–Joint Degree		
JD/MS–Juris Doctor/Master of Science–Joint-degree in Administrative Studies		

Law School Library has 5 professional staff members and contains more than 179,082 volumes and 2,074 periodicals. 227 seats are available in the library. When classes are in session, the library is open 96 hours per week.

WESTLAW and LEXIS-NEXIS are available, as are the World Wide Web and CD-ROM players.

First-Year Program Class size in the average section is 73.

Upper-Level Program Among the electives are:

Administrative Law
Business and Corporate Law
Commercial Law
Constitutional Law
Education Law

Environmental Law
Evidence
Family Law
Health Care/Human Services
Indian/Tribal Law
International/Comparative Law
Jurisprudence
Land Use Law/Natural Resources
Legal History/Philosophy
Probate Law
Professional Responsibility
Secure Transactions
Securities
Tax Law
Water Law

Clinical Courses Students receive degree credit for clinical courses.

THE UNIVERSITY OF MEMPHIS
CECIL C. HUMPHREYS SCHOOL OF LAW

Memphis, Tennessee

INFORMATION CONTACT
Donald J. Polden, Dean
Campus Box 526513
Memphis, TN 38152-6513

Phone: 901-678-2421   Fax: 901-678-5210
E-mail: uofmlaw@profnet.law.memphis.ed
Web site: http://www.people.memphis.edu/~law/

LAW STUDENT PROFILE [1997–98]

FULL-TIME   Enrollment: 479
Women: 43%   Men: 57%

PART-TIME   Enrollment: 31
Women: 52%   Men: 48%

RACIAL or ETHNIC COMPOSITION
African American, 9%; Asian/Pacific Islander, 1%; Hispanic, 1%; Nataive American, 0.4%

APPLICANTS and ADMITTEES
Number applied: 830
Admitted: 446
Percentage accepted: 54%
Seats available: 160
Average LSAT score: 155
Average GPA: 3.1

The University of Memphis Cecil C. Humphreys School of Law is a public institution that organizes classes on a semester calendar system. The campus is situated in an urban setting. Founded in 1962, first ABA approved in 1965, The University of Memphis Cecil C. Humphreys School of Law offers JD and JD/MBA degrees.

Faculty consists of 22 full-time and 31 part-time members in 1997–98. 6 full-time faculty members and 11 part-time faculty members are women. 100% of all faculty members have a JD; 50% have advanced law degrees. Of all faculty members, 4% are African American, 96% are white.

Application Information *Required:* LSAT, LSDAS, application form, application fee of $15, baccalaureate degree, 1 recommendation, personal statement. *Recommended:* resume. *Application deadline* for fall term is February 15.

Costs The 1997–98 tuition is $3654 full-time for state residents; $210 per credit hour part-time for state residents. Tuition is $8964 full-time for nonresidents; $505 per credit hour part-time for nonresidents.

Financial Aid In 1997–98, 72% of all students received some form of financial aid. 15 fellowships, totaling $108,000; 22 research assistantships, totaling

AT a GLANCE

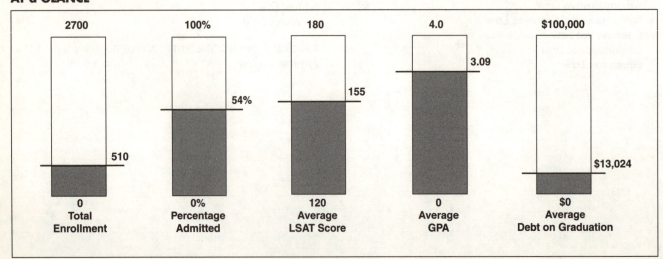

Degree Options

Degree	Total Credits Required	Length of Program
JD–Doctor of Law	90	3–4 yrs, full-time or part-time [day, summer]
JD/MBA–Juris Doctor/Master of Business Administration–Dual-degree Program	110	4–5 yrs, full-time or part-time [day, summer]

$88,434, were awarded. Fellowships, graduate assistantships, loans, merit-based grants/scholarships, and federal work-study loans are also available. The average student debt at graduation is $13,024. To apply for financial assistance, students must complete the Free Application for Federal Student Aid and institutional forms. Financial aid contact: Ms. Karen Smith, Assistant Director, Student Financial Aid, 312 Scates Hall, Memphis, TN 38152. Phone: 901-678-3687. Fax: 901-678-5210. E-mail: kasmith@cc.memphis.edu. Completed financial aid forms should be received by April 1.

Law School Library has 5 professional staff members and contains more than 267,566 volumes and 3,015 periodicals. 299 seats are available in the library. When classes are in session, the library is open 107 hours per week.

WESTLAW and LEXIS-NEXIS are available, as are the World Wide Web, online bibliographic services, and CD-ROM players. 30 computer workstations are available to students in the library.

First-Year Program Class size in the average section is 80; 100% of the first-year courses are taught by full-time faculty.

Upper-Level Program Class size in the average section is 50. Among the electives are:

Administrative Law

★ **Advocacy**
★ **Business and Corporate Law**
  Civil Rights
  Consumer Law
  Entertainment Law
  Environmental Law
  Family Law
  Federal Courts
  Insurance
  Intellectual Property
  International/Comparative Law
  Jurisprudence
  Labor Law
  Land Use Law/Natural Resources
  Lawyering Skills
  Litigation
  Mediation
  Probate Law
  Securities
★ **Tax Law**
(★ indicates an area of special strength)

Clinical Courses Students receive degree credit for clinical courses. (Clinical practicum is not required.) Among the clinical areas offered are:

Children's Advocacy
Civil Litigation
Elderly Advocacy

10% of the students participate in internship programs.

UNIVERSITY OF TENNESSEE, KNOXVILLE
COLLEGE OF LAW

Knoxville, Tennessee

INFORMATION CONTACT

Karen R. Britton, Director of Admissions and
Career Services
1505 West Cumberland Avenue
Knoxville, TN 37996-1810

Phone: 423-974-4131   Fax: 423-974-1572
E-mail: lawadmit@libra.law.utk.edu
Web site: http://www.law.utk.edu/

LAW STUDENT PROFILE [1997–98]

FULL-TIME   Enrollment: 494
Women: 45%   Men: 55%

RACIAL or ETHNIC COMPOSITION
African American, 8%; Asian/Pacific Islander, 0.4%; Hispanic,
1%; Native American, 1%

APPLICANTS and ADMITTEES
Number applied: 1,144
Admitted: 394
Percentage accepted: 34%
Seats available: 150
Average LSAT score: 155
Average GPA: 3.5

University of Tennessee, Knoxville College of Law
is a public institution. The campus is situated in an
urban setting. Founded in 1890, first ABA approved
in 1926, and an AALS member, University of
Tennessee, Knoxville College of Law offers JD,
JD/MBA, and JD/MPAd degrees.

Faculty consists of 31 full-time and 37 part-time
members in 1997–98. 9 full-time faculty members
and 11 part-time faculty members are women. 100%
of all faculty members have a JD; 10% have
advanced law degrees. Of all faculty members, 3%
are African American, 97% are white.

Application Information *Required:* LSAT, LSDAS,
application form, application fee of $15, baccalaure-
ate degree, 2 letters of recommendation, personal
statement, essay, college transcripts. *Application
deadline* for fall term is February 1.

Financial Aid In 1997–98, 77% of all students
received some form of financial aid. Loans, merit-
based grants/scholarships, need-based grants/
scholarships, and federal work-study loans are also
available. The average student debt at graduation is
$32,559. To apply for financial assistance, students
must complete the Free Application for Federal
Student Aid, institutional forms, and scholarship
specific applications. Financial aid contact: Janet S.
Hatcher, Admissions and Financial Aid Counselor,

AT a GLANCE

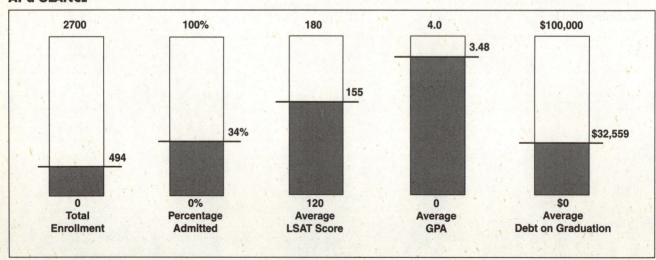

Degree Options

Degree	Total Credits Required	Length of Program
JD–Juris Doctor	89	3–5 yrs, full-time only [day]
JD/MBA–Juris Doctor/Master of Business Administration–Dual-degree Program		4–5 yrs, full-time only [day]
JD/MPAd–Juris Doctor/Master of Public Administration–Dual-degree Program		4–5 yrs, full-time only [day]

1505 West Cumberland Avenue, Suite 161, Knoxville, TN 37996-1810. Phone: 423-974-4131. Fax: 423-974-1572. E-mail: hatcher@libra.law.utk.edu. Completed financial aid forms should be received by February 14.

Law School Library University of Tennessee College of Law Library has 8 professional staff members and contains more than 436,128 volumes and 5,703 periodicals. 455 seats are available in the library. When classes are in session, the library is open 112 hours per week.

WESTLAW and LEXIS-NEXIS are available, as are the World Wide Web, online bibliographic services, and CD-ROM players. 88 computer workstations are available to students in the library. Special law collections include Special Collection of Rare and Autographed Books, Tennessee Collection, Audiovisual Collection, Microforms Collection.

First-Year Program Class size in the average section is 60; 90% of the first-year courses are taught by full-time faculty.

Upper-Level Program Class size in the average section is 40. Among the electives are:

Administrative Law
★ Advocacy

★ **Business and Corporate Law**
Entertainment Law
Environmental Law
Family Law
Intellectual Property
International/Comparative Law
Jurisprudence
Labor Law
Land Use Law/Natural Resources
Lawyering Skills
Litigation
Mediation
Probate Law
Public Interest
Securities
Tax Law
(★ indicates an area of special strength)

Clinical Courses Students receive degree credit for clinical courses. (Clinical practicum is not required.) Among the clinical areas offered are:

Civil Litigation
Criminal Defense
Criminal Prosecution
Mediation
Public Interest

1% of the students participate in internship programs.

VANDERBILT UNIVERSITY
SCHOOL OF LAW

Nashville, Tennessee

INFORMATION CONTACT
Kent D. Syverud, Dean
Nashville, TN 37240

Phone: 615-322-2615   Fax: 615-322-6631
Web site: http://www.vanderbilt.edu/

LAW STUDENT PROFILE [1997–98]

FULL-TIME   Enrollment: 542
Women: 40%   Men: 60%

RACIAL or ETHNIC COMPOSITION
African American, 10%; Asian/Pacific Islander, 5%; Hispanic,
2%; Nataive American, 0.2%; International, 4%

APPLICANTS and ADMITTEES
Seats available: 180
Median LSAT score: 163
Median GPA: 3.6

Vanderbilt University School of Law is a private
institution that organizes classes on a semester
calendar system. The campus is situated in an urban
setting. Founded in 1874, first ABA approved in
1925, and an AALS member, Vanderbilt University
School of Law offers JD, JD/MA, JD/MBA, JD/
MDiv, JD/MTS, and JD/PhD degrees.

Faculty consists of 30 full-time and 34 part-time
members in 1997–98. 7 full-time faculty members
and 10 part-time faculty members are women. 98%
of all faculty members have a JD degree. Of all
faculty members, 2% are Asian/Pacific Islander, 3%
are African American, 2% are Hispanic, 93% are
white.

Application Information *Required:* LSAT, LSDAS,
application form, application fee of $50, baccalaure-
ate degree, 2 letters of recommendation, personal
statement, college transcripts. *Application deadline*
for fall term is February 1.

Financial Aid Fellowships, loans, loan repayment
assistance program (LRAP), need-based grants/
scholarships, and federal work-study loans are
available. The average student debt at graduation is
$61,000. To apply for financial assistance, students
must complete the Free Application for Federal
Student Aid, institutional forms, and scholarship
specific applications. Financial aid contact: Anne M.

AT a GLANCE

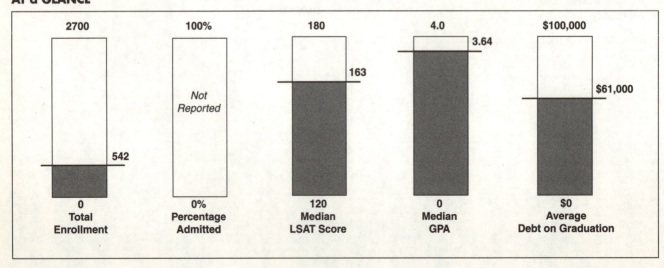

Degree Options

Degree	Total Credits Required	Length of Program
JD–Doctor of Laws	90	3–4 yrs, full-time only [day]
JD/MA–Juris Doctor/Master of Arts–Joint-degree Program		full-time only [day]
JD/MBA–Juris Doctor/Master of Business Administration–Joint-degree Program	110	4–5 yrs, full-time only [day]
JD/MDiv–Juris Doctor/Master of Divinity–Joint-degree Program		5 yrs, full-time only [day]
JD/MTS–Juris Doctor/Master of Theological Studies–Joint-degree Program		4 yrs, full-time only [day]
JD/PhD–Juris Doctor/Doctor of Philosophy–Joint-degree Program		full-time only [day]

Brandt, Assistant Dean, Vanderbilt Law School, Nashville, TN 37240. Phone: 615-322-6452. Fax: 615-322-6631. E-mail: admissions@law.vanderbilt.edu. Completed financial aid forms should be received by April 1.

Law School Library Alyne Queener Massey Law Library has 9 professional staff members and contains more than 510,348 volumes and 6,042 periodicals. 423 seats are available in the library. When classes are in session, the library is open 111 hours per week.

WESTLAW and LEXIS-NEXIS are available, as are the World Wide Web, online bibliographic services, and CD-ROM players. 64 computer workstations are available to students in the library. Special law collections include intellectual property, medico-legal, foreign/international law.

First-Year Program Class size in the average section is 90; 89% of the first-year courses are taught by full-time faculty.

Upper-Level Program Among the electives are:

Administrative Law
Advocacy
Business and Corporate Law
Consumer Law

Education Law
Entertainment Law
Environmental Law
Family Law
Government/Regulation
Health Care/Human Services
Intellectual Property
International/Comparative Law
Jurisprudence
Labor Law
Land Use Law/Natural Resources
Lawyering Skills
Legal History/Philosophy
Litigation
Media Law
Mediation
Probate Law
Public Interest
Securities
Tax Law

Clinical Courses Students receive degree credit for clinical courses. (Clinical practicum is not required.) Among the clinical areas offered are:

Civil Litigation
Criminal Defense
Juvenile Law

BAYLOR UNIVERSITY
SCHOOL OF LAW

Waco, Texas

INFORMATION CONTACT

Dr. Bradley J. B. Toben, Dean
PO Box 97288
Waco, TX 76798

Phone: 254-710-2316   Fax: 254-710-2316
E-mail: law_support@baylor.edu
Web site: http://law.baylor.edu/

LAW STUDENT PROFILE [1997–98]

FULL-TIME   Enrollment: 392
Women: 35%   Men: 65%

PART-TIME   Enrollment: 4
Women: 25%   Men: 75%

RACIAL or ETHNIC COMPOSITION

African American, 1%; Asian/Pacific Islander, 1%; Hispanic, 6%; Native American, 1%; International, 0%

APPLICANTS and ADMITTEES

Number applied: 797
Admitted: 302
Percentage accepted: 38%
Seats available: 75
Median LSAT score: 160
Median GPA: 3.5

Baylor University School of Law is a private institution that organizes classes on a quarter calendar system. The campus is situated in an urban setting. First ABA approved in 1931, and an AALS member, Baylor University School of Law offers JD, JD/MBA, JD/MPPA, and JD/MTAX degrees.

Faculty consists of 20 full-time and 35 part-time members in 1997–98. 6 full-time faculty members and 3 part-time faculty members are women. 99% of all faculty members have a JD; 14% have advanced law degrees. Of all faculty members, .2% are African American, .2% are Hispanic, 99.6% are white.

Application Information *Required:* LSAT, LSDAS, application form, application fee of $40, baccalaureate degree, recommendations, personal statement, college transcripts. *Recommended:* resume. *Application deadline* for fall term is March 1.

Costs The 1997–98 tuition is $11,357. Fees: $482.

Financial Aid In 1997–98, 97% of all students received some form of financial aid. 319 other awards were given. Loans, merit-based grants/scholarships, need-based grants/scholarships, and federal work-study loans are also available. The average student debt at graduation is $42,082. To apply for financial assistance, students must

AT a GLANCE

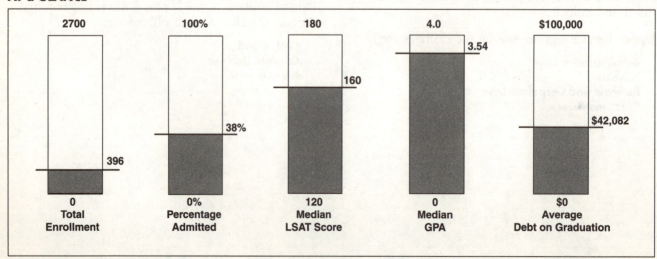

Degree Options

Degree	Total Credits Required	Length of Program
JD–Juris Doctor–Doctors of Laws	126	3 yrs, full-time only [day, summer]
JD/MBA–Juris Doctor/Master of Business Administration–Joint-degree Program		4 yrs, full-time only [day, summer]
JD/MPPA–Juris Doctor/Master of Public Policy and Administration–Joint-degree Program		4 yrs, full-time only
JD/MTAX–Juris Doctor/Master of Taxation–Joint-degree Program		4 yrs, full-time only [day, summer]

complete the Free Application for Federal Student Aid. Financial aid contact: Ms. Pat Lucas, Assistant Director of Loans, PO Box 97028, Waco, TX 76798-7028. Phone: 800-BAYLORU. Fax: 254-710-2316. E-mail: pat_lucas@baylor.edu.

Law School Library M. C. and Mattie Caston Law Library has 6 professional staff members and contains more than 178,096 volumes and 2,120 periodicals. 303 seats are available in the library. When classes are in session, the library is open 110 hours per week.

WESTLAW and LEXIS-NEXIS are available, as are the World Wide Web, online bibliographic services, and CD-ROM players. 25 computer workstations are available to students in the library.

First-Year Program Class size in the average section is 50; 100% of the first-year courses are taught by full-time faculty.

Upper-Level Program Class size in the average section is 40. Among the electives are:

- ★ Administrative Law
- ★ Advocacy
- ★ Business and Corporate Law
- Consumer Law
- ★ Criminal Law
- Entertainment Law
- Environmental Law
- Family Law
- Government/Regulation
- Health Care/Human Services
- Intellectual Property
- International/Comparative Law
- Jurisprudence
- Labor Law
- Land Use Law/Natural Resources
- Lawyering Skills
- ★ Litigation
- Mediation
- ★ Probate Law
- Securities
- Tax Law

(★ indicates an area of special strength)

Clinical Courses Students receive degree credit for clinical courses. (Clinical practicum is not required.) Among the clinical areas offered are:

Criminal Defense
Family Practice

4% of the students participate in internship programs.

ST. MARY'S UNIVERSITY OF SAN ANTONIO
SCHOOL OF LAW

San Antonio, Texas

INFORMATION CONTACT
Barbara Bader Aldave, Dean
1 Camino Santa Maria
San Antonio, TX 78228-8602

Phone: 210-436-3424
Web site: http://www.stmarytx.edu/acad/lawsch.htm

LAW STUDENT PROFILE [1997–98]

FULL-TIME   Enrollment: 702
Women: 46%   Men: 54%

PART-TIME   Enrollment: 70
Women: 59%   Men: 41%

RACIAL or ETHNIC COMPOSITION
African American, 3%; Asian/Pacific Islander, 3%; Hispanic, 25%; Native American, 1%; International, 0%

APPLICANTS and ADMITTEES
Seats available: 264

St. Mary's University of San Antonio School of Law is a private institution that organizes classes on a semester calendar system. The campus is situated in an urban setting. Founded in 1927, first ABA approved in 1948, and an AALS member, St. Mary's University of San Antonio School of Law offers JD, JD/MA, JD/MBA, JD/ME, JD/MEc, JD/MPAd, JD/MS, JD/MTS, and LLM degrees.

Faculty consists of 33 full-time and 31 part-time members in 1997–98. 8 full-time faculty members and 3 part-time faculty members are women.

Application Information *Required:* LSAT, LSDAS, application form, application fee of $45, baccalaureate degree. *Application deadline* for fall term is April 1.

Costs The 1997–98 tuition is $545 per credit hour. Fees: $235.

Financial Aid Merit-based grants/scholarships and need-based grants/scholarships are available. Completed financial aid forms should be received by March 31.

Law School Library Sarita Kennedy East Law Library has 9 professional staff members and

AT a GLANCE

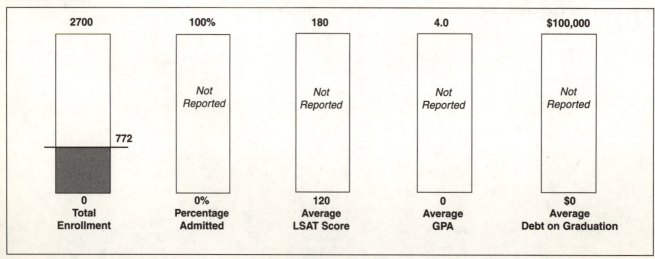

2700	100%	180	4.0	$100,000
	Not Reported	Not Reported	Not Reported	Not Reported
772				
0	0%	120	0	$0
Total Enrollment	**Percentage Admitted**	**Average LSAT Score**	**Average GPA**	**Average Debt on Graduation**

Degree Options

Degree	Total Credits Required	Length of Program
JD–Juris Doctor	90	full-time only
JD–Juris Doctor–Justice Administration		
JD/MA–Juris Doctor/Master of Arts–Economics Joint-degree Program		
JD/MA–Juris Doctor/Master of Arts–International Relations Dual-degree Program		
JD/MA–Juris Doctor/Master of Arts–Justice Administration Joint Degree		
JD/MBA–Juris Doctor/Master of Business Administration–Joint Degree		
JD/ME–Juris Doctor/Master of Engineering–Joint Degree		
JD/MEc–Juris Doctor/Master of Economics–Joint Degree		
JD/MPAd–Juris Doctor/Master of Public Administration–Joint Degree		
JD/MS–Juris Doctor/Master of Science–Computer Science Joint Degree		
JD/MTS–Juris Doctor/Master of Theological Studies–Joint Degree		
LLM–Master of Laws–International and Comparative Law		
LLM–Master of Laws–American Legal Studies		

contains more than 323,943 volumes and 3,529 periodicals. 446 seats are available in the library. When classes are in session, the library is open 110 hours per week.

WESTLAW and LEXIS-NEXIS are available. Special law collections include United Nations documents collection.

First-Year Program Class size in the average section is 88.

Clinical Courses Among the clinical areas offered are:

Civil Litigation
Criminal Defense
Family Practice
General Practice
Immigration
International Law

Internships are available.

SOUTHERN METHODIST UNIVERSITY
SCHOOL OF LAW

Dallas, Texas

INFORMATION CONTACT
Dr. Harvey Wingo, Interim Dean
PO Box 750116
Dallas, TX 75275-0116

Phone: 214-768-2620   Fax: 214-768-2549
Web site: http://ww.law.smu.edu/

LAW STUDENT PROFILE [1997–98]

FULL-TIME   Enrollment: 791
Women: 45%   Men: 55%

PART-TIME   Enrollment: 37
Women: 35%   Men: 65%

RACIAL or ETHNIC COMPOSITION
African American, 6%; Asian/Pacific Islander, 5%; Hispanic, 8%; Native American, 1%; International, 1%

APPLICANTS and ADMITTEES
Seats available: 238

Southern Methodist University School of Law is a private institution that organizes classes on a semester calendar system. The campus is situated in an urban setting. Founded in 1925, first ABA approved in 1927, and an AALS member, Southern Methodist University School of Law offers JD, JD/MA, JD/MBA, JSD, and LLM degrees.

Faculty consists of 42 full-time and 95 part-time members in 1997–98. 10 full-time faculty members and 20 part-time faculty members are women.

Application Information *Required:* LSAT, LSDAS, application form, application fee of $50, 2 letters of recommendation, personal statement, resume. *Application deadline* for fall term is February 1.

Financial Aid Loan repayment assistance program (LRAP), merit-based grants/scholarships, and need-based grants/scholarships are available. To apply for financial assistance, students must complete the Free Application for Federal Student Aid. Completed financial aid forms should be received by February 1.

Law School Library Underwood Law Library has 9 professional staff members and contains more than 497,265 volumes and 5,119 periodicals. 716 seats are available in the library. When classes are in session, the library is open 102 hours per week.

AT a GLANCE

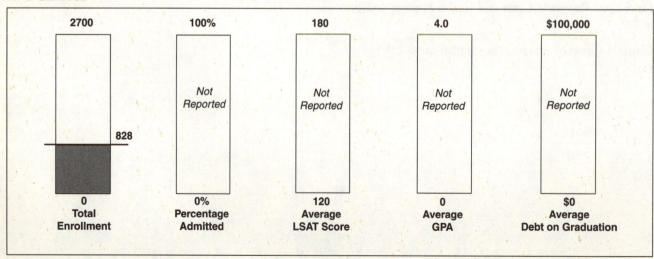

2700	100%	180	4.0	$100,000
	Not Reported	Not Reported	Not Reported	Not Reported
828				
0	0%	120	0	$0
Total Enrollment	**Percentage Admitted**	**Average LSAT Score**	**Average GPA**	**Average Debt on Graduation**

Degree Options

Degree	Total Credits Required	Length of Program
JD–Juris Doctor	90	3 yrs, full-time only
JD/MA–Juris Doctor/Master of Arts–Dual-degree Program in Economics	111	4 yrs, full-time or part-time
JD/MBA–Juris Doctor/Master of Business Administration	137	4.5 yrs, full-time only
JSD–Doctor of Juridical Science		2 yrs
LLM–Master of Laws–Taxation	24	full-time or part-time
LLM–Master of Laws	24	1–2 yrs, full-time or part-time
LLM–Master of Laws–Comparative and International Law	24	

WESTLAW and LEXIS-NEXIS are available, as is the World Wide Web.

First-Year Program Class size in the average section is 87.

Upper-Level Program Among the electives are:

Administrative Law
Advocacy
Aviation Law
Business and Corporate Law
Civil Procedure
Criminal Law
Criminal Procedure
Education Law
Environmental Law
Evidence
Family Law
Government/Regulation
Health Care/Human Services
Insurance
Intellectual Property
International/Comparative Law
Jurisprudence
Labor Law
Land Use Law/Natural Resources
Lawyering Skills
Legal History/Philosophy
Litigation
Maritime Law
Mediation
Oil and Gas
Probate Law
Property/Real Estate
Securities
Tax Law

Clinical Courses Students receive degree credit for clinical courses. Among the clinical areas offered are:

Civil Litigation
Criminal Defense
Criminal Prosecution
Family Practice
General Practice
Juvenile Law
Tax Law

Internships are available. International exchange programs permit students to visit United Kingdom.

SOUTH TEXAS COLLEGE OF LAW AFFILIATED WITH TEXAS A&M UNIVERSITY

Houston, Texas

INFORMATION CONTACT

Frank T. Read, President and Dean
1303 San Jacinto Street
Houston, TX 77002-7000

Phone: 713-659-8040   Fax: 713-659-2217
      Ext. 1819
E-mail: acramer@stcl.edu
Web site: http://www.stcl.tamu.edu/

LAW STUDENT PROFILE [1997–98]

FULL-TIME   Enrollment: 790
Women: 42%   Men: 58%

PART-TIME   Enrollment: 423
Women: 44%   Men: 56%

RACIAL or ETHNIC COMPOSITION
African American, 5%; Asian/Pacific Islander, 5%; Hispanic, 10%; Native American, 1%; International, 0%

APPLICANTS and ADMITTEES
Number applied: 1,686
Admitted: 1,037
Percentage accepted: 62%
Seats available: 354
Average LSAT score: 150
Average GPA: 3.0

South Texas College of Law Affiliated with Texas A&M University is a private nonprofit institution that organizes classes on a semester calendar system. The campus is situated in an urban setting. Founded in 1923, first ABA approved in 1959, and an AALS member, South Texas College of Law Affiliated with Texas A&M University offers a JD degree.

Faculty consists of 59 full-time and 30 part-time members in 1997–98. 15 full-time faculty members and 6 part-time faculty members are women. 100% of all faculty members have a JD; 22.4% have advanced law degrees. Of all faculty members, 1.2% are Native American, 1.2% are Asian/Pacific Islander, 3.5% are African American, 2.4% are Hispanic, 91.7% are white.

Application Information *Required:* LSAT, LSDAS, application form, application fee of $40, baccalaureate degree, 2 letters of recommendation, personal statement, resume. *Recommended:* minimum 2.9 GPA. *Application deadline* for fall term is March 1.

Financial Aid In 1997–98, 83% of all students received some form of financial aid. 880 other awards were given. Loans, merit-based grants/scholarships, need-based grants/scholarships, and

AT a GLANCE

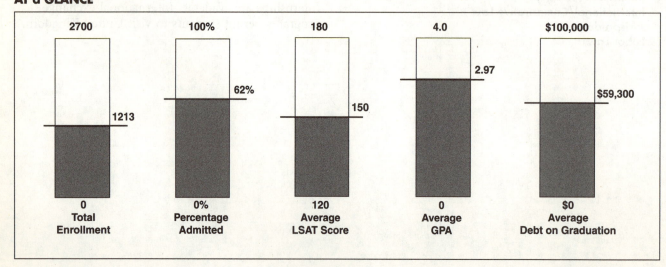

2700	100%	180	4.0	$100,000
			2.97	
	62%			$59,300
1213		150		
0	0%	120	0	$0
Total Enrollment	**Percentage Admitted**	**Average LSAT Score**	**Average GPA**	**Average Debt on Graduation**

Degree Options

Degree	Total Credits Required	Length of Program
JD–Doctor of Laws	90	2.5–6 yrs, full-time or part-time [day, evening, weekend, summer]

federal work-study loans are also available. The average student debt at graduation is $59,300. To apply for financial assistance, students must complete the Free Application for Federal Student Aid, institutional forms, scholarship specific applications, and prior year tax returns with attachments. Financial aid contact: Patricia Scheffe, Director of Scholarships and Financial Aid, 1303 San Jacinto Street, Houston, TX 77002-7000. Phone: 713-646-1820. Fax: 713-659-2217. E-mail: scheffe@stcl.edu. Completed financial aid forms should be received by May 1.

Law School Library South Texas College of Law Library has 9 professional staff members and contains more than 347,220 volumes and 4,083 periodicals. 586 seats are available in the library. When classes are in session, the library is open 103 hours per week.

WESTLAW and LEXIS-NEXIS are available, as are the World Wide Web, online bibliographic services, and CD-ROM players. 69 computer workstations are available to students in the library. Special law collections include maritime, Islamic law.

First-Year Program Class size in the average section is 63; 100% of the first-year courses are taught by full-time faculty.

Upper-Level Program Class size in the average section is 37. Among the electives are:

Administrative Law
★ Advocacy
Business and Corporate Law
Consumer Law
Education Law
Entertainment Law
★ Environmental Law
Family Law
Government/Regulation
★ Health Care/Human Services
Intellectual Property
★ International/Comparative Law
Jurisprudence
Labor Law
Land Use Law/Natural Resources
Lawyering Skills
Legal History/Philosophy
Litigation
Maritime Law
Media Law
★ Mediation
Probate Law
Public Interest
Securities
Tax Law
(★ indicates an area of special strength)

Clinical Courses Students receive degree credit for clinical courses. (Clinical practicum is not required.) Among the clinical areas offered are:

Civil Litigation
Criminal Defense
Criminal Prosecution
Family Practice
General Practice
Health
Mediation
Public Interest

3% of the students participate in internship programs. International exchange programs permit students to visit Denmark.

TEXAS SOUTHERN UNIVERSITY
THURGOOD MARSHALL SCHOOL OF LAW

Houston, Texas

INFORMATION CONTACT

L. Darnell Weeden, Acting Dean
3100 Cleburne Avenue
Houston, TX 77004

Phone: 713-313-7112   Fax: 713-313-1049
Web site: http://www.tsulaw.edu/

LAW STUDENT PROFILE [1997–98]

FULL-TIME   Enrollment: 10
Women: 40%   Men: 60%

PART-TIME   Enrollment: 1
Men: 100%

APPLICANTS and ADMITTEES

Seats available: 260
Average LSAT score: 143
Average GPA: 2.6

Texas Southern University Thurgood Marshall School of Law is a public institution that organizes classes on a semester calendar system. The campus is situated in an urban setting. Founded in 1947, first ABA approved in 1949, Texas Southern University Thurgood Marshall School of Law offers a JD degree.

Faculty consists of 22 full-time and 4 part-time members in 1997–98. 4 full-time faculty members and 1 part-time faculty members are women. 100% of all faculty members have a JD; 35% have advanced law degrees.

Application Information *Required:* LSAT, LSDAS, application form, application fee of $40, baccalaureate degree, personal statement, interview. *Recommended:* 2 letters of recommendation and resume. *Application deadline* for fall term is April 1.

Costs The 1997–98 tuition is $4480 full-time for state residents; $753 per semester (minimum) part-time for state residents. Tuition is $7576 full-time for nonresidents; $1140 per semester (minimum) part-time for nonresidents. Fees: $180.

Financial Aid Fellowships, loans, merit-based grants/scholarships, need-based grants/scholarships, and federal work-study loans are available. The average student debt at graduation is $55,500. To

AT a GLANCE

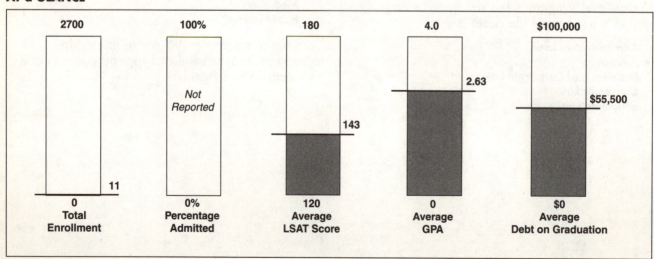

Degree Options

Degree	Total Credits Required	Length of Program
JD–Doctor of Laws	90	3 yrs, full-time only [day]

apply for financial assistance, students must complete the Free Application for Federal Student Aid and institutional forms. Financial aid contact: Andrea Williams, Director of Financial Aid, 3100 Cleburne Street, Houston, TX 77004. Phone: 713-313-7243. Fax: 713-313-1049. E-mail: awilliams@tsulaw.edu. Completed financial aid forms should be received by May 1.

Law School Library Law Library has 7 professional staff members and contains more than 379,979 volumes and 2,463 periodicals. 348 seats are available in the library. When classes are in session, the library is open 157 hours per week.

WESTLAW and LEXIS-NEXIS are available, as are the World Wide Web, online bibliographic services, and CD-ROM players. 23 computer workstations are available to students in the library.

First-Year Program Class size in the average section is 65; 92% of the first-year courses are taught by full-time faculty.

Upper-Level Program Class size in the average section is 30. Among the electives are:

Administrative Law
Advocacy
Business and Corporate Law
Consumer Law
Education Law
★ **Environmental Law**
Family Law
Intellectual Property
International/Comparative Law
Jurisprudence
Labor Law
Lawyering Skills
Litigation
Maritime Law
Media Law
Mediation
Probate Law
Securities
Tax Law
(★ *indicates an area of special strength*)

Clinical Courses Students receive degree credit for clinical courses. (Clinical practicum is not required.) Among the clinical areas offered are:

Environmental Law
Family Practice
Housing Law
Juvenile Law
Street Law

10% of the students participate in internship programs.

TEXAS TECH UNIVERSITY
SCHOOL OF LAW

Lubbock, Texas

INFORMATION CONTACT

W. Frank Newton, Dean
Box 40004
Lubbock, TX 79409-0004

Phone: 806-742-3791   Fax: 806-742-1629
Web site: http://www.law.ttu.edu/

LAW STUDENT PROFILE [1997–98]

FULL-TIME   Enrollment: 635
Women: 42%   Men: 58%

PART-TIME   Enrollment: 1
Men: 100%

RACIAL or ETHNIC COMPOSITION
African American, 2%; Asian/Pacific Islander, 1%; Hispanic, 8%; Native American, 1%; International, 0%

APPLICANTS and ADMITTEES
Number applied: 1,144
Admitted: 547
Percentage accepted: 48%
Seats available: 205
Average LSAT score: 155
Average GPA: 3.4

Texas Tech University School of Law is a public institution that organizes classes on a semester calendar system. The campus is situated in a small-town setting. Founded in 1967, first ABA approved in 1970, and an AALS member, Texas Tech University School of Law offers JD, JD/MBA, JD/MPAd, and JD/MS degrees.

Faculty consists of 27 full-time and 6 part-time members in 1997–98. 8 full-time faculty members are women. 100% of all faculty members have a JD; 38% have advanced law degrees. Of all faculty members, 4% are African American, 4% are Hispanic, 92% are white.

Application Information *Required:* LSAT, LSDAS, application form, application fee of $50, baccalaureate degree, personal statement, college transcripts. *Recommended:* 3 letters of recommendation and resume. *Application deadline* for fall term is February 1.

Costs The 1997–98 tuition is $3840 for state residents. Tuition is $7896 for nonresidents. Fees: $1457.

Financial Aid In 1997–98, 90% of all students received some form of financial aid. 8 research assistantships, totaling $36,013, were awarded. Loans, merit-based grants/scholarships, need-based

AT a GLANCE

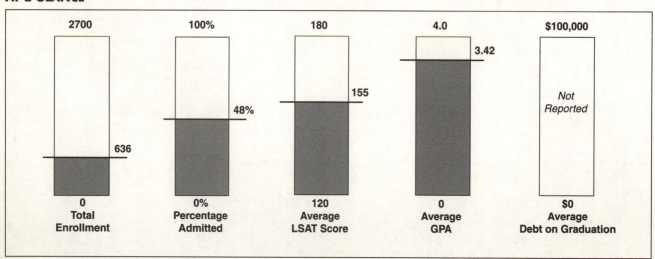

Degree Options

Degree	Total Credits Required	Length of Program
JD–Doctor of Law	90	3 yrs, full-time only [day, summer]
JD/MBA–Juris Doctor/Master of Business Administration	102	4 yrs, full-time only [day, summer]
JD/MPAd–Juris Doctor/Master of Public Administration	111	4 yrs, full-time only [day, summer]
JD/MS–Juris Doctor/Master of Science–Taxation	102	4 yrs, full-time only [day, summer]

grants/scholarships, and federal work-study loans are also available. To apply for financial assistance, students must complete the Free Application for Federal Student Aid, institutional forms, and financial aid transcripts. Financial aid contact: Director of Student Financial Aid, Texas Tech University, Box 4179, Lubbock, TX 79409. Fax: 806-742-1629. Completed financial aid forms should be received by May 15.

Law School Library Texas Tech Law School Library has 6 professional staff members and contains more than 259,426 volumes and 1,800 periodicals. 380 seats are available in the library. When classes are in session, the library is open 93 hours per week.

WESTLAW and LEXIS-NEXIS are available, as are the World Wide Web, online bibliographic services, and CD-ROM players. 232 computer workstations are available to students in the library.

First-Year Program Class size in the average section is 67; 100% of the first-year courses are taught by full-time faculty.

Upper-Level Program Among the electives are:

Administrative Law
★ **Advocacy**

Business and Corporate Law
Consumer Law
Education Law
Entertainment Law
★ **Environmental Law**
Family Law
Government/Regulation
Health Care/Human Services
Indian/Tribal Law
Intellectual Property
International/Comparative Law
Jurisprudence
Labor Law
Land Use Law/Natural Resources
Lawyering Skills
Legal History/Philosophy
Litigation
Media Law
Mediation
Probate Law
Public Interest
Tax Law
(★ *indicates an area of special strength*)

8% of the students participate in internship programs. International exchange programs permit students to visit Mexico.

TEXAS WESLEYAN UNIVERSITY
SCHOOL OF LAW

Fort Worth, Texas

INFORMATION CONTACT

Frank Walwer, Dean
1515 Commerce Street
Fort Worth, TX 76102

Phone: 817-212-4000   Fax: 817-212-4002
Web site: http://www.txwesleyan.edu/law/

LAW STUDENT PROFILE [1997–98]

FULL-TIME   Enrollment: 376
Women: 33%   Men: 67%

PART-TIME   Enrollment: 282
Women: 30%   Men: 70%

RACIAL or ETHNIC COMPOSITION
African American, 6%; Asian/Pacific Islander, 2%; Hispanic,
9%; Native American, 2%; International, 0%

APPLICANTS and ADMITTEES
Seats available: 198

Texas Wesleyan University School of Law is a
private institution that organizes classes on a
semester calendar system. The campus is situated in
an urban setting. Founded in 1989, first ABA
approved in 1994, Texas Wesleyan University School
of Law offers a JD degree.

Faculty consists of 24 full-time and 24 part-time
members in 1997–98. 6 full-time faculty members
and 8 part-time faculty members are women.

Application Information *Required:* LSAT, LSDAS,
application form, application fee of $50, baccalaure-
ate degree, 2 letters of recommendation, personal
statement. *Application deadline* for fall term is
May 1.

Costs The 1997–98 tuition is $450 per hour. Fees:
$200 per semester.

Financial Aid In 1997–98, 45% of all students
received some form of financial aid. Merit-based
grants/scholarships, need-based grants/scholarships,
and federal work-study loans are also available. To
apply for financial assistance, students must
complete the Free Application for Federal Student
Aid and institutional forms. Financial aid contact:
Texas Wesleyan University School of Law, Financial
Aid Office, 1515 Commerce Street, Fort Worth, TX

AT a GLANCE

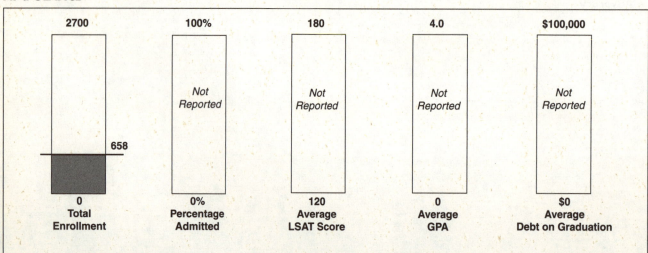

	2700	100%	180	4.0	$100,000
		Not Reported	Not Reported	Not Reported	Not Reported
	658				
	0	0%	120	0	$0
	Total Enrollment	Percentage Admitted	Average LSAT Score	Average GPA	Average Debt on Graduation

Degree Options

Degree	Total Credits Required	Length of Program
JD–Juris Doctor	88	full-time or part-time [day, evening]

76102. Phone: 800-733-9529 or toll-free 800-733-9529. Fax: 817-212-4002.

Law School Library has 7 professional staff members and contains more than 145,595 volumes and 2,747 periodicals. 234 seats are available in the library. When classes are in session, the library is open 112 hours per week.

WESTLAW and LEXIS-NEXIS are available, as are CD-ROM players. 12 computer workstations are available to students in the library.

Upper-Level Program Among the electives are:

Accounting
Administrative Law
Advocacy
Antitrust Law
Bankruptcy
Business and Corporate Law
Conflict of Laws
Constitutional Law
Consumer Law
Education Law

Employment Law
Environmental Law
Estate Planning
Evidence
Family Law
Government/Regulation
Insurance
Intellectual Property
International/Comparative Law
Jurisprudence
Labor Law
Land Use Law/Natural Resources
Legal History/Philosophy
Legislation
Litigation
Mediation
Oil and Gas
Property/Real Estate
Securities
Tax Law

Internships are available.

UNIVERSITY OF HOUSTON
LAW CENTER

Houston, Texas

INFORMATION CONTACT

Stephen Zamora, Dean
4800 Calhoun Street
Houston, TX 77204-2163

Phone: 713-743-2100   Fax: 713-743-2194
Web site: http://www.law.uh.edu/

LAW STUDENT PROFILE [1997–98]

FULL-TIME   Enrollment: 775
Women: 43%   Men: 57%

PART-TIME   Enrollment: 329
Women: 40%   Men: 60%

RACIAL or ETHNIC COMPOSITION
African American, 5%; Asian/Pacific Islander, 6%; Hispanic, 8%; Native American, 1%; International, 2%

APPLICANTS and ADMITTEES
Number applied: 2,149
Admitted: 861
Percentage accepted: 40%
Seats available: 308
Average LSAT score: 158
Average GPA: 3.3

University of Houston Law Center is a public institution that organizes classes on a semester calendar system. The campus is situated in an urban setting. Founded in 1947, first ABA approved in 1950, and an AALS member, University of Houston Law Center offers JD, JD/MA, JD/MBA, JD/MPH, and JD/PhD degrees.

Faculty consists of 47 full-time and 84 part-time members in 1997–98. 8 full-time faculty members and 13 part-time faculty members are women. 97% of all faculty members have a JD degree. Of all faculty members, 3% are African American, 97% are white.

Application Information *Required:* LSAT, LSDAS, application form, application fee of $50, baccalaureate degree, college transcripts. *Recommended:* recommendations, personal statement, resume. *Application deadline* for fall term is February 1.

Costs The 1997–98 tuition is $3840 full-time for state residents; $160 per credit hour part-time for state residents. Tuition is $7680 full-time for nonresidents; $320 per credit hour part-time for nonresidents. Fees: $1193 full-time; $119 per semester (minimum) part-time.

Financial Aid Loans, merit-based grants/scholarships, need-based grants/scholarships, and federal

AT a GLANCE

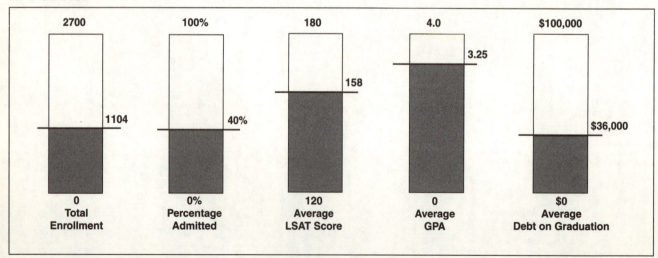

Degree Options

Degree	Total Credits Required	Length of Program
JD–Doctor of Laws	90	3–4 yrs, full-time or part-time [day, evening]
JD/MA–Juris Doctor/Master of Arts–Dual-degree Program in History		full-time or part-time [day, evening]
JD/MBA–Juris Doctor/Master of Business Administration–Dual-degree Program	115	4–5 yrs, full-time or part-time [day, evening]
JD/MPH–Juris Doctor/Master of Public Health–Dual-degree Program in Public Health		3–4 yrs, full-time or part-time [day, evening]
JD/PhD–Juris Doctor/Doctor of Philosophy–Dual-degree Program in Medical Humanities		5–6 yrs, full-time or part-time [day, evening]

work-study loans are available. The average student debt at graduation is $36,000. To apply for financial assistance, students must complete the Free Application for Federal Student Aid. Financial aid contact: Lillian Dixon, Financial Aid Coordinator, 4800 Calhoun, Houston, TX 77204-6391. Phone: 713-743-2269. Fax: 713-743-2194. E-mail: ldixon@uh.edu. Completed financial aid forms should be received by April 1.

Law School Library O. Quinn Law Library has 8 professional staff members and contains more than 451,569 volumes and 2,462 periodicals. 936 seats are available in the library. When classes are in session, the library is open 105 hours per week.

WESTLAW and LEXIS-NEXIS are available, as is the World Wide Web.

First-Year Program Class size in the average section is 80; 100% of the first-year courses are taught by full-time faculty.

Upper-Level Program Among the electives are:

Administrative Law
★ Advocacy
★ Business and Corporate Law
Constitutional Law
★ Consumer Law
Criminal Law
★ Education Law
Entertainment Law
★ Environmental Law
Family Law

Government/Regulation
★ Health Care/Human Services
Indian/Tribal Law
★ Intellectual Property
★ International/Comparative Law
Jurisprudence
Labor Law
Land Use Law/Natural Resources
Lawyering Skills
Legal History/Philosophy
Litigation
Maritime Law
★ Mediation
Probate Law
Public Interest
Securities
★ Tax Law
(★ indicates an area of special strength)

Clinical Courses Students receive degree credit for clinical courses. (Clinical practicum is not required.) Among the clinical areas offered are:

Criminal Defense
Criminal Prosecution
Environmental Law
Family Practice
Health
Immigration
Judicial Internship
Mediation
Public Interest

16% of the students participate in internship programs.

THE UNIVERSITY OF TEXAS AT AUSTIN
SCHOOL OF LAW

Austin, Texas

INFORMATION CONTACT

M. Michael Sharlot, Dean
727 East Dean Keeton Street
Austin, TX 78705

Phone: 512-232-1120   Fax: 512-471-6988
E-mail: admissions@mail.law.utexas.edu
Web site: http://www.utexas.edu/law/

LAW STUDENT PROFILE [1997–98]

FULL-TIME   Enrollment: 1,451
Women: 44%   Men: 56%

APPLICANTS and ADMITTEES
Number applied: 3,487
Admitted: 1,092
Percentage accepted: 31%
Seats available: 475
Average LSAT score: 163
Average GPA: 3.6

The University of Texas at Austin School of Law is a public institution that organizes classes on a semester calendar system. The campus is situated in an urban setting. Founded in 1883, first ABA approved in 1923, and an AALS member, The University of Texas at Austin School of Law offers JD, JD/MA, JD/MBA, JD/MPAf, JD/MURP, and LLM degrees.

Faculty consists of 73 full-time and 101 part-time members in 1997–98. 18 full-time faculty members and 22 part-time faculty members are women. 95% of all faculty members have a JD; 8% have advanced law degrees. Of all faculty members, 2.2% are Asian/Pacific Islander, 3.4% are African American, 4% are Hispanic, 87% are white, 3.4% are international.

Application Information *Required:* LSAT, LSDAS, application form, application fee of $65, baccalaureate degree, personal statement, college transcripts, resume. *Application deadline* for fall term is February 1.

Costs The 1997–98 tuition is $5468 for state residents. Tuition is $11,732 for nonresidents.

Financial Aid Loans, merit-based grants/scholarships, need-based grants/scholarships, and federal work-study loans are available. The average student debt at graduation is $36,000. To apply for financial assistance, students must complete the Free Applica-

AT a GLANCE

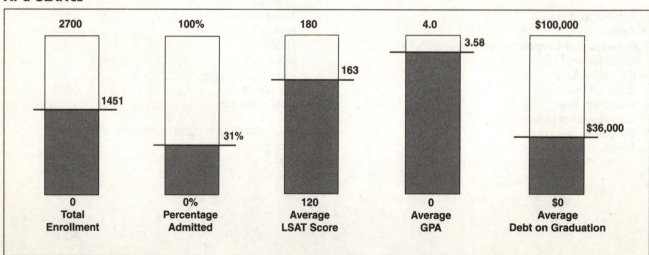

Degree Options

Degree	Total Credits Required	Length of Program
JD–Doctor of Laws	86	3 yrs, full-time only [day, summer]
JD/MA–Juris Doctor/Master of Arts–Joint-degree Program Latin American Studies	116	4 yrs, full-time only [day, summer]
JD/MA–Juris Doctor/Master of Arts–Joint-degree Program Middle Eastern Studies	119	4 yrs, full-time only [day, summer]
JD/MA–Juris Doctor/Master of Arts–Joint-degree Program Russian, East European, and Eurasian Studies	116	4 yrs, full-time only [day, summer]
JD/MBA–Juris Doctor/Master of Business Administration–Joint-degree Program	134	4–5 yrs, full-time only [day, summer]
JD/MPAf–Juris Doctor/Master of Public Affairs–Joint-degree Program	109	4 yrs, full-time only [day, summer]
JD/MURP–Juris Doctor/Masters of Urban and Regional Planning–Joint-degree Program	116	4 yrs, full-time only [day, summer]
LLM–Master of Laws	24	1 yr, full-time only [day, summer]

tion for Federal Student Aid. Financial aid contact: Anna Maria Saldana, Financial Aid Counselor, 727 East Dean Keeton Street, Austin, TX 78705. Phone: 512-232-1130. Fax: 512-471-6988. E-mail: lawfinaid@mail.law.utexas.edu. Completed financial aid forms should be received by March 31.

Law School Library Jamail Center for Legal Research has 19 professional staff members and contains more than 917,865 volumes and 8,817 periodicals. 1,200 seats are available in the library. When classes are in session, the library is open 103 hours per week.

WESTLAW and LEXIS-NEXIS are available, as are the World Wide Web, online bibliographic services, and CD-ROM players. 113 computer workstations are available to students in the library. Special law collections include European Union Documents Depository, Law in Popular Culture Collection, ABA Gavel Awards Archive, U.S. Supreme Court Justice Tom C. Clark Archives.

First-Year Program Class size in the average section is 113; 100% of the first-year courses are taught by full-time faculty.

Upper-Level Program Class size in the average section is 40. Among the electives are:

Administrative Law
Advocacy
Business and Corporate Law
Consumer Law
Education Law
Entertainment Law

Environmental Law
Family Law
Government/Regulation
Health Care/Human Services
Indian/Tribal Law
Intellectual Property
International/Comparative Law
Jurisprudence
Labor Law
Land Use Law/Natural Resources
Lawyering Skills
Legal History/Philosophy
Litigation
Maritime Law
Media Law
Mediation
Probate Law
Securities
Tax Law

Clinical Courses Students receive degree credit for clinical courses. (Clinical practicum is not required.) Among the clinical areas offered are:

Capital Punishment
Children's Advocacy
Criminal Defense
Domestic Violence
Elderly Advocacy
Health
Housing Law
Juvenile Law
Mediation

2% of the students participate in internship programs. International exchange programs available.

BRIGHAM YOUNG UNIVERSITY
J. REUBEN CLARK LAW SCHOOL

Provo, Utah

INFORMATION CONTACT

Dr. H. Reese Hansen, Dean
PO Box 28000
Provo, UT 84602-8000

Phone: 801-378-6383   Fax: 801-378-5897
E-mail: wilcockl@lawgate.byu.edu
Web site: http://www.byu.edu/

LAW STUDENT PROFILE [1997–98]

FULL-TIME   Enrollment: 445
Women: 33%   Men: 67%

RACIAL or ETHNIC COMPOSITION
African American, 0.5%; Asian/Pacific Islander, 5%; Hispanic, 5%; Native American, 2%; International, 2%

APPLICANTS and ADMITTEES
Number applied: 685
Admitted: 226
Percentage accepted: 33%
Seats available: 150
Average LSAT score: 160
Average GPA: 3.6

Brigham Young University J. Reuben Clark Law School is a private institution that organizes classes on a semester calendar system. The campus is situated in a suburban setting. Founded in 1973, first ABA approved in 1975, and an AALS member, Brigham Young University J. Reuben Clark Law School offers JD, JD/EdD, JD/MBA, JD/MED, JD/MOB, and JD/MPA degrees.

Faculty consists of 30 full-time and 27 part-time members in 1997–98. 6 full-time faculty members and 9 part-time faculty members are women. 100% of all faculty members have a JD degree. Of all faculty members, 2% are Native American, 2% are African American, 2% are Hispanic, 94% are white.

Application Information *Required:* minimum 145 LSAT score, LSDAS, application form, application fee of $30, baccalaureate degree, 3 letters of recommendation, personal statement, writing sample, college transcripts. *Application deadline* for fall term is February 1. Students are required to have their own computers.

Financial Aid Loans, merit-based grants/scholarships, and need-based grants/scholarships are available. The average student debt at graduation is $24,000. To apply for financial assistance, students must complete the Free Application for Federal Student Aid and institutional forms. Financial aid

AT a GLANCE

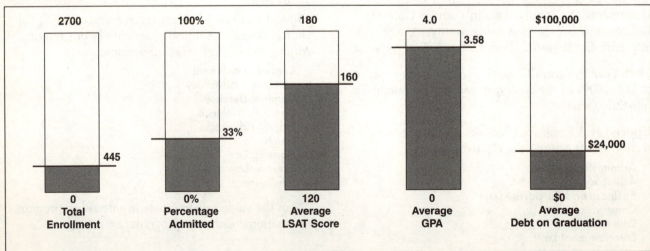

Degree Options

Degree	Total Credits Required	Length of Program
JD–Doctor of Laws	90	3–4 yrs, full-time only [day]
JD/EdD–Juris Doctor/Doctor of Education–Joint Degree	165	5 yrs, full-time only [day]
JD/MBA–Juris Doctor/Master of Business Administration–Joint Degree	131	4 yrs, full-time only [day]
JD/MED–Juris Doctor/Master of Education–Joint Degree	115	4 yrs, full-time only [day]
JD/MOB–Juris Doctor/Master of Organizational Behavior–Joint Degree	131	4 yrs, full-time only [day]
JD/MPA–Juris Doctor/Master of Professional Accountancy–Joint Degree	126	4 yrs, full-time only [day]

contact: Lola Wilcock, Director of Admissions, 340 JRCB Brigham Young University, Provo, UT 84602-8000. Phone: 801-378-4277. Fax: 801-378-5897. E-mail: wilcockl@lawgate.byu.edu. Completed financial aid forms should be received by June 1.

Law School Library Howard W. Hunter Library has 10 professional staff members and contains more than 415,732 volumes and 5,710 periodicals. 833 seats are available in the library. When classes are in session, the library is open 104 hours per week.

WESTLAW and LEXIS-NEXIS are available, as are the World Wide Web, online bibliographic services, and CD-ROM players. 96 computer workstations are available to students in the library. Special law collections include Biblical, Feminist, and Native American Law.

First-Year Program Class size in the average section is 110; 100% of the first-year courses are taught by full-time faculty.

Upper-Level Program Class size in the average section is 50. Among the electives are:

Administrative Law
Advocacy
Business and Corporate Law
★ Constitutional Law
Consumer Law
Education Law
Entertainment Law
Environmental Law
Family Law
Government/Regulation
Health Care/Human Services
Indian/Tribal Law
Intellectual Property
International/Comparative Law
Jurisprudence
Labor Law
Land Use Law/Natural Resources
Lawyering Skills
Legal History/Philosophy
Litigation
Maritime Law
Media Law
Mediation
Probate Law
Public Interest
Securities
Tax Law
(★ indicates an area of special strength)

Clinical Courses Students receive degree credit for clinical courses. (Clinical practicum is not required.) Among the clinical areas offered are:

Civil Litigation
Criminal Defense
Criminal Prosecution
Elderly Advocacy
Family Practice
Immigration
Mediation
Public Interest

25% of the students participate in internship programs. International exchange programs permit students to visit Czech Republic; Hungary; Poland; Romania; Russian Federation; and Yugoslavia.

UNIVERSITY OF UTAH
COLLEGE OF LAW

Salt Lake City, Utah

INFORMATION CONTACT
Lee E. Teitelbaum, Dean
332 South 1400 East Front
Salt Lake City, UT 84112-0730

Phone: 801-581-6571   Fax: 801-581-6897
E-mail: reyes.aguilar@law.utah.edu
Web site: http://www.utah.edu/

LAW STUDENT PROFILE [1997–98]

FULL-TIME   Enrollment: 371
Women: 35%   Men: 65%

RACIAL or ETHNIC COMPOSITION
African American, 1%; Asian/Pacific Islander, 5%; Hispanic, 5%; Native American, 1%; International, 2%

APPLICANTS and ADMITTEES
Number applied: 727
Admitted: 298
Percentage accepted: 41%
Seats available: 130
Average LSAT score: 160
Average GPA: 3.5

University of Utah College of Law is a public institution that organizes classes on a semester calendar system. The campus is situated in an urban setting. Founded in 1919, first ABA approved in 1927, and an AALS member, University of Utah College of Law offers JD, JD/MBA, JD/MPAd, and LLM degrees.

Faculty consists of 29 full-time and 36 part-time members in 1997–98. 10 full-time faculty members and 7 part-time faculty members are women. 100% of all faculty members have a JD; 17.6% have advanced law degrees. Of all faculty members, 2.94% are Native American, 2.94% are Asian/Pacific Islander, 8.82% are Hispanic, 85.3% are white.

Application Information *Required:* LSAT, LSDAS, application form, application fee of $40, baccalaureate degree, recommendations, personal statement, writing sample, college transcripts, resume. *Application deadline* for fall term is February 1.

Costs The 1997–98 tuition is $3333 for state residents. Tuition is $7361 for nonresidents.

Financial Aid In 1997–98, 80% of all students received some form of financial aid. 45 fellowships, 2 research assistantships were awarded. Fellowships, loans, loan repayment assistance program (LRAP), merit-based grants/scholarships, need-based

AT a GLANCE

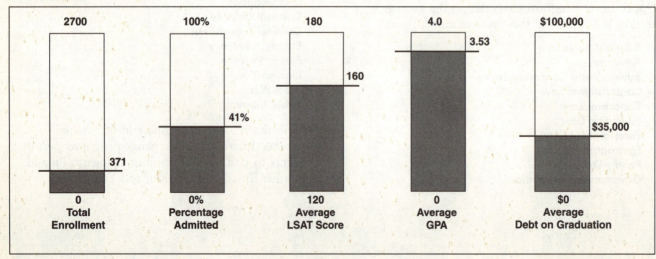

2700	100%	180	4.0	$100,000
			3.53	
		160		
	41%			$35,000
371				
0	0%	120	0	$0
Total Enrollment	Percentage Admitted	Average LSAT Score	Average GPA	Average Debt on Graduation

Degree Options

Degree	Total Credits Required	Length of Program
JD–Juris Doctor	88	3 yrs, full-time only [day, summer]
JD/MBA–Juris Doctor/Master of Business Administration–Joint-degree Program	137	3–4 yrs, full-time only [day, summer]
JD/MPAd–Juris Doctor/Master of Public Administration–Joint-degree Program	119	3–4 yrs, full-time only [day, summer]
LLM–Master of Laws–Environmental Law	24	1 yr, full-time only [day, summer]

grants/scholarships, and federal work-study loans are also available. The average student debt at graduation is $35,000. To apply for financial assistance, students must complete the Free Application for Federal Student Aid, institutional forms, and scholarship specific applications. Financial aid contact: Holly Green, Financial Aid Manager, 105 Student Services Building, Salt Lake City, UT 84112. Phone: 801-585-5828. Fax: 801-581-6897. E-mail: hgreen@ssb2.saff.utah.edu. Completed financial aid forms should be received by February 15.

Law School Library S. J. Quinney Law Library has 8 professional staff members and contains more than 290,000 volumes and 4,562 periodicals. 356 seats are available in the library. When classes are in session, the library is open 100 hours per week.

WESTLAW and LEXIS-NEXIS are available, as are the World Wide Web, online bibliographic services, and CD-ROM players. Special law collections include state and federal government documents.

First-Year Program Class size in the average section is 45; 100% of the first-year courses are taught by full-time faculty.

Upper-Level Program Class size in the average section is 30. Among the electives are:

Administrative Law
Advocacy
★ Business and Corporate Law
Consumer Law
★ Environmental Law
Estate Planning
Family Law
Government/Regulation
Health Care/Human Services

Indian/Tribal Law
Intellectual Property
★ International/Comparative Law
Jurisprudence
Labor Law
★ Land Use Law/Natural Resources
★ Lawyering Skills
Legal History/Philosophy
Litigation
Mediation
Probate Law
Property/Real Estate
Public Interest
Securities
Tax Law

(★ indicates an area of special strength)

Clinical Courses Students receive degree credit for clinical courses. (Clinical practicum is not required.) Among the clinical areas offered are:

Civil Litigation
Criminal Defense
Criminal Prosecution
Education
Elderly Advocacy
Environmental Law
Family Practice
Government Litigation
Health
Immigration
Indian/Tribal Law
Juvenile Law
Land Rights/Natural Resource
Mediation

60% of the students participate in internship programs. International exchange programs permit students to visit United Kingdom.

VERMONT LAW SCHOOL

South Royalton, Vermont

LAW STUDENT PROFILE [1997–98]

FULL-TIME   Enrollment: 25
Women: 40%   Men: 60%

RACIAL or ETHNIC COMPOSITION
African American, 12%; Hispanic, 4%; Native American, 20%; International, 20%

APPLICANTS and ADMITTEES
Number applied: 77
Admitted: 57
Percentage accepted: 74%
Seats available: 160
Average LSAT score: 153
Average GPA: 3.1

Vermont Law School is a private nonprofit institution that organizes classes on a semester calendar system. The campus is situated in a small-town setting. Founded in 1972, first ABA approved in 1975, and an AALS member, Vermont Law School offers JD, JD/MSEL, and MSEL degrees.

Faculty consists of 9 full-time and 8 part-time members in 1997–98. 3 full-time faculty members and 4 part-time faculty members are women. 100% of all faculty members have a JD; 20% have advanced law degrees. Of all faculty members, 4% are Native American, 2% are Asian/Pacific Islander, 2% are African American, 92% are white.

Application Information *Required:* LSAT, LSDAS, application form, application fee of $50, baccalaureate degree, 2 letters of recommendation, essay, college transcripts, resume. *Recommended:* interview. *Application deadline* for fall term is February 15.

Financial Aid 2 fellowships were awarded. Fellowships, loans, loan repayment assistance program (LRAP), merit-based grants/scholarships, need-based grants/scholarships, and federal work-study loans are also available. To apply for financial assistance, students must complete the Free Application for Federal Student Aid and institutional forms. Financial aid contact: Laura McClay, Director of Financial Aid, Chelsea Street, South Royalton, VT 05068-0096. Phone: 802-763-8303 Ext. 2235. Fax:

AT a GLANCE

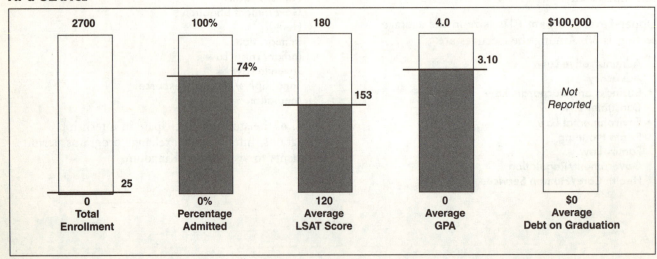

Degree Options

Degree	Total Credits Required	Length of Program
JD–Doctor of Law	84	3 yrs, full-time only [day]
JD/MSEL–Juris Doctor/Master of Studies in Environmental Law–Joint-degree Program	105	3–4 yrs, full-time only [day]
MSEL–Master of Studies in Environmental Law	30	1.5 yrs, full-time only [day]

802-763-7071. E-mail: finaid@vermontlaw.edu. Completed financial aid forms should be received by February 15.

Law School Library Cornell Library has 12 professional staff members and contains more than 215,000 volumes and 1,500 periodicals. 350 seats are available in the library. When classes are in session, the library is open 112 hours per week.

WESTLAW and LEXIS-NEXIS are available, as are the World Wide Web, online bibliographic services, and CD-ROM players. 50 computer workstations are available to students in the library. Special law collections include collection of Congressional publications, state sessions laws, US Supreme Court records and briefs, Federal register and Federal regulations.

First-Year Program Class size in the average section is 70; 100% of the first-year courses are taught by full-time faculty.

Upper-Level Program Class size in the average section is 35. Among the electives are:

Administrative Law
Advocacy
★ Business and Corporate Law
Consumer Law
Criminal Law
Entertainment Law
★ Environmental Law
Family Law
★ General Practice
Government/Regulation
Health Care/Human Services
★ Indian/Tribal Law
Intellectual Property
★ International/Comparative Law
Jurisprudence

★ Labor Law
★ Land Use Law/Natural Resources
Lawyering Skills
Legal History/Philosophy
Litigation
Mediation
Probate Law
★ Public Interest
Securities
Tax Law
★ Traditionally Disadvantaged Groups
(★ *indicates an area of special strength*)

Clinical Courses Students receive degree credit for clinical courses. (Clinical practicum is not required.) Among the clinical areas offered are:

Civil Litigation
Civil Rights
Corporate Law
Criminal Defense
Criminal Prosecution
Elderly Advocacy
Environmental Law
Family Practice
General Practice
Government Litigation
Indian/Tribal Law
Intellectual Property
International Law
Juvenile Law
Land Rights/Natural Resource
Mediation
Public Interest
Tax Law

50% of the students participate in internship programs. International exchange programs permit students to visit Canada; Italy; and Russian Federation.

COLLEGE OF WILLIAM AND MARY
SCHOOL OF LAW

Williamsburg, Virginia

LAW STUDENT PROFILE [1997–98]

FULL-TIME   Enrollment: 527
Women: 46%   Men: 54%

RACIAL or ETHNIC COMPOSITION
African American, 15%; Asian/Pacific Islander, 3%; Hispanic, 1%; Native American, 1%; International, 2%

APPLICANTS and ADMITTEES
Number applied: 2,363
Admitted: 722
Percentage accepted: 31%
Seats available: 170
Median LSAT score: 162
Average GPA: 3.3

College of William and Mary School of Law is a public institution that organizes classes on a semester calendar system. The campus is situated in a small-town setting. Founded in 1779, first ABA approved in 1932, and an AALS member, College of William and Mary School of Law offers JD, JD/MA, JD/MBA, JD/MPPo, and LLM degrees.

Faculty consists of 29 full-time and 19 part-time members in 1997–98. 9 full-time faculty members and 8 part-time faculty members are women. 100% of all faculty members have a JD; 20% have advanced law degrees. Of all faculty members, 3% are Asian/Pacific Islander, 8% are African American, 89% are white.

Application Information *Required:* LSAT, LSDAS, application form, application fee of $40, baccalaureate degree, recommendations, personal statement, writing sample, college transcripts. *Application deadline* for fall term is March 1.

Financial Aid In 1997–98, 43% of all students received some form of financial aid. 38 research assistantships, totaling $152,000; 24 teaching assistantships, totaling $114,000, were awarded. Fellowships, loans, merit-based grants/scholarships, need-based grants/scholarships, and federal work-study loans are also available. The average student debt at graduation is $35,234. To apply for financial

AT a GLANCE

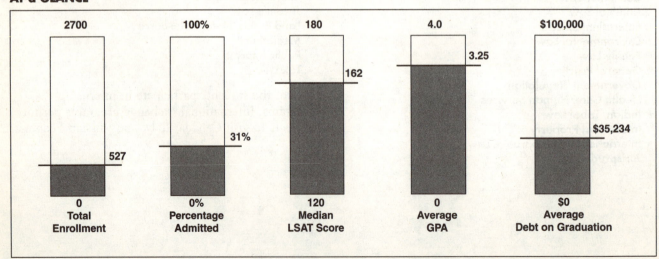

Degree Options

Degree	Total Credits Required	Length of Program
JD–Juris Doctor	90	3 yrs, full-time only [day, summer]
JD/MA–Juris Doctor/Master of Arts–Dual-degree Program in American Studies		3–4 yrs, full-time only [day, summer]
JD/MBA–Juris Doctor/Master of Business Administration–Dual-degree Program		4 yrs, full-time only [day, summer]
JD/MPPo–Juris Doctor/Master of Public Policy–Dual-degree Program		4 yrs, full-time only
LLM–Master of Laws–American Legal System	24	1 yr, full-time only [day]

assistance, students must complete the Free Application for Federal Student Aid and institutional forms. Financial aid contact: Faye Shealy, Associate Dean, William and Mary School of Law, PO Box 8795, Williamsburg, VA 23187-8795. Phone: 757-221-3785. Fax: 757-221-3261. E-mail: lawadm@facstaff.wm.edu. Completed financial aid forms should be received by February 15.

Law School Library Marshall-Wythe Law Library has 7 professional staff members and contains more than 340,000 volumes and 4,700 periodicals. 416 seats are available in the library. When classes are in session, the library is open 137 hours per week.

WESTLAW and LEXIS-NEXIS are available, as are the World Wide Web, online bibliographic services, and CD-ROM players. 67 computer workstations are available to students in the library. Special law collections include Roman Law, US Constitutional Law and Bill of Rights.

First-Year Program Class size in the average section is 85; 95% of the first-year courses are taught by full-time faculty.

Upper-Level Program Class size in the average section is 25. Among the electives are:

Administrative Law
★ Advocacy
Business and Corporate Law
Consumer Law
Education Law
Entertainment Law

★ Environmental Law
Family Law
Government/Regulation
Health Care/Human Services
Intellectual Property
International/Comparative Law
Jurisprudence
Labor Law
Land Use Law/Natural Resources
★ Lawyering Skills
Legal History/Philosophy
Litigation
Maritime Law
Media Law
Mediation
Probate Law
★ Professional Responsibility
Public Interest
Securities
Tax Law
(★ indicates an area of special strength)

Clinical Courses Students receive degree credit for clinical courses. (Clinical practicum is not required.) Among the clinical areas offered are:

Civil Litigation
Environmental Law
Family Practice
General Practice
Public Interest

20% of the students participate in internship programs. International exchange programs permit students to visit United Kingdom.

GEORGE MASON UNIVERSITY
SCHOOL OF LAW

Fairfax, Virginia

INFORMATION CONTACT
Dr. Mark F. Grady, Dean
3401 North Fairfax Drive
Arlington, VA 22201

Phone: 703-993-8085   Fax: 703-993-8088
Web site: http://www.gmu.edu/departments/law/

LAW STUDENT PROFILE [1997–98]

FULL-TIME   Enrollment: 379
Women: 43%   Men: 57%
PART-TIME   Enrollment: 336
Women: 33%   Men: 67%

RACIAL or ETHNIC COMPOSITION
African American, 4%; Asian/Pacific Islander, 5%; Hispanic,
2%; Nataive American, 0.3%; International, 0%

APPLICANTS and ADMITTEES
Number applied: 2,629
Admitted: 752
Percentage accepted: 29%
Seats available: 220
Average LSAT score: 157
Average GPA: 3.1

George Mason University School of Law is a public institution that organizes classes on a semester calendar system. The campus is situated in a suburban setting. Founded in 1979, first ABA approved in 1980, and an AALS member, George Mason University School of Law offers a JD degree.

Faculty consists of 25 full-time and 24 part-time members in 1997–98. 5 full-time faculty members and 3 part-time faculty members are women. 97% of all faculty members have a JD; 34% have advanced law degrees. Of all faculty members, 3% are Asian/Pacific Islander, 3% are African American, 94% are white.

Application Information *Required:* LSAT, LSDAS, application form, application fee of $35, baccalaureate degree, 2 letters of recommendation, personal statement. *Application deadline* for fall term is May 1.

Financial Aid Fellowships, graduate assistantships, loans, and merit-based grants/scholarships are available. To apply for financial assistance, students must complete the Free Application for Federal Student Aid. Financial aid contact: Jevita De Freitas, Financial Aid Counselor, George Mason University, Fairfax, VA 22030. Phone: 703-993-2353. Fax: 703-993-8088.

AT a GLANCE

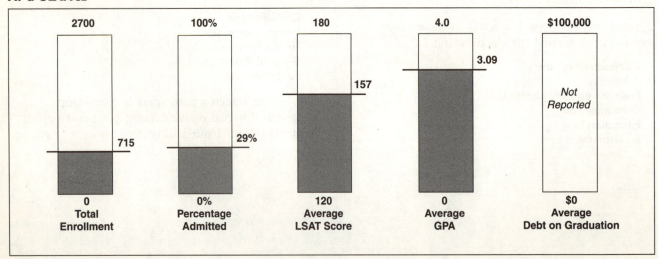

Degree Options

Degree	Total Credits Required	Length of Program
JD–Doctor of Laws	84	3–4 yrs, full-time or part-time [day, evening]

Law School Library has 6 professional staff members and contains more than 359,000 volumes and 4,600 periodicals. 250 seats are available in the library. When classes are in session, the library is open 92 hours per week.

WESTLAW and LEXIS-NEXIS are available, as are the World Wide Web, online bibliographic services, and CD-ROM players. 32 computer workstations are available to students in the library. Special law collections include federal government documents depository.

First-Year Program Class size in the average section is 105; 100% of the first-year courses are taught by full-time faculty.

Upper-Level Program Among the electives are:

   Administrative Law
   Advocacy
   Bankruptcy
★ Business and Corporate Law
   Consumer Law
   Environmental Law
   Family Law
★ Government/Regulation

   Health Care/Human Services
   Insurance
★ Intellectual Property
★ International/Comparative Law
   Jurisprudence
   Labor Law
   Land Use Law/Natural Resources
   Lawyering Skills
   Legal History/Philosophy
★ Litigation
   Probate Law
   Public Interest
★ Securities
   Tax Law
   Trusts and Estates
   Virginia Practice
(★ *indicates an area of special strength*)

Clinical Courses Students receive degree credit for clinical courses. (Clinical practicum is not required.) Among the clinical areas offered are:

   Civil Litigation
   Criminal Defense
   Criminal Prosecution

Internships are available.

REGENT UNIVERSITY
SCHOOL OF LAW

Virginia Beach, Virginia

INFORMATION CONTACT

J. Nelson Happy, Dean
1000 Regent University Drive
Virginia Beach, VA 23434

Phone: 757-226-4040   Fax: 757-579-4595
E-mail: lawschool@regent.edu
Web site: http://www.regent.edu/acad/schlaw/

LAW STUDENT PROFILE [1997–98]

FULL-TIME   Enrollment: 394
Women: 37%   Men: 63%

PART-TIME   Enrollment: 14
Women: 14%   Men: 86%

RACIAL or ETHNIC COMPOSITION
African American, 6%; Asian/Pacific Islander, 2%; Hispanic, 1%; Nataive American, 0.5%

APPLICANTS and ADMITTEES
Number applied: 308
Admitted: 115
Percentage accepted: 37%
Seats available: 143
Average LSAT score: 151
Average GPA: 3.0

Regent University School of Law is a private institution that organizes classes on a semester calendar system. The campus is situated in a suburban setting. Founded in 1986, first ABA approved in 1996, Regent University School of Law offers JD, JD/MA, and JD/MBA degrees.

Faculty consists of 20 full-time and 39 part-time members in 1997–98. 3 full-time faculty members and 7 part-time faculty members are women. 100% of all faculty members have a JD; 1% have advanced law degrees.

Application Information *Required:* LSAT, LSDAS, application form, application fee of $40, baccalaureate degree, 3 letters of recommendation, personal statement, interview, resume. *Recommended:* college transcripts. *Application deadline* for fall term is April 1. Students are required to have their own computers.

Costs The 1997–98 tuition is $495 per credit hour. Fees: $12 per semester.

Financial Aid In 1997–98, 73% of all students received some form of financial aid. Graduate assistantships, loans, merit-based grants/scholarships, and need-based grants/scholarships are also available. The average student debt at graduation is $60,000. To apply for financial assistance, students

AT a GLANCE

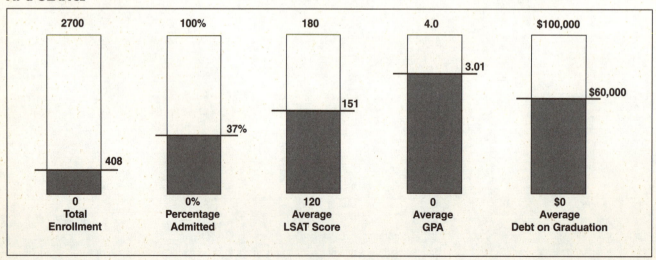

Degree Options

Degree	Total Credits Required	Length of Program
JD–Doctor of Laws	90	3–4 yrs, full-time or part-time [day, evening, summer]
JD/MA–Juris Doctor/Master of Arts–Public Policy or Public Administration	120	4 yrs, full-time only [day, summer]
JD/MA–Juris Doctor/Master of Arts–Communication Joint-degree Program	120	4 yrs, full-time only [day, summer]
JD/MBA–Juris Doctor/Master of Business Administration–Joint-degree Program	120	4 yrs, full-time only [day, summer]

must complete the Free Application for Federal Student Aid, institutional forms, and scholarship specific applications. Financial aid contact: Bonnie Creef, Assistant Director of Admissions and Financial Aid, 1000 Regent University Drive, Virginia Beach, VA 23464. Phone: 757-579-4559. Fax: 757-579-4595. E-mail: bonncre@regent.edu. Completed financial aid forms should be received by May 1.

Law School Library Law Library has 4 professional staff members and contains more than 300,000 volumes and 900 periodicals. 269 seats are available in the library. When classes are in session, the library is open 98 hours per week.

WESTLAW and LEXIS-NEXIS are available, as are the World Wide Web, online bibliographic services, and CD-ROM players. 11 computer workstations are available to students in the library. Special law collections include Transylvania Law School Collection.

First-Year Program Class size in the average section is 70.

Upper-Level Program Among the electives are:

* ★ **Biblical Law**
  Business and Corporate Law
* ★ **Common Law**
  Education
  Entertainment Law
  Environmental Law
  Family Law
  Health Care/Human Services
  Intellectual Property
  International/Comparative Law
  Jurisprudence
  Land Use Law/Natural Resources
  Lawyering Skills
  Legal History/Philosophy
  Litigation
  Maritime Law
  Media Law
  Mediation
  Public Interest
  Securities
* ★ **Tax Law**

(★ *indicates an area of special strength*)

Internships are available.

DEAN'S STATEMENT . . .

This nation needs more lawyers who have high ethical standards and who are committed to doing justice rather than pursuing selfish ambitions. These men and women understand the need to seek truth and demonstrate mercy, whether serving as advocates, counselors, mediators, or judges.

At Regent, we are looking for future lawyers who want to be the "salt of the earth" and the "light of the world" in our nation and beyond. We are committed to prepare these individuals with knowledge of the law and of the Bible so that they will be equipped to be ministers of reconciliation and justice.

It is my sincere hope that you will join the growing number of men and women who are making law both their career and their ministry. And there is no better place to prepare for this call than at Regent University School of Law.

I invite you to learn firsthand more about our unique program. Come to one of our Preview Weekends. Tour the campus. Talk to current students. The Admissions Office will be happy to assist you. Come see if you are being called to be part of what the Lord is doing at Regent University School of Law.

—J. Nelson Happy, Dean

HISTORY, CAMPUS, AND LOCATION

Since its founding in 1977 by Dr. M. G. "Pat" Robertson, Regent has grown to offer more than twenty-two master's and doctoral degrees from a Judeo-Christian worldview in the areas of law, business, communication, counseling, divinity, education, government, and organizational leadership. Regent University is accredited by the Commission on Colleges of the Southern Association of Colleges and Schools (1866 Southern Lane, Decatur, Georgia 30033-4097; Telephone: 404-679-4501) to award master's and doctoral degrees. The Regent University School of Law is fully accredited by the American Bar Association (ABA). Regent University is situated on a 700-acre suburban complex in Virginia Beach, Virginia. Virginia Beach is part of the Greater Hampton Roads metropolitan area, which encompasses Norfolk, Virginia Beach, Chesapeake, Portsmouth, Suffolk, Hampton, and Newport News. The total area population is more than 1 million. The School of Law is housed within Robertson Hall, a handsome blend of Georgian and Italian architecture, with accents in marble and stone. The facility provides an unparalleled environment for educational pursuits.

SPECIAL QUALITIES OF THE SCHOOL

The foremost distinction of Regent University School of Law is its Judeo-Christian perspective. No other law school in the nation offers the specific integration of faith and biblical principles in an accredited bar-approved study of law. Also high on the list of distinctions is Regent's affiliation with the American Center for Law and Justice (ACLJ), one of the country's foremost public interest firms, which is located on the Regent campus. This relationship provides internships as well as the opportunity to observe scholarly debates on current legal issues through a network of seminars and conferences. Regent also offers a part-time J.D. program for those who cannot accommodate a full-time program in law. Regent's joint-degree programs enable students to simultaneously earn a master's degree in the field of government, business, or communication. Also

offered is the Regent Summer Abroad Program in International Human Rights, held in Strasbourg, France.

TECHNOLOGY ON CAMPUS

Classrooms are fitted with large-screen video/data projection and electric and local area network (LAN) access. WESTLAW, LEXIS-NEXIS, the World Wide Web, and e-mail are available on the University LAN. Students may use their laptops to access the LAN from more than seventy-two connections in the School of Law and library buildings. A centrally located automated media delivery system provides high-quality transmission to and from the majority of classrooms over a fiber-optic network. Dozens of audio, video, film, and slide machines provide scheduled playback on demand by faculty in the equipped classrooms. Moot courtrooms and professional practice rooms feature remote cameras, microphones, and audiovisual equipment to allow students to sharpen their negotiation and arbitration skills. In addition, a large ceremonial courtroom features large-screen video/data projection. The University library provides more than 160,000 bound volumes, 560,000 microforms, and 1,425 journal subscriptions. Microforms include backfiles of many journals and special sets, such as the Library of American Civilization, the complete New York Times, NEWS-BANK, and Educational Resources Information Center (ERIC) documents.

SCHOLARSHIPS AND LOANS

Regent University's Central Financial Aid Office administers federal and private loans, Virginia Tuition Assistance Grant Program (TAGP), endowments, scholarships, and employee tuition remission. Students may also apply for institutional aid through the School of Law. Approximately 82 percent of the student body receives some form of scholarship. The Regent Tuition Installment Plan (TIP) enables students to pay tuition in installments over the course of the term. Graduate assistant positions are available throughout the campus (employee tuition remission does not apply).

STUDENT ACTIVITIES AND OPPORTUNITIES

Law Review The School of Law publishes the *Regent University Law Review*, a forum for a Christian perspective on law in a traditional legal periodical. Student editors and staff members, chosen on the basis of academic achievement and writing ability, gain valuable experience by writing and editing the *Law Review* under the guidance of the law faculty.

Moot Court The Moot Court Board serves to promote opportunities for student development of written and oral advocacy skills. The board organizes intramural competitions, which provide students with the opportunity to practice their courtroom advocacy skills before local attorneys and judges. It also serves to prepare teams for national moot court competitions, for which student teams are selected to represent Regent School of Law in competition against teams from other law schools. The Dispute Resolution and Client Counseling Board of the School of Law is an academic board committed to developing more effective personal negotiation and case settlement dynamics for resolving legal disputes outside the usual trial court process. The board is responsible for facilitating two annual intramural competitions as well as preparing teams to participate in both American Bar Association and regional law school competitions.

Extracurricular Activities Regent law students are among the nation's brightest and best, having won regional and national championships in student law competitions. The Regent Negotiations Team has maintained the regional championship for four consecutive years. Other recent honors include the 1996 National Championship of the 46th Annual Sutherland Moot Court Competition and the 1997 National Juvenile Law Competition—First Place Overall, Best Advocate, Second Best Advocate, and Runner-up for Best Brief. These achievements reflect the high caliber of students in Regent School of Law as well as the excellence of preparation the Regent law curriculum provides.

Special Opportunities There are numerous special opportunities for students, including such clubs and organizations as the Christian Legal Society, ABA/Law Student Division, Women's Legal Society, Council of Graduate Students, Black Law Students Association, Newman Club, Rutherford Institute Student Chapter, Law Student Advocate Association (ACLJ Student Chapter), and the Sports and Entertainment Legal Society.

Opportunities for Members of Minority Groups and Women Please see Special Opportunities section above for opportunities for members of minority groups and women.

BAR PASSAGE, CAREER SERVICES, AND PLACEMENT

The national first-time-takers' bar passage rate for the class of 1997 was 75 percent. The majority of the bar examinations were taken in Virginia (41.1 percent), followed by North Carolina (8.8 percent).

Regent University School of Law Career Services/ Alumni Office services include a bimonthly job bulletin mailed to graduates at their request, postcards of recent job openings, continued one-on-one counseling and resume/ cover letter review with assistance provided in job search strategies, reciprocity available with other law schools, bulletin boards with job announcements, and phone calls made to appropriate individuals for select positions. The School of Law also utilizes its growing Web site. The Regent Job Bulletin is posted there, along with many links to other job-related Web pages. Eighty-eight percent of the class of 1997 was employed within six months of graduation in the fields listed below.

Legal Field	Percentage of Graduates	Average Starting Salary
Academic	1.0%	n/a
Business	14.4%	$40,530
Government	11.3%	$33,315
Judicial Clerkship	6.2%	$34,638
Private Practice	39.0%	$34,488
Public Interest	10.3%	$38,778
Other	6.2%	n/a

CORRESPONDENCE AND INFORMATION

Admissions Office
Regent University School of Law
1000 Regent University Drive
Virginia Beach, Virginia 23464-9800
Telephone: 757-226-4584
800-373-5504 (toll-free)
Fax: 757-226-4595
E-mail: lawschool@regent.edu
World Wide Web: http://www.regent.edu/acad/schlaw

UNIVERSITY OF RICHMOND
SCHOOL OF LAW

University of Richmond, Virginia

INFORMATION CONTACT
John R. Pagan, Dean
University of Richmond, VA 23173

Phone: 804-289-8183   Fax: 804-289-8992
Web site: http://law.richmond.edu/

LAW STUDENT PROFILE [1997–98]

FULL-TIME   Enrollment: 471
Women: 46%   Men: 54%

PART-TIME   Enrollment: 1
Men: 100%

RACIAL or ETHNIC COMPOSITION
African American, 9%; Asian/Pacific Islander, 5%; Hispanic, 2%; Native American, 1%; International, 1%

APPLICANTS and ADMITTEES
Number applied: 1,314
Admitted: 554
Percentage accepted: 42%
Seats available: 167
Average LSAT score: 158
Average GPA: 3.1

University of Richmond School of Law is a private institution that organizes classes on a semester calendar system. The campus is situated in a suburban setting. Founded in 1830, first ABA approved in 1928, and an AALS member, University of Richmond School of Law offers JD, JD/MBA, JD/MHA, JD/MSW, and JD/MUP degrees.

Faculty consists of 27 full-time and 68 part-time members in 1997–98. 10 full-time faculty members and 25 part-time faculty members are women. 100% of all faculty members have a JD; 67% have advanced law degrees. Of all faculty members, 7% are African American, 93% are white.

Application Information *Required:* LSAT, LSDAS, application form, application fee of $35, baccalaureate degree, personal statement, college transcripts. *Recommended:* recommendations, writing sample, resume. *Application deadline* for fall term is February 1. Students are required to have their own computers.

Financial Aid Loans, merit-based grants/scholarships, need-based grants/scholarships, and federal work-study loans are available. The average student debt at graduation is $43,460. To apply for financial assistance, students must complete the Free Application for Federal Student Aid and institutional forms. Financial aid contact: Cindy Bolger, Director of

AT a GLANCE

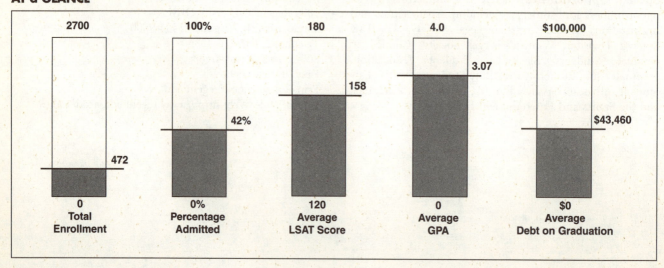

Degree Options

Degree	Total Credits Required	Length of Program
JD–Doctor of Laws	86	3–5 yrs, full-time only [day, summer]
JD/MBA–Juris Doctor/Master of Business Administration		4 yrs, full-time only [day]
JD/MHA–Juris Doctor/Master of Health Administration		4 yrs, full-time only [day]
JD/MSW–Juris Doctor/Master of Social Work		4 yrs, full-time only [day]
JD/MUP–Juris Doctor/Masters of Urban Planning		4 yrs, full-time only [day]

Financial Aid, Financial Aid Office, Sarah Brunet Hall, 2700 Sterncroft Drive, Richmond, VA 23225. Phone: 804-289-8438. Fax: 804-289-8992. Completed financial aid forms should be received by February 25.

Law School Library William Taylor Muse Law Library has 8 professional staff members and contains more than 257,837 volumes and 4,170 periodicals. 602 seats are available in the library. When classes are in session, the library is open 106 hours per week.

WESTLAW and LEXIS-NEXIS are available, as are the World Wide Web, online bibliographic services, and CD-ROM players. 15 computer workstations are available to students in the library. Special law collections include legal history, taxation.

First-Year Program Class size in the average section is 60; 100% of the first-year courses are taught by full-time faculty.

Upper-Level Program Class size in the average section is 30. Among the electives are:

Administrative Law
★ Advocacy
Business and Corporate Law
Education Law
Entertainment Law
Environmental Law
★ Family Law
Government/Regulation
Health Care/Human Services
Intellectual Property
International/Comparative Law
Jurisprudence
Labor Law
Land Use Law/Natural Resources
★ Lawyering Skills
Legal History/Philosophy
Litigation
Maritime Law
Mediation
Probate Law
★ Public Interest
Securities
Tax Law
(★ indicates an area of special strength)

Clinical Courses Students receive degree credit for clinical courses. (Clinical practicum is not required.) Among the clinical areas offered are:

Civil Litigation
Criminal Defense
Criminal Prosecution
Education
Environmental Law
Family Practice
Government Litigation
International Law
Juvenile Law
Labor and Employment
Land Rights/Natural Resource
Public Interest
Tax Law

45% of the students participate in internship programs. International exchange programs permit students to visit United Kingdom.

UNIVERSITY OF VIRGINIA
SCHOOL OF LAW

Charlottesville, Virginia

INFORMATION CONTACT
Robert E. Scott, Dean
580 Massie Road
Charlottesville, VA 22903-1789

Phone: 804-924-7343   Fax: 804-924-7536
Web site: http://www.law.virginia.edu/

LAW STUDENT PROFILE [1997–98]
FULL-TIME   Enrollment: 1,145
Women: 37%   Men: 63%

RACIAL or ETHNIC COMPOSITION
African American, 7%; Asian/Pacific Islander, 4%; Hispanic, 1%; Nataive American, 0.4%; International, 2%

APPLICANTS and ADMITTEES
Number applied: 3,188
Admitted: 988
Percentage accepted: 31%
Seats available: 360
Average LSAT score: 166
Average GPA: 3.6

University of Virginia School of Law is a public institution that organizes classes on a semester calendar system. The campus is situated in a suburban setting. Founded in 1826, first ABA approved in 1945, and an AALS member, University of Virginia School of Law offers JD, JD/MA, JD/MBA, JD/MPP, JD/MS, JD/PhD, JSD, and LLM degrees.

Faculty consists of 63 full-time and 3 part-time members in 1997–98. 14 full-time faculty members and 1 part-time faculty members are women. 100% of all faculty members have a JD degree. Of all faculty members, 1% are Asian/Pacific Islander, 6.5% are African American, 91% are white.

Application Information *Required:* LSAT, LSDAS, application form, application fee of $65, baccalaureate degree, 2 letters of recommendation, personal statement, college transcripts. *Application deadline* for fall term is January 15. Students are required to have their own computers.

Costs The 1997–98 tuition is $14,606 for state residents. Tuition is $20,706 for nonresidents.

Financial Aid Loans, loan repayment assistance program (LRAP), merit-based grants/scholarships, need-based grants/scholarships, and federal work-study loans are available. To apply for financial

AT a GLANCE

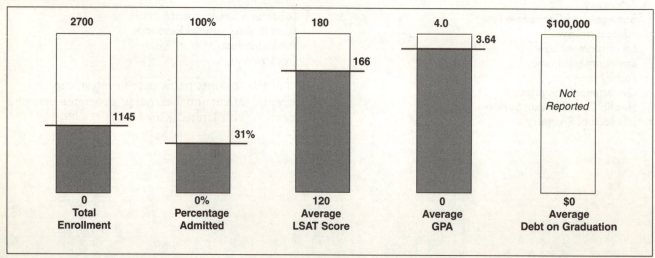

Degree Options

Degree	Total Credits Required	Length of Program
JD–Juris Doctor	86	3 yrs, full-time only [day]
JD/MA–Juris Doctor/Master of Arts–available in history, government, economics, English, philosophy, sociology, and marine affairs		
JD/MBA–Juris Doctor/Master of Business Administration		4 yrs, full-time only
JD/MPP–Juris Doctor/Master of Public Planning		
JD/MS–Juris Doctor/Master of Science–Accounting		
JD/PhD–Juris Doctor/Doctor of Philosophy–Government		
JSD–Doctor of Juridical Science		
LLM–Master of Laws	24	1 yr, full-time only [day]

assistance, students must complete the Free Application for Federal Student Aid and institutional forms. Financial aid contact: Jerome W. D. Stokes, Senior Assistant Dean for Admissions and Financial Aid, 580 Massie Road, Charlottesville, VA 22903-1789. Phone: 804-924-7805. Fax: 804-924-7536. E-mail: lawadmit@virginia.edu.

Law School Library Morris Law Library has 12 professional staff members and contains more than 769,196 volumes and 10,638 periodicals. 770 seats are available in the library. When classes are in session, the library is open 110 hours per week.

WESTLAW and LEXIS-NEXIS are available, as are the World Wide Web, online bibliographic services, and CD-ROM players. 123 computer workstations are available to students in the library. Special law collections include Oceans law, Commonwealth law.

First-Year Program 100% of the first-year courses are taught by full-time faculty.

Upper-Level Program Among the electives are:

Administrative Law
Advocacy
Business and Corporate Law
Consumer Law
Entertainment Law
Environmental Law
Evidence
Family Law
Feminist Jurisprudence
Government/Regulation
Health Care/Human Services

Human Rights
Indian/Tribal Law
Insurance
Intellectual Property
International/Comparative Law
Jurisprudence
Labor Law
Land Use Law/Natural Resources
Lawyering Skills
Legal History/Philosophy
Legislation
Litigation
Maritime Law
Media Law
Mediation
Probate Law
Public Interest
Race and Law
Securities
Tax Law

Clinical Courses Students receive degree credit for clinical courses. (Clinical practicum is not required.) Among the clinical areas offered are:

Appellate Litigation
Criminal Defense
Criminal Prosecution
Employment Law
Environmental Law
Family Practice
First Amendment
Human Rights
Local Government

Internships are available.

WASHINGTON AND LEE UNIVERSITY
SCHOOL OF LAW

Lexington, Virginia

INFORMATION CONTACT

Barry Sullivan, Dean
Sydney Lewis Hall
Lexington, VA 24450

Phone: 540-463-8502   Fax: 540-463-8488
Web site: http://www.wlu.edu/

LAW STUDENT PROFILE [1997–98]

FULL-TIME   Enrollment: 367
Women: 41%   Men: 59%

RACIAL or ETHNIC COMPOSITION
African American, 4%; Asian/Pacific Islander, 4%; Hispanic, 1%; Native American, 1%; International, 0%

APPLICANTS and ADMITTEES
Number applied: 1,389
Admitted: 500
Percentage accepted: 36%
Seats available: 120
Median LSAT score: 165
Median GPA: 3.4

Washington and Lee University School of Law is a private institution that organizes classes on a semester calendar system. The campus is situated in a small-town setting. Founded in 1849, first ABA approved in 1933, and an AALS member, Washington and Lee University School of Law offers a JD degree.

Faculty consists of 38 full-time and 16 part-time members in 1997–98. 11 full-time faculty members are women. 100% of all faculty members have a JD; 8.93% have advanced law degrees. Of all faculty members, 1.79% are Asian/Pacific Islander, 5.36% are African American, 92.85% are white.

Application Information *Required:* LSAT, LSDAS, application form, application fee of $40, baccalaureate degree, 2 letters of recommendation. *Application deadline* for fall term is February 1.

Financial Aid In 1997–98, 85% of all students received some form of financial aid. Fellowships, graduate assistantships, loans, merit-based grants/scholarships, need-based grants/scholarships, and federal work-study loans are also available. The average student debt at graduation is $50,485. To apply for financial assistance, students must complete the Free Application for Federal Student Aid. Financial aid contact: E. McClain Stradtner, Associate Director of Financial Aid, Gilliam House

AT a GLANCE

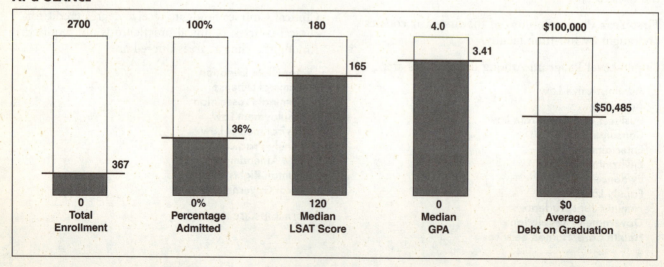

Degree Options

Degree	Total Credits Required	Length of Program
JD–Doctor of Laws	85	3 yrs, full-time only [day]

110, Washington and Lee University, Lexington, VA 24450. Phone: 540-463-8729. Fax: 540-463-8488. E-mail: emstradtner@wlu.edu. Completed financial aid forms should be received by February 15.

Law School Library Wilbur C. Hall Law Library has 7 professional staff members and contains more than 350,065 volumes and 4,460 periodicals. 551 seats are available in the library. When classes are in session, the library is open 168 hours per week.

WESTLAW and LEXIS-NEXIS are available, as are the World Wide Web and online bibliographic services. 78 computer workstations are available to students in the library. Special law collections include U.S. Document Depository, papers of Lewis F. Powell, Jr., papers of M. Caldwell Butler (Bankruptcy Reform and Impeachment of Richard M. Nixon).

First-Year Program Class size in the average section is 38; 100% of the first-year courses are taught by full-time faculty.

Upper-Level Program Class size in the average section is 24. Among the electives are:

Administrative Law
★ Advocacy
Business and Corporate Law
Consumer Law
Education Law
Entertainment Law
Environmental Law
Family Law
Government/Regulation

Health Care/Human Services
Indian/Tribal Law
Intellectual Property
International/Comparative Law
Jurisprudence
Labor Law
Land Use Law/Natural Resources
★ Lawyering Skills
Legal History/Philosophy
★ Litigation
Maritime Law
Media Law
Mediation
Probate Law
Public Interest
Securities
Tax Law
(★ indicates an area of special strength)

Clinical Courses Students receive degree credit for clinical courses. (Clinical practicum is not required.) Among the clinical areas offered are:

Black Lung
Capital Defense
Civil Litigation
Criminal Defense
Criminal Prosecution
General Practice
Judicial Clerkship
Mental Health and Law
Prison
Public Interest

Internships are available.

GONZAGA UNIVERSITY
SCHOOL OF LAW

Spokane, Washington

INFORMATION CONTACT
John E. Clute, Dean
PO Box 3528
Spokane, WA 99220

Phone: 509-328-4220   Fax: 509-324-5710
     Ext. 6090
E-mail: admissions@lawschool.gonzaga.e
Web site: http://www.law.gonzaga.edu/

LAW STUDENT PROFILE [1997–98]

FULL-TIME   Enrollment: 506
Women: 38%   Men: 62%

PART-TIME   Enrollment: 13
Women: 62%   Men: 38%

RACIAL or ETHNIC COMPOSITION
African American, 2%; Asian/Pacific Islander, 6%; Hispanic, 4%; Native American, 2%; International, 0%

APPLICANTS and ADMITTEES
Number applied: 1,005
Admitted: 752
Percentage accepted: 75%
Seats available: 175
Average LSAT score: 151
Average GPA: 3.0

Gonzaga University School of Law is a private institution that organizes classes on a semester calendar system. The campus is situated in a suburban setting. Founded in 1912, first ABA approved in 1955, and an AALS member, Gonzaga University School of Law offers JD, JD/MBA, and JD/MPA degrees.

Faculty consists of 35 full-time and 26 part-time members in 1997–98. 10 full-time faculty members and 5 part-time faculty members are women. 100% of all faculty members have a JD; 23% have advanced law degrees. Of all faculty members, 3.85% are African American, 7.69% are Hispanic, 88.46% are white.

Application Information *Required:* LSAT, LSDAS, application form, application fee of $40, baccalaureate degree, personal statement, college transcripts. *Recommended:* recommendations, essay, resume. *Application deadline* for fall term is March 15.

Costs The 1997–98 tuition is $610 per credit hour. Fees: $100.

Financial Aid 10 fellowships were awarded. Loans, merit-based grants/scholarships, need-based grants/scholarships, and federal work-study loans are also available. The average student debt at graduation is $80,000. To apply for financial assistance,

AT a GLANCE

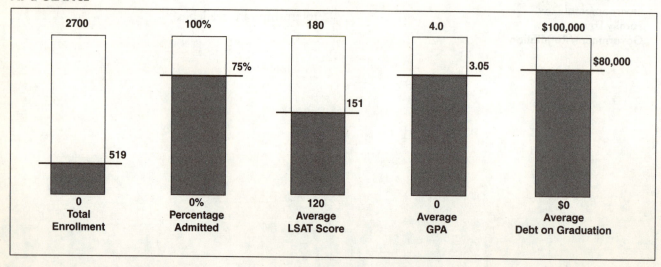

Degree Options

Degree	Total Credits Required	Length of Program
JD–Doctor of Laws	90	3–4 yrs, full-time or part-time [day]
JD/MBA–Juris Doctor/Master of Business Administration–Dual-degree Program	114	4–5 yrs, full-time or part-time [day, evening]
JD/MPA–Juris Doctor/Master of Professional Accountancy–Dual-degree Program	111	4–5 yrs, full-time or part-time [day, evening]

students must complete the Free Application for Federal Student Aid and scholarship specific applications. Financial aid contact: Joan Henning, Coordinator of Financial Services, PO Box 3528, Spokane, WA 99220. Phone: 509-323-3859. Fax: 509-324-5710. E-mail: jhenning@lawschool.gonzaga.edu. Completed financial aid forms should be received by March 15.

Law School Library Gonzaga University School of Law–Law Library has 11 professional staff members and contains more than 225,400 volumes and 5,733 periodicals. 468 seats are available in the library. When classes are in session, the library is open 108 hours per week.

WESTLAW and LEXIS-NEXIS are available, as are the World Wide Web, online bibliographic services, and CD-ROM players. 57 computer workstations are available to students in the library.

First-Year Program Class size in the average section is 167; 100% of the first-year courses are taught by full-time faculty.

Upper-Level Program Class size in the average section is 35. Among the electives are:

Administrative Law
Advocacy
★ Business and Corporate Law
Civil Rights
Community Property
Conflict of Laws
Constitutional Law
Consumer Law
Education Law
★ Environmental Law

Family Law
Government/Regulation
Indian/Tribal Law
Intellectual Property
International Law
Jurisprudence
Labor Law
★ Land Use Law/Natural Resources
Lawyering Skills
Litigation
Maritime Law
Media Law
Mediation
Probate Law
Product Liability
Property/Real Estate
★ Public Interest
Securities
Sports Law
Tax Law
(★ indicates an area of special strength)

Clinical Courses Students receive degree credit for clinical courses. (Clinical practicum is not required.) Among the clinical areas offered are:

Civil Rights
Criminal Defense
Elderly Advocacy
Family Practice
General Practice
Immigration
Indian/Tribal Law
Public Interest

25% of the students participate in internship programs.

SEATTLE UNIVERSITY
SCHOOL OF LAW

Seattle, Washington

INFORMATION CONTACT

James E. Bond, Dean
950 Broadway
Tacoma, WA 98402

Phone: 253-591-2273   Fax: 253-591-2902
E-mail: lawadmis@seattleu.edu
Web site: http://www.law.seattleu.edu/

LAW STUDENT PROFILE [1997–98]

FULL-TIME   Enrollment: 641
Women: 51%   Men: 49%

PART-TIME   Enrollment: 189
Women: 48%   Men: 52%

RACIAL or ETHNIC COMPOSITION
African American, 4%; Asian/Pacific Islander, 9%; Hispanic, 3%; Native American, 3%; International, 1%

APPLICANTS and ADMITTEES
Number applied: 1,213
Admitted: 790
Percentage accepted: 65%
Seats available: 265
Average LSAT score: 155
Average GPA: 3.3

Seattle University School of Law is a private institution that organizes classes on a semester calendar system. The campus is situated in an urban setting. Founded in 1972, first ABA approved in 1975, and an AALS member, Seattle University School of Law offers JD, JD/MA, JD/MBA, and JD/MS degrees.

Faculty consists of 37 full-time and 28 part-time members in 1997–98. 16 full-time faculty members and 10 part-time faculty members are women.

Application Information *Required:* LSAT, LSDAS, application form, application fee of $50, baccalaureate degree, 2 letters of recommendation, personal statement, college transcripts. *Recommended:* resume. *Application deadline* for fall term is April 1.

Costs The 1997–98 tuition is $17,880 full-time; $14,900 part-time. Fees: $46 full-time; $32 part-time.

Financial Aid In 1997–98, 97% of all students received some form of financial aid. Loans, merit-based grants/scholarships, and federal work-study loans are also available. The average student debt at graduation is $58,000. To apply for financial assistance, students must complete the Free Application for Federal Student Aid and institutional forms. Financial aid contact: Kathleen D. Koch, Associate

AT a GLANCE

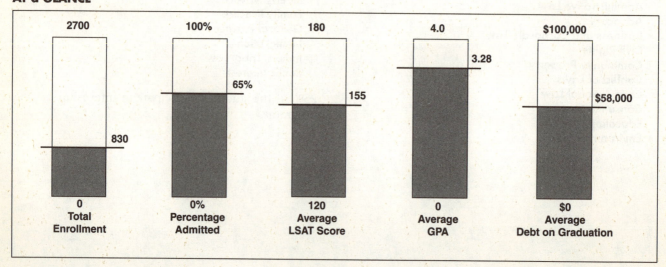

Degree Options

Degree	Total Credits Required	Length of Program
JD–Juris Doctor	90	3–4 yrs, full-time or part-time [day, evening, summer]
JD/MA–Juris Doctor/Master of Arts– Applied Economics		4–5 yrs, full-time or part-time [day, evening, summer]
JD/MBA–Juris Doctor/Master of Business Administration		4–5 yrs, full-time or part-time [day, evening, summer]
JD/MS–Juris Doctor/Master of Science–Finance		4–5 yrs, full-time or part-time [day, evening, summer]

Director of Financial Aid, 950 Broadway Plaza, Tacoma, WA 98402. Phone: 253-591-2261. Fax: 253-591-2902. E-mail: lawfa@seattleu.edu. Completed financial aid forms should be received by April 1.

Law School Library Seattle University Law Library has 14 professional staff members and contains more than 341,306 volumes and 3,606 periodicals. 589 seats are available in the library. When classes are in session, the library is open 119 hours per week.

WESTLAW and LEXIS-NEXIS are available, as are the World Wide Web, online bibliographic services, and CD-ROM players. 105 computer workstations are available to students in the library.

First-Year Program Class size in the average section is 75; 100% of the first-year courses are taught by full-time faculty.

Upper-Level Program Class size in the average section is 65. Among the electives are:

Administrative Law
Advocacy
Business and Corporate Law
Commercial Law
Constitutional Law
Consumer Law
Criminal Law
Education Law
Entertainment Law
Environmental Law
Family Law

Feminist Jurisprudence
Government/Regulation
Health Care/Human Services
Indian/Tribal Law
Intellectual Property
International/Comparative Law
Jurisprudence
Labor Law
Land Use Law/Natural Resources
Lawyering Skills
Legal History/Philosophy
Litigation
Maritime Law
Media Law
Mediation
Probate Law
Public Interest
Securities
Tax Law

Clinical Courses Students receive degree credit for clinical courses. (Clinical practicum is not required.) Among the clinical areas offered are:

Administrative Law
Bankruptcy
Civil Litigation
Criminal Defense
Education
Health
Immigration
Professional Responsibility

5% of the students participate in internship programs.

UNIVERSITY OF WASHINGTON
SCHOOL OF LAW

Seattle, Washington

INFORMATION CONTACT
Roland L. Hjorth, Dean
Campus Parkway, NE
Seattle, WA 98105-4078

Phone: 206-543-9476
E-mail: smadrid@u.washington.edu
Web site: http://www.law.washington.edu/

LAW STUDENT PROFILE [1997–98]

FULL-TIME Enrollment: 597
Women: 49% Men: 51%

PART-TIME Enrollment: 52
Women: 54% Men: 46%

RACIAL or ETHNIC COMPOSITION
African American, 2%; Asian/Pacific Islander, 15%; Hispanic, 7%; Native American, 3%; International, 6%

APPLICANTS and ADMITTEES
Number applied: 1,759
Admitted: 469
Percentage accepted: 27%
Seats available: 169

University of Washington School of Law is a public institution that organizes classes on a quarter calendar system. The campus is situated in an urban setting. Founded in 1899, first ABA approved in 1924, and an AALS member, University of Washington School of Law offers JD, JD/LLM, JD/MA, JD/MBA, and LLM degrees.

Faculty consists of 47 full-time and 46 part-time members in 1997–98. 19 full-time faculty members and 14 part-time faculty members are women.

Application Information *Required:* LSAT, LSDAS, application form, application fee of $50, 2 letters of recommendation. *Application deadline* for fall term is January 15.

Costs The 1997–98 tuition is $5763 for state residents. Tuition is $14,169 for nonresidents.

Financial Aid In 1997–98, 43% of all students received some form of financial aid. 3 fellowships, 6 research assistantships were awarded. Need-based grants/scholarships and federal work-study loans are also available. To apply for financial assistance, students must complete the Free Application for Federal Student Aid. Financial aid contact: Brenda Ringer Cote, Financial Aid Coordinator, 1100 Northeast Campus Parkway, Seattle, WA 98105-6617. Phone: 206-543-4552. E-mail:

AT a GLANCE

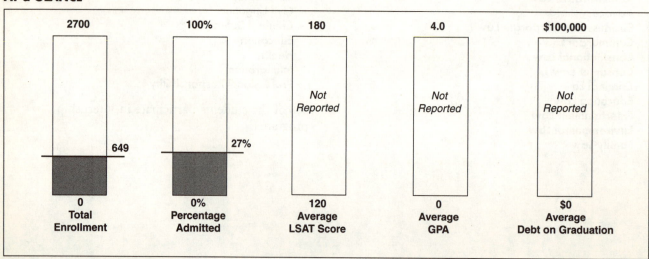

Degree Options

Degree	Total Credits Required	Length of Program
JD–Juris Doctor	86	full-time only
JD/LLM–Juris Doctor/Master of Laws–Marine Affairs	40	
JD/MA–Juris Doctor/Master of Arts–International Studies		
JD/MBA–Juris Doctor/Master of Business Administration		
LLM–Master of Laws–Taxation	24	1 yr, full-time or part-time [day, evening]
LLM–Master of Laws–East Asian Law	36	
LLM–Master of Laws–nternational Environmental Law	40	
LLM–Master of Laws–International Development	40	

uwlawaid@u.washington.edu. Completed financial aid forms should be received by February 28.

Law School Library Marian Gould Gallagher Law Library has 14 professional staff members and contains more than 482,173 volumes and 7,755 periodicals. 372 seats are available in the library. When classes are in session, the library is open 89 hours per week.

WESTLAW and LEXIS-NEXIS are available, as are the World Wide Web and CD-ROM players. Special law collections include East Asian Law collection.

First-Year Program Class size in the average section is 97.

Upper-Level Program Among the electives are:

Administrative Law
Advocacy
Business and Corporate Law
Conflict of Laws
Constitutional Law
Criminal Procedure
Education Law
Employment Law
Environmental Law
Estate Planning
Family Law
Government/Regulation

Health Care/Human Services
Indian/Tribal Law
Insurance
Intellectual Property
International/Comparative Law
Jurisprudence
Labor Law
Land Use Law/Natural Resources
Lawyering Skills
Legal History/Philosophy
Litigation
Maritime Law
Mediation
Public Interest
Securities
Tax Law

Clinical Courses Students receive degree credit for clinical courses. (Clinical practicum is required.) Among the clinical areas offered are:

Criminal Defense
Family Practice
General Practice
Immigration
Juvenile Law
Mediation
Unemployment Compensation

Internships are available.

WEST VIRGINIA UNIVERSITY
COLLEGE OF LAW

Morgantown, West Virginia

INFORMATION CONTACT

John W. Fisher II, Interim Dean
PO Box 6130
Morgantown, WV 26506-6130

Phone: 304-293-3199   Fax: 304-293-6891
Web site: http://www.wvu.edu/

LAW STUDENT PROFILE [1997–98]

FULL-TIME   Enrollment: 420
Women: 46%   Men: 54%

PART-TIME   Enrollment: 18
Women: 56%   Men: 44%

RACIAL or ETHNIC COMPOSITION
African American, 2%; Asian/Pacific Islander, 1%; Hispanic, 1%; Nataive American, 0.2%; International, 0%

APPLICANTS and ADMITTEES
Number applied: 511
Admitted: 255
Percentage accepted: 50%
Seats available: 145
Average LSAT score: 154
Average GPA: 3.3

West Virginia University College of Law is a public institution that organizes classes on a semester calendar system. The campus is situated in a small-town setting. Founded in 1894, first ABA approved in 1923, and an AALS member, West Virginia University College of Law offers a JD degree.

Faculty consists of 23 full-time and 15 part-time members in 1997–98. 8 full-time faculty members and 4 part-time faculty members are women. 100% of all faculty members have a JD; 34% have advanced law degrees.

Application Information *Required:* LSAT, LSDAS, application form, application fee of $45, baccalaureate degree, 3 letters of recommendation, personal statement, writing sample, college transcripts. *Recommended:* resume. *Application deadline* for fall term is March 1.

Costs The 1997–98 tuition is $5476 for state residents. Tuition is $12,748 for nonresidents.

Financial Aid In 1997–98, 81% of all students received some form of financial aid. 6 fellowships, 1 teaching assistantship was awarded. 7 other awards were given. Fellowships, graduate assistantships, loans, loan repayment assistance program (LRAP), merit-based grants/scholarships, need-based

AT a GLANCE

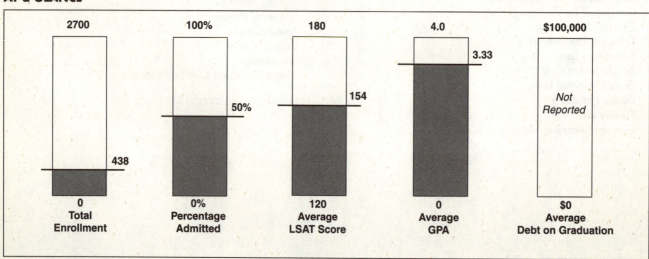

Total Enrollment	Percentage Admitted	Average LSAT Score	Average GPA	Average Debt on Graduation
2700	100%	180	4.0	$100,000
438	50%	154	3.33	Not Reported
0	0%	120	0	$0

Degree Options		
Degree	**Total Credits Required**	**Length of Program**
JD–Doctor of Laws	93	3–4 yrs, full-time or part-time [day]

grants/scholarships, and federal work-study loans are also available. To apply for financial assistance, students must complete the Free Application for Federal Student Aid. Financial aid contact: Joanna Hastings, Financial Aid Counselor, PO Box 6130, Morgantown, WV 26506-6130. Phone: 304-293-5302. Fax: 304-293-6891. E-mail: jhasting@wva.edu. Completed financial aid forms should be received by March 1.

Law School Library West Virginia University College of Law Library has 4 professional staff members and contains more than 246,000 volumes and 2,940 periodicals. 274 seats are available in the library. When classes are in session, the library is open 86 hours per week.

WESTLAW and LEXIS-NEXIS are available, as are the World Wide Web, online bibliographic services, and CD-ROM players. 35 computer workstations are available to students in the library. Special law collections include Andrew J. Colborn and Harry B. Colborn Rare book Room.

First-Year Program Class size in the average section is 70; 100% of the first-year courses are taught by full-time faculty.

Upper-Level Program Class size in the average section is 50. Among the electives are:

Administrative Law
★ Advocacy
Business and Corporate Law
Consumer Law
Entertainment Law
Environmental Law
Family Law
Government/Regulation
Health Care/Human Services
Intellectual Property
International/Comparative Law
Jurisprudence
Labor Law
Land Use Law/Natural Resources
★ Lawyering Skills
Legal History/Philosophy
★ Litigation
Media Law
Mediation
Probate Law
Public Interest
Securities
Tax Law
(★ indicates an area of special strength)

Clinical Courses Students receive degree credit for clinical courses. (Clinical practicum is not required.) Among the clinical areas offered are:

Civil Litigation
Family Practice
General Practice
Government Litigation
Immigration
Public Interest

International exchange programs permit students to visit France and Russian Federation.

MARQUETTE UNIVERSITY
LAW SCHOOL

Milwaukee, Wisconsin

INFORMATION CONTACT
Howard B. Eisenberg, Dean
Sensenbrenner Hall
PO Box 1881
Milwaukee, WI 53201-1881

Phone: 414-288-1765   Fax: 414-288-6403
Web site: http://www.marquette.edu/law/

LAW STUDENT PROFILE [1997–98]

FULL-TIME   Enrollment: 415
Women: 41%   Men: 59%

PART-TIME   Enrollment: 59
Women: 49%   Men: 51%

RACIAL or ETHNIC COMPOSITION
African American, 2%; Asian/Pacific Islander, 3%; Hispanic, 5%; Native American, 1%

APPLICANTS and ADMITTEES
Number applied: 961
Admitted: 507
Percentage accepted: 53%
Seats available: 187
Average LSAT score: 155
Average GPA: 3.1

Marquette University Law School is a private institution that organizes classes on a semester calendar system. The campus is situated in an urban setting. Founded in 1892, first ABA approved in 1925, and an AALS member, Marquette University Law School offers JD, JD/MA, and JD/MBA degrees.

Faculty consists of 23 full-time and 30 part-time members in 1997–98. 8 full-time faculty members and 6 part-time faculty members are women. 100% of all faculty members have a JD degree. Of all faculty members, 6.5% are African American, 3.2% are Hispanic, 90.3% are white.

Application Information *Required:* LSAT, LSDAS, application form, application fee of $40, baccalaureate degree, 2 letters of recommendation, essay, college transcripts. *Application deadline* for fall term is April 1.

Costs The 1997–98 tuition is $18,370 full-time; $760 per credit part-time.

Financial Aid In 1997–98, 80% of all students received some form of financial aid. Loans, merit-based grants/scholarships, and federal work-study loans are also available. The average student debt at graduation is $62,000. To apply for financial assistance, students must complete the Free Application for Federal Student Aid. Financial aid contact:

AT a GLANCE

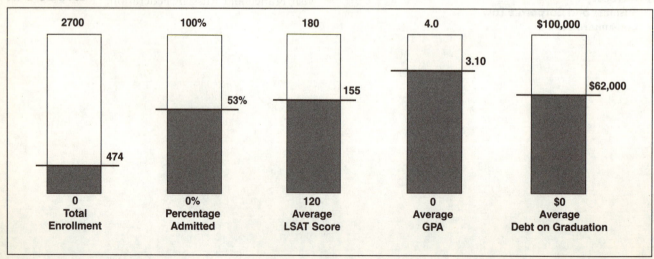

Degree Options

Degree	Total Credits Required	Length of Program
JD–Juris Doctor	90	3–6 yrs, full-time or part-time [day, evening, summer]
JD/MA–Juris Doctor/Master of Arts–Political Science		4 yrs, full-time or part-time [day, evening, summer]
JD/MA–Juris Doctor/Master of Arts–International Affairs		4 yrs, full-time or part-time [day, evening, summer]
JD/MBA–Juris Doctor/Master of Business Administration		4 yrs, full-time or part-time [day, evening, summer]

Law School Office of Admissions, Sensenbrenner Hall, PO Box 1881, Milwaukee, WI 53201-1881. Phone: 414-288-6767. Fax: 414-288-6403. E-mail: law.admission@marquette.edu. Completed financial aid forms should be received by March 1.

Law School Library Legal Research Center has 8 professional staff members and contains more than 255,349 volumes and 3,193 periodicals. 345 seats are available in the library. When classes are in session, the library is open 106 hours per week.

WESTLAW and LEXIS-NEXIS are available, as are the World Wide Web, online bibliographic services, and CD-ROM players. 20 computer workstations are available to students in the library. Special law collections include Japanese Language Legal Materials.

First-Year Program Class size in the average section is 70; 99% of the first-year courses are taught by full-time faculty.

Upper-Level Program Class size in the average section is 28. Among the electives are:

Administrative Law
Advocacy
★ Business and Corporate Law
★ Commercial Law
★ Criminal Law
Environmental Law
Family Law

Health Care/Human Services
Indian/Tribal Law
★ Intellectual Property
★ International/Comparative Law
Jurisprudence
Labor Law
Land Use Law/Natural Resources
★ Lawyering Skills
Legal History/Philosophy
★ Litigation
★ Mediation
★ Public Interest
★ Securities
★ Sports Law
★ Tax Law
(★ indicates an area of special strength)

Clinical Courses Students receive degree credit for clinical courses. (Clinical practicum is not required.) Among the clinical areas offered are:

Criminal Defense
Criminal Prosecution
Environmental Law
Immigration
Juvenile Law
Land Use Law/Natural Resources
Public Interest
Tax Law

Internships are available. International exchange programs permit students to visit Australia.

DEAN'S STATEMENT . . .

Marquette University Law School deserves your serious consideration. Our size—under 500 students—and our 15:1 student-faculty ratio enable Marquette to be a caring, supportive community of scholars. Our mission, as a Catholic Jesuit urban law school with a wonderfully diverse student body and faculty drawn from a wide range of academic, religious, and cultural settings, ensures that we are.

Our school is a short walk from Milwaukee's principal state and federal courthouses and from its downtown commercial, public interest, and government law offices. Formal clinical programs and internships and part-time and summer work opportunities are close at hand. They afford our students hands-on experience that both educates and builds competitive resumes. Our three law journals and Legal Writing Program provide a range of intensive experience in formal legal research and writing. These practical learning opportunities merely augment the School's underlying commitment to superior classroom teaching in an atmosphere mindful of the moral standards that separate a merely competent attorney from one who has a respect and compassion for all who need legal assistance and all who provide it skillfully and ethically.

Many things set our law school apart, including the presence of the National Sports Law Institute, the introduction last year of the Marquette Intellectual Property Law Review and other enhancements of our intellectual property law program, the recent inauguration of our joint summer program with Australia's University of Queensland, and increased opportunities for part-time study.

Marquette seeks women and men students who want to become engines of positive change in our society and who require outstanding teachers to challenge and instruct them. There are many excellent law schools across America. One of the best is to be found near the shores of Lake Michigan in Milwaukee, a vibrant, festive city proud of its heritage. We are Marquette, Wisconsin's largest private university. We welcome you to learn more about us. We welcome you to come and learn with us.

—Howard B. Eisenberg, Dean

HISTORY, CAMPUS, AND LOCATION

Marquette University, the largest private university in Wisconsin, was founded as a Jesuit college in 1881 and named for French missionary and explorer Pere Jacques Marquette who first set foot in this area in 1678. The University lies near the interchange of U.S. 43 and U.S. 94 at the western edge of downtown Milwaukee. It lies in sight of Lake Michigan on an 80-acre urban campus of more than 10,500 students, 90 minutes by car from Wisconsin's capital city of Madison to the west or Chicago to the south. Reconstructed on campus is a fifteenth-century French chapel with authentic connections to St. Joan of Arc.

The Law School was founded independently in 1892 and became part of the University in 1908. It was first accredited by the American Bar Association in 1925 and is a member of the Association of American Law Schools. It is housed in Sensenbrenner Hall, a 62,000 square-foot facility that dates back to 1924. The wing that houses the Legal Research Center was added in 1967; portions of each have been renovated since. Sensenbrenner lies close to several University parking facilities and includes two functioning courtrooms, all the School's administrative and faculty offices plus two student lounges and locker facilities, all Law School classrooms, a Career Planning Office and Library, and the National Sports Law Institute.

SPECIAL QUALITIES OF THE SCHOOL

Marquette University's Catholic Jesuit heritage informs the Law School's mission and provides a moral grounding for the lively, free, and open exchange of ideas from which more than 5,500 living Marquette Law School alumni have benefitted. More than 30 percent of its students come from outside the state, some from overseas. The School takes special pride in the informal interaction among its students, faculty, and administration and equal pride in its commitment to public interest law, encouraging and recognizing pro bono work by students and teachers alike. The School's proximity to Milwaukee's sports facilities, parks, Summerfest grounds, ethnic restaurants and festivals, breweries, State Fairgrounds, zoo, museums and cultural attractions, historic quarters, and neighborhoods ensure that hours away from study hold rich rewards of their own.

TECHNOLOGY ON CAMPUS

The Law Library and Legal Research Center, along with the University's main computer facility in nearby Cudahy Hall, provide students with extensive computer access. Available to law students performing research are WESTLAW and LEXIS-NEXIS, augmented by a wide range of word processing and other programs. The Law School Bulletin describes on-campus technology in greater detail and information about the School and its program, as well as access to its faculty and staff, can be had at any hour over the Internet at http://www.law.marquette.edu.

SCHOLARSHIPS AND LOANS

Most law students at Marquette finance their legal education through a combination of federal and private education loans. Some scholarship money is also available and is awarded to approximately 1 in 4 students on the basis of merit when offers are made. To apply for financial aid, students must complete the Federal Application for Federal Student Aid (FAFSA) and related materials.

STUDENT ACTIVITIES AND OPPORTUNITIES

Law Review The *Marquette Law Review*, the *Marquette Intellectual Property Law Review,* and the *Marquette Sports Law Journal* are all open to students based on academic standing and writing ability.

Moot Court Students are eligible to participate in a variety of moot court writing and advocacy competitions both at Marquette and interscholastically.

Extracurricular Activities Extracurricular activities span a wide variety of interests, including business, international, intellectual property, health, and public interest law; religious, ethnic, and cultural groups; and an active Student Bar Association. The pro bono and fund-raising activities of the School's Public Interest Law Society are especially notable.

Special Opportunities Special opportunities include Criminal Defense Clinics and Prosecutor Clinics; government, nonprofit, and public service internships; and judicial internships at local, state, and federal courthouses across the state.

Opportunities for Members of Minority Groups and Women Opportunities for members of minority groups and women are reflected by the presence at the School of a Black Law Students Association, Hispanic Law Students Association, Native American Law Students Association, Association of Women in the Law, and the flexible part-time day, part-time evening opportunities taught entirely by the regularly faculty in which members of minority groups and women scholars are represented. There is a staff to assist part-time applicants and students in planning their studies.

BAR PASSAGE, CAREER SERVICES, AND PLACEMENT

Graduates of Wisconsin's law schools who take the requisite courses (most are already required for gradua-tion) are admitted to the State Bar of Wisconsin on the Diploma Privilege, without having to sit for a bar examination. Those graduates who elect to practice in other jurisdictions routinely enjoy a high rate of passage on bar examinations.

The Career Planning Office at Marquette University Law School provides students with a library of materials on career planning, information on part-time and summer employment, and personal counseling on career selection, resumes, cover letters, and interviews. It sponsors panels on various job opportunities and coordinates on-campus interviews in the fall and spring semesters and publishes a biweekly newsletter that alerts all students of internship, clerkship, and other opportunities locally, across the country, and abroad. Graduates tend to settle in Wisconsin, although alumni can be found in every major legal center in America. Seven months after graduation, more than 91 percent of the class of 1997 had found employment in various fields, which are broken down below.

Legal Field	Percentage of Graduates	Average Salary
Academic	n/a	n/a
Business	14%	$41,075
Government	13%	$36,005
Judicial Clerkship	n/a	n/a
Private Practice	63%	$44,994
Public Interest	1%	$23,000
Other	n/a	n/a

CORRESPONDENCE AND INFORMATION

Office of Admissions
Sensenbrenner Hall, Room 116
Marquette University Law School
Milwaukee, Wisconsin 53201-1881
Telephone: 414-288-6767
Fax: 414-288-0676
E-mail: admissions@marquette.edu

UNIVERSITY OF WISCONSIN–MADISON
LAW SCHOOL

Madison, Wisconsin

INFORMATION CONTACT
Kenneth B. Davis Jr., Dean
975 Bascom Mall
Madison, WI 53706-1399

Phone: 608-262-0618   Fax: 608-262-5485
Web site: http://www.law.wisc.edu/

LAW STUDENT PROFILE [1997–98]

FULL-TIME   Enrollment: 808
Women: 45%   Men: 55%

PART-TIME   Enrollment: 65
Women: 54%   Men: 46%

RACIAL or ETHNIC COMPOSITION
African American, 9%; Asian/Pacific Islander, 3%; Hispanic, 7%; Native American, 3%

APPLICANTS and ADMITTEES
Number applied: 1,687
Admitted: 668
Percentage accepted: 40%
Seats available: 247
Average LSAT score: 158
Average GPA: 3.4

University of Wisconsin–Madison Law School is a public institution that organizes classes on a semester calendar system. The campus is situated in an urban setting. Founded in 1868, first ABA approved in 1923, and an AALS member, University of Wisconsin–Madison Law School offers JD, JD/MA, JD/MBA, JD/MPA, JD/MPAd, JD/MPAf, JD/MS, JD/PhD, JSD, and LLM degrees.

Faculty consists of 50 full-time members in 1997–98.

Application Information *Required:* LSAT, LSDAS, application form, application fee of $45, baccalaureate degree.

Costs The 1997–98 tuition is $4653 full-time for state residents; $776 per semester (minimum) part-time for state residents. Tuition is $12,231 full-time for nonresidents; $2039 per semester (minimum) part-time for nonresidents.

Financial Aid Fellowships, loans, and need-based grants/scholarships are available. To apply for financial assistance, students must complete the Free Application for Federal Student Aid. Financial aid contact: Dorothy Davis, 975 Bascom Mall, Suite 6224, Madison, WI 53706. Phone: 608-262-1815. Fax: 608-262-5485. E-mail: finaid@law.wisc.edu.

AT a GLANCE

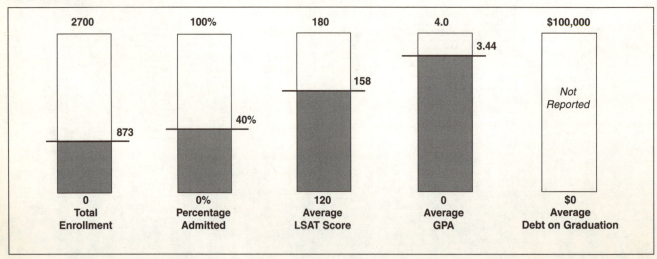

Degree Options

Degree	Total Credits Required	Length of Program
JD–Juris Doctor	90	
JD/MA–Juris Doctor/Master of Arts–Latin American and Iberian Studies	102	
JD/MBA–Juris Doctor/Master of Business Administration		
JD/MPA–Juris Doctor/Master of Professional Accountancy		
JD/MPAd–Juris Doctor/Master of Public Administration		
JD/MPAf–Juris Doctor/Master of Public Affairs		
JD/MS–Juris Doctor/Master of Science–Conservation Biology and Sustainable Development, Land Resources, Business, Water Resources Management, Environmental Monitoring		
JD/PhD–Juris Doctor/Doctor of Philosophy		
JD/PhD–Juris Doctor/Doctor of Philosophy–Environmental Monitoring, Land Resources		
JD/PhD–Juris Doctor/Doctor of Philosophy–Land Resources		
JSD–Doctor of Juridical Science		
LLM–Master of Laws		

Completed financial aid forms should be received by March 1.

Law School Library The University of Wisconsin Law Library has 13 professional staff members and contains more than 470,162 volumes and 4,937 periodicals. 589 seats are available in the library. When classes are in session, the library is open 107 hours per week.

WESTLAW and LEXIS-NEXIS are available, as are the World Wide Web, online bibliographic services, and CD-ROM players. 43 computer workstations are available to students in the library.

First-Year Program Class size in the average section is 75.

Upper-Level Program Among the electives are:

Accounting
Administrative Law
Advocacy
Appellate Litigation
Business and Corporate Law
Constitutional Law
Environmental Law
Evidence
Family Law
Government/Regulation
Health Care/Human Services
Intellectual Property
International/Comparative Law
Jurisprudence
Labor Law
Land Rights/Natural Resource
Lawyering Skills
Legal History/Philosophy
Litigation
Maritime Law
Mediation
Probate Law
Property/Real Estate
Securities
Tax Law

Clinical Courses Students receive degree credit for clinical courses. Among the clinical areas offered are:

Consumer Law
Criminal Defense
Criminal Prosecution
Family Practice
General Practice
Health
Immigration
Indian/Tribal Law

Internships are available. International exchange programs permit students to visit Peru.

UNIVERSITY OF WYOMING
COLLEGE OF LAW

Laramie, Wyoming

INFORMATION CONTACT
John M. Burman, Dean
PO Box 3035
Laramie, WY 82071-3035

Phone: 307-766-6416   Fax: 307-766-6417
Web site: http://www.uwyo.edu/law/law.htm

LAW STUDENT PROFILE [1997–98]

FULL-TIME   Enrollment: 209
Women: 44%   Men: 56%

RACIAL or ETHNIC COMPOSITION
African American, 0.5%; Hispanic, 3%; Native American, 1%

APPLICANTS and ADMITTEES
Number applied: 559
Admitted: 257
Percentage accepted: 46%
Seats available: 80

University of Wyoming College of Law is a public institution that organizes classes on a semester calendar system. Founded in 1920, first ABA approved in 1923, and an AALS member, University of Wyoming College of Law offers JD, JD/MBA, and JD/MPAd degrees.

Faculty consists of 15 full-time and 5 part-time members in 1997–98. 5 full-time faculty members and 1 part-time faculty members are women.

Application Information *Required:* LSAT, LSDAS, application form, application fee of $35, baccalaureate degree. *Application deadline* for fall term is April 1.

Financial Aid 7 teaching assistantships were awarded. Graduate assistantships, merit-based grants/scholarships, need-based grants/scholarships, and federal work-study loans are also available. To apply for financial assistance, students must complete the Free Application for Federal Student Aid. Financial aid contact: University of Wyoming College of Law, Office of Student Financial Aid, PO Box 3335, Laramie, WY 82071-3335. Phone: 307-766-2116. Fax: 307-766-6417. Completed financial aid forms should be received by March 15.

Law School Library The George William Hopper Law Library has 3 professional staff members and

AT a GLANCE

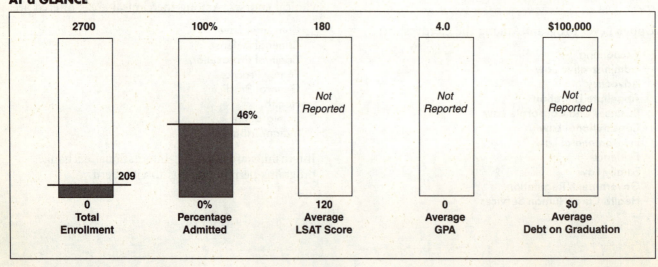

Degree Options

Degree	Total Credits Required	Length of Program
JD–Juris Doctor	88	3 yrs, full-time only
JD/MBA–Juris Doctor/Master of Business Administration–Joint Degree		
JD/MPAd–Juris Doctor/Master of Public Administration–Joint Degree		

contains more than 201,814 volumes and 2,481 periodicals. 248 seats are available in the library. When classes are in session, the library is open 107 hours per week.

WESTLAW and LEXIS-NEXIS are available, as is online bibliographic services.

First-Year Program Class size in the average section is 80.

Upper-Level Program Among the electives are:

Administrative Law
Advocacy
Agricultural Law
Business and Corporate Law
Consumer Law
Criminal Law
Environmental Law
Estate Planning
Family Law
Government/Regulation
Indian/Tribal Law
International/Comparative Law
Jurisprudence
Labor Law
Land Use Law/Natural Resources
Lawyering Skills
Legal History/Philosophy
Litigation
Mineral Rights
Oil and Gas
Probate Law
Pulic Lands
Securities
Tax Law
Water Law

Clinical Courses Students receive degree credit for clinical courses. Among the clinical areas offered are:

Civil Litigation
Criminal Defense
Criminal Prosecution
Family Practice
General Practice
Juvenile Law

INTER AMERICAN UNIVERSITY OF PUERTO RICO, METROPOLITAN CAMPUS
SCHOOL OF LAW

San Juan, Puerto Rico

INFORMATION CONTACT
Carlos E. Ramos-González, Dean
PO Box 70351
San Juan, PR 00936-8351

Phone: 787-751-1912   Fax: 787-751-2975
    Ext. 2001
Web site: http://www.inter.edu/law.html

LAW STUDENT PROFILE [1997–98]

FULL-TIME   Enrollment: 377
Women: 56%   Men: 44%
PART-TIME   Enrollment: 312
Women: 54%   Men: 46%

RACIAL or ETHNIC COMPOSITION
Hispanic, 100%

APPLICANTS and ADMITTEES
Number applied: 945
Admitted: 345
Percentage accepted: 37%
Seats available: 225
Average LSAT score: 140
Average GPA: 3.1

Inter American University of Puerto Rico, Metropolitan Campus School of Law is a private institution that organizes classes on a semester calendar system. The campus is situated in an urban setting. Founded in 1961, first ABA approved in 1978, Inter American University of Puerto Rico, Metropolitan Campus School of Law offers a JD degree.

Faculty consists of 23 full-time and 27 part-time members in 1997–98. 9 full-time faculty members and 8 part-time faculty members are women. 100% of all faculty members have a JD; 67% have advanced law degrees. Of all faculty members, 100% are Hispanic.

Application Information *Required:* LSAT, LSDAS, application form, application fee of $63, baccalaureate degree, minimum 2.5 GPA, college transcripts. *Recommended:* personal statement and essay. *Application deadline* for fall term is March 31.

Costs The 1997–98 tuition is $325 per credit. Fees: $322.

Financial Aid In 1997–98, 74% of all students received some form of financial aid. Fellowships, graduate assistantships, loans, loan repayment

AT a GLANCE

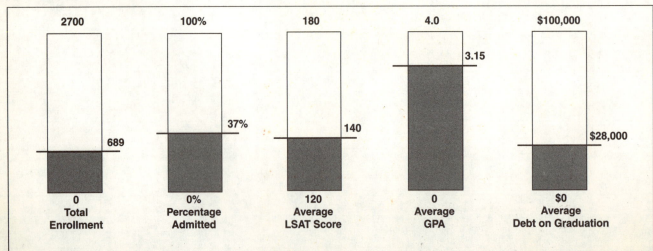

Degree Options

Degree	Total Credits Required	Length of Program
JD–Juris Doctor	92	3–4 yrs, full-time or part-time [day, evening]

assistance program (LRAP), merit-based grants/ scholarships, need-based grants/scholarships, and federal work-study loans are also available. The average student debt at graduation is $28,000. To apply for financial assistance, students must complete the Free Application for Federal Student Aid. Financial aid contact: Michael Ayala, Director of Financial Aid, PO Box 70351, San Juan, PR 00936-8351. Phone: 787-751-1912 Ext. 2014. Fax: 787-751-2975. E-mail: mayala@inter.edu. Completed financial aid forms should be received by April 30.

Law School Library Domingo Toledo-Alamo has 8 professional staff members and contains more than 172,749 volumes and 325 periodicals. 329 seats are available in the library. When classes are in session, the library is open 102 hours per week.

WESTLAW and LEXIS-NEXIS are available, as are the World Wide Web, online bibliographic services, and CD-ROM players. 29 computer workstations are available to students in the library. Special law collections include Hipolito Marcano, Jose Velez-Torres, Jose Echeverria-Yanez.

First-Year Program Class size in the average section is 50.

Upper-Level Program Among the electives are:

Administrative Law

Advocacy
Business and Corporate Law
★ Environmental Law
Family Law
Intellectual Property
International/Comparative Law
Labor Law
★ Lawyering Skills
Legal History/Philosophy
Litigation
Maritime Law
★ Mediation
★ Public Interest
(★ indicates an area of special strength)

Clinical Courses Students receive degree credit for clinical courses. (Clinical practicum is not required.) Among the clinical areas offered are:

Civil Litigation
Civil Rights
Criminal Defense
Environmental Law
Family Practice
General Practice
Juvenile Law
Mediation
Public Interest

PONTIFICAL CATHOLIC UNIVERSITY OF PUERTO RICO
SCHOOL OF LAW

Ponce, Puerto Rico

INFORMATION CONTACT

Charles Cuprill, Dean
2250 Las Americas Avenue
Suite 543
Ponce, PR 00731-6382

Phone: 787-841-2000
     Ext. 341
Web site: http://www.pucpr.edu/

LAW STUDENT PROFILE [1997–98]

FULL-TIME   Enrollment: 505
Women: 51%   Men: 49%

PART-TIME   Enrollment: 13
Women: 15%   Men: 85%

RACIAL or ETHNIC COMPOSITION
Hispanic, 100%

APPLICANTS and ADMITTEES
Number applied: 489
Admitted: 168
Percentage accepted: 34%
Seats available: 168
Median LSAT score: 137
Median GPA: 3.1

Pontifical Catholic University of Puerto Rico School of Law is a private institution that organizes classes on a semester calendar system. The campus is situated in an urban setting. Founded in 1961, first ABA approved in 1967, Pontifical Catholic University of Puerto Rico School of Law offers JD and JD/MBA degrees.

Faculty consists of 19 full-time and 12 part-time members in 1997–98. 8 full-time faculty members and 2 part-time faculty members are women.

Application Information *Required:* LSAT, application form, baccalaureate degree, minimum 2.5 GPA, interview. *Application deadline* for fall term is April 30.

Financial Aid Merit-based grants/scholarships, need-based grants/scholarships, and federal work-study loans are available. To apply for financial assistance, students must complete the Free Application for Federal Student Aid, institutional forms, and federal tax returns. Completed financial aid forms should be received by July 15.

Law School Library Monsieur Fremiot Torres Oliver Library has 4 professional staff members and contains more than 176,914 volumes and 2,225

AT a GLANCE

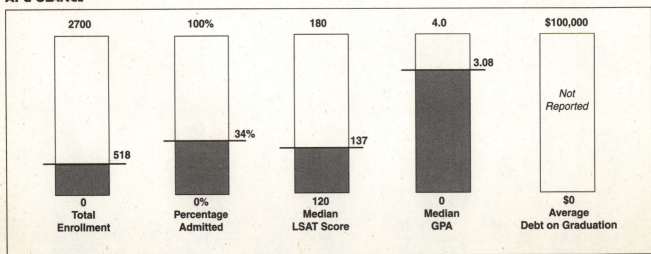

Degree Options		
Degree	**Total Credits Required**	**Length of Program**
JD–Juris Doctor	94	3–4 yrs, full-time or part-time [day, evening]
JD/MBA–Juris Doctor/Master of Business Administration		

periodicals. 169 seats are available in the library. When classes are in session, the library is open 92 hours per week.

WESTLAW and LEXIS-NEXIS are available, as are the World Wide Web and CD-ROM players.

First-Year Program Class size in the average section is 60.

Clinical Courses Among the clinical areas offered are:

Criminal Defense
Criminal Prosecution
Government Litigation
Judicial Clerkship
Tax Law

International exchange programs permit students to visit Spain.

UNIVERSITY OF PUERTO RICO, RÍO PIEDRAS
SCHOOL OF LAW

San Juan, Puerto Rico

INFORMATION CONTACT

Antonio García-Padilla, Dean
PO Box 23349
San Juan, PR 00931-3349

Phone: 809-763-8580   Fax: 787-764-2675
    Ext. 3829

LAW STUDENT PROFILE [1997–98]

FULL-TIME Enrollment: 467
Women: 58%   Men: 42%

PART-TIME Enrollment: 56
Women: 55%   Men: 45%

APPLICANTS and ADMITTEES

Seats available: 150
Average LSAT score: 147
Average GPA: 3.5

University of Puerto Rico, Río Piedras School of Law is a public institution that organizes classes on a semester calendar system. The campus is situated in an urban setting. Founded in 1913, first ABA approved in 1945, and an AALS member, University of Puerto Rico, Río Piedras School of Law offers JD, JD/Lic, and JD/MBA degrees.

Application Information *Required:* LSAT, LSDAS, application form, application fee of $15, baccalaureate degree, personal statement, college transcripts. *Application deadline* for fall term is February 21.

Financial Aid Graduate assistantships, loans, need-based grants/scholarships, and federal work-study loans are available. The average student debt at graduation is $6000. To apply for financial assistance, students must complete the Free Application for Federal Student Aid and institutional forms. Financial aid contact: Luz M. Santiago, Director of Financial Aid Program, University of Puerto Rico, PO Box 23353, San Juan, PR 00931-3353. Phone: 787-764-0000 Ext. 3148. Fax: 787-764-2675. Completed financial aid forms should be received by May 31.

Law School Library University of Puerto Rico Law Library has 10 professional staff members and

AT a GLANCE

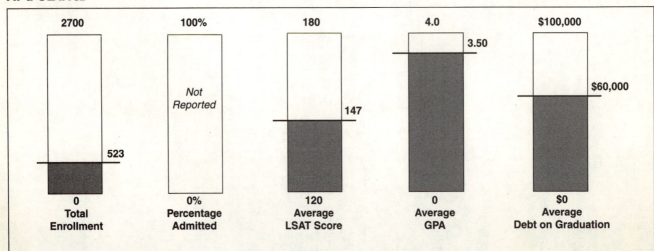

Degree Options

Degree	Total Credits Required	Length of Program
JD–Doctor of Laws	92	3–4 yrs, full-time or part-time [day, evening]
JD/Lic–Juris Doctor/Licenciatura	138	4 yrs, full-time only
JD/MBA–Juris Doctor/Master of Business Administration–Dual-degree Program	122	4 yrs, full-time only [day]

contains more than 290,387 volumes and 4,247 periodicals. 380 seats are available in the library. When classes are in session, the library is open 112 hours per week.

WESTLAW and LEXIS-NEXIS are available, as are the World Wide Web, online bibliographic services, and CD-ROM players. 24 computer workstations are available to students in the library. Special law collections include Caribbean Law Collection.

First-Year Program Class size in the average section is 45; 90% of the first-year courses are taught by full-time faculty.

Upper-Level Program Class size in the average section is 45. Among the electives are:

Administrative Law
Advocacy
Business and Corporate Law
Consumer Law
Education Law
Entertainment Law
Environmental Law
Family Law
Government/Regulation
Intellectual Property
International/Comparative Law
Jurisprudence

Labor Law
Land Use Law/Natural Resources
★ Lawyering Skills
Legal History/Philosophy
★ Litigation
Maritime Law
Mediation
Probate Law
Public Interest
Securities
Tax Law
(★ *indicates an area of special strength*)

Clinical Courses Students receive degree credit for clinical courses. 6 credit hours of clinical practicum are required. Among the clinical areas offered are:

Civil Litigation
Civil Rights
Criminal Defense
Environmental Law
Family Practice
General Practice
Immigration
Juvenile Law

10% of the students participate in internship programs. International exchange programs permit students to visit Spain.

INDEXES

SCHOOL NAME INDEX

The following index lists all of the law schools profiled in this book. The schools are listed alphabetically, with the page number of the school's profile appearing to the right of the school name. Those schools that also have an in-depth description appear in **bold type.**

EMPHASIZED UPPER-LEVEL COURSE INDEX

This index lists those upper-level courses that the schools have indicated are areas of special strength. The course titles are listed alphabetically, with the names of the schools that list that course as an area of special strength listed alphabetically under the course title, followed by the two-letter state abbreviation where the school resides and the school's profile page number.

Family Practice

Gender and the Law

General Practice

Global Legal Studies

Government Procurement

Government/Regulation

Great Lakes Law

Health

Health Care/Human Services

Legal History/Philosophy

Legal Writing

Legislation

Litigation

Local Government

Maritime Law

Media Law

Mediation

Mental Health and Law

CLINICAL COURSE INDEX

This index lists clinical course areas offered by the schools. The clinical course areas are listed alphabetically, with the names of the schools that offer those courses listed alphabetically followed by the two-letter state abbreviation where the school resides and the school's profile page number.

Criminal Defense

Criminal Law

Criminal Prosecution

Disability Law

Employment Law

Entertainment Law

Environmental Law

Government Litigation

Indian/Tribal Law

Intellectual Property

International Development

Mental Health and Law

Nonprofit Organizations

Ocean and Coastal Law

Pensions

Post-conviction Relief

Poverty/Welfare Law

Prison

Prisoners' Rights

Professional Responsibility

Public Benefits

Public Interest

Public Policy

Securities Law Arbitration

Small Business Counseling

Special Education Law

Sports Law

Street Law

Tax Law

Telecommunications Law

Tobacco Control

Unemployment Compensation

Welfare Rights

Wildlife Law

Women and the Law

Women's Rights

NOTES

NOTES

FIND A LIFETIME OF LEARNING AT PETERSON'S ON LINE!

Knowledge gives you the power to perform and to succeed— and petersons.com puts the power at your fingertips!

At **petersons.com** you can
- Explore graduate programs
- Discover distance learning programs
- Find out how to finance your education
- Search for career opportunities

Looking for advice on finding the right graduate program? Look no further than the **Enrollment Message Center at petersons.com!**

- Explore program options by discipline
- E-mail program contacts for more information
- Best of all? **It's FREE**

Peterson's gives you everything you need to start a lifetime of learning.

And it's all just a mouse click away!

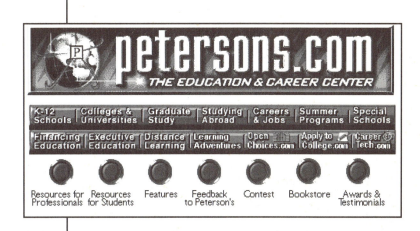

Wait! There's more!➡